economics
today

the micro view

THIRTEENTH EDITION

economics
today
the micro view

THIRTEENTH EDITION

Roger LeRoy Miller
Institute for University Studies, Arlington, Texas

PEARSON

Addison
Wesley

Boston San Francisco New York
London Toronto Sydney Tokyo Singapore Madrid
Mexico City Munich Paris Cape Town Hong Kong Montreal

Editor-in-Chief: Denise Clinton
Acquisitions Editor: Roxanne Hoch
Senior Development Editor: Rebecca Ferris-Caruso
Managing Editor: James Rigney
Senior Production Supervisor: Katherine Watson
Executive Marketing Manager: Stephen Frail
Senior Media Producer: Melissa Honig
Design Manager: Regina Hagen Kolenda
Executive Producer, Technology: Michelle Neil

Cover Designer: Regina Hagen Kolenda
Digital Assets Manager: Jason Miranda
Supplements Production Coordinator: Kirsten Dickerson
Senior Manufacturing Buyer: Hugh Crawford
Senior Media Buyer: Ginny Michaud
Cover Images: ©PictureQuest and Masterfile
Production House: Orr Book Services
Compostion: Nesbitt Graphics, Inc.

Photo Credits

Pages 1 and 12, © Ariel Skelley/CORBIS; Pages 25 and 42, © Photodisc/Getty Images; Pages 48 and 71, © Photodisc/Getty Images; Pages 77 and 93, ©Photodisc/Getty Images; Pages 98 and 118, © AFP/Getty Images; Pages 123 and 139, © Photodisc/Getty Images; Pages 465 and 478, © Javier Pierini/CORBIS; Pages 494 and 512, © Lawrence Manning/CORBIS; Pages 517 and 537, © Royalty-Free/CORBIS; Pages 542 and 563, © George D. Lepp/CORBIS; Pages 568 and 589, © Tom Stewart/CORBIS;

Pages 594 and 613, © Jose Luis Pelaez, Inc./CORBIS; Pages 637 and 654, © Getty Images; Pages 659 and 678, © Reuters/CORBIS; Pages 683 and 704, © Walter Hodges/CORBIS; Pages 709 and 726, © Reuters/CORBIS; Pages 730 and 753, © Rick Gomez/CORBIS; Pages 758 and 772, © Gavriel Jecan/CORBIS; Pages 777 and 793, © AFP/Getty Images; Pages 799 and 821, © Alan Schein Photography/CORBIS.

Library of Congress Cataloging-in-Publication Data

Miller, Roger LeRoy.
   Economics today/Roger LeRoy Miller—13th ed.
     p.cm.
   Includes bibliographical references and index.
   ISBN 0-321-27883-6 (main edition (hard cover) : alk. paper) —
   ISBN 0-321-27886-0 (the micro view (soft cover) : alk. paper) —
   ISBN 0-321-27885-2 (the macro view (soft cover) : alk. paper)
   I. Economics. 2. Microeconomics. 3. Macroeconomics. I. Title.
HB171.5.M642 2006
330—dc22   2004028936

ISBN: 0-321-27886-0
2 3 4 5 6 7 8 9 10—QWD—09 08 07 06 05

Dedication

To Aurélie and Frederic,

Always stay the newlyweds
that you are, making
sure to savor life along
the way.

— R. L. M.

The Addison-Wesley Series in Economics

Abel/Bernanke
Macroeconomics

Bade/Parkin
Foundations of Economics

Bierman/Fernandez
Game Theory with Economic Applications

Binger/Hoffman
Microeconomics with Calculus

Boyer
Principles of Transportation Economics

Branson
Macroeconomic Theory and Policy

Bruce
Public Finance and the American Economy

Byrns/Stone
Economics

Carlton/Perloff
Modern Industrial Organization

Caves/Frankel/Jones
World Trade and Payments

Chapman
Environmental Economics: Theory, Application, and Policy

Cooter/Ulen
Law and Economics

Downs
An Economic Theory of Democracy

Ehrenberg/Smith
Modern Labor Economics

Ekelund/Tollison
Economics

Fusfeld
The Age of the Economist

Gerber
International Economics

Ghiara
Learning Economics

Gordon
Macroeconomics

Gregory
Essentials of Economics

Gregory/Stuart
Russian and Soviet Economic Performance and Structure

Hartwick/Olewiler
The Economics of Natural Resource Use

Hoffman/Averett
Women and the Economy

Hubbard
Money, the Financial System, and the Economy

Hughes/Cain
American Economic History

Husted/Melvin
International Economics

Jehle/Reny
Advanced Microeconomic Theory

Johnson-Lans
A Health Care Economics Primer

Klein
Mathematical Methods for Economics

Krugman/Obstfeld
International Economics

Laidler
The Demand for Money

Leeds/von Allmen
The Economics of Sports

Leeds/von Allmen/Schiming
Economics

Lipsey/Courant/Ragan
Economics

Melvin
International Money and Finance

Miller
Economics Today

Miller/Benjamin/North
The Economics of Public Issues

Miller/Benjamin
The Economics of Macro Issues

Mills/Hamilton
Urban Economics

Mishkin
The Economics of Money, Banking, and Financial Markets

Murray
Econometrics

Parkin
Economics

Perloff
Microeconomics

Phelps
Health Economics

Riddell/Shackelford/Stamos/Schneider
Economics: A Tool for Critically Understanding Society

Ritter/Silber/Udell
Principles of Money, Banking, and Financial Markets

Rohlf
Introduction to Economic Reasoning

Ruffin/Gregory
Principles of Economics

Sargent
Rational Expectations and Inflation

Scherer
Industry Structure, Strategy, and Public Policy

Stock/Watson
Introduction to Econometrics

Studenmund
Using Econometrics

Tietenberg
Environmental and Natural Resource Economics

Tietenberg
Environmental Economics and Policy

Todaro/Smith
Economic Development

Waldman
Microeconomics

Waldman/Jensen
Industrial Organization

Weil
Economic Growth

Williamson
Macroeconomics

Contents in Brief

Contents in Detail

Chapter 3 DEMAND AND SUPPLY 48

Chapter 4 EXTENSIONS OF DEMAND AND SUPPLY ANALYSIS 77

Chapter 5 THE PUBLIC SECTOR AND PUBLIC CHOICE 98

Chapter 6   TAXES, TRANSFERS, AND PUBLIC SPENDING   123

PART V   DIMENSIONS OF MICROECONOMICS   465

Chapter 20   CONSUMER CHOICE   465

EXAMPLE

Newspaper Vending Machines versus Candy Vending Machines   470

e-Commerce EXAMPLE

Virtual 3D Pays Off at Lands' End   475

International EXAMPLE

Water in Saudi Arabia   476

Chapter 21 DEMAND AND SUPPLY ELASTICITY   494

EXAMPLES

The Price Elasticity of Demand for Six-Packs of Beer   497

What Do Real-World Price Elasticities of Demand Look Like?   505

When Incomes Rise, It's Easier to Believe Margarine Isn't Butter   508

e-Commerce EXAMPLE

The Cross Price Elasticity of Demand for Telescopes in Online Auctions   506

Policy EXAMPLE

Who Pays Higher Gasoline Taxes?   499

International EXAMPLE

French Truffle Production Takes a Nosedive   510

Chapter 22 RENTS, PROFITS, AND THE FINANCIAL ENVIRONMENT OF BUSINESS   517

EXAMPLES

Do Entertainment Superstars Make Super Economic Rents?   520

The Low Present Value of a Volunteer Soldier's Pay Package   531

How to Read the Financial Press: Stock Prices   534

International Policy EXAMPLE

Hoping for Some One-Yen Business Successes in Japan   524

International EXAMPLE

Is It Too Soon for a Pan-African Stock Exchange?   533

PART VI MARKET STRUCTURE, RESOURCE ALLOCATION, AND REGULATION 542

Chapter 23 THE FIRM: COST AND OUTPUT DETERMINATION 542

Chapter 24 PERFECT COMPETITION 568

International EXAMPLES

Chapter 34 EXCHANGE RATES AND THE BALANCE OF PAYMENTS 799

EXAMPLE

International EXAMPLES

Acknowledgments

I am the most fortunate of economics textbook writers, for I receive the benefit of literally hundreds of suggestions from those of you who use *Economics Today*. I continue to be fully appreciative of the constructive criticisms that you offer. There are some professors who have been asked by my publisher to participate in a more detailed reviewing process of this edition. I list them below. I hope that each one of you so listed accepts my sincere appreciation for the fine work that you have done.

Carlos Aguilar, El Paso Community College
Bruce W. Bellner, Ohio State University, Marion
Daniel K. Benjamin, Clemson University
Margaret M. Dalton, Frostburg State University
Diana Denison, Red Rocks Community College
Diana Fortier, Waubonsee Community College

M. James Kahiga, Georgia Perimeter College
Daniel Mizak, Frostburg State University
Judy Roobian-Mohr, Columbus State Community College
Paul Seidenstat, Temple University

Diane L. Stehman, Northeastern Illinois University
Anthony Uremovic, Joliet Junior College
David VanHoose, Baylor University
Mark A. Wilkening, Blinn College

I also thank the reviewers of previous editions:

Cinda J. Adams
Esmond Adams
John Adams
Bill Adamson
John R. Aidem
Mohammed Akacem
E. G. Aksoy
M. C. Alderfer
John Allen
Ann Al-Yasiri
Charles Anderson
Leslie J. Anderson
Fatma W. Antar
Mohammad Ashraf
Aliakbar Ataiifar
Leonard Atencio
John M. Atkins
Glen W. Atkinson
Thomas R. Atkinson
James Q. Aylesworth
John Baffoe-Bonnie
Kevin Baird
Charley Ballard
Maurice B. Ballabon
G. Jeffrey Barbour
Daniel Barszcz
Robin L. Bartlett
Kari Battaglia
Robert Becker
Charles Beem
Glen Beeson
Charles Berry
Abraham Bertisch
John Bethune
R.A. Blewett
Scott Bloom
M. L. Bodnar
Mary Bone
Karl Bonnhi
Thomas W. Bonsor
John M. Booth
Wesley F. Booth
Thomas Borcherding
Melvin Borland
Tom Boston
Barry Boyer
Maryanna Boynton
Ronald Brandolini
Fenton L. Broadhead
Elba Brown
William Brown
Michael Bull
Maureen Burton

Conrad P. Caligaris
Kevin Carey
James Carlson
Robert Carlsson
Dancy R. Carr
Scott Carson
Doris Cash
Thomas H. Cate
Richard J. Cebula
Catherine Chanbers
K. Merry Chambers
Richard Chapman
Ronald Cherry
Young Back Choi
Marc Chopin
Carol Cies
Joy L. Clark
Curtis Clarke
Gary Clayton
Marsha Clayton
Dale O. Cloninger
Warren L. Coats
Ed Coen
Pat Conroy
James Cox
Stephen R. Cox
Eleanor D. Craig
Peggy Crane
Jerry Crawford
Joanna Cruse
John P. Cullity
Will Cummings
Thomas Curtis
Andrew J. Dane
Mahmoud Davoudi
Edward Dennis
Carol Dimamro
William Dougherty
Barry Duman
Diane Dumont
Floyd Durham
G. B. Duwaji
James A. Dyal
Ishita Edwards
Robert P. Edwards
Alan E. Ellis
Mike Ellis
Steffany Ellis
Frank Emerson
Carl Enomoto
Zaki Eusufzai
Sandy Evans
John L. Ewing-Smith

Frank Falero
Frank Fato
Abdollah Ferdowsi
Grant Ferguson
David Fletcher
James Foley
John Foreman
Ralph G. Fowler
Arthur Friedberg
Peter Frost
Tom Fullerton
E. Gabriel
James Gale
Byron Gangnes
Steve Gardner
Peter C. Garlick
Neil Garston
Alexander Garvin
Joe Garwood
Doug Gehrke
J. P. Gilbert
Otis Gilley
Frank Glesber
Jack Goddard
Michael Goode
Allen C. Goodman
Richard J. Gosselin
Paul Graf
Edward Greenberg
Gary Greene
Nicholas Grunt
William Gunther
Kwabena Gyimah-Brempong
Demos Hadjiyanis
Martin D. Haney
Mehdi Haririan
Ray Harvey
E. L. Hazlett
Sanford B. Helman
William Henderson
John Hensel
Robert Herman
Gus W. Herring
Charles Hill
John M. Hill
Morton Hirsch
Benjamin Hitchner
Charles W. Hockert
R. Bradley Hoppes
James Horner
Grover Howard
Nancy Howe-Ford

Yu-Mong Hsiao
Yu Hsing
James Hubert
Joseph W. Hunt Jr.
Scott Hunt
John Ifediora
R. Jack Inch
Christopher Inya
Tomotaka Ishimine
E. E. Jarvis
Parvis Jenab
Allan Jenkins
Mark Jensen
S. D. Jevremovic
J. Paul Jewell
Frederick Johnson
David Jones
Lamar B. Jones
Paul A. Joray
Daniel A. Joseph
Craig Justice
Septimus Kai Kai
Devajyoti Kataky
Timothy R. Keely
Ziad Keilany
Norman F. Keiser
Randall G. Kesselring
Alan Kessler
E. D. Key
Saleem Khan
M. Barbara Killen
Bruce Kimzey
Philip G. King
Terrence Kinal
E. R. Kittrell
David Klingman
Charles Knapp
Jerry Knarr
Faik Koray
Janet Koscianski
Marie Kratochvil
Peter Kressler
Michael Kupilik
Larry Landrum
Margaret Landman
Richard LaNear
Keith Langford
Anthony T. Lee
Loren Lee
Bozena Leven
Donald Lien
George Lieu
Stephen E. Lile

Lawrence W. Lovick
Marty Ludlum
G. Dirk Mateer
Robert McAuliffe
James C. McBrearty
Howard J. McBride
Bruce McClung
John McDowell
E. S. McKuskey
James J. McLain
John L. Madden
Mary Lou Madden
Glen Marston
John M. Martin
Paul J. Mascotti
James D. Mason
Paul M. Mason
Tom Mathew
Warren Matthews
Warren T. Matthews
Akbar Marvasti
G. Hartley Mellish
Mike Melvin
Diego Mendez-Carbajo
Dan C. Messerschmidt
Michael Metzger
Herbert C. Milikien
Joel C. Millonzi
Glenn Milner
Khan Mohabbat
Thomas Molloy
Margaret D. Moore
William E. Morgan
Stephen Morrell
Irving Morrissett
James W. Moser
Thaddeaus Mounkurai
Martin F. Murray
Densel L. Myers
George L. Nagy
Solomon Namala
Jerome Neadly
James E. Needham
Claron Nelson
Douglas Nettleton
Gerald T. O'Boyle
Gregory Okoro
Richard E. O'Neill
Lucian T. Orlowski
Diane S. Osborne
Melissa A. Osborne
James O'Toole
Jan Palmer

Zuohong Pan
Gerald Parker
Ginger Parker
Randall E. Parker
Kenneth Parzych
Norm Paul
Wesley Payne
Raymond A. Pepin
Martin M. Perline
Timothy Perri
Jerry Petr
Bruce Pietrykowski
Maurice Pfannesteil
James Phillips
Raymond J. Phillips
I. James Pickl
Dennis Placone
Mannie Poen
William L. Polvent
Robert Posatko
Reneé Prim
Robert W. Pulsinelli
Rod D. Raehsler
Kambriz Raffiee
Sandra Rahman
Jaishankar Raman
John Rapp
Richard Rawlins
Gautam Raychaudhuri
Ron Reddall
Mitchell Redlo
Charles Reichhelu
Robert S. Rippey
Charles Roberts
Ray C. Roberts
Richard Romano
Duane Rosa
Richard Rosenberg
Larry Ross
Barbara Ross-Pfeiffer
Philip Rothman
John Roufagalas
Stephen Rubb
Henry Ryder
Patricia Sanderson
Thomas N. Schaap
William A. Schaeffer
William Schaniel
David Schauer
A. C. Schlenker
David Schlow
Scott J. Schroeder
William Scott

Dan Segebarth	Phil Smith	Rebecca Summary	William N. Trumbull	Wylie Whalthall	Whitney Yamamura
Swapan Sen	Steve Smith	Joseph L. Swaffar	Arianne K. Turner	James H. Wheeler	Donald Yankovic
Augustus Shackelford	William Doyle Smith	Thomas Swanke	Kay Unger	Everett E. White	Alex Yguado
Richard Sherman Jr.	Lee Spector	Frank D. Taylor	John Vahaly	Michael D. White	Paul Young
Liang-rong Shiau	George Spiva	Daniel Teferra	Jim Van Beek	Mark A. Wilkening	Shik Young
David Shorow	Richard L. Sprinkle	Lea Templer	Lee J. Van Scyoc	Raburn M. Williams	Mohammed Zaheer
Vishwa Shukla	Alan Stafford	Gary Theige	Roy Van Til	James Willis	Ed Zajicek
R. J. Sidwell	Herbert F. Steeper	Dave Thiessen	Craig Walker	George Wilson	Paul Zarembka
David E. Sisk	Columbus Stephens	Robert P. Thomas	Robert F. Wallace	Travis Wilson	William J. Zimmer Jr.
Alden Smith	William Stine	Deborah Thorsen	Henry C. Wallich	Mark Wohar	
Garvin Smith	Allen D. Stone	Richard Trieff	Milledge Weathers	Ken Woodward	
Howard F. Smith	Osman Suliman	George Troxler	Robert G. Welch	Tim Wulf	
Lynn A. Smith	J. M. Sullivan	William T. Trulove	Terence West	Peter R. Wyman	

When I undertake a major revision of *Economics Today*, I start the process almost immediately after I've published the previous edition. So, what you are about to read has its roots in editorial meetings that started almost three years ago.

I am fortunate to have an incredibly imaginative and knowledgeable editorial team at Addison-Wesley, with which I have worked during these last several years. They include Adrienne D'Ambrosio, Rebecca Ferris-Caruso, Roxanne Hoch, and Denise Clinton. Of course, they have accused me of monopolizing their time. In any event, I thank them for all of the meetings, phone calls, e-mails, and faxes that, if properly recorded, would fill up more pages than the resulting text.

On the design and production side, I feel fortunate to have worked with John Orr of Orr Book Services. I thank his staff and him for their creative and professional services as well as Katherine Watson, my production manager at Addison-Wesley, and Regina Kolenda, my talented designer. I also very much appreciate the efforts of Jason Miranda and Kirsten Dickerson in coordinating the production process of the many print supplements.

I had more than my deserved amount of constant comments and criticisms from my colleagues David VanHoose and Dan Benjamin. I hope they will accept this sentence of appreciation in the manner in which it is offered—with utmost sincerity.

I have been blessed with a powerhouse of talented colleagues who have created or revised the extensive supplements package. So, thank you David VanHoose of Baylor University for the Study Guides; Andrew J. Dane of Angelo State University for the Instructor's Manual; Debbie Mullin of the University of Colorado at Colorado Springs for the PowerPoint slides; Judy Roobian-Mohr, Columbus State Community College for Test Bank 1; Diane L. Stehman of Northeastern Illinois University for Test Bank 2; and G. Dirk Mateer of Penn State University for his critical role as editor of Test Bank 3 overseeing top-notch question contributions from Susan Glanz of St. Joseph's University and Bruce W. Bellner of Ohio State University, Marion, Marie Duggan of Keene State College, Teresa Laughlin of Pomona College, Debbie Mullin of the University of Colorado at Colorado Springs, Densel L. Myers of Oklahoma City Community College, and David Schlow of Penn State University.

I also must extend my gratitude to the multimedia developers who created and refined all of the online services for this edition of *Economics Today*. At Addison-Wesley, Melissa Honig and Michelle Neil deftly coordinated the efforts of the content and multimedia developers. I am especially appreciative of the efforts of the MyEconLab content development team. Key contributors include Scott Hunt of Columbus State Community College, Daniel Mizak of Frostburg State University, and Margaret M. Dalton of Frostburg State University.

Finally, Sue Jasin probably could teach a course in economics after typing, retyping, and even retyping again various drafts of this revision. Thank you, Sue, for everything, including the many weekends you worked on this project.

I welcome comments and ideas from professors and students. After all, by the time you read this, I will already be working on the next edition.

R. L. M.

Miller's Economics Today—
real-life economics for today's students

I have always challenged myself to deliver a textbook for principles of economics that would motivate students to take what they learn in this course into everyday life. I believe that the key to achieving this goal is to illustrate economic theory through attention-grabbing issues and applications that students are eager to read and discuss.

Clear presentation of theory ... examples, examples, and more examples ... plenty of opportunities to practice

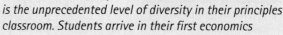

One of the major challenges economics instructors face today is the unprecedented level of diversity in their principles classroom. Students arrive in their first economics course with widely divergent skill sets, math abilities, academic interests, and personal backgrounds. Some students plan to major in economics, although many take the course to fulfill a college requirement.

If you accept the premise, as I do, that all students learn better when they're motivated through applications that tap into their personal interests, you will understand why I include such a breadth of examples—domestic and international, corporate and policy, consumer and celebrity—and why I update them in each new edition to make sure they stay current with students' interests. Each page offers instructors a new opportunity to connect with students, and a chance for students to connect economics to the world around them.

Balanced attention to a full range of modern and traditional theories

*And, as in previous editions, **Economics Today** provides balanced treatment of macroeconomic theories— including classical, Keynesian, monetarist, and real- business-cycle approaches—and it explores the arguments and evidence promoting active, discretionary versus passive, rules-based policymaking. In the realm of microeconomics, the text considers both time-tested approaches to perfect and imperfect competition, as well as more recent developments relating to information products and network effects.*

*In essence, my goals haven't changed since I wrote the first edition, but now I know that my priorities are in line with what students need. Millions of students have used my textbook. Feedback from those students and their instructors has convinced me that **Economics Today** focuses on what matters most: user friendliness; clear, modern theory; examples, examples, examples; and unlimited opportunities to practice via problem sets and online pedagogy.*

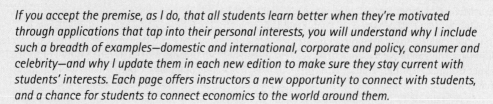

Roger LeRoy Miller

A significant revision—the latest public debates, a new Chapter 14, and recent data throughout

Building on the success of previous editions, the Thirteenth Edition offers thoroughly updated coverage throughout. Every example, table, and graph has been revised to reflect the most recent data available. You'll find major new material incorporating the latest public debates, research, and data in every part of the text, including:

▶ **New Chapter 14, "Deficit Spending and the Public Debt,"** addresses one of today's foremost public policy issues—the implications of higher deficits and a growing public debt. This timely chapter helps students understand why higher federal deficits may or may not pose problems for the U.S. economy. Major topics include the challenge of measuring the federal budget deficit; effects of government budget deficits on aggregate demand; and ways to reduce the government budget deficit.

▶ **Updated treatment of regulation and antitrust in Chapter 28** gives students the background required to evaluate the effects of regulatory and antitrust actions by U.S. and foreign policymakers. The chapter contrasts the benefits and costs of regulation, covers modern pricing techniques such as product versioning and bundling, and explains how U.S. and foreign policymakers have reacted differently to these pricing mechanisms.

▶ **Detailed coverage of the issue of labor outsourcing in Chapter 29** keys students in on this topic that has generated much public debate. Examples from both U.S. and foreign perspectives show why outsourcing has mixed near-term effects on wages and employment in U.S. labor markets but is beneficial on net for U.S. workers in the long run.

▶ **Enhanced coverage of labor union issues in Chapter 30** emphasizes the significant shift in U.S. unionization from manufacturing to services and highlights global unionization trends. The chapter provides complete coverage of the factors accounting for recent trends in and economic effects of labor unions. The discussion shows that unions are fundamental institutions in many nations, even though U.S. unionization rates are falling.

▶ **Expanded coverage of the role of international trade organizations in Chapter 33** highlights the increasing importance of regional trade blocs in affecting global trade flows and broadens the scope of coverage of the institutional framework governing world trade.

Chapter
Deficit Spending and the Public Debt

14

From the 1980s until the mid-1990s, the U.S. government spent more funds than it collected. So did the governments of many other nations, including Canada, France, Germany, and the

CHAPTER 29 *The Labor Market: Demand, Supply, and Outsourcing* **695**

ment and wages in the United States? Who loses and who gains from outsourcing? Let's consider each of these questions in turn.

Wage and Employment Effects of Outsourcing

Equilibrium wages and levels of employment in U.S. labor markets are determined by the demands for and supplies of labor in those markets. As you have learned, one of the determinants of the market demand for labor is the price of a substitute input. Availability of a lower-priced substitute, you also learned, causes the demand for labor to fall. Thus the *immediate* economic effects of labor outsourcing are straightforward. When a home industry's firms can obtain *foreign* labor services that are a close substitute for *home* labor services, the demand for labor services provided by foreign workers will increase. The demand for labor services provided by home workers will decrease. What this economic reasoning ultimately implies for U.S. labor markets, however, depends on whether we view the United States as the "home" country or the "foreign" country.

U.S. Labor Market Effects of Outsourcing by U.S. Firms. To begin, let's view the United States as the home country. Developments in computer, communications, and transportation technologies have enabled an increasing number of U.S. firms to regard the labor of foreign workers as a close substitute for labor provided by U.S. workers. Take a look at Figure 29-5. Panel (a) depicts demand and supply curves in the U.S. market for workers who handle calls for technical support for U.S. manufacturers of personal computers. Suppose that before technological change makes foreign labor substitutable for U.S. labor, point E_1 is the initial equilibrium. At this point, the market wage rate in this U.S. labor market is $19 per hour.

FIGURE 29-5
Outsourcing of U.S. Computer Technical-Support Services
Initially, the market wage for U.S. workers providing technical support for customers of U.S. computer manufacturers is $19 per hour at point E_1 in panel (a), while the market wage for Indian workers who provide the same service is $8 per hour in panel (b). This gives U.S. firms an incentive to substitute away from U.S. workers to Indian workers. The market demand for U.S. labor decreases in panel (a), generating a new equilibrium at point E_2 at a lower U.S. market wage and employment level. The market demand for Indian labor increases in panel (b), bringing about higher wages and employment at point E_2.

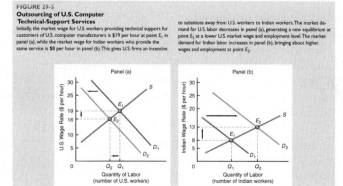

Demonstrating economic principles with examples from today's headlines

Economics Today captures interest through the infusion of dozens of new cases and 145 examples that reflect the vitality of economics—all selected to hold students' attention and to drive home the application of the theory just presented. Hard-hitting boxed features apply concepts to real-world situations. New examples throughout the text give immediate, common-sense reinforcement to economic concepts.

NEW "Economics Front and Center" Case Studies

These all-new cases—one in each chapter—place students in real-world situations requiring them to apply what they have studied in the chapter. The case in Chapter 3, for example, asks students to analyze the effects of a tornado on the supply and demand for the services of construction contractors.

Other cases include:

▶ Holding Out for a Better Salary Offer in an Improved Job Climate

▶ Confronting the Temptation to Collude in the Airline Industry

▶ Outsourcing Can Be a Win-Win Situation

Many new real-life examples highlight domestic topics and events

Effectively demonstrating economic principles, these new thought-provoking examples appear throughout the book, including:

▶ When Incomes Rise, It's Easier to Believe Butter Isn't Margarine

▶ The Low Present Value of a Volunteer Soldier's Pay Package

▶ Is Krispy Kreme Trying to Bake Too Many Doughnuts?

▶ Why You Pay a Different Price to Attend College Than Many of Your Fellow Students

Many added examples dealing with important policy questions

Students are exposed to policy questions on both domestic and international fronts in over 20 policy examples. This strong policy perspective helps students understand why economic concepts are important to them as citizens who seek to evaluate public debates surrounding the issues of the day. "Policy Examples" include:

▶ Does Imposing the Ultimate Legal Penalty Deter Homicides?

▶ How Pushing Prices Lower Can Violate Antitrust Laws

▶ State Government Spending Takes Off—Especially in One State

▶ The Discount Window Is Open, So Where Are the Banks?

CASE STUDY: Economics Front and Center

The Economics of a Tornado Cleanup Can Hit Close to Home

An early spring tornado has just rolled through a midwestern town, and more than 500 structures have experienced at least moderate damage. After recovering from the initial shock, one couple, the Richardsons, realize that they are lucky to have only blown-out windows and large holes in their roof, which they quickly cover with plastic sheeting. When they try to find a construction contractor to make permanent repairs, however, they do not feel so lucky any more. Most phone calls to contractors are producing either busy signals or unanswered voice mail messages. The few contractors who respond say that they are overwhelmed with requests for work and cannot possibly begin the Richardsons' repairs for at

nearly 25 percent higher than the usual prices charged to replace windows and a roof. How can demand and supply analysis explain the situation that the Richardsons are facing?

Points to Analyze

1. Has the structural damage inflicted on this town by the tornado resulted in changes in the demand for and supply of the services of construction contractors or changes in the quantities demanded and
relo-

EXAMPLE

Is Krispy Kreme Trying to Bake Too Many Doughnuts?

In 1937, the founder of Krispy Kreme Doughnuts, Vernon Rudolph, purchased a secret yeast-raised doughnut recipe from a French chef in New Orleans and opened a doughnut shop in Winston-Salem, North Carolina. Gradually, Krispy Kreme outlets spread across the southern tier of the United States. Then, in 2000, Krispy Kreme became a publicly traded company and embarked on a major expansion across most of the rest of the country.

The company calls many of its newest outlets "factory stores." These outlets are equipped with costly doughnut-making machinery that can churn out tens of thousands of doughnuts each day. An aim of the expansion strategy has been to reduce the long-run average cost of producing doughnuts. Some locales now have so many Krispy Kreme outlets in cl

urated" with doughnuts. Stores in these areas end up throwing away numerous one- and two-day-old doughnuts, which raises average costs of ingredients, labor, electricity, and wear and tear on machinery. For this reason, critics of Krispy Kreme's expansion strategy contend that the result has been higher long-run average costs for the company as a whole. The firm, they argue, has expanded beyond its minimum efficient scale.

For Critical Analysis

How might Krispy Kreme continue to expand geographically *into the four states that currently lack outlets while at the same time reducing its overall nationwide scale of doughnut*

Policy EXAMPLE

Does Imposing the Ultimate Legal Penalty Deter Homicides?

Figure 1-1 on the following page shows that a drop in the annual number of legally sanctioned executions in the United States between the late 1950s and early 1980s was accompanied by an increase in the U.S. murder rate. When the number of executions rose during the 1990s and early 2000s, the U.S. murder rate declined.

The extent to which the threat of receiving a death penalty actually contributes to lower murder rates depends on a host of other incentives, however. For instance, if more states reduce the chances of a convicted murderer receiving the death penalty, the disincentive to committing murders is reduced. In contrast, the disincentive effects of the death penalty are likely to be greater if prison conditions improve, thereby making the death penalty a much less desirable alternative punishment.

Economists have found that when these and other factors are taken into account, every *additional* legally sanctioned execution is associated with about five to six fewer homicides. Each judicial *reduction* of a death-penalty sentence to imprisonment is associated with the occurrence of one to two additional murders. Thus both the execution rate and the rate at which death-penalty sentences are reduced to long-term imprisonment have incentive effects on people contemplating murder.

For Critical Analysis

Why do you suppose that careful economic studies of the effects of the death penalty on homicide rates take into account whether people who committed murders might have been under the influence of alcohol or drugs?

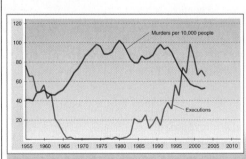

FIGURE 1-1
Murder Rates and Executions in the United States Since 1955
Since the mid-1950s, there has been an apparent negative relationship between the number of death-penalty sentences carried out and the U.S. murder rate.

Source: U.S. Department of Justice.

Economic stimulus for your classroom

International examples emphasize today's global economy

This edition features more than 40 international examples that broaden students' perspectives by showing that economic principles are applicable in other cultures and institutional environments. New "International Examples" include:

▶ The IMF's Cost to Taxpayers Is Surely "Not One Dime"

▶ Manufacturing Jobs Disappear Worldwide

▶ Hidden Costs of "Free" Canadian Health Care

▶ The European Union Starts a Food Fight

"E-Commerce Examples" explore the impact of advances in information technology

This edition's 15 new "E-Commerce Examples" demonstrate how advances in information technology are affecting virtually every area of the economy and students' personal lives. "E-Commerce Examples" include:

▶ Divorce Court Moves to the Internet

▶ U.S. Web Sellers Find Themselves Collecting Europe's Taxes

▶ Internet Packaging Tracking Cuts Marginal Costs at Federal Express

▶ Why Market Entries Have Been Followed by Market Exits at Online Auction Sites

Students get many opportunities to "think like economists"

At the end of each of this book's boxed examples, students are asked to "think like economists" as they answer **For Critical Analysis** questions. These probing questions are effective tools for sharpening students' analytical skills. Suggested answers to all questions are found in the *Instructor's Manual.*

International E X A M P L E

Hidden Costs of "Free" Canadian Health Care

Because physicians are unwilling to provide as many services as people wish to purchase at below-market fees dictated by the Canadian government, long waiting lists are a fixture of the Canadian system. The average waiting time to see a specialist after referral by a general practitioner is more than four months. Individuals experiencing debilitating back pain often must wait at least a year for neurosurgery. Even people diagnosed with life-threatening cancers typically have to wait six weeks before they have an initial examination by a cancer specialist.

The high opportunity costs associated with long waits for officially approved health care have led to the establishment of private health care clinics on Native American reservations, where physicians can legally accept private payments. (It is il-legal for Canadians to purchase private health insurance to pay for care received on these reservations, however.) In addition, rather than wait for years to obtain elective surgeries, about 20,000 Canadians fly to India each year at their own expense and pay physicians in that country to perform surgeries such as hip replacements. In actuality, the "free" Canadian health care system is very costly to that nation's residents.

For Critical Analysis
Why do you suppose that many Canadians who wish to have MRI scans travel to the United States and pay for scans out of their own pockets instead of waiting three months for a "free" MRI scan in Canada?

E-Commerce E X A M P L E

Divorce Court Moves to the Internet

At Web sites such as CompleteCase.com and LegalZoom.com, a couple desiring to amicably dissolve their marriage can pro-vide sufficient information to obtain fully completed legal di-vorce papers for fees ranging from $250 to $300. For another $50 to $100, they can also obtain all the information required to file their papers with a court to end their marriage legally. These online prices are much lower than the fees of $2,000 or so that divorce lawyers typically charge simply to fill out and process the same required legal forms.

When there are no child-custody or property-division is-sues to iron out, it is often in a couple's self-interest to bypass traditional lawyers to obtain a divorce. Not surprisingly, the total number of do-it-yourself divorces arranged online has more than doubled each year since Web-based preparers of di-vorce papers began operating in the early 2000s.

For Critical Analysis
Under what types of circumstances might a self-interested marriage partner be willing to pay an attorney much more than $2,000 to handle legal issues associated with obtaining a divorce?

For Critical Analysis
Under what types of circumstances might a self-interested marriage partner be willing to pay an attorney much more than $2,000 to handle legal issues associated with obtaining a divorce?

Provocative applications engage students in every chapter

Economics Today is based on the belief that students learn more when they are involved and engaged. The current applications in this book—all new to this edition—get students' attention right at the beginning of each chapter.

New chapter-opening issues present compelling examples ...

Each chapter-opening issue whets student interest in core chapter concepts with a compelling example. These openers engage students up front and involve them in the chapter material. New chapter-opening issues include:

▶ Increasing Obesity Rates Among U.S. Children

▶ Supply and Demand in the Market for Economics Instructors

▶ The Market for Online Music

▶ Collusive Price Fixing by Top Fashion-Modeling Agencies

... which are linked to corresponding chapter-end "Issues and Applications"

Located at the end of every chapter, the two-page "Issues and Applications" sections offer a more in-depth discussion of the issue introduced at the beginning of the chapter. These capstone applications feature current issues designed to encourage students to apply economic concepts to real-world situations. Each "Issues and Applications" concludes with "For Critical Analysis" questions, "Web Resources," and a suggested "Research Project" that give students opportunities for in-depth discussion and exploration of the application. (Suggested answers to critical thinking questions appear in the *Instructor's Manual*.)

Study tools guide students through each chapter

Economics Today provides a finely tuned teaching and learning system. Acknowledging that students learn in different ways and at different speeds, each of the following features has been carefully crafted to provide a sound structure to ground the student.

▶ **"Did You Know That . . .?" questions use current data to engage students in chapter topics**
Each chapter starts with a provocative question to engage students and to lead them into the content of the chapter. This new "Did You Know That . . .?" from Chapter 1 uses data about young Italians to show students how self-interest and incentives can be underpinnings for economic decisions.

> **Did You Know That** . . . more than half of all Italians aged 20 to 29 live with their parents? A labor law contributes to this state of affairs. Under the law, firing a worker who has been on a company's payroll longer than a three-month probationary period exposes the company to the risk that a judge will rule that the company did not have "just" cause to dismiss the employee. In this event, the company must reinstate the employee, reimburse the employee for back wages, and pay a fine to the government. Rather than expose themselves to this risk, the owners of many Italian companies have determined that it is in their self-interest *not* to keep new employees on their payrolls longer than three months. This response to Italy's labor law makes it difficult for many young Italians to earn steady incomes that would permit them to live independently from their parents.

"Learning Objectives" begin each chapter
A clear, numbered list of learning objectives on the first page of the chapter focuses students' studies.

▶ **Chapter-ending "Summary Discussion of Learning Objectives" reviews objectives**
To encourage students to retain important concepts, every chapter ends with a concise yet thorough summary of the key concepts. Each "Summary Discussion" paragraph is numbered to match its corresponding chapter-opening "Learning Objective."

SUMMARY DISCUSSION of Learning Objectives

1. **The Problem of Scarcity, Even for the Affluent:** Scarcity is very different from poverty. No one can obtain all one desires from nature without sacrifice. Thus even the richest people face scarcity because they have to make choices among alternatives. Despite their high levels of income or wealth, affluent people, like everyone else, want more than they can have (in terms of goods, power, prestige, and so on).

2. **Why Economists Consider Individuals' Wants but Not Their "Needs":** Goods are all things from which individuals derive satisfaction. Economic goods are those for which the desired quantity exceeds the amount that is directly available from nature at a zero price. To economists, the term *need* is undefinable, whereas humans have unlimited *wants*, which are defined as the goods and services on which we place a positive value.

3. **Why Scarcity Leads People to Evaluate Opportunity Costs:** We measure the opportunity cost of anything by the highest-valued alternative that one must give up to obtain it. The trade-offs that we face as individuals and as a society can be represented by a production possibilities curve (PPC), and moving from one point on a PPC to another entails incurring an opportunity cost. The reason is that along a PPC, all currently available resources and technology are being used, so obtaining more of one good requires shifting resources to production of that good and away from production of another. That is, there is an opportunity cost of allocating scarce resources toward producing one good instead of another good.

4. **Why Obtaining Increasing Increments of a Good Requires Giving Up More and More Units of Other Goods:** Typically, resources are specialized. Thus, when society allocates additional resources to producing more and more of a single good, it must increasingly employ resources that would be better suited for producing other goods. As a result, the law of increasing relative cost holds. Each additional unit of a good can be obtained only by giving up more and more of other goods, which means that the production possibilities curve that society faces is bowed outward.

5. **The Trade-Off Between Consumption Goods and Capital Goods:** If we allocate more resources to producing capital goods today, then, other things being equal, the economy will grow faster than it would have otherwise. Thus the production possibilities curve will shift outward by a larger amount in the future, which means that we can have more consumption goods in the future. The trade-off, however, is that producing more capital goods today entails giving up consumption goods today.

6. **Absolute Advantage versus Comparative Advantage:** A person has an absolute advantage if she can produce more of a specific good than someone else who uses the same amount of resources. Nevertheless, the individual may be better off producing a different good if she has a comparative advantage in producing that good, meaning that she can produce the good at a lower opportunity cost than someone else. By specializing in producing the good for which she has a comparative advantage, she assures herself of reaping gains from specialization in the form of a higher income.

CONCEPTS in Brief

- Scarcity exists because human wants always exceed what can be produced with the limited resources and time that nature makes available.

- We use scarce resources, such as land, labor, physical and human capital, and entrepreneurship, to produce economic goods—goods that are desired but are not directly obtainable from nature to the extent demanded or desired at a zero price.

- Wants are unlimited; they include all material desires and all nonmaterial desires, such as love, affection, power, and prestige.

- The concept of need is difficult to define objectively for every person; consequently, we simply consider every person's wants to be unlimited. In a world of scarcity, satisfaction of one want necessarily means nonsatisfaction of one or more other wants.

To test your understanding of the concepts covered in this section, go to the Online Review at www.myeconlab.com/miller.

▲ **"Concepts in Brief" offer review of each chapter section**
Encouraging students to review after reading each major section, "Concepts in Brief" summarize the main points of the section to reinforce learning and to encourage rereading of any difficult material. To further test their understanding of the concepts covered, students are encouraged to go to the Online Review at www.myeconlab.com/miller. Please turn to page xxix of this Preface for details on **MyEconLab.**

A variety of chapter-end "Problems"
At the end of each chapter students will find a variety of interesting "Problems" that offer many opportunities to test knowledge and review chapter concepts. Answers for all odd-numbered problems are provided at the back of the textbook.

Superb integration of online resources

Get Ahead of the Curve

Refer to the end of the chapter for a full listing of the multimedia learning materials available in MyEconLab.

"Media Resources" icons at the beginning of each chapter
These helpful prompts remind students to go to the end of the chapter for a full list of the multimedia materials available at **MyEconLab,** the full-featured online homework and tutorial system that accompanies *Economics Today.*

Chapter-end "Media Resources" sections correlated to MyEconLab
These helpful sections at the end of each chapter detail the many media resources—animations, videos, audio clips, and web links—available specifically for that chapter, which students can access by registering at **www.myeconlab.com/miller**.

URLs in the margins guide students to topic-related Web sites
Notes in the margins offer Web addresses—linking students to interesting Web sites that illustrate chapter topics and give students the opportunity to build their economic research skills as they access the latest information on the national and global economy.

"Economics on the Net" activities
These activities are designed to build student research skills and reinforce key concepts. The activities guide students to a Web site and provide structured assignments for both individual and group work.

If your exam were tomorrow, would you be ready? For each chapter, MyEconLab Practice Tests and Study Plans pinpoint which sections you have mastered and which ones you need to study. That way, you are more efficient with your study time, and you are better prepared for your exams.

Here is how it works:
1. Register and log in to www.myeconlab.com/miller.
2. Click on "Take a Test" and select Test A for this chapter.
3. Take the diagnostic test and MyEconLab will grade it automatically and create a personalized Study Plan, so you see which sections of the chapter you should study further.
4. The Study Plan will serve up additional practice problems and tutorials to help you master the specific areas where you need to focus. By practicing online, you can track your progress in the Study Plan.
5. After you have mastered the sections, "Take a Test" and select Test B for this chapter. Take the test, and see how you do!

In addition to Practice Tests and your personalized Study Plan, you'll find the following media resources in MyEcon-Lab:
1. *Graphs in Motion* animation of Figure A-8.
2. Videos featuring the author, Roger LeRoy Miller, on the following subjects:
   ● The Difference Between Microeconomics and Macro-economics
   ● Rational Self-Interest and the Rationality Assumption
   ● Positive versus Normative Economics
3. Links to the Web sites cited in the marginal Internet Resources, Issues and Applications feature, and Economics on the Net activity.
4. Audio clips of all key terms, additional practice problems, and a PDF version of the material from the print Study Guide.
5. eThemes of the Times, which is a New York Times arti-cle to help you understand the real-world applications

Go to www.econtoday.com/chap02 to find out from the World Trade Organization how much international trade takes place. Under "Resources," click on "Trade statistics."

COMPARATIVE ADVANTAGE AND TRADE AMONG NATIONS

Though most of our analysis of absolute advantage, comparative advantage, and special-ization has dealt with individuals, it is equally applicable to nations. First consider the United States. The Plains states have a comparative advantage in the production of grains and other agricultural goods. Relative to the Plains states, the states to the north and east tend to specialize in industrialized production, such as automobiles. Not surprisingly, grains are shipped from the Plains states to the northern states, and automobiles are shipped in the reverse direction. Such specialization and trade allow for higher incomes and standards of living. If both the Plains states and the northern states were separate na-tions, the same analysis would still hold, but we would call it international trade. Indeed, the European Union (EU) is comparable to the United States in area and population, but instead of one nation, the EU has 25. What U.S. residents call *interstate* trade, Europeans call *international* trade. There is no difference, however, in the economic results—both yield greater economic efficiency and higher average incomes.

ECONOMICS ON THE NET

The U.S. Nursing Shortage For some years media stories have discussed a shortage of qualified nurses in the United States. This application explores some of the factors that have caused the quantity of newly trained nurses de-manded to tend to exceed the quantity of newly trained nurses supplied.

Title: Nursing Shortage Resource Web Link

Navigation: Go to the Nursing Shortage Resource Web Link at **www.econtoday.com/chap03**, and click on *Enroll-ment Increase Insufficient to Meet the Projected Increase in Demand for New Nurses.*

Application Read the discussion, and answer the following questions.

1. Since 1995, what has happened to the demand for new nurses in the United States? What has happened to the supply of new nurses? Why has the result been a shortage?
2. If there is a free market for the skills of new nurses, what can you predict is likely to happen to the wage rate earned by individuals who have just completed their nursing training?

For Group Study and Analysis Discuss the pros and cons of high schools and colleges trying to factor predictions about future wages into student career counseling. How might this potentially benefit students? What problems might high schools and colleges face in trying to assist students in evaluating the future earnings prospects of various jobs?

Get Ahead of the Curve

MyEconLab:
The new standard in personalized online learning

MyEconLab—the innovative, resource-packed online homework and tutorial system that is packaged with every new copy of **Economics Today**—puts students in control of their own learning through a suite of study and practice tools correlated with the online, interactive version of the textbook and other media tools. Within **MyEconLab's** structured environment, students practice what they learn, test their understanding, and then pursue a Study Plan that MyEconLab generates for them based on their performance on practice tests.

At the core of MyEconLab are the following features:

Practice Tests—Practice tests for each chapter of the textbook enable students to test their understanding and identify the areas in which they need to do further work. Many practice test questions ask students to work with graphs: interpreting them, manipulating them, and even drawing them. Instructors can let students use the supplied pre-built tests or create their own tests.

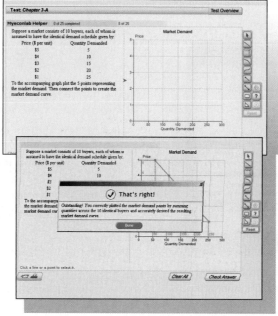

Personalized Study Plan—Using a student's performance on a practice test, a personal Study Plan MyEconLab generates shows where further study is needed. This study plan directs students to a series of additional exercises, including many graphing questions.

Additional Practice Exercises—Using their personalized study plan, students find additional exercises for each topic. These additional practice exercises, which are keyed to each section of the textbook, provide extensive practice and link students to the eText with animated graphs and to other tutorial instruction resources.

Tutorial Instruction—Launched from the additional practice exercises, tutorial instruction is provided in the form of solutions to problems, step-by-step explanations, and other media-based explanations.

Powerful Graphing Tool—Students can draw a graph, and **MyEconLab's** powerful graphing application will evaluate and grade it. Integrated into the practice tests and additional practice exercises, the graphing tool lets students manipulate and even draw graphs so that they get a better feel for how the concepts, numbers, and graphs are connected.

For additional MyEconLab resources, please turn the page ▶

Many time-saving tools for instructors:

MyEconLab provides flexible tools that enable instructors to easily and effectively customize online course materials to suit their needs. Instructors can create and assign tests, quizzes, or graded homework assignments. MyEconLab saves time by automatically grading all questions and tracking results in an online grade book. MyEconLab can even grade assignments that require students to draw a graph. Test Banks can also be used within **MyEconLab,** giving instructors ample material from which they can create assignments.

Once registered for **MyEconLab,** instructors have access to downloadable supplements such as instructor's manuals, PowerPoint® lecture notes, and Test Banks. Instructors can direct their students to the "Ask the Author" feature that allows them to connect directly with the author via e-mail.

For more information about **MyEconLab,** or to request an Instructor Access Code, visit http://www.myeconlab.com.

Get Ahead of the Curve

PLUS many additional MyEconLab resources

▶ **eText**—The entire textbook in electronic format with an audio clip for each glossary item.

▶ **eStudy guide**—The entire *Study Guide* in electronic format and printable.

▶ **Econ Tutor Center**—Staffed by qualified, experienced college economics instructors! The Econ Tutor Center is open five days a week, seven hours a day. Tutors can be reached by phone, fax, e-mail, or White Board technology. The Econ Tutor Center hours are designed to meet your students' study schedules, with evening hours Sunday through Thursday. Students receive one-on-one tutoring on examples, related exercises, and problems.

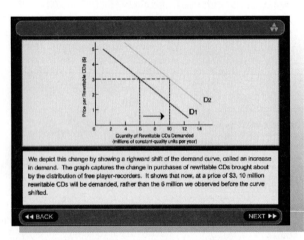

▶ **Animated figures**—145 figures from the textbook presented in step-by-step animations with audio explanations of the action.

▶ **Economics in Motion Animations**—In-depth animations of ten key economic ideas from the textbook—guiding students through precise graphical presentations with detailed audio explanations. A "Content Guide" in each animation allows students to zero in on ideas with which they are struggling.

▶ **Video clips**—Author Roger LeRoy Miller stresses key points in every chapter and further clarifies concepts that students find most difficult to grasp.

▶ **Audio clips**—Featuring an upbeat introduction to each chapter, discussing chapter topics, and focusing student attention on the most critical concepts.

▶ **Glossary Flashcards**—Every key term is available as a flashcard, allowing students to quiz themselves on vocabulary from one or more chapters at a time.

MyEconLab content resources:

▶ **Weekly News**—Featuring a new microeconomic and macroeconomic current events article with discussion questions posted online weekly by Andrew J. Dane of Angelo State University. Students can test their knowledge of current events in a five-question quiz posted each week. Instructor answer keys are available.

▶ **Economics and Your Everyday Life**—An online booklet offering numerous practical applications of economics and guidance for analyzing economic news.

▶ **eThemes of the Times**—Archived articles from *The New York Times*, correlated to each textbook chapter and paired with critical thinking questions.

▶ **Research Navigator**—Extensive help on the research process and four exclusive databases of accredited and reliable source material including The *New York Times*, *The Financial Times*, and peer-reviewed journals.

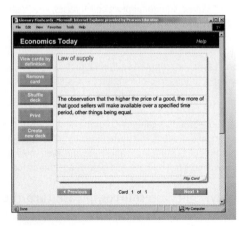

Essential teaching tools to help busy instructors maximize their time

Test Bank 1—This Test Bank provides more than 3,750 multiple-choice and 250 short-essay questions with answers. Revised by Judy Roobian-Mohr of Columbus State Community College and Michael Goode of Central Piedmont Community College, the questions have undergone extensive classroom testing for a number of years.

Test Bank 2—Revised by Diane L. Stehman of Northeastern Illinois University, this Test Bank includes more than 3,250 multiple-choice and 250 short-essay questions. All questions have been class-tested by many professors, including Clark G. Ross, coauthor of the National Competency Test for economics majors for the Educational Testing Service in Princeton, New Jersey.

Test Bank 3—This Test Bank features 3,250 test questions expertly assembled from a team of contributors by G. Dirk Mateer of Penn State University. *Test Bank 3* incorporates the best question-writing tactics and time-tested approaches of a number of dedicated and experienced instructors, including lead contributor Susan Glanz of St. Joseph's University and contributors Bruce W. Bellner of Ohio State University–Marion, Marie Duggan of Keene State College, Teresa Laughlin of Pomona College, Debbie Mullin of the University of Colorado at Colorado Springs, Densel L. Myers of Oklahoma City Community College, and David Schlow of Penn State University.

Instructor's Manual—Prepared by Andrew J. Dane of Angelo State University, the *Instructor's Manual* provides a new section featuring lecture-ready examples presented in the same format as the in-text examples. It also includes the following materials:

▶ Chapter overviews, objectives, and outlines
▶ Points to emphasize for instructors who wish to stress theory
▶ Answers to "Issues and Applications" critical thinking questions
▶ Further questions for class discussion
▶ Answers to all end-of-chapter problems (even and odd)
▶ Detailed step-by-step analyses of the end-of-chapter problems
▶ Suggested answers to "Economics Front and Center" case questions
▶ Annotated answers to selected student learning questions
▶ Selected references

Instructor's Resource Disk with PowerPoint Lecture Presentation.

Compatible with Windows and Macintosh computers, this CD-ROM provides numerous resources. The PowerPoint® Lecture Presentation was developed by Jeff Caldwell, Steve Smith, and Mark Mitchell of Rose State College and revised by Debbie Mullin of the University of Colorado at Colorado Springs. The PowerPoint® Lecture Presentation features graphs from the text and outlines key terms, concepts, and figures. For added convenience, the CD-ROM also includes Microsoft Word files for the entire content of the *Instructor's Manual* and computerized test bank files of *Test Banks 1, 2,* and *3*. The easy-to-use testing software (TestGen with QuizMaster for Windows and Macintosh) is a valuable test preparation tool that allows professors to view, edit, and add questions. *You will have 10,750 questions at your fingertips!*

Four-Color Overhead Transparencies—One hundred of the most important graphs from the textbook are reproduced as full-color transparency acetates. Many contain multiple overlays.

Proven resources guarantee student success—available for convenient packaging with this text

In addition to access to **MyEconLab,** the student's ultimate online tool, which is automatically packaged with each text, the following supplementary materials are available to aid and enhance students' mastery of concepts:

Micro-View and Macro-View Study Guides

Written by Roger LeRoy Miller and updated by David VanHoose, these valuable guides offer the practice and review students need to excel in this course. They have been thoroughly revised to take into account the significant changes in many of the chapters of the Thirteenth Edition. Each *Study Guide* is firmly oriented toward helping students learn what they need to know to succeed in the course—and in life. Electronic versions of the *Study Guides* are available on **MyEconLab.**

Economist.com Edition

The premier online source of economic news analysis, **Economist.com** provides your students with insight and opinion on current economic events. Through an agreement between Addison-Wesley and *The Economist,* students can receive a low-cost subscription to this premium Web site for three months, including the complete text of the current issue of *The Economist* and access to *The Economist's* searchable archives. Other features include Web-only weekly articles, news feeds with current world and business news, and stock market and currency data. Professors who adopt this special edition will receive a complimentary one-year subscription to **Economist.com.**

Wall Street Journal Edition

When packaged with the Miller text, Addison-Wesley offers students a reduced cost, 10- or 15-week subscription to the *Wall Street Journal* print edition and the *Wall Street Journal Interactive Edition.* Adopting professors will receive a complimentary one-year subscription to both the print and interactive versions.

Financial Times Edition

Featuring international news and analysis from journalists in more than 50 countries, *The Financial Times* will provide your students with insights and perspectives on economic developments around the world. For a small charge, a 15-week subscription to *The Financial Times* can be included with each new textbook. Adopting professors will receive a complimentary one-year subscription, as well as access to the online edition at **FT.com.**

The Dismal Scientist Edition

The Dismal Scientist provides real-time monitoring of the global economy allowing your students to go beyond theory and into application. For a nominal fee, a three-month subscription to *The Dismal Scientist* can be included with each new textbook. Each subscription includes complete access to all of *The Dismal Scientist's* award winning features. Professors adopting a book on this list receive a complimentary one-year subscription.

Pearson Choice Alternate Editions

With ever-increasing demands on time and resources, today's college faculty and students want greater value, innovation, and flexibility in products designed to meet teaching and learning goals. We've responded to that need by creating **PearsonChoices,** a unique program that allows faculty and students to choose from a range of text and media formats that match their teaching and learning styles—and, in the case of students, their budget.

Books à la Carte Edition

For today's student on the go, we've created highly portable versions of the **Economics Today** textbooks that are three-hole punched. Students can take only what they need to class, incorporate their own notes—and save money! Each *Books à la Carte* text arrives with a laminated study card, perfect for students to use when preparing for exams, plus access to **MyEconLab.**

MyEconLab Xpress Edition

The *Xpress Edition* contains access to all **MyEconLab** resources—including the eText—and a laminated study card. Students receive all the critical course content and powerful study tools included in **MyEconLab** at approximately half the cost of the full print textbook.

Chapter 1
The Nature of Economics

hirty years ago, only about 5 percent of all
U.S. residents between the ages of 2 and 19
were sufficiently overweight to be classified
as "obese." Since then, however, the obesity rate
among U.S. children and adolescents has increased to more than 15 percent. Why
are there so many more obese children and adolescents? It is tempting to look first
to the medical profession for an answer to this question. Most individuals who become overweight, however, consciously *choose* to consume more calories than
they use up through daily exercise. Increasingly, therefore, society is looking to
economists, who specialize in understanding how people make self-interested decisions in response to incentives—that is, rewards, or inducements—they face, to
develop a better understanding of why the rate of obesity among U.S. children has
increased.

LEARNING OBJECTIVES

After reading this chapter, you should be able to:

1. Discuss the difference between microeconomics and macroeconomics
2. Evaluate the role that rational self-interest plays in economic
   analysis
3. Explain why economics is a science
4. Distinguish between positive and normative economics

Media Resources

Refer to the end of the
chapter for a full listing of the
multimedia learning materials
available in MyEconLab.

Did You Know That ... more than half of all Italians aged 20 to 29 live with their parents? A labor law contributes to this state of affairs. Under the law, firing a worker who has been on a company's payroll longer than a three-month probationary period exposes the company to the risk that a judge will rule that the company did not have "just" cause to dismiss the employee. In this event, the company must reinstate the employee, reimburse the employee for back wages, and pay a fine to the government. Rather than expose themselves to this risk, the owners of many Italian companies have determined that it is in their self-interest *not* to keep new employees on their payrolls longer than three months. This response to Italy's labor law makes it difficult for many young Italians to earn steady incomes that would permit them to live independently from their parents.

In this chapter, you will learn why studying the nature of self-interested responses to **incentives** is the starting point for analyzing choices people make in all walks of life. After all, just as Italian companies have responded to legal incentives they face by limiting new workers' terms of employment, how much time you end up devoting to your study of economics depends in part on incentives established by your instructor's system of determining your grade. As you will see, self-interest and incentives are the underpinnings for all the decisions you and others around you make each day.

Incentives
Rewards for engaging in a particular activity.

THE POWER OF ECONOMIC ANALYSIS

Simply knowing that self-interest and incentives are central to any decision-making process is not sufficient for predicting the choices that people will actually make. You also have to develop a framework that will allow you to analyze solutions to each economic problem—whether you are trying to decide how much to study, which courses to take, whether to finish school, or whether the U.S. government should send troops abroad or raise taxes. The framework that you will learn in this text is the *economic way of thinking.*

This framework gives you power—the power to reach informed conclusions about what is happening in the world. You can, of course, live your life without the power of economic analysis as part of your analytical framework. Indeed, most people do. But economists believe that economic analysis can help you make better decisions concerning your career, your education, financing your home, and other important matters. In the business world, the power of economic analysis can help you increase your competitive edge as an employee or as the owner of a business. As a voter, for the rest of your life you will be asked to make judgments about policies that are advocated by political parties. Many of these policies will deal with questions related to international economics, such as whether the U.S. government should encourage or discourage immigration, prevent foreigners from investing in domestic TV stations and newspapers, or restrict other countries from selling their goods here.

Finally, just as taking an art, music, or literature appreciation class increases the pleasure you receive when you view paintings, listen to concerts, or read novels, taking an economics course will increase your understanding when watching the news on TV or reading articles in the newspaper or at Web sites.

DEFINING ECONOMICS

What is economics exactly? Some cynics have defined *economics* as "common sense made difficult." But common sense, by definition, should be within everyone's grasp. You will encounter in the following pages numerous examples that show that economics is, in fact, pure and simple common sense.

Economics is part of the social sciences and as such seeks explanations of real events. All social sciences analyze human behavior, as opposed to the physical sciences, which generally analyze the behavior of electrons, atoms, and other nonhuman phenomena.

Economics is the study of how people allocate their limited resources in an attempt to satisfy their unlimited wants. As such, economics is the study of how people make choices.

To understand this definition fully, two other words need explaining: *resources* and *wants*. **Resources** are things that have value and, more specifically, are used to produce things that satisfy people's wants. **Wants** are all of the things that people would purchase if they had unlimited income.

Whenever an individual, a business, or a nation faces alternatives, a choice must be made, and economics helps us study how those choices are made. For example, you have to choose how to spend your limited income. You also have to choose how to spend your limited time. You may have to choose how much of your company's limited funds to spend on advertising and how much to spend on new-product research. In economics, we examine situations in which individuals choose how to do things, when to do things, and with whom to do them. Ultimately, the purpose of economics is to explain choices.

Economics
The study of how people allocate their limited resources to satisfy their unlimited wants.

Resources
Things used to produce other things to satisfy people's wants.

Wants
What people would buy if their incomes were unlimited.

MICROECONOMICS VERSUS MACROECONOMICS

Economics is typically divided into two types of analysis: **microeconomics** and **macroeconomics.**

Microeconomics is the part of economic analysis that studies decision making undertaken by individuals (or households) and by firms. It is like looking through a microscope to focus on the small parts of our economy.

Macroeconomics is the part of economic analysis that studies the behavior of the economy as a whole. It deals with economywide phenomena such as changes in unemployment, the general price level, and national income.

Microeconomic analysis, for example, is concerned with the effects of changes in the price of gasoline relative to that of other energy sources. It examines the effects of new taxes on a specific product or industry. If price controls were reinstituted in the United States, how individual firms and consumers would react to them would be in the realm of microeconomics. The effects of higher wages brought about by an effective union strike would also be analyzed using the tools of microeconomics.

In contrast, issues such as the rate of inflation, the amount of economywide unemployment, and the yearly growth in the output of goods and services in the nation all fall into the realm of macroeconomic analysis. In other words, macroeconomics deals with **aggregates,** or totals—such as total output in an economy.

Be aware, however, of the blending of microeconomics and macroeconomics in modern economic theory. Modern economists are increasingly using microeconomic analysis—the study of decision making by individuals and by firms—as the basis of macroeconomic analysis. They do this because even though in macroeconomic analysis aggregates are being examined, those aggregates are the result of choices made by individuals and firms.

Microeconomics
The study of decision making undertaken by individuals (or households) and by firms.

Macroeconomics
The study of the behavior of the economy as a whole, including such economywide phenomena as changes in unemployment, the general price level, and national income.

Aggregates
Total amounts or quantities; aggregate demand, for example, is total planned expenditures throughout a nation.

Go to www.econtoday.com/chap01 to access the eCommerce Info Center and explore whether it is in a consumer's self-interest to shop on the Internet. Click on "To e-shoppers."

THE ECONOMIC PERSON: RATIONAL SELF-INTEREST

Economists assume that individuals act *as if* motivated by self-interest and respond predictably to opportunities for gain. This central insight of economics was first clearly articulated by Adam Smith in 1776. Smith wrote in his most famous book, *An Inquiry into the*

Nature and Causes of the Wealth of Nations, that "it is not from the benevolence of the butcher, the brewer, or the baker that we expect our dinner, but from their regard to their own interest." Thus the typical person about whom economists make behavioral predictions is assumed to act as though motivated by self-interest. Because monetary benefits and costs of actions are often the most easily measured, economists make behavioral predictions about individuals' responses to opportunities to increase their wealth, measured in money terms. Is it possible to apply the theory of rational self-interest to explain why many couples who mutually desire to end their marriages now use online divorce services?

E-Commerce EXAMPLE

Divorce Court Moves to the Internet

At Web sites such as CompleteCase.com and LegalZoom.com, a couple desiring to amicably dissolve their marriage can provide sufficient information to obtain fully completed legal divorce papers for fees ranging from $250 to $300. For another $50 to $100, they can also obtain all the information required to file their papers with a court to end their marriage legally. These online prices are much lower than the fees of $2,000 or so that divorce lawyers typically charge simply to fill out and process the same required legal forms.

When there are no child-custody or property-division issues to iron out, it is often in a couple's self-interest to bypass traditional lawyers to obtain a divorce. Not surprisingly, the total number of do-it-yourself divorces arranged online has more than doubled each year since Web-based preparers of divorce papers began operating in the early 2000s.

For Critical Analysis
Under what types of circumstances might a self-interested marriage partner be willing to pay an attorney much more than $2,000 to handle legal issues associated with obtaining a divorce?

The Rationality Assumption

Rationality assumption
The assumption that people do not intentionally make decisions that would leave them worse off.

The **rationality assumption** of economics, simply stated, is as follows:

> *We assume that individuals do not intentionally make decisions that would leave them worse off.*

The distinction here is between what people may think—the realm of psychology and psychiatry and perhaps sociology—and what they do. Economics does *not* involve itself in analyzing individual or group thought processes. Economics looks at what people actually do in life with their limited resources. It does little good to criticize the rationality assumption by stating, "Nobody thinks that way" or "I never think that way" or "How unrealistic! That's as irrational as anyone can get!"

Take the example of driving. When you consider passing another car on a two-lane highway with oncoming traffic, you have to make very quick decisions: You must estimate the speed of the car that you are going to pass, the speed of the oncoming cars, the distance between your car and the oncoming cars, and your car's potential rate of acceleration. If we were to apply a model to your behavior, we would use the rules of calculus. In actual fact, you and most other drivers in such a situation do not actually think of using the rules of calculus, but to predict your behavior, we could make the prediction *as if* you understood the rules of calculus.

How could experiments seeking to determine whether students are willing to trade coffee mugs for chocolate bars have led some researchers to question the rationality assumption?

EXAMPLE

Using Coffee Mugs to Attack the Rationality Assumption

Some researchers have challenged the rationality assumption based on results from numerous repetitions of the following experiment: Everyone in a group of university students is asked whether they would prefer to have a coffee mug or an identically priced chocolate bar. After recording the typical response that about half of the students prefer the chocolate bar, the experimenter randomly gives half of the students coffee mugs and the other half chocolate bars. Then the experimenter invites students who did not receive a preferred item to trade with other students who also failed to receive an item they desired. Only about half the students will have received their preferred items, so on average the other half should make trades. But in experiment after experiment, fewer than 10 percent typically do. According to some researchers, this provides evidence of irrational attachment to goods—and a contradiction to the rationality assumption of economics.

John List of the University of Maryland conducted the same experiment with people who commonly trade sports memorabilia, such as baseball cards, professional players' au-

tographs, and the like. In repeated experiments with these groups, about half of those who randomly received undesired coffee mugs and chocolate bars readily engaged in trades. Perhaps because they were less likely to suspect hidden motives by the experimenter, people who commonly engage in trade were more willing to do so. Thus the coffee mug-chocolate bar trading experiments have only shown that *inexperienced* traders are less likely to readily exchange items, while experienced traders are more likely to do so. The experiments have not disproved the rationality assumption.

For Critical Analysis

Why might it be rational for someone to be hesitant to trade a coffee mug for a more desirable chocolate bar when an experimenter offers an opportunity to do so? (Hint: Imagine yourself in the described experiment, and suppose that you have never before met either the person conducting the experiment or the other students participating in the experiment.)

Responding to Incentives

If it can be assumed that individuals never intentionally make decisions that would leave them worse off, then almost by definition they will respond to changes in incentives. Indeed, much of human behavior can be explained in terms of how individuals respond to changing incentives over time.

Schoolchildren are motivated to do better by a variety of incentive systems, ranging from gold stars and certificates of achievement when they are young, to better grades with accompanying promises of a "better life" as they get older. Of course, negative incentives affect our behavior, too. Punishments and other forms of negative incentives can raise the cost of engaging in criminal activities, for instance. This is why policymakers sometimes turn to economists for help with understanding the effects that alternative forms of punishment, such as the death penalty, are likely to have on crime rates. Does the death penalty actually affect murder rates?

Policy EXAMPLE

Does Imposing the Ultimate Legal Penalty Deter Homicides?

Figure 1-1 on the following page shows that a drop in the annual number of legally sanctioned executions in the United States between the late 1950s and early 1980s was accompa-

nied by an increase in the U.S. murder rate. When the number of executions rose during the 1990s and early 2000s, the U.S. murder rate declined.

The extent to which the threat of receiving a death penalty actually contributes to lower murder rates depends on a host of other incentives, however. For instance, if more states reduce the chances of a convicted murderer receiving the death penalty, the disincentive to committing murders is reduced. In contrast, the disincentive effects of the death penalty are likely to be greater if prison conditions improve, thereby making the death penalty a much less desirable alternative punishment.

Economists have found that when these and other factors are taken into account, every *additional* legally sanctioned execution is associated with about five to six fewer homicides. Each judicial *reduction* of a death-penalty sentence to imprisonment is associated with the occurrence of one to two additional murders. Thus both the execution rate and the rate at which death-penalty sentences are reduced to long-term imprisonment have incentive effects on people contemplating murder.

For Critical Analysis

Why do you suppose that careful economic studies of the effects of the death penalty on homicide rates take into account whether people who committed murders might have been under the influence of alcohol or drugs?

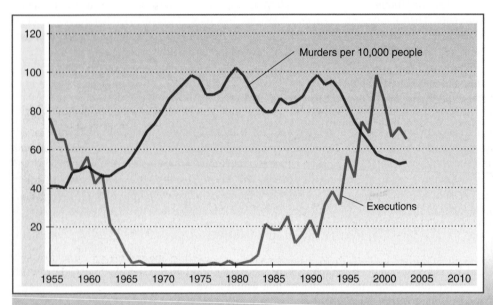

FIGURE 1-1

Murder Rates and Executions in the United States Since 1955

Since the mid-1950s, there has been an apparent negative relationship between the number of death-penalty sentences carried out and the U.S. murder rate.

Source: U.S. Department of Justice.

Defining Self-Interest

Self-interest does not always mean increasing one's wealth measured in dollars and cents. We assume that individuals seek many goals, not just increased wealth measured in monetary terms. Thus the self-interest part of our economic-person assumption includes goals relating to prestige, friendship, love, power, helping others, creating works of art, and many other matters. We can also think in terms of enlightened self-interest, whereby individuals, in the pursuit of what makes them better off, also achieve the betterment of others around them. In brief, individuals are assumed to want the right to further their goals by making decisions about how things around them are used. The head of a charitable organization will usually not turn down an additional contribution, because accepting it yields control over how those funds are used, even if it is for other people's benefit.

Thus charitable acts are not ruled out by self-interest. Giving gifts to relatives can be considered a form of charity that is nonetheless in the self-interest of the giver. But how efficient is such gift giving?

EXAMPLE

The Perceived Value of Gifts

Every holiday season, aunts, uncles, grandparents, mothers, and fathers give gifts to their college-aged loved ones. Joel Waldfogel, an economist at Yale University, surveyed several thousand college students after Christmas to find out the value of holiday gifts. He found that compact discs and outerwear (coats and jackets) had a perceived intrinsic value about equal to their actual cash equivalent. By the time he got down the list to socks, underwear, and cosmetics, the students' valu-

ation was only about 85 percent of the cash value of the gift. He found out that aunts, uncles, and grandparents gave the "worst" gifts and friends, siblings, and parents gave the "best."

For Critical Analysis
What argument could you use against the idea of substituting cash or gift certificates for physical gifts?

CONCEPTS in Brief

- Economics is a social science that involves the study of how individuals choose among alternatives to satisfy their wants, which are what people would buy if their incomes were unlimited.

- Microeconomics, the study of the decision-making processes of individuals (or households) and firms, and macroeconomics, the study of the performance of the economy as a whole, are the two main branches into which the study of economics is divided.

- In economics, we assume that people do not intentionally make decisions that will leave them worse off. This is known as the rationality assumption.

- Self-interest is not confined to material well-being but also involves any action that makes a person feel better off, such as having more friends, love, power, affection, or providing more help to others.

To test your understanding of the concepts covered in this section, go to the Online Review at www.myeconlab.com/miller.

ECONOMICS AS A SCIENCE

Economics is a social science that employs the same kinds of methods used in other sciences, such as biology, physics, and chemistry. Like these other sciences, economics uses models, or theories. Economic **models,** or **theories,** are simplified representations of the real world that we use to help us understand, explain, and predict economic phenomena in the real world. There are, of course, differences between sciences. The social sciences—especially economics—make little use of laboratory experiments in which changes in variables are studied under controlled conditions. Rather, social scientists, and especially economists, usually have to test their models, or theories, by examining what has already happened in the real world.

Models, or theories
Simplified representations of the real world used as the basis for predictions or explanations.

Models and Realism

At the outset it must be emphasized that no model in *any* science, and therefore no economic model, is complete in the sense that it captures *every* detail or interrelationship that exists. Indeed, a model, by definition, is an abstraction from reality. It is conceptually impossible to construct a perfectly complete realistic model. For example, in physics we cannot account for every molecule and its position and certainly not for every atom and subparticle. Not only is such a model impossibly expensive to build, but working with it would be impossibly complex.

The nature of scientific model building is that the model should capture only the *essential* relationships that are sufficient to analyze the particular problem or answer the particular question with which we are concerned. *An economic model cannot be faulted as unrealistic simply because it does not represent every detail of the real world.* A map of a city that shows only major streets is not necessarily unrealistic if, in fact, all you need to know is how to pass through the city using major streets. As long as a model is able to shed light on the *central* issue at hand or forces at work, it may be useful.

A map is the quintessential model. It is always a simplified representation. It is always unrealistic. But it is also useful in making predictions about the world. If the model—the map—predicts that when you take Campus Avenue to the north, you always run into the campus, that is a prediction. If our goal is to explain observed behavior, the simplicity or complexity of the model we use is irrelevant. If a simple model can explain observed behavior in repeated settings just as well as a complex one, the simple model has some value and is probably easier to use.

Assumptions

Every model, or theory, must be based on a set of assumptions. Assumptions define the set of circumstances in which our model is most likely to be applicable. When scientists predicted that sailing ships would fall off the edge of the earth, they used the *assumption* that the earth was flat. Columbus did not accept the implications of such a model because he did not accept its assumptions. He assumed that the world was round. The real-world test of his own model refuted the flat-earth model. Indirectly, then, it was a test of the assumption of the flat-earth model.

Is it possible to use our knowledge about assumptions to understand why driving directions sometimes contain very few details?

E X A M P L E

Getting Directions

Assumptions are a shorthand for reality. Imagine that you have decided to drive from your home in San Diego to downtown San Francisco. Because you have never driven this route, you decide to get directions from the local office of the American Automobile Association (AAA).

When you ask for directions, the travel planner could give you a set of detailed maps that shows each city through which you will travel—Oceanside, San Clemente, Irvine, Anaheim, Los Angeles, Bakersfield, Modesto, and so on—and then, opening each map, show you exactly how the freeway threads through each of these cities. You would get a nearly complete description of reality because the AAA travel planner will not have used many simplifying assumptions. It is more likely,

however, that the travel planner will simply say, "Get on Interstate 5 going north. Stay on it for about 500 miles. Follow the signs for San Francisco. After crossing the toll bridge, take any exit marked 'Downtown.'" By omitting all of the trivial details, the travel planner has told you all that you really need and want to know. The models you will be using in this text are similar to the simplified directions on how to drive from San Diego to San Francisco—they focus on what is relevant to the problem at hand and omit what is not.

For Critical Analysis
In what way do small talk and gossip represent the use of simplifying assumptions?

The *Ceteris Paribus* Assumption: All Other Things Being Equal. Everything in the world seems to relate in some way to everything else in the world. It would be impossible to isolate the effects of changes in one variable on another variable if we always had to worry about the many other variables that might also enter the analysis. Like other sciences, economics uses the ***ceteris paribus* assumption.** *Ceteris paribus* means "other things constant" or "other things equal."

Consider an example taken from economics. One of the most important determinants of how much of a particular product a family buys is how expensive that product is relative to other products. We know that in addition to relative prices, other factors influence decisions about making purchases. Some of them have to do with income, others with tastes, and yet others with custom and religious beliefs. Whatever these other factors are, we hold them constant when we look at the relationship between changes in prices and changes in how much of a given product people will purchase.

Deciding on the Usefulness of a Model

We generally do not attempt to determine the usefulness, or "goodness," of a model merely by evaluating how realistic its assumptions are. Rather, we consider a model "good" if it yields usable predictions and implications for the real world. In other words, can we use the model to predict what will happen in the world around us? Does the model provide useful implications of how things happen in our world?

Once we have determined that the model does predict real-world phenomena, the scientific approach to the analysis of the world around us requires that we consider evidence. Evidence is used to test the usefulness of a model. This is why we call economics an **empirical** science, *empirical* meaning that evidence (data) is looked at to see whether we are right. Economists are often engaged in empirically testing their models.

Consider two competing models for the way students act when doing complicated probability problems to choose the best gambles. One model predicts that based on the assumption of rational self-interest, students who are paid more money for better performance will perform better on average during the experiment. A competing model might be that students whose last names start with the letters *A* through *L* will do better than students with last names starting with *M* through *Z,* regardless of how much they are paid. Presumably, the model that consistently predicts more accurately is the model that we would normally choose if we wanted to understand the world. In this example, the "alphabet" model did not work well: The first letter of the last name of the students who actually did the experiment at UCLA was irrelevant in predicting how well they would perform the mathematical calculations necessary to choose the correct gambles. On average, students who received higher cash payments for better gambles did choose a higher percentage of better gambles. Thus the model based on rational self-interest predicted well.

Models of Behavior, Not Thought Processes

Take special note of the fact that economists' models do not relate to the way people *think;* they relate to the way people *act,* to what they do in life with their limited resources. Models tend to generalize human behavior. Normally, the economist does not attempt to predict how people will think about a particular topic, such as a higher price of oil products, accelerated inflation, or higher taxes. Rather, the task at hand is to predict how people will behave, which may be quite different from what they *say* they will do (much to the consternation of poll takers and market researchers). The people involved in examining thought processes are psychologists and psychiatrists, not typically economists.

If you ask people whether they like the routines in their lives, they usually say that they don't. But, then, why do so many people stick to so many routines in their day-to-day existences?

***Ceteris paribus* [KAY-ter-us PEAR-uh-bus] assumption**
The assumption that nothing changes except the factor or factors being studied.

Empirical
Relying on real-world data in evaluating the usefulness of a model.

Economics Front and Center

To see why thought processes regarding the pros and cons of sticking to a routine schedule ultimately amount to making choices about *actions* that are in one's self-interest, contemplate the case study,

Confronting a New Week—And Assessing Self-Interest,
on page 11.

E X A M P L E

The Costs and Benefits of Being Stuck in a Rut

Following a routine entails engaging in a customary or regular course of procedure from day to day. Routine is boring, and in random surveys, people claim to avoid it whenever possible. Nevertheless, there are benefits to routine scheduling of daily activities. People who work for a living are more likely to stick to set routines. Following similar daily and weekly routines can also allow spouses to spend more time together. Therefore, even though people consistently say in surveys that they avoid following routines, we can predict that married people with jobs are in fact likely, *ceteris paribus*, to follow relatively systematic daily schedules. In fact, studies of how people budget their time provide evidence supporting these predictions.

One *ceteris paribus* qualification concerning these predictions is extremely important. Irrespective of a person's involvement in the workplace or marital status, a key factor influencing just how much an individual tends to follow a routine is the person's income. Higher-income people have a greater ability than lower-income individuals to purchase more varied schedules in the form of evening dinners and weekend trips. Consequently, their schedules tend to include more nonroutine activities.

For Critical Analysis
What other factors, besides involvement in the workplace, marital status, and income, do you think are likely to influence whether an individual tends to follow a daily routine?

POSITIVE VERSUS NORMATIVE ECONOMICS

Positive economics
Analysis that is *strictly* limited to making either purely descriptive statements or scientific predictions; for example, "If A, then B." A statement of *what is*.

Normative economics
Analysis involving value judgments about economic policies; relates to whether things are good or bad. A statement of *what ought to be*.

Economics uses *positive analysis,* a value-free approach to inquiry. No subjective or moral judgments enter into the analysis. Positive analysis relates to statements such as "If A, then B." For example, "If the price of gasoline goes up relative to all other prices, then the amount of it that people will buy will fall." That is a positive economic statement. It is a statement of *what is*. It is not a statement of anyone's value judgment or subjective feelings. For many problems analyzed in the hard sciences such as physics and chemistry, the analyses are considered to be virtually value-free. After all, how can someone's values enter into a theory of molecular behavior? But economists face a different problem. They deal with the behavior of individuals, not molecules. That makes it more difficult to stick to what we consider to be value-free or **positive economics** without reference to our feelings.

When our values are interjected into the analysis, we enter the realm of **normative economics,** involving *normative analysis*. A positive economic statement is "If the price of gas rises, people will buy less." If we add to that analysis the statement "so we should not allow the price to go up," we have entered the realm of normative economics—we have expressed a value judgment. In fact, any time you see the word *should,* you will know that values are entering into the discussion. Just remember that positive statements are concerned with *what is,* whereas normative statements are concerned with *what ought to be*.

Each of us has a desire for different things. That means that we have different values. When we express a value judgment, we are simply saying what we prefer, like, or desire. Because individual values are diverse, we expect—and indeed observe—people expressing widely varying value judgments about how the world ought to be.

A Warning: Recognize Normative Analysis

It is easy to define positive economics. It is quite another matter to catch all unlabeled normative statements in a textbook, even though an author goes over the manuscript many times before it is printed. Therefore, do not get the impression that a textbook author will be able to keep all personal values out of the book. They will slip through. In fact, the very choice of which topics to include in an introductory textbook involves normative economics. There is no value-free way to decide which topics to use in a textbook. The author's values ultimately make a difference when choices have to be made. But from your own standpoint, you might want to be able to recognize when you are engaging in normative as opposed to positive economic analysis. Reading this text will help equip you for that task.

CONCEPTS in Brief

- A model, or theory, uses assumptions and is by nature a simplification of the real world. The usefulness of a model can be evaluated by bringing empirical evidence to bear on its predictions.

- Models are not necessarily deficient simply because they are unrealistic and use simplifying assumptions, because every model in every science requires simplification compared to the real world.

- Most models use the *ceteris paribus* assumption that all other things are held constant, or equal.

- Positive economics is value-free and relates to statements that can be refuted, such as "If A, then B." Normative economics involves people's values, and normative statements typically contain the word *should*.

To test your understanding of the concepts covered in this section, go to the Online Review at **www.myeconlab.com/miller**.

CASE STUDY: Economics Front and Center

Confronting a New Week—And Assessing Self-Interest

Stevenson, a first-semester college sophomore, awakens to a sunny Monday morning. As the cobwebs clear from his mind, he realizes that another week is beginning. Today he will face the same schedule as last Monday, and his schedule will be the same next Monday and the Monday after that. Furthermore, his basic schedule for the rest of the week will be essentially identical to last week's schedule and to the schedule for several weeks to come. He is sick of all this routine, and the thought of getting up to confront the same routine today and the rest of the week is almost unbearable. He contemplates sleeping in, skipping classes, and taking a one- or two-day mini-vacation.

Stevenson has observed, however, that his fellow students who attend all their classes each and every day and stick to a regular study schedule typically earn the highest grades and land the best jobs. In addition, a fellow student whom he hopes may eventually become his "significant other" will be at his 9 A.M. class.

The class meeting could prove his only opportunity to suggest studying together at the library a couple of nights each week. Stevenson does not have sufficient funds on hand to suggest discussing common interests over dinner at a nice restaurant.

What principle will guide Stevenson in deciding whether to stay stuck in a rut on this particular Monday? The answer, of course, is self-interest. The issue Stevenson faces now is determining how to *act* in his own self-interest.

Points to Analyze

1. What are the advantages and disadvantages to Stevenson of following his regular routine this week?

2. If Stevenson's roommate interrupts his thoughts to repay a $100 loan he had extended last week, how might this influence his decision about where his self-interest will lead him on this particular Monday?

Applying Economics to the Problem of Childhood Obesity

Concepts Applied
- Decision Making
- Rational Self-Interest
- Incentives

According to current medical standards, more than 65 percent of the U.S. population is overweight. This figure is about 20 percentage points higher than was true in 1980. More than 30 percent of the population is extremely overweight, or obese, which is more than double the 1980 figure.

It appears likely that even more people will be overweight or obese in future years because people are getting heavier at younger ages. As noted before, more than 15 percent of U.S. children and adolescents are obese today, compared to about 5 percent in the 1970s. Once body mass is gained, it is difficult to shed. Thus many of these children will probably remain obese and confront the associated health problems later when they reach maturity.

Like Most Things, Obesity Begins at Home

Children who gain weight consume more calories than they use up each day. Those who gain weight the fastest eat relatively larger amounts of high-calorie foods, such as hamburgers and french fries. They also spend more time watching television and playing video games rather than burning calories by playing in parks and participating in sports activities.

Traditionally, parents—in particular, mothers—have taken responsibility for making choices about children's food intake and the scope of their outdoor activities. Today parents are not allocating as much time to these duties as they once did. In the 1960s, fewer than half of all mothers had jobs, but today more than three-fourths of mothers work outside the home. These mothers have less time to spend keeping their children from eating too much or taking them to playgrounds for exercise. This undoubtedly helps explain why only about 8 percent of children whose mothers have never worked are obese, whereas the obesity rate rises to more than 17 percent among children whose mothers have worked full-time. Indeed, economists estimate that children with working mothers are roughly twice as likely to be obese as children with stay-at-home moms.

Schools Contribute to a Feeding Frenzy

Parents who choose to allocate more time to working than to overseeing their children entrust other caregivers—usually administrators and employees at day-care centers, preschools, and elementary and secondary schools—with providing that supervision. When it comes to planning a child's schedule, however, most caregivers have little incentive to include daily exercise that would burn off children's calories.

Furthermore, more than 25 percent of U.S. elementary schools give students access to vending machines with snacks, and 16 percent have contracts for delivery of lunch items from fast-food providers. Vending machines are present in 67 percent of middle schools and 96 percent of high schools. Furthermore, more than 25 percent of all middle schools and high schools contract with fast-food purveyors to provide a portion of the foods sold on school premises. Schools often earn a share of the profits from sales of snacks and fast-food lunches. Therefore, a number of school administrators have a strong economic incentive to encourage children to consume *more,* not fewer, high-calorie snacks and fast-food items.

Incentives, Incentives, Incentives

Incentives matter for children and adults alike. Children naturally have an incentive to consume sweet snacks and lunch on the best-tasting foods. Many children also prefer watching television or playing computer games in climate-controlled surroundings to working up a sweat on a playground. Parents increasingly have incentives to spend less time regulating their children's diets and activities. Few caregivers of children have an incentive to encourage exercise, and many have a strong financial incentive to encourage the consumption of high-calorie food and drinks.

Although children can engage in more activities while seated than in years past, they have always enjoyed eating sweets and lounging on sofas. What have changed are mainly the incentives faced by adult supervisors, who fail to encourage children to eat more healthful foods and to get more exercise. Parental choices about time allocations and school choices about daily schedules and availability of vending machines and fast-food items at schools are all economic decisions made in light of the incentives faced by parents and caregivers. Reducing the rate of child obesity, therefore, will require changes in the economic incentives confronting these adult supervisors of children.

For Critical Analysis

1. From an economic standpoint, is it possible that some parents effectively make a choice to have bigger, more expensive houses *and* overweight children? (Hint: To be able to purchase more expensive houses, parents must spend more time earning incomes and less time rearing their children.)
2. How might bans on the sale and consumption of snacks and fast foods on school grounds, which several states have begun to adopt, affect the incentives of children who have a taste for such items? (Hint: If there are convenience stores on busy streets within walking distance of schools with such bans, how are at least some students likely to respond?)

Web Resources

1. For basic facts and figures about child obesity, go to the link to the American Obesity Association's Web site at www.econtoday.com/chap01.
2. To learn about various ways states and the federal government are trying to combat child obesity, click on the link to the National Center for Chronic Disease Prevention and Health Promotion, available at www.econtoday.com/chap01.

Research Project

Health difficulties related to obesity clearly pose problems for an obese individual. From an economic standpoint, why might society at large care about a greater incidence of health problems resulting from increases in the rate of obesity among children? If one takes the stand that higher child obesity rates are a social problem, what are two possible actions that society might take to change the incentives of parents and caregivers in ways that might reverse the upward trend in child obesity? If your proposed actions require government spending, who would finance these expenditures?

SUMMARY DISCUSSION of Learning Objectives

1. **Microeconomics versus Macroeconomics:** In general, economics is the study of how individuals make choices to satisfy wants. Economics is usually divided into microeconomics, which is the study of individual decision making by households and firms, and macroeconomics, which is the study of nationwide phenomena, such as inflation and unemployment.

2. **Self-Interest in Economic Analysis:** Rational self-interest is the assumption that individuals never intentionally make decisions that would leave them worse off. Instead, they are motivated primarily by their self-interest, keeping in mind that self-interest can relate to monetary and nonmonetary objectives, such as love, prestige, and helping others.

3. **Economics as a Science:** Like other scientists, economists use models, or theories, that are simplified representations of the real world to analyze and make predictions about the real world. Economic models are never

completely realistic because by definition they are simplifications using assumptions that are not directly testable. Nevertheless, economists can subject the predictions of economic theories to empirical tests in which real-world data are used to decide whether or not to reject the predictions.

4. **Positive and Normative Economics:** Positive economics deals with *what is,* whereas normative economics deals with *what ought to be.* Positive economic statements are of the "if . . . then" variety; they are descriptive and predictive and are not related to what "should" happen. By contrast, whenever statements embodying values are made, we enter the realm of normative economics, or how individuals and groups think things ought to be.

KEY TERMS AND CONCEPTS

aggregates (3)	macroeconomics (3)	positive economics (10)
ceteris paribus assumption (9)	microeconomics (3)	rationality assumption (4)
economics (3)	models, or theories (7)	resources (3)
empirical (9)	normative economics (10)	wants (3)
incentives (2)		

PROBLEMS

Answers to the odd-numbered problems appear at the back of the book.

1-1. Define economics. Explain briefly how the economic way of thinking—in terms of rational, self-interested people responding to incentives—relates to each of the following situations.

    a. A student deciding whether to purchase a textbook for a particular class

    b. Government officials seeking more funding for mass transit through higher taxes

    c. A municipality taxing hotel guests to obtain funding for a new sports stadium

1-2. Some people claim that the "economic way of thinking" does not apply to issues such as health care. Explain how economics does apply to this issue by developing a "model" of an individual's choice.

1-3. Does the phrase "unlimited wants and limited resources" apply to both a low-income household and a middle-income household? Can the same phrase be applied to a very high-income household?

1-4. In a single sentence, contrast microeconomics and macroeconomics. Next, categorize each of the following issues as either a microeconomic issue, a macroeconomic issue, or not an economic issue.

    a. The national unemployment rate

    b. The decision of a worker to work overtime or not

    c. A family's choice of having a baby

    d. The rate of growth of the money supply

    e. The national government's budget deficit

    f. A student's allocation of study time across two subjects

1-5. One of your classmates, Sally, is a hardworking student, serious about her classes, and conscientious about her grades. Sally is also involved, however, in volunteer activities and an extracurricular sport. Is Sally displaying rational behavior? Based on what you read in this chapter, construct an argument supporting the conclusion that she is.

1-6. You have 10 hours in which to study for both a French test and an economics test. Construct a model to determine your allocation of study hours. Include as assumptions the points you "gain" from an hour of study time in each subject and your desired outcome on each test.

1-7. Suppose that a model constructed in answer to Problem 1-6 indicates that the student will earn 15 percentage points on an examination in each course for every hour spent studying. Suppose that you are taking these courses and desire to earn an "A" (90 percent) in economics and merely to pass (60 percent) in French. How much time does this model indicate that you should study each subject before taking the examinations?

1-8. Suppose you followed the model you constructed in Problem 1-6. Explain how you would "grade" the model.

1-9. Which of the following predictions appears to follow from a model based on the assumption that rational, self-interested individuals respond to incentives?

    a. For every 10 points Myrna must earn in order to pass her economics course and meet her graduation requirements, she will study one additional hour for her economics test next week.

    b. A coin toss will best predict Leonardo's decision about whether to purchase an expensive business suit or an inexpensive casual outfit to wear next week when he interviews for a high-paying job he is seeking.

    c. Celeste, who uses earnings from her regularly scheduled hours of part-time work to pay for her room and board at college, will decide to buy a newly released DVD this week only if she is able to work two additional hours.

1-10. Consider two models for estimating, in advance of an election, the shares of votes that will go to rival candidates. According to one model, pollsters' surveys of a randomly chosen set of registered voters before an election can be used to forecast the percentage of votes that each candidate will receive. This first model relies on the assumption that unpaid survey respondents will give truthful responses about how they will vote and that they will actually cast a ballot in the election. The other model uses prices of financial assets (legally binding I.O.U.s) issued by the Iowa Electronic Market, operated by the University of Iowa, to predict electoral outcomes. The final payments received by owners of these assets, which can be bought or sold during the weeks and days preceding an election, depend on the shares of votes the candidates actually end up receiving. This second model assumes that owners of these assets wish to earn the highest possible returns, and it indicates that the market prices of these assets provide an indication of the percentage of votes that each candidate will actually receive on the day of the election.

    a. Which of these two models for forecasting electoral results is more firmly based on the rationality assumption of economics?

    b. How would an economist evaluate which is the better model for forecasting electoral outcomes?

1-11. Write a sentence contrasting positive and normative economic analysis.

1-12. Based on your answer to Problem 1-11, categorize each of the following conclusions as being the result of positive analysis or normative analysis.

    a. A higher minimum wage will reduce employment opportunities for minimum wage workers.

    b. Increasing the earnings of minimum wage employees is desirable, and raising the minimum wage is the best way to accomplish this.

    c. Everyone should enjoy open access to health care.

    d. Heath care subsidies will increase the consumption of health care.

1-13. Consider the following statements, based on a positive economic analysis that assumes that all other things remain constant. For each, list one other thing that might change and thus offset the outcome stated.

    a. Increased demand for laptop computers will drive up their price.

    b. Falling gasoline prices will result in additional vacation travel.

    c. A reduction of income tax rates will result in more people working.

1-14. Alan Greenspan, chairman of the U.S. Federal Reserve, referred to the high stock market prices of the late 1990s as a result of "irrational exuberance." Counter this statement by considering the rationality of stock market investors.

ECONOMICS ON THE NET

The Usefulness of Studying Economics This application helps you see how accomplished people benefited from their study of economics. It also explores ways in which these people feel others of all walks of life can gain from learning more about the economics field.

Title: How Taking an Economics Course Can Lead to Becoming an Economist

Navigation: Go to www.econtoday.com/chap01 to visit the Federal Reserve Bank of Minneapolis home page. To access economists in *The Region* on their student experiences and the need for economic literacy, under Publications, click on *The Region*. Select the *Index by Issues*. Click on *December 1998,* and select the last article of the issue, Economists in *The Region* on Their Student Experiences and the Need for Economic Literacy.

Application Read the interviews of the six economists, and answer the following questions.

1. Based on your reading, what economists do you think other economists regard as influential? What educational institutions do you think are the most influential in economics?

2. Which economists do you think were attracted to micro-economics and which to macroeconomics?

For Group Study and Analysis Divide the class into three groups, and assign the groups the Blinder, Yellen, and Rivlin interviews. Have each group use the content of its assigned interview to develop a statement explaining why the study of economics is important, regardless of a student's chosen major.

If your exam were tomorrow, would you be ready? For each chapter, MyEconLab Practice Tests and Study Plans pinpoint which sections you have mastered and which ones you need to study. That way, you are more efficient with your study time, and you are better prepared for your exams.

Here is how it works:

1. Register and log in to www.myeconlab.com/miller.
2. Click on "Take a Test" and select Test A for this chapter.
3. Take the diagnostic test and MyEconLab will grade it automatically and create a personalized Study Plan, so you see which sections of the chapter you should study further.
4. The Study Plan will serve up additional practice problems and tutorials to help you master the specific areas where you need to focus. By practicing online, you can track your progress in the Study Plan.
5. After you have mastered the sections, "Take a Test" and select Test B for this chapter. Take the test, and see how you do!

In addition to Practice Tests and your personalized Study Plan, you'll find the following media resources in MyEcon-Lab:

1. *Graphs in Motion* animation of Figure A-8.
2. Videos featuring the author, Roger LeRoy Miller, on the following subjects:
   - The Difference Between Microeconomics and Macro-economics
   - Rational Self-Interest and the Rationality Assumption
   - Positive versus Normative Economics
3. Links to the Web sites cited in the marginal Internet Resources, Issues and Applications feature, and Economics on the Net activity.
4. Audio clips of all key terms, additional practice problems, and a PDF version of the material from the print Study Guide.
5. eThemes of the Times, which is a New York Times article to help you understand the real-world applications of what you are learning.

 www.myeconlab.com/miller.

Get Ahead of the Curve

Reading and Working with Graphs

A graph is a visual representation of the relationship between variables. In this appendix, we'll stick to just two variables: an **independent variable,** which can change in value freely, and a **dependent variable,** which changes only as a result of changes in the value of the independent variable. For example, if nothing else is changing in your life, your weight depends on your intake of calories. The independent variable is caloric intake and the dependent variable is weight.

A table is a list of numerical values showing the relationship between two (or more) variables. Any table can be converted into a graph, which is a visual representation of that list. Once you understand how a table can be converted to a graph, you will understand what graphs are and how to construct and use them.

Consider a practical example. A conservationist may try to convince you that driving at lower highway speeds will help you conserve gas. Table A-1 shows the relationship between speed—the independent variable—and the distance you can go on a gallon of gas at that speed—the dependent variable. This table does show a pattern. As the data in the first column get larger in value, the data in the second column get smaller.

Now let's take a look at the different ways in which variables can be related.

DIRECT AND INVERSE RELATIONSHIPS

Two variables can be related in different ways, some simple, others more complex. For example, a person's weight and height are often related. If we measured the height and weight of thousands of people, we would surely find that taller people tend to weigh more than shorter people. That is, we would discover that there is a **direct relationship** between height and weight. By this we simply mean that an *increase* in one variable is usually associated with an *increase* in the related variable. This can easily be seen in panel (a) of Figure A-1.

Let's look at another simple way in which two variables can be related. Much evidence indicates that as the price of a specific commodity rises, the amount purchased decreases—there is an **inverse relationship** between the variable's price per unit and

Independent variable
A variable whose value is determined independently of, or outside, the equation under study.

Dependent variable
A variable whose value changes according to changes in the value of one or more independent variables.

TABLE A-1
Gas Mileage as a Function of Driving Speed

Miles per Hour	Miles per Gallon
45	25
50	24
55	23
60	21
65	19
70	16
75	13

Direct relationship
A relationship between two variables that is positive, meaning that an increase in one variable is associated with an increase in the other and a decrease in one variable is associated with a decrease in the other.

Inverse relationship
A relationship between two variables that is negative, meaning that an increase in one variable is associated with a decrease in the other and a decrease in one variable is associated with an increase in the other.

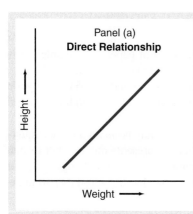
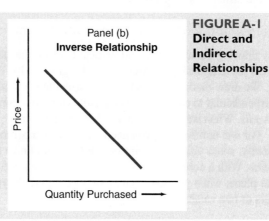

Panel (a)
Direct Relationship

Height — Weight —

Panel (b)
Inverse Relationship

Price — Quantity Purchased —

**FIGURE A-1
Direct and Indirect Relationships**

FIGURE A-2
Horizontal Number Line

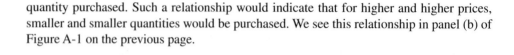

Number line
A line that can be divided into segments of equal length, each associated with a number.

FIGURE A-3
Vertical Number Line

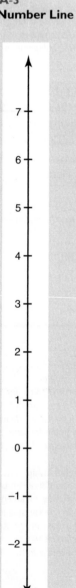

quantity purchased. Such a relationship would indicate that for higher and higher prices, smaller and smaller quantities would be purchased. We see this relationship in panel (b) of Figure A-1 on the previous page.

CONSTRUCTING A GRAPH

Let us now examine how to construct a graph to illustrate a relationship between two variables.

A Number Line

The first step is to become familiar with what is called a **number line.** One is shown in Figure A-2. There are two things that you should know about it.

1. The points on the line divide the line into equal segments.

2. The numbers associated with the points on the line increase in value from left to right; saying it the other way around, the numbers decrease in value from right to left. However you say it, what you're describing is formally called an *ordered set of points.*

On the number line, we have shown the line segments—that is, the distance from 0 to 10 or the distance between 30 and 40. They all appear to be equal and, indeed, are each equal to $\frac{1}{2}$ inch. When we use a distance to represent a quantity, such as barrels of oil, graphically, we are *scaling* the number line. In the example shown, the distance between 0 and 10 might represent 10 barrels of oil, or the distance from 0 to 40 might represent 40 barrels. Of course, the scale may differ on different number lines. For example, a distance of 1 inch could represent 10 units on one number line but 5,000 units on another. Notice that on our number line, points to the left of 0 correspond to negative numbers and points to the right of 0 correspond to positive numbers.

Of course, we can also construct a vertical number line. Consider the one in Figure A-3. As we move up this vertical number line, the numbers increase in value; conversely, as we descend, they decrease in value. Below 0 the numbers are negative, and above 0 the numbers are positive. And as on the horizontal number line, all the line segments are equal. This line is divided into segments such that the distance between −2 and −1 is the same as the distance between 0 and 1.

Combining Vertical and Horizontal Number Lines

By drawing the horizontal and vertical lines on the same sheet of paper, we are able to express the relationships between variables graphically. We do this in Figure A-4.

We draw them (1) so that they intersect at each other's 0 point and (2) so that they are perpendicular to each other. The result is a set of coordinate axes, where each line is called an *axis.* When we have two axes, they span a *plane.*

For one number line, you need only one number to specify any point on the line; equivalently, when you see a point on the line, you know that it represents one number or one value. With a coordinate value system, you need two numbers to specify a single point in the plane; when you see a single point on a graph, you know that it represents two numbers or two values.

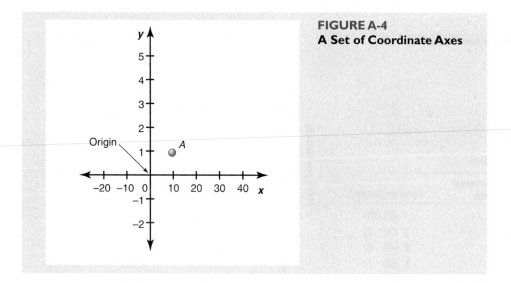

FIGURE A-4
A Set of Coordinate Axes

The basic things that you should know about a coordinate number system are that the vertical number line is referred to as the **y axis,** the horizontal number line is referred to as the **x axis,** and the point of intersection of the two lines is referred to as the **origin.**

Any point such as *A* in Figure A-4 represents two numbers—a value of *x* and a value of *y*. But we know more than that: We also know that point *A* represents a positive value of *y* because it is above the *x* axis, and we know that it represents a positive value of *x* because it is to the right of the *y* axis.

Point *A* represents a "paired observation" of the variables *x* and *y*; in particular, in Figure A-4, *A* represents an observation of the pair of values *x* = 10 and *y* = 1. Every point in the coordinate system corresponds to a paired observation of *x* and *y*, which can be simply written (*x*, *y*)—the *x* value is always specified first and then the *y* value. When we give the values associated with the position of point *A* in the coordinate number system, we are in effect giving the coordinates of that point. *A*'s coordinates are *x* = 10, *y* = 1, or (10, 1).

y axis
The vertical axis in a graph.

x axis
The horizontal axis in a graph.

Origin
The intersection of the *y* axis and the *x* axis in a graph.

GRAPHING NUMBERS IN A TABLE

Consider Table A-2. Column 1 shows different prices for T-shirts, and column 2 gives the number of T-shirts purchased per week at these prices. Notice the pattern of these numbers. As the price of T-shirts falls, the number of T-shirts purchased per week increases. Therefore, an inverse relationship exists between these two variables, and as soon as we represent it on a graph, you will be able to see the relationship. We can graph this relationship using a coordinate number system—a vertical and horizontal number line for each of these two variables. Such a graph is shown in panel (b) of Figure A-5 on the next page.

In economics, it is conventional to put dollar values on the *y* axis. We therefore construct a vertical number line for price and a horizontal number line, the *x* axis, for quantity of T-shirts purchased per week. The resulting coordinate system allows the plotting of each of the paired observation points; in panel (a), we repeat Table A-2, with a column added expressing these points in paired-data (*x*, *y*) form. For example, point *J* is the paired observation (30, 9). It indicates that when the price of a T-shirt is $9, 30 will be purchased per week.

If it were possible to sell parts of a T-shirt ($\frac{1}{2}$ or $\frac{1}{20}$ of a shirt), we would have observations at every possible price. That is, we would be able to connect our paired observations, represented as lettered points. Let's assume that we can make T-shirts perfectly divisible so that the

TABLE A-2
T-Shirts Purchased

(1) Price of T-Shirts	(2) Number of T-Shirts Purchased per Week
$10	20
9	30
8	40
7	50
6	60
5	70

FIGURE A-5
Graphing the Relationship Between T-Shirts Purchased and Price

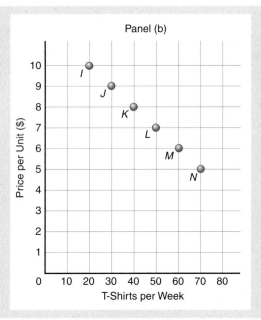

Panel (b)

Panel (a)

Price per T-Shirt	T-Shirts Purchased per Week	Point on Graph
$10	20	*I* (20, 10)
9	30	*J* (30, 9)
8	40	*K* (40, 8)
7	50	*L* (50, 7)
6	60	*M* (60, 6)
5	70	*N* (70, 5)

linear relationship shown in Figure A-5 also holds for fractions of dollars and T-shirts. We would then have a line that connects these points, as shown in the graph in Figure A-6.

In short, we have now represented the data from the table in the form of a graph. Note that an inverse relationship between two variables shows up on a graph as a line or curve that slopes *downward* from left to right. (You might as well get used to the idea that economists call a straight line a "curve" even though it may not curve at all. Much of economists' data turn out to be curves, so they refer to everything represented graphically, even straight lines, as curves.)

FIGURE A-6
Connecting the Observation Points

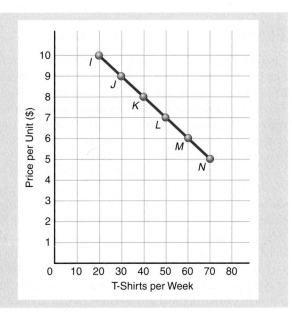

THE SLOPE OF A LINE (A LINEAR CURVE)

An important property of a curve represented on a graph is its *slope*. Consider Figure A-7, which represents the quantities of shoes per week that a seller is willing to offer at different prices. Note that in panel (a) of Figure A-7, as in Figure A-5, we have expressed the coordinates of the points in parentheses in paired-data form.

The **slope** of a line is defined as the change in the y values divided by the corresponding change in the x values as we move along the line. Let's move from point E to point D in panel (b) of Figure A-7. As we move, we note that the change in the y values, which is the change in price, is +$20, because we have moved from a price of $20 to a price of $40 per pair. As we move from E to D, the change in the x values is +80; the number of pairs of shoes willingly offered per week rises from 80 to 160 pairs. The slope calculated as a change in the y values divided by the change in the x values is therefore

$$\frac{20}{80} = \frac{1}{4}$$

It may be helpful for you to think of slope as a "rise" (movement in the vertical direction) over a "run" (movement in the horizontal direction). We show this abstractly in Figure A-8 (page 22). The slope is the amount of rise divided by the amount of run. In the example in Figure A-8, and of course in Figure A-7, the amount of rise is positive and so is the amount of run. That's because it's a direct relationship. We show an inverse relationship in Figure A-9 (page 22). The slope is still equal to the rise divided by the run, but in this case the rise and the run have opposite signs because the curve slopes downward. That means that the slope is negative and that we are dealing with an inverse relationship.

Now let's calculate the slope for a different part of the curve in panel (b) of Figure A-7. We will find the slope as we move from point B to point A. Again, we note that the slope, or rise over run, from B to A equals

$$\frac{20}{80} = \frac{1}{4}$$

A specific property of a straight line is that its slope is the same between any two points; in other words, the slope is constant at all points on a straight line in a graph.

Slope
The change in the y value divided by the corresponding change in the x value of a curve; the "incline" of the curve.

FIGURE A-7
A Positively Sloped Curve

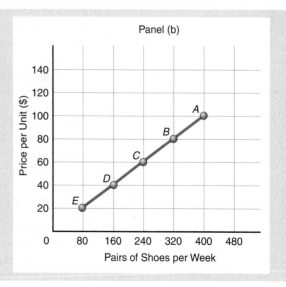

Panel (a)		
Price per Pair	Pairs of Shoes Offered per Week	Point on Graph
$100	400	A (400,100)
80	320	B (320, 80)
60	240	C (240, 60)
40	160	D (160, 40)
20	80	E (80, 20)

FIGURE A-8
Figuring Positive Slope

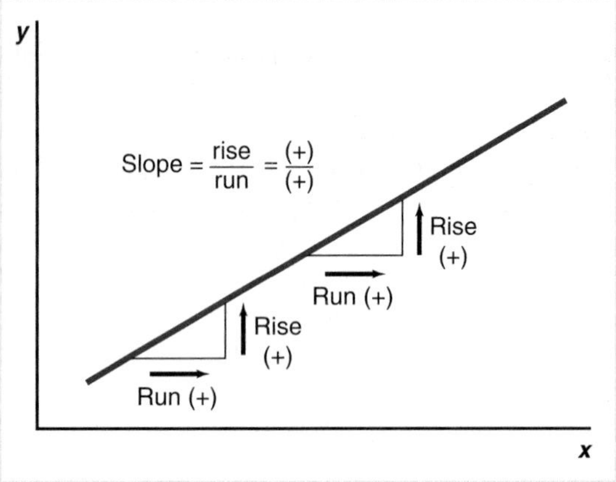

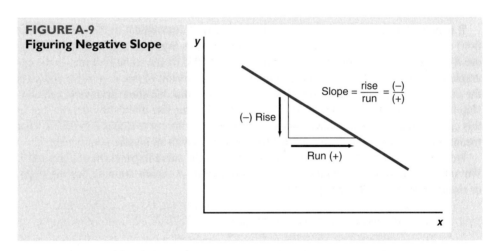

FIGURE A-9
Figuring Negative Slope

We conclude that for our example in Figure A-7 on the previous page, the relationship between the price of a pair of shoes and the number of pairs of shoes willingly offered per week is *linear*, which simply means "in a straight line," and our calculations indicate a constant slope. Moreover, we calculate a direct relationship between these two variables, which turns out to be an upward-sloping (from left to right) curve. Upward-sloping curves have positive slopes—in this case, the slope is $+\frac{1}{4}$.

We know that an inverse relationship between two variables shows up as a downward-sloping curve—rise over run will be negative because the rise and run have opposite signs, as shown in Figure A-9. When we see a negative slope, we know that increases in one variable are associated with decreases in the other. Therefore, we say that downward-sloping curves have negative slopes. Can you verify that the slope of the graph representing the relationship between T-shirt prices and the quantity of T-shirts purchased per week in Figure A-6 on page 20 is $-\frac{1}{10}$?

Slopes of Nonlinear Curves

The graph presented in Figure A-10 indicates a *nonlinear* relationship between two variables, total profits and output per unit of time. Inspection of this graph indicates that at first, increases in output lead to increases in total profits; that is, total profits rise as output increases. But beyond some output level, further increases in output cause decreases in total profits.

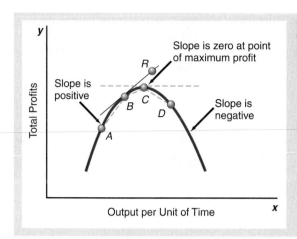

FIGURE A-10
The Slope of a Nonlinear Curve

Can you see how this curve rises at first, reaches a peak at point *C*, and then falls? This curve relating total profits to output levels appears mountain-shaped.

Considering that this curve is nonlinear (it is obviously not a straight line), should we expect a constant slope when we compute changes in *y* divided by corresponding changes in *x* in moving from one point to another? A quick inspection, even without specific numbers, should lead us to conclude that the slopes of lines joining different points in this curve, such as between *A* and *B*, *B* and *C*, or *C* and *D*, will *not* be the same. The curve slopes upward (in a positive direction) for some values and downward (in a negative direction) for other values. In fact, the slope of the line between any two points on this curve will be different from the slope of the line between any two other points. Each slope will be different as we move along the curve.

Instead of using a line between two points to discuss slope, mathematicians and economists prefer to discuss the slope *at a particular point*. The slope at a point on the curve, such as point *B* in the graph in Figure A-10, is the slope of a line *tangent* to that point. A tangent line is a straight line that touches a curve at only one point. For example, it might be helpful to think of the tangent at *B* as the straight line that just "kisses" the curve at point *B*.

To calculate the slope of a tangent line, you need to have some additional information besides the two values of the point of tangency. For example, in Figure A-10, if we knew that the point *R* also lay on the tangent line and we knew the two values of that point, we could calculate the slope of the tangent line. We could calculate rise over run between points *B* and *R*, and the result would be the slope of the line tangent to the one point *B* on the curve.

APPENDIX SUMMARY

1. Direct relationships involve a dependent variable changing in the same direction as the change in the independent variable.

2. Inverse relationships involve the dependent variable changing in the opposite direction of the change in the independent variable.

3. When we draw a graph showing the relationship between

two economic variables, we are holding all other things constant (the Latin term for which is *ceteris paribus*).

4. We obtain a set of coordinates by putting vertical and horizontal number lines together. The vertical line is called the *y* axis; the horizontal line, the *x* axis.

5. The slope of any linear (straight-line) curve is the change in the *y* values divided by the corresponding change in

the x values as we move along the line. Otherwise stated, the slope is calculated as the amount of rise over the amount of run, where rise is movement in the vertical direction and run is movement in the horizontal direction.

6. The slope of a nonlinear curve changes; it is positive when the curve is rising and negative when the curve is falling. At a maximum or minimum point, the slope of the nonlinear curve is zero.

KEY TERMS AND CONCEPTS

dependent variable (17)

direct relationship (17)

independent variable (17)

inverse relationship (17)

number line (18)

origin (19)

slope (21)

x axis (19)

y axis (19)

PROBLEMS

Answers to the odd-numbered problems appear at the back of the book.

A-1. Explain which is the independent variable and which is the dependent variable for each of the following examples.

    a. Once you determine the price of a notebook at the college bookstore, you will decide how many notebooks to buy.

    b. You will decide how many credit hours to register for this semester once the university tells you how many work-study hours you will be assigned.

    c. You anticipate earning a higher grade on your next economics exam grade because you studied more hours in the weeks preceding the exam.

A-2. For each of the following items, state whether a direct or an inverse relationship is likely to exist.

    a. The number of hours you study for an exam and your exam score

    b. The price of pizza and the quantity purchased

    c. The number of games the university basketball team won *last* year and the number of season tickets sold *this* year

A-3. Review Figure A-4, and then state whether each of the following paired observations is on, above, or below the x axis and on, to the left of, or to the right of the y axis.

    a. $(-10, 4)$

    b. $(20, -2)$

    c. $(10, 0)$

A-4. State whether each of the following functions is linear or nonlinear.

    a. $y = 5x$

    b. $y = 5x^2$

    c. $y = 3 + x$

    d. $y = -3x$

A-5. Given the function $y = 5x$, complete the following schedule and plot the curve.

y	x
	-4
	-2
	0
	2
	4

A-6. Given the function $y = 5x^2$, complete the following schedule and plot the curve.

y	x
	-4
	-2
	0
	2
	4

A-7. Calculate the slope of the function you graphed in Problem A-5.

A-8. Indicate at each ordered pair whether the slope of the curve you plotted in Problem A-6 is positive, negative, or zero.

A-9. State whether each of the following functions implies a positive or negative relationship between x and y.

    a. $y = 5x$

    b. $y = 3 + x$

    c. $y = -3x$

Chapter 2

Scarcity and the World of Trade-Offs

Since the early 2000s, law enforcement officials have noticed three disturbing trends concerning bank robberies. First, an increasing number of bank robberies are committed by women. Second, bank robberies in general are on an upswing—thieves of both genders are robbing more banks. Third, an increasing percentage of bank robbers are never caught. All three trends are linked to a common factor: Since the war on terrorism began in 2001, a greater share of the nation's law enforcement resources has been devoted to antiterrorism efforts. This has left fewer resources available to combat lesser crimes, such as bank robberies. In this chapter, you will learn about the fundamental trade-offs that society faces in the allocation of *all* scarce resources, including those relating to law enforcement.

LEARNING OBJECTIVES

After reading this chapter, you should be able to:

1. Evaluate whether even affluent people face the problem of scarcity
2. Understand why economics considers individuals' "wants" but not their "needs"
3. Explain why the scarcity problem induces individuals to consider opportunity costs
4. Discuss why obtaining increasing increments of any particular good typically entails giving up more and more units of other goods
5. Explain why society faces a trade-off between consumption goods and capital goods
6. Distinguish between absolute and comparative advantage

Media Resources

Refer to the end of the chapter for a full listing of the multimedia learning materials available in MyEconLab.

... a typical individual who commutes by automobile to and from a job in the 68 largest U.S. cities spends the equivalent of almost two more full workdays on the road each year, compared with a decade ago? A key reason is that the average amount of time that commuters spend at a complete stop in traffic each year has increased from just over 34 hours ten years ago to more than 50 hours today

The additional hours that people devote to commuting every year could otherwise be allocated to leisure activities with family or friends or perhaps simply staying in bed a few more minutes each morning. For many people, some of the hours stuck on highways and city streets could otherwise be spent on the job, where the average U.S. worker currently earns about $16 per hour. Every hour spent sitting in traffic imposes a cost on a commuter because time, like all other resources, is scarce.

SCARCITY

Scarcity
A situation in which the ingredients for producing the things that people desire are insufficient to satisfy all wants.

Whenever individuals or communities cannot obtain everything they desire simultaneously, they must make choices. Choices occur because of *scarcity*. **Scarcity** is the most basic concept in all of economics. Scarcity means that we do not ever have enough of everything, including time, to satisfy our *every* desire. Scarcity exists because human wants always exceed what can be produced with the limited resources and time that nature makes available.

What Scarcity Is Not

Scarcity is not a shortage. After a hurricane hits and cuts off supplies to a community, TV newscasts often show people standing in line to get minimum amounts of cooking fuel and food. A news commentator might say that the line is caused by the "scarcity" of these products. But cooking fuel and food are always scarce—we cannot obtain all that we want at a zero price. Therefore, do not confuse the concept of scarcity, which is general and all-encompassing, with the concept of shortages as evidenced by people waiting in line to obtain a particular product.

Scarcity is not the same thing as poverty. Scarcity occurs among the poor and among the rich. Even the richest person on earth faces scarcity because available time is limited. Low income levels do not create more scarcity. High income levels do not create less scarcity.

Scarcity is a fact of life, like gravity. And just as physicists did not invent gravity, economists did not invent scarcity—it existed well before the first economist ever lived. It has existed at all times in the past and will exist at all times in the future.

Scarcity and Resources

Production
Any activity that results in the conversion of resources into products that can be used in consumption.

Scarcity exists because resources are insufficient to satisfy our every desire. Resources are the inputs used in the production of the things that we want. **Production** can be defined as virtually any activity that results in the conversion of resources into products that can be used in consumption. Production includes delivering things from one part of the country to another. It includes taking ice from an ice tray to put it in your soft-drink glass. The resources used in production are called *factors of production,* and some economists use the terms *resources* and *factors of production* interchangeably. The total quantity of all resources that an economy has at any one time determines what that economy can produce.

Factors of production can be classified in many ways. Here is one such classification:

1. *Land.* **Land** encompasses all the nonhuman gifts of nature, including timber, water, fish, minerals, and the original fertility of land. It is often called the *natural resource.*

2. *Labor.* **Labor** is the *human resource,* which includes all productive contributions made by individuals who work, such as Web page designers, ballet dancers, and professional football players.

3. *Physical capital.* **Physical capital** consists of the factories and equipment used in production. It also includes improvements to natural resources, such as irrigation ditches.

4. *Human capital.* **Human capital** is the economic characterization of the education and training of workers. How much the nation produces depends not only on how many hours people work but also on how productive they are, and that in turn depends in part on education and training. To become more educated, individuals have to devote time and resources, just as a business has to devote resources if it wants to increase its physical capital. Whenever a worker's skills increase, human capital has been improved.

5. *Entrepreneurship.* The factor of production known as **entrepreneurship** (actually a subdivision of labor) involves human resources that perform the functions of organizing, managing, and assembling the other factors of production to create and operate business ventures. Entrepreneurship also encompasses taking risks that involve the possibility of losing large sums of wealth on new ventures. It includes new methods of doing common things and generally experimenting with any type of new thinking that could lead to making more money income. Without entrepreneurship, virtually no business organization could operate.

Goods versus Economic Goods

Goods are defined as all things from which individuals derive satisfaction or happiness. Goods therefore include air to breathe and the beauty of a sunset as well as food, cars, and MP3 players.

Economic goods are a subset of all goods—they are scarce goods about which we must constantly make decisions regarding their best use. By definition, the desired quantity of an economic good exceeds the amount that is directly available at a zero price. Virtually every example we use in economics concerns economic goods—cars, DVD players, computers, socks, baseball bats, and corn. Weeds are a good example of *bads*— goods for which the desired quantity is much *less* than what nature provides at a zero price.

Sometimes you will see references to "goods and services." **Services** are tasks that are performed for someone else, such as laundry, Internet access, hospital care, restaurant meal preparation, car polishing, psychological counseling, and teaching. One way of looking at services is thinking of them as *intangible goods.*

WANTS AND NEEDS

Wants are not the same as needs. Indeed, from the economist's point of view, the term *needs* is objectively undefinable. When someone says, "I need some new clothes," there is no way to know whether that person is stating a vague wish, a want, or a lifesaving necessity. If the individual making the statement were dying of exposure in a northern country during the winter, we might argue that indeed the person does need clothes—perhaps not new ones, but at least some articles of warm clothing. Typically, however, the term *need* is used very casually in conversation. What people mean, usually, is that they desire something that they do not currently have.

Land
The natural resources that are available from nature. Land as a resource includes location, original fertility and mineral deposits, topography, climate, water, and vegetation.

Labor
Productive contributions of humans who work, involving both mental and physical activities.

Physical capital
All manufactured resources, including buildings, equipment, machines, and improvements to land that is used for production.

Human capital
The accumulated training and education of workers.

Entrepreneurship
The factor of production involving human resources that perform the functions of raising capital, organizing, managing, assembling other factors of production, and making basic business policy decisions. The entrepreneur is a risk taker.

Goods
All things from which individuals derive satisfaction or happiness.

Economic goods
Goods that are scarce, for which the quantity demanded exceeds the quantity supplied at a zero price.

Services
Mental or physical labor or help purchased by consumers. Examples are the assistance of physicians, lawyers, dentists, repair personnel, housecleaners, educators, retailers, and wholesalers; things purchased or used by consumers that do not have physical characteristics.

Humans have unlimited wants. Just imagine if every single material want that you might have were satisfied. You can have all of the clothes, cars, houses, DVDs, yachts, and other things that you want. Does that mean that nothing else could add to your total level of happiness? Probably not, because you might think of new goods and services that you could obtain, particularly as they came to market. You would also still be lacking in fulfilling all of your wants for compassion, friendship, love, affection, prestige, musical abilities, sports abilities, and so on.

In reality, every individual has competing wants but cannot satisfy all of them, given limited resources. This is the reality of scarcity. Each person must therefore make choices. Whenever a choice is made to produce or buy something, something else that is also desired is not produced or not purchased. In other words, in a world of scarcity, every want that ends up being satisfied causes one or more other wants to remain unsatisfied or to be forfeited.

CONCEPTS in Brief

- Scarcity exists because human wants always exceed what can be produced with the limited resources and time that nature makes available.

- We use scarce resources, such as land, labor, physical and human capital, and entrepreneurship, to produce economic goods—goods that are desired but are not directly obtainable from nature to the extent demanded or desired at a zero price.

- Wants are unlimited; they include all material desires and all nonmaterial desires, such as love, affection, power, and prestige.

- The concept of need is difficult to define objectively for every person; consequently, we simply consider every person's wants to be unlimited. In a world of scarcity, satisfaction of one want necessarily means nonsatisfaction of one or more other wants.

To test your understanding of the concepts covered in this section, go to the Online Review at **www.myeconlab.com/miller.**

SCARCITY, CHOICE, AND OPPORTUNITY COST

The natural fact of scarcity implies that we must make choices. One of the most important results of this fact is that every choice made (or not made, for that matter) means that some opportunity had to be sacrificed. Every choice involves giving up an opportunity to produce or consume something else.

Consider a practical example. Every choice you make to study one more hour of economics requires that you give up the opportunity to engage in any of the following activities: study more of another subject, listen to music, sleep, browse at a local store, read a novel, or work out at the gym. The most highly valued of these opportunities is forgone also if you choose to study economics an additional hour.

Because there were so many alternatives from which to choose, how could you determine the value of what you gave up to engage in that extra hour of studying economics? First of all, no one else can tell you the answer because only *you* can put a value on the alternatives forgone. Only you know the value of another hour of sleep or of an hour looking for the latest DVDs. That means that only you can determine the highest-valued, next-best alternative that you had to sacrifice in order to study economics one more hour. Only you can determine the value of the next-best alternative.

For instance, when faced with alternative methods of moving from their parents' homes to their college dormitories, not all students will view the same methods as the next-best alternative. How has this given entrepreneurs an opportunity to profit from providing online mechanisms for arranging college moves?

E-Commerce EXAMPLE

Making the Big Move to College a Next-Best Alternative

If you live on campus, think back to your first days of college. Recall stuffing many of your personal items into your parent's car, perhaps a luggage-rack container on top of the car, and maybe even a trailer behind the car. In addition, remember all the efforts entailed in finding a parking place within walking distance of the dormitory and carrying everything to your room.

Now consider an alternative way to move into a college dorm room that is available to today's students: purchasing goods and services provided by AllDorm.com. At this Web site, which offers 6,000 common dorm room items, new students can buy items and arrange for advance delivery directly to their rooms.

For many students, moving numerous personal items from their home is the next-best alternative to paying AllDorm.com to handle delivery of desired items ahead of time. This is why AllDorm.com, which was founded by four college sophomores, now earns revenues of $25 million per year.

For Critical Analysis
Why might a student view purchasing the goods and services offered by AllDorm.com as the next-best alternative to moving all of her personal items to campus on her own?

The value of the next-best alternative is called **opportunity cost.** The opportunity cost of any action is the value of what is given up—the next-highest-ranked alternative—because a choice was made. When you study one more hour, there be many alternatives available for the use of that hour, but assume that you can do only one other thing in that hour—your next-highest-ranked alternative. What is important is the choice that you would have made if you hadn't studied one more hour. Your opportunity cost is the *next-highest-ranked* alternative, not *all* alternatives.

> **Opportunity cost**
> The highest-valued, next-best alternative that must be sacrificed to obtain something or to satisfy a want.

In economics, cost is always a forgone opportunity.

One way to think about opportunity cost is to understand that when you choose to do something, you lose something else. What you lose is being able to engage in your next-highest-valued alternative. The cost of your choice is what you lose, which is by definition your next-highest-valued alternative. This is your opportunity cost.

What do you think happens to the amount of time school bands play at basketball games when schools can receive large payments for short advertisements piped through their public address (PA) systems?

EXAMPLE

Why Today's College Bands Get Less Playing Time

With 25 seconds left in the college basketball game, the home team has scored and now trails by only one point. Following theft of the in-bound pass by the visiting team, the home team calls time out. The home pep band's director is preparing to lead a rousing chorus of the school sports fight song to get the crowd behind the team as it prepares to try to score a last-

second basket to win the game. But then the band director hears over her headset the words, "Sorry, but we've got one more commercial to do before the end of the game, so you can't play now." As the scoreboard flashes the name of a local bank, the gymnasium's 110-decibel sound system blares out a prerecorded voice describing the bank's low-interest loans and top-notch customer service. The commercial ends just before play resumes. Then a subdued crowd and the silent pep band watch the star player buckle under pressure and dribble the ball out of bounds just as time expires.

Across the nation, college athletic departments have discovered that each minute of time in front of crowds of thousands of fans can be worth as much as $15,000 to advertisers. When the opportunity cost of each minute of time taken by school songs played by pep bands amounts to thousands of dollars, it is little surprise that college bands are getting less playing time at sporting events. Many bands now fight to work

in 15-second snippets of school songs called "shorts" just before play resumes following timeouts that now are commonly allocated fully to commercial messages. At a number of colleges, however, even 15-second slots of time can command advertising revenues. Consequently, pep bands' "shorts" are also being heard less frequently at many college games.

For Critical Analysis
If the average minute of time at a college game can generate $10,000 in advertising revenues, what is the opportunity cost of a 15-second pep-band "short"?

THE WORLD OF TRADE-OFFS

Whenever you engage in any activity using any resource, even time, you are *trading off* the use of that resource for one or more alternative uses. The value of the trade-off is represented by the opportunity cost. The opportunity cost of studying economics has already been mentioned—it is the amount of the next-best alternative. When you think of any alternative, you are thinking of trade-offs.

Let's consider a hypothetical example of a trade-off between the results of spending time studying economics and history. For the sake of this argument, we will assume that additional time studying either economics or history will lead to a higher grade in the subject studied more. One of the best ways to examine this trade-off is with a graph. (If you would like a refresher on graphical techniques, study Appendix A at the end of Chapter 1 before going on.)

Graphical Analysis

Economics Front and Center

To consider how new technologies are affecting the opportunity costs that students face when deciding how to allocate their time, examine the case study, **Missing Class but Catching the Lecture,** on page 41.

In Figure 2-1, the expected grade in history is measured on the vertical axis of the graph, and the expected grade in economics is measured on the horizontal axis. We simplify the world and assume that you have a maximum of 12 hours per week to spend studying these two subjects and that if you spend all 12 hours on economics, you will get an A in the course. You will, however, fail history. Conversely, if you spend all of your 12 hours studying history, you will get an A in that subject, but you will flunk economics. Here the trade-off is a special case: one to one. A one-to-one trade-off means that the opportunity cost of receiving one grade higher in economics (for example, improving from a C to a B) is one grade lower in history (falling from a C to a D).

The Production Possibilities Curve (PPC)

Production possibilities curve (PPC)
A curve representing all possible combinations of total output that could be produced assuming (1) a fixed amount of productive resources of a given quality and (2) the efficient use of those resources.

The graph in Figure 2-1 illustrates the relationship between the possible results that can be produced in each of two activities, depending on how much time you choose to devote to each activity. This graph shows a representation of a **production possibilities curve (PPC)**.

Consider that you are producing a grade in economics when you study economics and a grade in history when you study history. Then the line that goes from A on one axis to A on the other axis therefore becomes a production possibilities curve. It is defined as the maximum quantity of one good or service that can be produced, given that a specific quantity of another is produced. It is a curve that shows the possibilities available for increasing the output of one good or service by reducing the amount of another. In the example in

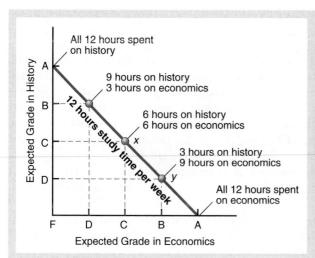

Production Possibilities Curve for Grades in History and Economics (Trade-Offs)
We assume that only 12 hours can be spent per week on studying. If the student is at point *x*, equal time (6 hours a week) is spent on both courses, and equal grades of C will be received. If a higher grade in economics is desired, the student may go to point *y*, thereby receiving a B in economics but a D in history. At point *y*, 3 hours are spent on history and 9 hours on economics.

Figure 2-1, your time for studying was limited to 12 hours per week. The two possible outputs were your grade in history and your grade in economics. The particular production possibilities curve presented in Figure 2-1 is a graphical representation of the opportunity cost of studying one more hour in one subject. It is a *straight-line production possibilities curve,* which is a special case. (The more general case will be discussed next.) If you decide to be at point *x* in Figure 2-1, you will devote 6 hours of study time to history and 6 hours to economics. The expected grade in each course will be a C. If you are more interested in getting a B in economics, you will go to point *y* on the production possibilities curve, spending only 3 hours on history but 9 hours on economics. Your expected grade in history will then drop from a C to a D.

Note that these trade-offs between expected grades in history and economics are the result of *holding constant* total study time as well as all other factors that might influence a student's ability to learn, such as computerized study aids. Quite clearly, if you wished to spend more total time studying, it would be possible to have higher grades in both economics and history. In that case, however, we would no longer be on the specific production possibilities curve illustrated in Figure 2-1. We would have to draw a new curve, farther to the right, to show the greater total study time and a different set of possible trade-offs.

CONCEPTS in Brief

- Scarcity requires us to choose. Whenever we choose, we lose the next-highest-valued alternative.
- Cost is always a forgone opportunity.
- Another way to look at opportunity cost is the trade-off that occurs when one activity is undertaken rather than the next-best alternative activity.
- A production possibilities curve (PPC) graphically shows the trade-off that occurs when more of one output is obtained at the sacrifice of another. The PPC is a graphical representation of, among other things, opportunity cost.

To test your understanding of the concepts covered in this section, go to the Online Review at www.myeconlab.com/miller.

THE CHOICES SOCIETY FACES

The straight-line production possibilities curve presented in Figure 2-1 can be generalized to demonstrate the related concepts of scarcity, choice, and trade-offs that our entire nation faces. As you will see, the production possibilities curve is a simple but powerful economic model because it can demonstrate these related concepts. The example we will use is the choice between the production of digital cameras and pocket personal computers (pocket PCs). We assume for the moment that these are the only two goods that can be produced in the nation. Panel (a) of Figure 2-2 gives the various combinations of digital cameras and pocket PCs that are possible. If all resources are devoted to camera production, 50 million per year can be produced. If all resources are devoted to production of pocket PCs, 60 million per year can be produced. In between are various possible combinations. These combinations are plotted as points *A, B, C, D, E, F,* and *G* in panel (b) of Figure 2-2. If these points are connected with a smooth curve, the nation's production possibilities curve is shown, demonstrating the trade-off between the production of digital cameras and pocket PCs. These trade-offs occur *on* the PPC.

Notice the major difference in the shape of the production possibilities curves in Figure 2-1 on page 31, and Figure 2-2. In Figure 2-1, there is a constant trade-off between grades in economics and in history. In Figure 2-2, the trade-off between digital camera production and pocket PC production is not constant, and therefore the PPC is a *bowed* curve. To understand why the production possibilities curve for a society is typically bowed outward, you must understand the assumptions underlying the PPC.

Go to www.econtoday.com/chap02 for one perspective, offered by the National Center for Policy Analysis, on whether society's production decisions should be publicly or privately coordinated.

FIGURE 2-2
Society's Trade-Off Between Digital Cameras and Pocket PCs

The production of digital cameras and pocket PCs is measured in millions of units per year. The various combinations are given in panel (a) and plotted in panel (b). Connecting the points A–G with a relatively smooth line gives the society's production possibilities curve for digital cameras and pocket PCs. Point *R* lies outside the production possibilities curve and is therefore unattainable at the point in time for which the graph is drawn. Point *S* lies inside the production possibilities curve and therefore entails unemployed or underemployed resources.

Panel (a)

Combination	Digital Cameras (millions per year)	Pocket PCs (millions per year)
A	50.0	0
B	48.0	10
C	45.0	20
D	40.0	30
E	33.0	40
F	22.5	50
G	0.0	60

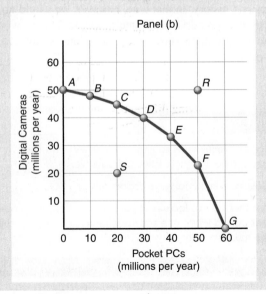

Panel (b)

Assumptions Underlying the Production Possibilities Curve

When we draw the curve that is shown in Figure 2-2, we make the following assumptions:

1. Resources are fully employed.
2. We are looking at production over a specific time period—for example, one year.
3. The resource inputs, in both quantity and quality, used to produce digital cameras or pocket PCs are fixed over this time period.
4. Technology does not change over this time period.

Technology is defined as society's pool of applied knowledge concerning how goods and services can be produced by managers, workers, engineers, scientists, and artisans, using land, physical and human capital, and entrepreneurship. You can think of technology as the formula or recipe used to combine factors of production. (When better formulas are developed, more production can be obtained from the same amount of resources.) The level of technology sets the limit on the amount and types of goods and services that we can derive from any given amount of resources. The production possibilities curve is drawn under the assumption that we use the best technology that we currently have available and that this technology doesn't change over the time period under study.

The land available to a town with established borders is an example of a fixed resource that is fully employed and used with available technology along a production possibilities curve. Why do you suppose that deciding how to allocate a fixed amount of land recently posed "grave" problems for a town in France?

Technology
Society's pool of applied knowledge concerning how goods and services can be produced.

International E X A M P L E

Making Death Illegal—At Least, Inside City Limits

Le Lavandou, France, a Riviera community known for breathtaking views of a rocky coastline along a clear-blue section of the Mediterranean Sea, recently drew international ridicule when it passed a law that appeared aimed at regulating death. Specifically, the law stated, "It is forbidden without a cemetery plot to die on the territory of the commune."

Of course, it is not possible for a law to prevent someone from dying inside a town. The purpose of the law was to indicate a permissible choice along a production possibilities curve. Land is a scarce resource with many alternative uses, so trade-offs involving different productive uses of land arise everywhere on the planet where people establish communities. Le Lavandou is no exception. The town's cemetery filled up, and the townspeople had to decide whether to allocate more land to cemetery plots, thereby providing a service for deceased individuals and for their family and friends, or to continue allocating remaining land resources to the production of other goods and services. The point of the legal requirement was to emphasize that the town had decided not to incur an opportunity cost by allocating more space to cemetery plots.

Nonetheless, it was still true that someone who happened to die in Le Lavandou without first buying an existing cemetery plot was technically breaking the law.

For Critical Analysis

What is likely to happen to the opportunity cost of cemetery services as the world's population continues to increase and spread over available land resources?

Being off the Production Possibilities Curve

Look again at panel (b) of Figure 2-2. Point *R* lies *outside* the production possibilities curve and is *impossible* to achieve during the time period assumed. By definition, the PPC indicates the *maximum* quantity of one good given some quantity of the other.

It is possible, however, to be at point *S* in Figure 2-2 on page 32. That point lies beneath the production possibilities curve. If the nation is at point *S,* it means that its resources are not being fully utilized. This occurs, for example, during periods of unemployment. Point *S* and all such points inside the PPC are always attainable but imply unemployed or underemployed resources.

Efficiency

The production possibilities curve can be used to define the notion of efficiency. Whenever the economy is operating on the PPC, at points such as *A, B, C,* or *D,* we say that its production is efficient. Points such as *S* in Figure 2-2, which lie beneath the PPC, are said to represent production situations that are not efficient.

Efficiency can mean many things to many people. Even in economics, there are different types of efficiency. Here we are discussing *productive efficiency*. An economy is productively efficient whenever it is producing the maximum output with given technology and resources.

A simple commonsense definition of efficiency is getting the most out of what we have. Clearly, we are not getting the most out of what we have if we are at point *S* in panel (b) of Figure 2-2 on page 32. We can move from point *S* to, say, point *C,* thereby increasing the total quantity of digital cameras produced without any decrease in the total quantity of pocket PCs produced. Alternatively, we can move from point *S* to point *E,* for example, and have both more digital cameras and more pocket PCs. Point *S* is called an **inefficient point,** which is defined as any point below the production possibilities curve.

Efficiency
The case in which a given level of inputs is used to produce the maximum output possible. Alternatively, the situation in which a given output is produced at minimum cost.

Inefficient point
Any point below the production possibilities curve at which the use of resources is not generating the maximum possible output.

The Law of Increasing Relative Cost

In the example in Figure 2-1 on page 31, the trade-off between a grade in history and a grade in economics was one to one. The trade-off ratio was constant. That is, the production possibilities curve was a straight line. The curve in Figure 2-2 on page 32 is a more general case. We have re-created the curve in Figure 2-2 as Figure 2-3. Each combination, *A* through *G,* of digital cameras and pocket PCs is represented on the production possibilities curve. Starting with the production of zero pocket PCs, the nation can produce 50 mil-

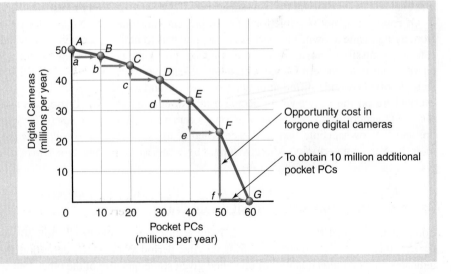

FIGURE 2-3
The Law of Increasing Relative Cost
Consider equal increments of production of pocket PCs, as measured on the horizontal axis. All of the horizontal arrows—*aB, bC,* and so on—are of equal length (10 million). The opportunity cost of going from 50 million pocket PCs per year to 60 million (*Ff*) is much greater than going from zero units to 10 million (*Aa*). The opportunity cost of each additional equal increase in production of pocket PCs rises.

lion digital cameras with its available resources and technology. When we increase production of pocket PCs from zero to 10 million per year, the nation has to give up in digital cameras an amount shown by that first vertical arrow, *Aa.* From panel (a) of Figure 2-2 on page 32 you can see that this is 2 million per year (50 million minus 48 million). Again, if we increase production of pocket PCs by 10 million units per year, we go from *B* to *C*. In order to do so, the nation has to give up the vertical distance *Bb,* or 3 million digital cameras per year. By the time we go from 50 million to 60 million pocket PCs, to obtain that 10 million increase, we have to forgo the vertical distance *Ff,* or 22.5 million digital cameras. In other words, we see that the opportunity cost of the last 10 million pocket PCs has increased to 22.5 million digital cameras, compared to 2 million digital comeras for an equivalent increase in pocket PCs when we started with none at all being produced.

What we are observing is called the **law of increasing relative cost.** When society takes more resources and applies them to the production of any specific good, the opportunity cost increases for each additional unit produced. The reason that as a nation we face the law of increasing relative cost (shown as a production possibilities curve that is bowed outward) is that certain resources are better suited for producing some goods than they are for other goods. Generally, resources are not *perfectly* adaptable for alternative uses. When increasing the output of a particular good, producers must use less suitable resources than those already used in order to produce the additional output. Hence the cost of producing the additional units increases. With respect to our hypothetical example here, at first the optical imaging specialists at digital camera firms would shift over to producing pocket PCs. After a while, though, lens-crafting technicians, workers who normally build cameras, and others would be asked to help design and manufacture pocket PC components. Clearly, they would be less effective in making pocket PCs than the people who specialize in this task.

As a rule of thumb, *the more specialized the resources, the more bowed the production possibilities curve.* At the other extreme, if all resources are equally suitable for digital camera production or production of pocket PCs, the curves in Figures 2-2 and 2-3 would approach the straight line shown in our first example in Figure 2-1 on page 31.

Law of increasing relative cost
The observation that the opportunity cost of additional units of a good generally increases as society attempts to produce more of that good. This accounts for the bowed-out shape of the production possibilities curve.

CONCEPTS in Brief

- Trade-offs are represented graphically by a production possibilities curve showing the maximum quantity of one good or service that can be produced, given a specific quantity of another, from a given set of resources over a specified period of time—for example, one year.

- A PPC is drawn holding the quantity and quality of all resources fixed over the time period under study.

- Points outside the production possibilities curve are unattainable; points inside are attainable but represent an inefficient use or underuse of available resouces.

- Because many resources are better suited for certain productive tasks than for others, society's production possibilities curve is bowed outward, following the law of increasing relative cost.

To test your understanding of the concepts covered in this section, go to the Online Review at www.myeconlab.com/miller.

ECONOMIC GROWTH AND THE PRODUCTION POSSIBILITIES CURVE

Over any particular time period, a society cannot be outside the production possibilities curve. Over time, however, it is possible to have more of everything. This occurs through economic growth. (An important reason for economic growth, capital accumulation, is discussed next. A more complete discussion of why economic growth occurs appears in Chapter 9.) Figure 2-4 on the following page shows the production possibilities curve for

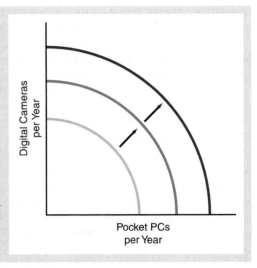

FIGURE 2-4
Economic Growth Allows for More of Everything
If the nation experiences economic growth, the production possibilities curve between digital cameras and pocket PCs will move out as shown. This takes time, however, and it does not occur automatically. This means, therefore, that we can have more digital cameras and more pocket PCs only after a period of time during which we have experienced economic growth.

digital cameras and pocket PCs shifting outward. The two additional curves shown represent new choices open to an economy that has experienced economic growth. Such economic growth occurs because of many things, including increases in the number of workers and productive investment in equipment.

Scarcity still exists, however, no matter how much economic growth there is. At any point in time, we will always be on some production possibilities curve; thus we will always face trade-offs. The more we want of one thing, the less we can have of others.

If a nation experiences economic growth, the production possibilities curve between digital cameras and pocket PCs will move outward, as shown in Figure 2-4. This takes time and does not occur automatically. One reason it will occur involves the choice about how much to consume today.

THE TRADE-OFF BETWEEN THE PRESENT AND THE FUTURE

Consumption
The use of goods and services for personal satisfaction.

The production possibilities curve and economic growth can be used to examine the trade-off between present **consumption** and future consumption. When we consume today, we are using up what we call consumption or consumer goods—food and clothes, for example.

Why We Make Capital Goods

Why would we be willing to use productive resources to make things—capital goods—that we cannot consume directly? For one thing, capital goods enable us to produce larger quantities of consumer goods or to produce them less expensively than we otherwise could. Before fish are "produced" for the market, equipment such as fishing boats, nets, and poles is produced first. Imagine how expensive it would be to obtain fish for market without using these capital goods. Catching fish with one's hands is not an easy task. The price per fish would be very high if capital goods weren't used.

Forgoing Current Consumption

Whenever we use productive resources to make capital goods, we are implicitly forgoing current consumption. We are waiting for some time in the future to consume the fruits that will be reaped from the use of capital goods. In effect, when we forgo current consumption to invest in capital goods, we are engaging in an economic activity that is forward-looking—we do not get instant utility or satisfaction from our activity. Indeed, if we were to produce only consumer goods now and no capital goods, our capacity to produce consumer goods in the future would suffer. Here we see a trade-off.

The Trade-Off Between Consumption Goods and Capital Goods

To have more consumer goods in the future, we must accept fewer consumer goods today. In other words, an opportunity cost is involved. Every time we make a choice for more goods today, we incur an opportunity cost of fewer goods tomorrow, and every time we make a choice of more goods in the future, we incur an opportunity cost of fewer goods today. With the resources that we don't use to produce consumer goods for today, we invest in capital goods that will produce more consumer goods for us later. The trade-off is shown in Figure 2-5. On the left in panel (a), you can see this trade-off depicted as a production possibilities curve between capital goods and consumption goods.

Assume that we are willing to give up $1 trillion worth of consumption today. We will be at point *A* in the left-hand diagram of panel (a). This will allow the economy to grow. We will have more future consumption because we invested in more capital goods today. In the right-hand diagram of panel (a), we see two goods represented, food and entertainment. The production possibilities curve will move outward if we collectively decide to restrict consumption each year and invest in capital goods.

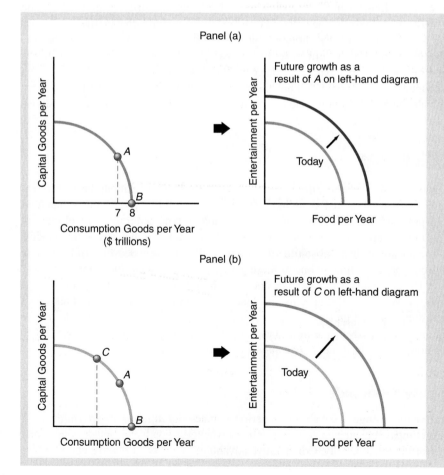

FIGURE 2-5
Capital Goods and Growth
In panel (a), the nation chooses not to consume $1 trillion, so it invests that amount in capital goods. In panel (b), it chooses even more capital goods (point *C*). The PPC moves even more to the right on the right-hand diagram in panel (b) as a result.

In panel (b), we show the results of our willingness to forgo even more current consumption. We move to point *C,* where we have many fewer consumer goods today but produce many more capital goods. This leads to more future growth in this simplified model, and thus the production possibilities curve in the right-hand side of panel (b) shifts outward more than it did in the right-hand side of panel (a).

In other words, the more we give up today, the more we can have tomorrow, provided, of course, that the capital goods are productive in future periods.

CONCEPTS in Brief

- The use of capital requires using productive resources to produce capital goods that will later be used to produce consumer goods.

- A trade-off is involved between current consumption and capital goods or, alternatively, between current consumption and future consumption. The more we invest in capital goods today, the greater the amount of consumer goods we can produce in the future and the smaller the amount of consumer goods we can produce today.

To test your understanding of the concepts covered in this section, go to the Online Review at **www.myeconlab.com/miller**.

SPECIALIZATION AND GREATER PRODUCTIVITY

Specialization
The division of productive activities among persons and regions so that no one individual or one area is totally self-sufficient. An individual may specialize, for example, in law or medicine. A nation may specialize in the production of coffee, computers, or cameras.

Specialization involves working at a relatively well-defined, limited endeavor, such as accounting or teaching. It involves a division of labor among different individuals and regions. Most individuals do specialize. For example, you could change the oil in your car if you wanted to. Typically, though, you take your car to a garage and let the mechanic change the oil. You benefit by letting the garage mechanic specialize in changing the oil and in doing other repairs on your car. The specialist normally will get the job finished sooner than you could and has the proper equipment to make the job go more smoothly. Specialization usually leads to greater productivity, not only for each individual but also for the nation.

Absolute Advantage

Absolute advantage
The ability to produce more units of a good or service using a given quantity of labor or resource inputs. Equivalently, the ability to produce the same quantity of a good or service using fewer units of labor or resource inputs.

Specialization occurs because different individuals and different nations have different skills. Sometimes it seems that some individuals are better at doing everything than anyone else. A president of a large company might be able to type better than any of the typists, file faster than any of the file clerks, and wash windows faster than any of the window washers. The president has an **absolute advantage** in all of these endeavors—if he were to spend a given amount of time in one of these activities, he could produce more than anyone else in the company. The president does not, however, spend his time doing those other activities. Why not? Because his absolute advantage in undertaking the president's managerial duties is even greater. The president specializes in one particular task in spite of having an absolute advantage in all tasks. Indeed, absolute advantage is irrelevant in predicting how he uses his time; only *comparative advantage* matters.

Comparative Advantage

Comparative advantage
The ability to produce a good or service at a lower opportunity cost compared to other producers.

Comparative advantage is the ability to perform an activity *at a lower opportunity cost.* You have a comparative advantage in one activity whenever you have a lower opportunity cost of performing that activity. Comparative advantage is always a *relative* concept. You may be able to change the oil in your car; you might even be able to change it faster than the local mechanic. But if the opportunity cost you face by changing the oil exceeds the mechanic's opportunity cost, the mechanic has a comparative advantage in changing the oil. The mechanic faces a lower opportunity cost for that activity.

You may be convinced that everybody can do everything better than you. In this extreme situation, do you still have a comparative advantage? The answer is yes. What you need to do to discover your comparative advantage is to find a job in which your *disadvantage* relative to others is smaller. You do not have to be a mathematical genius to figure this out. The market tells you very clearly by offering you the highest income for the job for which you have the smallest disadvantage compared to others. Stated differently, to find your comparative advantage, you simply find which job maximizes your income.

The coaches of sports teams are constantly faced with determining each player's comparative advantage. Babe Ruth was originally one of the best pitchers in professional baseball when he played for the Boston Red Sox. After he was traded to the New York Yankees, the owner and the coach decided to make him an outfielder, even though he was a better pitcher than anyone else on the team roster. They wanted "The Babe" to concentrate on his hitting. Good pitchers do not bring in as many fans as home-run kings. Babe Ruth's comparative advantage was clearly in hitting homers rather than in practicing and developing his pitching game.

Scarcity, Self-Interest, and Specialization

In Chapter 1, you learned about the assumption of rational self-interest. To repeat, for the purposes of our analyses we assume that individuals are rational in that they will do what is in their own self-interest. They will not consciously carry out actions that will make them worse off. In this chapter, you learned that scarcity requires people to make choices. We assume that they make choices based on their self-interest. When they make these choices, they attempt to maximize benefits net of opportunity cost. In so doing, individuals choose their comparative advantage and end up specializing. Ultimately, when people specialize, they increase the money income they make and therefore become richer. When all individuals and businesses specialize simultaneously, the gains are seen in greater material well-being. With any given set of resources, specialization will result in higher output.

THE DIVISION OF LABOR

In any firm that includes specialized human and nonhuman resources, there is a **division of labor** among those resources. The best-known example comes from Adam Smith, who in *The Wealth of Nations* illustrated the benefits of a division of labor in the making of pins, as depicted in the following example:

Division of labor
The segregation of a resource into different specific tasks; for example, one automobile worker puts on bumpers, another doors, and so on.

> One man draws out the wire, another straightens it, a third cuts it, a fourth points it, a fifth grinds it at the top for receiving the head; to make the head requires two or three distinct operations; to put it on is a peculiar business, to whiten the pins is another; it is even a trade by itself to put them into the paper.

Making pins this way allowed 10 workers without very much skill to make almost 48,000 pins "of a middling size" in a day. One worker, toiling alone, could have made perhaps 20 pins a day; therefore, 10 workers could have produced 200. Division of labor allowed for an increase in the daily output of the pin factory from 200 to 48,000! (Smith did not attribute all of the gain to the division of labor according to talent but credited also the use of machinery and the fact that less time was spent shifting from task to task.)

What we are discussing here involves a division of the resource called labor into different uses of labor. The different uses of labor are organized in such a way as to increase the amount of output possible from the fixed resources available. We can therefore talk about an organized division of labor within a firm leading to increased output.

COMPARATIVE ADVANTAGE AND TRADE AMONG NATIONS

Go to www.econtoday.com/chap02 to find out from the World Trade Organization how much international trade takes place. Under "Resources," click on "Trade statistics."

Though most of our analysis of absolute advantage, comparative advantage, and specialization has dealt with individuals, it is equally applicable to nations. First consider the United States. The Plains states have a comparative advantage in the production of grains and other agricultural goods. Relative to the Plains states, the states to the north and east tend to specialize in industrialized production, such as automobiles. Not surprisingly, grains are shipped from the Plains states to the northern states, and automobiles are shipped in the reverse direction. Such specialization and trade allow for higher incomes and standards of living. If both the Plains states and the northern states were separate nations, the same analysis would still hold, but we would call it international trade. Indeed, the European Union (EU) is comparable to the United States in area and population, but instead of one nation, the EU has 25. What U.S. residents call *interstate* trade, Europeans call *international* trade. There is no difference, however, in the economic results—both yield greater economic efficiency and higher average incomes.

Political problems that do not normally arise within a particular nation often do between nations. For example, if California avocado growers develop a cheaper method than growers in southern Florida to produce a tastier avocado, the Florida growers will lose out. They cannot do much about the situation except try to lower their own costs of production or improve their product. If avocado growers in Mexico, however, develop a cheaper method to produce better-tasting avocados, both California and Florida growers can (and likely will) try to raise political barriers that will prevent Mexican avocado growers from freely selling their product in the United States. U.S. avocado growers will use such arguments as "unfair" competition and loss of U.S. jobs. In so doing, they are only partly right: Avocado-growing jobs may decline in the United States, but there is no reason to believe that jobs will decline overall. If the argument of U.S. avocado growers had any validity, every time a region in the United States developed a better way to produce a product manufactured somewhere else in the country, U.S. employment would decline. That has never happened and never will.

When nations specialize where they have a comparative advantage and then trade with the rest of the world, the average standard of living in the world rises. In effect, international trade allows the world to move from inside the global production possibilities curve toward the curve itself, thereby improving worldwide economic efficiency. Thus all countries that engage in trade can benefit from comparative advantage.

Why might companies that assemble products from various components choose to include components manufactured in more than one country?

International EXAMPLE

Multiple Comparative Advantages in Dishwasher Production

Maytag workers assemble dishwashers in Jackson, Tennessee. Thus the dishwashers are officially "made in the U.S.A." International trade is nonetheless a fundamental aspect of Maytag's production of dishwashers.

Chinese workers and firms have a comparative advantage over the residents of most other nations in manufacturing small motors. Hence the motors bolted into the dishwashers are Chinese-made. Mexican producers have a comparative advantage over most countries in making small water pumps, so Mexican-manufactured water pumps are installed in the dishwashers. The workers in Maytag's Tennessee plant have the skills required to assemble dishwasher components more efficiently than workers in other nations. Consequently, the total production cost of a Maytag dishwasher that is *assembled* "in the U.S.A." actually reflects efficiencies arising from comparative advantages in more than one country.

For Critical Analysis
What would happen to the total cost of producing a Maytag dishwasher if the U.S. Congress were to pass a law requiring U.S. dishwasher manufacturers to use only U.S.-manufactured components?

Concepts in Brief

- With a given set of resources, specialization results in higher output; in other words, there are gains to specialization in terms of greater material well-being.

- Individuals and nations specialize in their areas of comparative advantage in order to reap the gains of specialization.

- Comparative advantages are found by determining which activities have the lowest opportunity cost—that is, which activities yield the highest return for the time and resources used.

- A division of labor occurs when different workers are assigned different tasks. Together, the workers produce a desired product.

To test your understanding of the concepts covered in this section, go to the Online Review at **www.myeconlab.com/miller.**

CASE STUDY: Economics Front and Center

Missing Class but Catching the Lecture

Hernandez attends a university that has an "instructional resources unit" that creates digital videos of all lectures for about 30 courses per semester and places them on the university's internal Web site for students to review if they miss class. She is enrolled in two of these courses.

Today Hernandez is trying to decide whether to attend one or both "live" lectures or view Internet videos tomorrow instead. One class meets in the morning, when Hernandez could be jogging instead. The other is in the afternoon, when she could be attending a lecture by a visiting senator. She has determined that even though she can view the videos at any time, she still will incur opportunity costs if she misses the actual class meeting. One is giving up the opportunity to ask questions of her professor. Another is sacrificing the chance to interact with other class members before, during, and after class. Finally, she will have to give up other activities that she could do instead of watching video lectures on the Web. Even though the availability of class videos has broadened Hernandez's opportunities, she still confronts trade-offs.

Points to Analyze

1. *What is the opportunity cost if Hernandez chooses to miss her morning class?*

2. *What is the opportunity cost if Hernandez attends her afternoon class?*

The Trade-Off Between Fighting Terrorism and Catching Bank Robbers

I n the United States, the responsibility for combating criminal activities is shared among local, state, and federal police authorities. The Federal Bureau of Investigation (FBI) is the main crime-fighting force of the federal government. Since its founding early in the twentieth century, the FBI's resources have supplemented those available to local police authorities, sheriff's departments, state police units, and other federal agencies. Together, these U.S. law enforcement agencies seek to catch bank robbers and kidnappers, enforce federal narcotics laws, and break up organized crime.

Concepts Applied

- Scarcity and Choice
- Opportunity Cost
- Law of Increasing Relative Cost

Altered Crime Enforcement Priorities

The 1993 bombing of the World Trade Center and the 1995 Oklahoma City bombing revealed that U.S. law enforcement officials faced a dangerous new criminal element. Nevertheless, few changes were made in the basic structure of the national law enforcement system. The FBI continued to focus on catching bank robbers, kidnappers, and Mafia kingpins.

Following the 2001 attacks that destroyed the World Trade Center and damaged the Pentagon, however, the FBI decided to attempt to stop terrorist attacks before they occur. The FBI found that pursuing preemptive strikes against domestic and international terrorists required considerable reallocation of its resources. Before 2001, fewer than 1,200 of the FBI's 9,000 agents based in the United States were directly or indirectly involved in antiterrorism activities. Within three years, nearly 2,000 FBI agents had been reassigned to counterterrorism duties.

Choosing a New Point on the Law Enforcement Production Possibilities Curve

The FBI's reassignment of agents suddenly shifted a significant portion of society's crime-fighting resources away from combating traditional lawbreakers. The number of FBI drug investigations fell by more than 50 percent between 2000 and 2004. Many local and state police detectives who had come to

rely on the FBI for assistance found themselves thrust into the unfamiliar role of lead investigators in cases involving drugs, kidnapping, and white-collar crimes. At the same time, municipal police agencies found themselves responding to occasional FBI calls for assistance in implementing counterterrorism measures to avert suspected threats to U.S. security.

Local and state law enforcement officials had to perform these new duties using the same amount of resources they had before the FBI's action. The result was predictable for anyone who has studied this chapter. As shown in Figure 2-6, there was a movement along a production possibilities curve relating the provision of antiterrorism services and the production of traditional law enforcement activities such as the depicted movement from point *A* to point *B*. Thus the FBI's reallocation of resources to increased counterterrorism activities entailed an opportunity cost. Society as a whole had to sacrifice the production of services aimed at reducing run-of-the-mill crimes in order to increase the production of services designed to prevent terrorist attacks.

Furthermore, because law enforcement resources are not equally suited to every type of policing task, the law of increasing relative cost applied. Each step-up in the production of antiterrorism services entailed an ever-higher opportunity cost in the form of reduced production of traditional law enforcement services. The result was a national law enforcement force better equipped to handle terrorists but less capable of dealing with bank robbers and kidnappers.

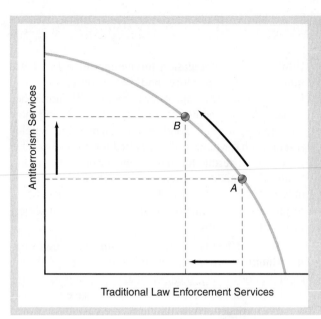

FIGURE 2-6
The Trade-Off Between the Provision of Antiterrorism Services and Traditional Law Enforcement Activities
Given available resources and technology, devoting more resources to producing antiterrorism services entails giving up the production of traditional law enforcement services.

Antiterrorism Services (vertical axis)
Traditional Law Enforcement Services (horizontal axis)

For Critical Analysis

1. Consider a production possibilities curve relating the production of all law enforcement services, including both antiterrorism and traditional policing activities, to the production of *all other* goods and services in the economy. What must happen if society continues to desire to boost counterterrorism efforts while maintaining the same level of traditional law enforcement services?

2. Terrorists seek to destroy both human lives and nonhuman resources and to make existing technology (such as airline passenger jets) less usable. In what sense, therefore, might society regard physical resources directed against terrorism, such as passenger- and baggage-screening devices at airports, as capital goods?

Web Resources

1. To learn more about the FBI resource reallocation that began after the 2001 terrorist attacks, go to www.econtoday.com/chap02.

2. For information about the financial resources the federal government commits to law enforcement efforts, follow the link to the U.S. Justice Department's Management Division available at www.econtoday.com/chap02, and click on the budget summary for the most recent year.

Research Project

Propose a plan of action for how society might shift out the production possibilities curve relating the provision of counterterrorism services to the production of traditional police services without increasing the total number of local, state, and federal law enforcement personnel. (Hint: What other types of resources and what types of technologies might be used instead of people to perform antiterrorism and regular law enforcement tasks?)

SUMMARY DISCUSSION of Learning Objectives

1. **The Problem of Scarcity, Even for the Affluent:** Scarcity is very different from poverty. No one can obtain all one desires from nature without sacrifice. Thus even the richest people face scarcity because they have to make choices among alternatives. Despite their high levels of income or wealth, affluent people, like everyone else, want more than they can have (in terms of goods, power, prestige, and so on).

2. **Why Economists Consider Individuals' Wants but Not Their "Needs":** Goods are all things from which individuals derive satisfaction. Economic goods are those for which the desired quantity exceeds the amount that is directly available from nature at a zero price. To economists, the term *need* is undefinable, whereas humans have unlimited *wants,* which are defined as the goods and services on which we place a positive value.

3. **Why Scarcity Leads People to Evaluate Opportunity Costs:** We measure the opportunity cost of anything by the highest-valued alternative that one must give up to obtain it. The trade-offs that we face as individuals and as a society can be represented by a production possibilities curve (PPC), and moving from one point on a PPC to another entails incurring an opportunity cost. The reason is that along a PPC, all currently available resources and technology are being used, so obtaining more of one good requires shifting resources to production of that good and away from production of another. That is, there is an opportunity cost of allocating scarce resources toward producing one good instead of another good.

4. **Why Obtaining Increasing Increments of a Good Requires Giving Up More and More Units of Other Goods:** Typically, resources are specialized. Thus, when society allocates additional resources to producing more and more of a single good, it must increasingly employ resources that would be better suited for producing other goods. As a result, the law of increasing relative cost holds. Each additional unit of a good can be obtained only by giving up more and more of other goods, which means that the production possibilities curve that society faces is bowed outward.

5. **The Trade-Off Between Consumption Goods and Capital Goods:** If we allocate more resources to producing capital goods today, then, other things being equal, the economy will grow faster than it would have otherwise. Thus the production possibilities curve will shift outward by a larger amount in the future, which means that we can have more consumption goods in the future. The trade-off, however, is that producing more capital goods today entails giving up consumption goods today.

6. **Absolute Advantage versus Comparative Advantage:** A person has an absolute advantage if she can produce more of a specific good than someone else who uses the same amount of resources. Nevertheless, the individual may be better off producing a different good if she has a comparative advantage in producing that good, meaning that she can produce the good at a lower opportunity cost than someone else. By specializing in producing the good for which she has a comparative advantage, she assures herself of reaping gains from specialization in the form of a higher income.

KEY TERMS AND CONCEPTS

absolute advantage (38)

comparative advantage (38)

consumption (36)

division of labor (39)

economic goods (27)

efficiency (34)

entrepreneurship (27)

goods (27)

human capital (27)

inefficient point (34)

labor (27)

land (27)

law of increasing relative cost (35)

opportunity cost (29)

physical capital (27)

production (26)

production possibilities curve (PPC) (30)

scarcity (26)

services (27)

specialization (38)

technology (33)

PROBLEMS

Answers to the odd-numbered problems appear at the back of the book.

2-1. Define opportunity cost. What is your opportunity cost of attending a class at 11:00 A.M.? How does it differ from your opportunity cost of attending a class at 8:00 A.M.?

2-2. If you receive a free ticket to a concert, what, if anything, is your opportunity cost of attending the concert? How does your opportunity cost change if miserable weather on the night of the concert requires you to leave much earlier for the concert hall and greatly extends the time it takes to get home afterward?

2-3. The following table illustrates the points a student can earn on examinations in economics and biology if the student uses all available hours for study.

Economics	Biology
100	40
90	50
80	60
70	70
60	80
50	90
40	100

Plot this student's production possibilities curve. Does the PPC illustrate increasing or decreasing opportunity costs?

2-4. Based on the information provided in Problem 2-3, what is the opportunity cost to this student of allocating enough additional study time on economics to move her grade up from a 90 to a 100?

2-5. Consider the following costs that a student incurs by attending a public university for one semester: $3,000 for tuition, $1,000 for room and board, $500 for books and $3,000 in after-tax wages lost that the student could have earned working. What is the total opportunity cost that the student incurs by attending college for one semester?

2-6. Consider a change in the table in Problem 2-3. The student's set of opportunities is now as follows:

Economics	Biology
100	40
90	60
80	75
70	85
60	93
50	98
40	100

Plot this student's production possibilities curve. Does the PPC illustrate increasing or decreasing opportunity costs? What is the opportunity cost to this student for the additional amount of study time on economics required to move her grade from 60 to 70? From 90 to 100?

2-7. Construct a production possibilities curve for a nation facing increasing opportunity costs for producing food and video games. Show how the PPC changes given the following events.

a. A new and better fertilizer is invented.
b. There is a surge in labor, which can be employed in both the agricultural sector and the video game sector.
c. A new programming language is invented that is less costly to code and is more memory-efficient, enabling the use of smaller game cartridges.
d. A heat wave and drought result in a 10 percent decrease in usable farmland.

2-8. The president of a university announces to the local media that the university was able to construct its sports complex at a lower cost than it had previously projected. The president argues that the university can now purchase a yacht for the president at no additional cost. Explain why this statement is false by considering opportunity cost.

2-9. You can wash, fold, and iron a basket of laundry in two hours and prepare a meal in one hour. Your roommate can wash, fold, and iron a basket of laundry in three hours and prepare a meal in one hour. Who has the absolute advantage in laundry, and who has an absolute advantage in meal preparation? Who has the comparative advantage in laundry, and who has a comparative advantage in meal preparation?

2-10. Based on the information in Problem 2-9, should you and your roommate specialize in a particular task?

Why? And if so, who should specialize in which task? Show how much labor time you save if you choose to "trade" an appropriate task with your roommate as opposed to doing it yourself.

2-11. On the one hand, Canada goes to considerable lengths to protect its television program and magazine producers from U.S. competitors. The United States, on the other hand, often seeks protection from food imports from Canada. Construct an argument showing that from an economywide viewpoint, these efforts are misguided.

2-12. Using only the concept of comparative advantage, evaluate this statement: "A professor with a Ph.D. in economics should never mow his or her own lawn, because this would fail to take into account the professor's comparative advantage."

2-13. Country A and country B produce the same consumption goods and capital goods and currently have *identical* production possibilities curves. They also have the same resources at present, and they have access to the same technology.

   a. At present, does either country have a comparative advantage in producing capital goods? Consumption goods?

   b. Currently, country A has chosen to produce more consumption goods, compared with country B. Other things being equal, which country will experience the larger outward shift of its PPC during the next year?

   c. Suppose that a year passes with no changes in technology or in factors other than the capital goods and consumption goods choices the countries initially made. In addition, suppose that both countries' PPCs have shifted outward from their initial positions, but not in a parallel fashion. Country B's opportunity cost of producing consumption goods will now be higher than country A's. Does either country have a comparative advantage in producing capital goods? Consumption goods?

Consider the following diagram when answering Problems 2-14, 2-15, and 2-16

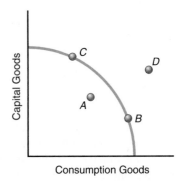

2-14. During a debate on the floor of the U.S. Senate, Senator Creighton makes the statement. "Our nation should not devote so many of its fully employed resources to producing capital goods, become we are already not producing enough consumption goods for our citizens." Compared with the other labled points on the diagram which one could be consistent with the *current* production combination choice that Senator Creighton believes the nation has made?

2-15. In response to Senator Creighton's statement reported in Problem 2-14, Senator Long replies, "We must remain at our current production combination if we want to be able to produce more consumption goods in the future." Of the labled points on the diagram, which one could depict the *future* production combination Senator Long has in mind?

2-16. Senator Borman interjects the following comment after the statements by Senators Creighton and Long reported in Problems 2-14 and 2-15: "In fact, both of my esteemed colleagues are wrong, because an unacceptably large portion of our nation's resources is currently unemployed." Of the labled points on the diagram, which one is consistent with Senator Borman's position?

ECONOMICS ON THE NET

Opportunity Cost and Labor Force Participation Many students choose to forgo full-time employment to concentrate on their studies, thereby incurring a sizable opportunity cost. This application explores the nature of this opportunity cost.

Title: College Enrollment and Work Activity of High School Graduates

Navigation: Go to www.econtoday.com/chap02 to visit the Bureau of Labor Statistics (BLS) home page. Select A–Z Index and then click on *Educational Attainment, Statistics.* Finally, under the heading "Economic News Releases," click on *College Enrollment and Work Activity of High School Graduates.*

Application Read the abbreviated report on college enrollment and work activity of high school graduates. Then answer the following questions.

1. Based on the article, explain who the BLS considers to be in the labor force and who it does not view as part of the labor force.

2. What is the difference in labor force participation rates between high school students entering four-year universities and those entering two-year universities? Using the concept of opportunity cost, explain the difference.

3. What is the difference in labor force participation rates between part-time college students and full-time college students? Using the concept of opportunity cost, explain the difference.

For Group Study and Analysis Read the last paragraph of the article. Then divide the class into two groups. The first group should explain, based on the concept of opportunity cost, the difference in labor force participation rates between youths not in school but with a high school diploma and youths not in school and without a high school diploma. The second half should explain, based on opportunity cost, the difference in labor force participation rates between men and women not in school but with a high school diploma and men and women not in school and without a high school diploma.

Media Resources

If your exam were tomorrow, would you be ready? For each chapter, MyEconLab Practice Tests and Study Plans pinpoint which sections you have mastered and which ones you need to study. That way, you are more efficient with your study time, and you are better prepared for your exams.

In addition to Practice Tests and your personalized Study Plan, you'll find the following media resources in MyEconLab:

1. *Graphs in Motion* animation of Figures 2-1, 2-3, and 2-4.

2. An *Economics in Motion* in-depth animation of the Production Possibilities Curve.

3. Videos featuring the author, Roger LeRoy Miller, on the following subjects:
   ● Scarcity, Resources, and Production
   ● Absolute versus Comparative Advantage

4. Links to the Web sites cited in the marginal Internet Resources, Issues and Applications feature, and Economics on the Net activity.

5. Audio clips of all key terms, additional practice problems, and a PDF version of the material from the print Study Guide.

6. eThemes of the Times, which is a New York Times article to help you understand the real-world applications of what you are learning.

myeconlab
Get Ahead of the Curve

To see how it works, turn to page 16 and then go to www.myeconlab.com/miller.

Chapter 3

Demand and Supply

The early 2000s were tough years for many job seekers, including those with a new Ph.D. in economics looking for jobs as college and university instructors. Many of these individuals were seeking positions at the same time that colleges and universities were cutting back on hiring. Their economics training had prepared the applicants to understand the nature of the problem they faced: The *supply* of economics instructors had increased at the same time that the *demand* for economics instructors had declined. As you will learn in this chapter, one outcome could be predicted with certainty: Other things being equal, the wages earned by economics instructors had to fall relative to wages available in other occupations.

LEARNING OBJECTIVES

After reading this chapter, you should be able to:

1. Explain the law of demand
2. Discuss the difference between money prices and relative prices
3. Distinguish between changes in demand and changes in quantity demanded
4. Explain the law of supply
5. Distinguish between changes in supply and changes in quantity supplied
6. Understand how the interaction of the demand for and supply of a commodity determines the market price of the commodity and the equilibrium quantity of the commodity that is produced and consumed

Media Resources

Refer to the end of the chapter for a full listing of the multimedia learning materials available in MyEconLab.

... even though the overall level of prices of goods and services has trended slightly upward during the past several decades, the prices of several consumer products have either held steady or declined? The average of all prices consumers pay for goods and services has risen by more than 30 percent since 1992, but the average price of an item of clothing has remained unchanged. The average price of a desktop personal computer has fallen by more than 50 percent.

Clearly, the prices of various items that consumers purchase can vary considerably *relative* to the prices of other goods and services. If we use the economist's primary set of tools, *demand* and *supply*, we can develop a better understanding of why we observe such variations in relative prices. Demand and supply are two ways of categorizing the influences on the price of goods that you buy and the quantities available. As such, demand and supply characterize virtually all economic analysis of the world around us.

As you will see throughout this text, the operation of the forces of demand and supply takes place in *markets*. A **market** is an abstract concept referring to all the arrangements individuals have for exchanging with one another. Goods and services are sold in markets, such as the automobile market, the health care market, and the compact disc market. Workers offer their services in the labor market. Companies, or firms, buy workers' labor services in the labor market. Firms also buy other inputs in order to produce the goods and services that you buy as a consumer. Firms purchase machines, buildings, and land. These markets are in operation at all times. One of the most important activities in these markets is the setting of the prices of all of the inputs and outputs that are bought and sold in our complicated economy. To understand the determination of prices, you first need to look at the law of demand.

Market
All of the arrangements that individuals have for exchanging with one another. Thus, for example, we can speak of the labor market, the automobile market, and the credit market.

THE LAW OF DEMAND

Demand has a special meaning in economics. It refers to the quantities of specific goods or services that individuals, taken singly or as a group, will purchase at various possible prices, other things being constant. We can therefore talk about the demand for microprocessor chips, french fries, CD players, children, and criminal activities.

Associated with the concept of demand is the **law of demand,** which can be stated as follows:

> *When the price of a good goes up, people buy less of it, other things being equal.*
> *When the price of a good goes down, people buy more of it, other things being equal.*

The law of demand tells us that the quantity demanded of any commodity is inversely related to its price, other things being equal. In an inverse relationship, one variable moves up in value when the other moves down. The law of demand states that a change in price causes a change in the quantity demanded in the *opposite* direction.

Notice that we tacked on to the end of the law of demand the statement "other things being equal." We referred to this in Chapter 1 as the *ceteris paribus* assumption. It means, for example, that when we predict that people will buy fewer DVD players if their price goes up, we are holding constant the price of all other goods in the economy as well as people's incomes. Implicitly, therefore, if we are assuming that no other prices change when we examine the price behavior of DVD players, we are looking at the *relative* price of DVD players.

The law of demand is supported by millions of observations of people's behavior in the marketplace. Theoretically, it can be derived from an economic model based on rational behavior, as was discussed in Chapter 1. Basically, if nothing else changes and the price of

Demand
A schedule of how much of a good or service people will purchase at any price during a specified time period, other things being constant.

Law of demand
The observation that there is a negative, or inverse, relationship between the price of any good or service and the quantity demanded, holding other factors constant.

a good falls, the lower price induces us to buy more over a certain period of time because we can enjoy additional net gains that were unavailable at the higher price. For the most part, if you examine your own behavior, you will see that it generally follows the law of demand.

Relative Prices versus Money Prices

Relative price
The price of one commodity divided by the price of another commodity; the number of units of one commodity that must be sacrificed to purchase one unit of another commodity.

Money price
The price that we observe today, expressed in today's dollars; also called the *absolute* or *nominal price.*

The **relative price** of any commodity is its price in terms of another commodity. The price that you pay in dollars and cents for any good or service at any point in time is called its **money price.** You might hear from your grandparents, "My first new car cost only fifteen hundred dollars." The implication, of course, is that the price of cars today is outrageously high because the average new car might cost $30,000. But that is not an accurate comparison. What was the price of the average house during that same year? Perhaps it was only $12,000. By comparison, then, given that the average price of houses today is close to $200,000, the price of a new car today doesn't sound so far out of line, does it?

The point is that money prices during different time periods don't tell you much. You have to calculate relative prices. Consider an example of the price of prerecorded DVDs versus prerecorded videocassettes from last year and this year. In Table 3-1, we show the money prices of DVDs and videocassettes for two years during which they have both gone up. That means that we have to pay out in today's dollars more for DVDs and more for videocassettes. If we look, though, at the relative prices of DVDs and videocassettes, we find that last year, DVDs were twice as expensive as videocassettes, whereas this year they are only $1\frac{3}{4}$ times as expensive. Conversely, if we compare videocassettes to DVDs, last year the price of videocassettes was half the price of DVDs, but today the price of videocassettes is about 57 percent higher. In the one-year period, though both prices have gone up in money terms, the relative price of DVDs has fallen (and equivalently, the relative price of videocassettes has risen).

When evaluating the effects of price changes, we must always compare *price per constant-quality unit.* Sometimes relative price changes occur because the quality of a product improves, thereby bringing about a decrease in the item's effective price per constant-quality unit.

Even though you are used to buying products that include multiple features, did you know that more and more products are being offered with different features sold separately? Read on.

TABLE 3-1
Money Price versus Relative Price
The money prices of both digital videodiscs (DVDs) and videocassettes have risen. But the relative price of DVDs has fallen (or conversely, the relative price of videocassettes has risen).

	Money Price		Relative Price	
	Price Last Year	Price This Year	Price Last Year	Price This Year
DVDs	$20	$28	$\frac{\$20}{\$10} = 2.0$	$\frac{\$28}{\$16} = 1.75$
Videocassettes	$10	$16	$\frac{\$10}{\$20} = 0.5$	$\frac{\$16}{\$28} = 0.57$

EXAMPLE

What's the Effective Price per Constant-Quality Unit? It Depends on Whether the Product Is "Bundled"

Consumers often pay a single price for products containing more than one feature. For instance, traditionally the price of a hotel room normally covered associated housekeeping services. Consequently, consumers could compare hotel prices per constant-quality unit, which included essential housekeeping services regarded as part of the overall package of amenities that hotels provided. Nowadays, however, a growing number of hotels offer guests a choice: the hotel room will not be cleaned each day unless the guest pays a fee ranging from $2 to $4 per day.

Likewise, in years past, the price of a durable good purchased from a retailer commonly included the privilege of returning the item if the purchaser chose not to keep it. Today many retailers charge customers for handling product returns. Electronics stores, for example, often charge consumers returning video cameras or DVD players restocking fees equal to 10 to 15 percent of the purchase price.

Such separate prices and fees are part of a growing trend toward product *unbundling* in hotel services, retailing, and various other industries. Individual features of products that sellers previously grouped together and sold as a set now are being offered as separately priced items. If this trend continues in these and other industries, consumers may ultimately find it easier to assess the effective price per constant-quality unit of the products. In the meantime, however, consumers seeking the lowest effective price must pay close attention to whether various product features are priced separately or as bundles.

For Critical Analysis
Why might some consumers be willing to pay an office supply store such as Office Depot or Staples a higher price for a pre-assembled desk, rather than paying a significantly lower price for an unassembled desk?

CONCEPTS in Brief

- The law of demand posits an inverse relationship between the quantity demanded of a good and its price, other things being equal.

- The law of demand applies when other things, such as income and the prices of all other goods and services, are held constant.

To test your understanding of the concepts covered in this section, go to the Online Review at www.myeconlab.com/miller.

THE DEMAND SCHEDULE

Let's take a hypothetical demand situation to see how the inverse relationship between the price and the quantity demanded looks (holding other things equal). We will consider the quantity of rewritable CDs demanded *per year*. Without stating the *time dimension*, we could not make sense out of this demand relationship because the numbers would be different if we were talking about the quantity demanded per month or the quantity demanded per decade.

In addition to implicitly or explicitly stating a time dimension for a demand relationship, we are also implicitly referring to *constant-quality units* of the good or service in question. Prices are always expressed in constant-quality units in order to avoid the problem of comparing commodities that are in fact not truly comparable.

In panel (a) of Figure 3-1 on the next page, we see that if the price were $1 apiece, 50 rewritable CDs would be bought each year by our representative individual, but if the price were $5 apiece, only 10 CDs would be bought each year. This reflects the law of demand. Panel (a) is also called simply demand, or a *demand schedule*, because it gives a schedule of alternative quantities demanded per year at different possible prices.

FIGURE 3-1
The Individual Demand Schedule and the Individual Demand Curve

In panel (a), we show combinations A through E of the quantities of rewritable CDs demanded, measured in constant-quality units at prices ranging from $5 down to $1 apiece. These combinations are points on the demand schedule. In panel (b), we plot combinations A through E on a grid. The result is the individual demand curve for rewritable CDs.

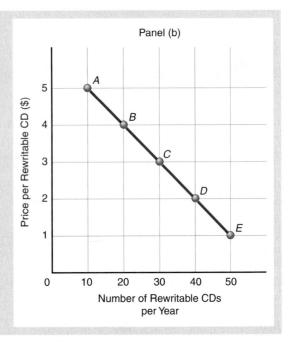

Panel (b)

Panel (a)

Combination	Price per Constant-Quality Rewritable CD	Quantity of Constant-Quality Rewritable CDs per Year
A	$5	10
B	4	20
C	3	30
D	2	40
E	1	50

The Demand Curve

Tables expressing relationships between two variables can be represented in graphical terms. To do this, we need only construct a graph that has the price per constant-quality rewritable CD on the vertical axis and the quantity measured in constant-quality rewritable CDs per year on the horizontal axis. All we have to do is take combinations A through E from panel (a) of Figure 3-1 and plot those points in panel (b). Now we connect the points with a smooth line, and *voilà*, we have a **demand curve.**[*] It is downward sloping (from left to right) to indicate the inverse relationship between the price of rewritable CDs and the quantity demanded per year. Our presentation of demand schedules and curves applies equally well to all commodities, including dental floss, bagels, textbooks, credit, and labor. Remember, the demand curve is simply a graphical representation of the law of demand.

Demand curve
A graphical representation of the demand schedule; a negatively sloped line showing the inverse relationship between the price and the quantity demanded (other things being equal).

Individual versus Market Demand Curves

The demand schedule shown in panel (a) of Figure 3-1 and the resulting demand curve shown in panel (b) are both given for an individual. As we shall see, the determination of price in the marketplace depends on, among other things, the **market demand** for a particular commodity. The way in which we measure a market demand schedule and derive a market demand curve for rewritable CDs or any other good or service is by summing (at each price) the individual quantities demanded by all buyers in the market. Suppose that the market demand for rewritable CDs consists of only two buyers: buyer 1, for whom we've already shown the demand schedule, and buyer 2, whose demand schedule is dis-

Market demand
The demand of all consumers in the marketplace for a particular good or service. The summation at each price of the quantity demanded by each individual.

---

[*]Even though we call them "curves," for the purposes of exposition we often draw straight lines. In many real-world situations, demand and supply curves will in fact be lines that do curve. To connect the points in panel (b) with a line, we assume that for all prices in between the ones shown, the quantities demanded will be found along that line.

FIGURE 3-2
The Horizontal Summation of Two Demand Curves

Panel (a) shows how to sum the demand schedule for one buyer with that of another buyer. In column 2 is the quantity demanded by buyer 1, taken from panel (a) of Figure 3-1. Column 4 is the sum of columns 2 and 3. We plot the demand curve for buyer 1 in panel (b) and the demand curve for buyer 2 in panel (c). When we add those two demand curves horizontally, we get the market demand curve for two buyers, shown in panel (d).

Panel (a)

(1) Price per Rewritable CD	(2) Buyer 1's Quantity Demanded	(3) Buyer 2's Quantity Demanded	(4) = (2) + (3) Combined Quantity Demanded per Year
$5	10	10	20
4	20	20	40
3	30	40	70
2	40	50	90
1	50	60	110

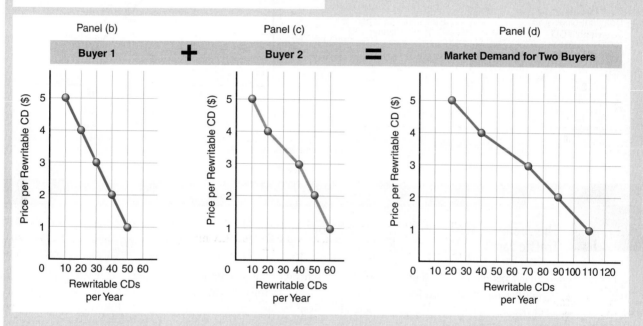

played in column 3 of panel (a) of Figure 3-2. Column 1 shows the price, and column 2 shows the quantity demanded by buyer 1 at each price. These data are taken directly from Figure 3-1. In column 3, we show the quantity demanded by buyer 2. Column 4 shows the total quantity demanded at each price, which is obtained by simply adding columns 2 and 3. Graphically, in panel (d) of Figure 3-2, we add the demand curves of buyer 1 [panel (b)] and buyer 2 [panel (c)] to derive the market demand curve.

There are, of course, numerous potential consumers of rewritable CDs. We'll simply assume that the summation of all of the consumers in the market results in a demand schedule, given in panel (a) of Figure 3-3 on the next page, and a demand curve, given in panel (b). The quantity demanded is now measured in millions of units per year. Remember, panel (b) in Figure 3-3 shows the market demand curve for the millions of users of rewritable CDs. The "market" demand curve that we derived in Figure 3-2 was undertaken assuming that there were only two buyers in the entire market. That's why we assume that the "market" demand curve for two buyers in panel (d) of Figure 3-2 is not a smooth line, whereas the true market demand curve in panel (b) of Figure 3-3 is a smooth line with no kinks.

Now that you know about the law of demand, what do you think happened in the last few years in Japan after the government raised the nation's highway tolls?

FIGURE 3-3
The Market Demand Schedule for Rewritable CDs

In panel (a), we add up the existing demand schedules for rewritable CDs. In panel (b), we plot the quantities from panel (a) on a grid; connecting them produces the market demand curve for rewritable CDs.

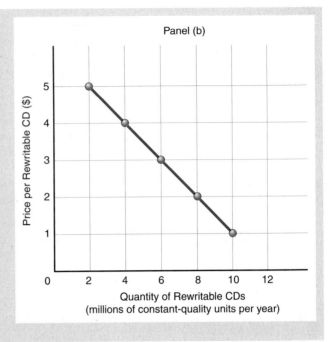

Panel (b)

Panel (a)

Price per Constant-Quality Rewritable CD	Total Quantity Demanded of Constant-Quality Rewritable CDs per Year (millions)
$5	2
4	4
3	6
2	8
1	10

International Policy EXAMPLE

The Japanese Government Discovers How to Prevent Traffic Jams on Expressways

In the United States, many people refer to auto expressways as "freeways." Applying the Japanese word for "free" to expressways would never occur to a resident of Japan, where all 4,350 miles of the nation's expressways are toll roads. The fee to make a two-hour trip on almost any stretch of a Japanese expressway is nearly $50. If the trip includes crossing a bridge, another $50 toll will apply. Someone who wishes to drive the entire length of Japan, a country slightly smaller in size than California, typically must pay at least $325 in tolls.

Since 1997, the average expressway toll in Japan has risen by about 8 percent *per mile*. Based on the law of demand, the result was predictable. Japanese trucking firms have instructed drivers to use expressways when necessary to meet delivery schedules but to keep to regular streets as much as possible to minimize tolls. Local delivery services prohibit their drivers from using expressways at all. Some Tokyo commuters even use global positioning systems in their cars to plot meandering trips on surface streets to avoid using expressways. As a consequence, the number of vehicles driving on Japanese expressways each day has dropped from 3.8 million in 1997 to below 3.6 million today.

For Critical Analysis
Why do you suppose that many Japanese drivers are still willing to pay higher tolls to drive on expressways?

CONCEPTS in Brief

- We measure the demand schedule in terms of a time dimension and in constant-quality units.

- The market demand curve is derived by summing the quantity demanded by individuals at each price. Graphically, we add the individual demand curves horizontally to derive the total, or market, demand curve.

To test your understanding of the concepts covered in this section, go to the Online Review at **www.myeconlab.com/miller.**

SHIFTS IN DEMAND

Assume that the federal government gives every student registered in a college, university, or technical school in the United States a rewritable CD drive (CD-RW drive) to use with personal computers. The demand curve presented in panel (b) of Figure 3-3 would no longer be an accurate representation of total market demand for rewritable CDs. What we have to do is shift the curve outward, or to the right, to represent the rise in demand that would result from this program. There will now be an increase in the number of rewritable CDs demanded at *each and every possible price*. The demand curve shown in Figure 3-4 will shift from D_1 to D_2. Take any price, say, $3 per rewritable CDs. Originally, before the federal government giveaway of CD-RW drives, the amount demanded at $3 was 6 million rewritable CDs per year. After the government giveaway of CD-RW drives, however, the new amount demanded at the $3 price is 10 million rewritable CDs per year. What we have seen is a shift in the demand for rewritable CDs.

Under different circumstances, the shift can also go in the opposite direction. What if colleges uniformly prohibited the use of personal computers by any of their students? Such a regulation would cause a shift inward—to the left—of the demand curve for rewritable CDs. In Figure 3-4, the demand curve would shift to D_3; the quantity demanded would now be less at each and every possible price.

The Other Determinants of Demand

The demand curve in panel (b) of Figure 3-3 is drawn with other things held constant, specifically all of the other factors that determine how much will be bought. There are many such determinants. We refer to these determinants as **ceteris paribus conditions,** and they include consumers' income; tastes and preferences; the prices of related goods; expectations regarding future prices, future incomes, and future product availability; and market size (number of buyers). Let's examine each determinant more closely.

Ceteris paribus conditions
Determinants of the relationship between price and quantity that are unchanged along a curve; changes in these factors cause the curve to shift.

Income. For most goods, an increase in income will lead to an increase in demand. The expression *increase in demand* always refers to a comparison between two different demand curves. Thus, for most goods, an increase in income will lead to a rightward shift in the position of the demand curve from, say, D_1 to D_2 in Figure 3-4 on the following page. You can avoid confusion about shifts in curves by always relating a rise in demand to a rightward shift in the demand curve and a fall in demand to a leftward shift in the demand curve. Goods for which the demand rises when consumer income rises are called **normal goods.** Most goods, such as shoes, computers, and DVDs, are "normal goods." For some goods, however, demand *falls* as income rises. These are called **inferior goods.** Beans might be an example. As households get richer, they tend to purchase fewer and fewer beans and purchase more and more meat. (The terms *normal* and *inferior* are merely part of the economist's lexicon; no value judgments are associated with them.)

Remember, a shift to the left in the demand curve represents a decrease in demand, and a shift to the right represents an increase in demand.

Normal goods
Goods for which demand rises as income rises. Most goods are normal goods.

Inferior goods
Goods for which demand falls as income rises.

Tastes and Preferences. A change in consumer tastes in favor of a good can shift its demand curve outward to the right. When Pokémon trading cards became the rage, the demand curve for them shifted outward to the right; when the rage died out, the demand curve shifted inward to the left. Fashions depend to a large extent on people's tastes and preferences. Economists have little to say about the determination of tastes; that is, they don't have any "good" theories of taste determination or why people buy one brand of

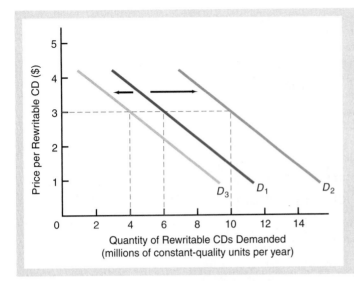

product rather than others. Advertisers, however, have various theories that they use to try to make consumers prefer their products over those of competitors.

What do you suppose happened to the demand for grapefruit when people learned that consumption of the fruit could, under certain circumstances, have adverse effects on their health?

E X A M P L E

Why Grapefruit Sales Have Gone Sour

Kids have never been known to like grapefruit, and many busy working people do not like to take the time to eat it. Consequently, grapefruit producers have found that many of their best customers are older, retired individuals.

Elderly people also tend to be the primary consumers of blood pressure and anticholesterol medications. In 1997, medical researchers discovered that grapefruit juice inhibits the production of an intestinal enzyme that breaks down such drugs, thereby amplifying their effects. Thus a person who drinks grapefruit juice while taking these drugs may experience side effects such as headaches and muscle pain. By the early 2000s, most physicians had begun suggesting that individuals taking

blood pressure and anti-cholesterol medications limit their intake of grapefruit juice.

Since the news of this discovery appeared in press reports in 1998, the demand for grapefruit has dropped significantly. In 1997, U.S. residents consumed about 4.6 billion pounds of grapefruit. Now they consume only about 3.4 billion pounds of grapefruit each year.

For Critical Analysis
How do you suppose that the recently publicized discovery that increased grapefruit juice consumption by younger people helps reduce cholesterol is likely to affect the demand for grapefruit?

Prices of Related Goods: Substitutes and Complements. Demand schedules are always drawn with the prices of all other commodities held constant. That is to say, when deriving a given demand curve, we assume that only the price of the good under study changes. For example, when we draw the demand curve for butter, we assume that the price of margarine is held constant. When we draw the demand curve for home cinema speakers, we assume that the price of surround-sound amplifiers is held constant. When we refer to *related goods*, we are talking about goods for which demand is interdependent. If a change in the price of one good shifts the demand for another good, those two goods have interdependent demands. There are two types of demand interdependencies: those in which goods are *substitutes* and those in which goods are *complements*. We can define and distinguish between substitutes and complements in terms of how the change in price of one commodity affects the demand for its related commodity.

Butter and margarine are **substitutes.** Either can be consumed to satisfy the same basic want. Let's assume that both products originally cost $2 per pound. If the price of butter remains the same and the price of margarine falls from $2 per pound to $1 per pound, people will buy more margarine and less butter. The demand curve for butter will shift inward to the left. If, conversely, the price of margarine rises from $2 per pound to $3 per pound, people will buy more butter and less margarine. The demand curve for butter will shift outward to the right. In other words, an increase in the price of margarine will lead to an increase in the demand for butter, and an increase in the price of butter will lead to an increase in the demand for margarine. For substitutes, a change in the price of a substitute will cause a change in demand *in the same direction*.

How do you think food-product manufacturers that can use either flavoring syrups or honey as sweeteners have responded to a recent rise in the price of honey?

Substitutes
Two goods are substitutes when either one can be used for consumption to satisfy a similar want—for example, coffee and tea. The more you buy of one, the less you buy of the other. For substitutes, the change in the price of one causes a shift in demand for the other in the same direction as the price change.

E X A M P L E

Higher Honey Prices Boost the Demand for Flavoring Syrup

The U.S. flavoring syrup industry processes a range of ingredients such as sugar, fruit, corn, and preservatives into concentrated syrups. Various food manufacturers use these flavoring syrups as sweetening ingredients in soft drinks, ice cream, and desserts.

Between 2000 and 2003, the price of honey, a substitute food-sweetening ingredient, increased from $0.60 per pound to just over $1.30 per pound. In 2001 and 2002, food manufacturers responded to the rising price of honey by continuing to buy honey, albeit in somewhat smaller quantities. By 2003, however, a number of food manufacturers had found ways to alter their recipes so that they could substitute flavoring syrups for honey. These manufacturers then reduced their orders for honey and boosted their orders for flavoring syrups. Thus the rise in the price of a substitute good, honey, caused the demand for flavoring syrups to increase, resulting in a rightward shift in the market demand curve for flavoring syrups.

For Critical Analysis
Why do you suppose that food manufacturers' substitution of flavoring syrups for honey did not occur instantaneously when the price of honey increased so much?

For **complements,** goods typically consumed together, the situation is reversed. Consider desktop computers and printers. We draw the demand curve for printers with the price of desktop computers held constant. If the price per constant-quality unit of computers decreases from, say, $2,000 to $1,000, that will encourage more people to purchase computer peripheral devices. They will now buy more printers, at any given printer price, than before. The demand curve for printers will shift outward to the right. If, by contrast, the price of desktop computers increases from $1,500 to $3,000, fewer people will purchase computer peripheral devices. The demand curve for printers will shift inward to the left. To summarize, a decrease in the price of computers leads to an increase in the demand for printers. An increase in the price of computers leads to a decrease in the demand for printers. Thus, for complements, a change in the price of a product will cause a change in demand *in the opposite direction*.

Complements
Two goods are complements if both are used together for consumption or enjoyment—for example, coffee and cream. The more you buy of one, the more you buy of the other. For complements, a change in the price of one causes an opposite shift in the demand for the other.

Why have higher cement prices induced builders to cut back on hiring construction workers?

EXAMPLE

Reduced Hiring of Construction Workers Is Set in Cement

Cement is an essential ingredient in the construction of building foundations. This is why U.S. builders purchase more than 100 million metric tons of cement every year.

In many parts of the United States, the price of cement has increased significantly in recent years. Builders have responded by redesigning buildings to use less cement and by hiring fewer workers to pour and shape cement. Thus the rise

in the price of cement has generated a decrease in the demand for complementary construction workers.

For Critical Analysis
How has the rise in the price of cement likely affected the demand for brick, which is a substitute for cement in certain construction applications?

Expectations. Consumers' expectations regarding future prices, future incomes, and future availability will prompt them to buy more or less of a particular good without a change in its current money price. For example, consumers getting wind of a scheduled 100 percent price increase in rewritable CDs next month will buy more of them today at today's prices. Today's demand curve for rewritable CDs will shift from D_1 to D_2 in Figure 3-4 on page 56. The opposite would occur if a decrease in the price of rewritable CDs were scheduled for next month.

Expectations of a rise in income may cause consumers to want to purchase more of everything today at today's prices. Again, such a change in expectations of higher future income will cause a shift in the demand curve from D_1 to D_2 in Figure 3-4.

Finally, expectations that goods will not be available at any price will induce consumers to stock up now, increasing current demand.

Market Size (Number of Buyers). An increase in the number of buyers (holding buyers' incomes constant) shifts the market demand curve outward. Conversely, a reduction in the number of buyers shifts the market demand curve inward.

Changes in Demand versus Changes in Quantity Demanded

We have made repeated references to demand and to quantity demanded. It is important to realize that there is a difference between a *change in demand* and a *change in quantity demanded*.

Demand refers to a schedule of planned rates of purchase and depends on a great many *ceteris paribus* conditions, such as incomes, expectations, and the prices of substitutes or complements. Whenever there is a change in a *ceteris paribus* condition, there will be a change in demand—a shift in the entire demand curve to the right or to the left.

A quantity demanded is a specific quantity at a specific price, represented by a single point on a demand curve. When price changes, quantity demanded changes according to the law of demand, and there will be a movement from one point to another along the same demand curve. Look at Figure 3-5. At a price of $3 per rewritable CD, 6 million CDs per year are demanded. If the price falls to $1, quantity demanded increases to 10 million per year. This movement occurs because the current market price for the product changes. In Figure 3-5, you can see the arrow pointing down the given demand curve *D*.

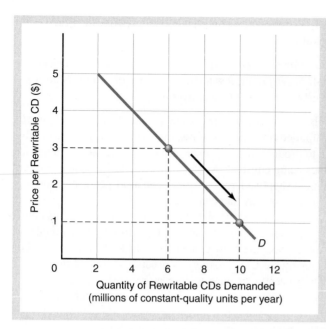

FIGURE 3-5
Movement Along a Given Demand Curve
A change in price changes the quantity of a good demanded. This can be represented as movement along a given demand schedule. If, in our example, the price of rewritable CDs falls from $3 to $1 apiece, the quantity demanded will increase from 6 million to 10 million units per year.

When you think of demand, think of the entire curve. Quantity demanded, in contrast, is represented by a single point on the demand curve.

A change or shift in demand is a movement of the **entire** *curve. The* **only** *thing that can cause the entire curve to move is a change in a determinant* **other than its own price.**

In economic analysis, we cannot emphasize too much the following distinction that must constantly be made:

A change in a good's own price leads to a change in quantity demanded for any given demand curve, other things held constant. This is a movement **on** *the curve.*

A change in any of the **ceteris paribus** *conditions for demand leads to a change in demand. This causes a movement* **of** *the curve.*

CONCEPT in Brief

- Demand curves are drawn with determinants other than the price of the good held constant. These other determinants, called *ceteris paribus* conditions, are (1) income; (2) tastes and preferences; (3) prices of related goods; (4) expectations about future prices, future incomes, and future availability of goods; and (5) market size (the number of buyers in the market). If any one of these determinants changes, the demand schedule will shift to the right or to the left.

- A change in demand comes about only because of a change in the *ceteris paribus* conditions of demand. This change in demand shifts the demand curve to the left or to the right.

- A change in the quantity demanded comes about when there is a change in the price of the good (other things held constant). Such a change in quantity demanded involves a movement along a given demand curve.

To test your understanding of the concepts covered in this section, go to the Online Review at www.myeconlab.com/miller.

THE LAW OF SUPPLY

The other side of the basic model in economics involves the quantities of goods and services that firms will offer for sale to the market. The **supply** of any good or service is the amount that firms will produce and offer for sale under certain conditions during a speci-

Supply
A schedule showing the relationship between price and quantity supplied for a specified period of time, other things being equal.

fied time period. The relationship between price and quantity supplied, called the **law of supply,** can be summarized as follows:

> *At higher prices, a larger quantity will generally be supplied than at lower prices, all other things held constant. At lower prices, a smaller quantity will generally be supplied than at higher prices, all other things held constant.*

There is generally a direct relationship between price and quantity supplied. For supply, as the price rises, the quantity supplied rises; as price falls, the quantity supplied also falls. Producers are normally willing to produce and sell more of their product at a higher price than at a lower price, other things being constant. At $5 per rewritable CD, manufacturers would almost certainly be willing to supply a larger quantity than at $1 per disc, assuming, of course, that no other prices in the economy had changed.

As with the law of demand, millions of instances in the real world have given us confidence in the law of supply. On a theoretical level, the law of supply is based on a model in which producers and sellers seek to make the most gain possible from their activities. For example, as a manufacturer of rewritable CDs attempts to produce more and more discs over the same time period, it will eventually have to hire more workers, pay overtime wages (which are higher), and overutilize its machines. Only if offered a higher price per disc will the manufacturer be willing to incur these higher costs. That is why the law of supply implies a direct relationship between price and quantity supplied.

THE SUPPLY SCHEDULE

Just as we were able to construct a demand schedule, we can construct a *supply schedule*, which is a table relating prices to the quantity supplied at each price. A supply schedule can also be referred to simply as *supply*. It is a set of planned production rates that depends on the price of the product. We show the individual supply schedule for a hypothetical producer in panel (a) of Figure 3-6. At $1 per rewritable CD, for example, this producer will supply 20,000 discs per year; at $5, this producer will supply 55,000 discs per year.

The Supply Curve

We can convert the supply schedule in panel (a) of Figure 3-6 into a **supply curve,** just as we earlier created a demand curve in Figure 3-1. All we do is take the price-quantity combinations from panel (a) of Figure 3-6 and plot them in panel (b). We have labeled these combinations *F* through *J*. Connecting these points, we obtain an upward-sloping curve that shows the typically direct relationship between price and quantity supplied. Again, we have to remember that we are talking about quantity supplied *per year*, measured in constant-quality units.

The Market Supply Curve

Just as we had to sum the individual demand curves to get the market demand curve, we need to sum the individual producers' supply curves to get the market supply curve. Look at Figure 3-7, in which we horizontally sum two typical supply curves for manufacturers of rewritable CDs. Supplier 1's data are taken from Figure 3-6; supplier 2 is added. The numbers are presented in panel (a). The graphical representation of supplier 1 is in panel (b), of supplier 2 in panel (c), and of the summation in panel (d). The result, then, is the supply curve for rewritable CDs for suppliers 1 and 2. We assume that there are more suppliers of rewritable CDs, however. The total market supply schedule and total market supply curve for rewritable CDs are represented in Figure 3-8 on the page 62, with the curve in panel (b) obtained by adding all of the supply curves such as those shown in panels (b)

FIGURE 3-6
The Individual Producer's Supply Schedule and Supply Curve for Rewritable CDs

Panel (a) shows that at higher prices, a hypothetical supplier will be willing to provide a greater quantity of rewritable CDs. We plot the various price-quantity combinations in panel (a) on the grid in panel (b). When we connect these points, we find the individual supply curve for rewritable CDs. It is positively sloped.

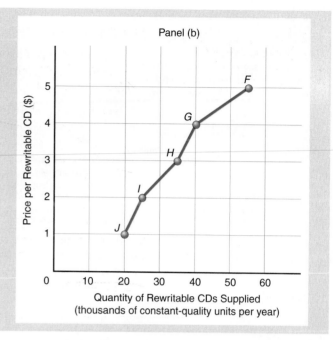

Panel (b)

Panel (a)		
Combination	Price per Constant-Quality Rewritable CD	Quantity of Rewritable CDs Supplied (thousands of constant-quality units per year)
F	$5	55
G	4	40
H	3	35
I	2	25
J	1	20

FIGURE 3-7
Horizontal Summation of Supply Curves

In panel (a), we show the data for two individual suppliers of rewritable CDs. Adding how much each is willing to supply at different prices, we come up with the combined quantities supplied in column 4. When we plot the values in columns 2 and 3 on grids in panels (b) and (c) and add them horizontally, we obtain the combined supply curve for the two suppliers in question, shown in panel (d).

Panel (a)			
(1) Price per Rewritable CD	(2) Supplier 1's Quantity Supplied (thousands)	(3) Supplier 2's Quantity Supplied (thousands)	(4) = (2) + (3) Combined Quantity Supplied per Year (thousands)
$5	55	35	90
4	40	30	70
3	35	20	55
2	25	15	40
1	20	10	30

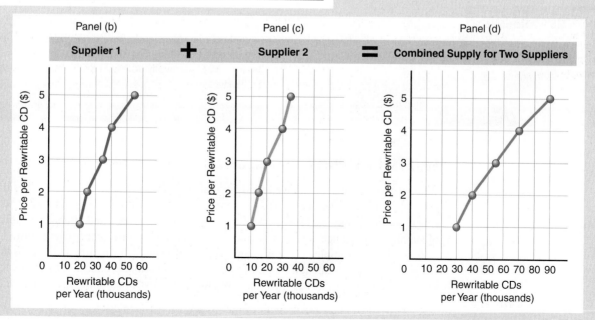

Panel (b)   Supplier 1   **+**   Panel (c)   Supplier 2   **=**   Panel (d)   Combined Supply for Two Suppliers

FIGURE 3-8
The Market Supply Schedule and the Market Supply Curve for Rewritable CDs

In panel (a), we show the summation of all the individual producers' supply schedules; in panel (b), we graph the resulting supply curve. It represents the market supply curve for rewritable CDs and is upward sloping.

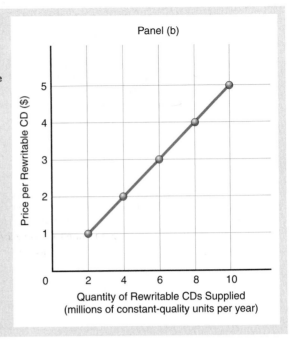
Panel (b)

Panel (a)

Price per Constant-Quality Rewritable CD	Quantity of Rewritable CDs Supplied (millions of constant-quality units per year)
$5	10
4	8
3	6
2	4
1	2

and (c) of Figure 3-7 on the previous page. Notice the difference between the market supply curve with only two suppliers in Figure 3-7 and the one with a large number of suppliers—the entire true market—in panel (b) of Figure 3-8. (For simplicity, we assume that the true total market supply curve is a straight line.)

Notice what happens at the market level when price changes. If the price is $3, the quantity supplied is 6 million. If the price goes up to $4, the quantity supplied increases to 8 million per year. If the price falls to $2, the quantity supplied decreases to 4 million per year. Changes in quantity supplied are represented by movements along the supply curve in panel (b) of Figure 3-8.

CONCEPTS in Brief

- There is normally a direct, or positive, relationship between price and quantity of a good supplied, other things held constant.

- The supply curve normally shows a direct relationship between price and quantity supplied. The market supply curve is obtained by horizontally adding individual supply curves in the market.

To test your understanding of the concepts covered in this section, go to the Online Review at www.myeconlab.com/miller.

SHIFTS IN SUPPLY

When we looked at demand, we found out that any change in anything relevant besides the price of the good or service caused the demand curve to shift inward or outward. The same is true for the supply curve. If something besides price changes and alters the willingness of suppliers to produce a good or service, we will see the entire supply curve shift.

Consider an example. There is a new method of manufacturing rewritable CDs that reduces the cost of production by 50 percent. In this situation, producers of rewritable CDs will supply more product at *all* prices because their cost of so doing has fallen dramatically. Competition among manufacturers to produce more at each and every price will shift the supply curve outward to the right from S_1 to S_2 in Figure 3-9. At a price of $3, the quantity supplied was originally 6 million per year, but now the quantity supplied (after the reduction in the costs of production) at $3 per rewritable CD will be 9 million a year. (This is similar to what has happened to the supply curve of personal computers and fax machines in recent years as computer memory chip prices have fallen.)

Consider the opposite case. If the cost of making rewritable CDs doubles, the supply curve in Figure 3-9 will shift from S_1 to S_3. At each and every price, the quantity of rewritable CDs supplied will fall due to the increase in the price of raw materials.

The Other Determinants of Supply

When supply curves are drawn, only the price of the good in question changes, and it is assumed that other things remain constant. The other things assumed constant are the *ceteris paribus* conditions of supply. They include the prices of resources (inputs) used to produce the product, technology and productivity, taxes and subsides, producers' price expectations, and the number of firms in the industry. If *any* of these *ceteris paribus* conditions changes, there will be a shift in the supply curve.

Cost of Inputs Used to Produce the Product. If one or more input prices fall, the supply curve will shift outward to the right; that is, more will be supplied at each and every price. The opposite will be true if one or more inputs become more expensive. For example, when we draw the supply curve of new laptop computers, we are holding the price of microprocessors (and other inputs) constant. When we draw the supply curve of blue jeans, we are holding the cost of cotton fabric fixed.

Technology and Productivity. Supply curves are drawn by assuming a given technology, or "state of the art." When the available production techniques change, the supply curve will shift. For example, when a better production technique for rewritable CDs becomes available, the supply curve will shift to the right. A larger quantity will be forthcoming at each and every price because the cost of production is lower.

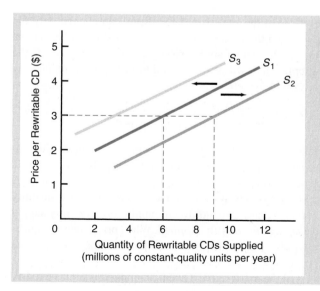

FIGURE 3-9
A Shift in the Supply Curve

If the cost of producing rewritable CDs were to fall dramatically, the supply curve would shift rightward from S_1 to S_2 such that at all prices, a larger quantity would be forthcoming from suppliers. Conversely, if the cost of production rose, the supply curve would shift leftward to S_3.

Subsidy
A negative tax; a payment to a producer from the government, usually in the form of a cash grant per unit.

Taxes and Subsidies. Certain taxes, such as a per-unit tax, are effectively an addition to production costs and therefore reduce the supply. If the supply curve were S_1 in Figure 3-9 on the previous page, a per-unit tax increase would shift it to S_3. A **subsidy** would do the opposite; it would shift the curve to S_2. Every producer would get a "gift" from the government for each unit produced.

How do you think that the supply of new housing in California has been affected by higher costs homebuilders face in meeting environmental regulations, which amount to a tax on each house they construct?

Policy EXAMPLE

Reducing the Supply of New Housing in California

To meet environmental regulations that have been added in recent years, developers and contractors must go through an approval process for new construction that is among the most complicated in the United States. According to some estimates, satisfying the regulations has added about $70,000 to the cost of building each new California home.

Naturally, builders have been willing to construct any given quantity of new houses only if they receive a price that is higher by $70,000 per house. This implies that, other things being equal, the supply curve for new-home construction has shifted upward by $70,000 per house. California's toughened environmental restrictions have, therefore, had the effect of reducing the supply of new houses in that state.

For Critical Analysis
On net, what would happen to the supply of housing if the state of California attempted to boost the production of new homes by granting every builder a $35,000 subsidy for each newly constructed house?

Price Expectations. A change in the expectation of a future relative price of a product can affect a producer's current willingness to supply, just as price expectations affect a consumer's current willingness to purchase. For example, suppliers of rewritable CDs may withhold from the market part of their current supply if they anticipate higher prices in the future. The current quantity supplied at each and every price will decrease.

Number of Firms in the Industry. In the short run, when firms can change only the number of employees they use, we hold the number of firms in the industry constant. In the long run, the number of firms (or the size of some existing firms) may change. If the number of firms increases, the supply curve will shift outward to the right. If the number of firms decreases, it will shift inward to the left.

Changes in Supply versus Changes in Quantity Supplied

We cannot overstress the importance of distinguishing between a movement along the supply curve—which occurs only when the price changes for a given supply curve—and a shift in the supply curve—which occurs only with changes in *ceteris paribus* conditions. A change in the price of the good in quesion always brings about a change in the quantity supplied along a given supply curve. We move to a different point on the existing supply curve. This is specifically called a *change in quantity supplied*. When price changes, quantity supplied changes, and there will be a movement from one point to another along the same supply curve.

When you think of *supply*, think of the entire curve. Quantity supplied is represented by a single point on the supply curve.

A change or shift in supply is a movement of the entire curve. The **only** *thing that can cause the entire curve to move is a change in one of the* **ceteris paribus** *conditions.*

Consequently,

A change in the price leads to a change in the quantity supplied, other things being constant. This is a movement **on** *the curve.*

A change in any **ceteris paribus** *conditon for supply leads to a change in supply. This causes a movement* **of** *the curve.*

CONCEPTS in Brief

● If the price changes, we *move along* a curve—there is a change in quantity demanded or supplied. If some other determinant changes, we *shift* a curve—there is a change in demand or supply.

● The supply curve is drawn with other things held constant. If these *ceteris paribus* conditions of supply change, the supply curve will shift. The major *ceteris paribus* conditions are (1) input prices, (2) technology and productivity, (3) taxes and subsidies, (4) expectations of future relative prices, and (5) the number of firms in the industry.

To test your understanding of the concepts covered in this section, go to the Online Review at www.myeconlab.com/miller.

PUTTING DEMAND AND SUPPLY TOGETHER

In the sections on demand and supply, we tried to confine each discussion to demand or supply only. But you have probably already realized that we can't view the world just from the demand side or just from the supply side. There is an interaction between the two. In this section, we will discuss how they interact and how that interaction determines the prices that prevail in our economy. Understanding how demand and supply interact is essential to understanding how prices are determined in our economy and other economies in which the forces of demand and supply are allowed to work.

Let's first combine the demand and supply schedules and then combine the curves.

Demand and Supply Schedules Combined

Let's place panel (a) from Figure 3-3 (the market demand schedule) on page 54 and panel (a) from Figure 3-8 (the market supply schedule) on page 62 together in panel (a) of Figure 3-10 on the next page. Column 1 shows the price; column 2, the quantity supplied per year at any given price; and column 3, the quantity demanded. Column 4 is the difference between columns 2 and 3, or the difference between the quantity supplied and the quantity demanded. In column 5, we label those differences as either excess quantity supplied (called a *surplus*, which we shall discuss shortly) or excess quantity demanded (commonly known as a *shortage*, also discussed shortly). For example, at a price of $1, only 2 million rewritable CDs would be supplied, but the quantity demanded would be 10 million. The difference would be −8 million, which we label excess quantity demanded (a shortage). At the other end, a price of $5 would elicit 10 million in quantity supplied, but quantity demanded would drop to 2 million, leaving a difference of +8 million units, which we call excess quantity supplied (a surplus).

Now, do you notice something special about the price of $3? At that price, both the quantity supplied and the quantity demanded per year are 6 million. The difference then is zero. There is neither excess quantity demanded (shortage) nor excess quantity supplied (surplus). Hence the price of $3 is very special. It is called the **market clearing price**—it clears the market of all excess quantities demanded or supplied. There are no willing con-

Go to www.econtoday.com/chap03 to see how the U.S. Department of Agriculture seeks to estimate demand and supply conditions for major agricultural products.

Market clearing, or equilibrium, price
The price that clears the market, at which quantity demanded equals quantity supplied; the price where the demand curve intersects the supply curve.

FIGURE 3-10
Putting Demand and Supply Together

In panel (a), we see that at the price of $3, the quantity supplied and the quantity demanded are equal, resulting in neither an excess quantity demanded nor an excess quantity supplied. We call this price the equilibrium, or market clearing, price. In panel (b), the intersection of the supply and demand curves is at *E*, at a price of $3 and a quantity of 6 million per year. At point *E*, there is neither an excess quantity demanded nor an excess quantity supplied. At a price of $1, the quantity supplied will be only 2 million per year, but the quantity demanded will be 10 million. The difference is excess quantity demanded at a price of $1. The price will rise, so we will move from point *A* up the supply curve and point *B* up the demand curve to point *E*. At the other extreme, $5 elicits a quantity supplied of 10 million but a quantity demanded of only 2 million. The difference is excess quantity supplied at a price of $5. The price will fall, so we will move down the demand curve and the supply curve to the equilibrium price, $3 per disc.

		Panel (a)		
(1)	(2)	(3)	(4) Difference (2) − (3)	(5)
Price per Constant-Quality Rewritable CD	Quantity Supplied (rewritable CDs per year)	Quantity Demanded (rewritable CDs per year)	(rewritable CDs per year)	Condition
$5	10 million	2 million	8 million	Excess quantity supplied (surplus)
4	8 million	4 million	4 million	Excess quantity supplied (surplus)
3	6 million	6 million	0	Market clearing price—equilibrium (no surplus, no shortage)
2	4 million	8 million	−4 million	Excess quantity demanded (shortage)
1	2 million	10 million	−8 million	Excess quantity demanded (shortage)

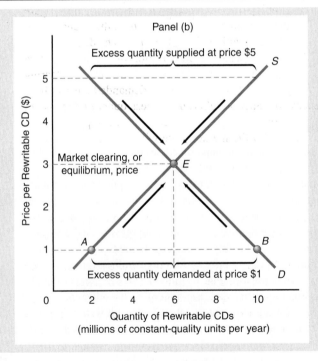

sumers who want to pay $3 per rewritable CD but are turned away by sellers, and there are no willing suppliers who want to sell rewritable CDs at $3 who cannot sell all they want at that price. Another term for the market clearing price is the **equilibrium price,** the price at which there is no tendency for change. Consumers are able to get all they want at that price, and suppliers are able to sell all they want at that price.

Equilibrium

We can define **equilibrium** in general as a point at which quantity demanded equals quantity supplied at a particular price. There tends to be no movement of the price or the quantity away from this point unless demand or supply changes. Any movement away from this point will set into motion forces that will cause movement back to it. Therefore, equilibrium is a stable point. Any point that is not at equilibrium is unstable and cannot be maintained.

Equilibrium
The situation when quantity supplied equals quantity demanded at a particular price.

The equilibrium point occurs where the supply and demand curves intersect. The equilibrium price is given on the vertical axis directly to the left of where the supply and demand curves cross. The equilibrium quantity is given on the horizontal axis directly underneath the intersection of the demand and supply curves. Equilibrium can change whenever there is a *shock* caused by a change in a *certeris peribus* condition for demand or supply.

A shock to the supply-and-demand system can be represented by a shift in the supply curve, a shift in the demand curve, or a shift in both curves. Any shock to the system will result in a new set of supply-and-demand relationships and a new equilibrium; forces will come into play to move the system from the old price-quantity equilibrium (now a disequilibrium situation) to the new equilibrium, where the new demand and supply curves intersect.

Panel (b) in Figure 3-3 and panel (b) in Figure 3-8 are combined as panel (b) in Figure 3-10. The only difference now is that the horizontal axis measures both the quantity supplied and the quantity demanded per year. Everything else is the same. The demand curve is labeled *D*, the supply curve *S*. We have labeled the intersection of the supply curve with the demand curve as point *E*, for equilibrium. That corresponds to a market clearing price of $3, at which both the quantity supplied and the quantity demanded are 6 million units per year. There is neither excess quantity supplied nor excess quantity demanded. Point *E*, the equilibrium point, always occurs at the intersection of the supply and demand curves. This is the price *toward which* the market price will automatically tend to gravitate.

Shortages

The demand and supply curves depicted in Figure 3-10 represent a situation of equilibrium. But a non-market-clearing, or disequilibrium, price will put into play forces that cause the price to change toward the market clearing price at which equilibrium will again be sustained. Look again at panel (b) in Figure 3-10. Suppose that instead of being at the market clearing price of $3, for some reason the market price is $1. At this price, the quantity demanded of 10 million per year exceeds the quantity supplied of 2 million per year. We have a situation of excess quantity demanded at the price of $1. This is usually called a **shortage.** Consumers of rewritable CDs would find that they could not buy all that they wished at $1 apiece. But forces will cause the price to rise: Competing consumers will bid up the price, and suppliers will increase output in response. (Remember, some buyers would pay $5 or more rather than do without rewritable CDs. They do not want to be left out.) We would move from points *A* and *B* toward point *E*. The process would stop when the price again reached $3 per disc.

Shortage
A situation in which quantity demanded is greater than quantity supplied at a price below the market clearing price.

**Economics
Front and Center**

To consider how a natural disaster
can create shortages of services
that can only be eliminated
speedily by a rapid price change,
consider the case study,
**The Economics of a Tornado
Cleanup Can Hit Close
to Home,** on page 70.

At this point, it is important to recall a distinction made in Chapter 2:

Shortages and scarcity are not the same thing.

A shortage is a situation in which the quantity demanded exceeds the quantity supplied at a price *below* the market clearing price. Our definition of scarcity was much more general and all-encompassing: a situation in which the resources available for producing output are insufficient to satisfy all wants. Any choice necessarily costs an opportunity, and the opportunity is lost. Hence we will always live in a world of scarcity because we must constantly make choices, but we do not necessarily have to live in a world of shortages.

Knowing what you do about why prices change, what do you think happened relatively recently when freight trains didn't have enough space to transport all of the grain that farmers wanted to supply?

E X A M P L E

The Price of Rail Transport Responds to a Rail Traffic Logjam

Recently, a big increase in the prices of grains such as wheat and corn, caused by a number of factors, induced farmers to grow more grain. When it came time to ship the grain to market on freight trains, which typically transport more than 40 percent of all U.S. grain, a problem arose. At prevailing rail shipping prices, railroad companies did not wish to provide enough freight cars to transport all the grain that farmers desired to ship. Farmers faced a shortage of rail transport services that led to some of the longest crop-shipping delays in years.

Within weeks, however, the price of rail transport of grain had risen, which induced some farmers to delay their grain shipments and gave railroad companies an incentive to put more freight cars into service. This equalized the quantities of rail freight services demanded and supplied and ended the shortage of grain transport services.

For Critical Analysis
What would have occurred if a government regulation had prevented the price of shipping grain by rail from rising to the equilibrium level?

Surpluses

Now let's repeat the experiment with the market price at $5 rather than at the market clearing price of $3. Clearly, the quantity supplied will exceed the quantity demanded at that price. The result will be an excess quantity supplied at $5 per unit. This excess quantity supplied is often called a **surplus.** Given the curves in panel (b) in Figure 3-10 on page 66, however, there will be forces pushing the price back down toward $3 per rewritable CD: Competing suppliers will cut prices and reduce output, and consumers will purchase more at these new lower prices. If the two forces of supply and demand are unrestricted, they will bring the price back to $3 per disc.

Surplus
A situation in which quantity supplied is greater than quantity demanded at a price above the market clearing price.

Shortages and surpluses are resolved in unfettered markets—markets in which price changes are free to occur. The forces that resolve them are those of competition: In the case of shortages, consumers competing for a limited quantity supplied drive up the price; in the case of surpluses, sellers compete for the limited quantity demanded, thus driving prices down to equilibrium. The equilibrium price is the only stable price, and all (unrestricted) market prices tend to gravitate toward it.

What happens when the price is set below the equilibrium price? Here come the scalpers.

Policy EXAMPLE

Should Shortages in the Ticket Market Be Solved by Scalpers?

If you have ever tried to get tickets to a playoff game in sports, a popular Broadway play, or a superstar's rap concert, you know about "shortages." The standard Super Bowl ticket situation is shown in Figure 3-11. At the face-value price of Super Bowl tickets (P_1), the quantity demanded (Q_2) greatly exceeds the quantity supplied (Q_1). Because shortages last only so long as prices and quantities do not change, markets tend to exhibit a movement out of this disequilibrium toward equilibrium. Obviously, the quantity of Super Bowl tickets cannot change, but the price can go as high as P_2.

Enter the scalper. This colorful term is used because when you purchase a ticket that is being resold at a price higher than face value, the seller is skimming an extra profit off the top ("taking your scalp"). If an event sells out and people who wished to purchase tickets at current prices were unable to do so, ticket prices by definition have been lower than market clearing prices. People without tickets may be willing to buy high-priced tickets because they place a greater value on the entertainment event than the face value of the ticket. Without scalpers, those individuals would not be able to attend the event. In the case of the Super Bowl, various forms of scalping occur nationwide. Tickets for a seat on the 50-yard line have been sold for more than $2,000 apiece. In front of every Super Bowl arena, you can find ticket scalpers hawking their wares.

In most states, scalping is illegal. In Pennsylvania, convicted scalpers are either fined $5,000 or sentenced to two years behind bars. For an economist, such legislation seems strange. As one New York ticket broker said, "I look at scalping like working as a stockbroker, buying low and selling high. If people are willing to pay me the money, what kind of problem is that?"

For Critical Analysis
What happens to ticket scalpers who are still holding tickets after an event has started?

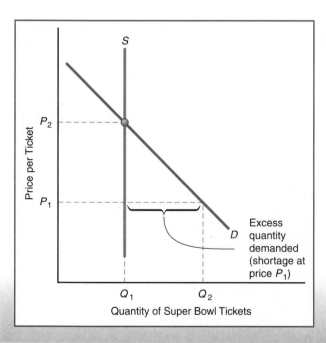

FIGURE 3-11
Shortages of Super Bowl Tickets
The quantity of tickets for any one Super Bowl is fixed at Q_1. At the price per ticket of P_1, the quantity demanded is Q_2, which is greater than Q_1. Consequently, there is an excess quantity demanded at the below–market clearing price. Prices can go as high as P_2 in the scalpers' market.

CONCEPTS in Brief

- The market clearing price occurs at the intersection of the market demand curve and the market supply curve. It is also called the equilibrium price, the price from which there is no tendency to change unless there is a change in demand or supply.

- Whenever the price is greater than the equilibrium price, there is an excess quantity supplied (a surplus).

- Whenever the price is less than the equilibrium price, there is an excess quantity demanded (a shortage).

To test your understanding of the concepts covered in this section, go to the Online Review at www.myeconlab.com/miller.

CASE STUDY: Economics Front and Center

The Economics of a Tornado Cleanup Can Hit Close to Home

An early spring tornado has just rolled through a midwestern town, and more than 500 structures have experienced at least moderate damage. After recovering from the initial shock, one couple, the Richardsons, realize that they are lucky to have only blown-out windows and large holes in their roof, which they quickly cover with plastic sheeting. When they try to find a construction contractor to make permanent repairs, however, they do not feel so lucky any more. Most phone calls to contractors are producing either busy signals or unanswered voice mail messages. The few contractors who respond say that they are overwhelmed with requests for work and cannot possibly begin the Richardsons' repairs for at least a couple of weeks. Meanwhile, temperatures are dropping, and rain is forecast for all of next week.

Finally, two contractors call back and say their companies will do the work, but only at prices that the Richardsons know to be nearly 25 percent higher than the usual prices charged to replace windows and a roof. How can demand and supply analysis explain the situation that the Richardsons are facing?

Points to Analyze

1. Has the structural damage inflicted on this town by the tornado resulted in changes in the demand for and supply of the services of construction contractors or changes in the quantities demanded and supplied of those services?

2. Why are the price quotes the Richardsons have received higher than the "usual" prices charged by local contractors?

Issues and Applications

Why Your Economics Instructor's Salary May Be Lagging

So far, the 2000s have been tough on young economists interested in teaching students like you at colleges and universities. Jobs have been more difficult to find than in years past. Salaries have been stagnant. The problem that prospective economics instructors face is one they would like to use as an example in an economics course—if only some of them could find teaching positions right away.

Concepts Applied
- Demand and Supply
- Surplus
- Market Clearing Price

A Sudden Spurt in the Supply of New Economists

The level of interest in advanced economics training has ebbed and flowed over the years. In the late 1970s and 1980s, many students became attracted to what is sometimes called the "queen of the social sciences." Enrollments in U.S. economics Ph.D. programs, where many new economics instructors are trained, surged. During the 1990s, enrollments in these programs declined when many people decided to enter the business world instead of becoming economics instructors.

Enrollments at U.S. graduate economics programs changed again in the early 2000s. More students chose careers as economists, which resulted in an increase in the number of individuals trained to teach the subject to college and university students. By 2004, nearly 250 more economics instructors per year were searching for teaching positions at any given price—in this case, a wage rate—than in 2000. Thus there was an increase in the supply of teaching services available from economics instructors.

Fewer Opportunities for New Economics Instructors

Unfortunately for all these budding teachers of economics, the early 2000s were also trying times for colleges and universities. Many publicly supported state institutions experienced funding cutbacks. Private colleges and universities also suffered from drops in stock prices that reduced the value of endowments provided by alumni and other benefactors.

Consequently, there was a fall in the revenues of the colleges and universities that employ economics instructors. These institutions responded to the decline in their revenues by cutting back on the number of job openings for new instructors. By 2004, colleges and universities were searching to fill about 400 fewer economics teaching positions per year than in 2000. That is, at any given wage rate for the services provided by economics instructors, the quantity of services demanded declined. There was a decrease in demand.

Pity Your Economics Instructor

Figure 3-12 on the next page summarizes the combined effects of the increase in the supply of and the decrease in the demand for the services of economics instructors. Following the rightward shift in supply, from S_1 to S_2, and the leftward shift in demand, from D_1 to D_2, there was an excess quantity of teaching services supplied at the initial price of these services, which was the wage rate W_1. Your current economics instructor has taught you how to reason out what had to happen to eliminate the market surplus: The market clearing price of the services economics instructors provided, their wage, had to decline, from W_1 to W_2. On net, the equilibrium quantity of services provided by new economics instructors declined. Hence, as shown in Figure 3-12, the equilibrium quantity fell from Q_1 at point E_1 to Q_2 at point E_2.

FIGURE 3-12

A Simultaneous Increase in the Supply of and Decrease in the Demand for Services of Economics Instructors

During the early 2000s, more individuals offered their services as economics instructors at any given price of their instructional services, or wage rate. At the same time, colleges and universities reduced the quantity of economics instructors' services demanded at each possible wage rate. Consequently, the equilibrium wage rate declined. The net effect was a decrease in the equilibrium quantity of services provided by economics instructors.

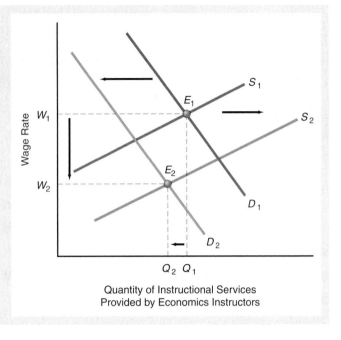

Quantity of Instructional Services
Provided by Economics Instructors

For Critical Analysis

1. How do you suppose that the decline in the relative wages earned by economics instructors during the early 2000s affected the demand for the services of graduate programs that train new economics instructors?
2. What would have happened to the equilibrium quantity of services provided by newly trained economics instructors if the revenues of colleges and universities had *increased* during this period?

Web Resources

1. Track jobs for new economics instructors at the links to academic position openings provided by the American Economic Association's "Job Openings for Economists" site by going to www.econtoday.com/chap03.
2. For the U.S. Department of Labor's outlook on career opportunities in college and university teaching, use the link provided at www.econtoday.com/chap03.

Research Project

Many of today's senior economics instructors are part of the relatively large "baby boom" generation born between the end of World War II and the late 1950s. A number of these individuals are now reaching retirement age. Evaluate what is likely to happen, other things being equal, to the relative wages of younger economics instructors if many of these older instructors retire from their positions during the next few years.

SUMMARY DISCUSSION of Learning Objectives

1. **The Law of Demand:** According to the law of demand, other things being equal, individuals will purchase fewer units of a good at a higher price, and they will purchase more units of a good at a lower price.

2. **Relative Prices versus Money Prices:** When determining the quantity of a good to purchase, people respond to

changes in its relative price, the price of the good in terms of other goods, rather than a change in the good's money price expressed in today's dollars. If the price of a CD rises by 50 percent next year while at the same time all other prices, including your wages, also increase by 50 percent, then the relative price of the CD has not changed. Thus, in a world of generally rising prices, you have to compare the price of one good with the general level of prices of other goods in order to decide whether the relative price of that one good has gone up, gone down, or stayed the same.

3. **A Change in Quantity Demanded versus a Change in Demand:** The demand schedule shows the relationship between various possible prices and respective quantities purchased per unit of time. Graphically, the demand schedule is a downward-sloping demand curve. A change in the price of the good generates a change in the quantity demanded, which is a movement along the demand curve. The determinants of the quantity of a good demanded other than the price of the good are (a) income, (b) tastes and preferences, (c) the prices of related goods, (d) expectations, and (e) market size (the number of buyers). Whenever any of these *ceteris paribus* conditions of demand changes, there is a change in the demand for the good, and the demand curve shifts to a new position.

4. **The Law of Supply:** According to the law of supply, sellers will produce and offer for sale more units of a good at a higher price, and they will produce and offer for sale fewer units of the good at a lower price.

5. **A Change in Quantity Supplied versus a Change in Supply:** The supply schedule shows the relationship between various possible prices and respective quantities produced and sold per unit of time. On a graph, the supply schedule is a supply curve that slopes upward. A change in the price of the good generates a change in the quantity supplied, which is a movement along the supply curve. The determinants of the quantity of a good supplied other than the price of the good are (a) input prices, (b) technology and productivity, (c) taxes and subsidies, (d) price expectations, and (e) the number of sellers. Whenever any of these *ceteris paribus* conditions changes, there is a change in the supply of the good, and the supply curve shifts to a new position

6. **Determining the Market Price and the Equilibrium Quantity:** The market price of a good and the equilibrium quantity of the good that is produced and sold are determined by the intersection of the demand and supply curves. At this intersection point, the quantity demanded by buyers of the good just equals the quantity supplied by sellers. At the market price at this point of intersection, the plans of buyers and sellers mesh exactly. Hence there is neither an excess quantity of the good supplied (surplus) nor an excess quantity of the good demanded (shortage) at this equilibrium point.

KEY TERMS AND CONCEPTS

ceteris paribus conditions (55)

complements (57)

demand (49)

demand curve (52)

equilibrium (67)

inferior goods (55)

law of demand (49)

law of supply (60)

market (49)

market clearing, or equilibrium, price (65)

market demand (52)

money price (50)

normal goods (55)

relative price (50)

shortage (67)

subsidy (64)

substitutes (57)

supply (59)

supply curve (60)

surplus (68)

PROBLEMS

Answers to the odd-numbered problems appear at the back of the book.

3-1. Suppose that in a recent market period, an industry-wide survey determined the following relationship between the price of rap music CDs and the quantity supplied and quantity demanded.

Price	Quantity Demanded	Quantity Supplied
$9	100 million	40 million
$10	90 million	60 million
$11	80 million	80 million
$12	70 million	100 million
$13	60 million	120 million

Illustrate the supply and demand curves for rap CDs given the information in the table. What are the equilibrium price and quantity? If the industry price is $10, is there a shortage or surplus of CDs? How much is the shortage or surplus?

3-2. Suppose that a survey for a later market period indicates that the quantities supplied in the table in Problem 3-1 are unchanged. The quantity demanded, however, has increased by 30 million at each price. Construct the resulting demand curve in the illustration you made for Problem 3-1. Is this an increase or a decrease in demand? What are the new equilibrium quantity and the new market price? Give two examples of changes in *ceteris paribus* conditions in each case that might cause such a change.

3-3. Consider the market for *DSL high-speed* Internet access services, which is a normal good. Explain whether the following events would cause an increase or a decrease in demand or an increase or a decrease in the quantity demanded.

   a. Firms providing cable Internet access services reduce their prices.
   b. Firms providing DSL high-speed Internet access services reduce their prices.
   c. There is a decrease in the incomes earned by consumers of DSL high-speed Internet access services.
   d. Consumers of DSL high-speed Internet access services anticipate a decline in the future price of these services.

3-4. In the market for rap music CDs, explain whether the following events would cause an increase or a decrease in demand or an increase or a decrease in the quantity demanded. Also explain what happens to the equilibrium quantity and the market price.

   a. The price of CD packaging material declines.
   b. The price of CD players declines.
   c. The price of cassette tapes increases dramatically.
   d. A booming economy increases the income of the typical CD buyer.
   e. Many rap fans suddenly develop a fondness for country music.

3-5. Give an example of a complement and a substitute in consumption for each of the following items.

   a. Bacon
   b. Tennis racquets
   c. Coffee
   d. Automobiles

3-6. At the end of the 1990s, the United States imposed high import taxes on a number of European goods due to a trade dispute. One of these goods was Roquefort cheese. Show how this tax affects the market for Roquefort cheese in the United States, shifting the appropriate curve and indicating a new equilibrium quantity and market price.

3-7. Problem 3-6 described a tax imposed on Roquefort cheese. Illustrate the effect of the tax on Roquefort cheese in the market for a similar cheese, such as blue cheese, shifting the appropriate curve and indicating a new equilibrium quantity and market price.

3-8. Consider the market for economics textbooks. Explain whether the following events would cause an increase or a decrease in supply or an increase or a decrease in the quantity supplied.

   a. The market price of paper increases.
   b. The market price of economics textbooks increases.
   c. The number of publishers of economics textbooks increases.
   d. Publishers expect that the market price of economics textbooks will increase next month.

3-9. Consider the market for laptop computers. Explain whether the following events would cause an increase or a decrease in supply or an increase or a decrease in the quantity supplied. Illustrate each, and show what would happen to the equilibrium quantity and the market price.

   a. The price of memory chips used in laptop computers declines.
   b. The price of machinery used to produce laptop computers increases.
   c. The number of manufacturers of laptop computers increases.
   d. There is a decrease in the demand for laptop computers.

3-10. The U.S. government offers significant per-unit subsidy payments to U.S. sugar growers. Describe the effects of the introduction of such subsidies on the market for sugar and the market for artificial sweeteners. Explain whether the demand curve or the supply curve shifts in each market, and if so, in which direction. Also explain what happens to the equilibrium quantity and the market price in each market.

3-11. The supply curve for season tickets for basketball games for your school's team is vertical because there are a fixed number of seats in the school's gymnasium. Before preseason practice sessions begin, your school's administration commits itself to selling season tickets the day before the first basketball game at a predetermined price that happens to equal the current market price. The school will not change that price at any time prior to and including the day tickets go on sale. Illustrate, within a supply and demand framework, the effect of each of the following events on the market for season tickets on the day the school opens ticket sales, and indicate whether a surplus or a shortage would result.

a. The school's star player breaks a leg during preseason practice.

b. During preseason practice, a published newspaper poll of coaches of teams in your school's conference surprises everyone by indicating that your school's team is predicted to win the conference championship.

c. At a preseason practice session that is open to the public, the school president announces that all refreshments served during games will be free of charge throughout the season.

d. Most of your school's basketball fans enjoy an up-tempo, "run and gun" approach to basketball, but after the team's coach quits following the first preseason practice, the school's administration immediately hires a new coach who believes in a deliberate style of play that relies heavily on slow-tempo, four-corners offense.

3-12. Advances in computer technology allow individuals to purchase and download music from the Internet. Buyers may download single songs or complete tracks of songs that are also sold on CDs. Explain the impact of this technological advance on the market for CDs sold in retail stores.

3-13. Ethanol is a motor fuel manufactured from corn, barley, or wheat, and it can be used to power the engines of many autos and trucks. Suppose that the government decides to provide a large per-unit subsidy to ethanol producers. Explain the effects in the markets for the following items:

a. Corn

b. Gasoline

c. Automobiles

3-14. If the price of processor chips used in manufacturing personal computers decreases, what will happen in the market for personal computers? How will the equilibrium price and equilibrium quantity of personal computers change?

3-15. Assume that the cost of aluminum used by soft-drink companies increases. Which of the following correctly describes the resulting effects in the market for canned soft drinks? (More than one statement may be correct.)

a. The demand for soft drinks decreases.

b. The quantity of soft drinks demanded decreases.

c. The supply of soft drinks decreases.

d. The quantity of soft drinks supplied decreases.

ECONOMICS ON THE NET

The U.S. Nursing Shortage For some years media stories have discussed a shortage of qualified nurses in the United States. This application explores some of the factors that have caused the quantity of newly trained nurses demanded to tend to exceed the quantity of newly trained nurses supplied.

Title: Nursing Shortage Resource Web Link

Navigation: Go to the Nursing Shortage Resource Web Link at www.econtoday.com/chap03, and click on *Enrollment Increase Insufficient to Meet the Projected Increase in Demand for New Nurses.*

Application Read the discussion, and answer the following questions.

1. Since 1995, what has happened to the demand for new nurses in the United States? What has happened to the supply of new nurses? Why has the result been a shortage?

2. If there is a free market for the skills of new nurses, what can you predict is likely to happen to the wage rate earned by individuals who have just completed their nursing training?

For Group Study and Analysis Discuss the pros and cons of high schools and colleges trying to factor predictions about future wages into student career counseling. How might this potentially benefit students? What problems might high schools and colleges face in trying to assist students in evaluating the future earnings prospects of various jobs?

If your exam were tomorrow, would you be ready? For each chapter, MyEconLab Practice Tests and Study Plans pinpoint which sections you have mastered and which ones you need to study. That way, you are more efficient with your study time, and you are better prepared for your exams.

In addition to Practice Tests and your personalized Study Plan, you'll find the following media resources in MyEconLab:

1. *Graphs in Motion* animation of Figures 3-2, 3-4, 3-5, 3-6, 3-7, 3-9, and 3-11.
2. An *Economics in Motion* in-depth animation of Demand, Supply, and Equilibrium.
3. Videos featuring the author, Roger LeRoy Miller, on the following subjects:
   - The Difference Between Relative and Absolute Prices and the Importance of Looking at Only Relative Prices
   - The Importance of Distinguishing Between a Shift in a Demand Curve and a Move Along the Demand Curve

- The Importance of Distinguishing Between a Change in Supply versus a Change in Quantity Supplied
4. Links to the Web sites cited in the marginal Internet Resources, Issues and Applications feature, and Economics on the Net activity.
5. Audio clips of all key terms, additional practice problems, and a PDF version of the material from the print Study Guide.
5. eThemes of the Times, which is a New York Times article to help you understand the real-world applications of what you are learning.

To see how it works, turn to page 16 and then go to **www.myeconlab.com/miller**.

Get Ahead of the Curve

Chapter 4

Extensions of Demand and Supply Analysis

Charleston (South Carolina), Jacksonville, New Orleans, and Los Angeles all share one common characteristic: they are seaports. Another shared characteristic is that available space for ships to navigate and dock is increasingly scarce in their ports. Indeed, shipping companies have complained in recent years that there has been a "shortage" of available space at many U.S. seaports. In this chapter, you will learn more about shortages and why a shortage eventually should disappear in an unregulated market. You will also learn, however, why the shortage of space at seaports has been a persistent problem in recent years.

LEARNING OBJECTIVES

After reading this chapter, you should be able to:

1. Discuss the essential features of the price system
2. Evaluate the effects of changes in demand and supply on the market price and equilibrium quantity
3. Understand the rationing function of prices
4. Explain the effects of price ceilings
5. Explain the effects of price floors
6. Describe various types of government-imposed quantity restrictions on markets

Media Resources

Refer to the end of the chapter for a full listing of the multimedia learning materials available in MyEconLab.

when there was an unexpected epidemic of a well-known variety of the influenza (or flu) virus in 2003 and 2004, manufacturers of flu vaccines failed to produce as much vaccine as people wanted to purchase? Indeed, on December 5, 2003, makers of flu vaccines announced that they had "run out" of doses and would not be manufacturing any more. People simply had to accept the absence of vaccines and hope that they and their children—who were particularly at risk from the flu—did not contract the virus. What led to this unresolved mismatch between the quantity of flu vaccines demanded and the quantity producers were willing to supply? As you will learn in this chapter, we can use the supply and demand analysis developed in Chapter 3 to answer this question. Similarly, we can use this analysis to examine the "shortage" of apartments in certain cities, the "surplus" of young workers in labor markets, and many other phenomena. All of these examples are part of our economy, which we characterize as a *price system*.

THE PRICE SYSTEM

Price system
An economic system in which relative prices are constantly changing to reflect changes in supply and demand for different commodities. The prices of those commodities are signals to everyone within the system as to what is relatively scarce and what is relatively abundant.

In a **price system,** otherwise known as a *market system,* relative prices are constantly changing to reflect changes in supply and demand for different commodities. The prices of those commodities are the signals to everyone within the system as to what is relatively scarce and what is relatively abundant. Indeed, it is the *signaling* aspect of the price system that provides the information to buyers and sellers about what should be bought and what should be produced. In a price system, there is a clear-cut chain of events in which any changes in demand and supply cause changes in prices that in turn affect the opportunities that businesses and individuals have for profit and personal gain. Such changes influence our use of resources. In this sense, prices provide information.

EXCHANGE AND MARKETS

Voluntary exchange
An act of trading, done on a voluntary basis, in which both parties to the trade are subjectively better off after the exchange.

Terms of exchange
The conditions under which trading takes place. Usually, the terms of exchange are equal to the price at which a good is traded.

The price system features **voluntary exchange,** acts of trading between individuals that make both parties to the trade subjectively better off. The **terms of exchange**—the prices we pay for the desired items—are determined by the interaction of the forces underlying supply and demand. In our economy, the majority of exchanges take place voluntarily in markets. A market encompasses the exchange arrangements of both buyers and sellers that underlie the forces of supply and demand. Indeed, one definition of a market is a low-cost institution for facilitating exchange. A market increases incomes by helping resources move to their highest-valued uses by means of prices.

Transaction Costs

Transaction costs
All of the costs associated with exchanging, including the informational costs of finding out price and quality, service record, and durability of a product, plus the cost of contracting and enforcing that contract.

Individuals turn to markets because markets reduce the cost of exchanges. These costs are sometimes referred to as **transaction costs,** which are broadly defined as the costs associated with finding out exactly what is being transacted as well as the cost of enforcing contracts. If you were Robinson Crusoe and lived alone on an island, you would never incur a transaction cost. For everyone else, transaction costs are just as real as the costs of production. High-speed computers have allowed us to reduce transaction costs by increasing our ability to process information and keep records.

Consider some simple examples of transaction costs. A club warehouse such as Sam's Club or Costco reduce the transaction costs of having to go to numerous specialty stores to obtain the items you desire. Financial institutions, such as commercial banks, have reduced transaction costs of directing funds from savers to borrowers. In general, the more organized the market, the lower the transaction costs. One group of individuals who constantly attempt to lower transaction costs are the much maligned middlemen.

The Role of Middlemen

As long as there are costs of bringing together buyers and sellers, there will be an incentive for intermediaries, normally called middlemen, to lower those costs. This means that middlemen specialize in lowering transaction costs. Whenever producers do not sell their products directly to the final consumer, by definition, one or more middlemen are involved. Farmers typically sell their output to distributors, who are usually called wholesalers, who then sell those products to retailers such as supermarkets.

How do you think that the Internet has changed the way middlemen work?

e-Commerce EXAMPLE

Shopbots: Middlemen of Choice on the Internet?

Just a few years ago, observers speculated that the Internet would be bad news for middlemen. People would just click their mouse to direct their computer's browser to a Web site where they could deal with a company directly. Nevertheless, software firms have developed *intelligent shopping agents,* sometimes called "shopbots." These are programs that search the Web to help consumers locate items and compare prices. Examples of Internet companies offering shopbots for consumer use are Shopping.com and Price.com, which are part of a shopbot industry that has grown by about 10 percent per year during the past five years.

Many consumers have found that shopbots do a good job of providing price comparisons for identical items. Nevertheless, many critics of shopbots argue that the industry will not continue to grow unless consumers can use shopbots to search for more than just the lowest price of an item. Companies that offer shopbot services have been working frantically to develop new versions that permit consumers to input desired product features in general product categories. In this way, consumers will be able to compare the items offered for sale by different companies based on both the item's price and its quality characteristics.

For Critical Analysis
Why has the massive growth in the number of Web pages broadened the potential market for the services of Internet middlemen such as shopbot companies?

CHANGES IN DEMAND AND SUPPLY

It is in markets that we see the results of changes in demand and supply. In certain situations, it is possible to predict what will happen to equilibrium price and equilibrium quantity when demand or supply changes. Specifically, whenever one curve is stable while the other curve shifts, we can tell what will happen to price and quantity. Consider the possibilities in Figure 4-1 on page 80. In panel (a), the supply curve remains unchanged, but demand increases from D_1 to D_2. Note that the results are an increase in the market clearing price from P_1 to P_2 and an increase in the equilibrium quantity from Q_1 to Q_2.

In panel (b), there is a decrease in demand from D_1 to D_3. This results in a decrease in both the relative price of the good and the equilibrium quantity. Panels (c) and (d) show the effects of a shift in the supply curve while the demand curve is unchanged. In panel (c), the supply curve has shifted rightward. The relative price of the product falls; the equi-

FIGURE 4-1
Shifts in Demand and in Supply: Determinate Results

In panel (a), the supply curve is unchanged at S. The demand curve shifts outward from D_1 to D_2. The equilibrium price and quantity rise from P_1, Q_1 to P_2, Q_2, respectively. In panel (b), again the supply curve is unchanged at S. The demand curve shifts inward to the left, showing a decrease in demand from D_1 to D_3. Both equilibrium price and equilibrium quantity fall. In panel (c), the demand curve now remains unchanged at D. The supply curve shifts from S_1 to S_2. The equilibrium price falls from P_1 to P_2. The equilibrium quantity increases, however, from Q_1 to Q_2. In panel (d), the demand curve is unchanged at D. Supply decreases as shown by a leftward shift of the supply curve from S_1 to S_3. The market clearing price increases from P_1 to P_3. The equilibrium quantity falls from Q_1 to Q_3.

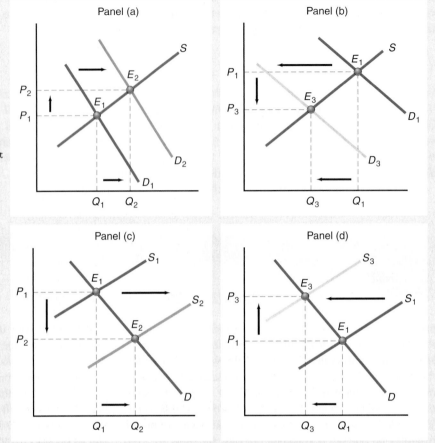

librium quantity increases. In panel (d), supply has shifted leftward—there has been a supply decrease. The product's relative price increases; the equilibrium quantity decreases.

When Both Demand and Supply Shift

The examples in Figure 4-1 show a theoretically determinate outcome of a shift in either the demand curve, holding the supply curve constant, or the supply curve, holding the demand curve constant. When both supply and demand curves change, the outcome is indeterminate for either equilibrium price or equilibrium quantity.

When both demand and supply increase, all we can be certain of is that equilibrium quantity will increase. We do not know what will happen to equilibrium price until we determine whether demand increased relative to supply (equilibrium price will rise) or supply increased relative to demand (equilibrium price will fall). The same analysis applies to decreases in both demand and supply, except that in this case equilibrium quantity falls.

We can be certain that when demand decreases and supply increases at the same time, the equilibrium price will fall, but we do not know what will happen to the equilibrium quantity unless we actually draw the new curves. If supply decreases and demand increases at the same time, we can be sure that equilibrium price will rise, but again we do not know what happens to equilibrium quantity without drawing the curves. In every situation in which both supply and demand change, you should always draw graphs to determine the resulting change in equilibrium price and quantity.

Why do you suppose that U.S. plywood prices rose considerably between 2001 and 2004, even though plywood production and consumption barely increased?

EXAMPLE

Why Plywood Prices Have Soared

In the mid-2000s, one builder said it was as if "all the galaxies had lined up perfectly" to generate a big increase in the equilibrium price of plywood. Of course, astronomical events had nothing to do with why the market clearing price of a 4-foot-by-8-foot sheet of plywood more than doubled between 2002 and 2004. Two forces were responsible for the big run-up in plywood prices: a simultaneous decrease in supply and an increase in demand.

Lower incomes associated with an economic downturn in 2001 had resulted in a decline in new-home construction from 2001 into 2002, and by 2003 a number of lumber sellers had exited the market. Furthermore, in the summer of 2003, unusually wet weather in forested areas of the United States slowed timber harvesting. By the fall of 2003, therefore, the plywood supply curve had shifted considerably leftward, as illustrated in Figure 4-2.

When U.S. incomes rose once again in 2002 and 2003, the demand for new houses increased, which generated an increase in the demand for plywood. Then, in the early autumn of 2003, the government unexpectedly ordered 766,000 sheets of plywood for the U.S. military. Together these factors caused the plywood demand curve to shift rightward, as shown in Figure 4-2. In the end, the total amount of plywood produced in the United States increased only slightly. The equilibrium price of plywood jumped, however, just as predicted in the figure.

For Critical Analysis
What do you suppose happened to the number of firms in the plywood industry in 2004 and 2005 in response to the large price increase between 2001 and 2004?

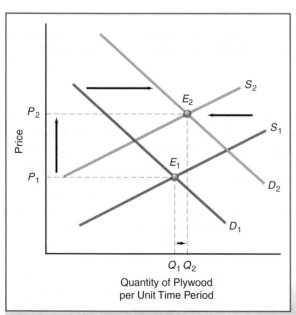

FIGURE 4-2
The Effects of a Simultaneous Decrease in Plywood Supply and Increase in Plywood Demand
In the mid-2000s, various factors contributed to a reduction in the supply of plywood in the United States, depicted by the leftward shift in the plywood supply curve from S_1 to S_2. At the same time, other factors contributed to an increase in the demand for plywood, as shown by the shift in the plywood demand curve from D_1 to D_2. On net, the equilibrium quantity of plywood produced and consumed rose only slightly, from Q_1 at point E_1, to Q_2 at point E_2, but the equilibrium price of plywood increased significantly, from P_1 to P_2.

PRICE FLEXIBILITY AND ADJUSTMENT SPEED

We have used as an illustration for our analysis a market in which prices are quite flexible. Some markets are indeed like that. In others, however, price flexibility may take the form of indirect adjustments such as hidden payments or quality changes. For example, although the published price of bouquets of flowers may stay the same, the freshness of the flowers may change, meaning that the price per constant-quality unit changes. The published price of French bread might stay the same, but the quality could go up or down, thereby changing the price per constant-quality unit. There are many ways to implicitly change prices without actually changing the published price for a *nominal* unit of a product or service.

We must also note that markets do not always return to equilibrium immediately. There may be a significant adjustment time. A shock to the economy in the form of an oil embargo, a drought, or a long strike will not be absorbed overnight. This means that even in unfettered market situations, in which there are no restrictions on changes in prices and quantities, temporary excess quantities supplied or excess quantities demanded may appear. Our analysis simply indicates what the market clearing price and equilibrium quantity ultimately will be, given a demand curve and a supply curve. Nowhere in the analysis is there any indication of the speed with which a market will get to a new equilibrium after a shock. The price may overshoot the equilibrium level. Remember this warning when we examine changes in demand and in supply due to changes in their *ceteris paribus* conditions.

CONCEPTS in Brief

- The terms of exchange in a voluntary exchange are determined by the interaction of the forces underlying demand and supply. These forces take place in markets, which tend to minimize transaction costs.

- When the demand curve shifts outward or inward with an unchanged supply curve, equilibrium price and quantity increase or decrease, respectively. When the supply curve

shifts outward or inward given an unchanged demand curve, equilibrium price moves in the direction opposite to equilibrium quantity.

- When there is a shift in demand or supply, the new equilibrium price is not obtained instantaneously. Adjustment takes time.

To test your understanding of the concepts covered in this section, go to the Online Review at www.myeconlab.com/miller.

THE RATIONING FUNCTION OF PRICES

A shortage creates forces that cause price to rise toward a market clearing, or equilibrium, level. A surplus brings into play forces that cause price to fall toward its market clearing level. The synchronization of decisions by buyers and sellers that leads to equilibrium is called the *rationing function of prices*. Prices are indicators of relative scarcity. An equilibrium price clears the market. The plans of buyers and sellers, given the price, are not frustrated.[*] It is the free interaction of buyers and sellers that sets the price that eventually clears the market. Price, in effect, rations a good to demanders who are willing and able to pay the highest price. Whenever the rationing function of prices is frustrated by government-enforced price ceilings that set prices below the market clearing level, a prolonged shortage results.

---

[*]There is a difference between frustration and unhappiness. You may be unhappy because you can't buy a Rolls Royce, but if you had sufficient income, you would not be frustrated in your attempt to purchase one at the current market price. By contrast, you would be frustrated if you went to your local supermarket and could get only two cans of your favorite soft drink when you had wanted to purchase a dozen and had the necessary funds.

Methods of Non-Price Rationing

There are ways other than price to ration goods. *First come, first served* is one method. *Political power* is another. *Physical force* is yet another. Cultural, religious, and physical differences have been and are used as rationing devices throughout the world.

Consider first come, first served as a rationing device. We call this *rationing by queues,* where *queue* means "line." Whoever is willing to wait in line the longest obtains the good that is being sold at less than the market clearing price. All who wait in line are paying a higher *total* price than the money price paid for the good. Personal time has an opportunity cost. To calculate the total price of the good, we must add up the money price plus the opportunity cost of the time spent waiting.

Random assignment is another way to ration goods. You may have been involved in a rationing-by-random-assignment scheme in college if you were assigned a housing unit. Sometimes rationing by random assignment is used to fill slots in popular classes.

Rationing by *coupons* has also been used, particularly during wartime. In the United States during World War II, families were allotted coupons that allowed them to purchase specified quantities of rationed goods, such as meat and gasoline. To purchase such goods, they had to pay a specified price *and* give up a coupon.

Rationing by waiting may occur in situations in which entrepreneurs are free to change prices to equate quantity demanded with quantity supplied but choose not to do so. This results in queues of potential buyers. It may seem to be that the price in the market is being held below equilibrium by some noncompetitive force. That is not true, however.

Such queuing may arise in a free market when the demand for a good is subject to large or unpredictable fluctuations, and the additional costs to firms (and ultimately to consumers) of constantly changing prices or of holding sufficient inventories or providing sufficient excess capacity to cover peak demands are greater than the costs to consumers of waiting for the good. Common examples are waiting in line to purchase a fast-food lunch and queuing to purchase a movie ticket a few minutes before the next show.

> **Economics Front and Center**
>
> When it comes time to allocate tickets for campus sporting events, colleges use a variety of rationing methods; see the case study, **A Full-Court Press for Season Tickets,** on page 92

The Essential Role of Rationing

In a world of scarcity, there is, by definition, competition for what is scarce. After all, any resources that are not scarce can be had by everyone at a zero price in as large a quantity as everyone wants, such as air to burn in internal combustion engines. Once scarcity arises, there has to be some method to ration the available resources, goods, and services. The price system is one form of rationing; the others that we mentioned are alternatives. Economists cannot say which system of rationing is "best." They can, however, say that rationing via the price system leads to the most efficient use of available resources. This means that generally in a freely functioning price system, all of the gains from mutually beneficial trade will be exhausted.

CONCEPTS in Brief

- Prices in a market economy perform a rationing function because they reflect relative scarcity, allowing the market to clear. Other ways to ration goods include first come, first served; political power; physical force; random assignment; and coupons.

- Even when businesspeople can change prices, some rationing by waiting may occur. Such queuing arises when there are large changes in demand coupled with high costs of satisfying those changes immediately.

To test your understanding of the concepts covered in this section, go to the Online Review at www.myeconlab.com/miller.

Price controls
Government-mandated minimum or maximum prices that may be charged for goods and services.

Price ceiling
A legal maximum price that may be charged for a particular good or service.

Price floor
A legal minimum price below which a good or service may not be sold. Legal minimum wages are an example.

Nonprice rationing devices
All methods used to ration scarce goods that are price-controlled. Whenever the price system is not allowed to work, nonprice rationing devices will evolve to ration the affected goods and services.

Black market
A market in which goods are traded at prices above their legal maximum prices or in which illegal goods are sold.

THE POLICY OF GOVERNMENT-IMPOSED PRICE CONTROLS

The rationing function of prices is prevented when governments impose price controls. **Price controls** often involve setting a **price ceiling**—the maximum price that may be allowed in an exchange. The world has had a long history of price ceilings applied to goods, wages, rents, and interest rates, among other things. Occasionally, a government will set a **price floor**—a minimum price below which a good or service may not be sold. These have most often been applied to wages and agricultural products. Let's first consider price ceilings.

Price Ceilings and Black Markets

As long as a price ceiling is below the market clearing price, imposing a price ceiling creates a shortage, as can be seen in Figure 4-3. At any price below the market clearing, or equilibrium, price of P_e, there will always be a larger quantity demanded than quantity supplied—a shortage, as you will recall from Chapter 3. Normally, whenever quantity demanded exceeds quantity supplied—that is, when a shortage exists—there is a tendency for the price to rise to its equilibrium level. But with a price ceiling, this tendency cannot be fully realized because everyone is forbidden to trade at the equilibrium price.

The result is fewer exchanges and **nonprice rationing devices.** In Figure 4-3, at an equilibrium price of P_e, the equilibrium quantity demanded and supplied (or traded) is Q_e. But at the price ceiling of P_1, the equilibrium quantity offered is only Q_s. Because frustrated consumers will be forced to purchase only Q_s units, there is a shortage. The most obvious nonprice rationing device to help clear the market is queuing, or long lines, which we have already discussed. To avoid physical lines, waiting lists may be established.

Typically, an effective price ceiling leads to a **black market.** A black market is a market in which the price-controlled good is sold at an illegally high price through various methods. For example, if the price of gasoline is controlled at lower than the market clearing price, drivers who wish to fill up their cars may offer the gas station attendant a cash

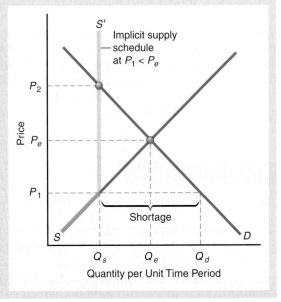

FIGURE 4-3
Black Markets
The demand curve is *D*. The supply curve is *S*. The equilibrium price is P_e. The government, however, steps in and imposes a maximum price of P_1 At that lower price, the quantity demanded will be Q_d, but the quantity supplied will be only Q_s. There is a "shortage." The implicit price (including time costs) tends to rise to P_2. If black markets arise, as they generally will, the equilibrium black market price will end up somewhere between P_1 and P_2. The actual quantity transacted will be between Q_s and Q_e.

payment on the side (as happened in the 1970s in the United States during price controls on gasoline). If the price of beef is controlled at below its market clearing price, the butcher may allocate otherwise unavailable beef to a customer who offers the butcher good tickets to an upcoming football game. Indeed, the true implicit price of a price-controlled good or service can be increased in an infinite number of ways, limited only by the imagination. (Black markets also occur when goods are made illegal.)

What explains the waiting lists that physicians now establish for access to vaccines intended to prevent illnesses such as whooping cough, diphtheria, chicken pox, and influenza?

EXAMPLE

Why Vaccines Can Sometimes Be So Hard to Obtain

In 1993, Congress established a federal program called Vaccines for Children, which required manufacturers of childhood vaccines to sell one-third of all vaccines to the federal government at a discount of 50 percent. The government then provided vaccines at no charge to children in households without private health insurance.

Later, the government began offering free vaccines to children in low-income families, even if the families had private health insurance. It also began requiring vaccine manufacturers to sell more of their output to the government at the discounted price. Manufacturers responded by cutting back on production. Some private physicians began to experience difficulties keeping vaccines in stock, so they used waiting lists to ration vaccines among children in families covered by private health insurance.

The government reacted to the growing problem of private vaccine shortages by providing vaccines to children in higher-income families deemed to be "underinsured." To provide these additional vaccines, of course, the government began obtaining even more vaccines at half price. Today the government purchases almost 60 percent of all childhood vaccines. Private vaccine shortages are worsening as manufacturers respond to lower prices and profits with further production cutbacks.

For Critical Analysis
What is likely to happen to the length of a typical private physician's vaccine waiting list if the federal government continues to require manufacturers to sell even more half-price vaccines to the Vaccines for Children program?

CONCEPTS in Brief

- Governments sometimes impose price controls in the form of price ceilings and price floors.

- An effective price ceiling is one that sets the legal price below the market clearing price and is enforced. Effective price ceilings lead to nonprice rationing devices and black markets.

To test your understanding of the concepts covered in this section, go to the Online Review at www.myeconlab.com/miller.

THE POLICY OF CONTROLLING RENTS

More than 200 U.S. cities and towns, including Berkeley, California, and New York City, operate under some kind of rent control. **Rent control** is a system under which the local government tells building owners how much they can charge their tenants in rent. In the United States, rent controls date back to at least World War II. The objective of rent control is to keep rents below levels that would be observed in a freely competitive market.

Rent control
The placement of price ceilings on rents in particular cities.

The Functions of Rental Prices

In any housing market, rental prices serve three functions: (1) to promote the efficient maintenance of existing housing and stimulate the construction of new housing, (2) to allocate existing scarce housing among competing claimants, and (3) to ration the use of existing housing by current demanders.

Rent Controls and Construction. Rent controls have discouraged the construction of new rental units. Rents are the most important long-term determinant of profitability, and rent controls have artificially depressed them. Consider some examples. In a recent year in Dallas, Texas, with a 16 percent rental vacancy rate but no rent control laws, 11,000 new rental housing units were built. In the same year in San Francisco, California, only 2,000 units were built, despite a mere 1.6 percent vacancy rate. The major difference? San Francisco has had stringent rent control laws. In New York City, until changes in the law in 1997 and 2003, the only rental units being built were luxury units, which were exempt from controls.

Effects on the Existing Supply of Housing. When rental rates are held below equilibrium levels, property owners cannot recover the cost of maintenance, repairs, and capital improvements through higher rents. Hence they curtail these activities. In the extreme situation, taxes, utilities, and the expenses of basic repairs exceed rental receipts. The result is abandoned buildings. Numerous buildings have been abandoned in New York City. Some owners have resorted to arson, hoping to collect the insurance on their empty buildings before the city claims them for back taxes.

Rationing the Current Use of Housing. Rent controls also affect the current use of housing because they restrict tenant mobility. Consider a family whose children have gone off to college. That family might want to live in a smaller apartment. But in a rent-controlled environment, giving up a rent-controlled unit can entail a substantial cost. In most rent-controlled cities, rents can be adjusted only when a tenant leaves. That means that a move from a long-occupied rent-controlled apartment to a smaller apartment can involve a hefty rent hike. This artificial preservation of the status quo became known in New York as "housing gridlock."

Attempts at Evading Rent Controls

Go to www.econtoday.com/chap04 to learn more about New York City's rent controls from Tenant.net.

The distortions produced by rent controls lead to efforts by both property owners and tenants to evade the rules. This leads to the growth of expensive government bureaucracies whose job it is to make sure that rent controls aren't evaded. In New York City, because rent can be raised only if the tenant leaves, property owners have had an incentive to make life unpleasant for tenants in order to drive them out or to evict them on the slightest pretense. The city has responded by making evictions extremely costly for property owners. Eviction requires a tedious and expensive judicial proceeding. Tenants, for their part, routinely try to sublet all or part of their rent-controlled apartments at fees substantially above the rent they pay to the owner. Both the city and the property owners try to prohibit subletting and typically end up in the city's housing courts—an entire judicial system developed to deal with disputes involving rent-controlled apartments. The overflow and appeals from the city's housing courts are now clogging the rest of New York's judicial system.

Who Gains and Who Loses from Rent Controls?

The big losers from rent controls are clearly property owners. But there is another group of losers—low-income individuals, especially single mothers, trying to find their first apartment. Some observers now believe that rent controls have worsened the problem of homelessness in such cities as New York.

Often, owners of rent-controlled apartments charge "key money" before a new tenant is allowed to move in. This is a large up-front cash payment, usually illegal but demanded nonetheless—just one aspect of the black market in rent-controlled apartments. Poor individuals cannot afford a hefty key money payment, nor can they assure the owner that their rent will be on time or even paid each month. Because controlled rents are usually below market clearing levels, apartment owners have little incentive to take any risk on low-income individuals as tenants. This is particularly true when a prospective tenant's chief source of income is a welfare check. Indeed, a large number of the litigants in the New York housing courts are welfare mothers who have missed their rent payments due to emergency expenses or delayed welfare checks. Their appeals commonly end in evictions and a new home in a temporary public shelter—or on the streets.

Who benefits from rent control? Ample evidence indicates that upper-income professionals benefit the most. These people can use their mastery of the bureaucracy and their large network of friends and connections to exploit the rent control system. Consider that in New York, actresses Mia Farrow and Cicely Tyson live in rent-controlled apartments, paying well below market rates. So do the director of the Metropolitan Museum of Art, the chairman of Pathmark Stores, and singer and children's book author Carly Simon.

CONCEPTS in Brief

- Rental prices perform three functions: (1) allocating existing scarce housing among competing claimants, (2) promoting efficient maintenance of existing houses and stimulating new housing construction, and (3) rationing the use of existing houses by current demanders.

- Effective rent controls impede the functioning of rental prices. Construction of new rental units is discouraged. Rent controls decrease spending on maintenance of existing ones and also lead to "housing gridlock."

- There are numerous ways to evade rent controls; key money is one.

To test your understanding of the concepts covered in this section, go to the Online Review at www.myeconlab.com/miller.

PRICE FLOORS IN AGRICULTURE

Another way that government can affect markets is by imposing price floors or price supports. In the United States, price supports are most often associated with agricultural products.

Price Supports

During the Great Depression, the federal government swung into action to help farmers. In 1933, it established a system of price supports for many agricultural products. Since then, there have been price supports for wheat, feed grains, cotton, rice, soybeans, sorghum, and dairy products, among other foodstuffs. The nature of the supports is quite simple: The government simply chooses a *support price* for an agricultural product and then acts to ensure that the price of the product never falls below the support level. Figure 4-4 on the following page shows the market demand for and supply of peanuts. Without a price support program, competitive forces would yield an equilibrium price of P_e and an equilibrium quantity of Q_e. Clearly, if the government were to set the support price at P_e or below, the quantity of peanuts demanded would equal the quantity of peanuts supplied at point E, because farmers could sell all they wanted at the market clearing price of P_e.

FIGURE 4-4
Agricultural Price Supports
Free market equilibrium occurs at E, with an equilibrium price of P_e and an equilibrium quantity of Q_e. When the government sets a support price at P_s, the quantity demanded is Q_d, and the quantity supplied is Q_s. The difference is the surplus, which the government buys. Note that farmers' total income is from consumers ($P_s \times Q_d$) plus taxpayers [($Q_s - Q_d$) $\times P_s$].

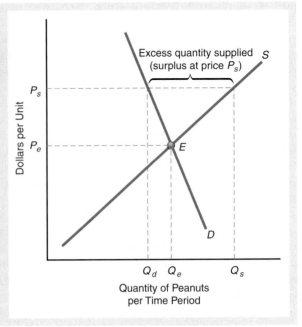

But what happens when the government sets the support price *above* P_e, at P_s? At a support price of P_s, the quantity demanded is only Q_d, but the quantity supplied is Q_s. The difference between them is called the *excess quantity supplied,* or *surplus.* As simple as this program seems, its existence creates a fundamental question: How can the government agency charged with administering the price-support program prevent market forces from pushing the actual price down to P_e?

If production exceeds the amount that consumers want to buy at the support price, what happens to the surplus? Quite simply, the government has to buy the surplus—the difference between Q_s and Q_d—if the price support program is to work. As a practical matter, the government acquires the quantity $Q_s - Q_d$ indirectly through a government agency. The government either stores the surplus or sells it to foreign countries at a greatly reduced price (or gives it away free of charge) under the Food for Peace program.

Who Benefits from Agricultural Price Supports?

Although agricultural price supports have traditionally been promoted as a way to guarantee a decent wage for low-income farmers, most of the benefits have in fact gone to the owners of very large farms. Price support payments are made on a per-bushel basis, not on a per-farm basis. Thus, traditionally, the larger the farm, the bigger the benefit from agricultural price supports. In addition, *all* of the benefits from price supports ultimately accrue to *landowners* on whose land price-supported crops could grow.

Back in the early 1990s, Congress indicated an intention to phase out most agricultural subsidies by the early 2000s. What Congress actually *did* throughout the 1990s, however, was to pass a series of "emergency laws" keeping farm subsidies alive. Then, in 2002, the legislative body enacted the Farm Security Act, which now commits the U.S. government to continued price supports for such farm products as wheat, corn, rice, cotton, and soybeans. All told, government payments for these and other products amount to about 20 percent of the annual market value of all U.S. farm production.

Nevertheless, European government price-support payments account for almost twice as much of the total value of European farm output. How do you suppose that the European Union has tried to link agricultural subsidies to governmental efforts to promote environmental protection and food safety?

International Policy EXAMPLE

France Convinces the European Union That Protecting the Environment Requires Agricultural Price Supports

The European Union (EU) allocates about $50 billion per year, or roughly half of its entire budget, to a subsidy program called the Common Agricultural Policy (CAP). In 2003, the French government proposed a new CAP system, which the EU has recently implemented. Under this system, the EU no longer *officially* pays farmers based on what they produce. Instead, the EU formally pays farmers for using agricultural production practices that help protect the environment and promote food safety. Furthermore, the EU has determined that in some cases, the most environmentally sound and safest practices involve no farming at all.

Under the new EU approach, as long as farmers use government-prescribed methods said to help the environment and make foods safer, the CAP program will make payments based on the "value of their production." If the EU determines that protecting the environment or promoting food safety entails not farming at all, then it will pay farmers based on the value of the products they otherwise *would* have grown. These values will be based on "fair prices" as determined by the government, not by the market. In short, the new EU program to promote environmentally friendly and safer agricultural techniques will essentially remain a program of agricultural price supports.

Who will benefit most from implementing this French system of "environmental and food-safety protection"? The answer is French farmers, who already receive about $10 billion per year under CAP, or about 20 percent of the entire EU farm-subsidy budget.

For Critical Analysis
Why will the new EU agricultural subsidy program continue to keep farm prices artificially above market levels?

PRICE FLOORS IN THE LABOR MARKET

The **minimum wage** is the lowest hourly wage rate that firms may legally pay their workers. Proponents want higher minimum wages to ensure low-income workers a "decent" standard of living. Opponents counter that higher minimum wages cause increased unemployment, particularly among unskilled minority teenagers.

The federal minimum wage started in 1938 at 25 cents an hour, about 40 percent of the average manufacturing wage at the time. Typically, its level has stayed at about 40 to 50 percent of average manufacturing wages. It was increased to $5.15 in 1997 and may be higher by the time you read this. Many states and cities have their own minimum wage laws that sometimes exceed the federal minimum.

What happens when the government establishes a floor on wages? The effects can be seen in Figure 4-5 on the following page. We start off in equilibrium with the equilibrium wage rate of W_e and the equilibrium quantity of labor equal to Q_e. A minimum wage, W_m, higher than W_e, is imposed. At W_m, the quantity demanded for labor is reduced to Q_d, and some workers now become unemployed. Note that the reduction in employment from Q_e to Q_d, or the distance from B to A, is less than the excess quantity of labor supplied at wage rate W_m. This excess quantity supplied is the distance between A and C, or the distance between Q_d and Q_s. The reason the reduction in employment is smaller than the excess quantity of labor supplied at the minimum wage is that the excess quantity of labor supplied also includes the *additional* workers who would like to work more hours at the new, higher minimum wage. Some workers may become unemployed as a result of the minimum wage, but others will move to sectors where minimum wage laws do not apply; wages will be pushed down in these uncovered sectors.

Minimum wage
A wage floor, legislated by government, setting the lowest hourly rate that firms may legally pay workers.

Go to www.econtoday.com/chap04 for information from the U.S. Department of Labor concerning recent developments concerning the federal minimum wage.

FIGURE 4-5
The Effect of Minimum Wages

The market clearing wage rate is W_e. The market clearing quantity of employment is Q_e, determined by the intersection of supply and demand at point E. A minimum wage equal to W_m is established. The quantity of labor demanded is reduced to Q_d. The reduction in employment from Q_e to Q_d is equal to the distance between B and A. That distance is smaller than the excess quantity of labor supplied at wage rate W_m. The distance between B and C is the increase in the quantity of labor supplied that results from the higher minimum wage rate.

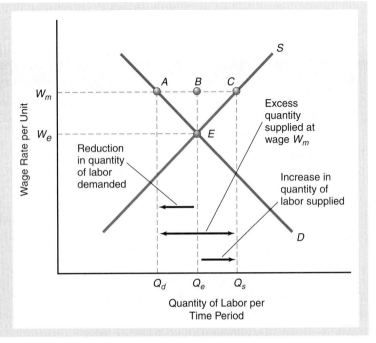

In the long run (a time period that is long enough to allow for full adjustment by workers and firms), some of the reduction in the quantity of labor demanded will result from a reduction in the number of firms, and some will result from changes in the number of workers employed by each firm. Economists estimate that a 10 percent increase in the minimum wage relative to the prices of goods and services decreases total employment of those affected by 1 to 2 percent.*

How has the relative minimum wage varied over time?

E X A M P L E

The Relative Minimum Wage Is What Matters

Recall from Chapter 3 that *relative* prices affect decisions. This is also true of wages, the prices of labor inputs. When a person decides whether to offer to work more hours, what matters is what the wage rate is relative to the overall prices of goods and services. If there is inflation over time without changes in the current wage, the *relative* wage rate declines.

Figure 4-6 shows that the money value of the U.S. minimum wage has increased from 25 cents per hour in October 1938 to $5.15 per hour. The inflation-adjusted minimum wage rose between 1938 and the 1960s, although it declined whenever inflation reduced the relative value of the minimum wage. Since the 1960s, the relative minimum wage has tended to decline, except following increases in the money value of the minimum wage. Nevertheless, the relative (or *real*, inflation-adjusted) value of the minimum wage is about 60 percent higher today than in the late 1930s.

For Critical Analysis
How could a government establish a system for keeping the relative value of the minimum wage from changing even in an inflationary environment?

---

*Because we are referring to a long-run analysis here, the reduction in the quantity of labor demanded would be demonstrated by an eventual shift inward to the left of the short-run demand curve, *D*, in Figure 4-5 as firms (the consumers of labor) went out of business.

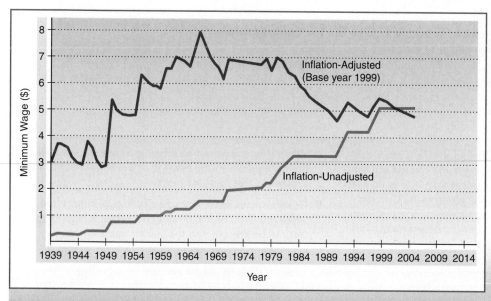

FIGURE 4-6
The Minimum Wage—Inflation-Adjusted versus Inflation-Unadjusted
The minimum wage has risen in steps. The inflation-adjusted value of the minimum wage has generally trended downward since the late 1960s, but it is still 60 percent higher than in 1939.

Source: U.S. Department of Labor.

QUANTITY RESTRICTIONS

Governments can impose quantity restrictions on a market. The most obvious restriction is an outright ban on the ownership or trading of a good. It is currently illegal to buy and sell human organs. It is also currently illegal to buy and sell certain psychoactive drugs such as cocaine, heroin, and marijuana. In some states, it is illegal to start a new hospital without obtaining a license for a particular number of beds to be offered to patients. This licensing requirement effectively limits the quantity of hospital beds in some states. From 1933 to 1973, it was illegal for U.S. citizens to own gold except for manufacturing, medicinal, or jewelry purposes.

Some of the most common quantity restrictions exist in the area of international trade. The U.S. government, as well as many foreign governments, imposes import quotas on a variety of goods. An **import quota** is a supply restriction that prohibits the importation of more than a specified quantity of a particular good in a one-year period. The United States has had import quotas on tobacco, sugar, and immigrant labor. For many years, there were import quotas on oil coming into the United States. There are also "voluntary" import quotas on certain goods. Japanese automakers have agreed since 1981 "voluntarily" to restrict the amount of Japanese cars they send to the United States.

What industry would you guess has the most products subject to U.S. import quotas?

Import quota
A physical supply restriction on imports of a particular good, such as sugar. Foreign exporters are unable to sell in the United States more than the quantity specified in the import quota.

Policy EXAMPLE

U.S. Textile Quotas Abound

The Office of Textiles and Apparel in the U.S. Department of Commerce oversees the enforcement of import quotas covering more than 140 categories of textile products. These include fabrics and clothing made of fibers derived from cotton, wool, silk, and synthetics.

For instance, in any given year imports of pairs of gloves and mittens from Pakistan cannot exceed 1,281,606 pairs, but up to 2,364,645 pairs can legally enter the United States from Cambodia. In addition, as many as 4,575 men's suit jackets can be imported from the Czech Republic, yet fewer than 3,746 jackets can arrive from the Philippines. Clearly, the U.S. government aims to apply very precise quotas to the textile products of different nations.

For Critical Analysis
Who in the United States stands to gain from restrictions on the quantities of textile imports?

CONCEPTS in Brief

- With a price support system, the government sets a minimum price at which, say, qualifying farm products can be sold. Any farmers who cannot sell at that price in the market can "sell" their surplus to the government. The only way a price support system can survive is for the government or some other entity to buy up the excess quantity supplied at the support price.

- When a floor is placed on wages at a rate that is above market equilibrium, the result is an excess quantity of labor supplied at that minimum wage.

- Quantity restrictions may take the form of import quotas, which are limits on the quantity of specific foreign goods that can be brought into the United States for resale purposes.

To test your understanding of the concepts covered in this section, go to the Online Review at www.myeconlab.com/miller.

CASE STUDY: Economics Front and Center

A Full-Court Press for Season Tickets

Last year, Chris purchased season tickets for her college's home basketball games with ease. When she registered for her classes, she received a ticket order form, which she dropped off at an athletic ticket office with her payment the same day. She received her tickets well in advance of the opening game and attended every game. Her college's team proceeded to surprise every sports prognosticator by winning its conference championship and advancing further than expected in the postseason tournament.

The price of tickets for the coming year's basketball season is the same as last year's price. Chris faces a much different situation than she did last year, however. No season ticket forms are offered when she registers for her classes. Instead, she is told that she must wait in a long line just to sign up to receive a ticket order form. The line moves so slowly that by the time she gets to the sign-up table, she is late for her next class. A college

representative then informs her that this year, once she receives and fills out a ticket order, she will have to wait in line again to make payment. In addition, she will be guaranteed tickets to only half of the home games, which the college will distribute to season ticket holders via a random lottery. This will all take time, so students will probably have to wait in more lines to pick up their tickets at the box office the day of the first game. Chris shakes her head and adds her name to the list of students requesting a ticket order form.

Points to Analyze

1. *What rationing method has Chris's college adopted to distribute this season's basketball tickets?*

2. *Is the price of a season ticket at Chris's college really "the same" as last year's price?*

Issues and Applications

Why Ships Face Traffic Jams

In recent years, the demand for pleasure cruises on passenger ships has increased considerably. Additionally, the number of companies operating cruise ships has increased, so the supply of pleasure cruises has also risen. The result has been a significant increase in the total number of passengers carried by cruise ships. As Figure 4-7 shows, in the early 1980s fewer than 2 million North American passengers traveled on cruise ships each year. Today the annual volume exceeds 8 million.

Concepts Applied
- Changes in Demand and Supply
- Price Ceiling
- Shortage

Government-Determined Prices at U.S. Seaports

To load and unload over 8 million passengers per year, cruise ships must be able to sail into ports and pull alongside docks. Hence the increase in the number of pleasure cruises has generated an increase in the demand for a complementary good—space at U.S. seaports. If there were an unregulated market, we would predict a resulting increase in the prices that ship owners pay to enter and dock at U.S. ports.

In fact, prices charged to use most U.S. port facilities are often regulated, or in some cases even directly set, by government agencies. At some U.S. seaports, such as the Port of Los Angeles, a city department oversees the prices of docking fa-

cilities. In others, such as the Port of Miami, pricing policies are supervised by a county agency. So far, government authorities have been slow to respond to the rising demand for port access by increasing the legally allowed prices for the use of port facilities.

Clogged Bays and Dock Delays

The failure of government agencies to allow the price of seaport usage to rise to the market clearing level has caused the quantity of port space demanded by ship owners to rise above—and to remain above—the quantity of port space

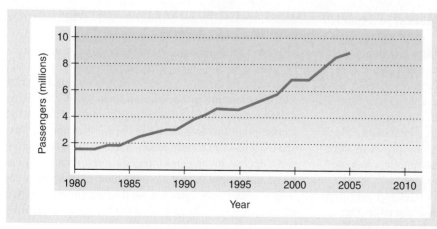

FIGURE 4-7

Annual North American Passenger Volumes on Cruise Ships

The number of North American residents traveling as passengers on cruise ships has more than quadrupled since the early 1980s.

Source: U.S. Department of Commerce.

supplied. The government agencies have effectively placed a ceiling price on port space. The results have been exactly what you might have predicted based on your study of this chapter: There is insufficient space in seaports to handle all the ships whose owners desire to use their facilities. Consequently, as ships near U.S. seaports, they are now required to give at least 24 hours' notice of their arrival so that port authorities can advise them if they need to delay their arrivals in light of space constraints. Even when ships arrive at their scheduled times, they often must wait for several minutes, or in some cases even several hours, before navigating toward their assigned docks.

While the many new cruise ships are moving in and out of harbors, freighters planning to load or unload merchandise at docks are among the ships forced to wait in line to use port facilities. As these freighters wait their turn, the ships' engines continue to burn fuel. In addition, their owners must pay wages to crews for the extra minutes or hours spent waiting in line. For the owner of a typical freighter, these and other costs can add up to considerable sums. According to current estimates, each hour a freighter must wait to arrive or depart entails a cost of nearly $1,000. Thus ship owners ultimately incur higher costs as a result of the shortage of port space at the government-determined prices.

For Critical Analysis

1. What nonprice rationing device are government port authorities using to ration channel passages and docking space?
2. If a cruise ship that requires as much space for safe passage as a freighter is the first to arrive at the point of entry to the only channel to a seaport, which ship's owner effectively "pays a price" for the failure of the government port authority to allow the price of port space to rise to the market clearing price?

Web Resources

1. To learn more about how the Port of Los Angeles establishes prices for the use of space and various port facilities, go to the link at www.econtoday.com/chap04.
2. For a comparative look at the rules governing pricing access to the Port of Miami, go to the link at www.econtoday.com/chap04.

Research Project

Suppose that a U.S. port authority decides to let the market determine the prices that should be charged for the right to enter the port and use its docking facilities. It implements this decision by auctioning rights to port space. All ships that are 48 hours from port must radio in bids for these rights, and the port authority establishes each ship's position in line through the channel to the port and a dock based on the size of its bid. Evaluate the pros and cons of such a system.

SUMMARY DISCUSSION of Learning Objectives

1. **Essential Features of the Price System:** The price system, otherwise called the market system, allows prices to respond to changes in supply and demand for different commodities. Consumers' and business managers' decisions on resource use depend on what happens to prices. In the price system, exchange takes place in markets. The terms of exchange are communicated by prices in the marketplace, where middlemen reduce transaction costs by bringing buyers and sellers together.

2. **How Changes in Demand and Supply Affect the Market Price and Equilibrium Quantity:** With a given supply curve, an increase in demand causes a rise in the market price and an increase in the equilibrium quantity, and a decrease in demand induces a fall in the market price and a decline in the equilibrium quantity. With a given demand curve, an increase in supply causes a fall in the market price and an increase in the equilibrium quantity, and a decrease in supply causes a rise in the market price and a decline in the equilibrium quantity. When both demand and supply shift at the same time, indeterminate results may occur. We must know the direction and degree of each shift in order to predict the change in the market price and the equilibrium quantity.

3. **The Rationing Function of Prices:** In the market system, prices perform a rationing function—they ration scarce goods and services. Other ways of rationing include first come, first served; political power; physical force; lotteries; and coupons.

4. **The Effects of Price Ceilings:** Government-imposed price controls that require prices to be no higher than a certain level are price ceilings. If a government sets a price ceiling below the market price, then at the ceiling price the quantity of the good demanded will exceed the quantity supplied. There will be a shortage of the good at the ceiling price. This can lead to nonprice rationing devices and black markets.

5. **The Effects of Price Floors:** Government-mandated price controls that require prices to be no lower than a certain level are price floors. If a government sets a price floor above the market price, then at the floor price the quantity of the good supplied will exceed the quantity demanded. There will be a surplus of the good at the floor price.

6. **Government-Imposed Restrictions on Market Quantities:** Quantity restrictions can take the form of outright government bans on the sale of certain goods, such as human organs or various psychoactive drugs. They can also arise from licensing requirements that limit the number of producers and thereby restrict the amount supplied of a good or service. Another example is an import quota, which limits the number of units of a foreign-produced good that can legally be sold domestically.

KEY TERMS AND CONCEPTS

black market (84)

import quota (91)

minimum wage (89)

nonprice rationing devices (84)

price ceiling (84)

price controls (84)

price floor (84)

price system (78)

rent control (85)

terms of exchange (78)

transaction costs (78)

voluntary exchange (78)

PROBLEMS

Answers to the odd-numbered problems appear at the back of the book.

4-1. Suppose that a rap band called the Raging Pyros has released its first CD with Polyrock Records at a list price of $14.99. Explain how price serves as a purveyor of information to the band, the producer, and the consumer of rap CDs.

4-2. The pharmaceutical industry has benefited from advances in research and development that enable manufacturers to identify potential cures more quickly and therefore at lower cost. At the same time, the aging of our society has increased the demand for new drugs. Construct a supply and demand diagram of the market for pharmaceutical drugs. Illustrate the impact of these developments, and evaluate the effects on the market price and the equilibrium quantity.

4-3. The following table depicts the quantity demanded and quantity supplied of one-bedroom apartments in a small college town.

Monthly Rent	Quantity Demanded	Quantity Supplied
$400	3,000	1,600
$450	2,500	1,800
$500	2,000	2,000
$550	1,500	2,200
$600	1,000	2,400

What are the market price and equilibrium quantity of apartments in this town? If this town imposes a rent control of $450 a month, how many apartments will be rented?

4-4. The U.S. government imposes a price floor that is above the market clearing price. Illustrate the U.S. sugar market with the price floor in place. Discuss the effects of the subsidy on conditions in the market for sugar in the United States.

4-5. The Canadian sugar industry has complained that U.S. sugar manufacturers "dump" sugar surpluses in the Canadian market. U.S. chocolate manufacturers have also complained about the high U.S. price of sugar. Explain how the imposition of a price floor for U.S. sugar, as described in Problem 4-4, affects these two markets. What are the changes in equilibrium quantities and market prices?

4-6. Suppose that the U.S. government places a ceiling on the price of Internet access and a black market for Internet providers arises, with Internet service providers developing hidden connections. Illustrate the black market for Internet access, including the implicit supply schedule, the legal price, the black market supply and demand, and the black market equilibrium price and quantity. Also show why there is a shortage of Internet access at the legal price.

4-7. The table below illustrates the demand and supply schedules for seats on air flights between two cities:

Price	Quantity Demanded	Quantity Supplied
$200	2,000	1,200
$300	1,800	1,400
$400	1,600	1,600
$500	1,400	1,800
$600	1,200	2,000

What are the market price and equilibrium quantity in this market? Now suppose that federal authorities limit the number of flights between the two cities to ensure that no more than 1,200 passengers can be flown. Evaluate the effects of this quota on air flights.

4-8. The consequences of decriminalizing illegal drugs have long been debated. Some claim that legalization will lower the price of these drugs and reduce related crime. Others claim that more people will use these drugs. Suppose that some of these drugs are legalized so that anyone may sell them and use them. Now consider the two claims—that price will fall and quantity demanded will increase. Based on positive economic analysis, are these claims sound?

4-9. Look back at Figure 4-4 on page 88. Suppose that the equilibrium price, P_e, is $1.00 per bushel of peanuts and the support price is $1.25. In addition, suppose that the equilibrium quantity, Q_e, is 5 million bushels and the quantity supplied, Q_s, and quantity demanded, Q_d, with the price support are 8 million and 4 million, respectively. What were farmers' total revenues before the

price support program? What are their total revenues afterward? What is the cost of this program to taxpayers?

4-10. Using the information in Problem 4-9, calculate the total expenditures of peanut consumers before and after the price support program. Explain why these answers make sense.

4-11. Labor is a key input at fast-food restaurants. Suppose that the government boosts the minimum wage above the equilibrium wage of fast-food workers.

a. How will the quantity of labor employed at restaurants respond to the increase in the minimum wage?

b. How will the market price and equilibrium quantity of fast-food hamburgers be affected by the increase in the minimum wage?

4-12. Suppose that owners of high-rise office buildings are the main employers of custodial workers in a city. The city has decided to impose rent controls, and it has established a rent ceiling below the previous equilibrium rental rate for offices throughout the city.

a. How will the quantity of offices the building owners lease change?

b. How will the market wage and equilibrium quantity of labor services provided by custodial workers be affected by the imposition of rent controls?

4-13. In 2003, the government of a nation established a price support for wheat. The government's support price has been above the equilibrium price each year since, and the government has purchased all wheat over and above the amounts that consumers have bought at the support price. Every year since 2003, there has been an increase in the number of wheat producers in the market. No other factors affecting the market for wheat have changed. Predict what has happened each year since 2003 to each of the following:

a. Quantity of wheat supplied by wheat producers

b. Quantity of wheat demanded by wheat consumers

c. Quantity of wheat purchased by the government

4-14. The government of a large U.S. city recently established a "living wage law" that, beginning January 1 of next year, will require all businesses operating within city limits to pay their workers a wage no lower than $8.50 per hour. The current equilibrium wage for fast-food workers is $7.50 per hour in this city. Predict what will happen to each of the following beginning on January 1 of next year:

a. The quantity of labor supplied by fast-food workers

b. The quantity of labor demanded by fast-food producers

c. The number of unemployed fast-food workers in this city

ECONOMICS ON THE NET

The Floor on Milk Prices At various times, the U.S. government has established price floors for milk. This application gives you an opportunity to apply what you have learned in this chapter to this real-world issue.

Title: Northeast Dairy Compact Commission

Navigation: Go to www.econtoday.com/chap04 to visit the Web site of the Northeast Dairy Compact Commission.

Application Read the contents and answer these questions.

1. Based on the government-set price control concepts discussed in Chapter 4, explain the Northeast Dairy Compact that was once in place in the northeastern United States.

2. Draw a diagram illustrating the supply of and demand for milk in the Northeast Dairy Compact and the supply of and demand for milk outside the Northeast Dairy Compact. Illustrate how the compact affected the quantities demanded and supplied for participants in the compact. In addition, show how this affected the market for milk produced by those producers outside the dairy compact.

3. Economists have found that while the Northeast Dairy Compact functioned, midwestern dairy farmers lost their dominance of milk production and sales. In light of your answer to Question 2, explain how this occurred.

For Group Discussion and Analysis Discuss the impact of congressional failure to reauthorize the compact based on your above answers. Identify which arguments in your debate are based on positive economic analysis and which are normative arguments.

Media Resources

If your exam were tomorrow, would you be ready? For each chapter, MyEconLab Practice Tests and Study Plans pinpoint which sections you have mastered and which ones you need to study. That way, you are more efficient with your study time, and you are better prepared for your exams.

In addition to Practice Tests and your personalized Study Plan, you'll find the following media resources in MyEconLab:

1. *Graphs in Motion* animation of Figures 4-1, 4-3, 4-4, and 4-5.

2. Videos featuring the author, Roger LeRoy Miller, on the following subjects:
   - Price Flexibility, the Essential Role of Rationing via Price and Alternative Rationing Systems
   - Minimum Wages

3. Links to the Web sites cited in the marginal Internet Resources, Issues and Applications feature, and Economics on the Net activity.

4. Audio clips of all key terms, additional practice problems, and a PDF version of the material from the print Study Guide.

5. eThemes of the Times, which is a New York Times article to help you understand the real-world applications of what you are learning.

myeconlab

Get Ahead of the Curve

To see how it works, turn to page 16 and then go to www.myeconlab.com/miller.

Chapter 5

The Public Sector and Public Choice

The governments of Japan, South Korea, and China have discussed a plan to promote the development of a new, "Asian" software system for operating personal computers. This proposed operating system would rival the world's main alternatives, the privately produced Microsoft Windows and Linux operating systems. According to some proponents of the governments' plan, computer operating systems are "public goods." Such goods, they contend, require governmental development, production, and distribution on behalf of the citizens of Asian nations. When you have completed this chapter, you will be able to evaluate the merits of this claim.

Media Resources

Refer to the end of the chapter for a full listing of the multimedia learning materials available in MyEconLab.

LEARNING OBJECTIVES

After reading this chapter, you should be able to:

1. Explain how market failures such as externalities might justify economic functions of government
2. Distinguish between private goods and public goods and explain the nature of the free-rider problem
3. Describe political functions of government that entail its involvement in the economy
4. Distinguish between average tax rates and marginal tax rates
5. Explain the structure of the U.S. income tax system
6. Discuss the central elements of the theory of public choice

... since passage of the 1986 tax act, which the Congress of that time indicated would be the last word in U.S. tax legislation for many years to come, more than 80 additional tax laws have been enacted? Just one of these contained 25 sections of tax changes, including 11 that were effective retroactively and 4 that applied within 90 days of the end of that tax year.

Thus Congress devotes considerable time and effort to determining new ways to fund the federal government's operations. The U.S. government collects more than $1 trillion annually in income taxes alone. Local, state, and federal governments additionally raise more than $1 trillion in miscellaneous other taxes, such as sales and excise taxes. Clearly, we cannot ignore the presence of government in our society. One of the reasons the government exists is to take care of the functions that people argue the price system does not do well.

WHAT A PRICE SYSTEM CAN AND CANNOT DO

Throughout the book so far, we have alluded to the benefits of a price system. High on the list is economic efficiency. In its most ideal form, a price system allows resources to move from lower-valued uses to higher-valued uses through voluntary exchange. A situation of economic efficiency arises when all mutually advantageous trades have taken place. In a price system, consumers are sovereign; that is to say, they have the individual freedom to decide what they wish to purchase. Politicians and even business managers do not ultimately decide what is produced; consumers decide. Some proponents of the price system argue that this is its most important characteristic. A market organization of economic activity generally prevents one person from illegally interfering with most of other people's activities. Competition among sellers protects consumers from coercion by one seller, and sellers are protected from coercion by one consumer because other consumers are available.

Sometimes the price system does not generate these results, and too few or too many resources go to specific economic activities. Such situations are called **market failures.** Market failures prevent the price system from attaining economic efficiency and individual freedom. Market failures offer one of the strongest arguments in favor of certain economic functions of government, which we now examine.

Market failure
A situation in which an unrestrained market economy leads to too few or too many resources going to a specific economic activity.

CORRECTING FOR EXTERNALITIES

In a pure market system, competition generates economic efficiency only when individuals know the true opportunity cost of their actions. In some circumstances, the price that someone actually pays for a resource, good, or service is higher or lower than the opportunity cost that all of society pays for that same resource, good, or service.

Consider a hypothetical world in which there is no government regulation against pollution. You are living in a town that until now has had clean air. A steel mill moves into town. It produces steel and has paid for the inputs—land, labor, capital, and entrepreneurship. The price the mill charges for the steel reflects, in this example, only the costs that it incurred. In the course of production, however, the mill gets one input—clean air—by simply taking it. This is indeed an input because in making steel, the furnaces emit smoke. The steel mill doesn't have to pay the cost of using the clean air; rather, it is the people in the community who pay that cost in the form of dirtier clothes, dirtier cars and houses, and more respiratory illnesses. The effect is similar to what would happen if the steel mill

Externality
A consequence of an economic activity that spills over to affect third parties. Pollution is an externality.

Third parties
Parties who are not directly involved in a given activity or transaction.

could take coal or oil or workers' services free. There is an **externality,** an external cost. Some of the costs associated with the production of the steel have "spilled over" to affect **third parties,** parties other than the buyer and the seller of the steel.

External Costs in Graphical Form

Look at panel (a) in Figure 5-1. Here we show the demand curve for steel as D. The supply curve is S_1. The supply curve includes only the costs that the firms have to pay. Equilibrium occurs at point E, with price P_1 and quantity Q_1. Let us take into account the fact that there are externalities—the external costs that you and your neighbors pay in the form of dirtier clothes, cars, and houses and increased respiratory disease due to the air pollution emitted from the steel mill; in this case, suppliers of steel use clean air without having to pay for it. Let's include these external costs in our graph to find out what the full cost of steel production really is. We do this by imagining that steel producers have to pay for the input—clean air—that they previously used at a zero price.

Recall from Chapter 3 that an increase in input prices shifts the supply curve. Thus, in panel (a) of the figure, the supply curve shifts from S_1 to S_2; the external costs equal the vertical distance between A and E_1. If steel firms had to take into account these external costs, the equilibrium quantity would fall to Q_2 and the price would rise to P_2. Equilibrium would shift from E to E_1. If the price of steel does not account for external costs, third parties bear those costs—represented by the distance between A and E_1—in the form of dirtier clothes, houses, and cars and increased respiratory illnesses.

FIGURE 5-1
External Costs and Benefits
In panel (a), we show a situation in which the production of steel generates external costs. If the steel mills ignore pollution, at equilibrium the quantity of steel will be Q_1. If the mills had to pay for the external costs borne by nearby residents that are caused by the steel mills' production, the supply curve would shift the vertical distance A–E_1, to S_2. If consumers of steel were forced to pay a price that reflected the spillover costs, the quantity demanded would fall to Q_2. In panel (b), we show a situation in which inoculations against communicable diseases generate external benefits to those individuals who may not be inoculated but who will benefit because epidemics will not occur. If each individual ignores the external benefit of inoculations, the market clearing quantity will be Q_1. If external benefits are taken into account by purchasers of inoculations, however, the demand curve would shift to D_2. The new equilibrium quantity would be Q_2, and the price would be higher, P_2.

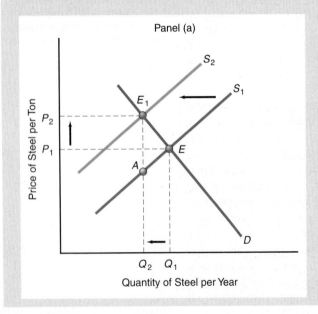

Panel (a)

Quantity of Steel per Year

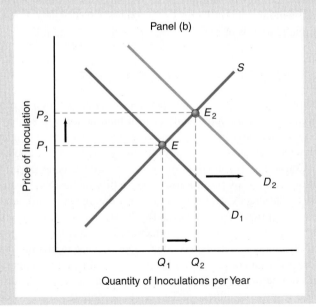

Panel (b)

Quantity of Inoculations per Year

How do you suppose that a French court sought to correct what it perceived to be a negative externality affecting every auction site on the Internet?

E-Commerce EXAMPLE

A French Court Finds a Way to Regulate the Entire Internet

A few year ago, several groups filed a joint lawsuit in a French court against Yahoo.com. The groups argued that the company's willingness to host Internet auctions of Nazi artifacts violated French laws prohibiting the display of any items that might incite racism. Yahoo had, they argued, illegally "polluted" the Internet by allowing photos and descriptions of Nazi artifacts to appear anywhere on the Internet.

The groups asked for judicial relief in the form of a ban on Yahoo's ability to offer auctions of Nazi artifacts on any Web site that French residents might visit. The judge responded by giving Yahoo an ultimatum: Either find a way to keep French residents from accessing any of its auction sites offering Nazi artifacts for sale, or bar the sale of these items on all of its auction sites around the world. Yahoo decided it would be less costly simply to bar all auctions of Nazi artifacts worldwide. Eventually, eBay and most other Web auction companies adopted similar policies.

For Critical Analysis
Under what circumstances might some collectors of World War II relics have preferred to have paid higher fees at Web auction sites in order to continue buying and selling Nazi artifacts?

External Benefits in Graphical Form

Externalities can also be positive. To demonstrate external benefits in graphical form, we will use the example of inoculations against communicable disease. In panel (b) of Figure 5-1, we show the demand curve as D_1 (without taking account of any external benefits) and the supply curve as S. The equilibrium price is P_1, and the equilibrium quantity is Q_1. We assume, however, that inoculations against communicable diseases generate external benefits to individuals who may not be inoculated but will benefit nevertheless because epidemics will not break out. If such external benefits were taken into account by those who purchase inoculations, the demand curve would shift from D_1 to D_2. The new equilibrium quantity would be Q_2, and the new equilibrium price would be P_2. If people who consider getting inoculations fail to take external benefits into account, this society is not devoting enough resources to inoculations against communicable diseases.

When there are external costs, the market will tend to *overallocate* resources to the production of the good or service in question, for those goods or services will be priced deceptively low. In the steel example, too much will be produced because the steel mill owners and managers are not required to take account of the external cost that steel production is imposing on the rest of society. In essence, the full cost of production is not borne by the owners and managers, so the price they charge the public for steel is lower than it would otherwise be. And, of course, the lower price means that buyers are willing and able to buy more. More steel is produced and consumed than if sellers were to bear external costs.

When there are external benefits, the market *underallocates* resources to the production of that good or service because the good or service is relatively too expensive (because the demand, which fails to reflect the external benefits, is relatively too low). In a market system, too many of the goods that generate external costs are produced, and too few of the goods that generate external benefits are produced.

How the Government Corrects Negative Externalities

The government can in theory correct externalities in a variety of ways in all situations that warrant such action. In the case of negative externalities, at least two avenues are open to the government: special taxes and legislative regulation or prohibition.

Special Taxes. In our example of the steel mill, the externality problem arises because using the air as a waste disposal place is costless to the firm but not to society. The government could make the steel mill pay a tax for dumping its pollutants into the air. The government could attempt to tax the steel mill commensurate with the cost to third parties from smoke in the air. This, in effect, would be a pollution tax or an **effluent fee.** The ultimate effect would be to reduce the supply of steel and raise the price to consumers, ideally making the price equal to the full cost of production to society.

Effluent fee
A charge to a polluter that gives the right to discharge into the air or water a certain amount of pollution; also called a *pollution tax.*

Go to www.econtoday.com/chap05 to learn more about how the Environmental Protection Agency uses regulations to try to protect the environment.

Regulation. Alternatively, to correct a negative externality arising from steel production, the government could specify a maximum allowable rate of pollution. This regulation would require that the steel mill install pollution abatement equipment at its facilities, reduce its rate of output, or some combination of the two. Note that the government's job would not be simple, for it would have to determine the appropriate level of pollution and then measure the pollutants emitted in order to enforce the regulation.

How the Government Corrects Positive Externalities

What can the government do when the production of one good spills *benefits* over to third parties? It has several policy options: financing the production of the good or producing the good itself, subsidies (negative taxes), and regulation.

Government Financing and Production. If the positive externalities seem extremely large, the government has the option of financing the desired additional production facilities so that the "right" amount of the good will be produced. Again consider inoculations against communicable diseases. The government could—and often does—finance campaigns to inoculate the population. It could (and does) even produce and operate inoculation centers where inoculations are given at no charge.

Subsidies. A subsidy is a negative tax; it is a payment made either to a business or to a consumer when the business produces or the consumer buys a good or a service. To generate more inoculations against communicable diseases, the government could subsidize everyone who obtains an inoculation by directly reimbursing those inoculated or by making payments to private firms that provide inoculations. Subsidies reduce the net price to consumers, thereby causing a larger quantity to be demanded.

Regulation. In some cases involving positive externalities, the government can require by law that individuals in the society undertake a certain action. For example, regulations require that all school-age children be inoculated before entering public and private schools. Some people believe that a basic school education itself generates positive externalities. Perhaps as a result of this belief, we have regulations—laws—that require all school-age children to be enrolled in a public or private school.

CONCEPTS in Brief

- External costs lead to an overallocation of resources to the specific economic activity. Two possible ways of correcting these spillovers are taxation and regulation.

- External benefits result in an underallocation of resources to the specific activity. Three possible government corrections are financing the production of the activity, subsidizing private firms or consumers to engage in the activity, and regulation.

To test your understanding of the concepts covered in this section, go to the Online Review at www.myeconlab.com/miller.

THE OTHER ECONOMIC FUNCTIONS OF GOVERNMENT

Besides correcting for externalities, the government performs many other economic functions that affect the way exchange is carried out. In contrast, the political functions of government have to do with deciding how income should be redistributed among households and selecting which goods and services have special merits and should therefore be treated differently. The economic and political functions of government can and do overlap.

Let's look at four more economic functions of government.

Providing a Legal System

The courts and the police may not at first seem like economic functions of government. Their activities nonetheless have important consequences for economic activities in any country. You and I enter into contracts constantly, whether they be oral or written, expressed or implied. When we believe that we have been wronged, we seek redress of our grievances through our legal institutions. Moreover, consider the legal system that is necessary for the smooth functioning of our economic system. Our system has defined quite explicitly the legal status of businesses, the rights of private ownership, and a method of enforcing contracts. All relationships among consumers and businesses are governed by the legal rules of the game. In its judicial function, then, the government serves as the referee for settling disputes in the economic arena. In this role, the government often imposes penalties for violations of legal rules.

Much of our legal system is involved with defining and protecting *property rights.* **Property rights** are the rights of an owner to use and to exchange his or her property. One might say that property rights are really the rules of our economic game. When property rights are well defined, owners of property have an incentive to use that property efficiently. Any mistakes in their decisions about the use of property have negative consequences that the owners suffer. Furthermore, when property rights are well defined, owners of property have an incentive to maintain that property so that if they ever desire to sell it, it will fetch a better price.

Property rights
The rights of an owner to use and to exchange property.

What populous country still ruled by the Communist Party do you suppose has awakened to the importance of the incentive effects of private property rights?

International EXAMPLE

Private Property Rights in China

In 1949, China officially became a "people's republic," in which all resources were owned by the government. For almost three decades, the Chinese government made all decisions concerning the production and distribution of goods and services.

Beginning in the 1980s, the Chinese government embarked on a gradual program of business privatization. This policy sparked an increase in economic growth. Nevertheless, government and business leaders eventually recognized that China's economy would be unable to attain its full potential in the absence of a formal declaration of private property rights. A constitutional amendment officially guaranteeing the right to private property was adopted in 2004.

For Critical Analysis
How might the establishment of private property rights have contributed to a burst of Chinese economic growth during the past few years? (Hint: Why might clearer rules about resource ownership make people more willing to start businesses?)

Promoting Competition

Antitrust legislation
Laws that restrict the formation of monopolies and regulate certain anticompetitive business practices.

Monopoly
A firm that has control over the price of a good. In the extreme case, a monopoly is the only seller of a good or service.

Many people believe that the only way to attain economic efficiency is through competition. One of the roles of government is to serve as the protector of a competitive economic system. Congress and the various state governments have passed **antitrust legislation.** Such legislation makes illegal certain (but not all) economic activities that might restrain trade—that is, that might prevent free competition among actual and potential rival firms in the marketplace. The avowed aim of antitrust legislation is to reduce the power of **monopolies**—firms that have great control over the price of the goods they sell. A large number of antitrust laws have been passed that prohibit specific anticompetitive actions. Both the Antitrust Division of the Department of Justice and the Federal Trade Commission attempt to enforce these antitrust laws. Various state judicial agencies also expend efforts at maintaining competition.

Providing Public Goods

Private goods
Goods that can be consumed by only one individual at a time. Private goods are subject to the principle of rival consumption.

Principle of rival consumption
The recognition that individuals are rivals in consuming private goods because one person's consumption reduces the amount available for others to consume.

Public goods
Goods for which the principle of rival consumption does not apply; they can be jointly consumed by many individuals simultaneously at no additional cost and with no reduction in quality or quantity. Also no one who fails to help pay for the good can be denied the benefit of the good.

The goods used in our examples up to this point have been **private goods**. When I eat a cheeseburger, you cannot eat the same one. So you and I are rivals for that cheeseburger, just as much as rivals for the title of world champion are. When I use a DVD player, you cannot play some other disc at the same time. When I use the services of an auto mechanic, that person cannot work at the same time for you. That is the distinguishing feature of private goods—their use is exclusive to the people who purchase or rent them. The **principle of rival consumption** applies to all private goods by definition. Rival consumption is easy to understand. With private goods, either you use them or I use them.

There is an entire class of goods that are not private goods. These are called **public goods.** The principle of rival consumption does not apply to them. That is, they can be consumed *jointly* by many individuals simultaneously. National defense, police protection, and the legal system, for example, are public goods. If you partake of them, you do not necessarily take away from anyone else's share of those goods.

Characteristics of Public Goods. Two fundamental characteristics of public goods set them apart from all other goods.[*]

1. *Public goods can be used by more and more people at no additional cost and without depriving others of any of the services of the goods.* Once money has been spent on national defense, the defense protection you receive does not reduce the amount of

[*]Sometimes a distinction is made between pure public goods, which have all the characteristics we have described here, and quasi- or near-public goods, which do not. The major feature of near-public goods is that they are jointly consumed, even though nonpaying customers can be, and often are, excluded—for example, movies, football games, and concerts.

protection bestowed on anyone else. The opportunity cost of your receiving national defense once it is in place is zero because once national defense is in place to protect you, it also protects others.

2. *It is difficult to design a collection system for a public good on the basis of how much individuals use it.* It is nearly impossible to determine how much any person uses or values national defense. No one can be denied the benefits of national defense for failing to pay for that public good. This is often called the **exclusion principle.**

Exclusion principle
The principle that no one can be excluded from the benefits of a public good, even if that person has not paid for it.

One of the problems of public goods is that the private sector has a difficult, if not impossible, time providing them. Individuals in the private sector have little or no incentive to offer public goods. It is difficult for them to make a profit doing so, because nonpayers cannot be excluded. Consequently, true public goods must necessarily be provided by government. Note, though, that economists do not necessarily categorize something as a public good simply because the government provides it.

Free Riders. The nature of public goods leads to the **free-rider problem,** a situation in which some individuals take advantage of the fact that others will assume the burden of paying for public goods such as national defense. Suppose that citizens were taxed directly in proportion to how much they tell an interviewer that they value national defense. Some people will probably tell interviewers that they are unwilling to pay for national defense because they don't want any of it—it is of no value to them. Such people are trying to be free riders. We may all want to be free riders if we believe that someone else will provide the commodity in question that we actually value.

Free-rider problem
A problem that arises when individuals presume that others will pay for public goods so that, individually, they can escape paying for their portion without causing a reduction in production.

The free-rider problem often arises when it comes to the international burden of defense sharing. A country may choose to belong to a multilateral defense organization, such as the North Atlantic Treaty Organization (NATO), but then consistently attempt to avoid contributing funds to the organization. The nation knows it would be defended by others in NATO if it were attacked but would rather not pay for such defense. In short, it seeks a free ride.

Why do you suppose that in some of the world's poorest regions, the inability of governments to deal with the free-rider problem has provided an opportunity for organizations that promote international terrorism?

International EXAMPLE

How Solving Free-Rider Problems May Help Combat Terrorism

During the 1990s, the Taliban government took control of Afghanistan and made it a haven for international terrorist organizations, including the Al Qaeda organization that launched attacks on the United States in 2001. A key to the Taliban's success was its ability to collect contributions from all residents—often under the threat of force—to fund a police force. Even though some in Afghanistan did not like the Taliban's strict rules, they appreciated its provision of public safety—a service the previous government had failed to provide. This enabled the Taliban to remain in power until ousted by the U.S. military in 2002.

Likewise, in the Palestinian territories, the government has often been unable to collect revenues from many Palestinians and hence has failed to provide many public services. This situation has fostered the growth of Hamas, an organization that both promotes terrorism against Israel and provides various public services to Palestinians. The ability of Hamas to collect funds from many Palestinian residents in order to coordinate these desirable public service activities has gained the group considerable popular support—plus a source of funds for terrorist operations.

The official Afghani government during the 1990s and the Palestinian government in the 2000s failed to deal with the free-rider problem. Terrorist organizations stepped in to address this government failure by providing public services the governments had been unable to fund. Thus many world leaders contend that establishing forms of government better equipped to tackle the free-rider problem will do much to diminish the strength of terrorist organizations.

For Critical Analysis
How might terrorist organizations themselves experience free-rider problems, and what might the world's governments do to exploit the free-rider problems these groups encounter?

Ensuring Economywide Stability

Our economy sometimes faces the problems of unemployment and rising prices. The government, especially the federal government, has made an attempt to solve these problems by trying to stabilize the economy by smoothing out the ups and downs in overall business activity. The notion that the federal government should undertake actions to stabilize business activity is a relatively new idea in the United States, encouraged by high unemployment rates during the Great Depression of the 1930s and subsequent theories about possible ways that government could reduce unemployment. In 1946, Congress passed the Full-Employment Act, a landmark law concerning government responsibility for economic performance. It established three goals for government stabilization policy: full employment, price stability, and economic growth. These goals have provided the justification for many government economic programs during the post–World War II period.

CONCEPTS in Brief

- The economic activities of government include (1) correcting for externalities, (2) providing a legal system, (3) promoting competition, (4) producing public goods, and (5) ensuring economywide stability.

- Public goods can be consumed jointly. The principle of rival consumption does not apply as it does with private goods.

- Public goods have two characteristics: (1) Once they are produced, there is no opportunity cost when additional consumers use them, because your use of a public good does not deprive others of its simultaneous use; and (2) consumers cannot conveniently be charged on the basis of use.

To test your understanding of the concepts covered in this section, go to the Online Review at www.myeconlab.com/miller.

THE POLITICAL FUNCTIONS OF GOVERNMENT

At least two functions of government are political or normative functions rather than economic ones like those discussed in the first part of this chapter. These two areas are (1) the regulation and provision of merit and demerit goods and (2) income redistribution.

Merit and Demerit Goods

Merit good
A good that has been deemed socially desirable through the political process. Museums are an example.

Certain goods are considered to have special merit. A **merit good** is defined as any good that the political process has deemed socially desirable. (Note that nothing inherent in any particular good makes it a merit good. The designation is entirely subjective.) Some examples of merit goods in our society are sports stadiums, museums, ballets, plays, and concerts. In these areas, the government's role is the provision of merit goods to the people in society who would not otherwise purchase them at market clearing prices or who would not purchase an amount of them judged to be sufficient. This provision may take the form of government production and distribution of merit goods. It can also take the form of reimbursement for payment on merit goods or subsidies to producers or consumers for part of the cost of merit goods. Governments do indeed subsidize such merit goods as professional sports, concerts, ballets, museums, and plays. In most cases, such merit goods would not be so numerous without subsidization.

Demerit goods are the opposite of merit goods. They are goods that, through the political process, are deemed socially undesirable. Heroin, cigarettes, gambling, and cocaine are examples. The government exercises its role in the area of demerit goods by taxing, regulating, or prohibiting their manufacture, sale, and use. Governments justify the relatively high taxes on alcohol and tobacco by declaring them demerit goods. The best-known example of governmental exercise of power in this area is the stance against certain psychoactive drugs. Most psychoactives (except nicotine, caffeine, and alcohol) are either expressly prohibited, as is the case for heroin, cocaine, and opium, or heavily regulated, as in the case of prescription psychoactives.

Income Redistribution

Another relatively recent political function of government has been the explicit redistribution of income. This redistribution uses two systems: the progressive income tax (described later in this chapter) and transfer payments. **Transfer payments** are payments made to individuals for which no services or goods are rendered in return. The three key money transfer payments in our system are welfare, Social Security, and unemployment insurance benefits. Income redistribution also includes a large amount of income **transfers in kind,** as opposed to money transfers. Some income transfers in kind are food stamps, Medicare and Medicaid, government health care services, and subsidized public housing.

The government has also engaged in other activities as a form of redistribution of income. For example, the provision of public education is at least in part an attempt to redistribute income by making sure that the poor have access to education.

Economics Front and Center

To evaluate a situation in which the consumption of publicly provided goods can generate externality effects, consider the real-world problem faced by a college student in **Too Few Opportunities to Play Table Tennis, or Too Many?**, on page 117.

Demerit good
A good that has been deemed socially undesirable through the political process. Heroin is an example.

Transfer payments
Money payments made by governments to individuals for which in return no services or goods are rendered. Examples are welfare, Social Security, and unemployment insurance benefits.

Transfers in kind
Payments that are in the form of actual goods and services, such as food stamps, subsidized public housing, and medical care, and for which in return no goods or services are rendered concurrently.

CONCEPTS in Brief

- Political, or normative, activities of the government include the provision and regulation of merit and demerit goods and income redistribution.

- Merit and demerit goods do not have any inherent characteristics that qualify them as such; rather, collectively, through the political process, we make judgments about which goods and services are "good" for society and which are "bad."

- Income redistribution can be carried out by a system of progressive taxation, coupled with transfer payments, which can be made in money or in kind, such as food stamps and Medicare.

> To test your understanding of the concepts covered in this section, go to the Online Review at www.myeconlab.com/miller.

PAYING FOR THE PUBLIC SECTOR

Jean-Baptiste Colbert, the seventeenth-century French finance minister, said the art of taxation was in "plucking the goose so as to obtain the largest amount of feathers with the least possible amount of hissing." In the United States, governments have designed a variety of methods of plucking the private-sector goose. To analyze any tax system, we must first understand the distinction between marginal tax rates and average tax rates.

Marginal and Average Tax Rates

If somebody says, "I pay 28 percent in taxes," you cannot really tell what that person means unless you know if he or she is referring to average taxes paid or the tax rate on the last dollars earned. The latter concept refers to the **marginal tax rate.***

The marginal tax rate is expressed as follows:

$$\text{Marginal tax rate} = \frac{\text{change in taxes due}}{\text{change in taxable income}}$$

It is important to understand that the marginal tax rate applies only to the income in the highest **tax bracket** reached, where a tax bracket is defined as a specified level of taxable income to which a specific and unique marginal tax rate is applied.

The marginal tax rate is not the same thing as the **average tax rate,** which is defined as follows:

$$\text{Average tax rate} = \frac{\text{total taxes due}}{\text{total taxable income}}$$

Taxation Systems

No matter how governments raise revenues—from income taxes, sales taxes, or other taxes—all of those taxes fit into one of three types of taxation systems: proportional, progressive, or regressive, according to the relationship between the tax rate and income. To determine whether a tax system is proportional, progressive, or regressive, we simply ask, What is the relationship between the average tax rate and the marginal tax rate?

Proportional Taxation. **Proportional taxation** means that regardless of an individual's income, taxes comprise exactly the same proportion. In a proportional taxation system, the marginal tax rate is always equal to the average tax rate. If every dollar is taxed at 20 percent, then the average tax rate is 20 percent, and so is the marginal tax rate.

Under a proportional system of taxation, taxpayers at all income levels end up paying the same *percentage* of their income in taxes. With a proportional tax rate of 20 percent, an individual with an income of $10,000 pays $2,000 in taxes, while an individual making $100,000 pays $20,000. The identical 20 percent rate, therefore, is levied on both taxpayers.

Progressive Taxation. Under **progressive taxation,** as a person's taxable income increases, the percentage of income paid in taxes increases. In a progressive system, the marginal tax rate is above the average tax rate. If you are taxed 5 percent on the first $10,000 you make, 10 percent on the next $10,000 you make, and 30 percent on the last $10,000 you make, you face a progressive income tax system. Your marginal tax rate is always above your average tax rate.

Regressive Taxation. With **regressive taxation,** a smaller percentage of taxable income is taken in taxes as taxable income increases. The marginal rate is *below* the average rate. As income increases, the marginal tax rate falls, and so does the average tax rate. The U.S.

Marginal tax rate
The change in the tax payment divided by the change in income, or the percentage of additional dollars that must be paid in taxes. The marginal tax rate is applied to the highest tax bracket of taxable income reached.

Tax bracket
A specified interval of income to which a specific and unique marginal tax rate is applied.

Average tax rate
The total tax payment divided by total income. It is the proportion of total income paid in taxes.

Proportional taxation
A tax system in which, regardless of an individual's income, the tax bill comprises exactly the same proportion.

Progressive taxation
A tax system in which, as income increases, a higher percentage of the additional income is taxed. The marginal tax rate exceeds the average tax rate as income rises.

Regressive taxation
A tax system in which as more dollars are earned, the percentage of tax paid on them falls. The marginal tax rate is less than the average tax rate as income rises.

---

*The word *marginal* means "incremental" (or "decremental") here.

Social Security tax is regressive. Once the legislative maximum taxable wage base is reached, no further Social Security taxes are paid. Consider a simplified hypothetical example: Suppose that every dollar up to $50,000 is taxed at 10 percent. After $50,000 there is no Social Security tax. Someone making $100,000 still pays only $5,000 in Social Security taxes. That person's average Social Security tax is 5 percent. The person making $50,000, by contrast, effectively pays 10 percent. The person making $1 million faces an average Social Security tax rate of only 0.5 percent in our simplified example.

CONCEPTS in Brief

- Tax rates are applied to tax brackets, defined as spreads of income over which the tax rate is constant.

- Tax systems can be proportional, progressive, or regressive, depending on whether the marginal tax rate is the same as, greater than, or less than the average tax rate as income rises.

To test your understanding of the concepts covered in this section, go to the Online Review at www.myeconlab.com/miller.

THE MOST IMPORTANT FEDERAL TAXES

The federal government imposes income taxes on both individuals and corporations and collects Social Security taxes and a variety of other taxes.

The Federal Personal Income Tax

The most important tax in the U.S. economy is the federal personal income tax, which accounts for about 43 percent of all federal revenues. All American citizens, resident aliens, and most others who earn income in the United States are required to pay federal income taxes on all taxable income. The rates that are paid rise as income increases, as can be seen in Table 5-1 on the next page. Marginal income tax rates at the federal level have varied from as low as 1 percent after the 1913 passage of the Sixteenth Amendment to as high as 94 percent (reached in 1944). There were 14 separate tax brackets prior to the Tax Reform Act of 1986, which reduced the number to three (now six). Advocates of a more progressive income tax system in the United States argue that such a system redistributes income from the rich to the poor, taxes people according to their ability to pay, and taxes people according to the benefits they receive from government. Although there is much controversy over the redistributional nature of our progressive tax system, there is no strong evidence that the tax system has actually ever done much income redistribution in this country. Currently, about 85 percent of all tax-paying U.S. residents pay roughly the same proportion of their total income in federal taxes.

Go to www.econtoday.com/chap05 to learn from the National Center for Policy Analysis about what distinguishes recent flat tax proposals from a truly proportional income tax system. Next, click on "Flat Tax Proposals."

The Treatment of Capital Gains

The difference between the buying and selling price of an asset, such as a share of stock or a plot of land, is called a **capital gain** if it is a profit and a **capital loss** if it is not. The federal government taxes capital gains, and as of 2005, there were several capital gains tax rates.

What appear to be capital gains are not always real gains. If you pay $100,000 for a financial asset in one year and sell it for 50 percent more 10 years later, your nominal capital gain is $50,000. But what if during those 10 years inflation has driven average asset prices up by 50 percent? Your *real* capital gain would be zero, but you would still have to

Capital gain
The positive difference between the purchase price and the sale price of an asset. If a share of stock is bought for $5 and then sold for $15, the capital gain is $10.

Capital loss
The negative difference between the purchase price and the sale price of an asset.

TABLE 5-1
Federal Marginal Income Tax Rates
These rates became effective in 2004. The highest rate includes a 10 percent surcharge on taxable income above $319,101.

Single Persons		Married Couples	
Marginal Tax Bracket	Marginal Tax Rate	Marginal Tax Bracket	Marginal Tax Rate
$0–$7,150	10%	$0–$14,300	10%
$7,151–$29,050	15%	$14,301–$58,100	15%
$29,051–$70,350	25%	$58,101–$117,250	25%
$70,351–$146,750	28%	$117,251–$178,650	28%
$146,751–$319,100	33%	$178,651–$319,100	33%
$319,101 and up	35%	$319,101 and up	35%

Source: U.S. Department of the Treasury.

pay taxes on that $50,000. To counter this problem, many economists have argued that capital gains should be indexed to the rate of inflation. This is exactly what is done with the marginal tax brackets in the federal income tax code. Tax brackets for the purposes of calculating marginal tax rates each year are expanded at the rate of inflation, or the rate at which the average of all prices is rising. So if the rate of inflation is 10 percent, each tax bracket is moved up by 10 percent. The same concept could be applied to capital gains and financial assets. So far, Congress has refused to enact such a measure.

The Corporate Income Tax

Corporate income taxes account for about 11 percent of all federal taxes collected and about 2 percent of all state and local taxes collected. Corporations are generally taxed on the difference between their total revenues (or receipts) and their expenses. The federal corporate income tax structure is given in Table 5-2.

Double Taxation. Because individual stockholders must pay taxes on the dividends they receive, which are paid out of *after-tax* profits by the corporation, corporate profits are taxed twice. If you receive $1,000 in dividends, you have to declare them as income, and

TABLE 5-2
Federal Corporate Income Tax Schedule
These corporate tax rates were in effect through 2005.

Corporate Taxable Income	Corporate Tax Rate
$0–$50,000	15%
$50,001–$75,000	25%
$75,001–$100,000	34%
$100,001–$335,000	39%
$335,001–$10,000,000	34%
$10,000,001–$15,000,000	35%
$15,000,001–$18,333,333	38%
$18,333,334 and up	35%

Source: Internal Revenue Service.

you must pay taxes on them. Before the corporation was able to pay you those dividends, it had to pay taxes on all its profits, including any that it put back into the company or did not distribute in the form of dividends. Eventually, the new investment made possible by those **retained earnings**—profits not given out to stockholders—along with borrowed funds will be reflected in the increased value of the stock in that company. When you sell your stock in that company, you will have to pay taxes on the difference between what you paid for the stock and what you sold it for. In both cases, dividends and retained earnings (corporate profits) are taxed twice. In 2003, Congress reduced the double taxation effect somewhat by enacting legislation that allows most dividends to be taxed at lower rates than are applied to regular income.

Retained earnings
Earnings that a corporation saves, or retains, for investment in other productive activities; earnings that are not distributed to stockholders.

Who Really Pays the Corporate Income Tax? Corporations can exist only as long as consumers buy their products, employees make their goods, stockholders (owners) buy their shares, and bondholders buy their bonds. Corporations per se do not do anything. We must ask, then, who really pays the tax on corporate income? This is a question of **tax incidence.** (The question of tax incidence applies to all taxes, including sales taxes and Social Security taxes.) The incidence of corporate taxation is the subject of considerable debate. Some economists suggest that corporations pass their tax burdens on to consumers by charging higher prices. Other economists argue that it is the stockholders who bear most of the tax. Still others contend that employees pay at least part of the tax by receiving lower wages than they would otherwise. Because the debate is not yet settled, we will not hazard a guess here as to what the correct conclusion may be. Suffice it to say that you should be cautious when you advocate increasing corporation income taxes. *People*—whether owners, consumers, or workers—ultimately end up paying the increase if they own shares in a corporation, buy its products, or work for it.

Tax incidence
The distribution of tax burdens among various groups in society.

CONCEPTS in Brief

- Because corporations must first pay an income tax on most earnings, the personal income tax shareholders pay on dividends received (or realized capital gains) constitutes double taxation.

- The corporate income tax is paid by people in one or more of the following groups: stockholder-owners, consumers of corporate-produced products, and employees of corporations.

To test your understanding of the concepts covered in this section, go to the Online Review at www.myeconlab.com/miller.

Social Security and Unemployment Taxes

Each year, payroll taxes levied on payrolls account for an increasing percentage of federal tax receipts. These taxes, which are distinct from personal income taxes, are for Social Security, retirement, survivors' disability, and old-age medical benefits (Medicare). Today the Social Security tax is imposed on earnings up to roughly $90,000 at a rate of 6.2 percent on employers and 6.2 percent on employees. That is, the employer matches your "contribution" to Social Security. (The employer's contribution is really paid, at least in part, in the form of a reduced wage rate paid to employees.) A Medicare tax is imposed on all wage earnings at a combined rate of 2.9 percent. These taxes and the base on which they are levied are slated to rise in the next decade. Social Security taxes came into existence when the Federal Insurance Contributions Act (FICA) was passed in 1935. The future of Social Security is addressed in Chapter 6.

There is also a federal unemployment tax, which helps pay for unemployment insurance. This tax rate is 0.8 percent on the first $7,000 of annual wages of each employee who earns more than $1,500. Only the employer makes the direct tax payment. This tax covers the costs of the unemployment insurance system and the costs of employment

FIGURE 5-2

Total Government Outlays over Time

Total government outlays (federal, state, and local combined) remained small until the 1930s, except during World War I. Since World War II, government outlays have not fallen back to their historical average.

Sources: *Facts and Figures on Government Finance*, various issues; *Economic Indicators*, various issues.

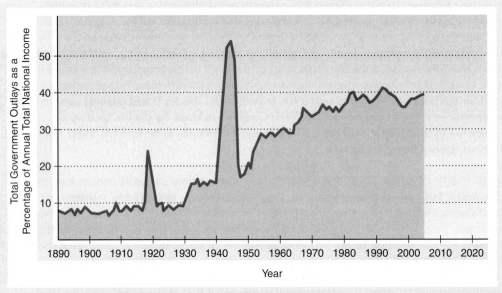

SPENDING, GOVERNMENT SIZE, AND TAX RECEIPTS

The size of the public sector can be measured in many different ways. One way is to count the number of public employees. Another is to look at total government outlays. Government outlays include all government expenditures on employees, rent, electricity, and the like. In addition, total government outlays include transfer payments, such as welfare and Social Security. In Figure 5-2, you see that government outlays prior to World War I did not exceed 10 percent of annual national income. There was a spike during World War I, a general increase during the Great Depression, and then a huge spike during World War II. Contrary to previous postwar periods, after World War II government outlays as a percentage of total national income rose steadily before dropping in the 1990s and rising slightly again in the 2000s.

Government Receipts

The main revenue raiser for all levels of government is taxes. We show in the two pie diagrams in Figure 5-3 the percentage of receipts from various taxes obtained by the federal government and by state and local governments.

Federal Government. The largest source of receipts for the federal government is the individual income tax. It accounts for 42.9 percent of all federal revenues. After that come social insurance taxes and contributions (Social Security), which account for 39.0 percent of total revenues. Next come corporate income taxes and then a number of other items, such as taxes on imported goods and excise taxes on such things as gasoline and alcoholic beverages.

State and Local Governments. As can be seen in Figure 5-3, there is quite a bit of difference in the origin of receipts for state and local governments and for the federal govern-

FIGURE 5-3
Sources of Government Tax Receipts

About 82 percent of federal revenues come from income and Social Security taxes (see in panel (a)), whereas state government revenues are spread more evenly across sources (see panel (b)), with less emphasis on taxes based on individual income.

Source: U.S. Department of Commerce, Bureau of Economic Analysis.

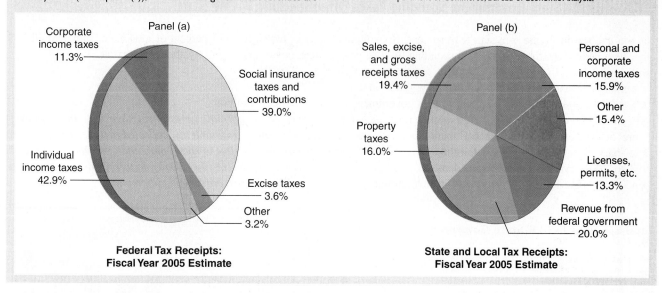

Panel (a)

Corporate income taxes 11.3%

Social insurance taxes and contributions 39.0%

Individual income taxes 42.9%

Excise taxes 3.6%

Other 3.2%

Federal Tax Receipts: Fiscal Year 2005 Estimate

Panel (b)

Sales, excise, and gross receipts taxes 19.4%

Personal and corporate income taxes 15.9%

Other 15.4%

Property taxes 16.0%

Licenses, permits, etc. 13.3%

Revenue from federal government 20.0%

State and Local Tax Receipts: Fiscal Year 2005 Estimate

ment. Personal and corporate income taxes account for only 15.9 percent of total state and local revenues. There are even a few states that collect no personal income tax. The largest sources of state and local receipts (other than from the federal government) are sales taxes, property taxes, and personal and corporate income taxes.

Figure 5-4 shows only the *distribution* of state government spending. How much has spending by state governments *changed* in recent years? See the next page.

Go to www.econtoday.com/ch05 to consider whether Internet sales should be taxed.

FIGURE 5-4
Federal Government Spending Compared to State and Local Spending

The federal government's spending habits are quite different from those of the states and cities. In panel (a), you can see that the categories of most importance in the federal budget are defense, income security, and Social Security, which make up 54.8 percent. In panel (b), the most important category at the state and local level is education, which makes up 34.7 percent. "Other" includes expenditures in such areas as waste treatment, garbage collection, mosquito abatement, and the judicial system.

Sources: *Budget of the United States Government; Government Finances.*

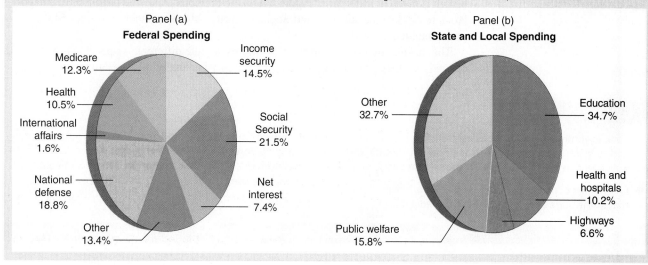

Panel (a)
Federal Spending

Medicare 12.3%

Income security 14.5%

Health 10.5%

International affairs 1.6%

Social Security 21.5%

National defense 18.8%

Net interest 7.4%

Other 13.4%

Panel (b)
State and Local Spending

Other 32.7%

Education 34.7%

Health and hospitals 10.2%

Highways 6.6%

Public welfare 15.8%

Policy EXAMPLE

State Government Spending Takes Off—Especially in One State

As you can see in Figure 5-5, state government expenditures have been increasing. Since 1997, total spending by state governments has risen by more than 39 percent.

Although all states have been spending more funds on items such as education and health care, one state's government in particular has contributed to the rise in expenditures depicted in Figure 5-5. California's government spending increased by more than 36 percent during just the three-year period from 1998 to 2001. For the entire period depicted in Figure 5-5, spending by California's government, which currently ac-

counts for close to 15 percent of total expenditures of all U.S. state governments, rose by about 50 percent.

For Critical Analysis

How could California's government have spent more on average in recent years than it has collected in taxes? (Hint: Unless a person who desires to spend more than the amount earned in a given year can convince someone to provide financial gifts, the individual must borrow the difference.)

FIGURE 5-5
Total Spending by U.S. State Governments Since 1997

State government expenditures have increased by about $150 billion, or more than 39 percent, since 1997.

Source: National Association of State Budget Officers.

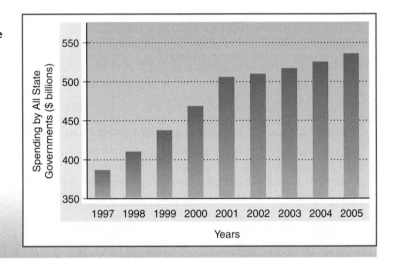

Comparing Federal with State and Local Spending. A typical federal government budget is given in panel (a) of Figure 5-4 on the previous page. The largest three categories are defense, income security, and Social Security, which together constitute 54.8 percent of the total federal budget.

The makeup of state and local expenditures is quite different. As panel (b) shows, education is the biggest category, accounting for 34.7 percent of all expenditures.

CONCEPTS in Brief

- Total government outlays including transfers have continued to grow since World War II and now account for about 38 percent of yearly total national output.

- Government spending at the federal level is different from that at the state and local levels. At the federal level,

defense, income security, and Social Security account for nearly 55 percent of the federal budget. At the state and local levels, education comprises almost 35 percent of all expenditures.

To test your understanding of the concepts covered in this section, go to the Online Review at **www.myeconlab.com/miller.**

COLLECTIVE DECISION MAKING: THE THEORY OF PUBLIC CHOICE

Governments consist of individuals. No government actually thinks and acts; rather, government actions are the result of decision making by individuals in their roles as elected representatives, appointed officials, and salaried bureaucrats. Therefore, to understand how government works, we must examine the incentives of the people in government as well as those who would like to be in government—avowed or would-be candidates for elective or appointed positions—and special-interest lobbyists attempting to get government to do something. At issue is the analysis of **collective decision making.** Collective decision making involves the actions of voters, politicians, political parties, interest groups, and many other groups and individuals. The analysis of collective decision making is usually called the **theory of public choice.** It has been given this name because it involves hypotheses about how choices are made in the public sector, as opposed to the private sector. The foundation of public-choice theory is the assumption that individuals will act within the political process to maximize their *individual* (not collective) well-being. In that sense, the theory is similar to our analysis of the market economy, in which we also assume that individuals are motivated by self-interest.

To understand public-choice theory, it is necessary to point out other similarities between the private market sector and the public, or government, sector; then we will look at the differences.

Collective decision making
How voters, politicians, and other interested parties act and how these actions influence nonmarket decisions.

Theory of public choice
The study of collective decision making.

Similarities in Market and Public-Sector Decision Making

In addition to the assumption of self-interest being the motivating force in both sectors, there are other similarities.

Scarcity.
At any given moment, the amount of resources is fixed. This means that for the private and the public sectors combined, there is a scarcity constraint. Everything that is spent by all levels of government plus everything that is spent by the private sector must add up to the total income available at any point in time. Hence every government action has an opportunity cost, just as in the market sector.

Competition.
Although we typically think of competition as a private-market phenomenon, it is also present in collective action. Given the scarcity constraint government faces, bureaucrats, appointed officials, and elected representatives will always be in competition for available government funds. Furthermore, the individuals within any government agency or institution will act as individuals do in the private sector: They will try to obtain higher wages, better working conditions, and higher job-level classifications. We assume that they will compete and act in their own interest, not society's.

Similarity of Individuals.
Contrary to popular belief, there are not two types of individuals, those who work in the private sector and those who work in the public sector; rather, individuals working in similar positions can be considered similar. The difference, as we shall see, is that the individuals in government face a different **incentive structure** than those in the private sector. For example, the costs and benefits of being efficient or inefficient differ in the private and public sectors.

One approach to predicting government bureaucratic behavior is to ask what incentives bureaucrats face. Take the United States Postal Service (USPS) as an example. The bureaucrats running that government corporation are human beings with IQs not dissimilar to those possessed by workers in similar positions at Microsoft or American Airlines. Yet

Incentive structure
The system of rewards and punishments individuals face with respect to their own actions.

the USPS does not function like either of these companies. The difference can be explained, at least in part, in terms of the incentives provided for managers in the two types of institutions. When the bureaucratic managers and workers at Microsoft make incorrect decisions, work slowly, produce shoddy products, and are generally "inefficient," the profitability of the company declines. The owners—millions of shareholders—express their displeasure by selling some of their shares of company stock. The market value, as tracked on the stock exchange, falls. But what about the USPS? If a manager, a worker, or a bureaucrat in the USPS gives shoddy service, the organization's owners—the taxpayers—have no straightforward mechanism for expressing their dissatisfaction. Despite the postal service's status as a "government corporation," taxpayers as shareholders do not really own shares of stock in the organization that they can sell.

Thus, to understand purported inefficiency in the government bureaucracy, we need to examine incentives and institutional arrangements—not people and personalities.

Differences Between Market and Collective Decision Making

There are probably more dissimilarities between the market sector and the public sector than there are similarities.

Government Goods at Zero Price. The majority of goods that governments produce are furnished to the ultimate consumers without payment required. **Government,** or **political, goods** can be either private or public goods. The fact that they are furnished to the ultimate consumer free of charge does *not* mean that the cost to society of those goods is zero, however; it only means that the price *charged* is zero. The full opportunity cost to society is the value of the resources used in the production of goods produced and provided by the government.

> **Government, or political, goods**
> Goods (and services) provided by the public sector; they can be either private or public goods.

For example, none of us pays directly for each unit of consumption of defense or police protection. Rather, we pay for all these things indirectly through the taxes that support our governments—federal, state, and local. This special feature of government can be looked at in a different way. There is no longer a one-to-one relationship between consumption of a government-provided good and payment for that good. Indeed, most taxpayers will find that their tax bill is the same whether or not they consume government-provided goods.

Use of Force. All governments may resort to using force in their regulation of economic affairs. For example, governments can use *expropriation*, which means that if you refuse to pay your taxes, your bank account and other assets may be seized by the Internal Revenue Service. In fact, you have no choice in the matter of paying taxes to governments. Collectively, we decide the total size of government through the political process, but individually, we cannot determine how much service we pay for just for ourselves during any one year.

> **Majority rule**
> A collective decision-making system in which group decisions are made on the basis of more than 50 percent of the vote. In other words, whatever more than half of the electorate votes for, the entire electorate has to accept.

Voting versus Spending. In the private market sector, a dollar voting system is in effect. This dollar voting system is not equivalent to the voting system in the public sector. There are at least three differences:

> **Proportional rule**
> A decision-making system in which actions are based on the proportion of the "votes" cast and are in proportion to them. In a market system, if 10 percent of the "dollar votes" are cast for blue cars, 10 percent of the output will be blue cars.

1. In a political system, one person gets one vote, whereas in the market system, each dollar one spends counts separately.
2. The political system is run by **majority rule,** whereas the market system is run by **proportional rule.**
3. The spending of dollars can indicate intensity of want, whereas because of the all-or-nothing nature of political voting, a vote cannot.

Ultimately, the main distinction between political votes and dollar votes is that political outcomes may differ from economic outcomes. Remember that economic efficiency is a situation in which, given the prevailing distribution of income, consumers get the economic goods they want. There is no corresponding situation using political voting. Thus we can never assume that a political voting process will lead to the same decisions that a dollar voting process will lead to in the marketplace.

Indeed, consider the dilemma every voter faces. Usually, a voter is not asked to decide on a single issue (although this happens); rather, a voter is asked to choose among candidates who present a large number of issues and state a position on each of them. Just consider the average U.S. senator, who has to vote on several thousand different issues during a six-year term. When you vote for that senator, you are voting for a person who must make thousands of decisions during the next six years.

CONCEPTS in Brief

- The theory of public choice examines how voters, politicians, and other parties collectively reach decisions in the public sector of the economy.

- As in private markets, scarcity and competition have incentive effects that influence public-sector decision making. In contrast to private market situations, however, there is not a one-to-one relationship between consumption of a publicly provided good and the payment for that good.

To test your understanding of the concepts covered in this section, go to the Online Review at www.myeconlab.com/miller.

CASE STUDY: Economics Front and Center

Too Few Opportunities to Play Table Tennis, or Too Many?

In Li's college dormitory, each floor has its own resident organization, which among other things enforces rules regarding student conduct and collects annual dues from each student resident. Each resident organization pools these funds, which are automatically deducted from each student's monthly rent, to purchase items intended to benefit all students who live on the floor. Most of the students who reside on Li's dormitory floor enjoy playing table tennis, but the nearest tables are some distance from the dormitory. Last month, Li and the other residents on his floor voted unanimously to use some of their resident association funds to purchase a ping-pong table. The table was placed in an open lounge area located just outside the entrance to Li's room, and each resident received his own paddle and ball.

Li now has a problem. Since the ping-pong table was purchased, other residents of his floor have been playing table tennis every night, sometimes until as late as 2:00 A.M. Consequently, he has had difficulty concentrating on his studies, and getting a good night's sleep has been even more problematical.

Points to Analyze

1. Is the ping-pong table an example of a public good or a merit good?

2. What is the term for the situation Li faces, and what might he propose that his resident association do to address it?

Can Computer Software Be a Public Good?

G overnments around the globe are actively involved in the production of numerous goods and services. All governments provide their citizens with national defense and law enforcement. Most governments today are also heavily involved in providing educational and health care services. Recently, some Asian governments have decided that computer software should join this list.

Concepts Applied

- Principle of Rival Consumption
- Public Goods
- Merit Goods

Governments and Computer Code

At a 2003 Asian economic summit, Japan's government formally proposed the formation of an intergovernmental software production project, to be conducted jointly with the governments of China, South Korea, and potentially other Asian nations. The Japanese government indicated that it would provide an initial amount exceeding 1.5 billion yen (more than $120 million) to fund preliminary work on an Asian-developed, Asian-owned, and Asian-distributed computer operating system.

To explain why Asian governments should become involved in the production of computer software, a Japanese government official described computer operating systems as "public goods." All residents of Japan and other Asian nations, he contended, "need" access to low-cost software to be able to function in today's "high-technology, twenty-first-century economy."

Is Computer Software a Public Good?

To evaluate whether Japanese government officials might be justified in viewing computer operating systems as public goods, let's consider whether such computer software satisfies the two characteristics of public goods. First, can computer operating systems be used by more and more people at no additional cost and without depriving others of any of the

systems' services? In principle, the answer is "yes." At present, a computer operating system such as Microsoft Windows can control flows of input and output commands on a personal computer only if it is installed on the computer's hard drive or some other storage medium. But, if operating systems could be downloaded at no charge from government Web sites, these computer programs truly could be used by additional people at no additional cost and without reducing anyone else's use of the product.

The second characteristic of a public good is that it must satisfy the exclusion principle. Is it difficult to devise a system for funding a computer operating system on the basis of how many individuals use it? The answer to this question is "no." Even if a computer operating system is made easily accessible on the Internet, it would be simple to require a user to pay before downloading the computer code for the system from an Internet site. Numerous private Web-based firms, such as manufacturers of antivirus software, have already proved that they can exclude people from using software if they fail to pay for it.

At best, therefore, computer operating systems might conceivably come close to possessing one of the two features of a public good. Such computer software is not, however, a public good. If Asian governments follow through with their plans to develop, produce, and distribute computer operating systems to their residents, they will actually have chosen to regard this specific form of computer software as a merit good.

1. Once it is posted on a Web site, can a downloadable digital music file, such as an MP3 file, be consumed by additional people without affecting its consumption by anyone else? If so, does this mean that the file is a public good?
2. "If computer operating systems are public goods, then Bill Gates (founder and former top officer of Microsoft) should have had a harder time accumulating a fortune from sales of Microsoft Windows." In light of the exclusion principle, does this statement make a legitimate point?

1. Learn about the development of the Microsoft Windows operating system at www.econtoday.com/chap05.
2. Find out more about the Linux operating system at www.econtoday.com/chap05.

Evaluate the following statement: "Anyone can be excluded from consuming a downloadable digital computer file if she or he fails to pay for it, so no digital file could ever be classified as a public good." Take a stand, and support your answer by reference to real-world examples such as commercial software for digital audio or video files.

SUMMARY DISCUSSION of Learning Objectives

1. **How Market Failures Such as Externalities Might Justify Economic Functions of Government:** A market failure is a situation in which an unhindered free market gives rise to too many or too few resources being directed to a specific form of economic activity. A good example of a market failure is an externality, which is a spillover effect on third parties not directly involved in producing or purchasing a good or service. In the case of a negative externality, firms do not pay for the costs arising from spillover effects that their production of a good imposes on others, so they produce too much of the good in question. Government may be able to improve on the situation by restricting production or by imposing fees on producers. In the case of a positive externality, buyers fail to take into account the benefits that their consumption of a good yields to others, so they purchase too little of the good. Government may be able to induce more consumption of the good by regulating the market or subsidizing consumption. It can also provide a legal system to adjudicate disagreements about property rights, conduct antitrust policies to discourage monopoly and promote competition, provide public goods, and engage in policies designed to promote economic stability.

2. **Private Goods versus Public Goods and the Free-Rider Problem:** Private goods are subject to the principle of rival consumption, meaning that one person's con-sumption of such a good reduces the amount available for another person to consume. This is not so for public goods, which can be consumed by many people simultaneously at no additional cost and with no reduction in the quality or quantity of the good. In addition, public goods are subject to the exclusion principle: No individual can be excluded from the benefits of a public good even if that person fails to help pay for it. This leads to the free-rider problem, which occurs when a person who thinks that others will pay for a public good seeks to avoid contributing to financing production of the good.

3. **Political Functions of Government That Lead to Its Involvement in the Economy:** Through the political process, people may decide that certain goods are merit goods, which they deem socially desirable, or demerit goods, which they feel are socially undesirable. They may call on government to promote the production of merit goods but to restrict or even ban the production and sale of demerit goods. In addition, the political process may determine that income redistribution is socially desirable, and governments may become involved in supervising transfer payments or in-kind transfers in the form of nonmoney payments.

4. **Average Tax Rates versus Marginal Tax Rates:** The average tax rate is the ratio of total tax payments to total income. By contrast, the marginal tax rate is the change

in tax payments induced by a change in total taxable income. Thus the marginal tax rate applies to the last dollar that a person earns.

5. **The U.S. Income Tax System:** The U.S. income tax system assesses taxes against both personal and business income. It is designed to be a progressive tax system, in which the marginal tax rate increases as income rises, so that the marginal tax rate exceeds the average tax rate. This contrasts with a regressive tax system, in which higher-income people pay lower marginal tax rates, resulting in a marginal tax rate that is less than the average tax rate. The marginal tax rate equals the average tax rate only under proportional taxation, in which the marginal tax rate does not vary with income.

6. **Central Elements of the Theory of Public Choice:** The theory of public choice is the study of collective decision making, or the process through which voters, politicians, and other interested parties interact to influence nonmarket choices. Public-choice theory emphasizes the incentive structures, or system of rewards or punishments, that affect the provision of government goods by the public sector of the economy. This theory points out that certain aspects of public-sector decision making, such as scarcity and competition, are similar to those that affect private-sector choices. Others, however, such as legal coercion and majority-rule decision making, differ from those involved in the market system.

KEY TERMS AND CONCEPTS

antitrust legislation (104)	incentive structure (115)	proportional taxation (108)
average tax rate (108)	majority rule (116)	public goods (104)
capital gain (109)	marginal tax rate (108)	regressive taxation (108)
capital loss (109)	market failure (99)	retained earnings (111)
collective decision making (115)	merit good (106)	tax bracket (108)
demerit good (107)	monopoly (104)	tax incidence (111)
effluent fee (102)	principle of rival consumption (104)	theory of public choice (115)
exclusion principle (105)	private goods (104)	third parties (100)
externality (100)	progressive taxation (108)	transfer payments (107)
free-rider problem (105)	property rights (103)	transfers in kind (107)
government, or political, goods (116)	proportional rule (116)	

PROBLEMS

Answers to the odd-numbered problems appear at the back of the book.

5-1. Many people who do not smoke cigars are bothered by the odor of cigar smoke. In the absence of any government involvement in the market for cigars, will too many or too few cigars be produced and consumed? From society's point of view, will the market price of cigars be too high or too low?

5-2. Suppose that repeated application of a pesticide used on orange trees causes harmful contamination of groundwater. The pesticide is produced by a large number of chemical manufacturers and is applied annually in orange groves throughout the world. Most orange growers regard the pesticide as a key input in their production of oranges.

a. Use a diagram of the market for the pesticide to illustrate the implications of a failure of pesticide manufacturers' costs to reflect the social costs of groundwater contamination.

b. Use your diagram from part (a) to explain a government policy that might be effective in achieving the amount of pesticide production that fully reflects all social costs.

5-3. Now draw a diagram of the market for oranges. Explain how the government policy you discussed in part (b) of Problem 5-2 is likely to affect the market price and equilibrium quantity in the orange market. In what sense do consumers of oranges "pay" for dealing with the spillover costs of pesticide production?

5-4. Suppose that the U.S. government determines that cigarette smoking creates social costs not reflected in the current market price and equilibrium quantity of cigarettes. A study has recommended that the government can correct for the externality effect of cigarette consumption by paying farmers *not* to plant tobacco used to manufacture cigarettes. It also recommends raising the funds to make these payments by increasing taxes on cigarettes. Assuming that the government is correct that cigarette smoking creates external costs, evaluate whether the study's recommended policies might help correct this negative externality.

5-5. The government of a major city in the United States has determined that mass transit, such as bus lines, helps alleviate traffic congestion, thereby benefiting both individual auto commuters and companies that desire to move products and factors of production speedily along streets and highways. Nevertheless, even though several private bus lines are in service, commuters in the city are failing to take the social benefits of the use of mass transit into account.

a. Discuss, in the context of demand-supply analysis, the essential implications of commuters' failure to take into account the social benefits associated with bus ridership.

b. Explain a government policy that might be effective in achieving the socially optimal use of bus services.

5-6. Draw a diagram of the market for automobiles, which are a substitute means of transit. Explain how the government policy you discussed in part (b) of Problem 5-5 is likely to affect the market price and equilibrium quantity in the auto market. How are auto consumers affected by this policy to attain the spillover benefits of bus transit?

5-7. A state government has determined that access to the Internet improves the learning skills of children, which it concluded would have external benefits. It has also concluded that in light of these external benefits, too few of the state's children have Internet access at their homes and in their school classrooms. Assuming that the state's judgments about the benefits of Internet access are correct, propose a policy that could address the situation.

5-8. Does a tennis court provided by a local government agency satisfy both key characteristics of a public good? Why or why not? Based on your answer, is a public tennis court a public good or a merit good?

5-9. To promote increased use of port facilities in a major coastal city, a state government has decided to construct a state-of-the-art lighthouse at a projected cost of $10 million. The state proposes to pay half this cost and asks the city to raise the additional funds. Rather than raise its $5 million in funds via an increase in city taxes and fees, however, the city's government asks major businesses in and near the port area to contribute voluntarily to the project. Discuss key problems that the city is likely to face in raising the funds.

5-10. A senior citizen gets a part-time job at a fast-food restaurant. She earns $8 per hour for each hour she works, and she works exactly 25 hours per week. Thus her total pretax weekly income is $200. Her total income tax assessment each week is $40, but she has determined that she is assessed $3 in taxes for the final hour she works each week.

a. What is this person's average tax rate each week?

b. What is the marginal tax rate for the last hour she works each week?

5-11. For purposes of assessing income taxes, there are three official income levels for workers in a small country: high, medium, and low. For the last hour on the job during a 40-hour workweek, a high-income worker pays a marginal income tax rate of 15 percent, a medium-income worker pays a marginal tax rate of 20 percent, and a low-income worker is assessed a 25 percent marginal income tax rate. Based only on this information, does this nation's income tax system appear to be progressive, proportional, or regressive?

5-12. Governments of country A and country B spend the same amount each year. Spending on functions relating to dealing with market externalities and public goods accounts for 25 percent of government expenditures in country A but makes up 75 percent of government expenditures in country B. Funding to provide merit goods and efforts to restrict the production of demerit goods account for 75 percent of government expenditures in country A but only 25 percent of government expenditures in country B. Which country's government is more heavily involved in the economy through economic functions of government as opposed to political functions? Explain.

5-13. A government agency is contemplating launching an effort to expand the scope of its activities. One rationale for doing so is that another government agency might make the same effort and, if successful, receive larger budget allocations in future years. Another rationale for expanding the agency's activities is that this will make the jobs of its workers more interesting, which may help the agency attract better-qualified employees. Nevertheless, to broaden its legal mandate, the agency will have to convince more than half of the House of Representatives and the Senate to approve a formal proposal to expand its activities. In addition, to expand its activities, the agency must have the authority to force private companies it does not currently regulate to be officially licensed by agency personnel. Identify which aspects of this problem are similar to those faced by firms that operate in private markets and which aspects are specific to the public sector.

ECONOMICS ON THE NET

Putting Tax Dollars to Work In this application, you will learn about how the U.S. government allocates its expenditures. This will enable you to conduct an evaluation of the current functions of the federal government.

Title: Historical Tables: Budget of the United States Government

Navigation: Go to www.econtoday.com/chap05 to visit the home page of the U.S. Government Printing Office. Select the most recent budget available, and then click on *Historical Tables*.

Application After the document downloads, examine Section 3, Federal Government Outlays by Function, and in particular Table 3.1, Outlays by Superfunction and Function. Then answer the following questions:

1. What government functions have been capturing growing shares of government spending in recent years? Which of these do you believe are related to the problem of addressing externalities, providing public goods, or dealing with other market failures? Which appear to be related to political functions instead of economic functions?

2. Which government functions are receiving declining shares of total spending? Are any of these related to the problem of addressing externalities, providing public goods, or dealing with other market failures? Are any related to political functions instead of economic functions?

For Group Study and Analysis Assign groups to the following overall categories of government functions: national defense, health, income security, and Social Security. Have each group prepare a brief report concerning long-term and recent trends in government spending on each category. Each group should take a stand on whether specific spending on items in its category is likely to relate to resolving market failures, public funding of merit goods, regulating the sale of demerit goods, and so on.

If your exam were tomorrow, would you be ready? For each chapter, MyEconLab Practice Tests and Study Plans pinpoint which sections you have mastered and which ones you need to study. That way, you are more efficient with your study time, and you are better prepared for your exams.

In addition to Practice Tests and your personalized Study Plan, you'll find the following media resources in MyEconLab:
1. *Graphs in Motion* animation of Figures 5-1, 5-2, and 5-5.
2. Videos featuring the author, Roger LeRoy Miller, on the following subjects:
   ● Private Goods and Public Goods
   ● Types of Tax Systems
   ● The Corporate Income Tax

3. Links to the Web sites cited in the marginal Internet Resources, Issues and Applications feature, and Economics on the Net activity.
4. Audio clips of all key terms, additional practice problems, and a PDF version of the material from the print Study Guide.
5. eThemes of the Times, which is a New York Times article to help you understand the real-world applications of what you are learning.

To see how it works, turn to page 16 and then go to www.myeconlab.com/miller.

Get Ahead of the Curve

Chapter 6

Taxes, Transfers, and Public Spending

I n Lake Oswego, Oregon, the family of a high school student who wants to participate in sports must pay fees as high as $900 per year. In Gurnee, Illinois, every student who wants to play in a middle school band or orchestra must pay a $60 membership fee. Parents or guardians of five-year-olds in Arlington, Massachusetts, must pay $1,500 before the children will be permitted to enroll in kindergarten. All of these fees are being charged by public schools. Yet just a few years ago public school students could participate in school activities at no additional cost to their families. Why are public schools now charging for various services that they once provided at no charge to students and their families? After you have completed your study of this chapter, you will know the answer to this question.

LEARNING OBJECTIVES

After reading this chapter, you should be able to:

1. Understand the key factors influencing the relationship between tax rates and the tax revenues governments collect
2. Explain how the taxes governments levy on purchases of goods and services affect market prices and equilibrium quantities
3. Analyze how Medicare affects the incentives to consume medical services
4. Explain why increases in government spending on public education have not been associated with improvements in measures of student performance
5. Understand how the Social Security system works and explain the nature of the problems it poses for today's students

Media Resources

Refer to the end of the chapter for a full listing of the multimedia learning materials available in MyEconLab.

...the first U.S. public school that provided education beyond the elementary school years was Boston Latin School, which began teaching male students in 1635? Throughout the seventeenth and eighteenth centuries, and well into the nineteenth century, nearly all middle schools and high schools were privately operated. As late as 1860, the United States had a total of only 40 public schools. Most of these were elementary schools, and most U.S. residents' formal education ended there. Students learned to read and to do simple arithmetic before going back to work on a farm or in a shop. Things began to change in the 1870s, when a handful of state supreme courts ruled that state taxes should support public education. State and local governments then began to finance public schools by granting subsidies, typically in the form of a specified dollar amount per enrolled student. Within a few years, public schools had spread throughout the nation, and by 1900 there were more than 6,000 public schools. Now there are about 90,000.

Public education is just one of a number of goods and services currently subsidized by government. Others include police protection, transportation services, and access to health care. To obtain all the funds required to provide these subsidies, state and local governments assess sales taxes, property taxes, income taxes, airline taxes, hotel occupancy taxes, and electricity, gasoline, water, and sewage taxes. At the federal level, there are income taxes, Social Security taxes, Medicare taxes, and so-called excise taxes. When a person dies, state and federal governments also collect estate and inheritance taxes. Clearly, as the subsidization role of governments has broadened, so has their role as tax collectors.

TAXATION FROM THE GOVERNMENT'S POINT OF VIEW

There are three sources of funding available to governments. One source is explicit fees, called user *charges,* for government services. The second and main source of government funding is taxes. Nevertheless, sometimes federal, state, and local governments spend more than they collect in taxes. To do this, they must rely on a third source of financing, which is borrowing. During a specific interval, the **government budget constraint** expresses this basic limitation on public expenditures. It states that the sum of public spending on goods and services and transfer payments during a given period cannot exceed tax revenues plus borrowed funds.

Government budget constraint
The limit on government spending and transfers imposed by the fact that every dollar the government spends, transfers, or uses to repay borrowed funds must ultimately be provided by the taxes it collects.

A government cannot borrow unlimited amounts, however. After all, a government, like an individual or a firm, can convince others to lend it funds only if it can provide evidence that it will repay its debts. A government must ultimately rely on taxation and user charges, the sources of its own current and future revenues, to repay its debts. Over the long run, therefore, taxes and user charges are any government's *fundamental* sources of revenues. This long-term constraint indicates that the total amount that a government plans to spend and transfer today and into the future cannot exceed the total taxes and user charges that it currently earns and can reasonably anticipate collecting in future years. Taxation dwarfs user charges as a source of government resources, so let's begin by looking at taxation from a government's perspective.

Tax Rates and Tax Revenues

In light of the government budget constraint, a major concern of any government is how to collect taxes. Governments commonly face two fundamental issues when they attempt to fund their operations by taxing market activities. One issue is how the tax rates that governments apply relate to the tax revenues they ultimately receive. Another is how the taxes governments impose on market transactions affect market prices and equilibrium quantities.

To collect a tax, a government typically establishes a **tax base,** which is a value of goods, services, incomes, or wealth subject to taxation. As a concrete example, let's consider a sales tax system.

Governments levy **sales taxes** on the prices that consumers pay to purchase each unit of a broad range of goods and services. Sellers collect sales taxes and transmit them to the government. Sales taxes are levied under a system of *ad valorem* **taxation,** which means that the tax is applied "to the value" of the good. Thus a government using a system of *ad valorem* taxation charges a tax rate equal to a fraction of the market price of each unit that a consumer buys. For instance, if the tax rate is 8 percent and the market price of an item is $100, then the amount of the tax on the item is $8.

A sales tax is therefore a proportional tax. The total amount of sales taxes a government collects equals the sales tax rate times the sales tax base, which is the market value of total purchases.

Governments of European nations also tax sales, but they use a form of sales taxation called a *value-added tax.* How have efforts by European governments to require U.S. Internet sellers to collect these taxes from their European customers complicated doing business on the Web?

Tax base
The value of goods, services, incomes, or wealth subject to taxation.

Sales taxes
Taxes assessed on the prices paid on a large set of goods and services.

Ad valorem taxation
Assessing taxes by charging a tax rate equal to a fraction of the market price of each unit purchased.

E-Commerce EXAMPLE

U.S. Web Sellers Find Themselves Collecting Europe's Taxes

Under the value-added tax systems used in most European nations, the total tax assessed on the sale of a particular item depends on tax rates applied at each stage of that item's production. Consider, for instance, the basic stages of bread production: harvesting of grains by farmers, processing of the grains by millers, production of the bread by bakers, and sale of the bread by grocers. Under a system of value-added taxation, the government taxes the final consumer for the market value added at each stage of production by the farmers, millers, bakers, and grocers. Thus the overall tax rate that a consumer pays on the purchase of a loaf of bread ultimately includes tax rates on values added at all stages of production.

Before 2003, U.S. firms selling products to European consumers on the Web treated them just like U.S. consumers. In the United States, a state assesses sales taxes on items sold on the Internet only if the firm from which a person buys an item has a physical presence in the state where the buyer resides. Europeans obviously did not reside in U.S. states, so they did not have to pay sales taxes.

In the summer of 2003, the nations of the European Union (EU) decided that U.S. companies wishing to sell products to European consumers on the Internet had to begin collecting value-added taxes for remittance to EU governments. A U.S. company with an office in a European nation is required to collect value-added taxes based on the specific system used by that nation. A U.S. firm without a European office, however, must figure out how to collect and remit value-added taxes for every nation in the EU. This is a complicated and costly undertaking, because each EU nation has its own tax-remittance procedures. Each country also has its own schedule of value-added tax rates—ranging from as low as 13 percent in Portugal to as high as 25 percent in Sweden.

For Critical Analysis
Why do you suppose that some U.S. firms selling items on the Web have responded to the EU tax change by collecting the required value-added taxes and also by charging additional fees to European consumers?

Static Tax Analysis. There are two approaches to evaluating how changes in tax rates affect government tax collections. **Static tax analysis** assumes that changes in the tax rate have no effect on the tax base. Thus this approach implies that if a state government desires to increase its sales tax collections, it can simply raise the tax rate. Multiplying the higher tax rate by the tax base thereby produces higher tax revenues.

Static tax analysis
Economic evaluation of the effects of tax rate changes under the assumption that there is no effect on the tax base, so that there is an unambiguous positive relationship between tax rates and tax revenues.

Governments often rely on static tax analysis. Sometimes this does not pay off. Consider, for instance, what happened in 1992 when Congress implemented a federal "luxury tax" on purchases of new pleasure boats priced at $100,000 or more. Applying the 10 percent luxury tax rate to the anticipated tax base—sales of new boats during previous years—produced a forecast of hundreds of million of dollars in revenues from the luxury tax. What actually happened, however, was an 80 percent plunge in sales of new luxury boats. People postponed boat purchases or bought used boats instead. Consequently, the tax base all but disappeared, and the federal government collected only a few tens of millions of dollars in taxes on boat sales. Congress repealed the tax a year later.

Dynamic Tax Analysis. The problem with static tax analysis is that it ignores incentive effects created by new taxes or hikes in existing tax rates. According to **dynamic tax analysis,** a likely response to an increase in a tax rate is a decrease in the tax base. When a government pushes up its sales tax rate, for example, consumers have an incentive to cut back on their purchases of goods and services subjected to the higher rate, perhaps by buying them in a locale where there is a lower sales tax rate or perhaps no tax rate at all. As shown in Figure 6-1, the maximum sales tax rate varies considerably from state to state. Someone who lives in a state bordering Oregon, where the sales tax rate can be as high as 8 percent, certainly has a strong incentive to buy higher-priced goods and services in Oregon, where there is no sales tax. Someone who lives in a high-tax county in Alabama has an incentive to buy an item online from an out-of-state firm and also avoid paying sales taxes. Such shifts in expenditures in response to higher relative tax rates can reduce a state's sales tax base and thereby result in lower sales tax collections than the levels predicted by static tax analysis.

Dynamic tax analysis recognizes that increasing the tax rate could actually cause the government's total tax collections to *decline* if a sufficiently large number of consumers react to the higher sales tax rate by cutting back on purchases of goods and services included in the state's tax base. Some residents who live close to other states with lower sales tax rates might, for instance, drive across the state line to do more of their shopping. Other residents might place more orders with catalog companies or online firms located in other legal jurisdictions where this state's sales tax does not apply.

Dynamic tax analysis
Economic evaluation of tax rate changes that recognizes that the tax base eventually declines with ever-higher tax rates, so that tax revenues may eventually decline if the tax rate is raised sufficiently.

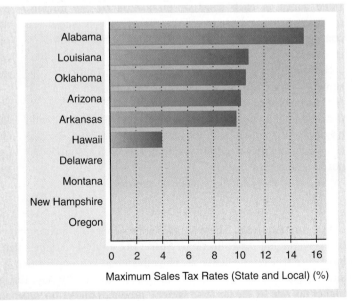

FIGURE 6-1
States with the Highest and Lowest Sales Tax Rates
A number of states allow counties and cities to collect their own sales taxes in addition to state sales taxes. This figure shows the maximum sales tax rates for selected states, including county and municipal taxes. Delaware, Montana, New Hampshire, and Oregon have no sales taxes. All other states and the District of Columbia have maximum sales tax rates between the 4 percent rate of Hawaii and the 9.875 percent rate in Arkansas.

Source: U.S. Department of Commerce.

Maximum Sales Tax Rates (State and Local) (%)

Did you know that even if you do not have to pay sales taxes on out-of-state purchases, your state may have a law requiring you to pay a "use tax" on items shipped to you from outside the state?

Policy EXAMPLE

Some States Make It More Difficult to Avoid Taxes on Out-of-State Purchases

In 18 states and Washington, D.C., state income tax forms now include a line for taxpayers to calculate and include *use taxes*, which apply to items purchased outside the home state but shipped to that state. A few other states also have separate forms that taxpayers are supposed to obtain for reporting and transmitting use taxes. Nevertheless, most states with use taxes currently do not expend sufficient resources to fully enforce these rules. Tax authorities in these locales most often try to collect unpaid use taxes from individuals only when evidence that they have avoided these taxes happens to emerge during

investigations of nonpayment of other taxes. Thus many individuals currently fail to pay use taxes even in states that have established this form of taxation.

For Critical Analysis

Why do you suppose that states with use taxes make more effort to collect these taxes from large companies than from individuals? (Hint: Are firms or individuals more likely to purchase large quantities of items from out-of-state producers?)

Maximizing Tax Revenues

Dynamic tax analysis indicates that whether a government's tax revenues ultimately rise or fall in response to a tax rate increase depends on exactly how much the tax base declines in response to the higher tax rate. On the one hand, the tax base may decline by a relatively small amount following an increase in the tax rate, or perhaps even imperceptibly, so that tax revenues rise. For instance, in the situation we imagine a government facing in Figure 6-2, a rise in the tax rate from 5 percent to 6 percent causes tax revenues to increase. In this situation, static tax analysis can provide a good approximation of the revenue effects of an increase in the tax rate. On the other hand, the tax base may decline so

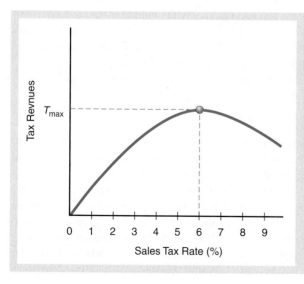

FIGURE 6-2
Maximizing the Government's Sales Tax Revenues
Dynamic tax analysis predicts that ever-higher tax rates bring about declines in the tax base, so that at sufficiently high tax rates the government's tax revenues begin to fall off. This implies that there is a tax rate, 6 percent in this example, at which the government can collect the maximum possible revenues, T_{max}.

much that total tax revenues decrease. In Figure 6-2 on the previous page, for example, increasing the tax rate from 6 percent to 7 percent causes tax revenues to *decline*.

What is most likely is that when the tax rate is already relatively low, increasing the tax rate causes relatively small declines in the tax base. Within a range of relatively low sales tax rates, therefore, increasing the tax rate generates higher sales tax revenues, as illustrated along the upward-sloping portion of the curve depicted in Figure 6-2. If the government continues to push up the tax rate, however, people increasingly have an incentive to find ways to avoid purchasing taxable goods and services. Eventually, the tax base decreases sufficiently that the government's tax collections decline with ever-higher tax rates.

Consequently, governments that wish to maximize their tax revenues should not assess a relatively high tax rate. In the situation illustrated in Figure 6-2, the government maximizes its tax revenues at T_{max} by establishing a sales tax rate of 6 percent. If the government were to raise the rate above 6 percent, it would induce a sufficient decline in the tax base that its tax collections would decline. If the government wishes to collect more than T_{max} in revenues to fund various government programs, it must somehow either expand its sales tax base or develop another tax.

CONCEPTS in Brief

- The static view of the relationship between tax rates and tax revenues implies that higher tax rates generate increased government tax collections.

- According to dynamic tax analysis, higher tax rates cause the tax base to decrease. Tax collections will rise less than predicted by static tax analysis.

- Dynamic tax analysis indicates that there is a tax rate that maximizes the government's tax collections. Setting the tax rate any higher would cause the tax base to fall sufficiently that the government's tax revenues will decline.

To test your understanding of the concepts covered in this section, go to the Online Review at www.myeconlab.com/miller.

TAXATION FROM THE POINT OF VIEW OF PRODUCERS AND CONSUMERS

Both the federal government and state and local governments impose taxes on a variety of market transactions. Take a look back at Figure 5-3 on page 113, and you will see that taxes on the sales of goods and services—sales taxes, gross receipts taxes, and excise taxes—generate almost one-fifth of the total funds available to state and local governments.

These taxes affect market prices and quantities. Let's consider why this is so.

Taxes and the Market Supply Curve

Governments collect taxes on product sales at the source. They require producers to charge these taxes when they sell their output. This means that imposing taxes on final sales of a good or service affects the position of the market supply curve.

Excise tax
A tax levied on purchases of a particular good or service.

Unit tax
A constant tax assessed on each unit of a good that consumers purchase.

To see why, consider panel (a) of Figure 6-3, which shows a gasoline market supply curve S_1 in the absence of taxation. At a price of $1.00 per gallon, gasoline producers are willing and able to supply 180,000 gallons of gasoline per week. If the price increases to $1.10 per gallon, firms increase production to 200,000 gallons of gasoline per week.

Both federal and state governments assess **excise taxes**—taxes on sales of particular commodities—on sales of gasoline. They levy gasoline excise taxes as a **unit tax,** or a

FIGURE 6-3

The Effects of Excise Taxes on the Market Supply and Equilibrium Price and Quantity of Gasoline

Panel (a) shows what happens if the government requires gasoline sellers to collect and transmit a $0.40 unit excise tax on gasoline. To be willing to continue supplying a given quantity, sellers must receive a price that is

$0.40 higher for each gallon they sell, so the market supply curve shifts vertically upward by the amount of the tax. As illustrated in panel (b), this decline in market supply causes a reduction in the equilibrium quantity of gasoline produced and purchased. It also causes a rise in the market price, so that consumers pay part of the tax. Sellers pay the rest in higher costs.

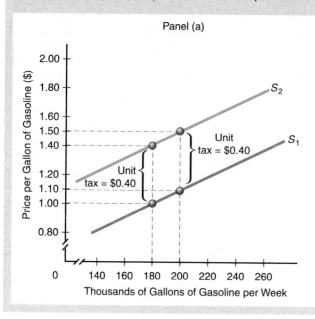

Panel (a)

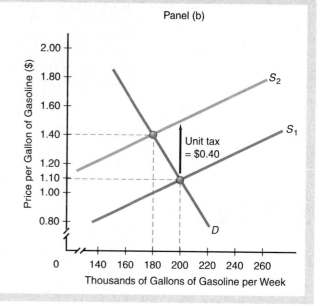

Panel (b)

constant tax per unit sold. On average, combined federal and state excise taxes on gasoline are about $0.40 per gallon.

Let's suppose, therefore, that a gasoline producer must transmit a total of $0.40 per gallon to federal and state governments for each gallon sold. Producers must continue to receive a net amount of $1.00 per gallon to induce them to supply 180,000 gallons each week, so they must now receive $1.40 per gallon to supply that weekly quantity. Likewise, gasoline producers now will be willing to supply 200,000 gallons each week only if they receive $0.40 more per gallon, or a total amount of $1.50 per gallon.

As you can see, imposing the combined $0.40 per gallon excise taxes on gasoline shifts the supply curve upward by exactly that amount to S_2. Thus the effect of levying excise taxes on gasoline is to shift the supply curve vertically upward by the total per-unit taxes levied on gasoline sales. Hence there is a decrease in supply. (In the case of an *ad valorem* sales tax, the supply curve would shift upward by a proportionate amount equal to the tax rate.)

How Taxes Affect the Market Price and Equilibrium Quantity

Panel (b) of Figure 6-3 shows how imposing $0.40 per gallon in excise taxes affects the market price of gasoline and the equilibrium quantity of gasoline produced and sold. In the absence of excise taxes, the market supply curve S_1 crosses the demand curve D at a market price of $1.10 per gallon. At this market price, the equilibrium quantity of gasoline is 200,000 gallons of gasoline per week.

The excise tax levy of $0.40 per gallon shifts the supply curve to S_2. At the original $1.10 per gallon price, there is now an excess quantity of gasoline demanded, so the market price of gasoline rises to $1.40 per gallon. At this market price, the equilibrium quantity of gasoline produced and consumed each week is 180,000 gallons.

What factors determine how much the equilibrium quantity of a good or service declines in response to taxation? The answer to this question depends on how responsive quantities demanded and supplied are to changes in price.

Who Pays the Tax?

In our example, imposing excise taxes of $0.40 per gallon of gasoline causes the market price to rise from $1.10 per gallon to $1.40 per gallon. Thus the price that each consumer pays is $0.30 per gallon higher. Consumers pay three-fourths of the excise tax levied on each gallon of gasoline produced and sold.

Gasoline producers must pay the rest of the tax. Their profits decline by $0.10 per gallon because costs have increased by $0.40 per gallon while consumers pay only $0.30 more per gallon.

In the gasoline market, as in other markets for products subject to excise taxes and other taxes on sales, the shapes of the market demand and supply curves determine who pays most of a tax. The reason is that the shapes of these curves reflect the price responsiveness of the quantity demanded by consumers and of the quantity supplied by producers.

In the example illustrated in Figure 6-3, the fact that consumers pay most of the excise taxes levied on gasoline reflects a relatively low responsiveness of quantity demanded by consumers to a change in the price of gasoline. Consumers pay most of the excise taxes on each gallon produced and sold because in this example the amount of gasoline they desire to purchase is relatively unresponsive to a change in the market price induced by excise taxes. We will revisit the issue of who pays excise taxes in Chapter 21.

CONCEPTS in Brief

- When the government levies a tax on sales of a particular product, firms must receive a higher price to continue supplying the same quantity as before, so the supply curve shifts vertically upward. If the tax is a unit excise tax, the supply curve shifts vertically upward by the amount of the tax.

- Imposing a tax on sales of an item reduces the equilibrium quantity produced and consumed and raises the market price.

- When a government assesses a unit excise tax, the market price of the good or service typically rises by an amount less than the per-unit tax. Hence consumers pay a portion of the tax, and firms pay the remainder.

To test your understanding of the concepts covered in this section, go to the Online Review at www.myeconlab.com/miller.

PUBLIC SPENDING AND TRANSFER PROGRAMS

Most state governments use sales and excise tax revenues, along with property and other taxes, to fund their spending and transfer programs. Likewise, the federal government uses excise taxes to supplement income tax collections that it uses to finance the bulk of federal purchases and transfers.

Governments use tax revenues to fund spending on public goods, such as the provision of public safety services and national defense. Some government programs subsidize the consumption of merit goods, such as education and health care. Others are pure transfer programs in which governments direct money payments to specific groups, such as when the federal government transfers funds from younger, healthy workers to the elderly and disabled via the Social Security system.

Publicly Subsidized Health Care: Medicare

Not surprisingly, medical expenses are a major concern for many elderly people. Since 1965, that concern has been reflected in the existence of the Medicare program, which pays hospital and physicians' bills for U.S. residents over the age of 65 (and for those younger than 65 in some instances). In return for paying a tax on their earnings while in the workforce (currently set at 2.9 percent of wages and salaries), retirees are ensured that the majority of their hospital and physicians' bills will be paid for with public monies.

Go to www.econtoday.com/chap06 to visit the U.S. government's official Medicare Web site.

The Simple Economics of Medicare. To understand how, in less than 40 years, Medicare became the second-biggest domestic spending program in existence, a bit of economics is in order. Consider Figure 6-4, which shows the demand for and supply of medical care.

The initial equilibrium price is P_0 and equilibrium quantity is Q_0. Perhaps because the government believes that Q_0 is not enough medical care for these consumers, suppose that the government begins paying a subsidy that eventually is set at M for each unit of medical care consumed. This will simultaneously tend to raise the price per unit of care received by providers (physicians, hospitals, and so on) and lower the perceived price per unit that consumers see when they make decisions about how much medical care to consume. As presented in the figure, the price received by providers rises to P_s, while the price paid by consumers falls to P_d. As a result, consumers of medical care want to purchase Q_m units, and suppliers are quite happy to provide it for them.

Medicare Incentives at Work. We can now understand the problems that plague the Medicare system today. First, one of the things that people observed during the 20 years after the founding of Medicare was a huge upsurge in physicians' incomes and medical school applications, the spread of private for-profit hospitals, and the rapid proliferation of

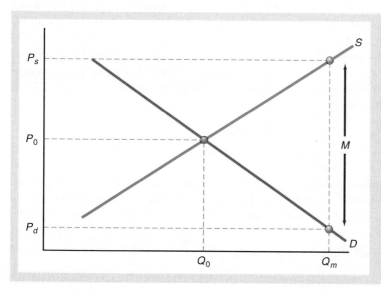

FIGURE 6-4
The Economic Effects of Medicare Subsidies
When the government pays a per-unit subsidy M for medical care, consumers pay the price of services P_d for the quantity of services Q_m. Providers receive the price P_s for supplying this quantity. Originally, the federal government projected its total spending on Medicare to equal an amount such as the area $Q_0 \times (P_0 - P_d)$. Because actual consumption equals Q_m, however, the government's total expenditures actual equal $Q_m \times M$.

new medical tests and procedures. All of this was being encouraged by the rise in the price of medical services from P_0 to P_s, which encouraged entry into this market.

Second, government expenditures on Medicare have routinely turned out to be far in excess of the expenditures forecast at the time the program was put in place or was expanded. The reasons for this are easy to see. Bureaucratic planners often fail to recognize the incentive effects of government programs. On the demand side, they fail to account for the huge increase in consumption (from Q_0 to Q_m) that will result from a subsidy like Medicare. On the supply side, they fail to recognize that the larger amount of services can only be extracted from suppliers at a higher price, P_s. Consequently, original projected spending on Medicare was an area like $Q_0 \times (P_0 - P_d)$, because original plans for the program only allowed for consumption of Q_0 and assumed that the subsidy would have to be only $P_0 - P_d$ per unit. In fact, consumption rises to Q_m, and marginal cost per unit of service rises to P_s, necessitating an increase in the per-unit subsidy to M. Hence actual expenditures turn out to be the far larger number $Q_m \times M$. The introduction of Medicare thus was more expensive than predicted, and every expansion of the program including the 2003 extension of Medicare to cover patients' prescription drug expenses, has followed the same pattern.

Third, total spending on medical services soars, consuming far more income than initially expected. Originally, total spending on medical services was $P_0 \times Q_0$. In the presence of Medicare, spending rises to $P_s \times Q_m$. This helps explain why current health care spending in the United States is about 15 percent of GDP—the largest percentage spent anywhere in the world.

How do you suppose that the prices charged by physicians who refuse to treat Medicare patients and patients covered by other public and private health plans compare with prices charged by physicians who accept such patients?

Economics Front and Center

To think about how government subsidies can sometimes create unintended incentives for producers of medications that doctors prescribe, consider the case study, **To Boost Drug Sales, Is It Time to Raise the Price?**, on page 138.

EXAMPLE

The Doctor Is In, but Insurance Is Out!

Quietly but steadily, a new type of health care clinic has emerged in recent years. What is different about these new clinics is that they will process neither Medicare nor private insurance claims. The clinics accept only cash, check, and credit- and debit-card payments, which they often require patients to tender *before* receiving a physician's care. By avoiding all the costs of handling the paperwork associated with health insurance, many of these clinics can operate with clerical staffs as much as 70 percent lower than clinics that accept Medicare and other forms of health insurance. Their physicians also avoid the headache of trying to convince insurers to reimburse for services already rendered to patients.

Because their costs are lower, physicians at these clinics can charge much lower prices than physicians at clinics that process health insurance claims. Currently, typical charges at clinics that will not accept payments through government and private health insurance companies are about $35 for an office visit and $20 for a basic blood test. In contrast, typical office-visit fees are $55 or more and blood-test charges start at $100 at clinics that devote considerable resources to handling the red tape associated with claims.

For Critical Analysis
Why might people who are covered by Medicare or private health insurance be willing to pay cash for treatment by physicians who will not accept payments from these insurers?

Economic Issues of Public Education

In the United States, government involvement in health care is a relatively recent phenomenon. In contrast, state and local governments have assumed primary responsibility for public education for many years. Currently, these governments spend well over $500 billion on education—more than 5 percent of total U.S. national income. State and local sales, excise, property, and income taxes finance the bulk of these expenditures. In addition, each year the federal government provides tens of billions of dollars of support for public education through grants and other transfers to state and local governments.

The Now-Familiar Economics of Public Education. State and local governments around the United States have developed a variety of complex mechanisms for funding public education. What all public education programs have in common, however, is the provision of educational services to primary, secondary, and college students at prices well below those that would otherwise prevail in the marketplace for these services.

So how do state and local governments accomplish this? The answer is that they operate public education programs that are very similar to government-subsidized health care programs such as Medicare. Analogously to Figure 6-4 on page 131, public schools provide educational services at a price below the market price. They are willing to produce the quantity of educational services demanded at this below-market price as long as they receive a sufficiently high per-unit subsidy from state and local governments.

For about a century, state and local governments in the United States have used this basic economic mechanism to provide public primary and secondary education. How do you suppose that the more recent involvement of the federal government in subsidizing college and university students has affected tuitions at these institutions?

Policy EXAMPLE

One Reason for College Tuition Hikes: Government Subsidies

Since the 1950s, the federal government has subsidized college and university students through various programs that offer grants, loans, and tax breaks directly to college students. The inflation-adjusted amount of these federal subsidies has increased by about 300 percent since then, partly because more students receive subsidies but also because each subsidized student receives more federal funding. In 1971, the average annual amount of federal aid per subsidized student was, in 2005 dollars, just over $2,600. Today, the average annual amount, in 2005 dollars, received by each federally subsidized student exceeds $5,600. Hence, today's federally subsidized student's willingness to pay for a year of higher education is $3,000

higher than it was in 1971. On top of that, the government transmits this higher average subsidy to many more students. The overall effect of federal support to students, therefore, has been an increase in the market demand for college and university training. This has contributed to the 120 percent increase in the average inflation-adjusted U.S. tuition rate that has taken place since 1971.

For Critical Analysis
What would happen to average tuition rates if federal subsidies were ended?

The Incentive Problems of Public Education. Since the 1960s, various measures of the performances of U.S. primary and secondary students have failed to increase even as public spending on education has risen. Some measures of student performance have even declined.

Many economists argue that the explanation for the failure of student performances to improve relates to the incentive effects that have naturally arisen as government subsidies for public education have increased. A higher per-pupil subsidy creates a difference between the relatively high costs to schools of providing the amount of educational services that parents and students are willing to purchase and the relatively lower valuations of those services by parents and students. As a consequence, schools may have provided services, such as after-school babysitting and various social services, which have contributed relatively little to student learning.

A factor that complicates assessing the effects of education subsidies is that the public school recipients often face little or no competition from unsubsidized providers of educational services. In addition, public schools rarely compete against each other. In most locales, therefore, parents who are unhappy with the quality of services provided at the subsidized price cannot transfer their child to a different public school.

CONCEPTS in Brief

- Medicare subsidizes the consumption of medical care by the elderly, thus increasing the amount of such care consumed. People tend to purchase large amounts of low-value, high-cost services in publicly funded health care programs such as Medicare, because they do not directly bear the full cost of their decisions.

- Basic economic analysis indicates that higher subsidies for public education have widened the differential between parents' and students' relatively low marginal valuations of the educational services of public schools and the higher costs that schools incur in providing those services.

To test your understanding of the concepts covered in this section, go to the Online Review at **www.myeconlab.com/miller**.

SOCIAL SECURITY

Medicare is one of two major federal transfer programs. The other is Social Security, the federal system that transfers portions of the incomes of working-age people to elderly and disabled individuals. If current laws are maintained, Medicare's share of total national income will double over the next 20 years, as will the number of "very old" people—those over 85 and most in need of care. When Social Security is also taken into account, probably *half* of all federal government spending will go to the elderly by 2025. In a nutshell, senior citizens are the beneficiaries of an expensive and rapidly growing share of all federal spending.

The Ticking Social Security Time Bomb

The federal government finances Social Security contributions with payroll taxes. It currently applies a tax rate of 12.4 percent to a tax base approximately equal to the first roughly $90,000 in wages earned by U.S. workers. If there is no change in the current structure of the Social Security system, the continuing retirements of large numbers of baby boomers, born between the late 1940s and early 1960s, will leave today's college students and their children with a potentially staggering bill to pay. For Social Security and Medicare to be maintained, the payroll (Social Security) tax rate will have to rise to 25 percent. And a payroll tax rate of 40 percent is not unlikely by 2050.

One way to think about the future bill that could face today's college students and their successors in the absence of fundamental changes in Social Security is to consider the number of workers available to support each retiree. In 1946, payroll taxes from 42 workers supported one Social Security recipient. By 1960, just 9 workers funded each retiree's Social Security benefits. Today, roughly 3 workers provide for each retiree's Social Security *and* Medicare benefits. Unless the current system is changed, by 2030 only 2 workers will be available to pay the Social Security and Medicare benefits due each recipient. In that event, a working couple would find themselves responsible for supporting not only themselves and their family, but also someone outside the family who is receiving Social Security and Medicare benefits.

These figures illustrate why efforts to reform these programs have begun to dominate the nation's public agenda. What remains to be seen is how the government will ultimately resolve them.

Good Times for the First Retirees

The Social Security system was founded in 1935, as the United States was recovering from the Great Depression. The decision was made to establish Social Security as a means of guaranteeing a minimum level of pension benefits to all residents. Today, many people regard Social Security as a kind of "social compact"—a national promise to successive generations that they will receive support in their old age.

Big Payoffs for the Earliest Recipients. The first Social Security taxes (called "contributions") were collected in 1937, but it was not until 1940 that retirement benefits were first paid. Ida May Fuller was the first person to receive a regular Social Security pension. She had paid a total of $25 in **Social Security contributions** before she retired. By the time she died in 1975 at age 100, she had received benefits totaling $23,000. Although Fuller did perhaps better than most, for the average retiree of 1940, the Social Security system was still more generous than any private investment plan anyone is likely to devise: After adjusting for inflation, the implicit **rate of return** on their contributions was an astounding 135 percent. (Roughly speaking, every $100 of combined employer and employee contributions yielded $135 *per year* during each and every year of that person's retirement. This is also called the **inflation-adjusted return**.)

> **Social Security contributions**
> The mandatory taxes paid out of workers' wages and salaries. Although half are supposedly paid by employers, in fact the net wages of employees are lower by the full amount.
>
> **Rate of return**
> The future financial benefit to making a current investment
>
> **Inflation-adjusted return**
> A rate of return that is measured in terms of real goods and services; that is, after the effects of inflation have been factored out.

Ever since the early days of Social Security, however, the rate of return has decreased. Nonetheless, Social Security was an excellent deal for most retirees during the twentieth century. Figure 6-5 on the next page shows the implicit rate of return for people retiring in different years.

Given that the inflation-adjusted long-term rate of return on the stock market is about 7 to 9 percent, it is clear that for retirees, Social Security was a good deal until at least 1970. In fact, because Social Security benefits are a lot less risky than stocks, Social Security actually remained a pretty good investment for many people until around 1990.

Slowing Membership Growth. Social Security has managed to pay such high returns because at each point in time, current retirees are paid benefits out of the contributions of individuals who are currently working. (The contributions of today's retirees were long ago used to pay the benefits of previous retirees.) As long as Social Security was pulling in growing numbers of workers, either through a burgeoning workforce or by expanding its coverage of individuals in the workforce, the impressive rates of return during the early years of the program were possible.

But as membership growth slowed as the post–World War II baby boom generation began to reach retirement age, the rate of return fell. Moreover, because the early participants received more than they contributed, it follows that if the number of participants stops growing, later participants must receive less—and that ultimately means a *negative* rate of return. And for today's college students—indeed for most people now under the age of 30 or so—that negative rate of return is what lies ahead, unless reforms are implemented.

What Will It Take to Salvage Social Security?

The United States now finds itself with a social compact—the Social Security system— that entails a flow of promised benefits that could exceed the inflow of taxes by about 2010. What, if anything, might be done about this? There are four relevant options to consider.

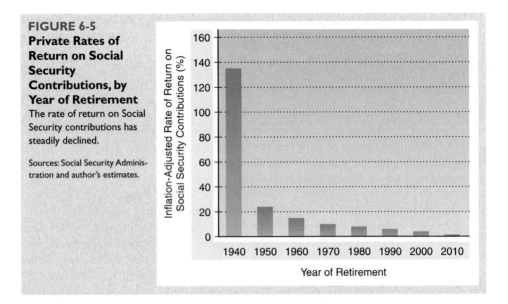

FIGURE 6-5
Private Rates of Return on Social Security Contributions, by Year of Retirement

The rate of return on Social Security contributions has steadily declined.

Sources: Social Security Administration and author's estimates.

(Chart: Inflation-Adjusted Rate of Return on Social Security Contributions (%) vs. Year of Retirement, from 1940 to 2010, showing a steady decline from about 135% in 1940.)

Go to www.econtoday.com/chap06 to learn more about Social Security at the official Web site of the Social Security Administration.

1. **Raise Taxes.** The history of Social Security has been one of steadily increasing tax rates applied to an ever-larger portion of workers' wages. In 1935, a Social Security payroll tax rate of 2 percent was applied to the first $3,000 of an individual's earnings (more than $35,000 in today's dollars). Now the Social Security payroll tax rate is 10.4 percentage points higher, and the government applies this tax rate to roughly an additional $55,000 of a worker's wages measured in today's dollars.

   One prominent proposal promises an $80 billion increase in contributions via a 2.2 percentage point hike in the payroll tax rate, to an overall rate of 14.6 percent. Another proposal is to eliminate the current cap on the level of wages to which the payroll tax is applied, which would also generate about $80 billion per year in additional tax revenues. Nevertheless, even a combined policy of eliminating the wage cap and implementing a 2.2 percentage-point tax increase would not, by itself, keep tax collections above benefit payments over the long run.

2. **Reduce Benefit Payouts.** Proposals are on the table to increase the age of full benefit eligibility, perhaps to as high as 70. Another option is to cut benefits to nonworking spouses. A third proposal is to impose "means testing" on some or all Social Security benefits. As things stand now, all individuals covered by the system collect benefits when they retire, regardless of their assets or other sources of retirement income. Under a system of means testing, individuals with substantial amounts of alternative sources of retirement income would receive reduced Social Security benefits.

3. **Reform Immigration Policies.** Many experts believe that significant changes in U.S. immigration laws could offer the best hope of dealing with the tax burdens and workforce shrinkage of the future. Currently, however, more than 90 percent of new immigrants are admitted on the basis of a selection system unchanged since 1952. This system ties immigration rights to family preference. That is why most people admitted to the United States happen to be the spouses, children, or siblings of earlier immigrants. Unless Congress makes skills or training that are highly valued in the U.S. workplace a criterion in the U.S. immigration preference system, new immigrants are unlikely to contribute significant resources to Social Security, because their incomes will remain relatively low. Without reforms, it is unlikely that immigration will relieve much of the pressure building due to our aging population.

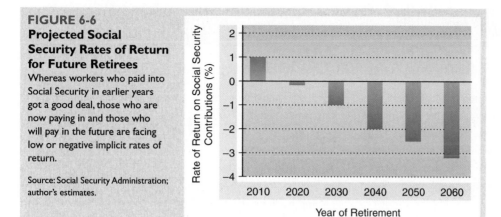

FIGURE 6-6
Projected Social Security Rates of Return for Future Retirees
Whereas workers who paid into Social Security in earlier years got a good deal, those who are now paying in and those who will pay in the future are facing low or negative implicit rates of return.

Source: Social Security Administration; author's estimates.

4. **Find a Way to Increase Social Security's Rate of Return.** As noted earlier, a major current problem for Social Security is a low implicit rate of return. Looking into the future, however, the situation looks even worse. As Figure 6-6 indicates, implicit rates of return for the system will be *negative* by 2020.

The long-term inflation-adjusted return available in the stock market has been 7 to 9 percent since the 1930s. It is not surprising, therefore, that some observers have advocated that the Social Security system purchase stocks rather than Treasury bonds with the current excess of payroll taxes over current benefit payments. (Because this would necessitate the Treasury's borrowing more from the public, this amounts to having the government borrow money from the public for purposes of investing in the stock market.)

Although the added returns on stock investments could help stave off tax increases or benefit cuts, there are a few potential problems with this proposal. Despite the stock market's higher long-term returns, the inherent uncertainty of those returns is not entirely consistent with the function of Social Security as a source of *guaranteed* retirement income. Another issue is what stocks would be purchased. Political pressure to invest in companies that happened to be politically popular and to refrain from investing in those that were unpopular, regardless of their returns, would reduce the expected returns from the government's stock portfolio—possibly even below the returns on Treasury bonds.

CONCEPTS in Brief

- Social Security and Medicare payments are using up a large and growing portion of the federal budget. Because of a shrinking number of workers available to support each retiree, the per capita expense for future workers to fund these programs will grow rapidly unless reforms are made.

- During the early years of the Social Security system, taxes were low relative to benefits, resulting in a high rate of return for retirees. As taxes have risen relative to

benefits, the rate of return on Social Security has fallen steadily.

- There are only four options—or combinations of these four options—for preserving the current social compact: raise taxes, reduce benefit payouts, reform immigration policies, or increase Social Security's rate of return.

To test your understanding of the concepts covered in this section, go to the Online Review at www.myeconlab.com/miller.

CASE STUDY : Economics Front and Center

To Boost Drug Sales, Is It Time to Raise the Price?

Robinson is an executive at a top pharmaceuticals company. She is in charge of determining the prices of medicines used in chemotherapy regimens for cancer patients. It is late in the evening and her subordinates have all gone home, but she is still in her office developing pricing plans for the company's newest chemotherapy drugs. She knows that under government-subsidy programs, reimbursements for chemotherapy treatments go to physicians instead of patients. This, she also knows, gives physicians an incentive to prescribe higher-priced medications. Thus the demand for her companies' drugs is likely to increase if the company raises its price.

Robinson posts a note to herself in an electronic file on her computer: "Tomorrow, find out the highest allowable reimbursement rates physicians can receive for chemotherapy prescriptions under Medicare and Medicaid rules. Then calculate how our drugs should be priced to generate those maximum physician reimbursements."

Points to Analyze

1. *Will the price paid by the Medicare patients receiving a chemotherapy drug produced by Robinson's company be above or below the price that would have prevailed in the absence of the Medicare program?*

2. *Will the price received by the doctors from the government for prescribing the company's chemotherapy drug be above or below the price that would have prevailed in the absence of the Medicare program?*

Issues and Applications

Why Activities Are No Longer "Free" at Many Public Schools

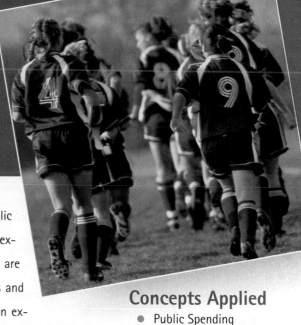

I n a growing number of communities across the United States, public schools are charging hundreds or even thousands of dollars for extracurricular activities, including music, clubs, and sports. Others are charging fees for preschool and kindergarten programs. When parents and guardians refuse to pay fees, school administrators are cutting back on extracurricular activities and offerings of preschool and kindergarten classes. Some schools are even eliminating these programs.

Concepts Applied
- Public Spending
- Public Subsidies

The Economics of School Subsidy Cutbacks

What has driven public schools to charge fees for extracurricular activities that they previously made available to students at no charge? The answer to this question can be inferred from Figure 6-7. As in Figure 6-4 on page 131, the government initially provides a per-unit subsidy, M, to public schools. Given this subsidy, students' families pay the very low price P_d for the quantity of educational services equal to Q_m. Schools receive the total price P_s for supplying this quantity.

In recent years, a number of state and local governments have cut back on the funds they provide for public education. Thus the per-unit subsidy has declined to an amount such as M' in Figure 6-7. At this lower subsidy, schools reduce the quantity of services they are willing to supply to Q'_m, because they receive a lower price, P'_s. Furthermore, families must pay a higher price, P'_d, for students to receive the smaller amount of educational services. Schools charge families the higher price by charging them service fees, such as band or orchestra admittance fees, fees to participate in sports, or fees for a child to attend kindergarten.

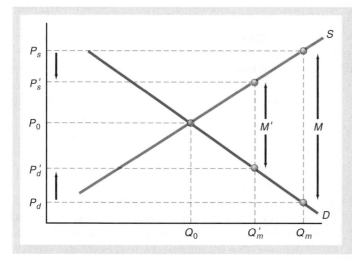

FIGURE 6-7
The Effects of a Reduction in Education Subsidies
A reduction in the per-unit subsidy that the government provides for educational services, from M to M', causes a reduction in the quantity of these services supplied, to Q'_m. In addition, the per-unit price that families must pay for the smaller quantity of services received rises to P'_d.

Paying for Band, Basketball, and Preschool

Why are schools choosing extracurricular activities and preschool and kindergarten programs for cutbacks? Recall that a higher per-pupil subsidy for public education widens the difference between the relatively high costs to schools of providing all the various services families are willing to purchase and the relatively lower family valuations of those services. As state and local governments have reduced school subsidies, this difference has narrowed. Consequently, schools are cutting back on services with the *lowest* value to families. Most families put higher values on reading, writing, and arithmetic than on band, basketball, and preschool. So these are the first programs that schools typically choose to reduce.

In some locales, proponents of these activities have found alternative ways to fund them. For instance, in some communities, parents, teachers, and administrators have formed groups with names such as "Save Our Sports," which conduct bake sales, car washes, and raffles aimed at raising funds to keep extracurricular programs from dying.

Irrespective of how funds to support extracurricular activities or other school programs are raised, there is no getting around a basic fact. Cutting back on school subsidies causes schools either to stop providing services with relatively low values to most families or to induce the families who place a relatively high value on these services to pay for them directly.

For Critical Analysis

1. In Figure 6-7, what price would families end up paying if state and local governments eliminated all school subsidies?
2. Why do you suppose that a number of high schools that previously offered "free" courses for preparation for college admissions tests are now charging fees for these courses?

Web Resources

1. For recent U.S. Department of Education data on education spending, go to **www.econtoday.com/chap06**.
2. To learn from the National Center for Policy Analysis about how special subsidies for schools providing services to disabled students have affected the number of students classified as "disabled," go to the link available at **www.econtoday.com/chap06**.

Research Project

Each year, the average U.S. public school spends approximately the following amounts per pupil: $4,300 for instructional services, $2,500 for various support services, and $300 for miscellaneous noninstructional expenses. Evaluate why government subsidization of public schools helps explain why they spend an average of $300 per student on items that are unrelated to their primary task of instructing students.

SUMMARY DISCUSSION of Learning Objectives

1. **The Relationship Between Tax Rates and Tax Revenues:** Static tax analysis assumes that the tax base does not respond significantly to an increase in the tax rate, so it seems to imply a tax rate hike boosts a government's total tax collections. Dynamic tax analysis reveals, however, increases in tax rates cause the tax base to decline. Thus there is a tax rate that maximizes the government's tax revenues. If the government pushes the tax rate higher, tax collections decline.

2. **How Taxes on Purchases of Goods and Services Affect Market Prices and Quantities:** When a government imposes a per-unit tax on a good or service, a seller is willing to supply any given quantity only if the seller receives a price that is higher by exactly the amount of the tax. Hence the supply curve shifts vertically upward by the amount of the tax per unit. In a market with typically shaped demand and supply curves, this results in a fall in the equilibrium quantity and an increase in the market price. To the extent that the market price rises, consumers pay a portion of the tax on each unit they buy. Sellers pay the remainder in higher per-unit production costs.

3. **The Effect of Medicare on the Incentives to Consume Medical Services:** Medicare subsidizes the consumption of medical services by the elderly. As a result, the quantity consumed is higher, as is the price sellers receive per unit of those services. As a result, the United States spends a larger portion of national income on medical care for the elderly than any other nation in the world. Medicare also encourages people to consume medical services that are very low in marginal value relative to

the cost of providing them. Medicare thereby places a substantial tax burden on other sectors of the economy.

4. **Why Bigger Subsidies for Public Schools Do Not Necessarily Translate into Improved Student Performance:** When governments subsidize public schools, the last unit of educational services provided by public schools is likely to cost more than its valuation by parents and students. Public schools therefore provide services in excess of those best suited to promoting student learning. This may help explain why measures of overall U.S. student performance have stagnated even as per-pupil subsidies to public schools have increased significantly.

5. **How Social Security Works and Why It Poses Problems for Today's Students:** Since its inception, Social Security benefits have been paid out of taxes. Because of the growing mismatch between elderly and younger citizens, future scheduled benefits vastly exceed future scheduled taxes, so some combination of higher taxes and lower benefits will have to be implemented to maintain the current system. The situation might also be eased a bit if more immigration of skilled workers were permitted and if Social Security contributions were invested in the stock market, where they could earn higher rates of return.

KEY TERMS AND CONCEPTS

ad valorem taxation (125)

dynamic tax analysis (126)

excise tax (128)

government budget constraint (124)

inflation-adjusted return (135)

rate of return (135)

sales taxes (125)

Social Security contributions (135)

static tax analysis (125)

tax base (125)

unit tax (128)

PROBLEMS

Answers to the odd-numbered problems appear at the back of the book.

6-1. Suppose that a state has enacted increases in its sales tax rate every other year since 1997. Assume that during this period, the static tax analysis was fully valid, and the state collected all sales taxes that residents legally owed. The following table summarizes its experience. What were total taxable sales in this state during each year displayed in the table?

Year	Sales Tax Rate	Sales Tax Collections
1997	0.03 (3 percent)	$9.0 million
1999	0.04 (4 percent)	$14.0 million
2001	0.05 (5 percent)	$20.0 million
2003	0.06 (6 percent)	$24.0 million
2005	0.07 (7 percent)	$29.4 million

6-2. The sales tax rate applied to all purchases within a state was 0.04 (4 percent) throughout 2004 but increased to 0.05 (5 percent) during all of 2005. The state government collected all taxes due, but its tax revenues were equal to $40 million each year. What

happened to the sales tax base between 2004 and 2005? What could account for this result?

6-3. A city government imposes a proportional income tax on all people who earn income within its city limits. In 2004, the city's income tax rate was 0.05 (5 percent), and it collected $20 million in income taxes. In 2005, it raised the income tax rate to 0.06 (6.0 percent), and its income tax collections declined to $19.2 million. What happened to the city's income tax base between 2004 and 2005? How could this have occurred?

6-4. The city government of a small town where a large college is located imposes a unit excise tax of $1 on each textbook purchased at local bookstores. If students are always willing to pay whatever price local bookstores charge in order to obtain the textbooks required for their courses, what will be the effect of this tax on the equilibrium textbook price?

6-5. Suppose that the federal government imposes a unit excise tax of $2 per month on the rates that Internet service providers charge for DSL high-speed Internet access in separate markets for the provision of these services to households and businesses.

a. Draw a diagram of normally shaped market demand and supply curves for DSL Internet access services. Use this diagram to make predictions about how the Internet service tax is likely to affect the market price and market quantity.

b. Suppose that in the market for DSL Internet access services provided to households, the market price increases by $2 per month after the unit excise tax is imposed. If the market supply curve slopes upward, what can you say about the shape of the market demand curve over the relevant ranges of prices and quantities? Who pays the excise tax in this market?

c. Suppose that in the market for DSL Internet access services provided to businesses, the market price does not change after the unit excise tax is imposed. If the market supply curve slopes upward, what can you say about the shape of the market demand curve over the relevant ranges of prices and quantities? Who pays the excise tax in this market?

6-6. A government offers to let a number of students at a public school transfer to a private school under two conditions: It will transmit to the private school the same per-pupil subsidy it currently provides the public school, and the private school will be required to admit the students at a below-market tuition rate. Will the economic outcome be the same as the one that would have arisen if the government instead simply provided students with grants to cover the current market tuition rate at the private school?

6-7. After a government implements a voucher program, numerous students in public schools switch to private schools, and parents' and students' valuations of the services provided at both private and public schools adjust to equality with the true market price of educational services. Is anyone likely to lose out nonetheless? If so, who?

6-8. Suppose that your employer is paying you a wage of $10 per hour, and you are working 40 hours per week. Now the government imposes a $2 per hour tax on your employment: $1 is collected from your employer, and $1 is collected from you. The proceeds of the tax are used by the government to buy for you groceries that you value at exactly $80 per week. You are eligible for the grocery program only as long as you continue to work 40 hours per week. Once the plan is in place, what hourly wage will the employer pay you?

6-9. Suppose that the current price of a DVD drive is $100 and that people are buying one million drives per year. In order to improve computer literacy, the government decides to begin subsidizing the purchase of new DVD drives. The government believes that the appropriate price is $60 per drive, so the program offers to send people cash for the difference between $60 and whatever the people pay for each drive they buy.

a. If no one changes his or her drive-buying behavior, how much will this program cost the taxpayers?

b. Will the subsidy cause people to buy more, less, or the same number of drives? Explain.

c. Suppose that people end up buying 1.5 million drives once the program is in place. If the market price of drives does not change, how much will this program cost the taxpayers?

d. Under the assumption that the program causes people to buy 1.5 million drives and also causes the market price of drives to rise to $120, how much will this program cost the taxpayers?

6-10. Scans of internal organs using magnetic resonance imaging (MRI) devices are often covered by subsidized health insurance programs such as Medicare. Consider the following table illustrating hypothetical quantities of individual MRI testing procedures demanded and supplied at various prices, and then answer the questions that follow.

Price	Quantity Demanded	Quantity Supplied
$100	100,000	40,000
$300	90,000	60,000
$500	80,000	80,000
$700	70,000	100,000
$900	60,000	120,000

a. In the absence of a government-subsidized health plan, what is the equilibrium price of MRI tests? What is the amount of society's total expense on MRI tests?

b. Suppose that the government establishes a health plan guaranteeing that all qualified participants can purchase MRI tests at an effective price (that is, out-of-pocket cost) to the individual of $100 per set of tests. How many MRI tests will people consume?

c. What is the per-unit cost incurred by producers to provide the amount of MRI tests demanded at the government-guaranteed price of $100? What is society's total expense on MRI tests?

   d. Under the government's coverage of MRI tests, what is the per-unit subsidy it provides? What is the total subsidy that the government pays to support MRI testing at its guaranteed price?

6-11. In the following situations, what is the rate of return on the investment? (Hint: In each case, what is the percentage by which next year's benefit exceeds—or falls short of—this year's cost?)

   a. You invest $100 today and receive in return $150 exactly one year from now.

   b. You invest $100 today and receive in return $80 exactly one year from now.

6-12. Suppose that the following Social Security reform became law: All current Social Security recipients will continue to receive their benefits, but no increase will be made other than cost-of-living adjustments; U.S. citizens between age 40 and retirement not yet on Social Security can opt to continue with the current system; those who opt out can place what they would have contributed to Social Security into one or more government-approved mutual funds; and those under 40 must place their contributions into one or more government-approved mutual funds.

Now answer the following questions:

   a. Who will be in favor of this reform and why?

   b. Who will be against this reform and why?

   c. What might happen to stock market indexes?

   d. What additional risk is involved for those who end up in the private system?

   e. What additional benefits are possible for the people in the private system?

   f. Which firms in the mutual fund industry might not be approved by the federal government and why?

ECONOMICS ON THE NET

Social Security Privatization There are many proposals for reforming Social Security, but only one fundamentally alters the nature of the current system: privatization. The purpose of this exercise is to learn more about what would happen if Social Security were privatized.

Title: Social Security Privatization

Navigation: Go to www.econtoday.com/chap06 to learn about Social Security privatization. Click on *FAQ* on *Social Security* in the left-hand column.

Application For each of the three entries noted here, read the entry and answer the question.

   1. Click on *How would individual accounts affect women?* According to this article, what are the likely consequences of Social Security privatization for women? Why?

   2. Click on *I'm a low-wage worker. How would individual accounts affect me?* What does this article contend are the likely consequences of Social Security privatization for low-wage workers? Why?

   3. Click on *I've heard that individual accounts would help minorities. Is that true?* Why does this article argue that African Americans in particular would benefit from a privatized Social Security system?

For Group Study and Analysis Taking into account the characteristics of your group as a whole, is it likely to be made better off or worse off if Social Security is privatized? Should your decision to support or oppose privatization be based solely on how it affects you personally? Or should your decision take into account how it might affect others in your group?

It will be worthwhile for those not nearing retirement age to examine what the "older" generation thinks about the idea of privatizing the Social Security system in the United States. So create two groups—one for and one against privatization. Each group will examine the following Web site and come up with arguments in favor or against the ideas expressed on it.

Go to www.econtoday.com/chap06 to read a proposal for Social Security reform. Accept or rebut the proposal, depending on the side to which you have been assigned. Be prepared to defend your reasons with more than just your feelings. At a minimum, be prepared to present arguments that are logical, if not entirely backed by facts.

Media Resources

If your exam were tomorrow, would you be ready? For each chapter, MyEconLab Practice Tests and Study Plans pinpoint which sections you have mastered and which ones you need to study. That way, you are more efficient with your study time, and you are better prepared for your exams.

In addition to Practice Tests and your personalized Study Plan, you'll find the following media resources in MyEconLab:

1. *Graphs in Motion* animation of Figures 6-2, 6-3, 6-4, and 6-6.
2. Video featuring the author, Roger LeRoy Miller, on the following subject:
   - Medicare

3. Links to the Web sites cited in the marginal Internet Resources, Issues and Applications feature, and Economics on the Net activity.
4. Audio clips of all key terms, additional practice problems, and a PDF version of the material from the print Study Guide.
5. eThemes of the Times, which is a New York Times article to help you understand the real-world applications of what you are learning.

Get Ahead of the Curve

To see how it works, turn to page 16 and then go to www.myeconlab.com/miller.

Chapter
20
Consumer Choice

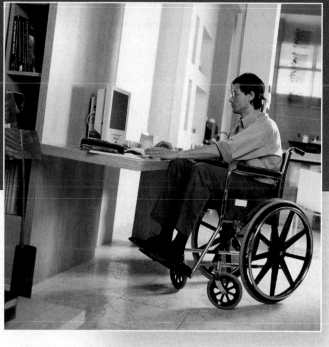

At present, fewer than 5 percent of Web sites are readily accessible by people with disabilities, even though estimates indicate that nearly a third of disabled U.S. residents regularly use the Internet. Cyberspace can be a particularly difficult place for people with visual impairments to navigate. To find the best buys on the Web, blind consumers often must rely on relatives and friends for assistance. The trouble entailed in engaging in assisted Internet shopping pushes up the effective price of each item that a visually disabled individual might purchase. In this chapter, you will learn about the theory of consumer choice, which helps to explain why this higher effective, or total, price of products for sale on the Internet discourages Web purchases by disabled consumers.

LEARNING OBJECTIVES

After reading this chapter, you should be able to:

1. Distinguish between total utility and marginal utility
2. Discuss why marginal utility at first rises but ultimately tends to decline as a person consumes more of a good or service
3. Explain why an individual's optimal choice of how much to consume of each good or service entails equalizing the marginal utility per dollar spent across all goods and services
4. Describe the substitution effect of a price change on quantity demanded of a good or service
5. Understand how the real-income effect of a price change affects the quantity demanded of a good or service
6. Evaluate why the price of diamonds is so much higher than the price of water even though people cannot survive long without water

Media Resources

Refer to the end of the chapter for a full listing of the multimedia learning materials available in MyEconLab.

Did You Know That ... during a typical year, manufacturers of consumer products introduce more than 30,000 new items, or more than twice as many as they did 20 years ago? Although most producers retire old products as they introduce new items, on net the variety of products available to consumers has increased. Hence there has been a proliferation of choices at U.S. grocery stores, which now stock an average of 40,000 items. Consumers today can choose among 16 flavors of frozen waffles; dozens of varieties of toothpaste; garbage bags with twist, draw-string, or handle ties; and wide varieties of other products.

In Chapter 3, you learned that a determinant of the quantity demanded of any particular item is the price of that item. The law of demand indicates that at a lower overall price, there will be a higher quantity demanded. Understanding the derivation of the law of demand is useful because it allows us to examine the relevant variables, such as price, income, and tastes, in such a way as to make better sense of the world and even perhaps generate predictions about it. One way of deriving the law of demand involves an analysis of the logic of consumer choice in a world of limited resources. In this chapter, therefore, we discuss what is called *utility analysis.*

UTILITY THEORY

When you buy something, you do so because of the satisfaction you expect to receive from having and using that good. For everything that you like to have, the more you have of it, the higher the level of total satisfaction you receive. Another term that can be used for satisfaction is **utility,** or want-satisfying power. This property is common to all goods that are desired. The concept of utility is purely subjective, however. There is no way that you or I can measure the amount of utility that a consumer might be able to obtain from a particular good, for utility does not imply "useful" or "utilitarian" or "practical." For this reason, there can be no accurate scientific assessment of the utility that someone might receive by consuming a frozen dinner or a movie relative to the utility that another person might receive from that same good or service.

Utility
The want-satisfying power of a good or service.

The utility that individuals receive from consuming a good depends on their tastes and preferences. These tastes and preferences are normally assumed to be given and stable for a particular individual. An individual's tastes determine how much utility that individual derives from consuming a good, and this in turn determines how that individual allocates his or her income to purchases of that good. But we cannot explain why tastes are different between individuals. For example, we cannot explain why some people like yogurt but others do not.

We can analyze in terms of utility the way consumers decide what to buy, just as physicists have analyzed some of their problems in terms of what they call force. No physicist has ever seen a unit of force, and no economist has ever seen a unit of utility. In both cases, however, these concepts have proved useful for analysis.

Utility analysis
The analysis of consumer decision making based on utility maximization.

Throughout this chapter, we will be discussing **utility analysis,** which is the analysis of consumer decision making based on utility maximization.

Utility and Utils

Economists once believed that utility could be measured. In fact, there is a philosophical school of thought based on utility theory called *utilitarianism,* developed by the English philosopher Jeremy Bentham (1748–1832). Bentham held that society should seek the greatest happiness for the greatest number. He sought to apply an arithmetic formula for measuring happiness. He and his followers developed the notion of measurable utility and invented the **util** to measure it. For the moment, we will also assume that we can measure satisfaction using this representative unit. Our assumption will allow us to quantify the way we examine consumer behavior.* Thus the first chocolate bar that you eat might yield you 4 utils of satisfaction; the first peanut cluster, 6 utils; and so on. Today, no one really believes that we can actually measure utils, but the ideas forthcoming from such analysis will prove useful in understanding how consumers choose among alternatives.

Util
A representative unit by which utility is measured.

Total and Marginal Utility

Consider the satisfaction, or utility, that you receive each time that you rent and watch a DVD. To make the example straightforward, let's say that there are hundreds of DVDs to choose from each year and that each of them is of the same quality. Let's say that you normally rent one DVD per week. You could, of course, rent two, or three, or four per week. Presumably, each time you rent another DVD per week, you will get additional satisfaction, or utility. The question, though, that we must ask is, given that you are already renting one per week, will the next one rented that week give you the same amount of additional utility?

That additional, or incremental, utility is called **marginal utility,** where *marginal* means "incremental" or "additional." (Marginal changes also refer to decreases, in which cases we talk about *decremental* changes.) The concept of marginality is important in economics because people make decisions *at the margin.* Thus we will think about people comparing additional (marginal) benefits with additional (marginal) costs.

Economics Front and Center

To contemplate why economists are skeptical about claims that utility can be measured and compared across individuals, consider the case study, **Can "Happiness Surveys" Reveal an Individual's Satisfaction?** on page 477.

Marginal utility
The change in total utility due to a one-unit change in the quantity of a good or service consumed.

Applying Marginal Analysis to Utility

The example in Figure 20-1 on the following page will clarify the distinction between total utility and marginal utility. The table in panel (a) shows the total utility and the marginal utility of watching DVDs each week. Marginal utility is the difference between total utility derived from one level of consumption and total utility derived from another level of consumption within a given time interval. A simple formula for marginal utility is this:

$$\text{Marginal utility} = \frac{\text{change in total utility}}{\text{change in number of units consumed}}$$

In our example, when a person has already watched two DVDs in one week and then watches another, total utility increases from 16 utils to 19. Therefore, the marginal utility (of watching one more DVD after already having watched two in one week) is equal to 3 utils.

GRAPHICAL ANALYSIS

We can transfer the information in panel (a) onto a graph, as we do in panels (b) and (c) of Figure 20-1. Total utility, which is represented in column 2 of panel (a), is transferred to panel (b).

Total utility continues to rise until four DVDs are watched per week. This measure of utility remains at 20 utils through the fifth DVD, and at the sixth DVD per week it falls to

---

*What follows is typically called *cardinal utility analysis* because it requires cardinal measurement. Numbers such as 1, 2, and 3 are cardinals. We know that 2 is exactly twice as many as 1 and that 3 is exactly three times as many as 1. You will see in Appendix E at the end of this chapter a type of consumer behavior analysis that requires only *ordinal* (ranked or ordered) measurement of utility. *First, second,* and *third* are ordinal numbers; nothing can be said about their exact size relationships; we can only talk about their importance relative to each other. Temperature, for example, is an ordinal ranking. One hundred degrees Celsius is not twice as warm as 50 degrees Celsius. All we can say is that 100 degrees Celsius is warmer than 50 degrees Celsius.

FIGURE 20-1
Total and Marginal Utility of Watching DVDs

If we were able to assign specific values to the utility derived from watching DVDs each week, we could obtain a marginal utility schedule similar in pattern to the one shown in panel (a). In column 1 is the number of DVDs watched per week; in column 2, the total utility derived from each quantity; and in column 3, the marginal utility derived from each additional quantity, which is defined as the change in total utility due to a change of one unit of watching DVDs per week. Total utility from panel (a) is plotted in panel (b). Marginal utility is plotted in panel (c), where you see that it reaches zero where total utility hits its maximum at between 4 and 5 units.

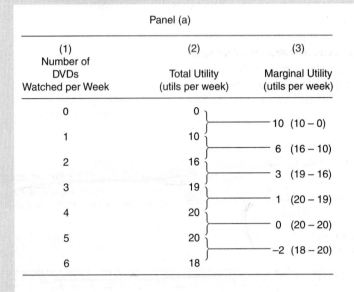

Panel (a)

(1) Number of DVDs Watched per Week	(2) Total Utility (utils per week)	(3) Marginal Utility (utils per week)
0	0	
		10 (10 − 0)
1	10	
		6 (16 − 10)
2	16	
		3 (19 − 16)
3	19	
		1 (20 − 19)
4	20	
		0 (20 − 20)
5	20	
		−2 (18 − 20)
6	18	

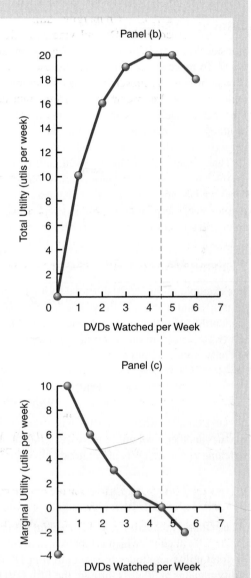

18 utils; we assume that at some quantity consumed per unit time period, boredom with consuming more DVDs begins to set in. This is shown in panel (b).

Marginal Utility

If you look carefully at panels (b) and (c) of Figure 20-1, the notion of marginal utility becomes very clear. In economics, the term *marginal* always refers to a *change* in the total. The marginal utility of watching three DVDs per week instead of two DVDs per week is the increment in total utility and is equal to 3 utils per week. All of the points in panel (c) are taken from column 3 of the table in panel (a). Notice that marginal utility falls throughout the graph. A special point occurs after four DVDs are watched per week because the total utility curve in panel (b) is unchanged after the consumption of the fourth DVD. That means that the consumer receives no additional (marginal) utility from watching the fifth DVD. This is shown in panel (c) as *zero* marginal utility. After that point, marginal utility becomes negative.

In our example, when marginal utility becomes negative, it means that the consumer is tired of watching DVDs and would require some form of compensation to watch any more. When marginal utility is negative, an additional unit consumed actually lowers total utility by becoming a nuisance. Rarely does a consumer face a situation of negative marginal utility. Whenever this point is reached, goods become in effect "bads." A rational consumer will stop consuming at the point at which marginal utility becomes negative, even if the good is available at a price of zero.

CONCEPTS in Brief

- Utility is defined as want-satisfying power; it is a power common to all desired goods and services.

- We arbitrarily measure utility in units called utils.

- It is important to distinguish between total utility and marginal utility. Total utility is the total satisfaction derived from the consumption of a given quantity of a good or service. Marginal utility is the *change* in total utility due to a one-unit change in the consumption of the good or service.

To test your understanding of the concepts covered in this section, go to the Online Review at www.myeconlab.com/miller.

DIMINISHING MARGINAL UTILITY

Notice that in panel (c) of Figure 20-1, marginal utility is continuously declining. This property has been named the principle of **diminishing marginal utility.** There is no way that we can prove diminishing marginal utility; nonetheless, economists and others have for years believed strongly in the notion. Diminishing marginal utility has even been called a law. This supposed law concerns a psychological, or subjective, utility that you receive as you consume more and more of a particular good. Stated formally, the law is as follows:

> *As an individual consumes more of a particular commodity, the total level of utility, or satisfaction, derived from that consumption usually increases. Eventually, however, the rate at which it increases diminishes as more is consumed.*

Take a hungry individual at a dinner table. The first serving is greatly appreciated, and the individual derives a substantial amount of utility from it. The second serving does not have quite as much pleasurable impact as the first one, and the third serving is likely to be even less satisfying. This individual experiences diminishing marginal utility of food until he or she stops eating, and this is true for most people. All-you-can-eat restaurants count on this fact; a second helping of ribs may provide some marginal utility, but the third helping would have only a little or even negative marginal utility. The fall in the marginal utility of other goods is even more dramatic.

Consider for a moment the opposite possibility—increasing marginal utility. Under such a situation, the marginal utility after consuming, say, one hamburger would increase. The second hamburger would be more valuable to you, and the third would be even more valuable yet. If increasing marginal utility existed, each of us would consume only one

Diminishing marginal utility
The principle that as more of any good or service is consumed, its extra benefit declines. Otherwise stated, increases in total utility from the consumption of a good or service become smaller and smaller as more is consumed during a given time period.

Go to www.econtoday.com/chap20 to learn from Finfact's Weekly Wine Page how diminishing marginal utility can complicate the task that wine tasters face when comparing different wines.

good or service! Rather than observing that "variety is the spice of life," we would see that monotony in consumption was preferred. We do not observe this, and therefore we have great confidence in the concept of diminishing marginal utility.

Consider an example. A student's birthday is on December 25, which the student also celebrates as the Christmas holiday. Suppose that the student derives utility from listening to new CDs each month. Even if the student receives exactly the same number of CDs as presents on December 25 that she would have if her birthday were six months later, her marginal utility from these combined presents will be lower. Why? Because of diminishing marginal utility. Let's say that the student's relatives and friends all give her CDs as birthday and Christmas presents. The marginal utility she receives from the twentieth CD on December 25 is less than if she had received only 10 CDs on December 25.

Can diminishing marginal utility explain why newspaper vending machines rarely prevent people from taking more than the one current issue they have paid to purchase?

E X A M P L E

Newspaper Vending Machines versus Candy Vending Machines

Have you ever noticed that newspaper vending machines nearly everywhere in the United States allow you to put in the correct change, lift up the door, and—if you were willing to violate the law—take as many newspapers as you want? Contrast this type of vending machine with candy machines. They are completely locked at all times. You must designate the candy that you wish, normally by using some type of keypad. The candy then drops down so that you can retrieve it but cannot grab any other candy.

The difference between these two types of vending machines is explained by diminishing marginal utility. Newspaper companies dispense newspapers from coin-operated boxes that allow dishonest people to take more copies than they pay for. What would a dishonest person do with more than one copy of a newspaper, however? The marginal utility

of a second newspaper is normally zero. The benefit of storing excessive newspapers is usually nil because yesterday's news has no value. But the same analysis does not hold for candy. The marginal utility of a second candy bar is certainly less than the first, but it is normally not zero. Moreover, one can store candy for relatively long periods of time at relatively low cost. Consequently, food vending machine companies have to worry about dishonest users of their equipment and must make that equipment more theftproof than newspaper companies do.

For Critical Analysis
Can you think of a circumstance under which a substantial number of newspaper purchasers might be inclined to take more than one newspaper out of a vending machine?

OPTIMIZING CONSUMPTION CHOICES

Every consumer has a limited income. Choices must be made. When a consumer has made all of his or her choices about what to buy and in what quantities, and when the total level of satisfaction, or utility, from that set of choices is as great as it can be, we say that the consumer has *optimized*. When the consumer has attained an optimum consumption set of goods and services, we say that he or she has reached **consumer optimum.***

Consider a simple two-good example. The consumer has to choose between spending income on the rental of DVDs at $5 each and on purchasing pizza slices at $3 each. Let's say that when the consumer has spent all income on DVD rentals and pizza slices, the last

Consumer optimum
A choice of a set of goods and services that maximizes the level of satisfaction for each consumer, subject to limited income.

---

*Optimization typically refers to individual decision-making processes. When we deal with many individuals interacting in the marketplace, we talk in terms of an equilibrium in the marketplace. Generally speaking, equilibrium is a property of markets rather than of individual decision making.

dollar spent on pizza yields 3 utils of utility but the last dollar spent on DVD rentals yields 10 utils. Wouldn't this consumer increase total utility if some dollars were taken away from pizza consumption and allocated to DVD rentals? The answer is yes. Given diminishing marginal utility, more dollars spent on DVD rentals will reduce marginal utility per last dollar spent, whereas fewer dollars spent on pizza consumption will increase marginal utility per last dollar spent. The optimum—where total utility is maximized—occurs when the satisfaction per last dollar spent on both pizza and DVD rentals per week is equal for the two goods. Thus the amount of goods consumed depends on the prices of the goods, the income of the consumers, and the marginal utility derived from each good.

Table 20-1 presents information on utility derived from consuming various quantities of DVD rentals and pizza slices. Columns 4 and 8 show the marginal utility per dollar spent on DVD rentals and pizza slices, respectively. If the prices of both goods are zero, individuals will consume each as long as their respective marginal utility is positive (at least five units of each and probably much more). It is also true that a consumer with infinite income will continue consuming goods until the marginal utility of each is equal to zero. When the price is zero or the consumer's income is infinite, there is no effective constraint on consumption.

Consumer optimum is attained when the marginal utility of the last dollar spent on each good yields the same utility and income is completely exhausted. The individual's income is $26. From columns 4 and 8 of Table 20-1, equal marginal utilities per dollar spent occur at the consumption level of four DVD rentals and two pizza slices (the marginal utility per dollar spent equals 7.3). Notice that the marginal utility per dollar spent for both goods is also (approximately) equal at the consumption level of three DVD rentals and one pizza slice, but here total income is not completely exhausted. Likewise, the marginal utility per dollar spent is (approximately) equal at five DVD rentals and three slices of pizza, but the expenditures necessary for that level of consumption ($34) exceed the individual's income.

Table 20-2 on the next page shows the steps taken to arrive at consumer optimum. The first DVD rental would yield a marginal utility per dollar of 10 (50 units of utility divided by

TABLE 20-1
Total and Marginal Utility from Consuming DVDs and Pizza Slices on an Income of $26

(1) DVD Rentals per Period	(2) Total Utility of DVD Rentals per Period (utils)	(3) Marginal Utility (utils) MU_d	(4) Marginal Utility per Dollar Spent (MU_d/P_d) (price = $5)	(5) Pizza Slices per Period	(6) Total Utility of Pizza Slices per Period (utils)	(7) Marginal Utility (utils) MU_p	(8) Marginal Utility per Dollar Spent (MU_p/P_p) (price = $3)
0	0	—	—	0	0	—	—
1	50.0	50.0	10.0	1	25	25	8.3
2	95.0	45.0	9.0	2	47	22	7.3
3	135.0	40.0	8.0	3	65	18	6.0
4	171.5	36.5	7.3	4	80	15	5.0
5	200.0	28.5	5.7	5	89	9	3.0

TABLE 20-2

Steps to Consumer Optimum

In each purchase situation described here, the consumer always purchases the good with the higher marginal utility per dollar spent (*MU/P*) For example, at the time of the third purchase, the marginal utility per last dollar spent on DVD rentals is 8, but it is 8.3 for pizza slices, and $16 of income remains, so the next purchase will be a slice of pizza. Here $P_d = \$5$, $P_p = \$3$, MU_d is the marginal utility of consumption of DVD rentals, and MU_p is the marginal utility of consumption of pizza slices.

		Choices				
	DVD Rentals		**Pizza Slices**			
Purchase	Unit	MU_d/P_d	Unit	MU_p/P_p	Buying Decision	Remaining Income
1	First	10.0	First	8.3	First DVD rental	$26 − $5 = $21
2	Second	9.0	First	8.3	Second DVD rental	$21 − $5 = $16
3	Third	8.0	First	8.3	First slice of pizza	$16 − $3 = $13
4	Third	8.0	Second	7.3	Third DVD rental	$13 − $5 = $8
5	Fourth	7.3	Second	7.3	Fourth DVD rental and	$8 − $5 = $3
					Second pizza slice	$3 − $3 = $0

$5 per DVD rental), while the first pizza slice would yield a marginal utility of only 8.3 per dollar (25 units of utility divided by $3 per slice). Because it yields the higher marginal utility per dollar, the DVD rental is purchased. This leaves $21 of income. The second DVD rental yields a higher marginal utility per dollar (9, versus 8.3 for pizza slices), so it is also purchased, leaving an unspent income of $16. At the third purchase, the first slice of pizza now yields a higher marginal utility per dollar than the next DVD rental (8.3 versus 8), so the first pizza slice is purchased. This leaves income of $13 to spend. The process continues until all income is exhausted and the marginal utility per dollar spent is equal for both goods.

To restate, consumer optimum requires the following:

> ***A consumer's money income should be allocated so that the last dollar spent on each good purchased yields the same amount of marginal utility (when all income is spent).***

A Little Math

We can state the rule of consumer optimum in algebraic terms by examining the ratio of marginal utilities and prices of individual products. This is sometimes called the *rule of equal marginal utilities per dollar spent* on a basket of goods. The rule simply states that a consumer maximizes personal satisfaction when allocating money income in such a way that the last dollars spent on good A, good B, good C, and so on, yield equal amounts of marginal utility. Marginal utility (*MU*) from good A is indicated by "*MU* of good A." For good B, it is "*MU* of good B." Our algebraic formulation of this rule, therefore, becomes

$$\frac{MU \text{ of good A}}{\text{Price of good A}} = \frac{MU \text{ of good B}}{\text{price of good B}} = \cdots = \frac{MU \text{ of good Z}}{\text{price of good Z}}$$

The letters A, B, . . . , Z indicate the various goods and services that the consumer might purchase.

We know, then, that the marginal utility of good A divided by the price of good A must equal the marginal utility of any other good divided by its price in order for the consumer to maximize utility. Note, though, that the application of the rule of equal marginal utility per dollar spent does not necessarily describe an explicit or conscious act on the part of consumers. Rather, this is a *model* of consumer optimum.

HOW A PRICE CHANGE AFFECTS CONSUMER OPTIMUM

Consumption decisions are summarized in the law of demand, which states that the amount purchased is inversely related to price. We can now see why by using the law of diminishing marginal utility.

When a consumer has optimally allocated all her income to purchases, the marginal utility per dollar spent at current prices of goods and services is the same for each good or service she buys. No consumer will, when optimizing, buy 10 units of a good per unit of time when the marginal utility per dollar spent on the tenth unit of that good is less than the marginal utility per dollar spent on some other item.

If we start out at a consumer optimum and then observe a good's price decrease, we can predict that consumers will respond to the price decrease by consuming more of that good. This is because before the price change, the marginal utility per dollar spent on each good or service consumed was the same. Now, when a specific good's price is lower, it is possible to consume more of that good while continuing to equalize the marginal utility per dollar spent on that good with the marginal utility per dollar spent on other goods and services. If the law of diminishing marginal utility holds, then the purchase and consumption of additional units of the lower-priced good will cause the marginal utility from consuming the good to fall. Eventually, it will fall to the point at which the marginal utility per dollar spent on the good is once again equalized with the marginal utility per dollar spent on other goods and services. At this point, the consumer will stop buying additional units of the lower-priced good.

A hypothetical demand curve for DVD rentals per week for a typical consumer is presented in Figure 20-2. Suppose that at point *A*, at which the rental price per DVD is $5, the marginal utility of the last DVD rented per week is MU_A. We represent the marginal utility at point *B*, at which the rental price is $4 per DVD per week, by MU_B. Because of the law

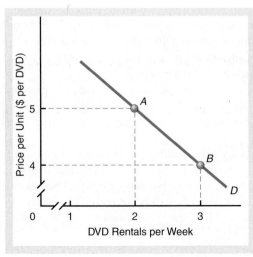

FIGURE 20-2
DVD Rental Prices and Marginal Utility
When consumers respond to a reduction in DVD rental prices from $5 per DVD to $4 per DVD by increasing consumption, marginal utility falls. This occurs because of the law of diminishing marginal utility. The movement from point *A* to point *B* thereby reduces marginal utility to bring about the equalization of the marginal utility per dollar spent across all purchases.

of diminishing marginal utility—with the consumption of more DVDs, the marginal utility of the last unit of these additional DVD rentals is lower—MU_B must be less than MU_A. What has happened is that at a lower price, the number of DVD rentals per week increased from two to three; marginal utility must have fallen. At a higher consumption rate, the marginal utility falls in response to the rise in DVD consumption so that the marginal utility per dollar spent is equalized across all purchases.

The Substitution Effect

Substitution effect
The tendency of people to substitute cheaper commodities for more expensive commodities.

What is happening as the price of DVD rentals falls is that consumers are substituting the now relatively cheaper DVD rentals for other goods and services, such as restaurant meals and live concerts. We call this the **substitution effect** of a change in price of a good because it occurs when consumers substitute relatively cheaper goods for relatively more expensive ones.

We assume that people desire a variety of goods and pursue a variety of goals. That means that few, if any, goods are irreplaceable in meeting demand. We are generally able to substitute one product for another to satisfy demand. This is commonly referred to as the **principle of substitution.**

Principle of substitution
The principle that consumers and producers shift away from goods and resources that become priced relatively higher in favor of goods and resources that are now priced relatively lower.

An Example. Let's assume now that there are several goods, not exactly the same, and perhaps even very different from one another, but all contributing to consumers' total utility. If the relative price of one particular good falls, we will most likely substitute in favor of the lower-priced good and against the other similar goods that we might have been purchasing. Conversely, if the price of that good rises relative to the price of the other similar goods, we will substitute in favor of them and not buy as much of the now higher-priced good. An example is the growth in purchases of personal computers since the late 1980s. As the relative price of computers has plummeted, people have substituted away from other, now relatively more expensive goods in favor of purchasing additional computers to use in their homes.

Purchasing power
The value of money for buying goods and services. If your money income stays the same but the price of one good that you are buying goes up, your effective purchasing power falls, and vice versa.

Purchasing Power and Real Income. If the price of some item that you purchase goes down while your money income and all other prices stay the same, your ability to purchase goods goes up. That is to say, your effective **purchasing power** has increased, even though your money income has stayed the same. If you purchase 20 gallons of gas a week at $2.60 per gallon, your total outlay for gas is $52. If the price goes down by 50 percent, to $1.30 cents a gallon, you would have to spend only $26 a week to purchase the same number of gallons of gas. If your money income and the prices of other goods remain the same, it would be possible for you to continue purchasing 20 gallons of gas a week *and* to purchase more of other goods. You will feel richer and will indeed probably purchase more of a number of goods, including perhaps even more gasoline.

The converse will also be true. When the price of one good you are purchasing goes up, without any other change in prices or income, the purchasing power of your income will drop. You will have to reduce your purchases of either the now higher-priced good or other goods (or a combination).

Real-income effect
The change in people's purchasing power that occurs when, other things being constant, the price of one good that they purchase changes. When that price goes up, real income, or purchasing power, falls, and when that price goes down, real income increases.

In general, this **real-income effect** is usually quite small. After all, unless we consider broad categories, such as housing or food, a change in the price of one particular item that we purchase will have a relatively small effect on our total purchasing power. Thus we expect the substitution effect usually to be more important than the real-income effect in causing us to purchase more of goods that have become cheaper and less of goods that have become more expensive.

THE DEMAND CURVE REVISITED

Linking the "law" of diminishing marginal utility and the rule of equal marginal utilities per dollar gives us a negative relationship between the quantity demanded of a good or service and its price. As the relative price of DVD rentals goes up, for example, the quantity demanded will fall; and as the relative price of DVD rentals goes down, the quantity demanded will rise. Figure 20-2 on page 473 showed this demand curve for DVD rentals. As the price of DVD rentals falls, the consumer can maximize total utility only by renting more DVDs, and vice versa. In other words, the relationship between price and quantity desired is simply a downward-sloping demand curve. Note, though, that this downward-sloping demand curve (the law of demand) is derived under the assumption of constant tastes and incomes. You must remember that we are keeping these important determining variables constant when we look at the relationship between price and quantity demanded.

Why do you suppose that Lands' End, the clothing retailer, found that adding virtual three-dimensional models to its Web site enabled it to raise prices of many items without inducing a net decrease in quantity consumed?

E-Commerce E X A M P L E

Virtual 3D Pays Off at Lands' End

When shopping at a mall, an individual can try on an item of clothing before purchasing it so that she can be sure that it fits. When shopping online, however, the individual cannot try on the item. If it does not fit, she will have to go to the trouble of returning it. This uncertainty about the fit lowers her anticipated marginal utility from buying online.

To address this problem, clothing retailer Lands' End added a "virtual 3D model" tool to its Web site. After clicking on "My Model" in the left-hand margin of the Lands' End home page, a shopper can enter her height, weight, and various size measurements. The model on the screen automatically adjusts to a shape matching the shape of the shopper's body. Then the shopper can see how well a particular blouse or dress she is considering buying is likely to fit.

Reducing uncertainty about how well clothing items will fit naturally increases an individual's anticipated marginal utility at any given quantity she might consider consuming—and at any price. Lands' End did not leave its online prices unchanged, however. In the first year after incorporating the virtual 3D model into its site, the retailer was able to raise the average price of an item of clothing sold at its site by 13 percent without a net fall in the quantity of clothing consumed. There was an unambiguous increase in Lands' End's revenues.

For Critical Analysis
If marginal utility increases at each possible quantity consumed at a given price, then does this cause a change in quantity demanded (a movement along the demand curve) or a change in demand (a shift in the demand curve)?

Marginal Utility, Total Utility, and the Diamond–Water Paradox

Even though water is essential to life and diamonds are not, water is cheap and diamonds are expensive. The economist Adam Smith in 1776 called this the "diamond-water paradox." The paradox is easily understood when we make the distinction between total utility and marginal utility. The total utility of water greatly exceeds the total utility derived from diamonds. What determines the price, though, is what happens on the margin. We have relatively few diamonds, so the marginal utility of the last diamond consumed is relatively high. The opposite is true for water. Total utility does not determine what people are willing to pay for a unit of a particular commodity; marginal utility does. Look at the situation

FIGURE 20-3
The Diamond-Water Paradox
We pick kilograms as a common unit of measurement for both water and diamonds. To demonstrate that the demand for and supply of water is immense, we have put a break in the horizontal quantity axis. Although the demand for water is much greater than the demand for diamonds, the marginal valuation of water is given by the marginal value placed on the *last* unit of water consumed. To find that, we must know the supply of water, which is given as S_1. At that supply, the price of water is P_{water}. But the supply for diamonds is given by S_2. At that supply, the price of diamonds is $P_{diamonds}$. The total valuation that consumers place on water is tremendous relative to the total valuation consumers place on diamonds. What is important for price determination, however, is the marginal valuation, or the marginal utility received.

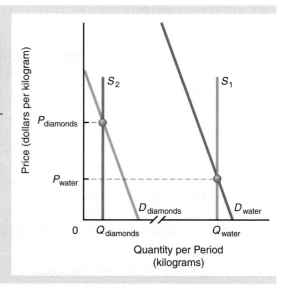

graphically in Figure 20-3. We show the demand curve for diamonds, labeled $D_{diamonds}$. The demand curve for water is labeled D_{water}. We plot quantity in terms of kilograms per unit time period on the horizontal axis. On the vertical axis, we plot price in dollars per kilogram. We use kilograms as our common unit of measurement for water and for diamonds. We could just as well have used gallons, acre-feet, or liters.

Notice that the demand for water is many, many times the demand for diamonds (even though we really can't show this in the diagram). We draw the supply curve of water as S_1 at a quantity of Q_{water}. The supply curve for diamonds is given as S_2 at quantity $Q_{diamonds}$. At the intersection of the supply curve of water with the demand curve of water, the price per kilogram is P_{water}. The intersection of the supply curve of diamonds with the demand curve of diamonds is at $P_{diamonds}$. Notice that $P_{diamonds}$ exceeds P_{water}. Diamonds sell at a higher price than water.

Based on this discussion, why does it make sense that in Saudi Arabia the price of gasoline is lower than the price of water?

International E X A M P L E

Water in Saudi Arabia

The diamond-water paradox deals with the situation in which water, although necessary for life, may be much cheaper than some luxury item. In Saudi Arabia, as you might expect, the contrary can be true. A liter of water costs five times as much as a liter of gasoline, whereas a pair of custom-made British wool dress pants costs only $20. These relative prices are quite different from what we are used to seeing in the United States. Water costs next to nothing, a liter of gas about 50 cents, and custom-

made wool pants at least $200. To understand what has happened in Saudi Arabia, simply substitute gasoline for water and water for diamonds in Figure 20-3.

For Critical Analysis
List some of the effects on human behavior that such a high relative price of water would cause.

CONCEPTS in Brief

- The law of diminishing marginal utility tells us that each successive marginal unit of a good consumed adds less extra utility.

- Each consumer with a limited income must make a choice about the basket of commodities to purchase; economic theory assumes that the consumer chooses the basket of commodities that yields optimum consumption. The consumer maximizes total utility by equating the marginal utility of the last dollar spent on one good with the marginal utility per last dollar spent on all other goods. That is the state of consumer optimum.

- To remain in consumer optimum, a price decrease requires an increase in consumption; a price increase requires a decrease in consumption.

- Each change in price has a substitution effect and a real-income effect. When price falls, the consumer substitutes in favor of the relatively cheaper good. When price falls, the consumer's real purchasing power increases, causing the consumer to purchase more of most goods. The opposite occurs when price increases. Assuming that the law of diminishing marginal utility holds, the demand curve must slope downward.

To test your understanding of the concepts covered in this section, go to the Online Review at www.myeconlab.com/miller.

CASE STUDY: Economics Front and Center

Can "Happiness Surveys" Reveal an Individual's Satisfaction?

In the economics course that Alcorn took last semester, he learned that utility is the satisfaction that an individual obtains from consuming a good or service. He also learned that the early nineteenth-century British philosopher Jeremy Bentham sought to measure *absolute* utility. Alcorn knows, however, that modern economists focus on examining *relative* levels of satisfaction for each individual distinct from others.

Alcorn has landed a summer work-study position with a professor who has been influenced by the research of a modern British economist, Andrew Oswald of Warwick University. As suggested by Oswald, Alcorn's supervisory professor has put Alcorn to work conducting "happiness surveys." Alcorn stands at the exit to a local shopping mall, and from time to time he successfully flags down shoppers to ask questions about items they have purchased. First, Alcorn asks how "happy," on a scale from 1 to 10, shoppers are with each item that they have purchased. Second, Alcorn asks the prices of the items.

Alcorn then divides the "happiness score" of each item by its price. His professor hypothesizes that if the theory of the consumer optimum is correct, then these ratios should be equal for all items purchased by each shopper. The professor also hopes to compare consumers' responses to determine how utilities they derive from similar items may differ. As he tabulates the data, Alcorn wonders if the professor's research really makes economic sense.

Points to Analyze

1. *Why might the "happiness scores" recorded by Alcorn be imperfect measures of utility?*

2. *Why might there be problems in comparing the "happiness scores" Alcorn has collected across different individuals?*

Altering the Marginal Utility of Web Shopping by Consumers with Disabilities

Disabled residents of the United States spend an estimated $175 billion per year on goods and services. Nevertheless, studies of Internet shopping by all consumers have revealed that in years past, disabled individuals have chosen to buy few products sold at Web sites.

Concepts Applied

- Consumer Optimum
- Marginal Utility
- Diminishing Marginal Utility

Trying to Navigate the Internet with a Disability

If you are not visually impaired, imagine the frustration a visually impaired person encounters when trying to shop on the Internet. Web pages advertising some of the lowest product prices available abound, but you would be unable to read most of them. Furthermore, more than 95 percent of Internet shopping sites lack audio files to assist visually impaired people in navigating their Web pages.

Alternatively, if you are not physically impaired, try to envision possessing a physical disability that prevents you from typing numerous keystrokes. In many cases, you might see something you would like to buy at the price posted at a Web site, but you would be unable to submit an online order form to buy it.

High Effective Prices Faced by Disabled Internet Shoppers

In years past, a disabled consumer interested in searching for the lowest available prices of goods and services on the Internet had to rely on someone else to help navigate through item descriptions and price lists. This imposed considerable additional costs on these consumers, which pushed up the *effective* price of purchasing a product via the Internet.

Recall that at a consumer optimum, the marginal utility per dollar spent to buy an item via the Internet will equal the marginal utility per dollar spent to buy a product in a physical retail store. The effective price of each item purchased on the

Internet was so high that the typical disabled consumer made Web purchases only to the point at which relatively high marginal utility was obtained. The law of diminishing marginal utility implies that the usual result was that consumers with visual or typing disabilities made very few Internet purchases.

Technological Change Alters the Consumer Optimum

Recent technological improvements have changed the consumer optimum calculation for many visually disabled individuals. Voice-dictation software now allows people to navigate the Internet by speaking phrases such as "Go to Amazon.com." The latest versions of many Web-development software packages provide Internet sellers with more capabilities for designing sites with audio links. Such packages also commonly include order-submit mechanisms that minimize or even eliminate the keystrokes that consumers must enter to buy a product.

Because many consumers with disabilities can hear an item description and price and submit an order without touching a keyboard, the effective prices of Internet-distributed products have dropped. Not surprisingly, disabled consumers are making more purchases on the Internet. Recent estimates indicate that the annual volume of Web purchases made by disabled consumers is currently increasing at more than twice the rate of growth of other consumers' Internet expenditures.

For Critical Analysis

1. At a consumer optimum for a disabled individual, why does an increase in the effective price of purchasing an item on the Internet result in a higher marginal utility of consuming that item, other things being equal?
2. At a disabled person's consumer optimum involving purchases of identical items offered on different Web sites at the same prices, why is the marginal utility likely to be higher for the item sold at the site with fewest accessibility features for disabled individuals?

Web Resources

1. Discover how a nonprofit organization called the Center for Applied Technology promotes the development of technologies that help disabled consumers via the link available at www.econtoday.com/chap20.
2. Learn about the latest in accessibility technologies for consumers with disabilities at the site of the IBM Accessibility Center, which can be accessed at www.econtoday.com/chap20.

Research Project

Suppose that developments in voice-recognition software permit anyone to dictate Web navigation commands and fill out Web order forms using spoken dictation, perhaps using handheld devices as well as computers. Discuss how this would be likely to affect the marginal utility gained from items bought on the Internet at a consumer optimum for *any* consumer, including a consumer without disabilities. Other things being equal, what effect do you predict that the widespread use of this voice-recognition technology would have on total purchases of products on the Internet? On purchases of goods and services at physical retail outlets?

SUMMARY DISCUSSION of Learning Objectives

1. **Total Utility versus Marginal Utility:** Total utility is the total satisfaction that an individual derives from consuming a given amount of a good or service during a given period. Marginal utility is the additional satisfaction that a person gains by consuming an additional unit of the good or service.

2. **The Law of Diminishing Marginal Utility:** For at least the first unit of consumption of a good or service, a person's total utility increases with increased consumption. Eventually, however, the rate at which an individual's utility rises with greater consumption tends to fall. Thus marginal utility ultimately declines as the person consumes more and more of the good or service.

3. **The Consumer Optimum:** An individual optimally allocates available income to consumption of all goods and services when the marginal utility per dollar spent on the last unit consumed of each good is equalized. Thus a consumer optimum occurs when (a) the ratio of the marginal utility derived from an item to the price of that item is equal across all goods and services that the person consumes and (b) when the person spends all available income.

4. **The Substitution Effect of a Price Change:** One effect of a change in the price of a good or service is that the price change induces people to substitute among goods. For example, if the price of a good rises, the individual will tend to consume some other good that has become relatively less expensive as a result. In addition, the individual will tend to reduce consumption of the good whose price increased.

5. **The Real-Income Effect of a Price Change:** Another effect of a price change is that it affects the purchasing power of an individual's available income. For instance, if the price of a good increases, a person must reduce purchases of either the now higher-priced good or other goods (or a combination of both of these responses). Normally, we anticipate that the real-income effect is smaller than the substitution effect, so that when the price of a good or service increases, people will purchase more of goods or services that have lower relative prices as a result.

6. **Why the Price of Diamonds Exceeds the Price of Water Even Though People Cannot Long Survive Without Water:** The reason for this price difference is that mar-

ginal utility, not total utility, determines how much people are willing to pay for any particular good. Because there are relatively few diamonds, the number of diamonds consumed by a typical individual is relatively small, which means that the marginal utility derived from consuming a diamond is relatively high. By contrast, water is abundant, so people consume relatively large volumes of water, and the marginal utility for the last unit of water consumed is relatively low. It follows that at a consumer optimum, in which the marginal utility per dollar spent is equalized for diamonds and water, people are willing to pay a much higher price for diamonds.

KEY TERMS AND CONCEPTS

consumer optimum (470)

diminishing marginal utility (469)

marginal utility (467)

principle of substitution (474)

purchasing power (474)

real-income effect (474)

substitution effect (474)

util (467)

utility (466)

utility analysis (466)

PROBLEMS

Answers to the odd-numbered problems appear at the back of the book.

20-1. The campus pizzeria sells a single pizza for $12. If you order a second pizza, however, its price is only $5. Explain how this relates to marginal utility.

20-2. As an individual consumes more units of an item, the person eventually experiences diminishing marginal utility. This means that to increase marginal utility, the person must often consume less of an item. Explain the logic of this behavior using the example in Problem 20-1.

20-3. Where possible, complete the missing cells in the table.

Number of Cheese-burgers	Total Utility of Cheese-burgers	Marginal Utility of Cheese-burgers	Bags of French Fries	Total Utility of French Fries	Marginal Utility of French Fries
0	0	—	0	0	—
1	20	—	1	—	8
2	36	—	2	—	6
3	—	12	3	—	4
4	—	8	4	20	—
5	—	4	5	20	—

20-4. From the data in Problem 20-3, if the price of a cheeseburger is $2, the price of a bag of french fries is $1, and you have $6 to spend (and you spend all of it), what is the utility-maximizing combination of cheeseburgers and french fries?

20-5. Suppose that you observe that total utility rises as more of an item is consumed. What can you say for certain about marginal utility? Can you say for sure that it is rising or falling or that it is positive or negative?

20-6. After monitoring your daily consumption patterns, you determine that your daily consumption of soft drinks is 3 and your daily consumption of tacos is 4 when the prices per unit are 50 cents and $1, respectively. Explain what happens to your consumption bundle, the marginal utility of soft drinks, and the marginal utility of tacos when the price of soft drinks rises to 75 cents.

20-7. At a consumer optimum, for all goods purchased, marginal utility per dollar spent is equalized. A high school student is deciding between attending Western State University and Eastern State University. The student cannot attend both universities simultaneously. Both are fine universities, but the reputation of Western is slightly higher, as is the tuition. Use the rule of consumer optimum to explain how the student will go about deciding which university to attend.

20-8. Suppose that 5 apples and 6 bananas generate a total utility of 50 for you. In addition, 4 apples and 8 bananas generate a total utility of 50. Given this information, what can you say about the marginal utility of apples relative to the marginal utility of bananas?

20-9. Return to Problem 20-4. Suppose that the price of cheeseburgers falls to $1. Determine the new utility-maximizing combination of cheeseburgers and french fries. Use this new combination of goods to explain the income and substitution effects.

20-10. Using your answers to Problems 20-4 and 20-9, illustrate a simple demand curve for cheeseburgers.

20-11. The table gives the marginal utilities a student obtains from weekly hours he spends playing sophisticated computer games at a Web site and attending professional baseball games. He is trying to decide how many hours per week he will devote to the two activities during a month that he is unemployed during the summer break. Assume that the student has sufficient funds to pay for all possible amounts of consumption time listed in the table.

Hours Playing Web Computer Games	Marginal Utility of Web Games (utils)	Hours at Baseball Games	Marginal Utility of Baseball Games (utils)
1	15	1	35
2	20	2	40
3	18	3	37
4	14	4	30
5	11	5	23
6	6	6	13
7	0	7	0

Suppose that at the beginning of his month of unemployment, the price of each hour the student spends playing computer games on the Internet is $10, and the price of a baseball ticket is $40 per baseball game. The student can purchase access to the Web computer game by the hour, and each baseball game lasts a hypothetical two hours. At the consumer optimum for all weekly hours of leisure activities the student buys,

he equalizes the marginal utility per dollar spent on each hour of activities at 2 utils per dollar. How many weekly hours will he plan to devote to playing the Web computer game and attending baseball games?

20-12. Reconsider the situation in Problem 20-11. One week into the student's one-month break from employment, the ticket price for baseball games falls to $30. Assume that the student continues to equalize the marginal utility per dollar spent at 2 utils per dollar. In addition, suppose that the student continues playing Web computer games the same number of weekly hours calculated in Problem 20-11. He does so by adjusting his time spent on other leisure activities as required to alter the number of hours he spends at the ballpark. How many hours will the student spend attending baseball games during the second week?

20-13. Proceeding from the situations laid out in Problems 20-11 and 20-12, after the second week, the company that sells access to the Web computer game sets a special discount access price of $3 per hour. The ticket price for each two-hour-long baseball game remains at $30. Assume that the student continues to equalize the marginal utility per dollar spent at 2 utils per dollar. In addition, suppose that the student continues attending baseball games the same number of hours calculated in Problem 20-12. He does so by adjusting his time spent on other leisure activities as necessary to alter the number of hours he spends playing games on the Internet. How many hours will the student spend playing Web computer games during the third week?

20-14. At a consumer optimum involving goods A and B, the marginal utility of good A is twice the marginal utility of good B. The price of good B is $3.50. What is the price of good A?

20-15. At a consumer optimum involving goods X and Y, the marginal utility of good X equals 3 utils. The price of good Y is three times the price of good X. What is the marginal utility of good Y?

ECONOMICS ON THE NET

Book Prices and Consumer Optimum This application helps you see how a consumer optimum can be attained when one engages in Internet shopping.

Title: Amazon.com Web site

Navigation: Go to www.econtoday.com/chap20 to start at Amazon.com's home page. Click on the *Books* tab.

Application

1. On the right-hand side of the page, find the list of the top books in the Amazon.com 100 section. Click on the number one book. Record the price of the book. Then locate the Search window. Type in "Roger LeRoy Miller." Scroll down until you find your class text listed. Record the price.

2. Suppose you are an individual who has purchased both the number one book and your class text through Amazon.com. Describe how economic analysis would explain this choice.

3. Using the prices you recorded for the two books, write an equation that relates the prices and your marginal utilities of the two books. Use this equation to explain verbally how you might quantify the magnitude of your marginal utility for the number one book relative to your marginal utility for your class text.

For Group Study and Analysis Discuss what changes might occur if the price of the number one book were lowered but the student remains enrolled in this course. Discuss what changes might take place regarding the consumer optimum if the student was not enrolled in this course.

Media Resources

If your exam were tomorrow, would you be ready? For each chapter, MyEconLab Practice Tests and Study Plans pinpoint which sections you have mastered and which ones you need to study. That way, you are more efficient with your study time, and you are better prepared for your exams.

In addition to Practice Tests and your personalized Study Plan, you'll find the following media resources in MyEconLab:

1. *Graphs in Motion* animation of Figures 20-1, 20-2, 20-3.

2. Videos featuring the author, Roger LeRoy Miller, on the following subjects:
   - Optimizing Consumption Choices
   - The Substitution Effect and the Real-Income Effect

3. Links to the Web sites cited in the marginal Internet Resources, Issues and Applications feature, and Economics on the Net activity.

4. Audio clips of all key terms, additional practice problems, and a PDF version of the material from the print Study Guide.

5. eThemes of the Times, which is a New York Times article to help you understand the real-world applications of what you are learning.

Get Ahead of the Curve

To see how it works, turn to page 16 and then go to www.myeconlab.com/miller.

More Advanced Consumer Choice Theory

It is possible to analyze consumer choice verbally, as we did for the most part in Chapter 20. The theory of diminishing marginal utility can be fairly well accepted on intuitive grounds and by introspection. If we want to be more formal and perhaps more elegant in our theorizing, however, we can translate our discussion into a graphical analysis with what we call *indifference curves* and the *budget constraint*. Here we discuss these terms and their relationship and demonstrate consumer equilibrium in geometric form.

ON BEING INDIFFERENT

What does it mean to be indifferent? It usually means that you don't care one way or the other about something—you are equally disposed to either of two alternatives. With this interpretation in mind, we will turn to two choices, playing golf and consuming restaurant meals. In panel (a) of Figure E-1, we show several combinations of golf outings and restaurant meals per week that a representative consumer considers equally satisfactory. That is to say, for each combination, *A*, *B*, *C*, and *D*, this consumer will have exactly the same level of total utility.

FIGURE E-I

Combinations That Yield Equal Levels of Satisfaction

A, B, C, and D represent combinations of golf outings and restaurant meals per week that give an equal level of satisfaction to this consumer. In other words, the consumer is indifferent among these four combinations.

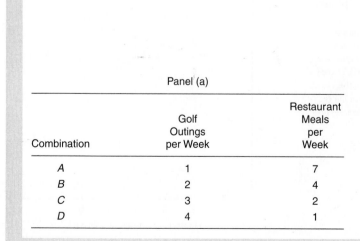

Panel (a)

Combination	Golf Outings per Week	Restaurant Meals per Week
A	1	7
B	2	4
C	3	2
D	4	1

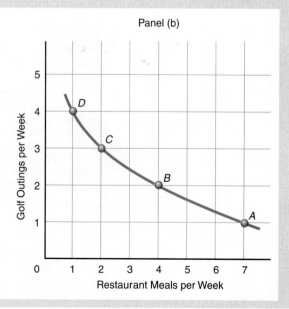

The simple numerical example that we have used happens to concern golf outings and the consumption of restaurant meals per week. This example is used to illustrate general features of indifference curves and related analytical tools that are necessary for deriving the demand curve. Obviously, we could have used any two commodities. Just remember that we are using a *specific* example to illustrate a *general* analysis.

We plot these combinations graphically in panel (b) of Figure E-1 on the previous page, with restaurant meals per week on the horizontal axis and golf outings per week on the vertical axis. These are our consumer's indifference combinations—the consumer finds each combination as acceptable as the others. These combinations lie along a smooth curve that is known as the consumer's **indifference curve.** Along the indifference curve, every combination of the two goods in question yields the same level of satisfaction. Every point along the indifference curve is equally desirable to the consumer. For example, four golf outings per week and one restaurant meal per week will give our representative consumer exactly the same total satisfaction as two golf outings per week and four restaurant meals per week.

Indifference curve
A curve composed of a set of consumption alternatives, each of which yields the same total amount of satisfaction.

PROPERTIES OF INDIFFERENCE CURVES

Indifference curves have special properties relating to their slope and shape.

Downward Slope

The indifference curve shown in panel (b) of Figure E-1 on the previous page slopes downward; that is, it has a negative slope. Now consider Figure E-2. Here we show two points, *A* and *B*. Point *A* represents four golf outings per week and two restaurant meals per week. Point *B* represents five golf outings per week and six restaurant meals per week. Clearly, *B* is always preferred to *A* because *B* represents more of everything. If *B* is always preferred to *A*, it is impossible for points *A* and *B* to be on the same indifference curve because the definition of the indifference curve is a set of combinations of two goods that are preferred equally.

FIGURE E-2
Indifference Curves: Impossibility of an Upward Slope
Point *B* represents a consumption of more golf outings per week and more restaurant meals per week than point *A*. *B* is always preferred to *A*. Therefore, *A* and *B* cannot be on the same *positively* sloped indifference curve. An indifference curve shows *equally preferred* combinations of the two goods.

Curvature

The indifference curve that we have drawn in panel (b) of Figure E-1 on page 483 is special. Notice that it is curved. Why didn't we just draw a straight line, as we have usually done for a demand curve? To find out why we don't posit straight-line indifference curves, consider the implications. We show such a straight-line indifference curve in Figure E-3. Start at point *A*. The consumer has no restaurant meals and five golf outings per week. Now the consumer wishes to go to point *B*. He or she is willing to give up only one golf outing in order to get one restaurant meal. Now let's assume that the consumer is at point *C*, playing golf once a week and consuming four restaurant meals per week. If the consumer wants to go to point *D*, he or she is again willing to give up one golf outing in order to get one more restaurant meal per week.

In other words, no matter how many times the consumer plays golf, he or she is willing to give up one golf outing to get one restaurant meal per week—which does not seem plausible. Doesn't it make sense to hypothesize that the more times the consumer plays golf each week, the less he or she will value an *additional* golf outing that week? Presumably, when the consumer has five golf outings and no restaurant meals per week, he or she should be willing to give up *more than* one golf outing in order to get one restaurant meal. Therefore, a straight-line indifference curve as shown in Figure E-3 no longer seems plausible.

In mathematical jargon, an indifference curve is convex with respect to the origin. Let's look at this in panel (a) of Figure E-1 on page 483. Starting with combination *A*, the consumer has one golf outing but seven restaurant meals per week. To remain indifferent, the consumer would have to be willing to give up three restaurant meals to obtain one more golf outing (as shown in combination *B*). To go from combination *C* to combination *D*, however, notice that the consumer would have to be willing to give up only one restaurant meal for an additional golf outing per week. The quantity of the substitute considered acceptable changes as the rate of consumption of the original item changes.

Consequently, the indifference curve in panel (b) of Figure E-1 will be convex when viewed from the origin.

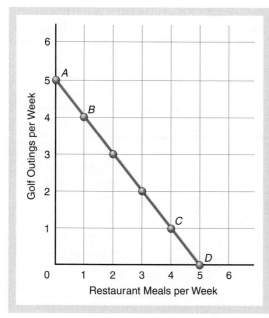

FIGURE E-3

Implications of a Straight-Line Indifference Curve

If the indifference curve is a straight line, the consumer will be willing to give up the same number of golf outings (one for one in this simple example) to get one more restaurant meal per week, whether the consumer has no restaurant meals or a lot of restaurant meals per week. For example, the consumer at point *A* plays golf five times and consumes no restaurant meals per week. He or she is willing to give up one golf outing in order to get one restaurant meal per week. At point *C*, however, the consumer has only one golf outing and four restaurant meals per week. Because of the straight-line indifference curve, this consumer is willing to give up the last golf outing in order to get one more restaurant meal per week, even though he or she already has four.

THE MARGINAL RATE OF SUBSTITUTION

Instead of using marginal utility, we can talk in terms of the *marginal rate of substitution* between restaurant meals and golf outings per week. We can formally define the consumer's marginal rate of substitution as follows:

> *The marginal rate of substitution is equal to the change in the quantity of one good that just offsets a one-unit change in the consumption of another good, such that total satisfaction remains constant.*

We can see numerically what happens to the marginal rate of substitution in our example if we rearrange panel (a) of Figure E-1 on page 483 into Table E-1. Here we show restaurant meals in the second column and golf outings in the third. Now we ask the question, what change in the number of golf outings per week will just compensate for a three-unit change in the consumption of restaurant meals per week and leave the consumer's total utility constant? The movement from *A* to *B* increases the number of weekly golf outings by one. Here the marginal rate of substitution is 3:1 —a three-unit decrease in restaurant meals requires an increase of one golf outing to leave the consumer's total utility unaltered. Thus the consumer values the three restaurant meals as the equivalent of one golf outing. We do this for the rest of the table and find that as restaurant meals decrease further, the marginal rate of substitution goes from 3:1 to 2:1 to 1:1. The marginal rate of substitution of restaurant meals for golf outings per week falls as the consumer plays more golf. That is, the consumer values successive golf outings less and less in terms of restaurant meals. The first golf outing is valued at three restaurant meals; the last (fourth) golf outing is valued at only one restaurant meal. The fact that the marginal rate of substitution falls is sometimes called the *law of substitution*.

In geometric language, the slope of the consumer's indifference curve (actually, the negative of the slope) measures the consumer's marginal rate of substitution. Notice that this marginal rate of substitution is purely subjective or psychological.

THE INDIFFERENCE MAP

Let's now consider the possibility of having both more golf outings *and* more restaurant meals per week. When we do this, we can no longer stay on the same indifference curve that we drew in Figure E-1. That indifference curve was drawn for equally satisfying combinations of golf outings and restaurant meals per week. If the individual can now obtain

TABLE E-1
Calculating the Marginal Rate of Substitution

As we move from combination *A* to combination *B*, we are still on the same indifference curve. To stay on that curve, the number of restaurant meals decreases by three and the number of golf outings increases by one. The marginal rate of substitution is 3:1. A three-unit decrease in restaurant meals requires an increase in one golf outing to leave the consumer's total utility unaltered.

(1) Combination	(2) Restaurant Meals per Week	(3) Golf Outings per Week	(4) Marginal Rate of Substitution of Restaurant Meals for Golf Outings
A	7	1	3:1
B	4	2	2:1
C	2	3	1:1
D	1	4	

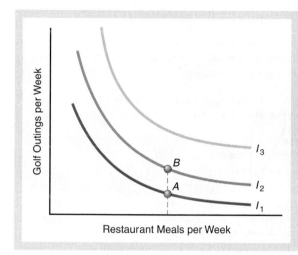

FIGURE E-4
A Set of Indifference Curves
An infinite number of indifference curves can be drawn. We show three possible ones. Realize that a higher indifference curve represents the possibility of higher rates of consumption of both goods. Hence a higher indifference curve is preferred to a lower one because more is preferred to less. Look at points A and B. Point B represents more golf outings than point A; therefore, bundles on indifference curve I_2 have to be preferred over bundles on I_1 because the number of restaurant meals per week is the same at points A and B.

more of both, a new indifference curve will have to be drawn, above and to the right of the one shown in panel (b) of Figure E-1. Alternatively, if the individual faces the possibility of having less of both golf outings and restaurant meals per week, an indifference curve will have to be drawn below and to the left of the one in panel (b) of Figure E-1 on page 483. We can map out a whole set of indifference curves corresponding to these possibilities.

Figure E-4 shows three possible indifference curves. Indifference curves that are higher than others necessarily imply that for every given quantity of one good, more of the other good can be obtained on a higher indifference curve. Looked at another way, if one goes from curve I_1 to I_2, it is possible to consume the same number of restaurant meals *and* be able to play more golf each week. This is shown as a movement from point A to point B in Figure E-4. We could do it the other way. When we move from a lower to a higher indifference curve, it is possible to play the same amount of golf *and* to consume more restaurant meals each week. Thus, the higher an indifference curve is for a consumer, the greater that consumer's total level of satisfaction.

THE BUDGET CONSTRAINT

Our problem here is to find out how to maximize consumer satisfaction. To do so, we must consult not only our *preferences*—given by indifference curves—but also our *market opportunities*, which are given by our available income and prices, called our **budget constraint.** We might want more of everything, but for any given budget constraint, we have to make choices, or trade-offs, among possible goods. Everyone has a budget constraint; that is, everyone faces a limited consumption potential. How do we show this graphically? We must find the prices of the goods in question and determine the maximum consumption of each allowed by our budget. For example, let's assume that there is a $10 fee for each golf outing and that a restaurant meal costs $20. Let's also assume that our representative consumer has a total budget of $60 per week. What is the maximum number of golf outings the consumer can make? Six. And the maximum number of restaurant meals per week he or she can consume? Three. So now, as shown in Figure E-5 on the following page, we have two points on our budget line, which is sometimes called the *consumption possibilities curve.* These anchor points of the budget line are obtained by dividing money income by the price of each product. The first point is at b on the vertical axis; the second, at b' on the horizontal axis. The budget line is linear because prices are constant.

Budget constraint
All of the possible combinations of goods that can be purchased (at fixed prices) with a specific budget.

FIGURE E-5
The Budget Constraint
The line *bb'* represents this individual's budget constraint. Assuming that golf outings cost $10 each, restaurant meals cost $20 each, and the individual has a budget of $60 per week, a maximum of six golf outings or three restaurant meals can be bought each week. These two extreme points are connected to form the budget constraint. All combinations within the colored area and on the budget constraint line are feasible.

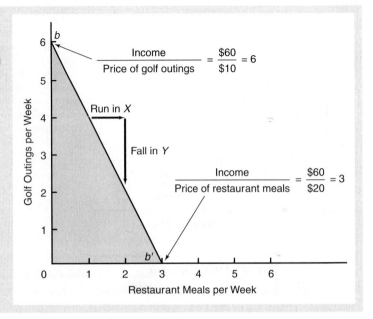

Any combination along line *bb'* is possible; in fact, any combination in the colored area is possible. We will assume, however, that the individual consumer completely uses up the available budget, and we will consider as possible only those points along *bb'*.

Slope of the Budget Constraint

The budget constraint is a line that slopes downward from left to right. The slope of that line has a special meaning. Look carefully at the budget line in Figure E-5. Remember from our discussion of graphs in Appendix A that we measure a negative slope by the ratio of the fall in *Y* over the run in *X*. In this case, *Y* is golf outings per week and *X* is restaurant meals per week. In Figure E-5, the fall in *Y* is −2 golf outings per week (a drop from 4 to 2) for a run in *X* of one restaurant meal per week (an increase from 1 to 2); therefore, the slope of the budget constraint is −2/1 or −2. This slope of the budget constraint represents the rate of exchange between golf outings and restaurant meals.

Now we are ready to determine how the consumer achieves the optimum consumption rate.

CONSUMER OPTIMUM REVISITED

Consumers will try to attain the highest level of total utility possible, given their budget constraints. How can this be shown graphically? We draw a set of indifference curves similar to those in Figure E-4, and we bring in reality—the budget constraint *bb'*. Both are drawn in Figure E-6. Because a higher level of total satisfaction is represented by a higher indifference curve, we know that the consumer will strive to be on the highest indifference curve possible. The consumer cannot get to indifference curve I_3, however, because the budget will be exhausted before any combination of golf outings and restaurant meals represented on indifference curve I_3 is attained. This consumer can maximize total utility, subject to the budget constraint, only by being at point *E* on indifference curve I_2 because

Go to www.econtoday.com/chap20 for a numerical example illustrating the consumer optimum.

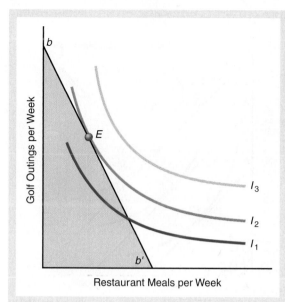

FIGURE E-6
Consumer Optimum
A consumer reaches an optimum when he or she ends up on the highest indifference curve possible, given a limited budget. This occurs at the tangency between an indifference curve and the budget constraint. In this diagram, the tangency is at E.

here the consumer's income is just being exhausted. Mathematically, point E is called the *tangency point* of the curve I_2 to the straight line bb'.

Consumer optimum is achieved when the marginal rate of substitution (which is subjective) is just equal to the feasible, or realistic, rate of exchange between golf outings and restaurant meals. This realistic rate is the ratio of the two prices of the goods involved. It is represented by the absolute value of the slope of the budget constraint (i.e., ignoring the negative signs). At point E, the point of tangency between indifference curve I_2 and budget constraint bb', the rate at which the consumer wishes to substitute golf outings for restaurant meals (the numerical value of the slope of the indifference curve) is just equal to the rate at which the consumer *can* substitute golf outings for restaurant meals (the slope of the budget line).

EFFECTS OF CHANGES IN INCOME

A change in income will shift the budget constraint bb' in Figure E-6. Consider only increases in income and no changes in price. The budget constraint will shift outward. Each new budget line will be parallel to the original one because we are not allowing a change in the relative prices of golf outings and restaurant meals. We would now like to find out how an individual consumer responds to successive increases in income when relative prices remain constant. We do this in Figure E-7 on the following page. We start out with an income that is represented by a budget line bb'. Consumer optimum is at point E, where the consumer attains the highest indifference curve I_1, given the budget constraint bb'. Now we let income increase. This is shown by a shift outward in the budget line to cc'. The consumer attains a new optimum at point E'. That is where a higher indifference curve, I_2, is reached. Again, the consumer's income is increased so that the new budget line is dd'. The new optimum now moves to E''. This is where indifference curve I_3 is reached. If we connect the three consumer optimum points, E, E', and E'', we have what is called an income-consumption curve. The **income-consumption curve** shows the optimum consumption points that would occur if income for that consumer were increased continuously, holding the prices of golf outings and restaurant meals constant.

Income-consumption curve
The set of optimal consumption points that would occur if income were increased, relative prices remaining constant.

FIGURE E-7
Income-Consumption Curve
We start off with income sufficient to yield budget constraint *bb'*. The highest attainable indifference curve is I_1, which is just tangent to *bb'* at E. Next we increase income. The budget line moves outward to *cc'*, which is parallel to *bb'*. The new highest indifference curve is I_2, which is just tangent to *cc'* at E'. We increase income again, which is represented by a shift in the budget line to *dd'*. The new tangency point of the highest indifference curve, I_3 with *dd'*, is at point E". When we connect these three points, we obtain the income-consumption curve.

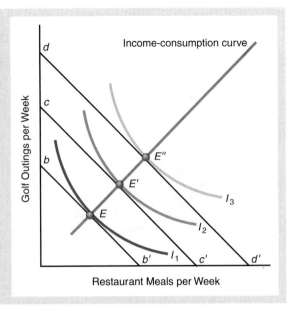

THE PRICE-CONSUMPTION CURVE

In Figure E-8, we hold money income and the price of golf outings constant while we lower the price of restaurant meals. As we keep lowering the price of restaurant meals, the quantity of meals that could be purchased if all income were spent on restaurant meals increases; thus the extreme points for the budget constraint keep moving outward to the right as the price of restaurant meals falls. In other words, the budget line rotates outward from *bb'* to *bb"* and *bb'''*. Each time the price of restaurant meals falls, a new budget line is formed. There has to be a new optimum point. We find it by locating on each new budget

FIGURE E-8
Price-Consumption Curve
As we lower the price of restaurant meals, income measured in terms of restaurant meals per week increases. We show this by rotating the budget constraint from *bb'* to *bb"* and finally to *bb'''*. We then find the highest indifference curve that is attainable for each successive budget constraint. For budget constraint *bb'*, the highest indifference curve is I_1, which is tangent to *bb'*, at point E. We do this for the next two budget constraints. When we connect the optimum points, E, E', and E", we derive the price-consumption curve, which shows the combinations of the two commodities that a consumer will purchase when money income and the price of one commodity remain constant while the other commodity's price changes.

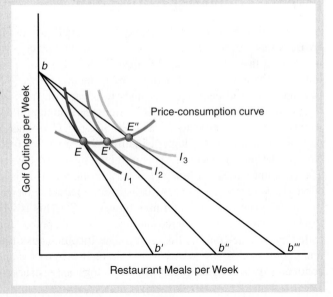

line the highest attainable indifference curve. This is shown at points E, E', and E''. We see that as price decreases for restaurant meals, the consumer purchases more restaurant meals per week. We call the line connecting points E, E' and E'' the **price-consumption curve.** It connects the tangency points of the budget constraints and indifference curves, thus showing the amounts of two goods that a consumer will buy when money income and the price of one commodity are held constant while the price of the remaining good changes.

Price-consumption curve
The set of consumer-optimum combinations of two goods that the consumer would choose as the price of one good changes, while money income and the price of the other good remain constant.

DERIVING THE DEMAND CURVE

We are now in a position to derive the demand curve using indifference curve analysis. In panel (a) of Figure E-9, we show what happens when the price of restaurant meals decreases, holding both the price of golf outings and income constant. If the price of

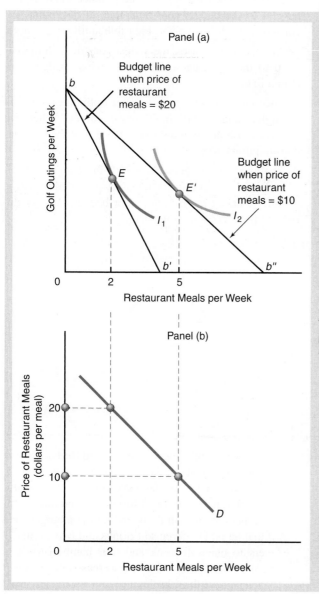

FIGURE E-9
Deriving the Demand Curve
In panel (a), we show the effects of a decrease in the price of restaurant meals from $20 to $10. At $20, the highest indifference curve touches the budget line bb' at point E. The quantity of restaurant meals consumed is two. We transfer this combination—price, $20; quantity demanded, 2—down to panel (b). Next we decrease the price of restaurant meals to $10. This generates a new budget line, or constraint, which is bb''. Consumer optimum is now at E'. The optimum quantity of restaurant meals demanded at a price of $10 is five. We transfer this point—price, $10; quantity demanded, 5—down to panel (b). When we connect these two points, we have a demand curve, D, for restaurant meals.

restaurant meals decreases, the budget line rotates from *bb'* to *bb"*. The two optimum points are given by the tangency at the highest indifference curve that just touches those two budget lines. This is at *E* and *E'*. But those two points give us two price-quantity pairs. At point *E*, the price of restaurant meals is $20; the quantity demanded is 2. Thus we have one point that we can transfer to panel (b) of Figure E-9. At point *E'*, we have another price-quantity pair. The price has fallen to $10; the quantity demanded has increased to 5. We therefore transfer this other point to panel (b). When we connect these two points (and all the others in between), we derive the demand curve for restaurant meals; it slopes downward.

APPENDIX SUMMARY

1. Along an indifference curve, the consumer experiences equal levels of satisfaction. That is to say, along any indifference curve, every combination of the two goods in question yields exactly the same level of satisfaction.

2. Indifference curves typically slope downward and are usually convex to the origin.

3. To measure the marginal rate of substitution, we find out how much of one good has to be given up in order to allow the consumer to consume one more unit of the other good while still remaining on the same indifference curve. The marginal rate of substitution falls as one moves down an indifference curve.

4. Indifference curves represent preferences. A budget constraint represents opportunities—how much can be purchased with a given level of income. Consumer optimum is obtained when the highest indifference curve is just tangent to the budget constraint line; at that point, the consumer reaches the highest feasible indifference curve.

5. When income increases, the budget constraint shifts outward to the right, parallel to the previous budget constraint line.

6. As income increases, the consumer optimum moves up to higher and higher indifference curves. When we connect those points with a line, we derive the income-consumption curve.

7. As the price of one good decreases, the budget line rotates. When we connect the tangency points of the highest indifference curves to these new budget lines, we derive the price-consumption curve.

KEY TERMS AND CONCEPTS

budget constraint (487)

income-consumption curve (489)

indifference curve (484)

price-consumption curve (491)

PROBLEMS

Answers to the odd-numbered problems appear at the back of the book.

E-1. Consider the indifference curve illustrated in Figure E-1 on page 483. Explain, in economic terms, why the curve is convex to the origin.

E-2. Your classmate tells you that he is indifferent between three soft drinks and two hamburgers or two soft drinks and three hamburgers.

a. Draw a rough diagram of an indifference curve containing your classmate's consumption choices.

b. Suppose that your classmate states that he is also indifferent between two soft drinks and three hamburgers or one soft drink and four hamburgers, but that he prefers three soft drinks and two hamburgers to one soft drink and four hamburgers. Use your diagram from Part (a) to reason out whether he can have these preferences.

E-3. The following table represents Sue's preferences for bottled water and soft drinks, which yield the same level of utility.

Combination of Bottled Water and Soft Drinks	Bottled Water per Month	Soft Drinks per Month
A	5	11
B	10	7
C	15	4
D	20	2
E	25	1

Calculate Sue's marginal rate of substitution of soft drinks for bottled water. Relate the marginal rate of substitution to marginal utility.

E-4. Using the information provided in Problem E-3, illustrate Sue's indifference curve, with water on the horizontal axis and soft drinks on the vertical axis.

E-5. Sue's monthly budget for bottled water and soft drinks is $23. The price of bottled water is $1 per bottle, and the price of soft drinks is $2 per bottle. Calculate the slope of Sue's budget constraint. Given this information and the information provided in Problem E-3, find the combination of goods that satisfies Sue's utility maximization problem in light of her budget constraint.

E-6. Using the indifference curve diagram you constructed in Problem E-4, add in Sue's budget constraint given the information in Problem E-5. Illustrate the utility-maximizing combination of bottled water and soft drinks.

E-7. Using the information provided in Problem E-5, suppose now that the price of a soft drink falls to $1. Now Sue's constant-utility preferences are as follows:

Combination of Bottled Water and Soft Drinks	Bottled Water per Month	Soft Drinks per Month
A	5	22
B	10	14
C	15	8
D	20	4
E	25	2

Calculate the slope of Sue's new budget constraint. Next, find the combination of goods that satisfies Sue's utility maximization problem in light of her budget constraint.

E-8. Illustrate Sue's new budget constraint and indifference curve in the diagram you constructed for Problem E-6. Illustrate also the utility-maximizing combination of goods. Finally, draw the price-consumption curve.

E-9. Given your answers to Problems E-5 and E-7, are Sue's preferences for soft drinks consistent with the law of demand?

E-10. Using your answer to Problem E-8, draw Sue's demand curve for soft drinks.

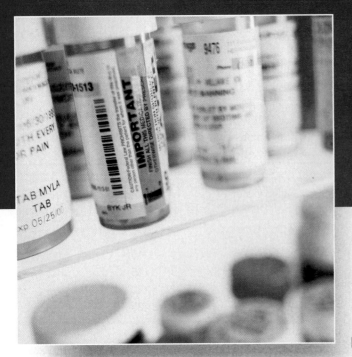

Chapter 21

Demand and Supply Elasticity

People suffering from physical illnesses often rely on physicians, hospitals, and prescription medications to maintain the quality of their lives—or perhaps to stay alive. Increases in the prices of physician services, hospital stays, or prescription drugs thereby tend to induce relatively small decreases in quantities demanded of these items. Mental health also has a major bearing on the quality of a person's life. Nevertheless, a rise in the price that consumers must pay for psychiatric services generates a relatively much larger decrease in the quantity of services demanded. Why is this so? How can we measure and compare the responsiveness of quantity demanded to price changes for various types of health care services? In this chapter, you will learn the answers to these questions.

Media Resources

Refer to the end of the chapter for a full listing of the multimedia learning materials available in MyEconLab.

LEARNING OBJECTIVES

After reading this chapter, you should be able to:

1. Express and calculate price elasticity of demand
2. Understand the relationship between the price elasticity of demand and total revenues
3. Discuss the factors that determine the price elasticity of demand
4. Describe the cross price elasticity of demand and how it may be used to indicate whether two goods are substitutes or complements
5. Explain the income elasticity of demand
6. Classify supply elasticities and explain how the length of time for adjustment affects the price elasticity of supply

...a fall in the price of beer helps explain why nearly one-third of the nearly 15 million U.S. college students are involved in some kind of campus violence each year? The law of demand indicates that a decline in the price of beer increases consumption. In turn, students who drink greater amounts of beer are more likely to have arguments and fights, to commit sexual assaults, and to get into altercations with college officials and police. Economists have found that a 10 percent reduction in the price of beer is associated with an increase in the incidence of campus violence of just over 3.5 percent. Since the early 1990s, the inflation-adjusted price of beer has declined by more than 10 percent, which helps explain why more than half a million additional instances of U.S. campus violence now occur each year.

College officials aren't alone in having to worry about how individuals respond to lower prices. Businesses must constantly take into account consumer response to changing prices. If Dell reduces its prices by 10 percent, will consumers respond by buying so many more computers that the company's revenues will rise? At the other end of the spectrum, can Rolls Royce dealers "get away" with a 2 percent increase in prices? That is, will Rolls Royce purchasers respond so little to the relatively small increase in price that the total revenues received for Rolls Royce sales will not fall and may actually rise? The only way to answer these questions is to know how responsive consumers in the real world will be to changes in prices. Economists have a special name for price responsiveness—*elasticity,* which is the subject of this chapter.

PRICE ELASTICITY

To begin to understand what elasticity is all about, just keep in mind that it means "responsiveness." Here we are concerned with the price elasticity of demand. We wish to know the extent to which a change in the price of, say, petroleum products will cause the quantity demanded to change, other things held constant. We want to determine the percentage change in quantity demanded in response to a percentage change in price.

Price Elasticity of Demand

We will formally define the **price elasticity of demand,** which we will label E_p as follows:

$$E_p = \frac{\text{percentage change in quantity demanded}}{\text{percentage change in price}}$$

Price elasticity of demand (E_p)
The responsiveness of the quantity demanded of a commodity to changes in its price; defined as the percentage change in quantity demanded divided by the percentage change in price.

What will price elasticity of demand tell us? It will tell us the *relative* amount by which the quantity demanded will change in response to a change in the price of a particular good.

Consider an example in which a 10 percent rise in the price of oil leads to a reduction in quantity demanded of only 1 percent. Putting these numbers into the formula, we find that the price elasticity of demand for oil in this case equals the percentage change in quantity demanded divided by the percentage change in price, or

$$E_p = \frac{-1\%}{+10\%} = -0.1$$

An elasticity of -0.1 means that a 1 percent *increase* in the price would lead to a mere 0.1 percent *decrease* in the quantity demanded. If you were now told, in contrast, that the price elasticity of demand for oil was -1, you would know that a 1 percent increase in the price of oil would lead to a 1 percent decrease in the quantity demanded.

Go to www.econtoday.com/chap21 for additional review of the price elasticity of demand.

Relative Quantities Only. Notice that in our elasticity formula, we talk about *percentage* changes in quantity demanded divided by *percentage* changes in price. Thus we are not interested in the absolute changes, only in relative amounts. This means that it doesn't matter if we measure price changes in terms of cents, dollars, or hundreds of dollars. It also doesn't matter whether we measure quantity changes in ounces, grams, or pounds. The percentage change will be independent of the units chosen.

Always Negative. The law of demand states that quantity demanded is *inversely* related to the relative price. An *increase* in the price of a good leads to a *decrease* in the quantity demanded. If a *decrease* in the relative price of a good should occur, the quantity demanded would *increase* by a certain percentage. The point is that price elasticity of demand will always be negative. By convention, however, *we will ignore the minus sign in our discussion from this point on.*

Basically, the greater the *absolute* price elasticity of demand (disregarding the sign), the greater the demand responsiveness to relative price changes—a small change in price has a great impact on quantity demanded. Conversely, the smaller the absolute price elasticity of demand, the smaller the demand responsiveness to relative price changes—a large change in price has little effect on quantity demanded.

CONCEPTS in Brief

- Elasticity is a measure of the price responsiveness of the quantity demanded and quantity supplied.

- The price elasticity of demand is equal to the percentage change in quantity demanded divided by the percentage change in price.

- Price elasticity of demand is calculated in terms of percentage changes in quantity demanded and in price. Thus it is expressed as a unitless, dimensionless number.

- The law of demand states that quantity demanded and price are inversely related. Therefore, the price elasticity of demand is always negative, because an increase in price will lead to a decrease in quantity demanded and a decrease in price will lead to an increase in quantity demanded. By convention, we ignore the negative sign in discussions of the price elasticity of demand.

To test your understanding of the concepts covered in this section, go to the Online Review at www.myeconlab.com/miller.

Calculating Elasticity

To calculate the price elasticity of demand, we must compute percentage changes in quantity demanded and in price. For the percentage change in quantity demanded, we might divide the change in the quantity demanded by the original quantity demanded:

$$\frac{\text{Change in quantity demanded}}{\text{Original quantity demanded}}$$

To find the percentage change in price, we might divide the change in price by the original price:

$$\frac{\text{Change in price}}{\text{Original price}}$$

There is an arithmetic problem, though, when we calculate percentage changes in this manner. The percentage change, say, from 2 to 3—50 percent—is not the same as the percentage change from 3 to 2—$33\frac{1}{3}$ percent. In other words, it makes a difference where you start. One way out of this dilemma is simply to use average values.

To compute the price elasticity of demand, we take the average of the two prices and the two quantities over the range we are considering and compare the change with these averages. For relatively small changes in price, the formula for computing the price elasticity of demand then becomes

$$E_p = \frac{\text{change in quantity}}{\text{sum of quantities}/2} \div \frac{\text{change in price}}{\text{sum of prices}/2}$$

We can rewrite this more simply if we do two things: (1) We can let Q_1 and Q_2 equal the two different quantities demanded before and after the price change and let P_1 and P_2 equal the two different prices. (2) Because we will be dividing a percentage by a percentage, we simply use the ratio, or the decimal form, of the percentages. Therefore,

$$E_p = \frac{\Delta Q}{(Q_1 + Q_2)/2} \div \frac{\Delta P}{(P_1 + P_2)/2}$$

where the Greek letter Δ (delta) stands for "change in."

How could we use actual price changes and associated changes in quantity demanded to calculate the price elasticity of demand using this formula?

E X A M P L E

The Price Elasticity of Demand for Six-Packs of Beer

Recently, the U.S. price of Lowenbrau, a beer imported from Germany, increased from about $4.67 to $7.00. The result was a decline in the amount of Lowenbrau beer sold in the United States each year, from the equivalent of about 25 million six-packs to 16.67 million six-packs.

We can calculate the price elasticity of demand for six-packs of Lowenbrau beer by using the formula presented earlier (under the assumption, of course, that all other things, such as the prices of substitute beers, were constant):

$$E_p = \frac{\text{change in } Q}{\text{sum of quantities}/2} \div \frac{\text{change in } P}{\text{sum of prices}/2}$$

$$= \frac{25 \text{ million} - 16.67 \text{ million}}{(25 \text{ million} + 16.67 \text{ million})/2} \div \frac{\$7.00 - \$4.67}{(\$7.00 + \$4.67)/2}$$

$$= \frac{8.33 \text{ million}}{41.67 \text{ million}/2} \div \frac{\$2.33}{\$11.67/2} = 1$$

The price elasticity of 1 means that a 1 percent increase in price generated a 1 percent decrease in the quantity of Lowenbrau beer demanded.

For Critical Analysis
Would the estimated price elasticity of demand for Lowenbrau beer have been different if we had not *used the average-values formula? How?*

PRICE ELASTICITY RANGES

We have names for the varying ranges of price elasticities, depending on whether a 1 percent change in price elicits more or less than a 1 percent change in the quantity demanded.

- We say that a good has an **elastic demand** whenever the price elasticity of demand is greater than 1. A 1 percent change in price causes a greater than 1 percent change in the quantity demanded.

Elastic demand
A demand relationship in which a given percentage change in price will result in a larger percentage change in quantity demanded. Total expenditures and price changes are inversely related in the elastic region of the demand curve.

Unit elasticity of demand
A demand relationship in which the quantity demanded changes exactly in proportion to the change in price. Total expenditures are invariant to price changes in the unit-elastic region of the demand curve.

Inelastic demand
A demand relationship in which a given percentage change in price will result in a less than proportionate percentage change in the quantity demanded. Total expenditures and price are directly related in the inelastic region of the demand curve.

Perfectly inelastic demand
A demand that exhibits zero responsiveness to price changes; no matter what the price is, the quantity demanded remains the same.

Perfectly elastic demand
A demand that has the characteristic that even the slightest increase in price will lead to zero quantity demanded.

- In a situation of **unit elasticity of demand,** a 1 percent change in price causes exactly a 1 percent change in the quantity demanded.
- In a situation of **inelastic demand,** a 1 percent change in price causes a change of less than 1 percent in the quantity demanded.

When we say that a commodity's demand is elastic, we are indicating that consumers are relatively responsive to changes in price. When we say that a commodity's demand is inelastic, we are indicating that its consumers are relatively unresponsive to price changes. When economists say that demand is inelastic, it does not mean that quantity demanded is *totally* unresponsive to price changes. Remember, the law of demand implies that there will be some responsiveness in quantity demanded to a price change. The question is how much. That's what elasticity attempts to determine.

Extreme Elasticities

There are two extremes in price elasticities of demand. One extreme represents total unresponsiveness of quantity demanded to price changes, which is referred to as **perfectly inelastic demand,** or zero elasticity. The other represents total responsiveness, which is referred to as infinitely or **perfectly elastic demand.**

We show perfect inelasticity in panel (a) of Figure 21-1. Notice that the quantity demanded per year is 8 million units, no matter what the price. Hence, for any price change, the quantity demanded will remain the same, and thus the change in the quantity demanded will be zero. Look back at our formula for computing elasticity. If the change in the quantity demanded is zero, the numerator is also zero, and a nonzero number divided into zero results in a value of zero too. This is true at any point along the demand curve. Hence there is perfect inelasticity.

At the opposite extreme is the situation depicted in panel (b) of Figure 21-1. Here we show that at a price of 30 cents, an unlimited quantity will be demanded. At a price that is only slightly above 30 cents, no quantity will be demanded. There is perfect, or infinite, responsiveness at each point along this curve, and hence we call the demand schedule in panel (b) perfectly elastic.

FIGURE 21-1
Extreme Price Elasticities
In panel (a), we show infinite price unresponsiveness. The demand curve is vertical at the quantity of 8 million units per year. This means that the price elasticity of demand is zero. In panel (b), we show complete price responsiveness. At a price of 30 cents, in this example, consumers will demand an unlimited quantity of the particular good in question. This is a case of infinite price elasticity of demand.

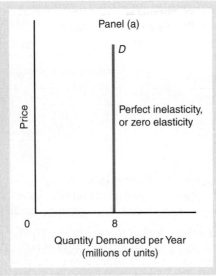

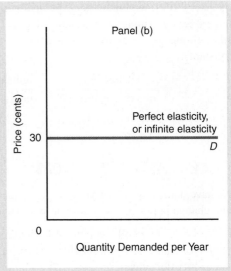

● One extreme elasticity occurs when a demand curve is vertical. It has zero price elasticity of demand; it is completely inelastic.

● Another extreme elasticity occurs when a demand curve is horizontal. It has completely elastic demand; its price elasticity of demand is infinite.

ELASTICITY AND TOTAL REVENUES

Suppose that you are in charge of the pricing decision for a cellular telephone service company. How would you know when it is better to raise or not to raise prices? The answer depends in part on the effect of your pricing decision on total revenues, or the total receipts of your company. (The rest of the equation is, of course, your cost structure, a subject we examine in Chapter 23.) It is commonly thought that the way to increase total receipts is to increase price per unit. But is it possible that a rise in price per unit could lead to a decrease in total revenues? The answer to this question depends on the price elasticity of demand. How does elasticity affect who pays gasoline taxes?

Policy EXAMPLE

Who Pays Higher Gasoline Taxes?

State and federal governments impose gasoline taxes, which are assessed as a flat amount per gallon sold. These taxes are paid by sellers of gasoline from the revenues they earn from their total sales. Thus, to receive the same effective price for selling a given quantity, a gasoline producer would have to receive a price that is higher by exactly the amount of the tax. As shown in panel (a) of Figure 21-2 on the next page, this means that imposing a gasoline tax shifts the supply curve upward by the amount of the tax. Sellers supply a given quantity of gasoline at a price that is higher by the amount of the tax that they will transmit to the government.

Who *truly* pays the tax depends on the price elasticity of demand, however. Take a look at panel (b) of Figure 21-2, which illustrates what happens to the market price in the case of perfectly inelastic demand for gasoline. In this instance, the market price rises by the full amount that the supply curve shifts

upward. This amount, of course, is the amount of the tax. Consequently, if gasoline consumers have a perfectly inelastic demand for gasoline, they effectively pay the entire tax in the form of higher prices. Panel (c) illustrates the opposite case, in which the demand for gasoline is perfectly elastic. In this situation, the market price is unresponsive to a tax-induced shift in the supply curve, so sellers must pay all the tax.

Realistically, the price elasticity of demand for gasoline is relatively low—most gasoline price elasticity estimates indicate values of 0.2 to 0.5. Thus the burden of gasoline taxes mainly falls on gasoline consumers.

For Critical Analysis
Based on the information in this example, if excise taxes on gasoline increase by 10 percent, by what range of percentages may desired gasoline purchases decline?

Let's look at Figure 21-3 on page 501. In panel (a), column 1 shows the price of cellular telephone service in cents per minute, and column 2 represents billions of minutes per year. In column 3, we multiply column 1 times column 2 to derive total revenue because total revenue is always equal to the number of units (quantity) sold times the price per unit. In column 4, we calculate values of elasticity. Notice what happens to total revenues throughout the schedule. They rise steadily as the price rises from 1 cent to 5 cents per minute; but when the price rises further to 6 cents per minute, total revenues remain con-

FIGURE 21-2
Price Elasticity and a Gasoline Tax

Placing a per-gallon tax on gasoline causes the supply curve to shift upward by the amount of the tax, as illustrated in panel (a), in order for sellers to receive the same effective price for any given quantity of gasoline they sell. If the demand for gasoline were perfectly inelastic, as depicted in panel (b), imposing the tax causes the market price of gasoline to rise by the amount of the tax, so that gasoline consumers would effectively pay all the tax. Conversely, if the demand for gasoline were perfectly elastic, as shown in panel (c), the market price would not change, and sellers would pay all the tax. The quantity demanded would fall to Q_2.

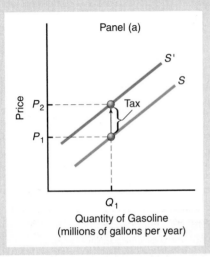

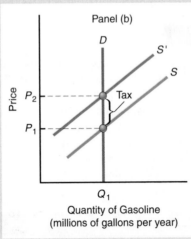

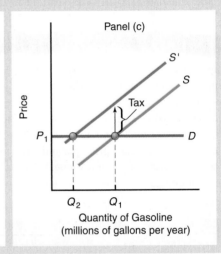

Go to www.econtoday.com/chap21 to participate in an Economics Interactive Tutorial at the University of South Carolina that provides further practice with elasticity.

stant at $3 billion. At prices per minute higher than 6 cents, total revenues fall as price increases. Indeed, if prices are above 6 cents per minute, total revenues can be increased only by *reducing* prices, not by raising them.

Labeling Elasticity

The relationship between price and quantity on the demand schedule is given in columns 1 and 2 of panel (a) in Figure 21-3 on the next page. In panel (b), the demand curve, *D*, representing that schedule is drawn. In panel (c), the total revenue curve representing the data in column 3 is drawn. Notice first the level of these curves at small quantities. The demand curve is at a maximum height, but total revenue is zero, which makes sense according to this demand schedule—at a price of 11 cents per minute and above, no units will be purchased, and therefore total revenue will be zero. As price is lowered, we travel down the demand curve, and total revenues increase until price is 6 cents per minute, remain constant from 6 cents to 5 cents per minute, and then fall at lower unit prices. Corresponding to those three sections, demand is elastic, unit-elastic, and inelastic. Hence we have three relationships among the three types of price elasticity and total revenues.

- *Elastic demand.* A negative relationship exists between small changes in price and changes in total revenues. That is to say, if price is lowered, total revenues will rise when the firm faces demand that is elastic, and if it raises price, total revenues will fall. Consider another example. If the price of Diet Coke were raised by 25 percent and the price of all other soft drinks remained constant, the quantity demanded of Diet Coke would probably fall dramatically. The decrease in quantity demanded due to the increase in the price of Diet Coke would lead in this example to a reduction in the total revenues of the Coca-Cola Company. Therefore, if demand is elastic, price and total revenues will move in *opposite* directions.

FIGURE 21-3

The Relationship Between Price Elasticity of Demand and Total Revenues for Cellular Phone Service

In panel (a), we show the elastic, unit-elastic, and inelastic sections of the demand schedule according to whether a reduction in price increases total revenues, causes them to remain constant, or causes them to decrease, respectively. In panel (b), we show these regions graphically on the demand curve. In panel (c), we show them on the total revenue curve.

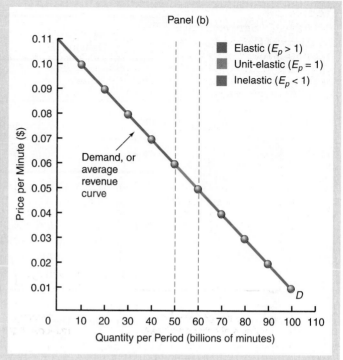

Panel (b)

Elastic ($E_p > 1$)
Unit-elastic ($E_p = 1$)
Inelastic ($E_p < 1$)

Demand, or average revenue curve

Price per Minute ($)
Quantity per Period (billions of minutes)

Panel (a)

(1) Price, P, per Minute of Cellular Phone Service	(2) Quantity Demanded, D (billions of minutes)	(3) Total Revenue ($ billions) = (1) x (2)	(4) Elasticity, $E_p = \dfrac{\text{Change in } Q}{(Q_1 + Q_2)/2} \div \dfrac{\text{Change in } P}{(P_1 + P_2)/2}$
$0.11	0	0	
0.10	10	1.0	21.000
0.09	20	1.8	6.330
0.08	30	2.4	3.400 } Elastic
0.07	40	2.8	2.143
0.06	50	3.0	1.144
0.05	60	3.0	1.000 } Unit-elastic
0.04	70	2.8	.692
0.03	80	2.4	.467 } Inelastic
0.02	90	1.8	.294
0.01	100	1.0	.158

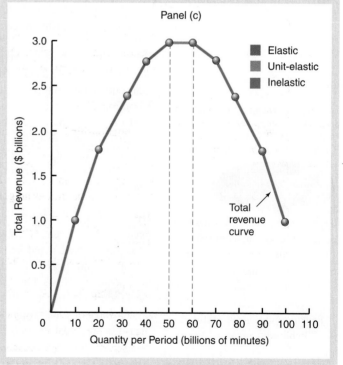

Panel (c)

Elastic
Unit-elastic
Inelastic

Total Revenue ($ billions)

Total revenue curve

Quantity per Period (billions of minutes)

- *Unit-elastic demand.* Changes in price do not change total revenues. When the firm is facing demand that is unit-elastic, if it increases price, total revenues will not change; if it decreases price, total revenues will not change either.

TABLE 21-1
Relationship Between Price Elasticity of Demand and Total Revenues

Price Elasticity of Demand (E_p)		Effect of Price Change on Total Revenues (TR)	
		Price Decrease	Price Increase
Inelastic	($E_p < 1$)	TR ↓	TR ↑
Unit-elastic	($E_p = 1$)	No change in TR	No change in TR
Elastic	($E_p > 1$)	TR ↑	TR ↓

● *Inelastic demand.* A positive relationship exists between changes in price and total revenues. When the firm is facing demand that is inelastic, if it raises price, total revenues will go up; if it lowers price, total revenues will fall. Consider another example. You have just invented a cure for the common cold that has been approved by the Food and Drug Administration for sale to the public. You are not sure what price you should charge, so you start out with a price of $1 per pill. You sell 20 million pills at that price over a year. The next year, you decide to raise the price by 25 percent, to $1.25. The number of pills you sell drops to 18 million per year. The price increase of 25 percent has led to a 10 percent decrease in quantity demanded. Your total revenues, however, will rise to $22.5 million because of the price increase. We therefore conclude that if demand is inelastic, price and total revenues move in the *same* direction.

Graphic Presentaion. The elastic, unit-elastic, and inelastic areas of the demand curve are shown in Figure 21-3 on the previous page. For prices from 11 cents per minute of cellular phone time to 6 cents per minute, as price decreases, total revenues rise from zero to $3 billion. Demand is price-elastic. When price changes from 6 cents to 5 cents, however, total revenues remain constant at $3 billion; demand is unit-elastic. Finally, when price falls from 5 cents to 1 cent, total revenues decrease from $3 billion to $1 billion; demand is inelastic. In panels (b) and (c) of Figure 21-3, we have labeled the sections of the demand curve accordingly, and we have also shown how total revenues first rise, then remain constant, and finally fall.

The Elasticity–Revenue Relationship. The relationship between price elasticity of demand and total revenues brings together some important microeconomic concepts. Total revenues, as we have noted, are the product of price per unit times number of units sold. The law of demand states that along a given demand curve, price and quantity changes will move in opposite directions: One increases as the other decreases. Consequently, what happens to the product of price times quantity depends on which of the opposing changes exerts a greater force on total revenues. But this is just what price elasticity of demand is designed to measure—responsiveness of quantity demanded to a change in price. The relationship between price elasticity of demand and total revenues is summarized in Table 21-1.

Economics Front and Center

To contemplate pricing issues that college textbook publishers face in light of different price elasticities of demand for textbooks in different subject areas, consider the case study, **Elasticities and Revenues in College Textbook Publishing,** on page 511.

CONCEPTS in Brief

● Price elasticity of demand is related to total revenues (and total consumer expenditures).

● When demand is *elastic*, the change in price elicits a change in total revenues in the direction opposite that of the price change.

- When demand is *unit-elastic*, a change in price elicits no change in total revenues (or in total consumer expenditures).

- When demand is *inelastic*, a change in price elicits a change in total revenues (and in consumer expenditures) in the same direction as the price change.

To test your understanding of the concepts covered in this section, go to the Online Review at **www.myeconlab.com/miller.**

DETERMINANTS OF THE PRICE ELASTICITY OF DEMAND

We have learned how to calculate the price elasticity of demand. We know that theoretically it ranges numerically from zero—completely inelastic—to infinity—completely elastic. What we would like to do now is come up with a list of the determinants of the price elasticity of demand. The price elasticity of demand for a particular commodity at any price depends, at a minimum, on the following factors:

- The existence, number, and quality of substitutes
- The percentage of a consumer's total budget devoted to purchases of that commodity
- The length of time allowed for adjustment to changes in the price of the commodity

Existence of Substitutes

The closer the substitutes for a particular commodity and the more substitutes there are, the greater will be its price elasticity of demand. At the limit, if there is a perfect substitute, the elasticity of demand for the commodity will be infinity. Thus even the slightest increase in the commodity's price will cause a significant reduction in the quantity demanded: Quantity demanded will fall to zero. We are really talking about two goods that the consumer believes are exactly alike and equally desirable, like dollar bills whose only difference is their serial numbers. When we talk about less extreme examples, we can speak only in terms of the number and the similarity of substitutes that are available. Thus we will find that the more narrowly we define a good, the closer and greater will be the number of substitutes available. For example, the demand for a Diet Coke may be highly elastic because consumers can switch to Diet Pepsi. The demand for diet drinks in general, however, is relatively less elastic because there are fewer substitutes.

Share of Budget

We know that the greater the share of a person's total budget that is spent on a commodity, the greater that person's price elasticity of demand is for that commodity. The demand for pepper is thought to be very inelastic merely because individuals spend so little on it relative to their total budgets. In contrast, the demand for items such as transportation and housing is thought to be far more elastic because they occupy a large part of people's budgets—changes in their prices cannot be ignored easily without sacrificing a lot of other alternative goods that could be purchased.

Consider a numerical example. A household spends $40,000 a year. It purchases $4 of pepper per year and $4,000 of transportation services. Now consider the spending power of this family when the price of pepper and the price of transportation both double. If the household buys the same amount of pepper, it will now spend $8. It will thus have to reduce other expenditures by $4. This $4 represents only 0.01 percent of the entire household budget. By contrast, a doubling of transportation costs requires that the family spend $8,000, or $4,000 more on transportation, if it is to purchase the same quantity. That increased expenditure on transportation of $4,000 represents 10 percent of total expenditures that must be switched from other purchases. We would therefore predict that the household will react differently to the doubling of prices for pepper than it will for a doubling of transportation prices. It will reduce its transportation purchases by a proportionately greater amount.

Time for Adjustment

When the price of a commodity changes and that price change persists, more people will learn about it. Further, consumers will be better able to revise their consumption patterns the longer the time period they have to do so. And in fact, the longer the time they do take, the less costly it will be for them to engage in this revision of consumption patterns. Consider a price decrease. The longer the price decrease persists, the greater will be the number of new uses that consumers will discover for the particular commodity, and the greater will be the number of new users of that particular commodity.

It is possible to make a very strong statement about the relationship between the price elasticity of demand and the time allowed for adjustment:

> *The longer any price change persists, the greater the elasticity of demand, other things held constant. Elasticity of demand is greater in the long run than in the short run.*

Let's consider an example. Suppose that the price of electricity goes up 50 percent. How do you adjust in the short run? You can turn the lights off more often, you can stop using the stereo as much as you usually do, and so on. Otherwise it's very difficult to cut back on your consumption of electricity. In the long run, though, you can devise methods to reduce your consumption. Instead of using electric heaters, the next time you have a house built you will install gas heaters. Instead of using an electric stove, the next time you move you will have a gas stove installed. You will purchase fluorescent bulbs because they use less electricity. The more time you have to think about it, the more ways you will find to cut your electricity consumption. We would expect, therefore, that the short-run demand curve for electricity would be relatively less elastic (in the price range around P_e), as demonstrated by D_1 in Figure 21-4. However, the long-run demand curve will exhibit more elasticity (in the neighborhood of P_e), as demonstrated by D_3. Indeed, we can think of an entire family of demand curves such as those depicted in the figure. The short-run demand curve is for the period when there is no time for adjustment. As more time is al-

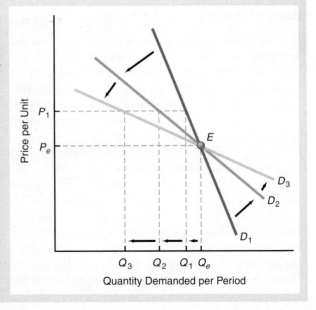

FIGURE 21-4
Short-Run and Long-Run Price Elasticity of Demand
Consider a situation in which the market price is P_e and the quantity demanded is Q_e. Then there is a price increase to P_1. In the short run, as evidenced by the demand curve D_1, we move from equilibrium quantity demanded, Q_e, to Q_1. After more time is allowed for adjustment, the demand curve rotates at original price P_e to D_2. Quantity demanded falls again, now to Q_2 After even more time is allowed for adjustment, the demand curve rotates at price to D_3. At the higher price P_1 in the long run, the quantity demanded falls all the way to Q_3.

lowed, the demand curve goes first to D_2 and then all the way to D_3. Thus, in the neighborhood of P_e, elasticity differs for each of these curves. It is greater for the less steep curves (but slope alone does not measure elasticity for the entire curve).

How to Define the Short Run and the Long Run. We've mentioned the short run and the long run. Is the short run one week, two weeks, one month, two months? Is the long run three years, four years, five years? The answer is that there is no single answer. What we mean by the long run is the period of time necessary for consumers to make a full adjustment to a given price change, all other things held constant. In the case of the demand for electricity, the long run will be however long it takes consumers to switch over to cheaper sources of heating, to buy houses that are more energy-efficient, to purchase appliances that are more energy-efficient, and so on. The long-run elasticity of demand for electricity therefore relates to a period of at least several years. The short run—by default—is any period less than the long run.

E X A M P L E

What Do Real-World Price Elasticities of Demand Look Like?

In Table 21-2, we present demand elasticities for selected goods. None of them is zero, and the largest is 4.6. Remember that even though we are leaving off the negative sign, there is an inverse relationship between price and quantity demanded, and the minus sign is understood. Also remember that these elasticities represent averages over given price ranges. Choosing different price ranges could yield different elasticity estimates for these goods.

Economists have consistently found that estimated price elasticities of demand are greater in the long run than in the short run, as seen in Table 21-2. There you see that all available estimates indicate that the long-run price elasticity of demand for vacation air travel is 2.7, whereas the estimate for the short run is 1.1. Throughout the table, you see that all estimates of long-run price elasticities of demand exceed their short-run counterparts.

For Critical Analysis
Explain the intuitive reasoning behind the difference between long-run and short-run price elasticity of demand.

TABLE 21-2
Price Elasticities of Demand for Selected Goods
Here are estimated demand elasticities for selected goods. All of them are negative, although we omit the minus sign. We have given some estimates of the long-run price elasticities of demand. The long run is associated with the time necessary for consumers to adjust fully to any given price change. (Note: "N.A." indicates that no estimate is available.)

| | Estimated Elasticity | |
Category	Short Run	Long Run
Air travel (business)	0.4	1.2
Air travel (vacation)	1.1	2.7
Beef	0.6	N.A.
Cheese	0.3	N.A.
Electricity	0.1	1.7
Fresh tomatoes	4.6	N.A.
Gasoline	0.2	0.5
Hospital services	0.1	0.7
Intercity bus service	0.6	2.2
Physician services	0.1	0.6
Private education	1.1	1.9
Restaurant meals	2.3	N.A.
Tires	0.9	1.2

CROSS PRICE ELASTICITY OF DEMAND

In Chapter 3, we discussed the effect of a change in the price of one good on the demand for a related good. We defined substitutes and complements in terms of whether a reduction in the price of one caused a decrease or an increase, respectively, in the demand for the other. If the price of compact discs is held constant, the number of CDs purchased (at any price) will certainly be influenced by the price of a close substitute such as audiocassettes. If the price of stereo speakers is held constant, the amount of stereo speakers demanded (at any price) will certainly be affected by changes in the price of stereo amplifiers.

Cross price elasticity of demand (E_{xy})
The percentage change in the demand for one good (holding its price constant) divided by the percentage change in the price of a related good.

What we now need to do is come up with a numerical measure of the price responsiveness of demand to the prices of related goods. This is called the **cross price elasticity of demand (E_{xy}),** which is defined as the percentage change in the demand for one good (a shift in the demand curve) divided by the percentage change in the price of the related good. In equation form, the cross price elasticity of demand for good X with good Y is

$$E_{xy} = \frac{\text{percentage change in demand for good X}}{\text{percentage change in price of good Y}}$$

Alternatively, the cross price elasticity of demand for good Y with good X would use the percentage change in the demand for good Y as the numerator and the percentage change in the price of good X as the denominator.

When two goods are substitutes, the cross price elasticity of demand will be positive. For example, when the price of zip disks goes up, the demand for rewritable CDs will rise too as consumers shift away from the now relatively more expensive zip disks to rewritable CDs. A producer of rewritable CDs could benefit from a numerical estimate of the cross price elasticity of demand between zip disks and rewritable CDs. For example, if the price of zip disks went up by 10 percent and the producer of rewritable CDs knew that the cross price elasticity of demand was 1, the CD producer could estimate that the demand for rewritable CDs would also go up by 10 percent at any given price. Plans for increasing production of rewritable CDs could then be made.

When two related goods are complements, the cross price elasticity of demand will be negative (and we will *not* disregard the minus sign). For example, when the price of personal computers declines, the demand for computer printers will rise. This is because as prices of computers decrease, the number of printers purchased at any given price of printers will naturally increase, because computers and printers are often used together. Any manufacturer of computer printers must take this into account in making production plans.

If goods are completely unrelated, their cross price elasticity of demand will, by definition, be zero.

To most people, backyard telescopes are all pretty much the same, but we might anticipate that certain telescopes are not close substitutes to serious astronomy enthusiasts. How could estimated cross price elasticities of demand for telescopes sold in Internet auctions be used to verify this expectation?

E-Commerce EXAMPLE

The Cross Price Elasticity of Demand for Telescopes in Online Auctions

Two economists at the U.S. Federal Trade Commission, Christopher Adams and Laura Bivins, used data from tele- scope auctions conducted on eBay's Web site to study the elasticity of demand for telescopes. They recorded prices and quantities demanded in 58 online auctions of telescopes with $3\frac{1}{2}$-inch, 5-inch, and 8-inch diameter mirrors. They found that the cross price elasticity of demand for telescopes with $3\frac{1}{2}$-inch and 5-inch diameter mirrors was equal to 13.33. In contrast, the cross price elasticities of demand for telescopes with $3\frac{1}{2}$-inch and 8-inch diameter mirrors and for telescopes with 5-inch and 8-inch diameter mirrors were equal to zero. The authors concluded, therefore, that telescopes with $3\frac{1}{2}$-inch and 5-inch diameter mirrors are substi-tutes, but that neither the $3\frac{1}{2}$-inch telescope nor the 5-inch telescope is a substitute for the 8-inch telescope.

For Critical Analysis
According to the authors' estimates, how will the demand for telescopes with $3\frac{1}{2}$-inch diameter mirrors change if there is a 1 percent decrease in the price of telescopes with 5-inch diameter mirrors?

INCOME ELASTICITY OF DEMAND

In Chapter 3, we discussed the determinants of demand. One of those determinants was in-come. Briefly, we can apply our understanding of elasticity to the relationship between changes in income and changes in demand. We measure the responsiveness of quantity purchased to income changes by the **income elasticity of demand (E_i):**

$$E_i = \frac{\text{percentage change in demand}}{\text{percentage change in income}}$$

holding relative price constant.

Income elasticity of demand (E_i)
The percentage change in demand for any good, holding its price constant, divided by the percentage change in income; the responsiveness of demand to changes in income, holding the good's relative price constant.

Income elasticity of demand refers to a *horizontal shift* in the demand curve in response to changes in income, whereas price elasticity of demand refers to a *movement along* the curve in response to price changes. Thus income elasticity of demand is calculated at a given price, and price elasticity of demand is calculated at a given income.

A simple example will demonstrate how income elasticity of demand can be computed. Table 21-3 gives the relevant data. The product in question is prerecorded DVDs. We as-sume that the price of DVDs remains constant relative to other prices. In period 1, six DVDs per month are purchased. Income per month is $4,000. In period 2, monthly income increases to $6,000, and the number of DVDs demanded per month increases to eight. We can apply the following calculation:

$$E_i = \frac{(8 - 6)/6}{(\$6,000 - \$4,000)/\$4,000} = \frac{1/3}{1/2} = \frac{2}{3} = 0.667$$

Hence measured income elasticity of demand for DVDs for the individual represented in this example is 0.667. Note that this holds only for the move from six DVDs to eight DVDs purchased per month. If the situation were reversed, with income decreasing from

Period	Number of DVDs Demanded per Month	Income per Month
1	6	$4,000
2	8	6,000

TABLE 21-3
How Income Affects Quantity of DVDs Demanded

$6,000 to $4,000 per month and DVDs purchased dropping from eight to six DVDs per month, the calculation becomes

$$E_i = \frac{(6 - 8)/8}{(\$4,000 - \$6,000)/\$6,000} = \frac{-2/8}{-1/3} = \frac{-1/4}{-1/3} = \frac{3}{4} = 0.75$$

In this case, the measured income elasticity of demand is equal to 0.75.

What can we infer from the fact that the income elasticity of demand for margarine is negative?

EXAMPLE

When Incomes Rise, It's Easier to Believe Margarine Isn't Butter

The U.S. Department of Agriculture regularly estimates income elasticities of demand for a wide variety of farm products. Among these are dairy products, such as butter, which has an estimated income elasticity of demand equal to 0.12. Thus, when consumers' incomes increase by 1 percent, their consumption of butter rises by 0.12 percent.

In contrast, the estimated income elasticity of demand for margarine is about −0.19, so a 1 percent increase in income induces consumers to *reduce* their consumption of margarine

by 0.19 percent. The fact that an income increase generates a decline in purchases of margarine means that margarine is an *inferior good.* Other things being equal, the demand for margarine declines as consumers' incomes rise.

For Critical Analysis
Can you think of any other item that might have a negative income elasticity of demand?

To get the same income elasticity of demand over the same range of values regardless of the direction of change (increase or decrease), we can use the same formula that we used in computing the price elasticity of demand. When doing so, we have

$$E_i = \frac{\text{change in quantity}}{\text{sum of quanties}/2} \div \frac{\text{change in income}}{\text{sum of incomes}/2}$$

You have just been introduced to three types of elasticities. All three elasticities are important in influencing the consumption of most goods. Reasonably accurate estimates of these elasticities can go a long way toward making accurate forecasts of demand for goods or services.

CONCEPTS in Brief

- Some determinants of price elasticity of demand are (1) the existence, number, and quality of substitutes; (2) the share of the total budget spent on the good in question; and (3) the length of time allowed for adjustment to a change in prices.

- Cross price elasticity of demand measures one good's demand responsiveness to another's price changes. For substitutes, it is positive; for complements, it is negative.

- Income elasticity of demand tells you by what percentage demand will change for a particular percentage change in income.

To test your understanding of the concepts covered in this section, go to the Online Review at **www.myeconlab.com/miller.**

ELASTICITY OF SUPPLY

The **price elasticity of supply** (E_s) is defined similarly to the price elasticity of demand. Supply elasticities are generally positive; this is because at higher prices, larger quantities will generally be forthcoming from suppliers. The definition of the price elasticity of supply is as follows:

$$E_s = \frac{\text{percentage change in quantity supplied}}{\text{percentage change in price}}$$

Classifying Supply Elasticities

Just as with demand, there are different ranges of supply elasticities. They are similar in definition to the ranges of demand elasticities.

If a 1 percent increase in price elicits a greater than 1 percent increase in the quantity supplied, we say that at the particular price in question on the supply schedule, *supply is elastic*. The most extreme elastic supply is called **perfectly elastic supply**—the slightest reduction in price will cause quantity supplied to fall to zero.

If, conversely, a 1 percent increase in price elicits a less than 1 percent increase in the quantity supplied, we refer to that as an *inelastic supply*. The most extreme inelastic supply is called **perfectly inelastic supply**—no matter what the price, the quantity supplied remains the same.

If the percentage change in the quantity supplied is just equal to the percentage change in the price, we call this *unit-elastic supply*.

Figure 21-5 shows two supply schedules, S and S'. You can tell at a glance, even without reading the labels, which one is perfectly elastic and which one is perfectly inelastic. As you might expect, most supply schedules exhibit elasticities that are somewhere between zero and infinity.

Price Elasticity of Supply and Length of Time for Adjustment

We pointed out earlier that the longer the time period allowed for adjustment, the greater the price elasticity of demand. It turns out that the same proposition applies to supply. The longer the time for adjustment, the more elastic the supply curve. Consider why this is true:

Price elasticity of supply (E_s)
The responsiveness of the quantity supplied of a commodity to a change in its price; the percentage change in quantity supplied divided by the percentage change in price.

Perfectly elastic supply
A supply characterized by a reduction in quantity supplied to zero when there is the slightest decrease in price.

Perfectly inelastic supply
A supply for which quantity supplied remains constant, no matter what happens to price.

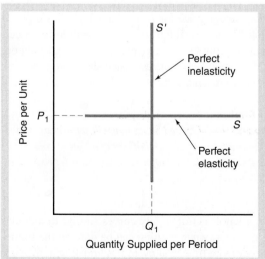

FIGURE 21-5
The Extremes in Supply Curves
Here we have drawn two extremes of supply schedules; S is a perfectly elastic supply curve; S' is a perfectly inelastic one. In the former, an unlimited quantity will be supplied at price P_1. In the latter, no matter what the price, the quantity supplied will be Q_1. An example of S' might be the supply curve for fresh (unfrozen) fish on the morning the boats come in.

1. The longer the time allowed for adjustment, the more resources can flow into (or out of) an industry through expansion (or contraction) of existing firms. As an example, suppose that there is a long-lasting, significant increase in the demand for gasoline. The result is a sustained rise in the market price of gasoline. Initially, gasoline refiners will not be able to expand their production with the operating refining equipment available to them. Over time, however, some refining companies might be able to recondition old equipment that had fallen into disuse. They can also place orders for construction of new gasoline-refining equipment, and once the equipment arrives, they can also put it into place to expand their gasoline production. Given sufficient time, therefore, existing gasoline refiners can eventually respond to higher gasoline prices by adding new refining operations.

2. The longer the time allowed for adjustment, the entry (or exit) of firms increases (or decreases) production in an industry. Consider what happens if the price of gasoline remains higher than before as a result of a sustained rise in gasoline demand. Even as existing refiners add to their capability to produce gasoline by retooling old equipment, purchasing new equipment, and adding new refining facilities, additional businesses may seek to earn profits at the now-higher gasoline prices. Over time, the entry of new gasoline-refining companies adds to the productive capabilities of the entire refining industry, and the quantity of gasoline supplied increases.

We therefore talk about short-run and long-run price elasticities of supply. The short run is defined as the time period during which full adjustment has not yet taken place. The long run is the time period during which firms have been able to adjust fully to the change in price.

What do you suppose was the proportionate response in the quantity of truffles supplied by French farmers to a 30 percent drop in price?

International EXAMPLE

French Truffle Production Takes a Nosedive

Some of the best truffles in the world come from the seven *départements* (counties) in the middle of France that make up the Périgord region. Black truffles are often called "black diamonds" because they are so expensive and also because they have a faceted skin. Their official name is *Tuber melanosporum*. Ranging in size from as small as a hazelnut to as large as a baseball, truffles are sliced fine and used in cooking as a pungent addition to many refined dishes. Their prices range from $250 to $500 a pound wholesale to as much as $1,000 a pound retail. Yet things are not well in the French truffle industry. The Chinese have started exporting their version of truffles, considered inferior by the French but popular nonetheless in the open market. A few years ago, the average price for French-grown truffles dropped by 30 percent. Many French farmers, fed up with lower prices, simply gave up on truffles. French production subsequently decreased by 25 percent. Hence the estimated short-run price elasticity of supply of French truffles was 0.83. (Why?)

For Critical Analysis
There is a company in the United States that will sell you trees inoculated with the truffle organism so that you can "grow your own." How will this affect the price of truffles and thus French production?

A Graphic Presentation. We can show a whole set of supply curves similar to the ones we generated for demand. As Figure 21-6 shows, when nothing can be done in the immediate run, the supply curve is vertical, S_1. As more time is allowed for adjustment, the supply curve rotates to S_2 and then to S_3, becoming more elastic as it rotates.

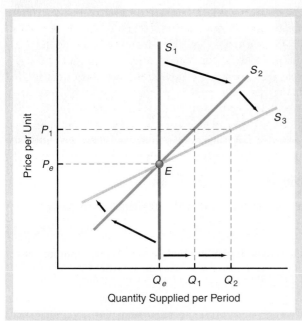

FIGURE 21-6
Short-Run and Long-Run Price Elasticity of Supply
Consider a situation in which the price is P_e and the quantity supplied is Q_e. In the immediate run, we hypothesize a vertical supply curve, S_1. With the price increase to P_1, therefore, there will be no change in the short run in quantity supplied; it will remain at Q_e. Given some time for adjustment, the supply curve will rotate to S_2. The new amount supplied will increase to Q_1. The long-run supply curve is shown by S_3. The amount supplied again increases to Q_2.

CONCEPTS in Brief

- Price elasticity of supply is calculated by dividing the percentage change in quantity supplied by the percentage change in price.

- Usually, price elasticities of supply are positive—higher prices yield larger quantities supplied.

- Long-run supply curves are more elastic than short-run supply curves because the longer the time allowed, the more resources can flow into or out of an industry when price changes.

To test your understanding of the concepts covered in this section, go to the Online Review at www.myeconlab.com/miller.

CASE STUDY : Economics Front and Center

Elasticities and Revenues in College Textbook Publishing

Donovan recently landed a position as a marketing researcher with a textbook publishing company. Her first assignment is to review the company's textbook prices and recommend price adjustments aimed at increasing the firm's total revenues. After spending a few days studying current conditions in the textbook market, Donovan is convinced that the company should consider price adjustments for most of its books.

As Donovan reads a recent research report prepared by the company's marketing staff, she jots down the following estimated price elasticities of demand for texts in various subjects: Accounting: 0.61; American History: 1.23; Astronomy: 0.55; Chemistry: 0.76; Economics: 0.99; French Literature: 1.32; Ger-

man Language: 0.92; Psychology: 1.01; and Trigonometry: 0.28. It is clear, she concludes, that price changes in most subjects will boost the company's revenues. Now it is time to write a report making specific recommendations.

Points to Analyze

1. *For which subjects is textbook demand inelastic? For which subjects is textbook demand elastic?*

2. *For which textbook subjects should Donovan recommend price increases? For which should she recommend price decreases? Are there any subjects for which textbook price changes are unlikely to have much of an effect on total revenues?*

The Inelastic Demand for Health Care—With One Striking Exception

A s we all know, both physical and mental health contribute to overall life satisfaction. One consequence is that U.S. residents purchase significant amounts of health care services. Today, U.S consumers allocate about 15 percent of their total income to health care expenditures each year. Another consequence is that the demands for many—but not all—health care services and products are very inelastic.

Concepts Applied

- Price Elasticity of Demand
- Inelastic Demand
- Elastic Demand

Inelastic Demands for Most Health Care Services and Products

Figure 21-7 displays estimated price elasticities of demand for various types of health care services and products. Each price elasticity estimate gives the proportionate response of quantity demanded to a proportionate change in the out-of-pocket price paid by consumers.

Although an individual can purchase tests to evaluate certain physical conditions, such as pregnancy, in many instances a person who experiences physical symptoms and wishes to obtain a diagnosis must visit a physician. Likewise, an individ-

ual with a condition requiring surgery normally has few alternatives to outpatient or inpatient hospital services. Hence, it is not surprising that the price elasticities of demand for physician and hospital services reported in Figure 21-7 are very low.

For conditions not requiring surgeries or other hospital-provided treatments, drugs are a commonly prescribed treatment. This is particularly true of internal illnesses affecting the cardiovascular system or organs such as the lungs or stomach. For problems ranging from high blood pressure to allergies and digestive disorders, there often are few close substitutes for medications. This is why the price elasticity of demand for prescription drugs has been so low.

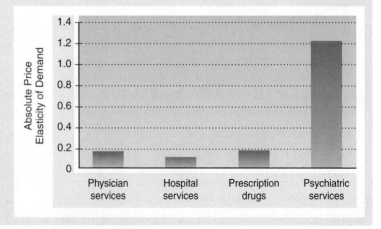

FIGURE 21-7
Estimated Price Elasticities of Demand for Selected Health Care Services and Products
These elasticity estimates apply to the response of quantity demanded to a change in the out-of-pocket prices paid by consumers of health care services and products. The estimated price elasticity of demand for psychiatric services is much higher than for other health care services and products.

Source: U.S. Department of Health and Human Services.

The Notable Exception: Psychiatric Services

What clearly stands out in Figure 21-7 is the estimated price elasticity of demand for psychiatric services. This price elasticity is more than six times greater than the next-highest price elasticity in the figure, which is the price elasticity of demand for prescription drugs. A 1 percent increase in the price of a unit of psychiatric services, therefore, causes a percentage decrease in quantity demanded that is more than six times larger than the percentage decrease in the quantity of prescription drugs demanded resulting from a 1 percent rise in drug prices.

Why is the demand for psychiatric services so much more elastic than the demands for other health care services and products? The answer is that people who experience many mental health problems, such as anxiety and depression, can choose from a relatively large range of strategies for diagnosis and treatment. In lieu of visiting a psychiatrist, for instance, an individual experiencing a mood disorder can instead seek a diagnosis from a physician, who may be able to prescribe medications to treat physically based elements of the problem. Alternatively, the individual may be able to seek help from psychologists, social workers, or family counselors. Because people have more substitutes for psychiatric services, the price elasticity of demand for these services is much higher.

For Critical Analysis

1. What would happen to the price elasticity of demand for psychiatric services if a law was enacted permitting only qualified psychiatrists to prescribe psychiatric medications?
2. Based on the elasticity estimates reported in Figure 21-7, if the market prices of 30-minute office visits for physicians and psychiatrists both increase by the same percentage this year, will the revenues earned by each type of health care provider rise or fall, other things being equal?

Web Resources

1. For information about economic issues facing physicians, go to the American Medical Association's home page via www.econtoday.com/chap21.
2. To see how the American Psychiatric Association seeks to influence the economic and legal environment its members face, go to the link at www.econtoday.com/chap21, and click on "Advocacy Action Center."

Research Project

Suppose that a state government currently exempts all health care services from taxes, but it is considering applying special excise taxes to all services provided by physicians and psychiatrists. If the state were to impose a $1 excise tax on each 30-minute time period that a patient spends with each type of health care professional, would the providers or their patients end up paying most of the tax? Explain your reasoning for each type of health care provider. [Hint: Recall that the supply curve for each health care service shifts up along each demand curve by the amount of the $1 excise tax.]

SUMMARY DISCUSSION of Learning Objectives

1. **Expressing and Calculating the Price Elasticity of Demand:** The price elasticity of demand is the responsiveness of the quantity demanded of a good to a change in the price of the good. It is the percentage change in quantity demanded divided by the percentage change in price. To calculate the price elasticity of demand for relatively small changes in price, the percentage change in quantity demanded is equal to the change in the quantity resulting from a price change divided by the average of the initial and final quantities, and the percentage change

in price is equal to the price change divided by the average of the initial and final prices.

2. **The Relationship Between the Price Elasticity of Demand and Total Revenues:** Demand is elastic when the price elasticity of demand exceeds 1, and over the elastic range of a demand curve, an increase in price reduces total revenues. Demand is inelastic when the price elasticity of demand is less than 1, and over this range of a demand curve, an increase in price raises total revenues.

Finally, demand is unit-elastic when the price elasticity of demand equals 1, and over this range of a demand curve, an increase in price does not affect total revenues.

3. **Factors That Determine the Price Elasticity of Demand:** Three factors affect the price elasticity of demand. If there are more close substitutes for a good, the price elasticity of demand increases. The price elasticity of demand for a good also tends to be higher when a larger portion of a person's budget is spent on the good. In addition, if people have a longer period of time to adjust to a price change and change their consumption patterns, the price elasticity of demand tends to be higher.

4. **The Cross Price Elasticity of Demand and Using It to Determine Whether Two Goods Are Substitutes or Complements:** The cross price elasticity of demand for a good is the percentage change in the demand for that good divided by the percentage change in the price of a related good. If two goods are substitutes in consumption, an increase in the price of one of the goods induces an increase in the demand for the other good, so that the cross price elasticity of demand is positive. In contrast, if two goods are complements in consumption, an increase in the price of one of the goods brings about a decrease in the demand for the other good, so that the cross price elasticity of demand is negative.

5. **The Income Elasticity of Demand:** The income elasticity of demand for any good is the responsiveness of the demand for the good to a change in income, holding the good's relative price unchanged. It is equal to the percentage change in demand for the good divided by the percentage change in income.

6. **Classifying Supply Elasticities and How the Length of Time for Adjustment Affects the Price Elasticity of Supply:** The price elasticity of supply is equal to the percentage change in quantity supplied divided by the percentage change in price. If the price elasticity of supply is greater than 1, supply is elastic, and if the price elasticity of supply is less than 1, supply is inelastic. Supply is unit-elastic if the price elasticity of supply equals 1. Supply is more likely to be elastic when sellers have more time to adjust to price changes. One reason for this is that the more time sellers have to adjust, the more resources can flow into (or out of) an industry via expansion (or contraction) of firms. Another reason is that the longer the time allowed for adjustment, the entry (or exit) of firms increases (or decreases) production in response to a price increase (or decrease).

KEY TERMS AND CONCEPTS

cross price elasticity of demand (E_{xy}) (506)

elastic demand (497)

income elasticity of demand (E_i) (507)

inelastic demand (498)

perfectly elastic demand (498)

perfectly elastic supply (509)

perfectly inelastic demand (498)

perfectly inelastic supply (509)

price elasticity of demand (E_p) (495)

price elasticity of supply (E_s) (509)

unit elasticity of demand (498)

PROBLEMS

Answers to the odd-numbered problems appear at the back of the book.

21-1. A student organization finds that when it prices shirts emblazoned with the college logo at $10, the organization sells 150 per week. When the price is reduced to $9, the organization sells 200 per week. Based on this information, calculate the price elasticity of demand for logo-emblazoned shirts.

21-2. Table 21-2 on page 505 indicates that the short-run price elasticity of demand for tires is 0.9. If a tire store raises the price of a tire from $50 to $60, by

what percentage should it expect the quantity of tires sold to change?

21-3. When Joe's Campus Grill priced its famous hamburgers at $1, it sold 200 a week. When the price was $2, Joe's sold only 100 a week. What is the price elasticity of demand for Joe's hamburgers? Is demand elastic, unit-elastic, or inelastic?

21-4. In a local market, the monthly price of Internet access service decreases from $20 to $10, and the total quantity of monthly accounts across all Internet access providers increases from 100,000 to 200,000. What is the price elasticity of demand? Is demand elastic, unit-elastic, or inelastic?

21-5. At a price of $17.50 to play 18 holes on a golf course, 120 consumers pay to play a game of golf each day. Increasing the price to $22.50 causes the number of consumers to decline to 80. What is the price elasticity of demand? Is demand elastic, unit-elastic, or inelastic?

21-6. It is very difficult to find goods with perfectly elastic or perfectly inelastic demand. We can, however, find goods that lie near these extremes. Characterize demands for the following goods as being near perfectly elastic or near perfectly inelastic.

    a. Corn grown and harvested by a small farmer in Iowa
    b. Heroin for a drug addict
    c. Water for a desert hiker
    d. One of several optional textbooks in a pass-fail course.

21-7. A craftsman who makes guitars by hand finds that when he prices his guitars at $800, his annual revenue is $64,000. When he prices his guitars at $700, his annual revenue is $63,000. Over this range of guitar prices, does the craftsman face elastic, unit-elastic, or inelastic demand?

21-8. Suppose that over a range of prices, the price elasticity of demand varies from 15.0 to 2.5. Over another range of prices, price elasticity of demand varies from 1.5 to 0.75. What can you say about total revenue and the total revenue curve over these two ranges of the demand curve as price falls?

21-9. Based on the information provided alone, characterize the demands for the following goods as being more elastic or more inelastic.

    a. A 45-cent box of salt that you buy once a year
    b. A type of high-powered ski boat that you can rent from any one of a number of rental agencies
    c. A specific brand of bottled water
    d. Automobile insurance in a state that requires autos to be insured but has few insurance companies
    e. A 75-cent guitar pick for the lead guitarist of a major rock band

21-10. The value of cross price elasticity of demand between goods X and Y is 1.25, while the cross price elasticity of demand between goods X and Z is −2.0. Characterize X and Y and X and Z as substitutes or complements.

21-11. Suppose that the cross price elasticity of demand between eggs and bacon is −0.5. What would you expect to happen to the sales of bacon if the price of eggs rises by 10 percent?

21-12. Assume that the income elasticity of demand for hot dogs is −1.25 and that the income elasticity of demand for lobster is 1.25. Explain why the measure for hot dogs is negative while that for lobster is positive. Based on this information alone, are these normal or inferior goods? (Hint: You may want to refer to the discussion of normal and inferior goods in Chapter 3.)

21-13. At a price of $25,000, producers of midsized automobiles are willing to manufacture and sell 75,000 cars per month. At a price of $35,000, they are willing to produce and sell 125,000 a month. Using the same type of calculation method used to compute the price elasticity of demand, what is the price elasticity of supply? Is supply elastic, unit-elastic, or inelastic?

21-14. The price elasticity of supply of a basic commodity that a nation produces domestically and that it also imports is 2. What would you expect to happen to the volume of imports if the price of this commodity rises by 10 percent?

21-15. A 20 percent increase in the price of skis induces ski manufacturers to increase production of skis by 10 percent in the short run. In the long run, other things being equal, the 20 percent price increase generates a production increase of 40 percent. What is the short-run price elasticity of supply? What is the long-run price elasticity of supply?

21-16. An increase in the market price of men's haircuts, from $15 per haircut to $25 per haircut, initially causes a local barbershop to have its employees work overtime to increase the number of daily haircuts provided from 35 to 45. When the $25 market price remains unchanged for several weeks and all other things remain equal as well, the barbershop hires additional employees and provides 65 haircuts per day. What is the short-run price elasticity of supply? What is the long-run price elasticity of supply?

ECONOMICS ON THE NET

Price Elasticity and Consumption of Illegal Drugs Making the use of certain drugs illegal drives up their market prices, so the price elasticity of demand is a key factor affecting the use of illegal drugs. This application applies concepts from this chapter to analyze how price elasticity of demand affects drug consumption.

Title: The Demand for Illicit Drugs

Navigation: Go to www.econtoday.com/chap21, and follow the link to the summary of this paper published by the National Bureau of Economic Research.

Application Read the summary of the results of this study of price elasticities of participation in use of illegal drugs, and answer the following questions.

1. Based on the results of the study, is the demand for cocaine more or less price elastic than the demand for heroin? For which drug, therefore, will quantity demanded fall by a greater percentage in response to a proportionate increase in price?

2. The study finds that decriminalizing currently illegal drugs would bring about sizable increases both in overall consumption of heroin and cocaine and in the price elasticity of demand for both drugs. Why do you suppose that the price elasticity of demand would rise? (Hint: At present, users of cocaine and heroin are restricted to only a few illegal sources of the drugs, but if the drugs could legally be produced and sold there would be many more suppliers providing a variety of different types of both drugs.)

For Group Study and Analysis Discuss ways that government officials might use information about the price elasticities of demand for illicit drugs to assist in developing policies intended to reduce the use of these drugs. Which of these proposed policies might prove most effective? Why?

Media Resources

If your exam were tomorrow, would you be ready? For each chapter, MyEconLab Practice Tests and Study Plans pinpoint which sections you have mastered and which ones you need to study. That way, you are more efficient with your study time, and you are better prepared for your exams.

In addition to Practice Tests and your personalized Study Plan, you'll find the following media resources in MyEcon-Lab:

1. *Graphs in Motion* animation of Figures 21-1, 21-2, 21-4, and 21-6.
2. An *Economics in Motion* in-depth animation of the Price Elasticity of Demand.
3. Videos featuring the author, Roger LeRoy Miller, on the following subjects:
   - The Determinants of the Price Elasticity of Demand
   - Cross Price Elasticity of Demand
   - Income Elasticity of Demand

4. Links to the Web sites cited in the marginal Internet Resources, Issues and Applications feature, and Economics on the Net activity.
5. Audio clips of all key terms, additional practice problems, and a PDF version of the material from the print Study Guide.
6. eThemes of the Times, which is a New York Times article to help you understand the real-world applications of what you are learning.

Get Ahead of the Curve

To see how it works, turn to page 16 and then go to www.myeconlab.com/miller.

Chapter 22

Rents, Profits, and the Financial Environment of Business

Since 2000, annual inflation rates in the United States, Hungary, and Brazil have averaged 1.8 percent, 6.9 percent, and 8.7 percent, respectively. For savings accounts, bonds, or other financial assets, the inflation-adjusted interest rate that a person receives ultimately will depend on what the inflation rate turns out to be. Holding assets that all have about the same risk, such as nearly risk-free government securities, generates very different inflation-adjusted rates of return in these three nations. One important exception in the United States is *Treasury Inflation-Protection Securities*, or *TIPS*, which provide a fixed inflation-adjusted return. This chapter will help you understand why investors have recently started holding more TIPS.

LEARNING OBJECTIVES

After reading this chapter, you should be able to:

1. Understand the concept of economic rent
2. Distinguish among the main organizational forms of business and explain the chief advantages and disadvantages of each
3. Explain the difference between accounting profits and economic profits
4. Discuss how the interest rate performs a key role in allocating resources
5. Calculate the present discounted value of a payment to be received at a future date
6. Identify the three main sources of corporate funds and differentiate between stocks and bonds

Media Resources

Refer to the end of the chapter for a full listing of the multimedia learning materials available in MyEconLab.

Did You Know That ...the world's first bonds with inflation-adjusted returns were issued by the Commonwealth of Massachusetts during the Revolutionary War? In 1780, the Massachusetts government created the bonds in response to severe wartime inflation, which was eroding the purchasing power of the earnings of Massachusetts soldiers serving in the colonial army. The commonwealth issued the bonds, which it called "depreciation notes," to its soldiers as deferred compensation for their service.

Bonds offering fixed inflation-adjusted rates of return are now commonplace, although they are no longer given to soldiers to supplement their regular pay. In addition to the U.S. Treasury, governments of numerous countries issue these bonds to investors who desire to protect the interest payments they receive from the effects of inflation. Increasingly, profit-seeking private companies, such as SLM Corporation, Merrill Lynch, Morgan Stanley, and Bear Stearns, also offer inflation-indexed bonds. Why do some investors desire to hold these bonds? Indeed, why do governments and businesses issue interest-bearing bonds at all? Before we can consider these questions, you must first learn about the important economic functions of rents, profits, and interest.

RENT

Economic rent
A payment for the use of any resource over and above its opportunity cost.

When you hear the term *rent,* you are accustomed to having it mean the payment made to property owners for the use of land or dwellings. The term *rent* has a different meaning in economics. **Economic rent** is payment to the owner of a resource in excess of its opportunity cost—the minimum payment that would be necessary to call forth production of that amount of the resource.

Determining Land Rent

Economists originally used the term *rent* to designate payment for the use of land. What was thought to be important about land was that its supply is completely inelastic. That is, the supply curve for land was thought to be a vertical line, so that no matter what the prevailing market price for land, the quantity supplied would remain the same.

The concept of economic rent is associated with the British economist David Ricardo (1772–1823). Here is how Ricardo analyzed economic rent for land. He first simplified his model by assuming that all land is equally productive. Then Ricardo assumed that the quantity of land in a country is *fixed*. Graphically, then, in terms of supply and demand, we draw the supply curve for land vertically (zero price elasticity). In Figure 22-1, the supply curve for land is represented by S. If the demand curve is D_1, it intersects the supply curve, S, at price P_1. The entire amount of revenues obtained, $P_1 \times Q_1$, is labeled "Economic rent." If the demand for land increases to D_2, the equilibrium price will rise to P_2. Additions to economic rent are labeled "More economic rent." Notice that the quantity of land remains insensitive to the change in price. Another way of stating this is that the supply curve is perfectly inelastic.

Economic Rent to Labor

Land and natural resources are not the only factors of production to which the analysis of economic rent can be applied. In fact, the analysis is probably more often applicable to labor. Here is a list of people who provide different labor services, some of whom probably receive large amounts of economic rent:

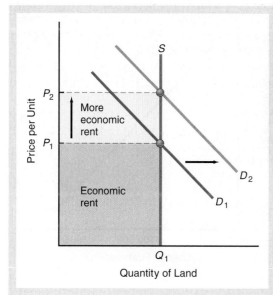

FIGURE 22-1
Economic Rent

If indeed the supply curve of land were completely price-inelastic in the long run, it would be depicted by S. At the quantity in existence, Q_1, any and all revenues are economic rent. If demand is D_1, the price will be P_1; if demand is D_2, price will rise to P_2. Economic rent would be $P_1 \times Q_1$, and $P_2 \times Q_1$, respectively.

- Professional sports superstars
- Rock stars
- Movie stars
- World-class models
- Successful inventors and innovators
- World-famous opera stars

Just apply the definition of economic rent to the phenomenal earnings that these people make. They would undoubtedly work for much, much less than they earn. Therefore, much of their earnings constitutes economic rent (but not all, as we shall see). Economic rent occurs because specific resources cannot be replicated exactly. No one can duplicate today's most highly paid entertainment figures, and therefore they receive economic rent.

Economic Rent and the Allocation of Resources

If a highly paid movie star would make the same number of movies at half his or her current annual earnings, does that mean that 50 percent of his or her income is unnecessary? To evaluate the question, consider first why the superstar gets such a high income. The answer can be found in Figure 22-1. Substitute *entertainment activities of the superstars* for the word *land*. The high "price" received by the superstar is due to the demand for his or her services. If Halle Berry announces that she will work for a measly $1 million a movie and do two movies a year, how is she going to know which production company values her services the most highly? Roberts and other movie stars let the market decide where their resources should be used. In this sense, we can say the following:

Economic rent allocates resources to their highest-valued use.

Otherwise stated, economic rent directs resources to the people who can use them most efficiently.

A common counterexample involves rock stars who claim that promoters try to overprice their tickets. Suppose that an artist agrees to perform, say, five concerts with all tickets being sold at the same price, $55. Assume that the star performs these concerts in halls with 20,000 seats. A total of 100,000 individuals per year will be able to see this particular performer. This is represented by point *A* in Figure 22-2 on the next page. By assumption,

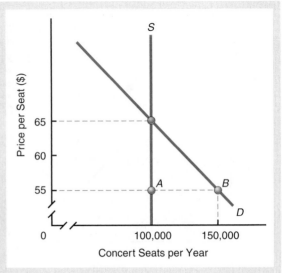

FIGURE 22-2
The Allocative Function of Rent

If the performer agrees to give five concerts a year "at any price" and there are 20,000 seats in each concert hall, the supply curve of concerts, S, is vertical at 100,000 seats per year. The demand curve is given by D. The performer wants a price of only $55 to be charged. At that price, the quantity of seats demanded per year is 150,000. The excess quantity demanded is equal to the horizontal distance between points A and B, or 50,000 seats per year.

this performer is still receiving some economic rent because the supply curve of concerts is vertical at 100,000 seats per year. At a price per ticket of $55, however, the annual quantity of seats demanded will be 150,000, represented by point *B*. The difference between points *A* and *B* is the excess quantity of tickets demanded at the below-market-clearing price of $55 a seat. The *additional* economic rent that could be earned by this performer by charging the clearing price of $65 per seat in this graph would serve as the rationing device that would make the quantity demanded equal to the quantity supplied.

If the tickets are sold at only $55, part of the economic rent that could have been earned is dissipated—it is captured, for example, by radio station owners in the form of promotional gains when they are allowed to give away a certain number of tickets on the air (even if they have to pay $55 per ticket) because the tickets are worth $65. Ticket holders who resell tickets at higher prices ("scalpers") also capture part of the rent. Conceivably, at 100,000 seats per year, this performer could charge the market clearing price of $65 per ticket and give away to charity the portion of the economic rent ($10 per ticket) that would have been dissipated. In such a manner, the performer could make sure that the recipients of the rent are worthy in his or her own view. How much do top performers earn?

E X A M P L E

Do Entertainment Superstars Make Super Economic Rents?

Superstars certainly do well financially. Table 22-1 shows the earnings of selected individuals in the entertainment industry as estimated by *Forbes* magazine. Earnings are totaled for a two-year period. How much of these earnings can be called economic rent? The question is not easy to answer, because an entertainment newcomer would almost certainly work for much less than he or she earns, thereby making high economic rent. The same cannot necessarily be said for entertainers who

have been raking in millions for years. They probably have very high accumulated wealth and also a more jaded outlook about their work. It is therefore not clear how much they would work if they were not offered those huge sums of money.

For Critical Analysis
Even if some superstar entertainers would work for less, what forces cause them to make so much income anyway?

Name	Occupation	Two-Year Earnings
Steven Spielberg	Director, producer, studio owner	$200,000,000
George Lucas	Director, producer, studio owner	185,000,000
Oprah Winfrey	Talk show host and owner, author	180,000,000
Rolling Stones	Rock group	66,500,000
Will Smith	Actor	60,000,000
Paul McCartney	Rock singer	59,000,000
David Copperfield	Magician	55,000,000
Tom Hanks	Actor	55,000,000
Eddie Murphy	Actor	45,000,000
Jim Carrey	Actor	40,000,000

TABLE 22-1
Superstar Earnings

Source: *Forbes*, 2004.

CONCEPTS in Brief

● Economic rent is defined as payment for a factor of production that is completely inelastic in supply.

● Economic rent serves an allocative function by guiding available supply to the most efficient use.

To test your understanding of the concepts covered in this section, go to the Online Review at **www.myeconlab.com/miller**

FIRMS AND PROFITS

Firms or businesses, like individuals, seek to earn the highest possible returns. We define a **firm** as follows:

A firm is an organization that brings together factors of production—labor, land, physical capital, human capital, and entrepreneurial skill—to produce a product or service that it hopes can be sold at a profit.

A typical firm will have an organizational structure consisting of an entrepreneur, managers, and workers. The entrepreneur is the person who takes the risks, mainly of losing his or her personal wealth. In compensation, the entrepreneur will get any profits that are made. Recall from Chapter 2 that entrepreneurs take the initiative in combining land, labor, and capital to produce a good or a service. Entrepreneurs are the ones who innovate in the form of new production and new products. The entrepreneur also decides whom to hire to manage the firm. Some economists maintain that the true quality of an entrepreneur becomes evident with his or her selection of managers. Managers, in turn, decide who should be hired and fired and how the business generally should be set up. The workers ultimately use the other inputs to produce the products or services that are being sold by the firm. Workers and managers are paid contractual wages. They receive a specified amount of income for a specified time period. Entrepreneurs are not paid contractual wages. They receive no reward specified in advance. The entrepreneurs make profits if there are any, for profits accrue to those who are willing to take risks. (Because the entrepreneur gets only

Firm
A business organization that employs resources to produce goods or services for profit. A firm normally owns and operates at least one "plant" in order to produce.

what is left over after all expenses are paid, he or she is often referred to as a *residual claimant.* The entrepreneur lays claim to the residual—whatever is left.)

The Legal Organization of Firms

We all know that firms differ from one another. Some sell frozen yogurt, others make automobiles; some advertise, some do not; some have annual sales of a few thousand dollars, others have sales in the billions of dollars. The list of differences is probably endless. Yet for all this diversity, the basic organization of *all* firms can be thought of in terms of a few simple structures, the most important of which are the proprietorship, the partnership, and the corporation.

Proprietorship
A business owned by one individual who makes the business decisions, receives all the profits, and is legally responsible for the debts of the firm.

Proprietorship. The most common form of business organization is the **proprietorship;** as shown in Table 22-2 close to 72 percent of all firms in the United States are proprietorships. Each is owned by a single individual who makes the business decisions, receives all the profits, and is legally responsible for all the debts of the firm. Although proprietorships are numerous, they are generally rather small businesses, with annual sales typically not much more than $57,000. For this reason, even though there are nearly 18 million proprietorships in the United States, they account for less than 5 percent of all business revenues.

Advantages of Proprietorships. Proprietorships offer several advantages as a form of business organization. First, they are *easy to form and to dissolve.* In the simplest case, all one must do to start a business is to start working; to dissolve the firm, one simply stops working. Second, *all decision-making power resides with the sole proprietor.* No partners, shareholders, or board of directors need be consulted. The third advantage is that its *profit is taxed only once.* All profit is treated by law as the net income of the proprietor and as such is subject only to personal income taxation.

Unlimited liability
A legal concept whereby the personal assets of the owner of a firm can be seized to pay off the firm's debts.

Disadvantages of Proprietorships. The most important disadvantage of a proprietorship is that the proprietor faces **unlimited liability** *for the debts of the firm.* This means that the owner is personally responsible for all of the firm's debts. The second disadvantage is that it has *limited ability to raise funds,* to expand the business or even simply to help it survive bad times. Because of this, many lenders are reluctant to lend large sums to a proprietorship. The third disadvantage of proprietorships is that they normally *end with the death of the proprietor,* which creates added uncertainty for prospective lenders or employees.

TABLE 22-2
Forms of Business Organization

Type of Firm	Percentage of U.S. Firms	Average Size (annual sales in dollars)	Percentage of Total Business Revenues
Proprietorship	71.6	57,000	4.5
Partnership	8.2	1,125,000	10.1
Corporation	20.2	3,884,000	85.4

Sources: U.S. Bureau of the Census; *2004 Statistical Abstract.*

Partnership. The second important form of business organization is the **partnership.** As shown in Table 22-2, partnerships are far less numerous than proprietorships but tend to be significantly larger, with annual sales about twenty times greater on average. A partnership differs from a proprietorship chiefly in that there are two or more co-owners, called partners. They share the responsibilities of operating the firm and its profits, and they are *each* legally responsible for *all* of the debts incurred by the firm. In this sense, a partnership may be viewed as a proprietorship with more than one owner.

Advantages of Partnerships. The first advantage of a partnership is that it is *easy to form.* In fact, it is almost as easy as forming a proprietorship. Second, partnerships, like proprietorships, often help *reduce the costs of monitoring job performance.* This is particularly true when interpersonal skills are important for successful performance and in lines of business in which, even after the fact, it is difficult to measure performance objectively. Thus attorneys and physicians often organize themselves as partnerships. A third advantage of the partnership is that it *permits more effective specialization* in occupations in which, for legal or other reasons, the multiple talents required for success are unlikely to be uniform across individuals. Finally, the income of the partnership is treated as personal income and thus is *subject only to personal taxation.*

Disadvantages of Partnerships. Partnerships also have their disadvantages. First, the *partners each have unlimited liability.* Thus the personal assets of *each* partner are at risk due to debts incurred on behalf of the partnership by *any* of the partners. Second, *decision making is generally more costly* in a partnership than in a proprietorship; more people are involved in making decisions, and they may have differences of opinion that must be resolved before action is possible. Finally, *dissolution of the partnership is generally necessary* when a partner dies or voluntarily withdraws or when one or more partners wish to remove someone from the partnership. This creates potential uncertainty for creditors and employees.

Corporation. A **corporation** is a legal entity that may conduct business in its own name just as an individual does. The owners of a corporation are called *shareholders* because they own shares of the profits earned by the firm. By law, shareholders enjoy **limited liability,** meaning that if the corporation incurs debts that it cannot pay, the shareholders' personal property is shielded from claims by the firm's creditors. As shown in Table 22-2, corporations are far less numerous than proprietorships, but because of their large size, they are responsible for more than 85 percent of all business revenues in the United States.

Advantages of Corporations. Perhaps the greatest advantage of corporations is that their owners (the shareholders) enjoy *limited liability.* The liability of shareholders is limited to the value of their shares. The second advantage is that, legally, the corporation *continues to exist* even if one or more owners cease to be owners. A third advantage of the corporation stems from the first two: Corporations are well positioned to *raise large sums of financial capital.* People are able to buy ownership shares or lend funds to the corporation knowing that their liability is limited to the amount of funds they invest and confident that the corporation's existence does not depend on the life of any one of the firm's owners.

Disadvantages of Corporations. The chief disadvantage of the corporation is that corporate income is subject to *double taxation.* The profits of the corporation are subject first to corporate taxation. Then, if any of the after-tax profits are distributed to shareholders as **dividends,** such payments are treated as personal income to the shareholders and subject to personal taxation, although the dividends may be taxed at lower rates than other personal income. Despite the lower tax rates on dividends, owners of corporations generally

Partnership
A business owned by two or more joint owners, or partners, who share the responsibilities and the profits of the firm and are individually liable for all the debts of the partnership.

Corporation
A legal entity that may conduct business in its own name just as an individual does; the owners of a corporation, called shareholders, own shares of the firm's profits and enjoy the protection of limited liability.

Limited liability
A legal concept whereby the responsibility, or liability, of the owners of a corporation is limited to the value of the shares in the firm that they own.

Dividends
Portion of a corporation's profits paid to its owners (shareholders).

pay higher taxes on corporate income than on other forms of income because the corporate income is also taxed at the corporate level.

A second disadvantage of the corporation is that corporations are potentially subject to problems associated with the *separation of ownership and control.* The owners and managers of a corporation are typically different persons and may have different incentives. The problems that can result are discussed later in the chapter.

Why do you suppose that the Japanese government has been trying hard to promote the formation of more business start-ups?

International Policy EXAMPLE

Hoping for Some One-Yen Business Successes in Japan

Japanese economic activity was stagnant throughout the 1990s and early 2000s. A contributing factor, the Japanese government decided, was the fact that entrepreneurial activity was much lower in Japan than in most other Asian nations, including Thailand, South Korea, Singapore, and Taiwan. So the government decided to try to encourage new business formation. It exempted new companies from rules requiring corporations to start with at least 10 million yen (about $95,000) on hand and partnerships to possess at least 3 million yen (about $28,600) before opening for business. The government announced that until 2008, a "one-yen policy" would be in effect: new companies could begin operations with only one yen on hand—or the equivalent of less than a penny.

The Japanese government had hoped that the new policy would encourage the formation of 10,000 new businesses annually. Over the next two years, however, the government could credit the law with contributing to only about 6,000 additional business start-ups per year. Critics of the government's effort to promote new business formations contended that the problem was that the one-yen policy had ignored other impediments to establishing new businesses. Among these are a 250,000-yen (about $2,400) business registration tax and government policies making it difficult for new companies to fire employees that the owners find to be incompetent.

For Critical Analysis
What other legal changes could the Japanese government make to encourage more business start-ups?

The Profits of a Firm

Explicit costs
Costs that business managers must take account of because they must be paid; examples are wages, taxes, and rent.

Accounting profit
Total revenues minus total explicit costs.

Implicit costs
Expenses that managers do not have to pay out of pocket and hence do not normally explicitly calculate, such as the opportunity cost of factors of production that are owned; examples are owner-provided capital and owner-provided labor.

Most people think of a firm's profit as the difference between the amount of revenues the firm takes in and the amount it spends for wages, materials, and so on. In a bookkeeping sense, the following formula could be used:

$$\text{Accounting profit} = \text{total revenue} - \text{explicit costs}$$

where **explicit costs** are expenses that must actually be paid out by the firm. This definition of profit is known as **accounting profit.** It is appropriate when used by accountants to determine a firm's taxable income. Economists are more interested in how firm managers react not just to changes in explicit costs but also to changes in **implicit costs,** defined as expenses that business managers do not have to pay out of pocket but are costs to the firm nonetheless because they represent an opportunity cost. They do not involve any direct cash outlay by the firm and must therefore be measured by the *opportunity cost principle.* That is to say, they are measured by what the resources (land, capital) currently used in producing a particular good or service could earn in other uses. Economists use the full opportunity cost of all resources (including both explicit and implicit costs) as the figure to subtract from revenues to obtain a definition of profit. Therefore, another definition of implicit cost is the opportunity cost of using factors that a producer does not buy or hire but already owns.

Opportunity Cost of Capital

Firms enter or remain in an industry if they earn, at minimum, a **normal rate of return.** People will not invest their wealth in a business unless they obtain a positive normal (competitive) rate of return—that is, unless their invested wealth pays off. Any business wishing to attract capital must expect to pay at least the same rate of return on that capital as all other businesses (of similar risk) are willing to pay. Put another way, when a firm requires the use of a resource in producing a particular product, it must bid against alternative users of that resource. Thus the firm must offer a price that is at least as much as other potential users are offering to pay. For example, if individuals can invest their wealth in almost any publishing firm and get a rate of return of 10 percent per year, each firm in the publishing industry must *expect* to pay 10 percent as the normal rate of return to present and future investors. This 10 percent is a *cost to the firm,* the **opportunity cost of capital.** The opportunity cost of capital is the amount of income, or yield, that could have been earned by investing in the next-best alternative. Capital will not stay in firms or industries in which the expected rate of return falls below its opportunity cost, that is, what could be earned elsewhere. If a firm owns some capital equipment, it can either use it or lease it and earn a return. If the firm uses the equipment for production, part of the cost of using that equipment is the forgone revenue that the firm could have earned had it leased out that equipment.

Normal rate of return
The amount that must be paid to an investor to induce investment in a business; also known as the *opportunity cost of capital.*

Opportunity cost of capital
The normal rate of return, or the available return on the next-best alternative investment. Economists consider this a cost of production, and it is included in our cost examples.

Opportunity Cost of Owner-Provided Labor and Capital

Single-owner proprietorships often grossly exaggerate their profit rates because they understate the opportunity cost of the labor that the proprietor provides to the business. Here we are referring to the opportunity cost of labor. For example, you may know people who run a small grocery store. These people will sit down at the end of the year and figure out what their "profits" are. They will add up all their sales and subtract what they had to pay to other workers, what they had to pay to their suppliers, what they had to pay in taxes, and so on. The end result they will call "profit." They normally will not, however, have figured into their costs the salary that they could have made if they had worked for somebody else in a similar type of job. By working for themselves, they become residual claimants—they receive what is left after all explicit costs have been accounted for. Part of the costs, however, should include the salary the owner-operator could have received working for someone else.

Consider a simple example of a skilled auto mechanic working 14 hours a day at his own service station, six days a week. Compare this situation to how much he could earn working 84 hours a week as a trucking company mechanic. This self-employed auto mechanic might have an opportunity cost of about $25 an hour. For his 84-hour week in his own service station, he is forfeiting $2,100. Unless his service station shows accounting profits of more than that per week, he is incurring losses in an economic sense.

Another way of looking at the opportunity cost of running a business is that opportunity cost consists of all explicit and implicit costs. Accountants only take account of explicit costs. Therefore, accounting profit ends up being the residual after only explicit costs are subtracted from total revenues.

This same analysis can apply to owner-provided capital, such as land or buildings. The fact that the owner owns the building or the land with which he or she operates a business does not mean that it is "free." Rather, use of the building and land still has an opportunity cost—the value of the next-best alternative use for those assets.

Go to www.econtoday.com/chap22 for a link to Internal Revenue Service reports on U.S. annual revenues and expenses of proprietorships, partnerships, and corporations based on tax returns. Click on recent quarters and choose relevant reports.

Accounting Profits versus Economic Profits

The term *profits* in economics means the income that entrepreneurs earn, over and above all costs including their own opportunity cost of time, plus the opportunity cost of the capital they have invested in their business. Profits can be regarded as total revenues minus total costs—which is how accountants think of them—but we must now include *all* costs. Our definition of **economic profits** will be the following:

Economic profits
Total revenues minus total opportunity costs of all inputs used, or the total of all implicit and explicit costs.

$$\text{Economic profits} = \text{total revenues} - \text{total opportunity cost of all inputs used}$$

or

$$\text{Economic profits} = \text{total revenues} - (\text{explicit} + \text{implicit costs})$$

Remember that implicit costs include a normal rate of return on invested capital. We show this relationship in Figure 22-3.

The Goal of the Firm: Profit Maximization

When we examined the theory of consumer demand, utility (or satisfaction) maximization by the individual provided the basis for the analysis. In the theory of the firm and production, *profit maximization* is the underlying hypothesis of our predictive theory. The goal of the firm is to maximize economic profits, and the firm is expected to try to make the positive difference between total revenues and total costs as large as it can.

Our justification for assuming profit maximization by firms is similar to our assumption concerning utility maximization by individuals (see Chapter 20). To obtain labor, capital, and other resources required to produce commodities, firms must first obtain financing from investors. In general, investors are indifferent about the details of how a firm uses the funds they provide. They are most interested in the earnings on these funds and the risk

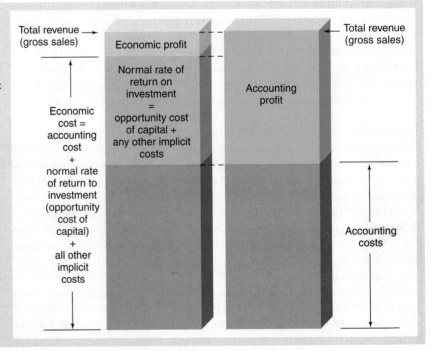

FIGURE 22-3
Simplified View of Economic and Accounting Profit
We see on the right column that accounting profit is the difference between total revenues and total explicit accounting costs. Conversely, we see on the left column that economic profit is equal to total revenues minus economic costs. Economic costs equal explicit accounting costs plus all implicit costs, including a normal rate of return on invested capital.

of obtaining lower returns or losing the funds they have invested. Firms that can provide relatively higher risk-corrected returns will therefore have an advantage in obtaining the financing needed to continue or expand production. Over time, we would expect a policy of profit maximization to become the dominant mode of behavior for firms that survive.

CONCEPTS in Brief

- Proprietorships are the most common form of business organization, comprising close to 72 percent of all firms. Each is owned by a single individual who makes all business decisions, receives all the profits, and has unlimited liability for the firm's debts.

- Partnerships are much like proprietorships, except that two or more individuals, or partners, share the decisions and the profits of the firm. In addition, each partner has unlimited liability for the debts of the firm.

- Corporations are responsible for the largest share of business revenues. The owners, called shareholders, share in the firm's profits but normally have little responsibility for the firm's day-to-day operations. They enjoy limited liability for the debts of the firm.

- Accounting profits differ from economic profits. Economic profits are defined as total revenues minus total costs, where costs include the full opportunity cost of all of the factors of production plus all other implicit costs.

- The full opportunity cost of capital invested in a business is generally not included as a cost when accounting profits are calculated. Thus accounting profits often overstate economic profits. We assume throughout that the goal of the firm is to maximize economic profits.

To test your understanding of the concepts covered in this section, go to the Online Review at www.myeconlab.com/miller.

INTEREST

The term *interest* is used to mean two different things: (1) the price paid by debtors to creditors for the use of loanable funds and (2) the market return earned by (nonfinancial) capital as a factor of production. Owners of capital, whether directly or indirectly, obtain interest income. Often businesses go to credit markets to obtain so-called **financial capital** in order to invest in physical capital and rights to patents and trademarks from which they hope to make a satisfactory return. In other words, in our complicated society, the production of capital goods often occurs because of the existence of credit markets in which borrowing and lending take place. For the moment, we will look only at the credit market.

Financial capital
Funds used to purchase physical capital goods, such as buildings and equipment, and patents and trademarks.

Interest and Credit

When you obtain credit, you actually obtain funds to have command over resources today. We can say, then, that **interest** is the payment for current rather than future command over resources. Thus interest is the payment for obtaining credit. If you borrow $100 from me, you have command over $100 worth of goods and services today. I no longer have that command. You promise to pay me back $100 plus interest at some future date. The interest that you pay is usually expressed as a percentage of the total loan, calculated on an annual basis. If at the end of one year you pay me back $105, the annual interest rate is $5 ÷ $100, or 5 percent. When you go out into the marketplace to obtain credit, you will find that the interest rate charged differs greatly. A loan to buy a house (a mortgage) may cost you 6 to 9 percent in annual interest. An installment loan to buy an automobile may cost you 7 to 10 percent in annual interest. The federal government, when it wishes to obtain credit (issue U.S. Treasury securities), may have to pay only 2 to 6 percent in annual interest. Variations in the rate of annual interest that must be paid for credit depend on the following factors.

Interest
The payment for current rather than future command over resources; the cost of obtaining credit. Also, the return paid to owners of capital.

1. *Length of loan.* In some (but not all) cases, the longer the loan will be outstanding, other things being equal, the greater will be the interest rate charged.
2. *Risk.* The greater the risk of nonrepayment of the loan, other things being equal, the greater the interest rate charged. Risk is assessed on the basis of the creditworthiness of the borrower and whether the borrower provides collateral for the loan. Collateral consists of any asset that will automatically become the property of the lender should the borrower fail to comply with the loan agreement.
3. *Handling charges.* It takes resources to set up a loan. Papers have to be filled out and filed, credit references have to be checked, collateral has to be examined, and so on. The larger the amount of the loan, the smaller the handling (or administrative) charges as a percentage of the total loan. Therefore, we would predict that, other things being equal, the larger the loan, the lower the interest rate.

Go to www.econtoday.com/chap22 for Federal Reserve data on U.S. interest rates.

Real versus Nominal Interest Rates

We have been assuming that there is no inflation. In a world of inflation—a persistent rise in an average of all prices—the **nominal rate of interest** will be higher than it would be in a world with no inflation. Basically, nominal, or market, rates of interest rise to take account of the anticipated rate of inflation. If, for example, there is no inflation and no inflation is expected, the nominal rate of interest might be 5 percent for home mortgages. If the rate of inflation goes to 4 percent a year and stays there, everybody will anticipate that inflation rate. The nominal rate of interest will rise to about 9 percent to take account of the anticipated rate of inflation. If the interest rate did not rise to 9 percent, the principal plus interest earned at 5 percent would be worth less in the future because inflation would have eroded its purchasing power. We can therefore say that the nominal, or market, rate of interest is approximately equal to the real rate of interest plus the anticipated rate of inflation, or

Nominal rate of interest
The market rate of interest expressed in today's dollars.

Economics Front and Center

To think about circumstances in which a firm that wishes to raise funds might find it advantageous to borrow at an inflation-adjusted rate of interest, read the case study, **A Hometown Bank Considers Joining the Inflation-Adjusted Bandwagon,** on page 536.

Real rate of interest
The nominal rate of interest minus the anticipated rate of inflation.

$$i_n = i_r + \text{anticipated rate of inflation}$$

where i_n equals the nominal rate of interest and i_r equals the real rate of interest. In short, you can expect to see high nominal rates of interest in periods of high inflation rates. The **real rate of interest** may not necessarily be high, though. We must first correct the nominal rate of interest for the anticipated rate of inflation before determining whether the real interest rate is in fact higher than normal.

The Allocative Role of Interest

In Chapter 4, we talked about the price system and the role that prices play in the allocation of resources. Interest is a price that allocates loanable funds (credit) to consumers and to businesses. Within the business sector, interest allocates funds to different firms and therefore to different investment projects. Investment, or capital, projects with rates of return higher than the market rate of interest in the credit market will be undertaken, given an unrestricted market for loanable funds. For example, if the expected rate of return on the purchase of a new factory in some industry is 10 percent and funds can be acquired for 6 percent, the investment project may proceed. If, however, that same project had an expected rate of return of only 4 percent, it would not be undertaken. In sum, the interest rate allocates funds to industries whose investments yield the highest (risk-adjusted) returns—where resources will be the most productive.

It is important to realize that the interest rate performs the function of allocating financial capital and that this ultimately allocates real physical capital to various firms for investment projects.

Interest Rates and Present Value

Businesses make investments in which they often incur large costs today but don't make any profits until some time in the future. Somehow they have to be able to compare their investment cost today with a stream of future profits. How can they relate present cost to future benefits?

Interest rates are used to link the present with the future. After all, if you have to pay $105 at the end of the year when you borrow $100, that 5 percent interest rate gives you a measure of the premium on the earlier availability of goods and services. If you want to have things today, you have to pay the 5 percent interest rate in order to have current purchasing power.

The question could be put this way: What is the present value (the value today) of $105 that you could receive one year from now? That depends on the market rate of interest, or the rate of interest that you could earn in some appropriate savings institution, such as in a savings account. To make the arithmetic simple, let's assume that the rate of interest is 5 percent. Now you can figure out the **present value** of $105 to be received one year from now. You figure it out by asking the question, What sum must I put aside today at the market interest rate of 5 percent to receive $105 one year from now? Mathematically, we represent this equation as

$$(1 + 0.05)PV_1 = \$105$$

where PV_1 is the sum that you must set aside now.

Let's solve this simple equation to obtain PV_1:

$$PV_1 = \frac{\$105}{1.05} = \$100$$

That is, $100 will accumulate to $105 at the end of one year with a market rate of interest of 5 percent. Thus the present value of $105 one year from now, using a rate of interest of 5 percent, is $100. The formula for present value of any sums to be received one year from now thus becomes

$$PV_1 = \frac{FV_1}{1 + i}$$

where

$$PV_1 = \text{present value of a sum one year hence}$$
$$FV_1 = \text{future sum of money paid or received one year hence}$$
$$i = \text{market rate of interest}$$

Present Values for More Distant Periods. The present-value formula for figuring out today's worth of dollars to be received at a future date can now be determined. How much would have to be put in the same savings account today to have $105 two years from now if the account pays a rate of 5 percent per year compounded annually?

After one year, the sum that would have to be set aside, which we will call PV_2, would have grown to $PV_2 \times 1.05$. This amount during the second year would increase to $PV_2 \times 1.05 \times 1.05$, or $PV_2 \times (1.05)^2$. To find the PV_2 that would grow to $105 over two years, let

$$PV_2 \times (1.05)^2 = \$105$$

and solve for PV_2:

Go to www.econtoday.com/chap22 to utilize an MFM Communication Software, Inc. manual providing additional review of present value.

Present value
The value of a future amount expressed in today's dollars; the most that someone would pay today to receive a certain sum at some point in the future.

$$PV_2 = \frac{\$105}{(1.05)^2} = \$95.24$$

Thus the present value of $105 to be paid or received two years hence, discounted at an interest rate of 5 percent per year compounded annually, is equal to $95.24. In other words, $95.24 put into a savings account yielding 5 percent per year compounded interest would accumulate to $105 in two years.

The General Formula for Discounting. The general formula for **discounting** becomes

$$PV_t = \frac{PV_t}{(1 + i)^t}$$

Discounting
The method by which the present value of a future sum or a future stream of sums is obtained.

Rate of discount
The rate of interest used to discount future sums back to present value.

where *t* refers to the number of periods in the future the money is to be paid or received.

Table 22-3 gives the present value of $1 to be received in future years at various interest rates. The interest rate used to derive the present value is called the **rate of discount.**

Each individual has his or her own *personal rate of discount,* which is the annual rate at which the individual discounts values to be received in future years. People with relatively low personal rates of discount are more willing to save funds today, because they subjectively perceive a higher present value on future interest payments. Those with relatively high personal rates of discount are more likely to borrow, because they perceive a lower present value on future interest payments. The market interest rate, therefore, lies between the upper and lower ranges of personal rates of discount.

Why do you think that U.S. military personnel who receive an average of about $38,000 *per year* in deferred benefits perceive the present value of those payments to be much lower?

TABLE 22-3
Present Value of a Future Dollar
This table shows how much a dollar received at the end of a certain number of years in the future is worth today. For example, at 5 percent a year, a dollar to be received 20 years in the future is worth 37.7 cents; if received in 50 years, it isn't even worth a dime today. To find out how much $10,000 would be worth a certain number of years from now, just multiply the figures in the table by 10,000. For example, $10,000 received at the end of 10 years discounted at a 5 percent rate of interest would have a present value of $6,140.

| Year | Compounded Annual Interest Rate | | | | |
	3%	5%	8%	10%	20%
1	.971	.952	.926	.909	.833
2	.943	.907	.857	.826	.694
3	.915	.864	.794	.751	.578
4	.889	.823	.735	.683	.482
5	.863	.784	.681	.620	.402
6	.838	.746	.630	.564	.335
7	.813	.711	.583	.513	.279
8	.789	.677	.540	.466	.233
9	.766	.645	.500	.424	.194
10	.744	.614	.463	.385	.162
15	.642	.481	.315	.239	.0649
20	.554	.377	.215	.148	.0261
25	.478	.295	.146	.0923	.0105
30	.412	.231	.0994	.0573	.00421
40	.307	.142	.0460	.0221	.000680
50	.228	.087	.0213	.00852	.000109

EXAMPLE

The Low Present Value of a Volunteer Soldier's Pay Package

U.S. taxpayers pay each member of the nation's all-volunteer military a package of salary and benefits equal to an average of about $99,000 per year. About $42,500 of this amount is direct pay. Approximately $38,000 of the remaining $56,500 consists of health care and pension benefits that a person in the military will not actually receive until at least 20 years of service have been completed.

Studies of choices that officers and enlisted personnel have made when allowed to choose between lump-sum and annual payments have revealed that officers discount future benefits at an annual rate of 10 to 19 percent. Enlisted personnel have even higher rates of discount, ranging from 35 to 54 percent per year.

From the point of view of taxpayers using market interest rates to discount the value of a dollar to be paid to a soldier 20

years from now, the present value of that dollar of deferred benefits is 36 cents. In contrast, a soldier discounting at an annual rate of 35 percent perceives the present value to be less than a fifth of a cent. This helps explain why, even as U.S. taxpayers accumulate an unfunded military pension liability approaching $600 billion, many of the nation's military personnel perceive themselves to be seriously underpaid.

For Critical Analysis

From today's perspective, why might taxpayers view the current military pay package as a "bargain"? (Hint: Compare the present value of a dollar in deferred pension benefits noted above to the cost of paying military personnel a dollar in wages today.)

CONCEPTS in Brief

- Interest is the price paid for the use of financial capital. It is also the cost of obtaining credit. In the credit market, the rate of interest paid depends on the length of the loan, the risk, and the handling charges, among other things.

- Nominal, or market, interest rates include a factor to take account of the anticipated rate of inflation. Therefore, dur-

ing periods of high anticipated inflation, nominal interest rates will be relatively high.

- Payments received or costs incurred in the future are worth less than those received or incurred today. The present value of any future sum is lower the further it occurs in the future and the greater the discount rate used.

To test your understanding of the concepts covered in this section, go to the Online Review at **www.myeconlab.com/miller.**

CORPORATE FINANCING METHODS

When the Dutch East India Company was founded in 1602, it raised financial capital by selling shares of its expected future profits to investors. The investors thus became the owners of the company, and their ownership shares eventually became known as "shares of stock," or simply *stocks.* The company also issued notes of indebtedness, which involved borrowing funds in return for interest paid on the funds, plus eventual repayment of the principal amount borrowed. In modern parlance, these notes of indebtedness are called *bonds.* As the company prospered over time, some of its revenues were used to pay lenders the interest and principal owed them; of the profits that remained, some were paid to shareholders in the form of dividends, and some were retained by the company for reinvestment in further enterprises. The methods of financing used by the Dutch East India Company four centuries ago—stocks, bonds, and reinvestment—remain the principal methods of financing for today's corporations.

A **share of stock** in a corporation is simply a legal claim to a share of the corporation's future profits. If there are 100,000 shares of stock in a company and you own 1,000 of them, you own the right to 1 percent of that company's future profits. If the stock you own

Share of stock
A legal claim to a share of a corporation's future profits; if it is *common stock,* it incorporates certain voting rights regarding major policy decisions of the corporation; if it is *preferred stock,* its owners are accorded preferential treatment in the payment of dividends.

is *common stock,* you also have the right to vote on major policy decisions affecting the company, such as the selection of the corporation's board of directors. Your 1,000 shares would entitle you to cast 1 percent of the votes on such issues. If the stock you own is *preferred stock,* you own a share of the future profits of the corporation but do *not* have regular voting rights. You do, however, get something in return for giving up your voting rights: preferential treatment in the payment of dividends. Specifically, the owners of preferred stock generally must receive at least a certain amount of dividends in each period before the owners of common stock can receive *any* dividends.

Bond
A legal claim against a firm, usually entitling the owner of the bond to receive a fixed annual coupon payment, plus a lump-sum payment at the bond's maturity date. Bonds are issued in return for funds lent to the firm.

A **bond** is a legal claim against a firm, entitling the owner of the bond to receive a fixed annual *coupon* payment, plus a lump-sum payment at the maturity date of the bond.* Bonds are issued in return for funds lent to the firm; the coupon payments represent interest on the amount borrowed by the firm, and the lump-sum payment at maturity of the bond generally equals the amount originally borrowed by the firm. Bonds are *not* claims on the future profits of the firm; legally, bondholders must be paid whether the firm prospers or not. To help ensure this, bondholders generally receive their coupon payments each year, along with any principal that is due, before *any* shareholders can receive dividend payments.

Reinvestment
Profits (or depreciation reserves) used to purchase new capital equipment.

Reinvestment takes place when the firm uses some of its profits to purchase new capital equipment rather than paying the profits out as dividends to shareholders. Although sales of stock are an important source of financing for new firms, reinvestment and borrowing are the primary means of financing for existing firms. Indeed, reinvestment by established firms is such an important source of financing that it dominates the other two sources of corporate finance, amounting to roughly 75 percent of new financial capital for corporations in recent years. Also, small businesses, which are the source of much current growth, often cannot rely on the stock market to raise investment funds.

THE MARKETS FOR STOCKS AND BONDS

Securities
Stocks and bonds.

Economists often refer to the "market for wheat" or the "market for labor," but these are concepts rather than actual places. For **securities** (stocks and bonds), however, there really are markets—centralized, physical locations where exchange takes place. The most prestigious of these markets are the New York Stock Exchange (NYSE) and the New York Bond Exchange, both located in New York City. Numerous other stock and bond markets, or exchanges, exist throughout the United States and in various financial capitals of the world, such as London and Tokyo. Although the exact process by which exchanges are conducted in these markets varies slightly from one to another, the process used on the NYSE is representative of the principles involved.[†]

More than 2,500 stocks are traded on the NYSE, which is sometimes called the "Big Board." Leading brokerage firms—about 600 of them—own seats on the NYSE. These seats, which are actually rights to buy and sell stocks on the floor of the Big Board, are themselves regularly exchanged. In recent years, their value has fluctuated between $350,000 and $2 million each. These prices reflect the fact that stock trades on the NYSE are ultimately handled by the firms owning these seats, and the firms earn commissions on each trade.

---

*Coupon payments on bonds get their name from the fact that bonds once had coupons attached to them when they were issued. Each year, the owner would clip a coupon off the bond and send it to the issuing firm in return for that year's interest on the bond.
†A number of stocks and bonds are traded in so-called over-the-counter (OTC) markets, which, although not physically centralized, otherwise operate in much the same way as the NYSE and so are not treated separately in this text.

The second-largest U.S. stock exchange is the National Association of Securities Dealers Automated Quotation (Nasdaq) system, which began in 1971 as a tiny electronic network linking about 100 securities firms. Today, the Nasdaq market links about 500 dealers, and Nasdaq is home to nearly 5,500 stocks, including those of such companies as Microsoft, Intel, and Cisco.

Can you deduce why many businesspeople in Africa believe that establishing a single African stock exchange could help to reinvigorate stock trading in that part of the world?

International E X A M P L E

Is It Too Soon for a Pan-African Stock Exchange?

Johannesburg, South Africa, is home to the world's sixteenth-largest stock exchange. Until the 1980s, close to 95 percent of all stock trades in Africa took place there. Since 1990, numerous new stock exchanges have been established throughout Africa. Today, a total of 20 African stock exchanges outside Johannesburg now handle about one-fourth of all stock trades in the region. All of these new stock exchanges have faced a common problem, however: a lack of liquidity. Each exchange lists only about a few dozen stocks, so orders to buy or sell stocks arrive relatively infrequently on days when the exchanges are open. At the same time, the migration of some companies' stocks away from the Johannesburg exchange to the newer exchanges has also sapped some of the liquidity from that stock exchange. As a result, someone who wants to sell shares of stock in a company using an African stock exchange often has to wait for days for an interested buyer to place an order.

In an effort to make African stock trading more liquid, an attempt has been under way to combine stock exchanges throughout Africa into a single, continent-spanning stock exchange system. So far, progress toward this goal has been slow. Stock exchanges in developed nations are linked by Internet-based auction systems, but Africa's telecommunications networks lag behind those in the rest of the world. Thus technological handicaps are hindering efforts to broaden the liquidity of the market for African stocks.

For Critical Analysis
Why might low liquidity in a stock market induce prospective investors to regard the stocks traded in that market as risky propositions?

The Theory of Efficient Markets

At any point in time, there are tens of thousands, even millions, of persons looking for any bit of information that will enable them to forecast correctly the future prices of stocks. Responding to any information that seems useful, these people try to buy low and sell high. The result is that all publicly available information that might be used to forecast stock prices gets taken into account by those with access to the information and the knowledge and ability to learn from it, leaving no forecastable profit opportunities. And because so many people are involved in this process, it occurs quite swiftly. Indeed, there is some evidence that *all* information entering the market is fully incorporated into stock prices within less than a minute of its arrival. One view is that any information about specific stocks will prove to have little value by the time it reaches you.

Consequently, stock prices tend to follow a *random walk,* which is to say that the best forecast of tomorrow's price is today's price. This is called the **random walk theory.** Although large values of the random component of stock price changes are less likely than small values, nothing else about the magnitude or direction of a stock price change can be predicted. Indeed, the random component of stock prices exhibits behavior much like what

Random walk theory
The theory that there are no predictable trends in securities prices that can be used to "get rich quick."

would occur if you rolled two dice and subtracted 7 from the resulting total. On average, the dice will show a total of 7, so after you subtract 7, the average result will be zero. It is true that rolling a 12 or a 2 (resulting in a total of +5 or −5) is less likely than rolling an 8 or a 6 (yielding a total of +1 or −1). Nevertheless, positive and negative totals are equally likely, and the expected total is zero.

Inside Information

Inside information
Information that is not available to the general public about what is happening in a corporation.

Go to www.econtoday.com/chap22 to explore how the U.S. Securities and Exchange Commission seeks to prevent the use of inside information.

Isn't there any way to "beat the market"? The answer is yes—but normally only if you have **inside information** that is not available to the public. Suppose that your best friend is in charge of new product development at the world's largest software firm, Microsoft Corporation. Your friend tells you that the company's smartest programmer has just come up with major new software that millions of computer users will want to buy. No one but your friend and the programmer—and now you—is aware of this. You could indeed make a killing using this information by purchasing shares of Microsoft and then selling them (at a higher price) as soon as the new product is publicly announced. There is one problem: Stock trading based on inside information such as this is illegal, punishable by substantial fines and even imprisonment. So unless you happen to have a stronger-than-average desire for a long vacation in a federal prison, you might be better off investing in Microsoft after the new program is publicly announced.

It is, of course, possible for people to influence stock or bond prices through the accidental release of inside information. For instance, when the U.S. Treasury decided it would discontinue issuing 30-year bonds, it decided to announce its decision on October 31, 2001. Treasury officials told the media that the information of the bond's demise would be public as of 10 AM. Nevertheless, as a courtesy officials informed reporters in advance in an impromptu 9 AM meeting so that the reporters would have some time to write stories to release at that time. Officials failed to check the credentials of everyone who attended the meeting, however, and one of those individuals was a financial consultant who did not understand that this early news of the bond's end was "embargoed" until 10 AM. After the news conference ended just before 9:30 AM, the consultant called some of his clients and told them of the media announcement. Within a very few minutes, word of the Treasury's plans had spread widely. Ten minutes before the Treasury's formal announcement, stock and bond prices had already reacted to the news.

What can learn from stock quotes available from the financial media?

EXAMPLE

How to Read the Financial Press: Stock Prices

Table 22-4, reproduced from the *Wall Street Journal,* contains information about the stocks of four companies. Across the top of the financial page are a series of column headings. Under the heading "Stock" we find the name of the company—in the second row, for example, is Nike. The first column gives the year-to-date percentage change in the price of the company's stock. The next two columns to the left of the company's name show the highest and lowest prices at which shares of that company's stock traded during the past 52 weeks.

Immediately to the right of the company's name you will find the company's *symbol* on the NYSE. This symbol (omitted by some newspapers) is simply the unique identifier used by the exchange when it reports information about the stock. For example, the designation NKE is used by the exchange as the unique identifier for the firm Nike.

The last two columns of information for each firm summarize the behavior of the firm's stock price on the latest trading day. On this particular day, the last (or closing) price at which

TABLE 22-4
Reading Stock Quotes

YTD % CHG	52 – WEEK HI	52 – WEEK LO	STOCK(SYM)	DIV	YLD %	PE	VOL 100s	CLOSE	NET CHG
−5.2	28.60	19.58	Nidec ADS **NJ** s	.07e	.3	...	45	22.59	0.39
4.6	78.56	54.07	Nike B **NKE**	.80	1.1	20	6768	71.60	−0.20
−52.9	36.07	12.10	99cOnlyStr **NDN**		...	23	10216	12.82	0.31
−3.7	30.20	20.39	Nippon ADS **NTT**	.23e	1.0	...	418	23.65	0.04

The summary of stock market information presented on the financial pages of many newspapers reveals the following:

YTD %CHG: The percentage change in the stock price since the beginning of the year

52 Week Hi/Lo: The highest and lowest prices, in dollars per share, of the stock during the previous 52 weeks

STOCK: The name of the company (frequently abbreviated)

(SYM):   Highly abbreviated name of the company, as it appears on the stock exchange ticker tape

DIV: Dividend paid, in dollars per share ("e" means estimated)

YLD %:   Yield in percent per year; the dividend divided by the price of the stock

PE: Price-earnings ratio; the price of the stock divided by the earnings (profits) per share of the company

VOL 100s: Number of shares traded during the day, in hundreds of shares

CLOSE: Last price at which the stock traded that day

NET CHG: Net change in the stock's price from the previous day's closing price

it traded was $71.60 per share. The net change in the price of Nike stock was −0.20 which means that it *closed* the day at a price about $0.20 per share below the price at which it closed the day before.

The dividend column, headed "DIV," shows the annual dividend (in dollars and cents) that the company has paid over the preceding year on each share of its stock. In Nike's case, this amounts to $0.80 a share. If the dividend is divided by the closing price of the stock ($0.80 ÷ $71.60), the result is 1.1 percent, which is shown in the yield percentage ("YLD %") column in Nike's stock price listing. In a sense, the company is paying interest on the stock at a rate of about 1.1 percent. At first glance, this seems like a relatively low amount; after all, at the time this issue of the *Wall Street Journal* was printed, ordinary checking accounts were paying about this much. The reason people tolerate this seemingly low yield on Nike's stock (or any other

firm's stock) is that they expect that the price of the stock will rise over time, yielding capital gains.

The column heading "PE" stands for *price-earnings ratio*. To obtain the entries for this column, the firm's total earnings (profits) for the year are divided by the number of the firm's shares in existence to give the earnings per share. When the price of the stock is divided by the earnings per share, the result is the price-earnings ratio.

The column to the right of the PE ratio shows the total *volume* of the shares of the stock traded that day, measured in hundreds of shares.

For Critical Analysis

Is there necessarily any relationship between the net change in a stock's price and how many shares have been sold on a particular day?

CONCEPTS in Brief

- The three primary sources of corporate funds are stocks, bonds, and reinvestment of profits.

- A share of stock is a share of ownership providing a legal claim to a corporation's future profits. A bond is a legal claim entitling the owner to a fixed annual coupon payment and to a lump-sum payment on the date the bond matures.

- Many economists believe that asset markets, especially the stock market, are efficient, meaning that one cannot make a higher-than-normal rate of return without having inside information (information that the general public does not possess). Stock prices normally follow a random walk, meaning that you cannot predict changes in future stock prices based on information about stock price behavior in the past.

To test your understanding of the concepts covered in this section, go to the Online Review at www.myeconlab.com/miller.

CASE STUDY: Economics Front and Center

A Hometown Bank Considers Joining the Inflation-Adjusted Bandwagon

After finishing a business degree at a local college, Fleming has begun a management training program with his hometown bank, First Municipal Bank. The bank has charted a path for significant growth, with the goal of becoming the top institutional lender to businesses in its part of the state. To do this, however, the bank must raise sufficient deposit funds to fuel its intended loan expansion.

In his college economics courses, Fleming learned that an increasing number of companies are offering bonds with inflation-adjusted rates of return. After spending some time searching the Internet, he has discovered that several banks have extended inflation protection to certificates of deposit (CDs). LaSalle Bank, Bank of New York, Mellon Bank, and others now issue certificates paying inflation-adjusted interest rates in $1,000 denominations and with maturities of 5 to 10 years. Fleming is ready to go to his boss with a proposal to take to the bank's sen-

ior management: offer inflation-protected CDs in denominations as small as $500 and with one- to five-year maturities. This proposal, Fleming is convinced, would attract both new depositors and additional funds from existing depositors.

Points to Analyze

1. *At present, with non-inflation-adjusted rates paid on its deposits, does First Municipal Bank gain or lose if the inflation rate turns out to be higher than anticipated during the coming year? Explain.*

2. *If the bank's senior management implements Fleming's suggestion, what will happen to the nominal interest rate on deposits if the inflation rate unexpectedly rises? What will happen to the real interest rate on deposits?*

Investors Line Up to Get More TIPS from the U.S. Treasury

Suppose that you anticipate that the U.S. inflation rate will be a little below 2 percent per year during the next decade. If you purchase a 10-year U.S. Treasury note that pays a nominal rate of interest equal to 6 percent per year, you expect that the annual real interest rate for this security issued by the U.S. government will be just over 4 percent. If the annual inflation rate in the United States were to unexpectedly rise to nearly 4 percent, however, your actual real annual rate of return would be cut in half, to only a little over 2 percent (before taxes).

Concepts Applied
- Securities
- Nominal Rate of Interest
- Real Rate of Interest

Treasury Inflation-Protection Securities

Those who purchase 10-year notes from the U.S. Treasury can avoid the possibility that the above scenario might apply to them. Instead of buying regular 10-year Treasury notes, they can buy Treasury Inflation-Protection Securities, or TIPS. These securities have *nominal* returns that automatically adjust to changes in the Consumer Price Index. A TIPS note that offers a real rate of interest equal to 4 percent per year will pay this real rate of return no matter what the rate of consumer price inflation turns out to be in future years.

The British government was the first to offer inflation-protection securities during the modern period, beginning in 1981. The governments of Australia, Canada, and Sweden followed suit. The U.S. Treasury began offering TIPS as 5- and 10-year notes and 30-year bonds in 1997. By that time, U.S. inflation rates had declined relative to previous years. Consequently, there was little investor interest in the securities, so the Treasury stopped issuing TIPS as 5-year notes and 30-year bonds.

The Rising Demand for TIPS—A Signal of Inflation Fears?

Until 2002, the volume of TIPS and other inflation-protected securities held by investors worldwide averaged about $250 billion, and traders exchanged about $500 million of such securities each year. Since 2003, however, the outstanding amount of inflation-protected securities issued and purchased worldwide has risen to $450 billion, and an estimated $5 billion in annual trading of these securities now takes place among investors. By 2004, investor interest in TIPS had increased so much that the U.S. Treasury made plans to reintroduce 5-year notes and 30-year bonds with inflation protection.

This led many media commentators to speculate that investors' inflation fears were on the rise. Indeed, the difference between market rates on regular 10-year Treasury notes and inflation-protected 10-year notes rose in 2003 and 2004, which indicated a slight increase in the expected U.S. inflation rate.

Another factor helped explain the rise in demand for inflation-protected securities, however. Traditionally, investors have regarded stocks as "hedges" against inflation because average rates of return on stocks, including capital gains, have increased nearly in proportion with inflation. Since the early 2000s, however, average rates of return on stocks have been much lower. Thus a growing number of investors no longer view stocks as inflation hedges. More of these investors are turning to TIPS as an alternative form of inflation protection.

For Critical Analysis

1. Why might changes in the difference between the market interest rates on a regular 10-year Treasury note and an inflation-protected 10-year Treasury note indicate a change in the anticipated rate of inflation?
2. How might an investor who holds a regular 10-year Treasury note end up earning higher real interest returns over a decade than someone who holds an inflation-protected 10-year Treasury note for the same period?

Web Resources

1. To obtain detailed information about Treasury Inflation-Protection Securities from the Treasury's Bureau of the Public Debt, go to www.econtoday.com/chap22.
2. To learn about how to buy Treasury securities online, go to the U.S. Treasury's Treasury-Direct Web site via the link at www.econtoday.com/chap22.

Research Project

Discuss various incentives that investors have to hold TIPS. Why does the U.S. Treasury also have an incentive to *issue* these securities to help finance government deficits? Explain your reasoning.

SUMMARY DISCUSSION of Learning Objectives

1. **Economic Rent and Resource Allocation:** Owners of a resource in fixed supply, meaning that the resource supply curve is perfectly inelastic, are paid economic rent. Originally, this term was used to refer to payment for the use of land or any other natural resource that is considered to be in fixed supply. More generally, however, economic rent is a payment for use of any resource that exceeds the opportunity cost of the resource. People who provide labor services that are difficult for others to provide, such as sports superstars, movie stars, and the like, typically receive earnings well in excess of the earnings that would otherwise have been sufficient to induce them to provide their services. Nevertheless, the economic rents that they earn reflect the maximum market valuation of their value, so economic rent allocates resources to their highest-valued use.

2. **The Main Organizational Forms of Business and the Chief Advantages and Disadvantages of Each:** The primary organizational forms businesses take are the proprietorship, the partnership, and the corporation. The proprietorship is owned by a single person, the proprietor, who makes the business decisions, is entitled to all the profits, and is subject to unlimited liability—that is, is personally responsible for all debts incurred by the firm. The partnership differs from the proprietorship chiefly in that there are two or more owners, called partners. They share the responsibility for decision making, share the firm's profits, and individually bear unlimited liability for the firm's debts. The net income, or profits, of both proprietorships and partnerships is subject only to personal income taxes. Both types of firms legally cease to exist when the proprietor or a partner gives up ownership or dies. The corporation differs from proprietorships and partnerships in three important dimensions. Owners of corporations enjoy limited liability; that is, their responsibility for the debts of the corporation is limited to the value of their ownership shares. In addition, the income from corporations is subject to double taxation—corporate taxation when income is earned by the corporation and personal taxation when after-tax profits are paid as dividends to the owners. Finally, corporations do not legally cease to exist due to a change of ownership or the death of an owner.

3. **Accounting Profits versus Economic Profits:** A firm's accounting profits equal its total revenues minus its total explicit costs, which are expenses directly paid out by the firm. Economic profits equal accounting profits minus implicit costs, which are expenses that managers do not have to pay out of pocket, such as the opportunity cost of factors of production dedicated to the firm's production process. Owners of a firm seek to maximize the firm's economic profits to ensure that they earn at least a normal rate of return, meaning that the firm's total revenues at least cover explicit costs and implicit opportunity costs.

4. **Interest Rates:** Interest is a payment for the ability to use resources today instead of in the future. Factors that influence interest rates are the length of the term of a loan, the loan's risk, and handling charges. The nominal interest rate includes a factor that takes into account the anticipated inflation rate. Therefore, during periods of high anticipated inflation, current market (nominal) interest

rates are high. Comparing the market interest rate with the rate of return on prospective capital investment projects enables owners of funds to determine the highest-valued uses of the funds. Thus the interest rate allocates funds to industries whose investments yield the highest (risk-adjusted) returns, thereby ensuring that available resources will be put to their most productive uses.

5. **Calculating the Present Discounted Value of a Payment to Be Received at a Future Date:** The present value of a future payment is the value of the future amount expressed in today's dollars, and it is equal to the most that someone would pay today to receive that amount in the future. The method by which the present value of a future sum is calculated is called *discounting.* This method implies that the present value of a sum to be received a year from now is equal to the future amount divided by 1 plus the appropriate rate of interest, which is called the *rate of discount.*

6. **The Three Main Sources of Corporate Funds:** The main sources of financial capital for corporations are stocks, bonds, and reinvestment of profits. Stocks are ownership shares, promising a share of profits, sold to investors. Common stocks also embody voting rights regarding the major decisions of the firm; preferred stocks typically have no voting rights but enjoy priority status in the payment of dividends. Bonds are notes of indebtedness, issued in return for the loan of money. They typically promise to pay interest in the form of annual coupon payments, plus repayment of the original principal amount upon maturity. Bondholders are generally promised payment before any payment of dividends to shareholders, and for this reason bonds are less risky than stocks. Reinvestment involves the purchase of assets by the firm, using retained profits or depreciation reserves it has set aside for this purpose. No new stocks or bonds are issued in the course of reinvestment, although the firm's value is fully reflected in the price of existing shares of stock.

KEY TERMS AND CONCEPTS

accounting profit (524)	firm (521)	present value (529)
bond (532)	implicit costs (524)	proprietorship (522)
corporation (523)	inside information (534)	random walk theory (533)
discounting (530)	interest (527)	rate of discount (530)
dividends (523)	limited liability (523)	real rate of interest (528)
economic profits (526)	nominal rate of interest (528)	reinvestment (532)
economic rent (518)	normal rate of return (525)	securities (532)
explicit costs (524)	opportunity cost of capital (525)	share of stock (531)
financial capital (527)	partnership (523)	unlimited liability (522)

PROBLEMS

Answers to the odd-numbered problems appear at the back of the book.

22-1. Which of the following would you expect to have a high level of economic rent, and which would you expect to have a low level of economic rent? Explain why for each.

   a. Bob has a highly specialized medical skill that is in great demand.

   b. Sally has never attended school. She is 25 years old and is an internationally known supermodel.

   c. Tim is a high school teacher and sells insurance part time.

22-2. Though he has retired from hockey, Wayne Gretzky still earns a sizable annual income from endorsements. Explain why, in economic terms, his level of economic rent is so high.

22-3. Michael Jordan once retired from basketball to play baseball. As a result, his annual dollar income dropped from the millions to the thousands. Eventually, Jordan quit baseball and returned to basketball. What can be said about the role of economic rents in his situation?

22-4. A British pharmaceutical company spent several years and considerable funds on the development of a treatment for HIV patients. Now, with the protection afforded by patent rights, the company has the potential to reap enormous gains. The government, in response, has threatened to tax away any rents the company may earn. Is this an advisable policy? Why or why not?

22-5. Write a brief explanation of the differences between a sole proprietorship, a partnership, and a corporation. In addition, list one advantage and one disadvantage of a sole proprietorship, a partnership, and a corporation.

22-6. After graduation, you face a choice. One option is to work for a multinational consulting firm and earn a starting salary (benefits included) of $40,000. The other option is to use $5,000 in savings to start your own consulting firm. You could earn an interest return of 5 percent on your savings. You choose to start your own consulting firm. At the end of the first year, you add up all of your expenses and revenues. Your total includes $12,000 in rent, $1,000 in office supplies, $20,000 for office staff, and $4,000 in telephone expenses. What are your total explicit costs and total implicit costs?

22-7. Suppose, as in Problem 22-6, that you have now operated your consulting firm for a year. At the end of the first year, your total revenues are $77,250. Based on the information in Problem 22-6, what is the accounting profit, and what is your economic profit?

22-8. An individual leaves a college faculty, where she was earning $40,000 a year, to begin a new venture. She invests her savings of $10,000, which were earning 10 percent annually. She then spends $20,000 on office equipment, hires two students at $30,000 a year each, rents office space for $12,000, and has other variable expenses of $40,000. At the end of the year, her revenues were $200,000. What are her accounting profit and her economic profit for the year?

22-9. Classify the following items as either financial capital or physical capital.

   a. A drill press owned by a manufacturing company
   b. $100,000 set aside in an account to purchase a drill press
   c. Funds raised through a bond offer to expand plant and equipment
   d. A warehouse owned by a shipping company

22-10. Explain the difference between the dividends of a corporation and the profits of a sole proprietorship or partnership, particularly in their tax treatment.

22-11. The owner of WebCity is trying to decide whether to remain a proprietorship or to incorporate. Suppose that the corporate tax rate on profits is 20 percent and the personal income tax rate is 30 percent. For simplicity, assume that all corporate profits (after corporate taxes are paid) are distributed as dividends in the year they are earned and that such dividends are subject to tax at the personal income tax rate.

   a. If the owner of WebCity expects to earn $100,000 in before-tax profits this year, regardless of whether the firm is a proprietorship or a corporation, which method of organization should be chosen?
   b. What is the dollar value of the after-tax advantage of that form of organization?
   c. Suppose that the corporate form of organization has cost advantages that will raise before-tax profits by $50,000. Should the owner of WebCity incorporate?
   d. By how much will after-tax profits change due to incorporation?
   e. Suppose that tax policy is changed to completely exempt from personal taxation the first $40,000 per year in dividends. Would this change in policy affect the decision made in part (a)?
   f. How can you explain the fact that even though corporate profits are subject to double taxation, most business in America is conducted by corporations rather than by proprietorships or partnerships?

22-12. Explain how the following events would likely affect the relevant interest rate.

   a. A major bond-rating agency has improved the risk rating of a developing nation.
   b. To regulate and protect the public, the government has passed legislation that requires a considerable increase in the reporting paperwork when a bank makes a loan.

22-13. Suppose that the interest rate in Japan is only 2 percent, while the comparable rate in the United States is 4 percent. Japan's rate of inflation is 0.5 percent, while the U.S. inflation rate is 3 percent. Which economy has the higher real interest rate?

22-14. You expect to receive a payment of $104 one year from now. Your discount rate is 4 percent. What is the present value of the payment to be received? Suppose that the discount rate is 5 percent. What is the present value of the payment to be received?

22-15. Outline the differences between common stock and preferred stock.

22-16. Explain the basic differences between a share of stock and a bond.

22-17. Suppose that one of your classmates informs you that he has developed a method of forecasting stock market returns based on past trends. With a monetary investment by you, he claims that the two of you could profit handsomely from this forecasting method. How should you respond to your classmate?

22-18. Suppose that you are trying to decide whether to spend $1,000 on stocks issued by WildWeb or on bonds issued by the same company. There is a 50 percent chance that the value of the stock will rise to $2,200 at the end of the year and a 50 percent chance that the stock will be worthless at the end of the year. The bonds promise an interest rate of 20 percent per year, and it is certain that the bonds and interest will be repaid at the end of the year.

a. Assuming that your time horizon is exactly one year, will you choose the stocks or the bonds?

b. By how much is your expected end-of-year wealth reduced if you make the wrong choice?

c. Suppose the odds of success improve for Wild-Web: Now there is a 60 percent chance that the value of the stock will be $2,200 at year's end and only a 40 percent chance that it will be worthless. Should you now choose the stocks or the bonds?

d. By how much did your expected end-of-year wealth rise as a result of the improved outlook for WildWeb?

ECONOMICS ON THE NET

How the New York Stock Exchange Operates This application gives you the chance to learn about how the New York Stock Exchange functions.

Title: The New York Stock Exchange: How the NYSE Operates

Navigation: Follow the link at www.econtoday.com/chap22 to visit the New York Stock Exchange. In the left margin in the pop-up menu next to "About the NYSE," click on *Education*. Along the top, select the tab named *Educational Publications*. Then under the heading, "The New York Stock Exchange: A Guide to the World's Leading Securities Market," click on "Chapter Two: The Trading Floor."

Application Read the chapter; then answer the following questions.

1. What characteristics distinguish the two types of floor brokers?

2. List the key functions of a stock exchange specialist. Why is the "Point-of-Sale Display Book" likely to be particularly useful for a specialist?

For Group Study and Analysis Divide the class into groups, and have each group examine and discuss the description of how NYSE trades are executed. Ask each group to compose a listing of the various points at which Internet trading may be a more efficient way to execute a trade, as compared with trading via a traditional brokerage firm. Then go through these as a class, and discuss the following issue: In the New York Stock Exchange, which people cannot be replaced by new information technologies?

If your exam were tomorrow, would you be ready? For each chapter, MyEconLab Practice Tests and Study Plans pinpoint which sections you have mastered and which ones you need to study. That way, you are more efficient with your study time, and you are better prepared for your exams.

In addition to Practice Tests and your personalized Study Plan, you'll find the following media resources in MyEconLab:
1. *Graphs in Motion* animation of Figures 22-1 and 22-2.
2. Videos featuring the author, Roger LeRoy Miller, on the following subjects:
   ● Economic Rent and the Allocation of Resources
   ● The Goal of the Firm Is Profit Maximization
   ● Interest Rates and Present Value
   ● The Theory of Efficient Markets and Inside Information

3. Links to the Web sites cited in the marginal Internet Resources, Issues and Applications feature, and Economics on the Net activity.
4. Audio clips of all key terms, additional practice problems, and a PDF version of the material from the print Study Guide.
5. eThemes of the Times, which is a New York Times article to help you understand the real-world applications of what you are learning.

To see how it works, turn to page 16 and then go to www.myeconlab.com/miller.

Get Ahead of the Curve

Chapter 23

The Firm: Cost and Output Determination

F reight trains still move goods down many of the same railroad tracks they have used for years. Nevertheless, today's train dispatchers no longer use pencils and 3-foot-long paper "train sheets" to plot the positions of freight cars (normally called rolling stock). Dispatchers are now surrounded by computer screens transmitting real-time information about each train, and they communicate with engineers via nationwide intercom networks. Even though the basic techniques for moving locomotives and rolling stock along the rails have not dramatically changed, technological advances in information processing and communications have revolutionized the economics of rail transportation. In this chapter, you will learn how these new technologies have made rail companies more productive and, simultaneously, more cost efficient.

Media Resources

Refer to the end of the chapter for a full listing of the multimedia learning materials available in MyEconLab.

LEARNING OBJECTIVES

After reading this chapter, you should be able to:

1. Discuss the difference between the short run and the long run from the perspective of a firm
2. Understand why the marginal physical product of labor eventually declines as more units of labor are employed
3. Explain the short-run cost curves a typical firm faces
4. Describe the long-run cost curves a typical firm faces
5. Identify situations of economies and diseconomies of scale and define a firm's minimum efficient scale

... since 1999, U.S. power companies have added more than 200,000 megawatts of new electricity-generating capacity? To bring about this increase in output, power companies constructed about 400 new power plants. On the hottest midsummer day this year, power companies are able to produce nearly 25 percent more electricity than they could on an equally hot day a decade ago. They can also generate all this additional electricity at a lower cost per unit.

How could a major expansion in electricity-generating capacity simultaneously *reduce* the average cost of producing power? By the time you have finished this chapter, you will know the answer to this question.

SHORT RUN VERSUS LONG RUN

In Chapter 21, we discussed short-run and long-run price elasticities of supply and demand. For consumers, the long run meant the time period during which all adjustments to a change in price could be made, and anything shorter than that was considered the short run. For suppliers, the long run was the time in which all adjustments could be made, and anything shorter than that was the short run.

Now that we are discussing firms only, we will maintain a similar distinction between the short and the long run, but we will be more specific. In the theory of the firm, the **short run** is defined as any time period that is so short that there is at least one input, such as current **plant size,** that the firm cannot alter.[*] In other words, during the short run, a firm makes do with whatever big machines and factory size it already has, no matter how much more it wants to produce because of increased demand for its product. We consider the plant and heavy equipment, the size or amount of which cannot be varied in the short run, as fixed resources. In agriculture and in some other businesses, land may be a fixed resource.

There are, of course, variable resources that the firm can alter when it wants to change its rate of production. These are called *variable inputs* or *variable factors of production.* Typically, the variable inputs of a firm are its labor and its purchases of raw materials. In the short run, in response to changes in demand, the firm can, by definition, change only the amounts of its variable inputs.

The **long run** can now be considered the period of time in which *all* inputs can be varied. Specifically, in the long run, the firm can alter its plant size. How long is the long run? That depends on each individual industry. For Wendy's or McDonald's, the long run may be four or five months, because that is the time it takes to add new franchises. For a steel company, the long run may be several years, because that's how long it takes to plan and build a new plant. An electric utility might need over a decade to build a new plant, as another example.

Short run and *long run* in our discussion are terms that apply to planning decisions made by managers. The firm can operate only in the short run in the sense that decisions must be made in the present. The same analysis applies to your own behavior. You may have many long-run plans about graduate school, vacations, and the like, but you always operate in the short run—you make decisions every day about what you do every day.

Short run
The time period during which at least one input, such as plant size, cannot be changed.

Plant size
The physical size of the factories that a firm owns and operates to produce its output. Plant size can be defined by square footage, maximum physical capacity, and other physical measures.

Long run
The time period during which all factors of production can be varied.

Economics Front and Center

To contemplate why labor might be a variable input even for a firm that sells its product exclusively on the Internet, read the case study, **Short-Run Adjustments at a Web-Based Firm,** on page 562.

---

[*]There can be many short runs but only one long run. For ease of analysis, in this section we simplify the case to one short run and talk about short-run costs.

THE RELATIONSHIP BETWEEN OUTPUT AND INPUTS

A firm takes numerous inputs, combines them using a technological production process, and ends up with an output. There are, of course, a great many factors of production, or inputs. Ignoring land, we classify production inputs into two broad categories—labor and capital. The relationship between output and these two inputs is as follows:

Output per time period = some function of capital and labor inputs

In simple math, the production relationship can be written $Q = f(K, L)$, where Q = output per time period, K = capital, and L = labor.

Production
Any activity that results in the conversion of resources into products that can be used in consumption.

We have used the word *production* but have not defined it. **Production** is any process by which resources are transformed into goods or services. Production includes not only making things but also transporting them, retailing, repackaging them, and so on. Notice that if we know that production occurs, we do not necessarily know the value of the output. The production relationship tells nothing about the worth or value of the inputs or the output.

The Production Function: A Numerical Example

Production function
The relationship between inputs and maximum physical output. A production function is a technological, not an economic, relationship.

The relationship between maximum physical output and the quantity of capital and labor used in the production process is sometimes called the **production function.** The production function is a technological relationship between inputs and output. Firms that are inefficient or wasteful in their use of capital and labor will obtain less output than the production function in theory will show. No firm can obtain more output than the production function shows, however. The production function specifies the maximum possible output that can be produced with a given amount of inputs. It also specifies the minimum amount of inputs necessary to produce a given level of output. The production function depends on the technology available to the firm. It follows that an improvement in technology that allows the firm to produce more output with the same amount of inputs (or the same output with fewer inputs) results in a new production function.

For many firms, a big part of the production process involves distributing manufactured items to the retail outlets where they ultimately are sold to customers. Why do you think that some producers have found that loading trucks as fully as possible does not necessarily maximize the total amount of output that can be transported using given inputs?

E X A M P L E

Filling a Truck Is Less Productive Than Sending It Half Full

For years, managers at Procter & Gamble, the consumer-products company, told warehouse workers to pack a truck full of detergent and send it out to make deliveries to retailers, then pack the next truck full of boxes of toothpaste, and so on. Then, in the early 2000s, the company invested in inventory-tracking software that allowed managers to determine how many workers and how much time were required to get products to their ultimate destinations. What they discovered at first seemed counterintuitive. Sending out trucks fully loaded with a single product required the use of more inputs per unit of time than shipping a mix of products on trucks that were less full.

Packing trucks as fully as possible, the data revealed, often left warehouse workers idle for long stretches between trucks. Also, filling individual trucks with boxes of a single product to be dropped off at many locations ultimately required driving trucks more miles—and using more fuel—than loading a variety of products onto trucks driven to fewer final destinations. Based on this information, Procter & Gamble began sending out rerouted and less full trucks carrying more than one product at a time. The company was able to ship 30 percent more output per unit of time using the same truck, labor, and fuel inputs as before.

For Critical Analysis
If Procter & Gamble continued to manufacture and ship as much output each week after the change in its distribution system, did it require the same amount of trucks, fuel, and workers to accomplish this task?

Look at panel (a) of Figure 23-1 on the next page. It shows a production function relating total output in column 2 to the quantity of labor measured in workers per week in column 1. When there are zero workers per week of input, there is no output. When there are 5 workers per week of input (given the capital stock), there is a total output of 50 computer printers per week. (Ignore for the moment the rest of that panel.) Panel (b) of Figure 23-1 shows this particular hypothetical production function graphically. Note again that it relates to the short run, because plant size is fixed, and that it is for an individual firm.

Panel (b) shows a total physical product curve, or the maximum amount of physical output that is possible when we add successive equal-sized units of labor while holding all other inputs constant. The graph of the production function in panel (b) is not a straight line. In fact, it peaks at 7 workers per week and then starts to go down. To understand why it starts to go down with an individual firm in the short run, we have to analyze in detail the **law of diminishing (marginal) returns.**

But before that, let's examine the meaning of columns 3 and 4 of panel (a) of Figure 23-1—that is, average and marginal physical product.

Average and Marginal Physical Product

The definition of **average physical product** is straightforward: It is the total product divided by the number of worker-weeks. You can see in column 3 of panel (a) of Figure 23-1 that the average physical product of labor first rises and then steadily falls after two workers are hired.

Remember that *marginal* means "additional." Hence the **marginal physical product** of labor is the change in total product that occurs when a worker joins an existing production process. (The term *physical* here emphasizes the fact that we are measuring in terms of physical units of production, not in dollar terms.) It is also the *change* in total product that occurs when that worker quits or is laid off an existing production process. The marginal physical product of labor therefore refers to the *change in output caused by a one-unit change in the labor input.* (Marginal physical product is also referred to as *marginal product* and *marginal return.*)

DIMINISHING MARGINAL RETURNS

The concept of diminishing marginal returns—also known as diminishing marginal product—applies to many situations. If you put a seat belt across your lap, a certain amount of safety is obtained. If you add another seat belt over your shoulder, some additional safety is obtained, but less than when the first belt was secured. When you add a third seat belt over the other shoulder, the amount of *additional* safety obtained is even smaller.

The same analysis holds for firms in their use of productive inputs. When the returns from hiring more workers are diminishing, it does not necessarily mean that more workers won't be hired. In fact, workers will be hired until the returns, in terms of the *value* of the *extra* output produced, are equal to the additional wages that have to be paid for those workers to produce the extra output. Before we get into that decision-making process, let's

Law of diminishing (marginal) returns
The observation that after some point, successive equal-sized increases in a variable factor of production, such as labor, added to fixed factors of production, will result in smaller increases in output.

Average physical product
Total product divided by the variable input.

Marginal physical product
The physical output that is due to the addition of one more unit of a variable factor of production; the change in total product occurring when a variable input is increased and all other inputs are held constant; also called *marginal product* or *marginal return.*

FIGURE 23-1

Diminishing Returns, the Production Function, and Marginal Product: A Hypothetical Case

Marginal product is the addition to the total product that results when one additional worker is hired. Thus, in panel (a), the marginal product of the fourth worker is eight computer printers. With four workers, 44 printers are produced, but with three workers, only 36 are produced; the difference is 8. In panel (b), we plot the numbers from columns 1 and 2 of panel (a). In panel (c), we plot the numbers from columns 1 and 4 of panel (a). When we go from 0 to 1, marginal product is 10. When we go from one worker to two workers, marginal product increases to 16. After two workers, marginal product declines, but it is still positive. Total product (output) reaches its peak at seven workers, so after seven workers, marginal product is negative. When we move from seven to eight workers, marginal product becomes −1 printer.

Panel (a)

(1) Input of Labor (number of worker-weeks)	(2) Total Product (output in computer printers per week)	(3) Average Physical Product (total product ÷ number of worker-weeks) [printers per week]	(4) Marginal Physical Product (output in printers per week)
0	—	—	
1	10	10.00	10
2	26	13.00	16
3	36	12.00	10
4	44	11.00	8
5	50	10.00	6
6	54	9.00	4
7	56	8.00	2
8	55	6.88	−1
9	53	5.89	−2
10	50	5.00	−3
11	46	4.18	−4

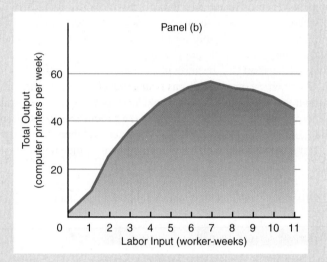

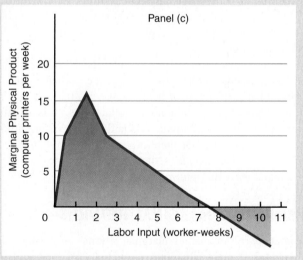

demonstrate that diminishing returns can be represented graphically and can be used in our analysis of the firm.

Measuring Diminishing Returns

How do we measure diminishing returns? First, we limit the analysis to only one variable factor of production (or input)—let's say the factor is labor. Every other factor of production, such as machines, must be held constant. Only in this way can we calculate the marginal returns from using more workers and know when we reach the point of diminishing marginal returns.

The marginal productivity of labor may increase rapidly at the very beginning. A firm starts with no workers, only machines. The firm then hires one worker, who finds it difficult to get the work started. But when the firm hires more workers, each is able to *specialize* in performing different tasks, and the marginal product of those additional workers may actually be greater than the marginal product of the previous few workers. Beyond some point, however, diminishing returns must set in—*not* because new workers are less qualified but because each worker has, on average, fewer machines with which to work (remember, all other inputs are fixed). In fact, eventually the firm's plant will become so crowded that workers will start to get in each other's way. At that point, marginal physical product becomes negative, and total production declines.

Using these ideas, we can define the law of diminishing returns as follows:

> *As successive equal increases in a variable factor of production are added to fixed factors of production, there will be a point beyond which the extra, or marginal, product that can be attributed to each additional unit of the variable factor of production will decline.*

Note that the law of diminishing returns is a statement about the *physical* relationships between inputs and outputs that we have observed in many firms. If the law of diminishing returns were not a fairly accurate statement about the world, what would stop firms from hiring additional workers forever?

An Example of the Law of Diminishing Returns

Production of computer printers provides an example of the law of diminishing returns. With a fixed amount of factory space, assembly equipment, and quality-control diagnostic software, the addition of more workers eventually yields decreasing increases in output. After a while, when all the assembly equipment and quality-control diagnostic software are being used, additional workers will have to start assembling and troubleshooting quality problems manually. They obviously won't be as productive as the first workers who had access to other productive inputs. The marginal physical product of an additional worker, given a specified amount of capital, must eventually be less than that for the previous workers.

A hypothetical set of numbers illustrating the law of diminishing marginal returns is presented in panel (a) of Figure 23-1 on the previous page. The numbers are presented graphically in panel (c). Marginal productivity (returns from adding more workers) first increases, then decreases, and finally becomes negative.

When one worker is hired, total output goes from 0 to 10. Thus marginal physical product is 10 computer printers per week. When the second worker is hired, total product goes from 10 to 26 printers per week. Marginal physical product therefore increases to 16 printers per week. When a third worker is hired, total product again increases, from 26 to 36 printers per week. This represents a marginal physical product of only 10 printers per week. Therefore, the point of diminishing marginal returns occurs after two workers are hired.

Notice that after 7 workers per week, marginal physical product becomes negative. That means that the hiring of an eighth worker would create a situation that reduces total product. Sometimes this is called the *point of saturation,* indicating that given the amount of fixed inputs, there is no further positive use for more of the variable input. We have entered the region of negative marginal returns.

CONCEPTS in Brief

- The technological relationship between output and inputs is called the production function. It relates output per time period to several inputs, such as capital and labor.

- After some rate of output, the firm generally experiences diminishing marginal returns.

- The law of diminishing returns states that if all factors of production are held constant except one, equal increments in that one variable factor will eventually yield decreasing increments in output.

To test your understanding of the concepts covered in this section, go to the Online Review at www.myeconlab.com/miller.

SHORT-RUN COSTS TO THE FIRM

You will see that costs are the extension of the production ideas just presented. Let's consider the costs the firm faces in the short run. To make this example simple, assume that there are only two factors of production, capital and labor. Our definition of the short run will be the time during which capital is fixed but labor is variable.

Total costs
The sum of total fixed costs and total variable costs.

In the short run, a firm incurs certain types of costs. We label all costs incurred **total costs.** Then we break total costs down into total fixed costs and total variable costs, which we will explain shortly. Therefore,

$$\text{Total costs (TC)} = \text{total fixed costs (TFC)} + \text{total variable costs (TVC)}$$

Remember that these total costs include both explicit and implicit costs, including the normal rate of return on investment.

After we have looked at the elements of total costs, we will find out how to compute average and marginal costs.

Total Fixed Costs

Let's look at an ongoing business such as Dell, Inc. The decision makers in that corporate giant can look around and see big machines, thousands of parts, huge buildings, and a multitude of other components of plant and equipment that have already been bought and are in place. Dell has to take account of the technological obsolescence of this equipment, no matter how many computers it produces. The payments on the loans taken out to buy the equipment will all be exactly the same. The opportunity costs of any land that Dell owns will all be exactly the same. In the short run, these costs are more or less the same for Dell no matter how many computers it produces.

We also have to point out that the opportunity cost (or normal rate of return) of capital must be included along with other costs. Remember that we are dealing in the short run, during which capital is fixed. If investors in Dell have already put $100 million into a new factory addition, the opportunity cost of that capital invested is now, in essence, a *fixed cost.* Why? Because in the short run, nothing can be done about that cost; the investment has already been made. This leads us to a very straightforward definition of fixed costs: All costs that do not vary—that is, all costs that do not depend on the rate of production— are called **fixed costs.**

Fixed costs
Costs that do not vary with output. Fixed costs typically include such things as rent on a building. These costs are fixed for a certain period of time (in the long run, though, they are variable).

Let's now take as an example the fixed costs incurred by an assembler of recordable DVDs. This firm's total fixed costs will usually include the cost of the rent on its equipment and the insurance it has to pay. We see in panel (a) of Figure 23-2 that total fixed costs per day are $10. In panel (b), these total fixed costs are represented by the horizontal line at $10 per day. They are invariant to changes in the output of recordable DVDs per day—no matter how many are produced, fixed costs will remain at $10 per day.

FIGURE 23-2

Cost of Production: An Example

In panel (a), the derivations of columns 4 through 9 are given in parentheses in each column heading. For example, column 6, average variable costs, is derived by dividing column 3, total variable costs, by column 1, total output per day. Note that marginal cost (MC) in panel (c) intersects average variable costs (AVC) at the latter's minimum point. Also, MC intersects average total costs (ATC) at that latter's minimum point. It is a little more difficult to see that MC equals AVC and ATC at their respective minimum points in panel (a) because we are using discrete one-unit changes. You can see, though, that the marginal cost of going from 4 units per day to 5 units per day is $2 and increases to $3 when we move to 6 units per day. Somewhere between it equals AVC of $2.60, which is in fact the minimum average variable cost. The same analysis holds for ATC, which hits minimum at 7 units per day at $4.28 per unit. MC goes from $4 to $5 and just equals ATC somewhere in between.

Panel (a)

(1) Total Output (Q/day)	(2) Total Fixed Costs (TFC)	(3) Total Variable Costs (TVC)	(4) Total Costs (TC) (4) = (2) + (3)	(5) Average Fixed Costs (AFC) (5) = (2) ÷ (1)	(6) Average Variable Costs (AVC) (6) = (3) ÷ (1)	(7) Average Total Costs (ATC) (7) = (4) ÷ (1)	(8) Total Costs (TC) (4)	(9) Marginal Cost (MC) (9) = Change in (8) / Change in (1)
0	$10	$ 0	$10	—	—	—	$10	
1	10	5	15	$10.00	$5.00	$15.00	15	$5
2	10	8	18	5.00	4.00	9.00	18	3
3	10	10	20	3.33	3.33	6.67	20	2
4	10	11	21	2.50	2.75	5.25	21	1
5	10	13	23	2.00	2.60	4.60	23	2
6	10	16	26	1.67	2.67	4.33	26	3
7	10	20	30	1.43	2.86	4.28	30	4
8	10	25	35	1.25	3.12	4.38	35	5
9	10	31	41	1.11	3.44	4.56	41	6
10	10	38	48	1.00	3.80	4.80	48	7
11	10	46	56	.91	4.18	5.09	56	8

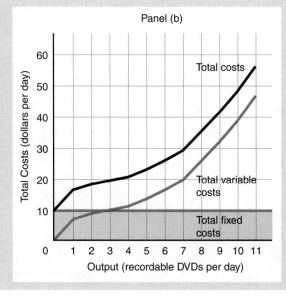

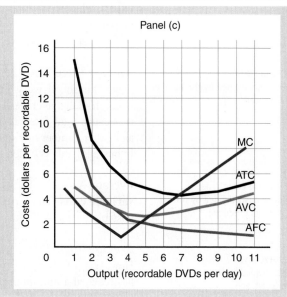

549

Total Variable Costs

Variable costs
Costs that vary with the rate of production. They include wages paid to workers and purchases of materials.

Total **variable costs** are costs whose magnitude varies with the rate of production. Wages are an obvious variable cost. The more the firm produces, the more labor it has to hire; therefore, the more wages it has to pay. Parts are another variable cost. To assemble recordable DVDs, for example, microchips must be bought. The more DVDs that are made, the greater the number of chips that must be bought. A portion of the rate of depreciation (wear and tear) on machines that are used in the assembly process can also be considered a variable cost if depreciation depends partly on how long and how intensively the machines are used. Total variable costs are given in column 3 in panel (a) of Figure 23-2 on the previous page. These are translated into the total variable cost curve in panel (b). Notice that the total variable cost curve lies below the total cost curve by the vertical distance of $10. This vertical distance represents, of course, total fixed costs.

Short-Run Average Cost Curves

In panel (b) of Figure 23-2, we see total costs, total variable costs, and total fixed costs. Now we want to look at average cost. With the average cost concept, we are measuring cost per unit of output. It is a matter of simple arithmetic to figure the averages of these three cost concepts. We can define them as follows:

$$\text{Average total costs (ATC)} = \frac{\text{total costs (TC)}}{\text{output } (Q)}$$

$$\text{Average variable costs (AVC)} = \frac{\text{total variable costs (TVC)}}{\text{output } (Q)}$$

$$\text{Average fixed costs (AFC)} = \frac{\text{total fixed costs (TFC)}}{\text{output } (Q)}$$

The arithmetic is done in columns 5, 6, and 7 in panel (a) of Figure 23-2. The numerical results are translated into a graphical format in panel (c). Because total costs (TC) equal variable costs (TVC) plus fixed costs (TFC), the difference between average total costs (ATC) and average variable costs (AVC) will always be identical to average fixed costs (AFC). That means that average total costs and average variable costs move together as output expands.

Now let's see what we can observe about the three average cost curves in Figure 23-2.

Average fixed costs
Total fixed costs divided by the number of units produced.

Average Fixed Costs (AFC). **Average fixed costs** continue to fall throughout the output range. In fact, if we were to continue panel (c) of Figure 23-2 farther to the right, we would find that average fixed costs would get closer and closer to the horizontal axis. That is because total fixed costs remain constant. As we divide this fixed number by a larger and larger number of units of output, the resulting AFC has to become smaller and smaller. In business, this is called "spreading the overhead."

Average variable costs
Total variable costs divided by the number of units produced.

Average Variable Costs (AVC). We assume a particular form of the curve for **average variable costs.** The form that it takes is U-shaped: First it falls; then it starts to rise. It is possible for the AVC curve to take other shapes in the long run.

Average total costs
Total costs divided by the number of units produced; sometimes called *average per-unit total costs.*

Average Total Costs (ATC). This curve has a shape similar to that of the AVC curve. However, it falls even more dramatically in the beginning and rises more slowly after it has reached a minimum point. It falls and then rises because **average total costs** are the summation of the AFC curve and the AVC curve. Thus, when AFC and AVC are both falling, ATC must fall too. At some point, however, AVC starts to increase while AFC continues to fall. Once the increase in the AVC curve outweighs the decrease in the AFC curve, the ATC curve will start to increase and will develop a U shape, just like the AVC curve.

Marginal Cost

We have stated repeatedly that the basis of decisions is always on the margin—movement in economics is always determined at the margin. This dictum also holds true within the firm. Firms, according to the analysis we use to predict their behavior, are very interested in their **marginal costs.** Because the term *marginal* means "additional" or "incremental" (or "decremental," too) here, *marginal costs* refer to costs that result from a one-unit change in the production rate. For example, if the production of 10 recordable DVDs per day costs a firm $48 and the production of 11 recordable DVDs costs it $56 per day, the marginal cost of producing 11 rather than 10 DVDs per day is $8.

> **Marginal costs**
> The change in total costs due to a one-unit change in production rate.

Marginal costs can be measured by using the formula

$$\text{Marginal cost} = \frac{\text{change in total cost}}{\text{change in output}}$$

We show the marginal costs of production of recordable DVDs per day in column 9 of panel (a) in Figure 23-2 on page 549, computed according to the formula just given. In our example, we have changed output by one unit every time, so we can ignore variations in the denominator in that particular formula.

This marginal cost schedule is shown graphically in panel (c) of Figure 23-2. Just like average variable costs and average total costs, marginal costs first fall and then rise. The U shape of the marginal cost curve is a result of increasing and then diminishing marginal returns. At lower levels of output, the marginal cost curve declines. The reasoning is that as marginal physical product increases with each addition of output, the marginal cost of this last unit of output must fall. Conversely, when diminishing marginal returns set in, marginal physical product decreases (and eventually becomes negative); it follows that the marginal cost must rise when the marginal product begins its decline. These relationships are clearly reflected in the geometry of panels (b) and (c) of Figure 23-2.

In summary:

> *As long as marginal physical product rises, marginal cost will fall, and when marginal physical product starts to fall (after reaching the point of diminishing marginal returns), marginal cost will begin to rise.*

Have you ever thought about how much delivery-service companies such as FedEx have reduced their marginal costs by making it easy for you to track a package on the Internet instead of checking on its status by telephone?

E-Commerce EXAMPLE

Internet Package Tracking Cuts Marginal Cost at FedEx

At FedEx, the marginal cost incurred in delivering packages speedily often encompasses more than just the expense of physically transporting a package from one location to another. The additional cost of delivering one more package also includes the cost of providing information to senders or recipients checking on the status of the package. Before most people had access to the Internet, FedEx provided tracking services only by telephone. Hundreds of thousands of customers would call each day and give the tracking numbers of their packages to FedEx representatives, who would check their status using the company's internal computer system. The additional cost entailed in providing this service exceeded $2 per package.

Today, a customer can go to www.fedex.com on the Internet, enter a package's tracking number, and view its current status. Maintaining this service to respond to the three million tracking requests received at the Web site each day costs

FedEx about 4 cents per package. Because only a few thousand people per day now phone in tracking requests, the company's cost of delivering one more package is now much lower. The company's marginal cost curve, therefore, has shifted downward.

For Critical Analysis
How has FedEx's Internet tracking system affected the company's average total cost curve?

The Relationship Between Average and Marginal Costs

Let us now examine the relationship between average costs and marginal costs. There is always a definite relationship between averages and marginals. Consider the example of 10 football players with an average weight of 200 pounds. An eleventh player is added. His weight is 250 pounds. That represents the marginal weight. What happens now to the average weight of the team? It must increase. Thus, when the marginal player weighs more than the average, the average must increase. Likewise, if the marginal player weighs less than 200 pounds, the average weight will decrease.

There is a similar relationship between average variable costs and marginal costs. When marginal costs are less than average costs, the latter must fall. Conversely, when marginal costs are greater than average costs, the latter must rise. When you think about it, the relationship makes sense. The only way average variable costs can fall is if the extra cost of the marginal unit produced is less than the average variable cost of all the preceding units. For example, if the average variable cost for two units of production is $4.00 a unit, the only way for the average variable cost of three units to be less than that of two units is for the variable costs attributable to the last unit—the marginal cost—to be less than the average of the past units. In this particular case, if average variable cost falls to $3.33 a unit, total variable cost for the three units would be three times $3.33, or almost exactly $10.00. Total variable cost for two units is two times $4.00 (average variable cost), or $8.00. The marginal cost is therefore $10.00 minus $8.00, or $2.00, which is less than the average variable cost of $3.33.

A similar type of computation can be carried out for rising average variable costs. The only way average variable costs can rise is if the average variable cost of additional units is more than that for units already produced. But the incremental cost is the marginal cost. In this particular case, the marginal costs have to be higher than the average variable costs.

There is also a relationship between marginal costs and average total costs. Remember that average total cost is equal to total cost divided by the number of units produced. Also remember that marginal cost does not include any fixed costs. Fixed costs are, by definition, fixed and cannot influence marginal costs. Our example can therefore be repeated substituting *average total cost* for *average variable cost.*

These rising and falling relationships can be seen in panel (c) of Figure 23-2 on page 549, where MC intersects AVC and ATC at their respective minimum points.

Minimum Cost Points

At what rate of output of recordable DVDs per day does our representative firm experience the minimum average total costs? Column 7 in panel (a) of Figure 23-2 shows that the minimum average total cost is $4.28, which occurs at an output rate of seven DVDs per day. We can also find this minimum cost by finding the point in panel (c) of Figure 23-2 where the marginal cost curve intersects the average total cost curve. This should not be surprising. When marginal cost is below average total cost, average total cost falls. When marginal cost is above average total cost, average total cost rises. At the point where average total cost is neither falling nor rising, marginal cost must then be equal to average total cost. When we represent this graphically, the marginal cost curve will intersect the average total cost curve at the latter's minimum.

The same analysis applies to the intersection of the marginal cost curve and the average variable cost curve. When are average variable costs at a minimum? According to panel (a) of Figure 23-2, average variable costs are at a minimum of $2.60 at an output rate of five recordable DVDs per day. This is where the marginal cost curve intersects the average variable cost curve in panel (c) of Figure 23-2.

Why do you think that cost minimization helps explain why bathrooms in many office buildings are stocked with a new type of toilet paper dispenser?

E X A M P L E

How Building Owners Are Winning the Toilet Paper Tug-of-War

Most firms in the United States do not own their own office buildings. Instead, they rent space from landlords that own and maintain the buildings. Landlords charge rents that cover heating, cooling, plumbing, and other basic services, such as restroom maintenance and supplies, including toilet paper. All told, commercial restrooms account for about 20 percent of all U.S. toilet paper consumption, or about 600,000 tons per year.

Years ago, restrooms in office buildings stocked the same toilet paper rolls commonly used in homes. This, of course, gave some office employees an incentive to steal entire rolls of toilet paper to carry home. This small-time larceny increased the landlords' expense of keeping buildings' restrooms stocked. In an effort to reduce their costs, between the late 1980s and early 2000s landlords gradually replaced most standard toilet paper dispensers with "controlled-delivery" dispensers. These mechanisms include gears that provide resistance to efforts to pull out more than small amounts of toilet paper. Locked inside the dispensers are jumbo rolls of paper as large as 13 inches in diameter, which cut down on the number of visits that custodians have to make to restock building restrooms. Many landlords even have their custodial staffs carefully track toilet paper usage so that they can pressure specific tenants to cut down on consumption. Estimates indicate that controlled delivery has reduced landlords' toilet paper costs by about 20 percent per year.

For Critical Analysis
Has the installation of controlled-delivery toilet paper dispensers reduced landlords' fixed or variable costs?

CONCEPTS in Brief

- Total costs equal total fixed costs plus total variable costs.

- Fixed costs are those that do not vary with the rate of production; variable costs are those that do vary with the rate of production.

- Average total costs equal total costs divided by output (ATC = TC/Q).

- Average variable costs equal total variable costs divided by output (AVC = TVC/Q).

- Average fixed costs equal total fixed costs divided by output (AFC = TFC/Q).

- Marginal cost equals the change in total cost divided by the change in output (MC = ΔTC/ΔQ, where the Greek letter Δ, delta, means "change in").

- The marginal cost curve intersects the minimum point of the average total cost curve and the minimum point of the average variable cost curve.

To test your understanding of the concepts covered in this section, go to the Online Review at **www.myeconlab.com/miller.**

THE RELATIONSHIP BETWEEN DIMINISHING MARGINAL RETURNS AND COST CURVES

There is a unique relationship between output and the shape of the various cost curves we have drawn. Let's consider specifically the relationship between marginal cost and the example of diminishing physical returns in panel (a) of Figure 23-3 on page 556. It turns out that if wage rates are constant, the shape of the marginal cost curve in panel (d) of Figure 23-3 is both a reflection of and a consequence of the law of diminishing returns.

Let's assume that each unit of labor can be purchased at a constant price. Further assume that labor is the only variable input. We see that as more workers are hired, marginal physical product first rises and then falls after the point at which diminishing returns are encountered. Thus the marginal cost of each extra unit of output will first fall as long as marginal physical product is rising, and then it will rise as long as marginal physical product is falling. Recall that marginal cost is defined as

$$\text{MC} = \frac{\text{change in total cost}}{\text{change in output}}$$

Because the price of labor is assumed to be constant, the change in total cost depends solely on the unchanged price of labor, *W*. The change in output is simply the marginal physical product (MPP) of the one-unit increase in labor. Therefore, we see that

$$\text{Marginal cost} = \frac{W}{\text{MPP}}$$

This means that initially, when there are increasing returns, marginal cost falls (we are dividing *W* by increasingly larger numbers), and later, when diminishing returns set in and marginal physical product is falling, marginal cost must increase (we are dividing *W* by smaller numbers). So, as marginal physical product increases, marginal cost decreases, and as marginal physical product decreases, marginal cost must increase. Thus, when marginal physical product reaches its maximum, marginal cost necessarily reaches its minimum.

To illustrate this, let's return to Figure 23-1 on page 546 and consider specifically panel (a). Assume that a skilled printer-assembly worker is paid $1,000 a week. When we go from zero labor input to one unit, output increases by 10 computer printers. Each of those 10 printers has a marginal cost of $100. Now the second unit of labor is hired, and it too costs $1,000 per week. Output increases by 16. Thus the marginal cost is $1,000 ÷ 16 = $62.50. We continue the experiment. We see that the next unit of labor yields only 10 additional computer printers, so marginal cost starts to rise again back to $100. The following unit of labor increases marginal physical product by only 8, so marginal cost becomes $1,000 ÷ 8 = $125.

All of the foregoing can be restated in relatively straightforward terms:

Firms' short-run cost curves are a reflection of the law of diminishing marginal returns. Given any constant price of the variable input, marginal costs decline as long as the marginal physical product of the variable resource is rising. At the point at which diminishing marginal returns begin, marginal costs begin to rise as the marginal physical product of the variable input begins to decline.

The result is a marginal cost curve that slopes down, hits a minimum, and then slopes up. Of course, the average total cost curve and average variable cost curve are affected. They will have their familiar U shape in the short run. Again, to see this, recall that

$$\text{AVC} = \frac{\text{total variable costs}}{\text{total output}}$$

As we move from zero labor input to one unit in panel (a) of Figure 23-1 on page 546, output increases from zero to 10 computer printers. The total variable costs are the price per worker, W ($1,000), times the number of workers (1). Because the average product of one worker (column 3) is 10, we can write the total product, 10, as the average product, 10, times the number of workers, 1. Thus we see that

$$\text{AVC} = \frac{\$1{,}000 \times 1}{10 \times 1} = \frac{\$1{,}000}{10} = \frac{W}{\text{AP}}$$

From column 3 in panel (a) of Figure 23-1, we see that the average product increases, reaches a maximum, and then declines. Because AVC = W/AP, average variable cost decreases as average product increases and increases as average product decreases. AVC reaches its minimum when average product reaches its maximum. Furthermore, because ATC = AVC + AFC, the average total cost curve inherits the relationship between the average variable cost and diminishing returns.

To illustrate, consider an Internet service provider that employs skilled technicians to provide access services within a given geographic area. Panel (a) of Figure 23-3 on the next page presents in column 2 the total number of Internet access accounts serviced as the number of technicians increases. Notice that the total product first increases at an increasing rate and later increases at a decreasing rate. This is reflected in column 4, which shows that the marginal physical product increases at first and then falls. The average physical product too first rises and then falls. The marginal and average physical products are graphed in panel (c) of Figure 23-3. Our immediate interest here is the average variable and marginal costs. Because we can define average variable cost as $1,000/AP (assuming that the wage paid is constant at $1,000), as the average product rises from 50 to 55 to 60 Internet access accounts, the average variable cost falls from $20.00 to $18.18 to $16.67. Conversely, as average product falls from 60 to 51, average variable cost rises from $16.67 to $19.61. Likewise, because marginal cost can also be defined as W/MPP, we see that as marginal physical product rises from 50 to 70, marginal cost falls from $20.00 to $14.29. As marginal physical product falls to 30, marginal cost rises to $33.33. These relationships are also expressed in panels (b), (c), and (d) of Figure 23-3.

LONG-RUN COST CURVES

The long run is defined as a time period during which full adjustment can be made to any change in the economic environment. Thus, in the long run, *all* factors of production are variable. Long-run curves are sometimes called *planning curves,* and the long run is sometimes called the **planning horizon.** We start our analysis of long-run cost curves by considering a single firm contemplating the construction of a single plant. The firm has three alternative plant sizes from which to choose on the planning horizon. Each particular plant size generates its own short-run average total cost curve. Now that we are talking about the difference between long-run and short-run cost curves, we will label all short-run curves with an S and long-run curves with an L; short-run average (total) costs will be labeled SAC; and long-run average cost curves will be labeled LAC.

Panel (a) of Figure 23-4 on page 557 shows short-run average cost curves for three successively larger plants. Which is the optimal size to build, if we can only choose among these three? That depends on the anticipated normal, sustained rate of output per time period. Assume for a moment that the anticipated normal, sustained rate is Q_1. If a plant of size 1 is built, the average costs will be C_1. If a plant of size 2 is built, we see on SAC$_2$ that the average costs will be C_2. which is greater than C_1. Thus, if the anticipated rate of output is Q_1, the appropriate plant size is the one from which SAC$_1$ was derived.

Planning horizon
The long run, during which all inputs are variable.

Panel (a)

(1) Labor Input	(2) Total Product (number of Internet access accounts serviced)	(3) Average Physical Product (accounts per technician) (3) = (2) ÷ (1)	(4) Marginal Physical Product	(5) Average Variable Cost (5) = W ($1,000) ÷ (3)	(6) Marginal Cost (6) = W ($1,000) ÷ (4)
0	0	—	—	—	—
1	50	50	50	$20.00	$20.00
2	110	55	60	18.18	16.67
3	180	60	70	16.67	14.29
4	240	60	60	16.67	16.67
5	290	58	50	17.24	20.00
6	330	55	40	18.18	25.00
7	360	51	30	19.61	33.33

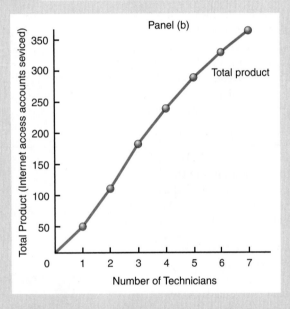

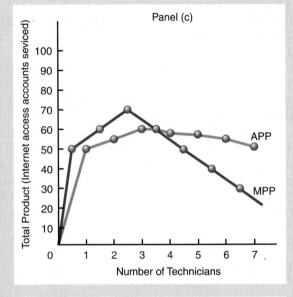

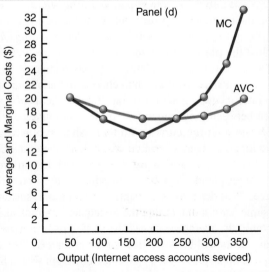

FIGURE 23-3

The Relationship Between Output and Costs

As the number of skilled technicians increases, the total number of Internet access accounts serviced each month rises, as shown in panels (a) and (b). In panel (c), marginal physical product (MPP) first rises and then falls. Average physical product (APP) follows. The near mirror image of panel (c) is shown in panel (d), in which MC and AVC first fall and then rise.

FIGURE 23-4
Preferable Plant Size and the Long-Run Average Cost Curve

If the anticipated permanent rate of output per unit time period Q_1, is the optimal plant to build is the one corresponding to SAC_1 in panel (a) because average costs are lower. However, if the permanent rate of output increases to Q_2, it will be more profitable to have a plant size corresponding to SAC_2. Unit costs fall to C_3.

If we draw all the possible short-run average cost curves that correspond to different plant sizes and then draw the envelope (a curve tangent to each member of a set of curves) to these various curves, SAC_1–SAC_8, we obtain the long-run average cost curve, or the planning curve, as shown in panel (b).

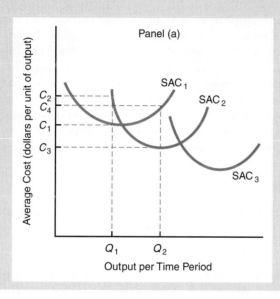

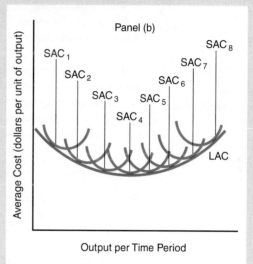

However, if the anticipated permanent rate of output per time period increases from Q_1 to Q_2 and a plant of size 1 is selected, average costs will be C_4. If a plant of size 2 is chosen, average costs will be C_3, which is clearly less than C_4.

In choosing the appropriate plant size for a single-plant firm during the planning horizon, the firm will pick the size whose short-run average cost curve generates an average cost that is lowest for the expected rate of output.

Long-Run Average Cost Curve

If we now assume that the entrepreneur faces an infinite number of choices of plant sizes in the long run, we can conceive of an infinite number of SAC curves similar to the three in panel (a) of Figure 23-4. We are not able, of course, to draw an infinite number, but we have drawn quite a few in panel (b) of Figure 23-4. We then draw the "envelope" to all these various short-run average cost curves. The resulting envelope is the **long-run average cost curve.** This long-run average cost curve is sometimes called the **planning curve,** for it represents the various average costs attainable at the planning stage of the firm's decision making. It represents the locus (path) of points giving the least unit cost of producing any given rate of output. Note that the LAC curve is *not* tangent to each individual SAC curve at the latter's minimum points, except at the minimum point of the LAC curve. Then and only then are minimum long-run average costs equal to minimum short-run average costs.

Long-run average cost curve
The locus of points representing the minimum unit cost of producing any given rate of output, given current technology and resource prices.

Planning curve
The long-run average cost curve.

WHY THE LONG-RUN AVERAGE COST CURVE IS U-SHAPED

Notice that the long-run average cost curve, LAC, in panel (b) of Figure 23-4 on the previous page is U-shaped, similar to the U shape of the short-run average cost curve developed earlier in this chapter. The reason behind the U shape of the two curves is not the same, however. The short-run average cost curve is U-shaped because of the law of diminishing marginal returns. But the law cannot apply to the long run, because in the long run, all factors of production are variable; there is no point of diminishing marginal returns because there is no fixed factor of production.

Why, then, do we see the U shape in the long-run average cost curve? The reasoning has to do with economies of scale, constant returns to scale, and diseconomies of scale. When the firm is experiencing **economies of scale,** the long-run average cost curve slopes downward—an increase in scale and production leads to a fall in unit costs. When the firm is experiencing **constant returns to scale,** the long-run average cost curve is at its minimum point, such that an increase in scale and production does not change unit costs. When the firm is experiencing **diseconomies of scale,** the long-run average cost curve slopes upward—an increase in scale and production increases unit costs. These three sections of the long-run average cost curve are broken up into panels (a), (b), and (c) in Figure 23-5.

Reasons for Economies of Scale

We shall examine three of the many reasons why a firm might be expected to experience economies of scale: specialization, the dimensional factor, and improved productive equipment.

Specialization. As a firm's scale of operation increases, the opportunities for specialization in the use of resource inputs also increase. This is sometimes called *increased division*

Economies of scale
Decreases in long-run average costs resulting from increases in output.

Constant returns to scale
No change in long-run average costs when output increases.

Diseconomies of scale
Increases in long-run average costs that occur as output increases.

FIGURE 23-5
Economies of Scale, Constant Returns to Scale, and Diseconomies of Scale Shown with Long-Run Average Cost Curve

The long-run average cost curve will fall when there are economies of scale, as shown in panel (a). It will be constant (flat) when the firm is ex-periencing constant returns to scale, as shown in panel (b). It will rise when the firm is experiencing diseconomies of scale, as shown in panel (c).

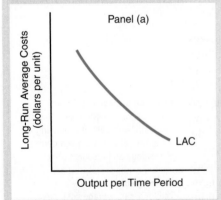

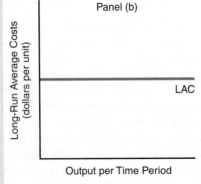

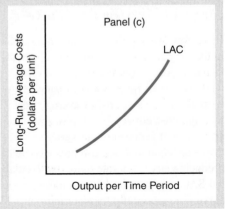

of tasks or *operations*. Gains from such division of labor or increased specialization are well known. When we consider managerial staffs, we also find that larger enterprises may be able to put together more highly specialized staffs.

Dimensional Factor. Large-scale firms often require proportionately less input per unit of output simply because certain inputs do not have to be physically doubled in order to double the output. Consider the cost of storage of oil. The cost of storage is basically related to the cost of steel that goes into building the storage container; however, the amount of steel required goes up less than in proportion to the volume (storage capacity) of the container (because the volume of a container increases more than proportionately with its surface area).

Improved Productive Equipment. The larger the scale of the enterprise, the more the firm is able to take advantage of larger-volume (output capacity) types of machinery. Small-scale operations may not be able profitably to use large-volume machines that can be more efficient per unit of output. Also, smaller firms often cannot use technologically more advanced machinery because they are unable to spread out the high cost of such sophisticated equipment over a large output.

For any of these reasons, the firm may experience economies of scale, which means that equal percentage increases in output result in a decrease in average cost. Thus output can double, but total costs will less than double; hence average cost falls. Note that the factors listed for causing economies of scale are all *internal* to the firm; they do not depend on what other firms are doing or what is happening in the economy.

Why a Firm Might Experience Diseconomies of Scale

One of the basic reasons that a firm can expect to run into diseconomies of scale is that there are limits to the efficient functioning of management. Moreover, as more workers are hired, a more than proportionate increase in managers and staff people may be needed, and this could cause increased costs per unit. This is so because larger levels of output imply successively larger *plant* size, which in turn implies successively larger *firm* size. Thus, as the level of output increases, more people must be hired, and the firm gets bigger. As this happens, however, the support, supervisory, and administrative staff and the general paperwork of the firm all increase. As the layers of supervision grow, the costs of information and communication grow more than proportionately; hence the average unit cost will start to increase.

Some observers of corporate giants claim that many of them have been experiencing some diseconomies of scale. Witness the problems that General Motors and International Business Machines (IBM) had in the early 1990s. Some analysts say that the financial problems they encountered were at least partly a function of their size relative to their smaller, more flexible competitors, who could make decisions more quickly and then take advantage of changing market conditions more rapidly. This was particularly true for IBM. Initially, the company adapted very slowly to the fact that the large mainframe computer business was declining as micro- and minicomputers became more and more powerful. Finally, by the end of the 1990s, IBM had adjusted to a more appropriate scale.

What situation must have existed before recent cutbacks in the sizes of many large Chinese companies generated reductions in long-run average cost at those firms?

International EXAMPLE

Chinese Enterprises Reduce Their Scale—And Average Costs

In the 1980s, many firms in China were *government-sponsored enterprises* that were either owned by the government or received large government subsidies. Since the 1990s, the Chinese government has been selling off many of the companies it once owned and has been reducing the subsidies previously granted to other firms.

As a consequence, many former government-sponsored enterprises have had to make some long-run adjustments.

Most of these adjustments have involved downsizing plant sizes, cutting levels of employment, and reducing rates of output. The payoffs for most companies have been reductions in long-run average total costs ranging from 25 to 50 percent.

For Critical Analysis
Prior to the end of government sponsorship, were Chinese companies experiencing economies of scale or diseconomies of scale?

MINIMUM EFFICIENT SCALE

Minimum efficient scale (MES)
The lowest rate of output per unit time at which long-run average costs for a particular firm are at a minimum.

Economists and statisticians have obtained actual data on the relationship between changes in all inputs and changes in average cost. It turns out that for many industries, the long-run average cost curve does not resemble that shown in panel (b) of Figure 23-4 on page 557. Rather, it more closely resembles Figure 23-6. What you can observe there is a small portion of declining long-run average costs (economies of scale) and then a wide range of outputs over which the firm experiences relatively constant economies of scale. At the output rate when economies of scale end and constant economies of scale start, the **minimum efficient scale (MES)** for the firm is encountered. It occurs at point *A*. The minimum efficient scale will always be the lowest rate of output at which long-run average costs are minimized. In any industry with a long-run average cost curve similar to the one in Figure 23-6, larger firms will have no cost-saving advantage over smaller firms as long as the smaller firms have at least obtained the minimum efficient scale at point *A*.

Why do you suppose that some critics of a major expansion of the Krispy Kreme doughnut chain worry that the company's efforts to attain a larger scale may actually be making the firm less cost-efficient?

FIGURE 23-6
Minimum Efficient Scale
This long-run average cost curve reaches a minimum point at *A*. After that point, long-run average costs remain horizontal, or constant, and then rise at some later rate of output. Point *A* is called the minimum efficient scale for the firm because that is the point at which it reaches minimum costs. It is the lowest rate of output at which average long-run costs are minimized. At point *B*, diseconomies of scale arise, so long-run average cost begins to increase with further increases in output.

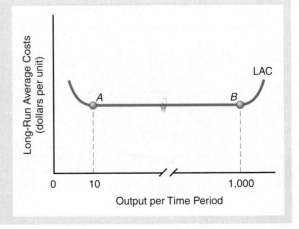

EXAMPLE

Is Krispy Kreme Trying to Bake Too Many Doughnuts?

In 1937, the founder of Krispy Kreme Doughnuts, Vernon Rudolph, purchased a secret yeast-raised doughnut recipe from a French chef in New Orleans and opened a doughnut shop in Winston-Salem, North Carolina. Gradually, Krispy Kreme outlets spread across the southern tier of the United States. Then, in 2000, Krispy Kreme became a publicly traded company and embarked on a major expansion across most of the rest of the country.

The company calls many of its newest outlets "factory stores." These outlets are equipped with costly doughnut-making machinery that can churn out tens of thousands of doughnuts each day. An aim of the expansion strategy has been to reduce the long-run average cost of producing doughnuts. Some locales now have so many Krispy Kreme outlets in close proximity, however, that they regularly become "sat-

urated" with doughnuts. Stores in these areas end up throwing away numerous one- and two-day-old doughnuts, which raises average costs of ingredients, labor, electricity, and wear and tear on machinery. For this reason, critics of Krispy Kreme's expansion strategy contend that the result has been higher long-run average costs for the company as a whole. The firm, they argue, has expanded beyond its minimum efficient scale.

For Critical Analysis
How might Krispy Kreme continue to expand geographically into the four states that currently lack outlets while at the same time reducing its overall nationwide scale of doughnut production?

Among its uses, the minimum efficient scale gives us a rough measure of the degree of competition in an industry. If the MES is small relative to industry demand, the extent of competition in that industry is likely to be high because there is room for many efficiently sized plants. Conversely, when the MES is large relative to industry demand, the degree of competition is likely to be small because there is room for a relatively small number of efficiently sized plants or firms. Looked at another way, if it takes a very large scale of plant to obtain minimum long-run average cost, the output of just a few of these very large firms can fully satisfy total market demand. This means that there isn't room for a large number of smaller plants if maximum efficiency is to be obtained in the industry.

CONCEPTS in Brief

- The long run is often called the planning horizon. The long-run average cost curve is the planning curve. It is found by drawing a curve tangent to one point on a series of short-run average cost curves, each corresponding to a different plant size.

- The firm can experience economies of scale, diseconomies of scale, or constant returns to scale, all according to whether the long-run average cost curve slopes downward, slopes upward, or is horizontal (flat). Economies of scale refer to what happens to average cost when all factors of production are increased.

- We observe economies of scale for a number of reasons, including specialization, improved productive equipment, and the dimensional factor, because large-scale firms require proportionately less input per unit of output. The firm may experience diseconomies of scale primarily because of limits to the efficient functioning of management.

- The minimum efficient scale occurs at the lowest rate of output at which long-run average costs are minimized.

To test your understanding of the concepts covered in this section, go to the Online Review at www.myeconlab.com/miller.

CASE STUDY: Economics Front and Center

Short-Run Adjustments at a Web-Based Firm

During the rapid growth of Internet commerce in the late 1990s, Morales and two partners started an Internet bank. They leased corporate servers and other capital equipment and hired 20 employees to operate the bank, which conducts all of its operations electronically. Customers transmit funds for deposit using PayPal and other Web-based payment services, and the bank also makes loans and bond purchases via the Internet.

Between 1999 and 2001, the bank earned economic profits. Since 2001, however, the bank's economic profits have shrunk, as depositors have closed accounts and borrowers have failed to renew loans. Morales recollects that during the late 1990s, some economists speculated that Internet-based firms such as his would respond to tough times by reducing capital instead of labor. If the bank were to break leases on some of its capital equipment, however, it would have to pay large lease-termination penalties. In addition, it would be difficult for the

bank to handle its normal daily volumes of financial transactions as speedily, which might lead to the loss of even more customers. Morales is very reluctant to lay off or terminate any of the bank's lending officers or programmers. Nevertheless, employee layoffs or terminations appear to be the best short-term options available to the partners. Morales begins typing an e-mail to his partners proposing that they consider laying off, or perhaps even firing, two or three employees.

Points to Analyze

1. *Why is a typical firm more likely to regard labor, rather than capital, as a variable factor of production?*

2. *Is it possible that given sufficient time, Morales and his partners might have chosen to end leases on some capital equipment instead of laying off or terminating employees?*

Issues and Applications

The Latest Thing in High-Tech Gadgets: Railroad Locomotives?

The scene is one of classic heavy industry: A Santa Fe freight train is hauling more than 18,000 tons of low-sulfur coal across the Texas plains. Three locomotives—two in front pulling the lengthy train and one applying extra push at the rear—are required to move this huge load. Of course, these locomotives have the latest 4,000-horsepower diesel engines, but aside from some retooling here and there, the basic technology for powering trains has not changed dramatically in recent decades. What is new is some other technology inside these locomotives.

Concepts Applied

- Production
- Average Physical Product
- Average Total Cost

Working on the Railroad, but with Only One Fellow Employee

Moving a 130-car freight train from the coal-rich Powder River Basin of Wyoming to the Dallas–Ft. Worth metropolitan area of north-central Texas has always required three or four locomotives to propel rolling stock up steep grades. At one time, the task also entailed the efforts of half a dozen rail workers on each train, plus coordination by a 600-member crew-dispatching center.

Since the late 1990s, however, train transportation has moved into the information age. Built into the consoles of the lead locomotive of a freight train is a computer that sends packets of radio signals to the other locomotives that are pushing or pulling its cars. This allows the lead locomotive to automatically blend all the engines' outputs to achieve maximum combined efficiency. When the train, which is now staffed by only two people, reaches Ft. Worth, the locomotives are uncoupled and moved to another track to begin hauling freight to a new location. Two switch operators then take over moving the newly arrived freight cars to separate tracks for distribution to their ultimate destinations. They use an old switching locomotive refitted with a new wireless computer that they can operate remotely using handheld devices. Coordinating the tasks of the switch operators and the work of the engineers driving incoming and outgoing trains is a dispatch center now staffed by fewer than 100 people on any given day. This smaller staff can do more than 1,000 people could have accomplished a decade ago.

A Higher Marginal Product of Labor Translates into Cost Efficiencies

Clearly, there has been a dramatic increase in the average physical product and marginal product of labor in the rail transportation industry. Even though rail transport has increased in recent years, rail freight companies employ fewer workers to produce each additional unit of freight transportation services. At Burlington Northern Santa Fe, for instance, in 1997 the average employee utilized locomotives and other equipment to move about 19 gross tons of freight per mile. Today, this figure is more than 21 percent higher at nearly 24 gross tons per mile per employee.

As you learned in this chapter, the average product of labor is a key determinant of any firm's average total cost. It should be no surprise, therefore, to learn that the use of new information technologies by rail freight operators has resulted in a significant increase in the cost efficiency of rail transportation. Even though labor remains the largest expense item for the nations' railroads, companies have shed thousands of jobs in recent years. The result has been a significant reduction in the average total cost of moving items by rail.

563

For Critical Analysis

1. If the average product of labor curve has shifted upward at a typical rail freight company, what must have happened to the marginal product of labor curve?
2. Based on your answer to question 1, what has also happened to the marginal cost curve at a typical railroad firm?

Web Resources

1. Learn more about efficiency improvements in the rail industry by following the link to the Web site of Burlington Northern Santa Fe at **www.econtoday.com/chap23** and clicking on "Service and Efficiency" under the heading, "Additional railroad industry information."
2. To see how CSX Corporation has integrated information technologies into its rail operations, use the link available at **www.econtoday.com/chap23**.

Research Project

Some smaller railroad firms have found that the use of information technologies allows them to operate smaller trains and shorter lines of track at lower long-run average total cost than some of the largest operators, such as Burlington Northern Santa Fe and CSX. If further technological advances make this common for all smaller railroad operators, what would this imply about the shape of the long-run average total cost curve? What would it mean for minimum efficient scale in the rail transportation industry? Assuming no change in the demand for rail transportation services, would you predict that there would be more or fewer railroad companies in the future?

S U M M A R Y   D I S C U S S I O N   of Learning Objectives

1. **The Short Run versus the Long Run from a Firm's Perspective:** The short run for a firm is a period during which at least one input, such as plant size, cannot be altered. Inputs that cannot be changed in the short run are fixed inputs, whereas factors of production that may be adjusted in the short run are variable inputs. The long run is a period in which a firm may vary all factors of production.

2. **The Law of Diminishing Marginal Returns:** The production function is the relationship between inputs and the maximum physical output, or total product, that a firm can produce. Typically, a firm's marginal physical product—the physical output resulting from the addition of one more unit of a variable factor of production—increases with the first few units of the variable factor of production that it employs. Eventually, however, as the firm adds more and more units of the variable input, the marginal physical product begins to decline. This is the law of diminishing returns.

3. **A Firm's Short-Run Cost Curves:** The expenses for a firm's fixed inputs are its fixed costs, and the expenses for its variable inputs are variable costs. The total costs of a firm are the sum of its fixed costs and variable costs. Dividing fixed costs by various possible output levels traces out the firm's average fixed cost curve, which

slopes downward because dividing fixed costs by a larger total product yields a lower average fixed cost. Average variable cost equals total variable cost divided by total product, and average total cost equals total cost divided by total product. For the latter two, doing these computations at various possible output levels yields U-shaped curves. Finally, marginal cost is the change in total cost resulting from a one-unit change in production. A firm's marginal costs typically decline as the firm produces the first few units of output, but at the point of diminishing marginal returns, the marginal cost curve begins to slope upward. The marginal cost curve also intersects the minimum points of the average variable cost curve and average total cost curve.

4. **A Firm's Long-Run Cost Curves:** Over a firm's long-run, or planning, horizon, it can choose all factors of production, including plant size. Thus it can choose a long-run scale of production along a long-run average cost curve. The long-run average cost curve, which for most firms is U-shaped, is traced out by the short-run average cost curves corresponding to various plant sizes.

5. **Economies and Diseconomies of Scale and a Firm's Minimum Efficient Scale:** Along the downward-sloping range of a firm's long-run average cost curve, the firm experiences economies of scale, meaning that its long-

run production costs decline as it increases its plant size and thereby raises its output scale. In contrast, along the upward-sloping portion of the long-run average cost curve, the firm encounters diseconomies of scale, so that its long-run costs of production rise as it increases its output scale. The minimum point of the long-run average cost curve occurs at the firm's minimum efficient scale, which is the lowest rate of output at which the firm can achieve minimum long-run average cost.

KEY TERMS AND CONCEPTS

average fixed costs (550)

average physical product (545)

average total costs (550)

average variable costs (550)

constant returns to scale (558)

diseconomies of scale (558)

economies of scale (558)

fixed costs (548)

law of diminishing (marginal) returns (545)

long run (543)

long-run average cost curve (557)

marginal costs (551)

marginal physical product (545)

minimum efficient scale (MES) (560)

planning curve (557)

planning horizon (555)

plant size (543)

production (544)

production function (544)

short run (543)

total costs (548)

variable costs (550)

PROBLEMS

Answers to the odd-numbered problems appear at the back of the book.

23-1. The academic calendar for a university is August 15 through May 15. A professor commits to a contract that binds her to a teaching position at this university for this period. Based on this information, explain the short run and long run that the professor faces.

23-2. The short-run production function for a manufacturer of DVD drives is as follows:

Input of Labor (workers per week)	Total Output of DVD Drives
0	0
1	25
2	60
3	85
4	105
5	115
6	120

Based on this information, calculate the average physical product at each quantity of labor.

23-3. Using the information provided in Problem 23-2, calculate the marginal physical product of labor at each quantity of labor.

23-4. For the manufacturer of DVD drives in Problems 23-2 and 23-3, at what point do diminishing marginal returns set in?

23-5. At the end of the year, a firm produced 10,000 laptop computers. Its total costs were $5 million, and its fixed costs were $2 million. What are the average variable costs of this firm?

23-6. The cost structure of a manufacturer of cable modems is described in the following table. The firm's fixed costs equal $10 per day.

Output (cable modems per day)	Total Cost of Output ($ thousands)
0	10
25	60
50	95
75	150
100	220
125	325
150	465

Calculate the average variable cost, average fixed cost, and average total cost at each output level.

23-7. Calculate the marginal cost that the manufacturer of cable modems in Problem 23-6 faces at each daily output rate, including the first cable modem it produces. At what production rate do diminishing marginal returns set in?

23-8. A watch manufacturer finds that at 1,000 units of output, its marginal costs are below average total costs. If it produces an additional watch, will its average total costs rise, fall, or stay the same?

23-9. At its current short-run level of production, a firm's average variable costs equal $20 per unit, and its average fixed costs equal $30 per unit. Its total costs at this production level equal $2,500.

    a. What is the firm's current output level?

    b. What are its total variable costs at this output level?

    c. What are its total fixed costs?

23-10. In the short run, a firm's total costs of producing the hundredth unit of output equal $10,000. If it produces one more unit, its total costs will increase to $10,150.

    a. What is the marginal cost of the 101st unit of output?

    b. What is the firm's average total cost of producing 100 units?

    c. What is the firm's average total cost of producing 101 units?

23-11. Suppose that a firm's only variable input is labor, and the constant hourly wage rate is $20 per hour. The last unit of labor hired enabled the firm to increase its hourly production from 250 units to 251 units. What was the marginal cost of the 251st unit of output?

23-12. Suppose that a firm's only variable input is labor. The firm increases the number of employees from four to five, thereby causing weekly output to rise by two units and total costs to increase from $3,000 per week to $3,300 per week.

    a. What is the marginal physical product of the fifth worker?

    b. What is the weekly wage rate earned by the fifth worker?

23-13. Suppose that a company currently employs 1,000 workers and produces 1 million units of output per month. Labor is its only variable input, and the company pays each worker the same monthly wage. The company's current total variable costs equal $2 million.

a. What are average variable costs at this firm's current output level?

b. What is the average physical product of labor?

c. What monthly wage does the firm pay each worker?

23-14. A manufacturing firm with a single plant is contemplating changing its plant size. It must choose from among seven alternative plant sizes. In the table, plant size A is the smallest it might build, and size G is the largest. Currently, the firm's plant size is B.

Plant Size	Average Total Cost ($)
A (smallest)	5,000
B	4,000
C	3,500
D	3,100
E	3,000
F	3,250
G (largest)	4,100

a. Is this firm currently experiencing economies of scale or diseconomies of scale?

b. What is the firm's minimum efficient scale?

23-15. An electricity-generating company confronts the following long-run average total costs associated with alternative plant sizes. It is currently operating at plant size G.

Plant Size	Average Total Cost ($)
A (smallest)	2,000
B	1,800
C	1,600
D	1,550
E	1,500
F	1,500
G (largest)	1,500

a. What is this firm's minimum efficient scale?

b. If a state representative is successful in winning passage of a bill requiring this firm to reduce its plant size from its current size to B, would there be a leftward or rightward movement along the firm's long-run average total cost curve?

ECONOMICS ON THE NET

Industry-Level Capital Expenditures In this chapter, you learned about the explicit and implicit costs that firms incur in the process of producing goods and services. This Internet application gives you an opportunity to consider one type of cost—expenditures on capital goods.

Title: U.S. Census Bureau's Annual Capital Expenditures Survey

Navigation: Follow the link at www.econtoday.com/chap23, and select *PDF Download*. Then click on the most recent *Annual Capital Expenditures Survey*.

Application: Read the Introduction in the report, and then answer the following questions:

1. What types of business expenditures does the Census Bureau include in this report?

2. Are the inputs that generate these business expenditures more likely to be inputs that firms can vary in the short run or in the long run?

3. Which inputs account for the largest portion of firms' capital expenditures? Why do you suppose this is so?

For Group Discussion and Analysis Review reports for the past several years. Do capital expenditures vary from year to year? What factors might account for such variations? Are there noticeable differences in capital expenditures from industry to industry?

Media Resources

If your exam were tomorrow, would you be ready? For each chapter, MyEconLab Practice Tests and Study Plans pinpoint which sections you have mastered and which ones you need to study. That way, you are more efficient with your study time, and you are better prepared for your exams.

In addition to Practice Tests and your personalized Study Plan, you'll find the following media resources in MyEconLab:
1. *Graphs in Motion* animation of Figures 23-1, 23-3, 23-5, and 23-6.
2. An *Economics in Motion* in-depth animation of the Production Function and Marginal Physical Product.
3. Videos featuring the author, Roger LeRoy Miller, on the following subjects:
   ● Short-Run Costs to the Firm
   ● Reasons for Economies of Scale

4. Links to the Web sites cited in the marginal Internet Resources, Issues and Applications feature, and Economics on the Net activity.
5. Audio clips of all key terms, additional practice problems, and a PDF version of the material from the print Study Guide.
6. eThemes of the Times, which is a New York Times article to help you understand the real-world applications of what you are learning.

Get Ahead of the Curve

To see how it works, turn to page 16 and then go to www.myeconlab.com/miller.

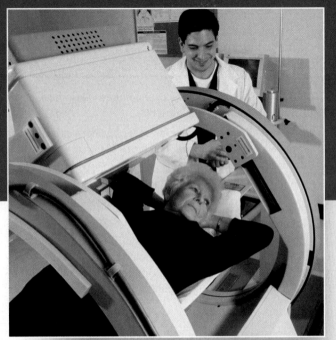

M any people pay to have computed tomography (CT) scans of their entire bodies, simply to be reassured that they are
free of disease. Each CT-scanning device yields vir-
tually an identical scan of a person's body. Thus individuals are usually willing to
have any qualified provider perform a scan, as long as a scan is not available from
another provider at a lower price. In fact, someone shopping around for a full-body
CT scan will typically find that providers charge very nearly the same price.

A person who last had a scan in 1999 and arranged to have another in 2004 received some good news: The price of a scan had fallen by more than two-thirds. In
this chapter, you will learn why providers typically charged the same prices for CT
scans and why the prices they charged fell so dramatically.

Media Resources

Refer to the end of the
chapter for a full listing of the
multimedia learning materials
available in MyEconLab.

LEARNING OBJECTIVES

After reading this chapter, you should be able to:

1. Identify the characteristics of a perfectly competitive market structure
2. Discuss the process by which a perfectly competitive firm decides how much output to produce
3. Understand how the short-run supply curve for a perfectly competitive firm is determined
4. Explain how the equilibrium price is determined in a perfectly competitive market
5. Describe what factors induce firms to enter or exit a perfectly competitive industry
6. Distinguish among constant-, increasing-, and decreasing-cost industries based on the shape of the long-run industry supply curve

... over the past decade, bad weather was the top reason U.S. clothing retailers cited to explain declining profits? Company reports to corporate shareholders have blamed lower-than-anticipated returns on weather that was alleged to have been "too cool," "too warm," "too wet," or "too dry" to induce consumers to shop at their stores. Undoubtedly, from time to time, unexpected variations in weather do affect consumer clothing preferences. But most economists think that what has really happened is that clothing retailers have faced greater competition in recent years as more firms have entered the clothing market. Some of the new entrants have come from abroad, as European retailers have opened stores in major U.S. cities, but most of the increased competition has been homegrown.

In common speech, *competition* simply means "rivalry." In perfectly competitive situations, individual buyers and sellers cannot affect the market price—it is determined by the market forces of demand and supply. In addition, economic profits that perfectly competitive firms may earn for a time ultimately disappear as other firms respond by entering the industry. In this chapter, we examine these and other implications of the theory of perfect competition.

CHARACTERISTICS OF A PERFECTLY COMPETITIVE MARKET STRUCTURE

We are interested in studying how a firm acting within a perfectly competitive market structure makes decisions about how much to produce. In a situation of **perfect competition,** each firm is such a small part that it cannot affect the price of the product in question. That means that each **perfectly competitive firm** in the industry is a **price taker**—the firm takes price as a given, something determined *outside* the individual firm.

This definition of a competitive firm is obviously idealized, for in one sense the individual firm *has* to set prices. How can we ever have a situation in which firms regard prices as set by forces outside their control? The answer is that even though every firm sets its own prices, a firm in a perfectly competitive situation will find that it will eventually have no customers at all if it sets its price above the competitive price. The best example is in agriculture. Although the individual farmer can set any price for a bushel of wheat, if that price doesn't coincide with the market price of a bushel of similar-quality wheat, no one will purchase the wheat at a higher price; nor would the farmer be inclined to reduce revenues by selling below the market price.

Let's examine why a firm in a perfectly competitive industry is a price taker.

Perfect competition
A market structure in which the decisions of *individual* buyers and sellers have no effect on market price.

Perfectly competitive firm
A firm that is such a small part of the total *industry* that it cannot affect the price of the product it sells.

Price taker
A competitive firm that must take the price of its product as given because the firm cannot influence its price.

1. *There are a large number of buyers and sellers.* When this is the case, the quantity demanded by one buyer or the quantity supplied by one seller is negligible relative to the market quantity. No one buyer or seller has any influence on price.
2. *The product sold by the firms in the industry is homogeneous.* The product sold by each firm in the industry is a perfect substitute for the product sold by every other firm. Buyers are able to choose from a large number of sellers of a product that the buyers believe to be the same.
3. *Both buyers and sellers have equal access to information.* Consumers are able to find out about lower prices charged by competing firms. Firms are able to find out about cost-saving innovations that can lower production costs and prices, and they are able to learn about profitable opportunities in other industries.
4. *Any firm can enter or leave the industry without serious impediments.* Firms in a competitive industry are not hampered in their ability to get resources or reallocate resources. They move labor and capital in pursuit of profit-making opportunities to whatever business venture gives them their highest expected rate of return on their investment.

What do you supposed happened in Chile's market for educational services when its government allowed families to use public funds at both private and public schools?

International EXAMPLE

Chile Verifies That Free Entry Can Shift Educational Resources

For many years, Chile's public schools were operated by a single authority, the national government's Ministry of Education. About 85 percent of all Chilean children attended public schools, which could be opened or closed only with the permission of this institution.

In 1981, the government decided to decentralize the public funding of education. Under the revamped national educational system, which remains in place, the government shifted oversight of public schools to individual municipal governments throughout the country. The government also allowed parents to choose which schools their children would attend, and it broadened the list of schools to include private institutions. If a child's parents decided to enroll their child at a private school willing to accept public funds in full or partial

payment of tuition, the government transmitted payment to the school.

Opening Chile's market for educational services to competition generated a dramatic flow of resources into the provision of education. Since the late 1980s, more than 1,200 additional private schools have opened their doors. As a consequence, public schools now enroll fewer than 58 percent of the nation's school-aged children.

For Critical Analysis
What factors do you suppose account for the failure of the number of public schools in Chile to increase very much even though the number of private schools has grown considerably since 1981?

THE DEMAND CURVE OF THE PERFECT COMPETITOR

When we discussed substitutes in Chapter 21, we pointed out that the more substitutes there are and the more similar they are to the commodity in question, the greater is the price elasticity of demand. Here we assume that the perfectly competitive firm is producing a homogeneous commodity that has perfect substitutes. That means that if the individual firm raises its price one penny, it will lose all of its business. This, then, is how we characterize the demand schedule for a perfectly competitive firm: It is the going market price as determined by the forces of market supply and market demand—that is, where the market demand curve intersects the market supply curve. The demand curve for the product of an individual firm in a perfectly competitive industry is perfectly elastic at the going market price. Remember that with a perfectly elastic demand curve, any increase in price leads to zero quantity demanded.

We show the market demand and supply curves in panel (a) of Figure 24-1. Their intersection occurs at the price of $5. The commodity in question is recordable DVDs. Assume for the purposes of this exposition that all recordable DVDs are perfect substitutes for all others. At the going market price of $5 apiece, a hypothetical individual demand curve for a producer of recordable DVDs who sells a very, very small part of total industry production is shown in panel (b). At the market price, this firm can sell all the output it wants. At the market price of $5 each, which is where the demand curve for the individual producer lies, consumer demand for the recordable DVDs of that one producer is perfectly elastic. This can be seen by noting that if the firm raises its price, consumers, who are assumed to know that this supplier is charging more than other producers, will buy elsewhere, and the producer in question will have no sales at all. Thus the demand curve for that producer is

FIGURE 24-1
The Demand Curve for a Producer of Recordable DVDs
At $5—where market demand, D, and market supply, S, intersect—the individual firm faces a perfectly elastic demand curve, d. If it raises its price even one penny, it will sell no DVDs at all. Notice the difference in the quantities of recordable DVDs represented on the horizontal axis of panels (a) and (b).

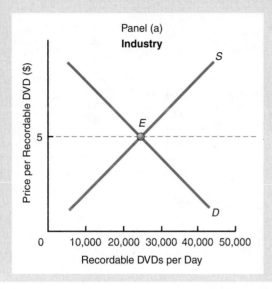

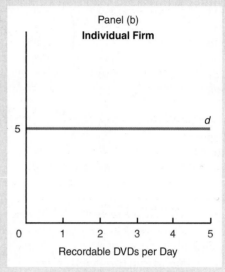

perfectly elastic. We label the individual producer's demand curve *d*, whereas the *market* demand curve is always labeled *D*.

HOW MUCH SHOULD THE PERFECT COMPETITOR PRODUCE?

As we have shown, a perfect competitor has to accept the price of the product as a given. If the firm raises its price, it sells nothing; if it lowers its price, it earns lower revenues per unit sold than it otherwise could. The firm has one decision left: How much should it produce? We will apply our model of the firm to this question to come up with an answer. We'll use the *profit-maximization model,* which assumes that firms attempt to maximize their total profits—the positive difference between total revenues and total costs. This also means that firms seek to minimize any losses that arise in times when total revenues may be less than total costs.

Total Revenues

Every firm has to consider its *total revenues*. **Total revenues** are defined as the quantity sold multiplied by the price. (They are the same as total receipts from the sale of output.) The perfect competitor must take the price as a given.

Total revenues
The price per unit times the total quantity sold.

Look at Figure 24-2. The information in panel (a) comes from panel (a) of Figure 23-2 on page 549, but we have added some essential columns for our analysis. Column 3 is the market price, *P*, of $5 per recordable DVD. Column 4 shows the total revenues, or TR, as equal to the market price, *P*, times the total output per day, or *Q*. Thus TR = *PQ*.

For the perfect competitor, price is also equal to average revenue (AR) because

Panel (a)

(1) Total Output and Sales per Day (Q)	(2) Total Costs (TC)	(3) Market Price (P)	(4) Total Revenue (TR) (4) = (3) x (1)	(5) Total Profit (TR – TC) (5) = (4) – (2)	(6) Average Total Cost (ATC) (6) = (2) ÷ (1)	(7) Average Variable Cost (AVC)	(8) Marginal Cost (MC) (8) = Change in (2) / Change in (1)	(9) Marginal Revenue (MR) (9) = Change in (4) / Change in (1)
0	$10	$5	$ 0	–$10	—	—		
							$5	$5
1	15	5	5	– 10	$15.00	$5.00		
							3	5
2	18	5	10	– 8	9.00	4.00		
							2	5
3	20	5	15	– 5	6.67	3.33		
							1	5
4	21	5	20	– 1	5.25	2.75		
							2	5
5	23	5	25	2	4.60	2.60		
							3	5
6	26	5	30	4	4.33	2.67		
							4	5
7	30	5	35	**5**	4.28	2.86		
							5	5
8	35	5	40	**5**	4.38	3.12		
							6	5
9	41	5	45	4	4.56	3.44		
							7	5
10	48	5	50	2	4.80	3.80		
							8	5
11	56	5	55	– 1	5.09	4.18		

FIGURE 24-2
Profit Maximization
Profit maximization occurs where marginal revenue equals marginal cost. Panel (a) indicates that this point occurs at a rate of sales of between seven and eight recordable DVDs per day. In panel (b), we find maximum profits where total revenues exceed total costs by the largest amount. This occurs at a rate of production and sales per day of seven or eight DVDs. In panel (c), the marginal cost curve, MC, intersects the marginal revenue curve at a rate of output and sales of somewhere between seven and eight DVDs per day.

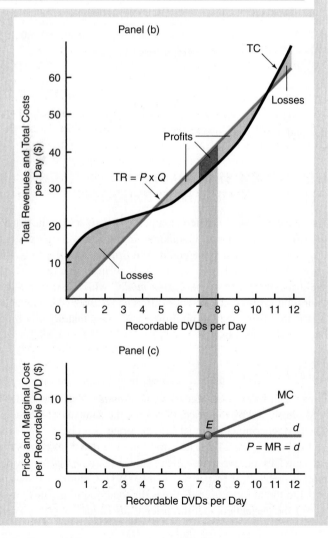

$$AR = \frac{TR}{Q} = \frac{PQ}{Q} = P$$

where Q stands for quantity. If we assume that all units sell for the same price, it becomes apparent that another name for the demand curve is the *average revenue curve* (this is true regardless of the type of market structure under consideration).

We are assuming that the market supply and demand schedules intersect at a price of $5 and that this price holds for all the firm's production. We are also assuming that because our maker of DVDs is a small part of the market, it can sell all that it produces at that price. Thus panel (b) of Figure 24-2 shows the total revenue curve as a straight green line. For every additional DVD sold, total revenue increases by $5.

Comparing Total Costs with Total Revenues

Total costs are given in column 2 of panel (a) of Figure 24-2 and plotted in panel (b). Remember, the firm's costs always include a normal rate of return on investment. So, whenever we refer to total costs, we are talking not about accounting costs but about economic costs. When the total cost curve is above the total revenue curve, the firm is experiencing losses. When it is below the total revenue curve, the firm is making profits.

By comparing total costs with total revenues, we can figure out the number of recordable DVDs the individual competitive firm should produce per day. Our analysis rests on the assumption that the firm will attempt to maximize total profits. In panel (a) of Figure 24-2, we see that total profits reach a maximum at a production rate of either seven or eight DVDs per day. We can see this graphically in panel (b) of the figure. The firm will maximize profits where the total revenue curve lies above the total cost curve by the greatest amount. That occurs at a rate of output and sales of either seven or eight recordable DVDs per day; this rate is called the **profit-maximizing rate of production.** (If output were continuously divisible or we were dealing with extremely large numbers of recordable DVDs, we would get a unique profit-maximizing output.)

We can also find the profit-maximizing rate of production for the individual competitive firm by looking at marginal revenues and marginal costs.

Profit-maximizing rate of production
The rate of production that maximizes total profits, or the difference between total revenues and total costs; also, the rate of production at which marginal revenue equals marginal cost.

USING MARGINAL ANALYSIS TO DETERMINE THE PROFIT-MAXIMIZING RATE OF PRODUCTION

It is possible—indeed, preferred—to use marginal analysis to determine the profit-maximizing rate of production. We end up with the same results derived in a different manner, one that focuses more on where decisions are really made—on the margin. Managers examine changes in costs and relate them to changes in revenues. In fact, whether the question is how much more or less to produce, how many more workers to hire or fire, or how much more to study or not study, we almost always compare changes in costs with changes in benefits, where change is occurring at the margin.

Marginal revenue represents the change in total revenues attributable to changing production of an item by one unit. Hence a more formal definition of marginal revenue is

$$\text{Marginal revenue} = \frac{\text{change in total revenues}}{\text{change in output}}$$

Marginal revenue
The change in total revenues resulting from a change in output (and sale) of one unit of the product in question.

In a perfectly competitive market, the marginal revenue curve is exactly equivalent to the price line or the individual firm's demand curve. Each time the firm produces and sells one more unit, total revenues rise by an amount equal to the (constant) market price of the good. Thus, in Figure 24-1 on page 571, the demand curve, *d*, for the individual producer is at a price of $5—the price line is coincident with the demand curve. But so is the marginal revenue curve, for marginal revenue in this case also equals $5.

The marginal revenue curve for our competitive producer of recordable DVDs is shown as a line at $5 in panel (c) of Figure 24-2 on page 572. Notice again that the marginal revenue curve is the price line, which is the firm's demand, or average revenue, curve, *d*.

When Are Profits Maximized?

Now we add the marginal cost curve, MC, taken from column 8 in panel (a) of Figure 24-2. As shown in panel (c) of that figure, the marginal cost curve first falls and then starts to rise because of the law of diminishing returns, eventually intersecting the marginal revenue curve and then rising above it. Notice that the numbers for both the marginal cost schedule, column 8 in panel (a), and the marginal revenue schedule, column 9 in panel (a), are printed *between* the rows on which the quantities appear. This indicates that we are looking at a *change* between one rate of output and the next rate of output.

In panel (c), the marginal cost curve intersects the marginal revenue curve somewhere between seven and eight recordable DVDs per day. The firm has an incentive to produce and sell until the amount of the additional revenue received from selling one more recordable DVD just equals the additional costs incurred for producing and selling that DVD. This is how the firm maximizes profit. Whenever marginal cost is less than marginal revenue, the firm will always make more profit by increasing production.

Now consider the possibility of producing at an output rate of 10 recordable DVDs per day. The marginal cost curve at that output rate is higher than the marginal revenue (or *d*) curve. The firm would be spending more to produce that additional output than it would be receiving in revenues; it would be foolish to continue producing at this rate.

But how much should it produce? It should produce at point *E*, where the marginal cost curve intersects the marginal revenue curve from below.[*] The firm should continue production until the cost of increasing output by one more unit is just equal to the revenues obtainable from that extra unit. This is a fundamental rule in economics:

> *Profit maximization occurs at the rate of output at which marginal revenue equals marginal cost.*

For a perfectly competitive firm, this is at the intersection of the demand schedule, *d*, and the marginal cost curve, MC. When MR exceeds MC, each additional unit of output adds more to total revenues than to total costs, so the additional unit should be produced. When MC is greater than MR, each unit produced adds more to total cost than to total revenues, so this unit should not be produced. Therefore, profit maximization occurs when MC equals MR. In our particular example, our profit-maximizing, perfectly competitive producer of recordable DVDs will produce at a rate of either seven or eight DVDs a day. (If we were dealing with a very large rate of output, we would come up with an exact profit-maximizing rate.)

CONCEPTS in Brief

● Four fundamental characteristics of the market in perfect competition are (1) a large number of buyers and sellers, (2) a homogeneous product, (3) good information in the hands of both buyers and sellers, and (4) unrestrained exit from and entry into the industry by other firms.

---

[*]The marginal cost curve, MC, also cuts the marginal revenue curve, *d*, from above at an output rate of less than 1 in this example. This intersection should be ignored because it is irrelevant to the firm's decisions; profit is always greater at point *E*.

- A perfectly competitive firm is a price taker. It has no control over price and consequently has to take price as a given, but it can sell all that it wants at the going market price.

- The demand curve for a perfect competitor is perfectly elastic at the going market price. The demand curve is also the perfect competitor's marginal revenue curve because marginal revenue is defined as the change in total revenue due to a one-unit change in output.

- Profit is maximized at the rate of output at which the positive difference between total revenues and total costs is the greatest. This is the same level of output at which marginal revenue equals marginal cost. The perfectly competitive firm produces at an output rate at which marginal cost equals the price per unit of output, because MR is always equal to P

To test your understanding of the concepts covered in this section, go to the Online Review at www.myeconlab.com/miller.

SHORT-RUN PROFITS

To find what our competitive individual producer of recordable DVDs is making in terms of profits in the short run, we have to add the average total cost curve to panel (c) of Figure 24-2 on page 572. We take the information from column 6 in panel (a) and add it to panel (c) to get Figure 24-3. Again the profit-maximizing rate of output is between seven and eight recordable DVDs per day. If we have production and sales of seven DVDs per day, total revenues will be $35 a day. Total costs will be $30 a day, leaving a profit of $5 a day. If the rate of output and sales is eight recordable DVDs per day, total revenues will be $40 and total costs will be $35, again leaving a profit of $5 a day. In Figure 24-3, the lower boundary of the rectangle labeled "Profits" is determined by the intersection of the profit-maximizing quantity line represented by vertical dashes and the average total cost curve. Why? Because

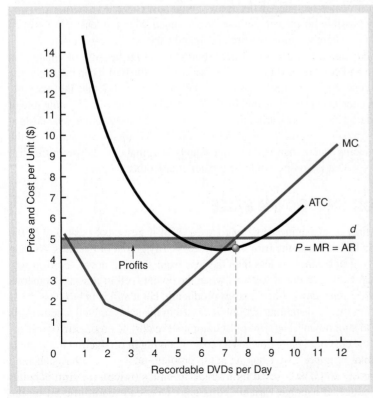

FIGURE 24-3
Measuring Total Profits
Profits are represented by the shaded area. The height of the profit rectangle is given by the difference between average total costs and price ($5), where price is also equal to average revenue. This is found by the vertical difference between the ATC curve and the price, or average revenue, line *d*, at the profit-maximizing rate of output of between seven and eight recordable DVDs per day.

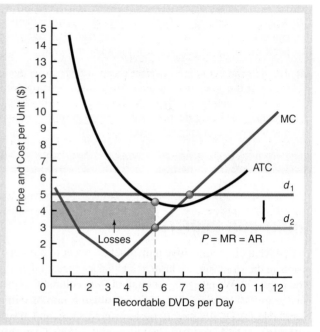

FIGURE 24-4
Minimization of Short-Run Losses

In situations in which average total costs exceed price, which in turn is greater than or equal to average variable cost, profit maximization is equivalent to loss minimization. This again occurs where marginal cost equals marginal revenue. Losses are shown in the shaded area.

the ATC curve gives us the cost per unit, whereas the price ($5), represented by *d*, gives us the revenue per unit, or average revenue. The difference is profit per unit. So the height of the rectangular box representing profits equals profit per unit, and the length equals the amount of units produced. When we multiply these two quantities, we get total profits. Note, as pointed out earlier, that we are talking about *economic profits* because a normal rate of return on investment is included in the average total cost curve, ATC.

It is also certainly possible for the competitive firm to make short-run losses. We give an example in Figure 24-4, where we show the firm's demand curve shifting from d_1 to d_2. The going market price has fallen from $5 to $3 per recordable DVDs because of changes in market supply or demand conditions (or both). The firm will do the best it can by producing where marginal revenue equals marginal cost. We see in Figure 24-4 that the marginal revenue (d_2) curve is intersected (from below) by the marginal cost curve at an output rate of about $5\frac{1}{2}$ DVDs per day. The firm is clearly not making profits because average total costs at that output rate are greater than the price of $3 per DVD. The losses are shown in the shaded area. By producing where marginal revenue equals marginal cost, however, the firm is minimizing its losses; that is, losses would be greater at any other output.

THE SHORT-RUN SHUTDOWN PRICE

In Figure 24-4, the firm is sustaining economic losses. Will it go out of business? In the long run it will, but in the short run the firm will not necessarily go out of business. As long as the loss from staying in business is less than the loss from shutting down, the firm will continue to produce. A firm *goes out of business* when the owners sell its assets to someone else. A firm temporarily *shuts down* when it stops producing, but it still is in business.

Now how can a firm that is sustaining economic losses in the short run tell whether it is still worthwhile not to shut down? The firm must compare the cost of producing (while incurring losses) with the cost of closing down. The cost of staying in production in the short run is given by the total *variable* cost. Looking at the problem on a per-unit basis, as long as average variable cost (AVC) is covered by average revenues (price), the firm is better off continuing to produce. If average variable costs are exceeded even a little bit by the price of the product, staying in production produces some revenues in excess of variable costs that can be applied toward covering fixed costs.

A simple example will demonstrate this situation. Suppose that the price of some product is \$8, and average total costs equal \$9 at an output of 100. In this example, we assume that average total costs are broken up into average variable costs of \$7 and average fixed costs of \$2. Total revenues, then, equal \$8 × 100, or \$800, and total costs equal \$9 × 100, or \$900. Total losses therefore equal \$100. However, this does not mean that the firm will shut down. After all, if it does shut down, it still has fixed costs to pay. And in this case, because average fixed costs equal \$2 at an output of 100, the fixed costs are \$200. Thus the firm has losses of \$100 if it continues to produce, but it has losses of \$200 (the fixed costs) if it shuts down. The logic is fairly straightforward:

> *As long as the price per unit sold exceeds the average variable cost per unit produced, the earnings of the firm's owners will be higher if it continues to produce in the short run than if it shuts down.*

Calculating the Short-Run Break-Even Price

Look at demand curve d_1 in Figure 24-5. It just touches the minimum point of the average total cost curve, which, as you will remember, is exactly where the marginal cost curve intersects the average total cost curve. At that price, which is about \$4.30, the firm will be making exactly zero short-run *economic* profits. That price is called the **short-run break-even price,** and point E_1 therefore occurs at the short-run break-even price for a competitive firm. It is the point at which marginal revenue, marginal cost, and average total cost are all equal (that is, at which $P = MC$ and $P = ATC$). The break-even price is the one that yields zero short-run economic profits or losses.

Short-run break-even price
The price at which a firm's total revenues equal its total costs. At the break-even price, the firm is just making a normal rate of return on its capital investment. (It is covering its explicit and implicit costs.)

Calculating the Short-Run Shutdown Price

To calculate the firm's shutdown price, we must introduce the average variable cost (AVC) to our graph. In Figure 24-5 on the previous page, we have plotted the AVC values from

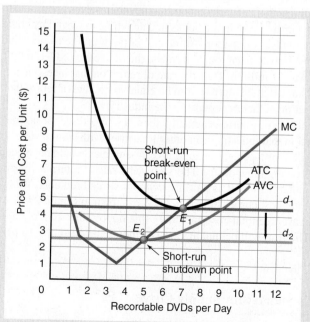

FIGURE 24-5
Short-Run Shutdown and Break-Even Prices
We can find the short-run break-even price and the short-run shutdown price by comparing price with average total costs and average variable costs. If the demand curve is d_1, profit maximization occurs at output E_1, where MC equals marginal revenue (the d_1 curve). Because the ATC curve includes all relevant opportunity costs, point E_1 is the break-even point, and zero economic profits are being made. The firm is earning a normal rate of return. If the demand curve falls to d_2, profit maximization (loss minimization) occurs at the intersection of MC and MR (the d_2 curve), or E_2. Below this price, it does not pay for the firm to continue in operation because its average variable costs are not covered by the price of the product.

column 7 in panel (a) of Figure 24-2 on page 572. For the moment, consider two possible demand curves, d_1 and d_2. which are also the firm's respective marginal revenue curves. Therefore, if demand is d_1, the firm will produce at E_1, where that curve intersects the marginal cost curve. If demand falls to d_2, the firm will produce at E_2. The special feature of the hypothetical demand curve, d_2, is that it just touches the average variable cost curve at the latter's minimum point, which is also where the marginal cost curve intersects it. This price is the **short-run shutdown price.** Why? Below this price, the firm would be paying out more in variable costs than it is receiving in revenues from the sale of its product. Each unit it sold would add to its losses. Clearly, the way to avoid incurring these additional losses, if price falls below the shutdown point, is in fact to shut down operations.

Short-run shutdown price
The price that covers average variable costs. It occurs just below the intersection of the marginal cost curve and the average variable cost curve.

The intersection of the price line, the marginal cost curve, and the average variable cost curve is labeled E_2. The resulting short-run shutdown price is valid only for the short run because, of course, in the long run the firm will not stay in business at a yield less than a normal rate of return (zero economic profits).

THE MEANING OF ZERO ECONOMIC PROFITS

The fact that we labeled point E_1 in Figure 24-5 the break-even point may have disturbed you. At point E_1, price is just equal to average total cost. If this is the case, why would a firm continue to produce if it were making no profits whatsoever? If we again make the distinction between accounting profits and economic profits, you will realize that at that price, the firm has zero economic profits but positive accounting profits. Recall that accounting profits are total revenues minus total explicit costs. But such accounting ignores the reward offered to investors—the opportunity cost of capital—plus all other implicit costs.

Go to www.econtoday.com/chap24 for a Congressional Budget Office analysis of whether the model of perfect competition applies to the market for pharmaceuticals.

In economic analysis, the average total cost curve includes the full opportunity cost of capital. Indeed, the average total cost curve includes the opportunity cost of *all* factors of production used in the production process. At the short-run break-even price, economic profits are, by definition, zero. Accounting profits at that price are not, however, equal to zero; they are positive. Consider an example. A baseball bat manufacturer sells bats at some price. The owners of the firm have supplied all the funds in the business. They have borrowed no money from anyone else, and they explicitly pay the full opportunity cost to all factors of production, including any managerial labor that they themselves contribute to the business. Their salaries show up as a cost in the books and are equal to what they could have earned in the next-best alternative occupation. At the end of the year, the owners find that after they subtract all explicit costs from total revenues, they have earned $100,000. Let's say that their investment was $1 million. Thus the rate of return on that investment is 10 percent per year. We will assume that this turns out to be equal to the rate of return that, on average, all other baseball bat manufacturers make in the industry.

This $100,000, or 10 percent rate of return, is actually, then, a competitive, or normal, rate of return on invested capital in that industry or in other industries with similar risks. If the owners had made only $50,000, or 5 percent on their investment, they would have been able to make higher profits by leaving the industry. The 10 percent rate of return is the opportunity cost of capital. Accountants show it as a profit; economists call it a cost. We include that cost in the average total cost curve, similar to the one shown in Figure 24-5. At the short-run break-even price, average total cost, including this opportunity cost of capital, will just equal that price. The firm will be making zero economic profits but a 10 percent *accounting* rate of return.

Now we are ready to derive the firm's supply curve.

The Perfect Competitor's Short-Run Supply Curve

What does the supply curve for the individual firm look like? Actually, we have been looking at it all along. We know that when the price of recordable DVDs is $5, the firm will supply seven or eight of them per day. If the price falls to $3, the firm will supply five or six DVDs per day. And if the price falls below $3, the firm will shut down in the short run. Hence, in Figure 24-6, the firm's supply curve is the marginal cost curve above the short-run shutdown point. This is shown as the solid part of the marginal cost curve. ***By definition, then, a firm's short-run supply curve in a competitive industry is its marginal cost curve at and above the point of intersection with the average variable cost curve.***

The Short-Run Industry Supply Curve

In Chapter 3, we indicated that the market supply curve was the summation of individual supply curves. At the beginning of this chapter, we drew a market supply curve in Figure 24-1 on page 571. Now we want to derive more precisely a market, or industry, supply curve to reflect individual producer behavior in that industry. First we must ask, What is an industry? It is merely a collection of firms producing a particular product. Therefore, we have a way to figure out the total supply curve of any industry: As discussed in Chapter 3, we add the quantities that each firm will supply at every possible price. In other words, we sum the individual supply curves of all the competitive firms *horizontally*. The individual supply curves, as we just saw, are simply the marginal cost curves of each firm.

Consider doing this for a hypothetical world in which there are only two producers of recordable DVDs in the industry, firm A and firm B. These two firms' marginal cost curves are given in panels (a) and (b) of Figure 24-7 on the next page. The marginal cost curves for the two separate firms are presented as MC_A in panel (a) and MC_B in panel (b). Those two marginal cost curves are drawn only for prices above the minimum average variable cost for each respective firm. Hence we are not including any of the marginal cost curves below minimum average variable cost. In panel (a), for firm A, at price P_1, the quantity supplied would be q_{A1}. At price P_2, the quantity supplied would be q_{A2}. In panel (b), we see the two different quantities that would be supplied by firm B corresponding to those two prices. Now for price P_1, we add horizontally the quantities of q_{A1} and q_{B1}. This gives us one point, F, for our short-run **industry supply curve**, S. We obtain the other point, G, by doing the same horizontal adding of quantities at P_2. When we connect all points such as F and G, we obtain the industry supply curve S, which is also marked ΣMC, indicating that it is the horizontal summation of the marginal cost curves (at and above the respective

Industry supply curve
The locus of points showing the minimum prices at which given quantities will be forthcoming; also called the *market supply curve*.

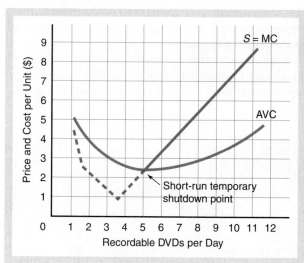

FIGURE 24-6
The Individual Firm's Short-Run Supply Curve
The individual firm's short-run supply curve is the portion of its marginal cost curve at and above the minimum point on the average variable cost curve.

FIGURE 24-7
Deriving the Industry Supply Curve
Marginal cost curves at and above minimum average variable cost are presented in panels (a) and (b) for firms A and B. We horizontally sum the two quantities supplied, q_{A1} and q_{B1}, at price P_1. This gives us point F in

panel (c). We do the same thing for the quantities at price P_2. This gives us point G. When we connect those points, we have the industry supply curve, S, which is the horizontal summation—represented by the Greek letter sigma (Σ)—of the firms' marginal cost curves above their respective minimum average variable costs.

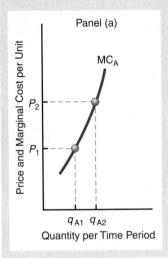

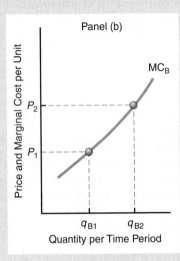

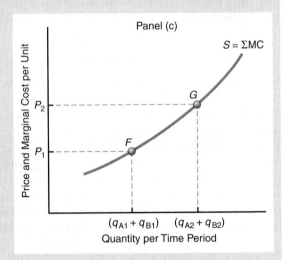

minimum average variable cost of each firm).* Because the law of diminishing returns makes marginal cost curves rise, the short-run supply curve of a perfectly competitive industry must be upward sloping.

Factors That Influence the Industry Supply Curve

As you have just seen, the industry supply curve is the horizontal summation of all of the individual firms' marginal cost curves at and above their respective minimum average variable cost points. This means that anything that affects the marginal cost curves of the firm will influence the industry supply curve. Therefore, the individual factors that will influence the supply schedule in a competitive industry can be summarized as the factors that cause the variable costs of production to change. These are factors that affect the individual marginal cost curves, such as changes in the individual firm's productivity, in factor costs (such as wages paid to labor and prices of raw materials), in taxes, and in anything else that would influence the individual firm's marginal cost curve.

All of these are *ceteris paribus* conditions of supply (see page 63). Because they affect the position of the marginal cost curve for the individual firm, they affect the position of the industry supply curve. A change in any of these will shift the industry supply curve.

CONCEPTS in Brief

● Short-run average profits or losses are determined by comparing average total costs with price (average revenue) at the profit-maximizing rate of output. In the short run,

the perfectly competitive firm can make economic profits or economic losses.

---

*The capital Greek sigma, Σ, is the symbol for summation.

- The competitive firm's short-run break-even price equals the firm's minimum average total cost, which is at the point where the marginal cost curve intersects the average total cost curve.

- The competitive firm's short-run shutdown price equals the firm's minimum average variable cost, which is at the point where the marginal cost curve intersects the average variable cost curve. Shutdown will occur if price falls below average variable cost.

- The firm will continue production at a price that exceeds average variable costs because revenues exceed total variable costs of producing with variable inputs.

- At the short-run break-even price, the firm is making zero economic profits, which means that it is just making a normal rate of return in that industry.

- The firm's short-run supply curve is the portion of its marginal cost curve at and above its minimum average variable cost. The industry short-run supply curve is a horizontal summation of the individual firms' marginal cost curves at and above their respective minimum average variable costs.

To test your understanding of the concepts covered in this section, go to the Online Review at www.myeconlab.com/miller.

COMPETITIVE PRICE DETERMINATION

How is the market, or "going," price established in a competitive market? This price is established by the interaction of all the suppliers (firms) and all the demanders. The market demand schedule, *D,* in panel (a) of Figure 24-8 on the following page represents the demand schedule for the entire industry, and the supply schedule, *S,* represents the supply schedule for the entire industry. Price P_e is established by the forces of supply and demand at the intersection of *D* and the short-run industry supply curve, *S.* Even though each individual firm has no control or effect on the price of its product in a competitive industry, the interaction of *all* the producers and buyers determines the price at which the product will be sold. We say that the price P_e and the quantity Q_e in panel (a) of Figure 24-8 constitute the competitive solution to the resource allocation problem in that particular industry. It is the equilibrium at which quantity demanded equals quantity supplied, and both suppliers and demanders are doing as well as they can. The resulting individual firm demand curve, *d,* is shown in panel (b) of Figure 24-8 at the price P_e.

In a purely competitive industry, the individual producer takes price as a given and chooses the output level that maximizes profits. (This is also the equilibrium level of output from the producer's standpoint.) We see in panel (b) of Figure 24-8 that this is at q_e. If the producer's average costs are given by AC_1, the short-run break-even price arises at q_e (see Figure 24-5 on page 577); if its average costs are given by AC_2, at q_e, AC exceeds price (average revenue), and the firm is incurring losses. Alternatively, if average costs are given by AC_3, the firm will be making economic profits at q_e. In the former case, we would expect, over time, that some firms will cease production (exit the industry), causing supply to shift inward, whereas in the latter case, we would expect new firms to enter the industry to take advantage of the economic profits, thereby causing supply to shift outward. We now turn to these long-run considerations.

THE LONG-RUN INDUSTRY SITUATION: EXIT AND ENTRY

In the long run in a competitive situation, firms will be making zero economic profits. We surmise, therefore, that in the long run a perfectly competitive firm's price (marginal revenue) curve will just touch its average total cost curve. How does this occur? It is through an adjustment process that depends on economic profits and losses.

FIGURE 24-8
Industry Demand and Supply Curves and the Individual Firm Demand Curve
The industry demand curve is represented by D in panel (a). The short-run industry supply curve is S and is equal to ΣMC. The intersection of the demand and supply curves at E determines the equilibrium or market clearing price at P_e. The individual firm demand curve in panel (b) is perfectly elastic at the market clearing price determined in panel (a). If the producer has a marginal cost curve MC, this producer's individual profit-maximizing output level is at q_e. For AC_1, economic profits are zero; for AC_2, profits are negative; and for AC_3, profits are positive.

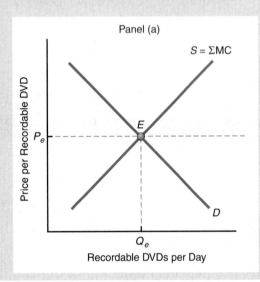

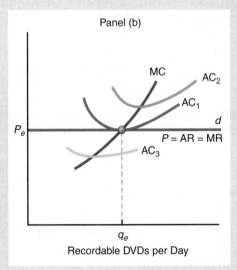

Exit and Entry of Firms

Look back at Figure 24-3 on page 575 and Figure 24-4 on page 576. The existence of either profits or losses is a signal to owners of capital both inside and outside the industry. If the industry is characterized by firms showing economic profits as represented in Figure 24-3, this will signal owners of capital elsewhere in the economy that they, too, should enter this industry. If, by contrast, there are firms in the industry suffering economic losses as represented in Figure 24-4, this signals resource owners outside the industry to stay out. It also signals resource owners within the industry not to reinvest and if possible to leave the industry. It is in this sense that we say that profits direct resources to their highest-valued use. In the long run, capital will flow into industries in which profitability is highest and will flow out of industries in which profitability is lowest.

Allocation of Capital and Market Signals. The price system therefore allocates capital according to the relative expected rates of return on alternative investments. Entry restrictions will thereby hinder economic efficiency by not allowing resources to flow to their highest-valued use. Similarly, exit restrictions (such as laws that require firms to give advance notice of closings) will act to trap resources (temporarily) in sectors in which their value is below that in alternative uses. Such laws will also inhibit the ability of firms to respond to changes in the domestic and international marketplaces.

Not every industry presents an immediate source of opportunity for every firm. In a brief period of time, it may be impossible for a firm that produces tractors to switch to the production of computers, even if there are very large profits to be made. Over the long run, however, we would expect to see such a change, whether or not the tractor producers want to change over to another product. In a market economy, investors supply firms in the more profitable industry with more investment funds, which they take from firms in less profitable industries. (Also, profits induce existing firms to use internal investment funds for expansion.) Consequently, resources useful in the production of more profitable goods, such as labor, will be bid away from lower-valued opportunities. Investors and other suppliers of resources respond to market **signals** about their highest-valued opportunities.

Tendency Toward Equilibrium. Market adjustment to changes in demand will occur regardless of the wishes of the managers of firms in less profitable markets. They can either attempt to adjust their product line to respond to the new demands, be replaced by managers who are more responsive to new conditions, or see their firms go bankrupt as they find themselves unable to replace worn-out plant and equipment.

In addition, when we say that in a competitive long-run equilibrium situation firms will be making zero economic profits, we must realize that at a particular point in time it would be pure coincidence for a firm to be making *exactly* zero economic profits. Real-world information is not as precise as the curves we use to simplify our analysis. Things change all the time in a dynamic world, and firms, even in a very competitive situation, may for many reasons not be making exactly zero economic profits. We say that there is a *tendency* toward that equilibrium position, but firms are adjusting all the time to changes in their cost curves and in their individual demand curves.

Sometimes adjustments toward long-run equilibrium take several years. Why do you suppose that long-run adjustments sometimes occur more rapidly in markets for items sold on the Internet?

Signals
Compact ways of conveying to economic decision makers information needed to make decisions. A true signal not only conveys information but also provides the incentive to react appropriately. Economic profits and economic losses are such signals.

Economics Front and Center

To contemplate a case study of how entry of new firms into a market can affect an existing firm, read the case study, **Cardiologists Give Heart Surgeons Chest Pains,** on page 588.

E-Commerce EXAMPLE

Why Exits Have Followed Entries at Online Auction Sites

Since the mid-1990s, individuals have been using online auction sites, such as those operated by eBay, uBid, and Yahoo, to sell off old clothes, collectibles, and other used items that they find when cleaning out closets and attics. During the early 2000s, manufacturers and retailers discovered that online auction sites were useful for selling unsold inventories of items such as digital cameras, lawn mowers, and laptop computers. Sharper Image, Sears, and Hewlett-Packard are among the companies that regularly sell off inventories of outdated products in online auctions.

In 2002, a few companies, with names like "ReturnBuy" and "Connection to eBay" (owned by global management consulting firm Accenture), began buying large quantities of out-

dated models of various items from manufacturers and selling them at higher prices in online auctions. The significant profits they earned signaled more firms to enter this line of business. But with the sharp increase in the supplies of "like new," yet outdated items offered for sale in online auctions, prices began to fall significantly. Consequently, the profits earned by firms such as "ReturnBuy" and "Connection to eBay" declined. By 2004, these and a few other firms had exited the market.

For Critical Analysis
Why would you guess that it is not unusual for a big burst of new entrants into a market to be followed by the eventual exit from the market by several of those same firms?

Long-Run Industry Supply Curves

In panel (a) of Figure 24-8 on page 582, we drew the summation of all of the portions of the individual firms' marginal cost curves at and above each firm's respective minimum average variable costs as the upward-sloping supply curve of the entire industry. We should be aware, however, that a relatively steep upward-sloping supply curve may be appropriate only in the short run. After all, one of the prerequisites of a competitive industry is free entry.

Remember that our definition of the long run is a period of time in which all adjust-

Long-run industry supply curve
A market supply curve showing the relationship between prices and quantities after firms have been allowed the time to enter into or exit from an industry, depending on whether there have been positive or negative economic profits.

ments can be made. The **long-run industry supply curve** is a supply curve showing the relationship between quantities supplied by the entire industry at different prices after firms have been allowed to either enter or leave the industry, depending on whether there have been positive or negative economic profits. Also, the long-run industry supply curve is drawn under the assumption that entry and exit have been completed. This means that along the long-run industry supply curve, firms in the industry earn zero economic profits.

The long-run industry supply curve can take one of three shapes, depending on whether input prices stay constant, increase, or decrease as the number of firms in the industry changes. In Chapter 23, we assumed that input prices remained constant to the firm regardless of the firm's rate of output. When we look at the entire industry, however, when all firms are expanding and new firms are entering, they may simultaneously bid up input prices.

Constant-Cost Industries. In principle, there are industries that use such a small percentage of the total supply of inputs required for industrywide production that firms can enter the industry without bidding up input prices. In such a situation, we are dealing with a **constant-cost industry.** Its long-run industry supply curve is therefore horizontal and is represented by S_L in panel (a) of Figure 24-9.

Constant-cost industry
An industry whose total output can be increased without an increase in long-run per-unit costs; its long-run supply curve is horizontal.

We can work through the case in which constant costs prevail. We start out in panel (a) with demand curve D_1 and supply curve S_1. The equilibrium price is P_1. Market demand shifts rightward to D_2. In the short run, the equilibrium price rises to P_2. This generates positive economic profits for existing firms in the industry. Such economic profits induce capital to flow into the industry. The existing firms expand or new firms enter (or both). The short-run supply curve shifts outward to S_2. The new intersection with the new demand curve is at E_3. The new equilibrium price is again P_1. The long-run supply curve is obtained by connecting the intersections of the corresponding pairs of demand and supply curves, E_1 and E_3. Labeled S_L, it is horizontal; its slope is zero. In a constant-cost industry, long-run supply is perfectly elastic. Any shift in demand is eventually met by just enough entry or exit of suppliers that the long-run price is constant at P_1.

FIGURE 24-9
Constant-Cost, Increasing-Cost, and Decreasing-Cost Industries

In panel (a), we show a situation in which the demand curve shifts from D_1 to D_2. Price increases from P_1 to P_2. In time, the short-run supply curve shifts outward because positive profits are being earned, and the equilibrium shifts from E_2 to E_3. The market clearing price is again P_1. If we connect points such as E_1 and E_3, we come up with the long-run supply curve S_L. This is a constant-cost industry. In panel (b), costs are increasing for the industry, and therefore the long-run supply curve, S_L', slopes upward and long-run prices rise from P_1 to P_2. In panel (c), costs are decreasing for the industry as it expands, and therefore the long-run supply curve, S_L'', slopes downward such that long-run prices decline from P_1 to P_2.

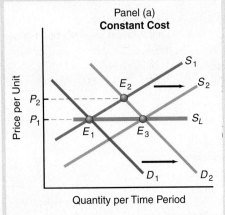

Panel (a)
Constant Cost

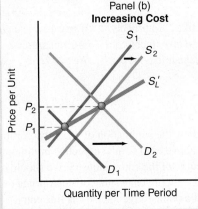

Panel (b)
Increasing Cost

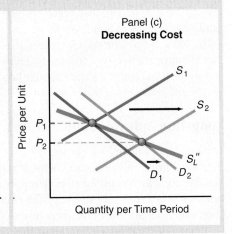

Panel (c)
Decreasing Cost

Retail trade is often given as an example of such an industry because output can be expanded or contracted without affecting input prices. Banking is another example.

Increasing–Cost Industries.
In an **increasing-cost industry,** expansion by existing firms and the addition of new firms cause the price of inputs specialized within that industry to be bid up. As costs of production rise, the ATC curve and the firms' MC curves shift upward, causing short-run supply curves (each firm's marginal cost curve) to shift upward. Hence, industry supply shifts out by less than in a constant-cost industry. The result is a long-run industry supply curve that slopes upward, as represented by S_L' in panel (b) of Figure 24-9. Examples are residential construction and coal mining—both use specialized inputs that cannot be obtained in ever-increasing quantities without causing their prices to rise.

> **Increasing–cost industry**
> An industry in which an increase in industry output is accompanied by an increase in long-run per-unit costs, such that the long-run industry supply curve slopes upward.

Decreasing–Cost Industries.
An expansion in the number of firms in an industry can lead to a reduction in input costs and a downward shift in the ATC and MC curves. When this occurs, the long-run industry supply curve will slope downward. An example, S_L'', is given in panel (c) of Figure 24-9. This is a **decreasing-cost industry.**

Based on this discussion, what evidence would support a conclusion that the firms that manufacture electronic transistors operate within a decreasing-cost industry?

> **Decreasing–cost industry**
> An industry in which an increase in output leads to a reduction in long-run per-unit costs, such that the long-run industry supply curve slopes downward.

EXAMPLE

Decreasing Costs and the Market for Transistors

Figure 24-10 shows that the world's output of transistors, the main components of microprocessors used in computers, has exploded, from just over 1 billion in the late 1960s to more than 1 quintillion (a million trillions) today. During this same period, the average price of a transistor has plummeted, from about $1 to less than $0.00002, or two one-thousandths of a cent. Thus the transistor industry is an example of a decreasing-cost industry.

For Critical Analysis
How does the decrease in transistor prices help to explain why average (constant-quality) computer prices have declined by 99 percent since the 1960s?

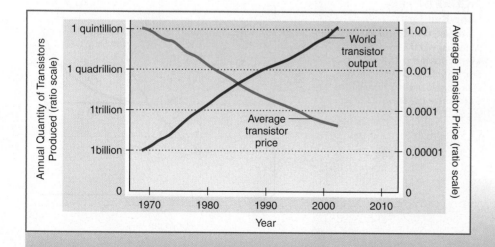

FIGURE 24-10
World Transistor Production and Prices Since 1968
As global output of transistors has increased, the average market price of transistors has decreased.

Source: *Organization for Economic Cooperation and Development.*

LONG-RUN EQUILIBRIUM

In the long run, the firm can change the scale of its plant, adjusting its plant size in such a way that it has no further incentive to change. It will do so until profits are maximized. Figure 24-11 shows the long-run equilibrium of the perfectly competitive firm. Given a price of P and a marginal cost curve, MC, the firm produces at output q_e. Because profits must be zero in the long run, the firm's short-run average costs (SAC) must equal P at q_e, which occurs at minimum SAC. In addition, because we are in long-run equilibrium, any economies of scale must be exhausted, so we are on the minimum point of the long-run average cost curve (LAC). In other words, the long-run equilibrium position is where "everything is equal," which is at point E in Figure 24-11. There, *price* equals *marginal revenue* equals *marginal cost* equals *average cost* (minimum, short-run, and long-run).

Perfect Competition and Minimum Average Total Cost

Look again at Figure 24-11. In long-run equilibrium, the perfectly competitive firm finds itself producing at output rate q_e. At that rate of output, the price is just equal to the minimum long-run average cost as well as the minimum short-run average cost. In this sense, perfect competition results in the production of goods and services using the least costly combination of resources. This is an important attribute of a perfectly competitive long-run equilibrium, particularly when we wish to compare the market structure of perfect competition with other market structures that are less than perfectly competitive. We will examine these other market structures in later chapters.

COMPETITIVE PRICING: MARGINAL COST PRICING

In a perfectly competitive industry, each firm produces where its marginal cost curve intersects its marginal revenue curve from below. Thus perfectly competitive firms always sell their goods at a price that just equals marginal cost. This represents an optimal pricing situation because the price that consumers pay reflects the opportunity cost to society of producing the good. Recall that marginal cost is the amount that a firm must spend to purchase the additional resources needed to expand output by one unit. Given competitive

FIGURE 24-11
Long-Run Firm Competitive Equilibrium
In the long run, the firm operates where price, marginal revenue, marginal cost, short-run minimum average cost, and long-run minimum average cost are all equal. This occurs at point E.

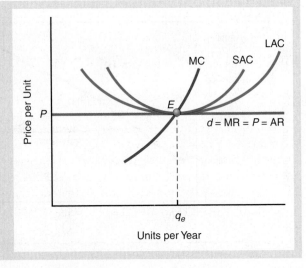

markets, the amount paid for a resource will be the same in all of its alternative uses. Thus MC reflects relative resource input use; that is, if the MC of good 1 is twice the MC of good 2, one more unit of good 1 requires twice the resource input of one more unit of good 2. Because price equals marginal cost under perfect competition, the consumer, in determining her or his allocation of income on purchases on the basis of relative prices, is actually allocating income on the basis of relative resource input use.

Marginal Cost Pricing

The competitive firm produces up to the point at which the market price just equals the marginal cost. Herein lies the element of the optimal nature of a competitive solution. It is called **marginal cost pricing.** The competitive firm sells its product at a price that just equals the cost to society—the opportunity cost—for that is what the marginal cost curve represents. (But note here that it is the self-interest of firm owners that causes price to equal the additional cost to society.) In other words, the marginal benefit to consumers, given by the price that they are willing to pay for the last unit of the good purchased, just equals the marginal cost to society of producing the last unit. (If the marginal benefit exceeds the marginal cost, that is, if $P > $ MC, too little is being produced in that people value additional units more than the cost to society of producing them; if $P < $ MC, the opposite is true.)

When an individual pays a price equal to the marginal cost of production, the cost to the user of that product is equal to the sacrifice or cost to society of producing that quantity of that good as opposed to more of some other good. (We are assuming that all marginal social costs are accounted for.) The competitive solution, then, is called *efficient,* in the economic sense of the word. Economic efficiency means that it is impossible to increase the output of any good without lowering the *value* of the total output produced in the economy. No juggling of resources, such as labor and capital, will result in an output that is higher in total value than the value of all of the goods and services already being produced. In an efficient situation, it is impossible to make one person better off without making someone else worse off. All resources are used in the most advantageous way possible, and society therefore enjoys an efficient allocation of productive resources. All goods and services are sold at their opportunity cost, and marginal cost pricing prevails throughout.

How do you suppose that competition from abroad has helped to push price closer to marginal cost for Japanese retail goods?

Marginal cost pricing
A system of pricing in which the price charged is equal to the opportunity cost to society of producing one more unit of the good or service in question. The opportunity cost is the marginal cost to society.

Go to www.econtoday.com/chap24 to find out how the Congressional Budget Office tries to judge whether banks engage in marginal cost pricing with automated teller machines.

International E X A M P L E

Pressuring Japanese Retailers to Equalize Price and Average Total Cost

Since the late 1990s, discount retailers based outside Japan, such as Wal-Mart and Costco from the United States and Carrefour from France, have entered the Japanese discount-store industry. To be able to reduce their prices to the levels charged by these companies, Japanese retailers have had to become more cost-efficient. This has required Japanese retailers to downsize traditionally complex and expensive distribution networks. By establishing direct links to manufacturers, they have also reduced their reliance on intermediaries in the distribution chain. Now Japanese retailers are selling their products at the same prices as their U.S. and French competitors—and operating at very close to the same average total cost. In this way, the entry of the foreign firms has induced retailers in Japan to identify and employ the least costly combinations of resources.

For Critical Analysis
Would U.S. companies have as much incentive to minimize long-run average total cost if non-U.S. firms were prevented from selling their products in this country?

Market Failure

Market failure
A situation in which an unrestrained market operation leads to either too few or too many resources going to a specific economic activity.

Although perfect competition does offer many desirable results, situations arise when perfectly competitive markets cannot efficiently allocate resources. Either too many or too few resources are used in the production of a good or service. These situations are instances of **market failure.** Externalities and public goods are examples. For reasons discussed in later chapters, perfectly competitive markets cannot efficiently allocate resources in these situations, and alternative allocation mechanisms are called for. In some cases, alternative market structures or government intervention *may* improve the economic outcome.

CONCEPTS in Brief

- The competitive price is determined by the intersection of the market demand curve and the market supply curve; the market supply curve is equal to the horizontal summation of the portions of the individual marginal cost curves above their respective minimum average variable costs.

- In the long run, competitive firms make zero economic profits because of entry and exit whenever there are industrywide economic profits or losses.

- A constant-cost industry has a horizontal long-run supply curve. An increasing-cost industry has an upward-sloping

long-run supply curve. A decreasing-cost industry has a downward-sloping long-run supply curve.

- In the long run, a competitive firm produces where price, marginal revenue, marginal cost, short-run minimum average cost, and long-run minimum average cost are all equal.

- Competitive pricing is essentially marginal cost pricing. Therefore the competitive solution is called efficient because marginal cost represents the social opportunity cost of producing one more unit of the good.

To test your understanding of the concepts covered in this section, go to the Online Review at **www.myeconlab.com/miller.**

CASE STUDY : Economics Front and Center

Cardiologists Give Heart Surgeons Chest Pains

About two years ago, Banerjee completed her surgical residency and joined a heart surgery practice in a medium-sized U.S. metropolitan area. Until last year, she and her seven surgical partners had a thriving practice. Several of them earned more than $1 million per year. In a typical month, they performed about 120 major heart operations, including many lucrative bypass surgeries. In the past few months, however, the practice's caseload has dropped to an average of just 45 surgeries per month. Last month, the partners performed only 30 surgeries.

A group of cardiologists has been using specially coated stents, or tiny metal scaffolds, to prop open arteries after clearing them with angioplasty balloons. Physicians in this cardiology group hand their patients off to surgeons they have hired as part of their own practice for major operations only in particularly serious situations. Since the cardiology group began their prac-

tice, the market price for a heart bypass operation has dropped by 50 percent. The combined effects of this price reduction and the decrease in surgeries she is performing have dramatically reduced Banerjee's income. She and her partners are having a meeting this afternoon to contemplate how much longer their heart surgery practice is likely to remain a viable business.

Points to Analyze

1. *Has the market price of heart surgeries in Banerjee's local area recently been above or below the short-run shutdown price?*

2. *What will determine whether Banerjee and her partners decide to maintain their surgical practice as an ongoing business?*

In the 1950s, science-fiction authors envisioned a twenty-first-century world in which people could get regular "body scans" conducted using sophisticated computer-controlled imaging equipment. In futuristic stories of the time, body scans would provide reassurance that no diseases were in the process of developing or would give an early warning of a condition requiring medical treatment. It turns out that the stories of five decades ago were on the mark. Doctors have long used computed tomography (CT) scans, which provide cross-section views of specific areas of the body. In recent years, however, many companies have offered full-body CT scans to anyone willing to pay the price of imaging cross sections of the entire body. As in the old science-fiction stories, people willing to pay for full-body CT scans can verify that no hidden ailments exist or get a head start on combating previously undetected diseases.

Concepts Applied

- Perfect Competition
- Signals
- Short-Run Shutdown Price

Responding to the Lure of Economic Profits

In the late 1990s, the market price of a full-body CT scan was about $1,500. This price was well above the average total cost that companies offering full-body CT scans incurred in providing this service. Consequently, companies specializing in this service earned significant economic profits.

In the early 2000s, numerous medical entrepreneurs responded to this signal by opening CT-scan centers around the country. In some states, such as California, Florida, Illinois, and New York, firms opened entire chains of centers offering full-body CT scans. As predicted by the theory of perfect competition, significant positive economic profits earned by previously existing firms induced the speedy entry of new firms into the industry.

A Painful Adjustment to Long-Run Equilibrium

This rapid increase in the number of producers of full-body CT scans, of course, generated an increase in market supply.

Furthermore, about the same time that the supply was increasing, many physicians began advising outwardly healthy patients *against* obtaining the sophisticated procedures. In a series of interviews that received wide distribution in print and on television, prominent physicians contended that the tests often yield ambiguous results, which induce people to purchase even more tests, only to learn that there is absolutely nothing wrong with their bodies. This bad publicity led to a fall in the market demand for full-body CT scans.

Naturally, the simultaneous rise in supply and decline in demand generated a decline in the market price. By 2004, the market price of a full-body CT scan had dropped to below $400. For many companies, this market price of a full-body CT scan was less than the average variable cost of providing the service; that is, the market price was below their short-run shutdown price. Among the firms that shut down their operations were several of the new industry entrants that had been in operation for only a few months. For a while, some companies held out hope that the demand for full-body scans would recover and push the market price back toward previous levels. But

589

when the market price stabilized at just above $400 in early 2004, they closed their operations permanently. The CT-scan- ning industry had reached a long-run equilibrium, in which firms remaining in the industry were earning a normal profit.

For Critical Analysis

1. What do you think would have happened in the market for full-body CT scans during 2003 and 2004 if these medical tests had instead received highly favorable recommen- dations from physicians?
2. Why did the market price of a full-body CT stabilize at about $400 in early 2004?

Web Resources

1. For links to sites surveying the costs and benefits of full-body CT scans, follow the Body Scan News link at www.econtoday.com/chap24.
2. To learn from the Food and Drug Administration why the demand for full-body CT scans declined in the early 2000s even as new providers entered the industry, go to www.econtoday.com/chap24.

Research Project

Recent developments in CT-scanning technology promise to bring about both a major re- duction in ambiguous test results and a significant decrease in the average total cost of conducting full-body scans. Evaluate the effects that each of these factors individually would be likely to have on long-run equilibrium in the market for full-body CT scans. Can you predict, other things being equal, whether the market price of a full-body CT scan is likely, on net, to rise or fall if these technological developments pan out?

Summary Discussion of Learning Objectives

1. **The Characteristics of a Perfectly Competitive Market Structure:** A perfectly competitive industry has four fun- damental characteristics: (1) There are a large number of buyers and sellers, (2) firms in the industry produce and sell a homogeneous product, (3) information is equally accessible to both buyers and sellers, and (4) there are in- significant barriers to industry entry or exit. These char- acteristics imply that each firm in a perfectly competitive industry is a price taker, meaning that the firm takes the market price as given and outside its control.

2. **How a Perfectly Competitive Firm Decides How Much to Produce:** Because a perfectly competitive firm sells the amount that it wishes at the market price, the addi- tional revenue it earns from selling an additional unit of output is the market price. Thus the firm's marginal rev- enue equals the market price, and its marginal revenue curve is the firm's own perfectly elastic demand curve. The firm maximizes economic profits when marginal cost equals marginal revenue, as long as the market price is not below the short-run shutdown price, where the marginal cost curve crosses the average variable cost curve.

3. **The Short-Run Supply Curve of a Perfectly Competi- tive Firm:** If the market price is below the short-run shut-

down price, the firm's total revenues fail to cover its vari- able costs. Then the firm would be better off halting pro- duction, thereby minimizing its economic loss in the short run. If the market price is above the short-run shut- down price, however, the firm produces the rate of output where marginal revenue, the market price, equals mar- ginal cost. Thus the range of the firm's marginal cost curve above the short-run shutdown price gives combina- tions of market prices and production choices of the per- fectly competitive firm. This range of the firm's marginal cost curve is therefore the firm's short-run supply curve.

4. **The Equilibrium Price in a Perfectly Competitive Market:** The short-run supply curve for a perfectly com- petitive industry is obtained by summing the quantities supplied at each price by all firms in the industry. At the equilibrium market price, the total amount of output sup- plied by all firms is equal to the total amount of output demanded by all buyers.

5. **Incentives to Enter or Exit a Perfectly Competitive In- dustry:** In the short run, a perfectly competitive firm will continue to produce output as long as the market price exceeds the short-run shutdown price. This is so even if the market price is below the short-run break-even point where the marginal cost curve crosses the firm's average

total cost curve. Even though the firm earns an economic loss, it minimizes the amount of the loss by continuing to produce in the short run. In the long run, however, an economic loss is a signal that the firm is not engaged in the highest-value activity available to its owners, and continued economic losses in the long run will induce the firm to exit the industry. Conversely, persistent economic profits induce new firms to enter a perfectly competitive industry. In long-run equilibrium, the market price is equal to the minimum average total cost of production for the firms in the industry, because at this point firms earn zero economic profits.

6. **The Long-Run Industry Supply Curve and Constant-, Increasing-, and Decreasing-Cost Industries:** The long-run industry supply curve in a perfectly competitive industry shows the relationship between prices and quantities after firms have the opportunity to enter or leave the industry in response to economic profits or losses. In a constant-cost industry, total output can increase without a rise in long-run per-unit production costs, so the long-run industry supply curve is horizontal. In an increasing-cost industry, however, per-unit costs increase with a rise in industry output, so the long-run industry supply curve slopes upward. In contrast, in a decreasing-cost industry per-unit costs decline as industry output increases, and the long-run industry supply curve slopes downward.

KEY TERMS AND CONCEPTS

constant-cost industry (584)

decreasing-cost industry (585)

increasing-cost industry (585)

industry supply curve (579)

long-run industry supply curve (584)

marginal cost pricing (587)

marginal revenue (573)

market failure (588)

perfect competition (569)

perfectly competitive firm (569)

price taker (569)

profit-maximizing rate of production (573)

short-run break-even price (577)

short-run shutdown price (578)

signals (583)

total revenues (571)

PROBLEMS

Answers to the odd-numbered problems appear at the back of the book.

24-1. Explain why each of the following examples is *not* a perfectly competitive industry.

   a. Even though one firm produces a large portion of the industry's total output, there are many firms in the industry, and their products are indistinguishable. Firms can easily exit and enter the industry.

   b. There are many buyers and sellers in the industry. Consumers have equal information about the prices of firms' products, which differ slightly in quality from firm to firm.

   c. Many taxicabs compete in a city. The city's government requires all taxicabs to provide identical service. Taxicabs are virtually identical, and all drivers must wear a designated uniform. The government also limits the number of taxicab companies that can operate within the city's boundaries.

24-2. Illustrate the following situation in the market for DVD rentals, which is perfectly competitive: The supply curve slopes upward, the demand curve slopes downward, and the equilibrium rental price equals $3.50. Next, illustrate the demand curve that a single independent DVD rental store faces. Finally, illustrate how an increase in the market demand for DVD rentals affects the market price and the demand curve faced by the individual rental store.

24-3. The campus barber faces stiff competition from the large number of shops that surround the campus area, and for all practical purposes the market is perfectly competitive. He charges $12 for a haircut and cuts hair for 15 people a day. His shop is open five days a week. Calculate his weekly total revenue, average revenue, and marginal revenue.

24-4. The following table represents the hourly output and cost structure for a local pizza shop. The market is perfectly competitive, and the market price of a pizza in the area is $10. Total costs include all implicit opportunity costs.

a. Calculate the total revenue and total economic profit for this pizza shop at each rate of output.

b. Assuming that the pizza shop always produces and sells at least one pizza per hour, does this appear to be a situation of short-run or long-run equilibrium?

Total Hourly Output and Sales of Pizzas	Total Hourly Cost ($)
0	5
1	9
2	11
3	12
4	14
5	18
6	24
7	32
8	42
9	54
10	68

24-5. Using the information provided in Problem 24-4, calculate the pizza shop's marginal cost and marginal revenue at each rate of output. Based on marginal analysis, what is the profit-maximizing rate of output for the pizza shop?

24-6. Based on the information in Problems 24-4 and 24-5 and your answers to them, draw a diagram depicting the short-run marginal revenue and marginal cost curves for this pizza shop, and illustrate the determination of its profit-maximizing output rate.

24-7. Consider the information provided in Problem 24-4. Suppose the market price drops to only $5 per pizza. In the short run, should this pizza shop continue to make pizzas, or will it maximize its economic profits (that is, minimize its economic loss) by shutting down?

24-8. Yesterday, a perfectly competitive producer of construction bricks manufactured and sold 10,000 bricks at a market price that was just equal to the minimum average variable cost of producing each brick. Today, all the firm's costs are the same, but the market price of bricks has declined.

a. Assuming that this firm has positive fixed costs, did the firm earn economic profits, economic losses, or zero economic profits yesterday?

b. To maximize economic profits today, how many bricks should this firm produce today?

24-9. Suppose that a perfectly competitive firm faces a market price of $5 per unit, and at this price the upward-sloping portion of the firm's marginal cost curve crosses its marginal revenue curve at an output level of 1,500 units. If the firm produces 1,500 units, its average variable costs equal $5.50 per unit, and its average fixed costs equal 50 cents per unit. What is the firm's profit-maximizing (or loss-minimizing) output level? What is the amount of its economic profits (or losses) at this output level?

24-10. Suppose that the price of a service sold in a perfectly competitive market is $25 per unit. For a firm in this market, the output level corresponding to a marginal cost of $25 per unit is 2,000 units. Average variable costs at this output level equal $15 per unit, and average fixed costs equal $5 per unit. What is the firm's profit-maximizing (or loss-minimizing) output level? What is the amount of its economic profits (or losses) at this output level?

24-11. Suppose that a firm in a perfectly competitive industry finds that at its current output rate, marginal revenue exceeds the minimum average total cost of producing any feasible rate of output. Furthermore, the firm is producing an output rate at which marginal cost is less than the average total cost at that rate of output. Is the firm maximizing its economic profits? Why or why not?

24-12. A perfectly competitive industry is initially in a short-run equilibrium in which all firms are earning zero economic profits but in which firms are operating below their minimum efficient scale. Explain the long-run adjustments that will take place for the industry to attain long-run equilibrium with firms operating at their minimum efficient scale.

24-13. Two years ago, a large number of firms entered a market in which existing firms had been earning positive economic profits. By the end of last year, the typical firm in this industry had begun earning negative economic profits. No other events occurred in this market during the past two years.

a. Explain the adjustment process that occurred last year.

b. Predict what adjustments will take place in this market beginning this year, other things being equal.

ECONOMICS ON THE NET

The Cost Structure of the Movie Theater Business A key idea in this chapter is that competition among firms in an industry can influence the long-run cost structure within the industry. Here you get a chance to apply this concept to a multinational company that owns movie theaters.

Title: AMC International

Navigation: Follow the link at www.econtoday.com/chap24 to visit American Multi-Cinema's home page.

Application Answer the following questions.

1. Click on *Investor Resources.* What is the average number of screens in an AMC theater? How many theaters does it own and manage?

2. Click on *Locations Worldwide,* and use the map to select the theater in Toyohashi City, Japan. This is the largest megaplex theater in Japan. How many screens does the megaplex have?

3. Based on the average number of screens at an AMC theater and the number of screens at the Japanese facility, what can you conclude about the cost structure of this industry? Illustrate the long-run average cost curve for this industry.

For Group Discussion and Analysis Is the Japanese facility the largest multiplex? What do you think constrains the size of a multiplex in Japan? Given the location of AMC's headquarters, how does that affect the cost structure of the firm? Is it easier for AMC to have fewer facilities that are larger in size?

Media Resources

If your exam were tomorrow, would you be ready? For each chapter, MyEconLab Practice Tests and Study Plans pinpoint which sections you have mastered and which ones you need to study. That way, you are more efficient with your study time, and you are better prepared for your exams.

In addition to Practice Tests and your personalized Study Plan, you'll find the following media resources in MyEconLab:

1. *Graphs in Motion* animation of Figures 24-1, 24-2, 24-3, 24-4, 24-5, 24-6, 24-7, 24-8, and 24-11.
2. An *Economics in Motion* in-depth animation of Costs, Revenues, and Profit Maximization.
3. Videos featuring the author, Roger LeRoy Miller, on the following subjects:
   - The Short-Run Shutdown Price
   - The Meaning of Zero Economic Profits

4. Links to the Web sites cited in the marginal Internet Resources, Issues and Applications feature, and Economics on the Net activity.
5. Audio clips of all key terms, additional practice problems, and a PDF version of the material from the print Study Guide.
6. eThemes of the Times, which is a New York Times article to help you understand the real-world applications of what you are learning.

Get Ahead of the Curve

To see how it works, turn to page 16 and then go to www.myeconlab.com/miller.

Chapter 25

Monopoly

I magine being the owner of a company that, after months of preparations, is ready to sell digital music files on the Web. You have just received notice, however, that a firm holding a *business method patent* has filed a lawsuit against your company. The firm claims that its patent applies to online sales of *any* audio recording and demands that you either pay royalties or close your business before it even opens. You have only two options: Pay the royalties, or fight the legal claim in court. Either way, the cost of doing business is now going to be higher than you had anticipated, and profits are going to be lower. Already, the viability of your new company is in doubt. This true story depicts a situation in which a company has encountered a *barrier to entry*, a concept that you will learn about in this chapter.

Media Resources

Refer to the end of the chapter for a full listing of the multimedia learning materials available in MyEconLab.

LEARNING OBJECTIVES

After reading this chapter, you should be able to:

1. Identify situations that can give rise to monopoly
2. Describe the demand and marginal revenue conditions a monopolist faces
3. Discuss how a monopolist determines how much output to produce and what price to charge
4. Evaluate the profits earned by a monopolist
5. Understand price discrimination
6. Explain the social cost of monopolies

... the average price that an individual must pay to obtain a set of hearing aids is $2,200, even though the technology exists to produce hearing aid sets that could be priced close to an average total cost of no more than $200? Since 1977, the Food and Drug Administration has permitted only state-licensed hearing-aid specialists and audiologists to sell hearing aids. These government-approved providers have worked together to establish rules requiring consumers to complete batteries of tests and undergo lengthy fitting sessions before they can purchase hearing aids. This helps drive up the overall price of obtaining a hearing aid by $2,000.

In this chapter, you will learn how restricting the sale of an item such as hearing aids to a limited set of providers can push up the item's price. By coordinating their actions, the providers can search for the price that maximizes their combined profits. This creates a situation called *monopoly*.

DEFINITION OF A MONOPOLIST

The word *monopoly* probably brings to mind notions of a business that gouges the consumer, sells faulty products, and gets unconscionably rich in the process. But if we are to succeed in analyzing and predicting the behavior of noncompetitive firms, we will have to be more objective in our definition. Although most monopolies in the United States are relatively large, our definition will be equally applicable to small businesses: A **monopolist** is the *single supplier* of a good or service for which there is no close substitute.

In a monopoly market structure, the firm (the monopolist) and the industry are one and the same. Occasionally, there may be a problem in identifying an industry and therefore determining if a monopoly exists. For example, should we think of aluminum and steel as separate industries, or should we define the industry in terms of basic metals? Our answer depends on the extent to which aluminum and steel can be substituted in the production of a wide range of products.

As we shall see in this chapter, a seller prefers to have a monopoly than to face competitors. In general, we think of monopoly prices as being higher than prices under perfect competition and of monopoly profits as being higher than profits under perfect competition (which are, in the long run, merely equivalent to a normal rate of return). How does a firm obtain a monopoly in an industry? Basically, there must be *barriers to entry* that enable firms to receive monopoly profits in the long run. Barriers to entry are restrictions on who can start a business or who can stay in a business.

Monopolist
The single supplier of a good or service for which there is no close substitute. The monopolist therefore constitutes its entire industry.

BARRIERS TO ENTRY

For any amount of monopoly power to continue to exist in the long run, the market must be closed to entry in some way. Either legal means or certain aspects of the industry's technical or cost structure may prevent entry. We will discuss several of the barriers to entry that have allowed firms to reap monopoly profits in the long run (even if they are not pure monopolists in the technical sense).

Ownership of Resources Without Close Substitutes

Preventing a newcomer from entering an industry is often difficult. Indeed, some economists contend that no monopoly acting without government support has been able to prevent entry into the industry unless that monopoly has had the control of some essential natural resource. Consider the possibility of one firm's owning the entire supply of a raw material input that is essential to the production of a particular commodity. The exclusive ownership of such a vital resource serves as a barrier to entry until an alternative source of the raw material input is found or an alternative technology not requiring the raw material in question is developed. A good example of control over a vital input is the Aluminum Company of America (Alcoa), a firm that prior to World War II controlled world stocks of bauxite, the essential raw material in the production of aluminum. Such a situation is rare, though, and is ordinarily temporary.

Problems in Raising Adequate Capital

Certain industries require a large initial capital investment. The firms already in the industry can, according to some economists, obtain monopoly profits in the long run because no competitors can raise the large amount of capital needed to enter the industry. This argument, called the "imperfect" capital market argument, is employed to explain long-run, relatively high rates of return in certain industries. Firms in these industries generally must incur large fixed costs merely to start production. Their fixed costs are normally for expensive machines necessary to the production process.

Economies of Scale

Sometimes it is not profitable for more than one firm to exist in an industry. This is so if one firm would have to produce such a large quantity in order to realize lower unit costs that there would not be sufficient demand to warrant a second producer of the same product. Such a situation may arise because of a phenomenon we discussed in Chapter 23, economies of scale. When economies of scale exist, total costs increase less than proportionately to the increase in output. That is, proportional increases in output yield proportionately smaller increases in total costs, and per-unit costs drop. When economies of scale exist, larger firms (with larger output) have an advantage in that they have lower costs that enable them to charge lower prices and thereby drive smaller firms out of business.

> **Natural monopoly**
> A monopoly that arises from the peculiar production characteristics in an industry. It usually arises when there are large economies of scale relative to the industry's demand such that one firm can produce at a lower average cost than can be achieved by multiple firms.

When economies of scale occur over a wide range of outputs, a **natural monopoly** may develop. A natural monopoly is the first firm to take advantage of persistent declining long-run average costs as scale increases. The natural monopolist is able to underprice its competitors and eventually force all of them out of the market.

Figure 25-1 shows a downward-sloping long-run average cost curve (LAC). Recall that when average costs are falling, marginal costs are less than average costs. Thus, when the long-run average cost curve (LAC) slopes downward, the long-run marginal cost curve (LMC) will be below the LAC.

In our example, long-run average costs are falling over such a large range of production rates that we would expect only one firm to survive in such an industry. That firm would be the natural monopolist. It would be the first one to take advantage of the decreasing average costs; that is, it would construct the large-scale facilities first. As its average costs fell, it would lower prices and get an ever larger share of the market. Once that firm had driven all other firms out of the industry, it would set its price to maximize profits.

Legal or Governmental Restrictions

Governments and legislatures can also erect barriers to entry. These include licenses, franchises, patents, tariffs, and specific regulations that tend to limit entry.

Licenses, Franchises, and Certificates of Convenience. It is illegal to enter many industries without a government license, or a "certificate of convenience and public neces-

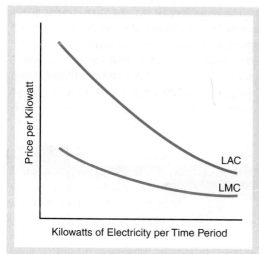

FIGURE 25-1
The Cost Curves That Might Lead to a Natural Monopoly: The Case of Electricity
Whenever long-run average costs are falling, the same will be true of long-run marginal costs. Also, long-run marginal costs (LMC) will always be below long-run average costs (LAC). A natural monopoly might arise in such a situation. The first firm to establish low-unit-cost capacity would be able to take advantage of the lower average total cost curve. This firm would drive out all rivals by charging a lower price than the others could sustain at their higher average costs.

sity." For example, in some states you cannot form an electrical utility to compete with the electrical utility already operating in your area. You would first have to obtain a certificate of convenience and public necessity from the appropriate authority, which is usually the state's public utility commission. Yet public utility commissions in these states rarely, if ever, issue a certificate to a group of investors who want to compete directly in the same geographic area as an existing electrical utility; hence entry into the industry in a particular geographic area is prohibited, and long-run monopoly profits could conceivably be earned by the electrical utility already serving the area.

To enter interstate (and also many intrastate) markets for pipelines, television and radio broadcasting, and transmission of natural gas, to cite a few such industries, it is often necessary to obtain similar permits. Because these franchises or licenses are restricted, long-run monopoly profits might be earned by the firms already in the industry.

Did you realize that in Louisiana, it is against the law to sell two or more kinds of flowers in a single bouquet unless you have a license?

E X A M P L E

It's No Rose Garden Trying to Be a Florist in Louisiana

To sell two or more varieties of flowers together or to sell even the same type of flowers in a vase in Louisiana, an individual must become a licensed florist. This requires paying a $150 fee to apply to take a practical examination proving your ability to arrange flowers. The judges are other licensed florists, who regularly give failing grades to more than 40 percent of the people who take the exam. In this way, people who are already licensed florists can restrict entry into the market for floral arrangements.

For Critical Analysis
Why do Louisiana florists who already possess a license have an incentive to give florist-license applicants failing grades on their practical exams?

Patents. A patent is issued to an inventor to provide protection from having the invention copied or stolen for a period of 20 years. Suppose that engineers working for Ford Motor

Go to www.econtoday.com/chap25 to learn more about patents and trademarks from the U.S. Patent and Trademark Office and to learn all about copyrights from the U.S. Copyright Office.

Company discover a way to build an engine that requires half the parts of a regular engine and weighs only half as much. If Ford is successful in obtaining a patent on this discovery, it can (in principle) prevent others from copying it. The patent holder has a monopoly. It is the patent holder's responsibility to defend the patent, however. That means that Ford—like other patent owners—must expend resources to prevent others from imitating its invention. If the costs of enforcing a particular patent are greater than the benefits, though, the patent may not bestow any monopoly profits on its owner. The policing costs would be just too high.

Tariffs
Taxes on imported goods.

Tariffs. **Tariffs** are special taxes that are imposed on certain imported goods. Tariffs make imports more expensive relative to their domestic counterparts, encouraging consumers to switch to the relatively cheaper domestically made products. If the tariffs are high enough, domestic producers gain monopoly advantage as the sole suppliers. Many countries have tried this protectionist strategy by using high tariffs to shut out foreign competitors.

Regulations. Throughout the twentieth century, government regulation of the U.S. economy increased, especially along the dimensions of safety and quality. For example, pharmaceutical quality-control regulations enforced by the Food and Drug Administration may require that each pharmaceutical company install a $200 million computerized testing system that requires elaborate monitoring and maintenance. Presumably, this large fixed cost can be spread over a greater number of units of output by greater firms than by smaller firms, thereby putting the smaller firms at a competitive disadvantage. It will also deter entry to the extent that the scale of operation of a potential entrant must be sufficiently large to cover the average fixed costs of the required equipment. We examine regulation in more detail in Chapter 28.

Economics Front and Center

To contemplate how colleges can maintain sports cartels, read the case study, **Collegiate Cartel Restricts Output of Postseason Games,** on page 612.

Cartels

"Being the only game in town" is preferable because such a monopoly position normally allows the monopolist to charge higher prices and make greater profits. Not surprisingly, manufacturers and sellers have frequently attempted to form an organization (which often is international) that acts as one. This is called a **cartel.** Cartels are an attempt by their members to earn higher-than-competitive profits. They set common prices and output quotas for their members. The key to the success of a cartel is keeping one member from competing against other members by expanding production and thereby lowering price.

Why do you think that oil production rose in late 2003 and 2004 even though the Organization of Petroleum Exporting Countries (OPEC) twice reduced production quotas for member nations during those years?

Cartel
An association of producers in an industry that agree to set common prices and output quotas to prevent competition.
Go to www.econtoday.com/chap25 to find out from WTRG Economics how effective OPEC has been in trying to act as an oil market monopolist.

International EXAMPLE

No Matter What OPEC Says, the Oil Keeps Pumping

The media issue reports whenever the so-called OPEC cartel announces planned cuts in oil production. The media rarely follow up, however, to see if member nations actually follow through with the reductions. As you can see in Figure 25-2, following an announced reduction in OPEC's official production quota in November 2003, oil production by OPEC members actually increased. Production steadily increased after OPEC announced another reduction in its target production quota in April 2004. Beginning in July 2004, the organization abandoned its effort to depress oil production. Even though the world's biggest

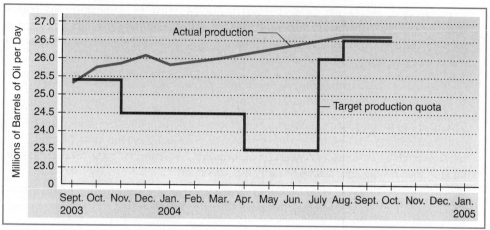

FIGURE 25-2
OPEC Targets for Oil Production Quotas and Actual Production Levels
Even though OPEC announced reductions in its quota targets in 2003 and 2004, actual oil production by OPEC nations increased.

Source: International Energy Agency.

group of oil-producing nations claims to function as a coordinated cartel, its members regularly violate OPEC production limits.

For Critical Analysis
What gives individual members of OPEC an incentive to violate the organization's production quotas?

CONCEPTS in Brief

● A monopolist is the single seller of a product or good for which there is no close substitute.

● To maintain a monopoly, there must be barriers to entry. Barriers to entry include ownership of resources without

close substitutes; large capital requirements in order to enter the industry; economies of scale; legally required licenses, franchises, and certificates of convenience; patents; tariffs; and safety and quality regulations.

To test your understanding of the concepts covered in this section, go to the Online Review at **www.myeconlab.com/miller.**

THE DEMAND CURVE A MONOPOLIST FACES

A *pure monopolist* is the sole supplier of *one* product, good, or service. A pure monopolist faces a demand curve that is the demand curve for the entire market for that good.

> **The monopolist faces the industry demand curve because the monopolist is the entire industry.**

Because the monopolist faces the industry demand curve, which is by definition downward sloping, its decision-making process with respect to how much to produce is not the same as for a perfect competitor. When a monopolist changes output, it does not automatically receive the same price per unit that it did before the change.

Profits to Be Made from Increasing Production

How do firms benefit from changing production rates? What happens to price in each case? Let's first review the situation among perfect competitors.

Marginal Revenue for the Perfect Competitor. Recall that a perfectly competitive firm faces a perfectly elastic demand curve. That is because the competitive firm is such a small part of the market that it cannot influence the price of its product. It is a *price taker.*

If the forces of supply and demand establish that the price per constant-quality pair of shoes is $50, the individual firm can sell all the pairs of shoes it wants to produce at $50 per pair. The average revenue is $50, the price is $50, and the marginal revenue is also $50.

Let us again define marginal revenue:

> *Marginal revenue equals the change in total revenue due to a one-unit change in the quantity produced and sold.*

In the case of a competitive industry, each time a single firm changes production by one unit, total revenue changes by the going price, and price is always the same. Marginal revenue never changes; it always equals price, or average revenue. Average revenue was defined as total revenue divided by quantity demanded, or

$$\text{Average revenue} = \frac{\text{TR}}{Q} = \frac{PQ}{Q} = P$$

Hence marginal revenue, average revenue, and price are all the same for the price-taking firm.

Marginal Revenue for the Monopolist.

What about a monopoly firm? Because a monopoly is the entire industry, the monopoly firm's demand curve is the market demand curve. The market demand curve slopes downward, just like the other demand curves that we have seen. Therefore, to sell more of a particular product, given the industry demand curve, the monopoly firm must lower the price. Thus the monopoly firm moves *down* the demand curve. If all buyers are to be charged the same price, the monopoly must lower the price on *all* units sold in order to sell more. It cannot lower the price on just the *last* unit sold in any given time period in order to sell a larger quantity.

Put yourself in the shoes of a monopoly ferryboat owner. You have a government-bestowed franchise, and no one can compete with you. Your ferryboat goes between two islands. If you are charging $1 per crossing, a certain quantity of your services will be demanded. Let's say that you are ferrying 100 people a day each way at that price. If you decide that you would like to ferry more individuals, you must lower your price to all individuals—you must move *down* the existing demand curve for ferrying services. To calculate the marginal revenue of your change in price, you must first calculate the total revenues you received at $1 per passenger per crossing and then calculate the total revenues you would receive at, say, 90 cents per passenger per crossing.

Competition versus Monopoly.

It is sometimes useful to compare monopoly markets with perfectly competitive markets. The monopolist is constrained by the demand curve for its product, just as a competitive firm is constrained by its demand. The key difference is the nature of the demand each type of firm faces. We see this in Figure 25-3, which compares the demand curves of the perfect competitor and the monopolist.

Here we see the fundamental difference between the monopolist and the competitor. The competitor doesn't have to worry about lowering price to sell more. In a purely competitive situation, the competitive firm accounts for such a small part of the market that it can sell its entire output, whatever that may be, at the same price. The monopolist cannot. The more the monopolist wants to sell, the lower the price it has to charge on the last unit (and on *all* units put on the market for sale). To sell the last unit, the monopolist has to lower the price because it is facing a downward-sloping demand curve, and the only way to move down the demand curve is to lower the price on all units. Consequently, the extra revenues the monopolist receives from selling one more unit are going to be smaller than the extra revenues received from selling the next-to-last unit.

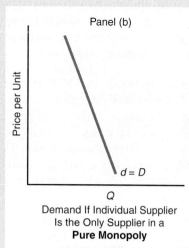

FIGURE 25-3
Demand Curves for the Perfect Competitor and the Monopolist
The perfect competitor in panel (a) faces a perfectly elastic demand curve, *d*. The monopolist in panel (b) faces the entire industry demand curve, which slopes downward.

The Monopolist's Marginal Revenue: Less Than Price

An essential point is that for the monopolist, marginal revenue is always less than price. To understand why, look at Figure 25-4, which shows a unit increase in output sold due to a reduction in the price of a commodity from P_1 to P_2. After all, the only way that the firm can sell more output, given a downward-sloping demand curve, is to reduce the price. Price P_2 is the price received for the last unit. Thus if previous units sell at the price P_1, the price P_2 times the last unit sold represents revenues received from the last unit sold. That is equal to the vertical column (area A). Area A is one unit wide by P_2 high.

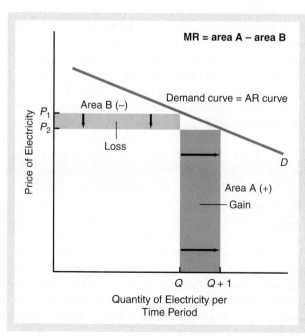

FIGURE 25-4
Marginal Revenue: Always Less Than Price
The price received for the last unit sold is equal to P_2. The revenues received from selling this last unit are equal to P_2 times one unit, or the area of the vertical column. However, if a single price is being charged for all units, total revenues do not go up by the amount of the area represented by that column. The price had to be reduced on all the previous Q units that were being sold at price P_1. Thus we must subtract area B—the rectangle between P_1 and P_2 from the origin to Q—from area A in order to derive marginal revenue. Marginal revenue is therefore always less than price.

But price times the last unit sold is *not* the addition to *total* revenues received from selling that last unit. Why? Because price had to be reduced on all previous units sold (Q) in order to sell the larger quantity $Q + 1$. The reduction in price is represented by the vertical distance from P_1 to P_2 on the vertical axis. We must therefore subtract area B from area A to come up with the *change* in total revenues due to a one-unit increase in sales. Clearly, the change in total revenues—that is, marginal revenue—must be less than price because marginal revenue is always the difference between areas A and B in Figure 25-4 on the previous page. For example, if the initial price is $8 and quantity demanded is 3, to increase quantity to 4 units, it is necessary to decrease price to $7, not just for the fourth unit, but on all three previous units as well. Thus, at a price of $7, marginal revenue is $7 − $3 = $4 because there is a $1 per unit price reduction on three previous units. Hence marginal revenue, $4, is less than price, $7.

ELASTICITY AND MONOPOLY

The monopolist faces a downward-sloping demand curve (its average revenue curve). That means that it cannot charge just *any* price with no changes in quantity (a common misconception) because, depending on the price charged, a different quantity will be demanded.

Earlier we defined a monopolist as the single seller of a well-defined good or service with no *close* substitute. This does not mean, however, that the demand curve for a monopoly is vertical or exhibits zero price elasticity of demand. (Indeed, as we shall see, the profit-maximizing monopolist will never operate in a price range in which demand is inelastic.) After all, consumers have limited incomes and unlimited wants. The downward slope of a monopolist's demand curve occurs because individuals compare the marginal satisfaction they will receive to the cost of the commodity to be purchased. Take the example of telephone service. Even if miraculously there were absolutely no substitutes whatsoever for telephone service, the market demand curve would still slope downward. At lower prices, people will add more phones and separate lines for different family members.

Furthermore, the demand curve for telephone service slopes downward because there are at least several *imperfect* substitutes, such as letters, e-mail, in-person conversations, and Internet telephony. Thus, even though we defined a monopolist as a single seller of a commodity with no *close* substitutes, we can talk about the range of *imperfect* substitutes. The more such imperfect substitutes there are, and the better these substitutes are, the more elastic will be the monopolist's demand curve, all other things held constant.

Why do you think that your college library may pay a different price for an online subscription to a scholarly journal than the library of another college?

E-Commerce EXAMPLE

Online Journal Subscriptions and Demand Elasticity

JSTOR (Journal Storage) is a nonprofit organization that sells subscriptions for Internet access to back issues of scholarly journals in fields such as chemistry, literature, and business and economics. To determine the fees that it charges institutions for online subscriptions, JSTOR analyzes the electronic data it accumulates on how often faculty and students access articles in different journals. Intensive downloading of large numbers of articles in physics journals at any given price, for instance, indicates that the price elasticity of demand for JSTOR subscriptions to physics journals is likely to be relatively low. JSTOR takes such data into account when it sets the price it charges a college library for its physics journal subscriptions. In this way, it can charge a higher price to colleges where faculty and students have more inelastic demand.

For Critical Analysis
What might data that show a large proportionate rise in downloads of sociology articles in response to a relatively small price reduction indicate about the price elasticity of demand for subscriptions to sociology journals, other things being equal?

CONCEPTS in Brief

- The monopolist estimates its marginal revenue curve, where marginal revenue is defined as the change in total revenues due to a one-unit change in quantity sold.

- For the perfect competitor, price equals marginal revenue equals average revenue. For the monopolist, marginal revenue is always less than price because price must be reduced on all units to sell more.

- The price elasticity of demand for the monopolist depends on the number and similarity of substitutes. The more numerous and more similar the substitutes, the greater the price elasticity of demand of the monopolist's demand curve.

To test your understanding of the concepts covered in this section, go to the Online Review at www.myeconlab.com/miller.

COSTS AND MONOPOLY PROFIT MAXIMIZATION

To find out the rate of output at which the perfect competitor would maximize profits, we had to add cost data. We will do the same thing now for the monopolist. We assume that profit maximization is the goal of the pure monopolist, just as it is for the perfect competitor. The perfect competitor, however, has only to decide on the profit-maximizing rate of output because price is given. The competitor is a price taker. For the pure monopolist, we must seek a profit-maximizing *price-output combination* because the monopolist is a **price searcher.** We can determine this profit-maximizing price-output combination with either of two equivalent approaches—by looking at total revenues and total costs or by looking at marginal revenues and marginal costs. We shall examine both approaches.

Price searcher
A firm that must determine the price-output combination that maximizes profit because it faces a downward-sloping demand curve.

The Total Revenues–Total Costs Approach

We show hypothetical demand (rate of output and price per unit), revenues, costs, and other data in panel (a) of Figure 25-5 on page 604. In column 3, we see total revenues for our hypothetical monopolist, and in column 4, we see total costs. We can transfer these two columns to panel (b). The only difference between the total revenue and total cost diagram in panel (b) and the one we showed for a perfect competitor in Chapter 24 is that the total revenue line is no longer straight. Rather, it curves. For any given demand curve, in order to sell more, the monopolist must lower the price. Thus the basic difference between a monopolist and a perfect competitor has to do with the demand curve for the two types of firms. Monopoly market power is derived from facing a downward-sloping demand curve.

Profit maximization involves maximizing the positive difference between total revenues and total costs. This occurs at an output rate of between 9 and 10 units.

The Marginal Revenue–Marginal Cost Approach

Profit maximization will also occur where marginal revenue equals marginal cost. This is as true for a monopolist as it is for a perfect competitor (but the monopolist will charge a higher price). When we transfer marginal cost and marginal revenue information from columns 6 and 7 in panel (a) of Figure 25-5 to panel (c), we see that marginal revenue

FIGURE 25-5

Monopoly Costs, Revenues, and Profits

In panel (a), we give hypothetical demand (rate of output and price per unit), revenues, costs, and other relevant data. As shown in panel (b), the monopolist maximizes profits where the positive difference between TR and TC is greatest. This is at an output rate of between 9 and 10. Put another way, profit maximization occurs where marginal revenue equals marginal cost, as shown in panel (c). This is at the same output rate of between 9 and 10. (The MC curve must cut the MR curve from below.)

Panel (a)

(1) Output (units)	(2) Price per Unit	(3) Total Revenues (TR) (3) = (2) x (1)	(4) Total Costs (TC)	(5) Total Profit (5) = (3) − (4)	(6) Marginal Cost (MC)	(7) Marginal Revenue (MR)
0	$8.00	$ .00	$10.00	−$10.00		
					$4.00	$7.80
1	7.80	7.80	14.00	−6.20		
					3.50	7.40
2	7.60	15.20	17.50	−2.30		
					3.25	7.00
3	7.40	22.20	20.75	1.45		
					3.05	6.60
4	7.20	28.80	23.80	5.00		
					2.90	6.20
5	7.00	35.00	26.70	8.30		
					2.80	5.80
6	6.80	40.80	29.50	11.30		
					2.75	5.40
7	6.60	46.20	32.25	13.95		
					2.85	5.00
8	6.40	51.20	35.10	16.10		
					3.20	4.60
9	6.20	55.80	38.30	17.50		
					4.40	4.20
10	6.00	60.00	42.70	17.30		
					6.00	3.80
11	5.80	63.80	48.70	15.10		
					9.00	3.40
12	5.60	67.20	57.70	9.50		

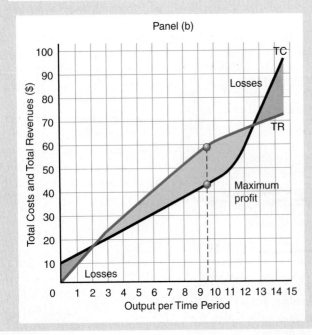

Panel (b)

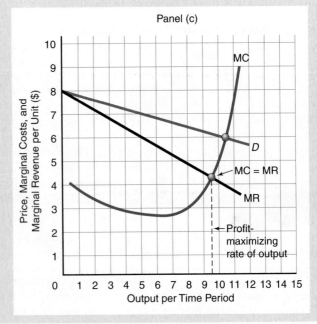

Panel (c)

equals marginal cost at an output rate of between 9 and 10 units. Profit maximization occurs at the same output as in panel (b).

Why Produce Where Marginal Revenue Equals Marginal Cost? If the monopolist goes past the point where marginal revenue equals marginal cost, marginal cost will exceed marginal revenue. That is, the incremental cost of producing any more units will exceed the incremental revenue. It just would not be worthwhile, as was true also in perfect competition. But if the monopolist produces less than that, it is also not making maximum profits. Look at output rate Q_1 in Figure 25-6 on the following page. Here the monopolist's marginal revenue is at *A,* but marginal cost is at *B.* Marginal revenue exceeds marginal cost on the last unit sold; the profit for that *particular* unit, Q_1, is equal to the vertical difference between *A* and *B,* or the difference between marginal revenue and marginal cost. The monopolist would be foolish to stop at output rate Q_1 because if output is expanded, marginal revenue will still exceed marginal cost, and therefore total profits will rise. In fact, the profit-maximizing monopolist will continue to expand output and sales until marginal revenue equals marginal cost, which is at output rate Q_m. The monopolist won't produce at rate Q_2 because here, as we see, marginal costs are *C* and marginal revenues are *F.* The difference between *C* and *F* represents the *reduction* in total profits from producing that additional unit. Total profits will rise as the monopolist reduces its rate of output back toward Q_m.

Why do manufacturers of computer printers, fax machines, and copiers try so hard to prevent other companies from selling replacement ink and toner cartridges to owners of their machines?

E X A M P L E

Stifling Competition for Replacement Ink and Toner Cartridges

There are numerous manufacturers of similar computer printers, fax machines, and copiers, so the markets for these business machines are far from monopolistic. Nevertheless, manufacturers are careful to design each model so that it will accept only ink and toner cartridges with a very specific size and shape. In this way, once the consumer has purchased a machine, the manufacturer can operate as a monopolistic seller of replacement ink and toner cartridges. For many business machine manufacturers, sales of these cartridges, which generate about $40 billion in worldwide revenues each year, account for more than 50 percent of total revenues.

In recent years, however, thousands of firms have entered the market for ink and toner cartridges. These firms collect used, empty cartridges, which they repair, refill with ink and toner, and resell at lower prices than those charged by the original manufacturers. Estimates indicate that since 1998, their share of sales in the market for ink and toner cartridges has increased from 5 percent to 20 percent.

In an effort to stifle this competition, many manufacturers of business machines now produce ink and toner cartridges containing microchips. When a cartridge is replaced, the microchips cease to function, and the cartridge can no longer communicate with the host machine. Enterprising competitors responded by figuring out how to repair or replace the microchips. Now several court battles are under way to determine whether these outside competitors have violated copyright protections of digital codes imprinted on microchips. As these legal cases proceed, business machine manufacturers are busily working to develop new microchips that will be more difficult to repair or reproduce.

For Critical Analysis
Why do you suppose that manufacturers of printers, fax machines, and copiers are currently fighting to overturn a European Union environmental protection rule requiring all ink and toner cartridges to be recyclable by the end of 2006?

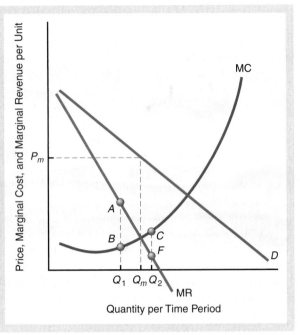

FIGURE 25-6
Maximizing Profits
The profit-maximizing production rate is Q_m, and the profit-maximizing price is P_m. The monopolist would be unwise to produce at the rate Q_1 because here marginal revenue would be Q_1A, and marginal costs would be Q_1B. Marginal revenue would exceed marginal cost. The firm will keep producing until the point Q_m, where marginal revenue just equals marginal cost. It would be foolish to produce at the rate Q_2, for here marginal cost exceeds marginal revenue. It behooves the monopolist to cut production back to Q_m.

What Price to Charge for Output?

How does the monopolist set prices? We know the quantity is set at the point at which marginal revenue equals marginal cost. The monopolist then finds out how much can be charged—how much the market will bear—for that particular quantity, Q_m, in Figure 25-6. We know that the demand curve is defined as showing the *maximum* price for which a given quantity can be sold. That means that our monopolist knows that to sell Q_m, it can charge only P_m because that is the price at which that specific quantity, Q_m, is demanded. This price is found by drawing a vertical line from the quantity, Q_m, to the market demand curve. Where that line hits the market demand curve, the price is determined. We find that price by drawing a horizontal line from the demand curve over to the price axis; that gives us the profit-maximizing price, P_m.

In our detailed numerical example, at a profit-maximizing rate of output of between 9 and 10 in Figure 25-5 on page 604, the firm can charge a maximum price of about $6 and still sell all the goods produced, all at the same price.

The basic procedure for finding the profit-maximizing short-run price-quantity combination for the monopolist is first to determine the profit-maximizing rate of output, by either the total revenue–total cost method or the marginal revenue–marginal cost method, and then to determine by use of the demand curve, *D,* the maximum price that can be charged to sell that output.

Don't get the impression that just because we are able to draw an exact demand curve in Figures 25-5 and 25-6, real-world monopolists have such perfect information. The process of price searching by a less than perfect competitor is just that—a process. A monopolist can only estimate the actual demand curve and therefore can only make an educated guess when it sets its profit-maximizing price. This is not a problem for the perfect competitor because price is given already by the intersection of market demand and market supply. The monopolist, in contrast, reaches the profit-maximizing output-price combination by trial and error.

CALCULATING MONOPOLY PROFIT

We have talked about the monopolist's profit, but we have yet to indicate how much profit the monopolist makes. We have actually shown total profits in column 5 of panel (a) in Figure 25-5 on page 604. We can also find total profits by adding an average total cost curve to panel (c) of that figure. We do that in Figure 25-7. When we add the average total cost curve, we find that the profit that a monopolist makes is equal to the shaded area—or total revenues ($P \times Q$) minus total costs (ATC $\times$ Q). Given the demand curve and a uniform pricing system (that is, all units sold at the same price), there is no way for a monopolist to make greater profits than those shown by the shaded area. The monopolist is maximizing profits where marginal cost equals marginal revenue. If the monopolist produces less than that, it will be forfeiting some profits. If the monopolist produces more than that, it will also be forfeiting some profits.

The same is true of a perfect competitor. The competitor produces where marginal revenues equal marginal costs because it produces at the point where the marginal cost curve intersects the perfectly elastic firm demand curve. The perfectly elastic firm demand curve represents the marginal revenue curve for the pure competitor, because the same average revenues are obtained on all the units sold. Perfect competitors maximize profits at MR = MC, as do pure monopolists. But the perfect competitor makes no true economic profits in the long run; rather, all it makes is a normal, competitive rate of return.

In Chapter 24, we talked about companies experiencing short-run economic profits because they had, for example, invented something new. Competition, though, gradually eroded those higher-than-normal profits. The fact that a firm experiences higher-than-normal profits today does not mean that it will have a monopoly forever. Try as companies may, keeping competitors away is never easy.

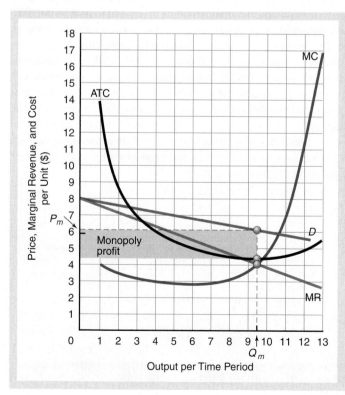

FIGURE 25-7
Monopoly Profit
We find monopoly profit by subtracting total costs from total revenues at an output rate of between 9 and 10, labeled Q_m, which is the profit-maximizing rate of output for the monopolist. The profit-maximizing price is therefore about $6 and is labeled P_m. Monopoly profit is given by the shaded area, which is equal to total revenues ($P \times Q$) minus total costs (ATC $\times$ Q). This diagram is similar to panel (c) of Figure 25-5, with the short-run average total cost curve (ATC) added.

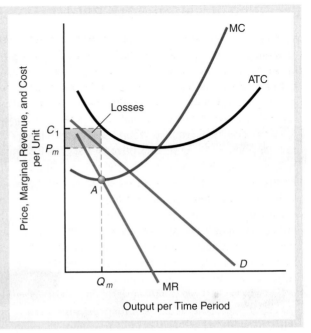

FIGURE 25-8
Monopolies: Not Always Profitable
Some monopolists face the situation shown here. The average total cost curve, ATC, is everywhere above the average revenue, or demand, curve, D. In the short run, the monopolist will produce where MC = MR at point A. Output Q_m will be sold at price P_m, but average total cost per unit is C_1, Losses are the shaded rectangle. Eventually, the monopolist will go out of business.

No Guarantee of Profits

The term *monopoly* conjures up the notion of a greedy firm ripping off the public and making exorbitant profits. However, the mere existence of a monopoly does not guarantee high profits. Numerous monopolies have gone bankrupt. Figure 25-8 shows the monopolist's demand curve as *D* and the resultant marginal revenue curve as MR. It does not matter at what rate of output this particular monopolist operates; total costs cannot be covered. Look at the position of the average total cost curve. It lies everywhere above *D* (the average revenue curve). Thus there is no price-output combination that will allow the monopolist even to cover costs, much less earn profits. This monopolist will, in the short run, suffer economic losses as shown by the shaded area. The graph in Figure 25-8 depicts a situation for millions of typical monopolies that exist; it applies to many inventions. The owner of a patented invention or discovery has a pure legal monopoly, but the demand and cost curves are such that production is not profitable. Every year at inventors' conventions, one can see many inventions that have never been put into production because they were deemed "uneconomic" by potential producers and users.

ON MAKING HIGHER PROFITS: PRICE DISCRIMINATION

In a perfectly competitive market, each buyer is charged the same price for every unit of the particular commodity (corrected for differential transportation charges). Because the product is homogeneous and we also assume full knowledge on the part of the buyers, a difference in price cannot exist. Any seller of the product who tried to charge a price higher than the going market price would find that no one would purchase it from that seller.

In this chapter, we have assumed until now that the monopolist charged all consumers the same price for all units. A monopolist, however, may be able to charge different people different prices or different unit prices for successive units sought by a given buyer. When there is no cost difference, either one or a combination of these strategies is called **price discrimination.** A firm will engage in price discrimination whenever feasible to increase profits. A price-discriminating firm is able to charge some customers more than other customers.

It must be made clear at the outset that charging different prices to different people or for different units to reflect differences in the cost of service does not amount to price discrimination. This is **price differentiation:** differences in price that reflect differences in marginal cost.

We can also say that a uniform price does not necessarily indicate an absence of price discrimination. Charging all customers the same price when production costs vary by customer is actually a case of price discrimination.

Price discrimination
Selling a given product at more than one price, with the price difference being unrelated to differences in marginal cost.

Price differentiation
Establishing different prices for similar products to reflect differences in marginal cost in providing those commodities to different groups of buyers.

Necessary Conditions for Price Discrimination

Three conditions are necessary for price discrimination to exist:

1. The firm must face a downward-sloping demand curve.
2. The firm must be able to readily (and cheaply) identify buyers or groups of buyers with predictably different elasticities of demand.
3. The firm must be able to prevent resale of the product or service.

Has it ever occurred to you that most of the other students seated in your college classroom pay different overall tuition rates than you do because your college and others use financial aid packages to engage in price discrimination?

EXAMPLE

Why Students Pay Different Prices to Attend College

Out-of-pocket tuition rates for any two college students can differ by considerable amounts, even if the students happen to major in the same subjects and enroll in many of the same courses. The reason is that colleges offer students diverse financial aid packages depending on their "financial need."

To document their "need" for financial aid, students must provide detailed information about family income and wealth. This information, of course, helps the college determine the prices that different families are most likely to be willing and able to pay, so that it can engage in price discrimination. Figure 25-9 (p. 610) shows how this collegiate price-discrimination process works. Colleges charge the price P_7, which is the college's official posted "tuition rate," to students with families judged to be most willing and able to pay the highest price. Students whose families have the lowest levels of income and wealth are judged to be willing and able to pay a much lower price, such as P_1. To charge these students this lower tuition rate, the college provides them with a financial aid package that reduces the price they pay by the difference

FIGURE 25-9

Toward Perfect Price Discrimination in College Tuition Rates

Students that a college determines to be "neediest" and least able to pay the full tuition price, P_7, receive a financial aid package equal to $P_7 - P_1$. These students effectively pay only the price P_1. The college groups the remaining students into categories on the basis of their willingness and ability to pay a higher price, and each group receives a progressively smaller financial aid package. Those students who are willing and able to pay the full price, P_7, receive no financial aid from the college.

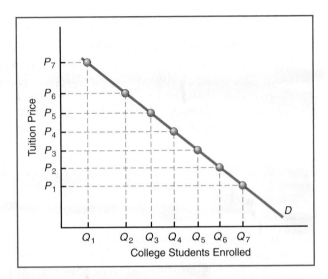

between P_7, the full tuition price, and P_1. In this way, the actual price paid by these "neediest" students is only P_1.

Likewise, the college groups other, somewhat less "needy" students into a slightly higher income-and-wealth category and determines that they are likely to be willing to pay a somewhat higher price, P_2. Hence it grants them a smaller financial aid package, equal to $P_7 - P_2$, so that the students

actually pay the price P_2. The college continues this process for other groups, thereby engaging in price discrimination in its tuition charges.

For Critical Analysis
Does the educational product supplied by colleges satisfy all three conditions necessary for price discrimination?

THE SOCIAL COST OF MONOPOLIES

Let's run a little experiment. We will start with a purely competitive industry with numerous firms, each one unable to affect the price of its product. The supply curve of the industry is equal to the horizontal sum of the marginal cost curves of the individual producers above their respective minimum average variable costs. In panel (a) of Figure 25-10, we show the market demand curve and the market supply curve in a perfectly competitive situation. The competitive price in equilibrium is equal to P_e, and the equilibrium quantity at that price is equal to Q_e. Each competitor faces a demand curve (not shown) that is coincident with the price line P_e. No individual supplier faces the market demand curve, D.

Comparing Monopoly with Perfect Competition

Now let's assume that a monopolist comes in and buys up every single competitor in the industry. In so doing, we'll assume that monopolization does not affect any of the marginal cost curves or demand. We can therefore redraw D and S in panel (b) of Figure 25-10, exactly the same as in panel (a).

How does this monopolist decide how much to charge and how much to produce? If the monopolist is profit maximizing, it is going to look at the marginal revenue curve and produce at the output where marginal revenue equals marginal cost. But what is the marginal cost curve in panel (b) of Figure 25-10? It is merely S, because we said that S was equal to the horizontal summation of the portions of the individual marginal cost curves above each firm's respective minimum average variable cost. The monopolist therefore produces quantity Q_m, and sells it at price P_m. Notice that Q_m is less than Q_e and that P_m is greater

FIGURE 25-10
The Effects of Monopolizing an Industry

In panel (a), we show a competitive situation in which equilibrium is established at the intersection of *D* and *S* at point *E*. The equilibrium price is P_e and the equilibrium quantity is Q_e. Each individual competitive producer faces a demand curve that is perfectly elastic at the market clearing price, P_e. What happens if the industry is suddenly monopolized? We assume

that the costs stay the same; the only thing that changes is that the monopolist now faces the entire downward-sloping demand curve. In panel (b), we draw the marginal revenue curve. Marginal cost is *S* because that is the horizontal summation of all the individual marginal cost curves. The monopolist therefore produces at Q_m and charges price P_m. This price P_m in panel (b) is higher than P_e in panel (a), and Q_m is less than Q_e.

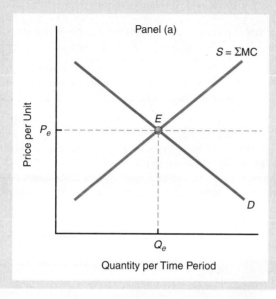

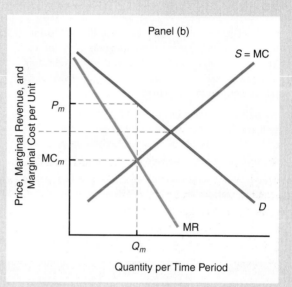

than P_e. A monopolist therefore produces a smaller quantity and sells it at a higher price. This is the reason usually given when economists criticize monopolists. Monopolists raise the price and restrict production, compared to a competitive situation. For a monopolist's product, consumers are forced to pay a price that exceeds the marginal cost of production. Resources are misallocated in such a situation—too few resources are being used in the monopolist's industry, and too many are used elsewhere.

Implications of Higher Monopoly Prices

Notice from Figure 25-10 that by setting MR = MC, the monopolist produces at a rate of output where $P >$ MC (compare P_m to MC_m). The marginal cost of a commodity (MC) represents what society had to give up in order to obtain the last unit produced. Price, by contrast, represents what buyers are willing to pay to acquire that last unit. Thus the price of a good represents society's valuation of the last unit produced. The monopoly outcome of $P >$ MC means that the value to society of the last unit produced is greater than its cost (MC); hence not enough of the good is being produced. As we have pointed out before, these differences between monopoly and competition arise not because of differences in costs but rather because of differences in the demand curves the individual firms face. The monopolist has monopoly power because it faces a downward-sloping demand curve. The individual perfect competitor faces a perfectly elastic demand curve.

Before we leave the topic of the cost to society of monopolies, we must repeat that our analysis is based on a heroic assumption. That assumption is that the monopolization of the perfectly competitive industry does not change the cost structure. If monopolization results in higher marginal cost, the net cost of monopoly to society is even greater.

Conversely, if monopolization results in cost savings, the net cost of monopoly to society is less than we infer from our analysis. Indeed, we could have presented a hypothetical example in which monopolization led to such a dramatic reduction in average cost that society actually benefited. Such a situation is a possibility in industries in which economies of scale exist for a very great range of outputs.

CONCEPTS in Brief

- Three conditions are necessary for price discrimination: (1) The firm must face a downward-sloping demand curve, (2) the firm must be able to identify buyers with predictably different price elasticities of demand, and (3) resale of the product or service must be preventable.

- A monopolist can make higher profits if it can price-discriminate. Price discrimination requires that two or more identifiable classes of buyers exist whose price elasticities of demand for the product or service are different,

that these two classes of buyers can be distinguished at little cost, and that resales between them can be prevented.

- Price discrimination should not be confused with price differentiation, which occurs when differences in price reflect differences in marginal cost.

- Monopoly tends to result in a lower quantity being sold, because the price is higher than it would be in an ideal perfectly competitive industry in which the cost curves were essentially the same as the monopolist's.

To test your understanding of the concepts covered in this section, go to the Online Review at **www.myeconlab.com/miller.**

CASE STUDY: Economics Front and Center

The Collegiate Cartel Restricts Output of Postseason Games

Zambrano has become the youngest-ever athletic director at his alma mater, where he was once an All-American football linebacker and defensive team captain for two years running. Now he faces a tougher problem than he did back in the days when he was trying to guess the next play an offensive team would run against his defense. The university, which is a member of the organization of large universities that operate the Bowl Championship Series (BCS), has assigned Zambrano as its representative in negotiations with other colleges outside this organization. These colleges are upset about the rules that the BCS has established to determine which schools' football teams qualify to participate in end-of-season bowl games. These games generate considerable amounts of revenue, most of which goes to BCS members. Some colleges that are not BCS members have threatened to establish new bowl games that would compete with existing bowl games for television time and payments from advertisers.

Under Zambrano's leadership, the BCS negotiators have developed an arrangement aimed at satisfying non-BCS universities and colleges. BCS schools already share some of the revenues earned from bowl games with non-BCS schools. Provided that the non-BCS schools promise not to establish competing bowl games, the BCS universities will increase these payments by more than 50 percent. After the BCS negotiators' proposal is accepted, Zambrano decides that this accomplishment tops the game-winning end-zone fumble recovery he made to win a bowl game back when he was a star college football player.

Points to Analyze

1. *What do BCS universities gain if they are able to limit the number of postseason college bowl games?*

2. *Under the arrangement Zambrano has helped establish, are BCS schools the only members of the college football postseason bowl cartel?*

I n 1998, a federal court ruled in a case involving a bank that an invention is entitled to a patent as long as it produces a "useful, concrete, and tangible" result. Shortly thereafter, another federal court used this ruling to uphold the patent eligibility of a process for enhancing records of long-distance phone calls simply by adding a data field to a computer file. The court remarked that its new interpretation of patent law reflected a "sea change" in the legal environment for patents. Indeed, this new interpretation of patent law opened the floodgate for *business method patents*, or patents that typically combine computer software with business methodologies.

Concepts Applied
- Patents
- Barriers to Entry

The Race to Obtain Business Method Patents Creates Barriers to Entry

Since the advent of business method patents, the annual volume of patent applications received by the U.S. Patent and Trademark Office (USPTO) has more than doubled. To keep up with the deluge of new patent applications, the USPTO has increased its staff of patent examiners by more than one-third since 1998. Still, waits of a year or longer for judgments on the merits of business method patent applications remain commonplace.

Furthermore, pressure on patent examiners to keep up may have led them to approve business methods of doubtful "novelty." For instance, the USPTO recently granted a patent for a system for managing bank payments on the Web, even though banks had employed the technique since the 1960s. Indeed, banks were already applying this well-known business method on their own Web sites before the patent application was submitted to the USPTO.

Following this error, the USPTO promised to do better. By the mid-2000s it had reduced its rate of approval of applications for business method patents to 45 percent, down from nearly 60 percent in the late 1990s.

A Patent Covering All Web-Based International Trade?

Recently, however, the USPTO sent notice of pending approval of an application that a company had filed in the early 1990s for a patent covering "a process for carrying out an international transaction . . . using computer-to-computer communication." The company promptly mailed letters to every firm it could think of that might be using, or contemplating the use of, any type of online process aimed at helping firms coordinate international exchanges of goods and services. The letters threatened legal action against anyone providing such services without paying royalties.

Dozens of legal challenges to the validity of the USPTO's patent judgment in this case promise to tie up a number of courts for years. In the meantime, the company holding the patent will have prevented some potential competitors from entering the market for services to firms engaging in international trade.

For Critical Analysis

1. Why do you suppose that companies are sometimes willing to pay patent attorneys millions of dollars to fight the validity of another firm's patent claims?
2. Why might it be in society's long-term interest for the government to issue patents for truly novel inventions, even if this gives patent owners monopolies for a time?

Web Resources

1. To learn about how to apply for a USPTO patent, go to www.econtoday.com/chap25.
2. For more on business method patents, access the USPTO's site at www.econtoday.com/chap25.

Research Project

Commentators have criticized the USPTO's decision to issue a patent to a DVD rental company for a method of using computers to log customer requests for rental DVDs, and to track DVDs. They argued that the DVD rental company sought to patent this business method to discourage new firms from entering the industry. How might an existing firm use its ownership of such a patent to discourage the entry of other firms?

SUMMARY DISCUSSION of Learning Objectives

1. **Why Monopoly Can Occur:** Monopoly, a situation in which a single firm produces and sells a good or service that has no close substitute, can occur when there are significant barriers to market entry by other firms. Examples of barriers to entry include (1) ownership of important resources for which there are no close substitutes, (2) problems in raising adequate capital to begin production, (3) economies of scale for even large ranges of output, or natural monopoly conditions, (4) legal or governmental restrictions, and (5) associations of producers called cartels that work together to stifle competition.

2. **Demand and Marginal Revenue Conditions a Monopolist Faces:** Because a monopolist constitutes the entire industry, it faces the entire market demand curve. When it reduces the price of its product, it is able to sell more units at the new price, which pushes up its revenues, but it also sells other units at this lower price, which pushes its revenues down somewhat. For this reason, the monopolist's marginal revenue at any given quantity is less than the price at which it sells that quantity of output. Hence the monopolist's marginal revenue curve slopes downward and lies below the demand curve it faces.

3. **How a Monopolist Determines How Much Output to Produce and What Price to Charge:** A monopolist is a price searcher, meaning that it seeks to charge the price consistent with the production level that maximizes its economic profits. It maximizes its profits by producing to the point at which marginal revenue equals marginal cost. The monopolist then charges the maximum price for this amount of output, which is the price that consumers are willing to pay for that quantity of output.

4. **A Monopolist's Profits:** The amount of profit earned by a monopolist is equal to the difference between the price it charges and its average production cost times the amount of output it produces and sells. At the profit-maximizing output rate, the monopolist's price is at the point on the demand curve corresponding to this output rate, and its average total cost of producing this output rate is at the corresponding point on the monopolist's average total cost curve. A monopolist commonly earns positive economic profits, but situations can arise in which average total cost exceeds the profit-maximizing price. In this case, the maximum profit is negative.

5. **Price Discrimination:** If a monopolist engages in price discrimination, it sells its product at more than one price, with the price difference being unrelated to differences in production costs. To be able to engage successfully in price discrimination, a monopolist must be able to identify and separate buyers with different price elasticities of demand. This allows the monopolist to sell some of its output at higher prices to consumers with less elastic demand. Even then, however, the monopolist must be able to prevent resale of its product by those with more elastic demand to those with less elastic demand.

6. **Social Cost of Monopolies:** Because a monopoly is a price searcher, it is able to charge the highest price that people are willing to pay for the amount of output it produces. This price exceeds the marginal cost of producing the output. In addition, if the monopolist's marginal cost curve corresponds to the sum of the marginal cost curves for the number of firms that would exist if the industry were perfectly competitive instead, then the monopolist produces and sells less output than perfectly competitive firms would have produced and sold.

KEY TERMS AND CONCEPTS

cartel (598)

monopolist (595)

natural monopoly (596)

price differentiation (609)

price discrimination (609)

price searcher (603)

tariffs (598)

PROBLEMS

Answers to the odd-numbered problems appear at the back of the book.

25-1. An international coffee cartel has established a price above the perfectly competitive price. Discuss the prospects for maintaining a successful cartel if new coffee producers are choosing not to join.

25-2. Discuss the price elasticity of demand for a perfectly competitive firm and a monopolist. Explain why the price elasticities are different.

25-3. The following table depicts the daily output, price, and costs of a monopoly dry cleaner located near the campus of a remote college town.

    a. Compute revenues and profits at each output level.
    b. What is the profit-maximizing level of output?

Output (suits cleaned)	Price per Suit ($)	Total Costs ($)
0	8.00	3.00
1	7.50	6.00
2	7.00	8.50
3	6.50	10.50
4	6.00	11.50
5	5.50	13.50
6	5.00	16.00
7	4.50	19.00
8	4.00	24.00

25-4. Given the information in Problem 25-3, calculate the dry cleaner's marginal revenue and marginal cost at each output level. Based on marginal analysis, what is the profit-maximizing level of output?

25-5. A manager of a monopoly firm notices that the firm is producing output at a rate at which average total cost is falling but is not at its minimum feasible point. The manager argues that surely the firm must not be maximizing its economic profits. Is this argument correct?

25-6. Use the graph to answer the following questions.

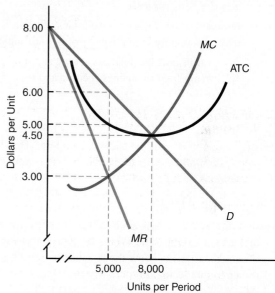

    a. What is the monopolist's profit-maximizing output?
    b. At the profit-maximizing output rate, what are the monopolist's average total cost and average revenue?
    c. At the profit-maximizing output rate, what are the monopolist's total cost and total revenue?
    d. What is the maximum profit?

25-7. Using the diagram for Problem 25-6, suppose that the marginal cost and average total cost curves also illustrate the horizontal summation of the firms in a competitive industry in the long run. What would the market price and equilibrium output be if the market were competitive? Explain the economic cost to society of allowing a monopoly to exist in this industry.

25-8. The marginal revenue curve of a monopoly crosses its marginal cost curve at $30 per unit, and an output of 2 million units. The price that consumers are willing and able to pay for this output is $40 per unit. If it produces this output, the firm's average total cost is $43 per unit, and its average fixed cost is $8 per unit.

What is this producer's profit-maximizing (loss-minimizing) output level? What are the firm's economic profits (or economic losses)?

25-9. A monopolist's marginal revenue curve crosses its marginal cost curve at $20 per unit and 1 million units. The price that consumers are willing to pay is $30 per unit. If it produces this output, the firm's average total cost is $35 per unit, and its average fixed cost is $4 per unit. What is this producer's profit-maximizing (loss-minimizing) output? What are its economic profits (or losses)?

25-10. For each of the following examples, explain how and why a monopoly would try to price-discriminate.

   a. Air transport for business people and tourists
   b. Serving food to business people and retired people

   c. A theater that shows the same movie to large families and to individuals and couples

25-11. A monopolist's revenues vary directly with price. Is it maximizing its economic profits? Why or why not?

25-12. A new competitor enters the industry and competes with a second firm, which had been a monopolist. The second firm finds that although demand is not perfectly elastic, it is now relatively more elastic. What will happen to the second firm's marginal revenue curve and to its profit-maximizing price?

25-13. A monopolist's marginal cost curve has shifted upward. What is likely to happen to the monopolist's price, output rate, and economic profits?

25-14. Demand has fallen. What is likely to happen to the monopolist's price, output rate, and economic profits?

ECONOMICS ON THE NET

Patents, Trademarks, and Intellectual Property This Internet application allows you to explore a firm's view on legal protections.

Title: Intellectual Property

Navigation: Follow the link at www.econtoday.com/chap25 to the GlaxoWellcome Web site. Select *Investors,* then *Financial Reports.* View the Annual Report 2003. Scroll down to Intellectual Property (page 24).

Application Read the statement and table; then answer the following questions:

1. What are the differences between patents, trademarks, and registered designs and copyrights?

2. What are GlaxoWellcome's intellectual property goals? Do patents or trademarks seem to be more important?

For Group Discussion and Analysis In 1969, GlaxoWellcome developed Ventolin, a treatment for asthma symptoms. Though the patent and trademark have long expired, the company still retains over a third of the market in this treatment. Explain, in economic terms, the source of GlaxoWellcome's strength in this area. Discuss whether patents and trademarks are beneficial for the development and discovery of new treatments.

Media Resources

If your exam were tomorrow, would you be ready? For each chapter, MyEconLab Practice Tests and Study Plans pinpoint which sections you have mastered and which ones you need to study. That way, you are more efficient with your study time, and you are better prepared for your exams.

In addition to Practice Tests and your personalized Study Plan, you'll find the following media resources in MyEconLab:

1. *Graphs in Motion* animation of Figures 25-3, 25-4, 25-6, 25-8, and 25-10.

2. Videos featuring the author, Roger LeRoy Miller, on the following subjects:
   ● Barriers to Entry
   ● The Demand Curve Facing a Monopoly is Not Vertical
   ● Price Discrimination

3. Links to the Web sites cited in the marginal Internet Resources, Issues and Applications feature, and Economics on the Net activity.

4. Audio clips of all key terms, additional practice problems, and a PDF version of the material from the print Study Guide.

5. eThemes of the Times, which is a New York Times article to help you understand the real-world applications of what you are learning.

myeconlab
Get Ahead of the Curve

To see how it works, turn to page 16 and then go to www.myeconlab.com/miller.

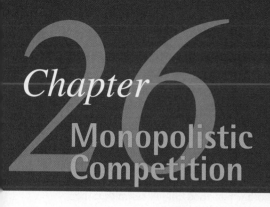

What do Hewlett-Packard, Wal-Mart, Microsoft, Sony, MTV, Yahoo, and Amazon all have in common? The answer is that recently these and other companies have rushed to enter the market for online music. The goal of each of these companies is to earn profits from downloadable digital music files. They offer many of the same musical recordings for sale, but each firm provides its own particular method to enable consumers to download, store, and play the recordings. Given that sellers of online music face competition from numerous other firms but provide online music in different formats, how do they determine the prices to charge consumers to download songs from their Web sites? In this chapter, you will learn the answer provided by the theory of monopolistic competition.

LEARNING OBJECTIVES

After reading this chapter, you should be able to:

1. Discuss the key characteristics of a monopolistically competitive industry

2. Contrast the output and pricing decisions of monopolistically competitive firms with those of perfectly competitive firms

3. Explain why brand names and advertising are important features of monopolistically competitive industries

4. Describe the fundamental properties of information products and evaluate how the prices of these products are determined under monopolistic competition

Media Resources

Refer to the end of the chapter for a full listing of the multimedia learning materials available in MyEconLab.

Did You Know That . . . there are now nearly 278,000 fast-food restaurants in the United States? Thus there is one fast-food restaurant for every 1,000 U.S. residents, compared with one for every 1,400 residents in 1990 and one for every 2,000 residents in 1980. Almost all of these restaurants offer at least one salad item. The salads are similar, but each differs from the others in some specific way. Burger King's menu, for instance, includes the Chicken Caesar Salad. Wendy's offers the Chicken Bacon-Lettuce-Tomato "Garden Sensations" Salad. At McDonald's, a consumer can purchase the Grilled Chicken Bacon Ranch "Premium" Salad. Not to be outdone, Jack in the Box offers the Chicken Club "Ultimate" Salad. In media advertisements from coast to coast, each of these and other fast-food chains claim that their particular salad is biggest, best tasting, and lowest in calories and carbohydrates.

Advertising did not show up in our analysis of perfect competition. Nevertheless, it plays a large role in industries that cannot be described as perfectly competitive but cannot be described as pure monopolies either. A combination of consumers' preferences for variety and competition among producers has led to similar but *differentiated* products in the marketplace. This situation has been described as *monopolistic competition,* the subject of this chapter.

MONOPOLISTIC COMPETITION

In the 1920s and 1930s, economists became increasingly aware that there were many industries for which both the perfectly competitive model and the pure monopoly model did not apply and did not seem to yield very accurate predictions. Theoretical and empirical research was instituted to develop some sort of middle ground. Two separately developed models of **monopolistic competition** resulted. At Harvard, Edward Chamberlin published *Theory of Monopolistic Competition* in 1933. The same year, Britain's Joan Robinson published *The Economics of Imperfect Competition.* In this chapter, we will outline the theory as presented by Chamberlin.

> **Monopolistic competition**
> A market situation in which a large number of firms produce similar but not identical products. Entry into the industry is relatively easy.

Chamberlin defined monopolistic competition as a market structure in which a relatively large number of producers offer similar but differentiated products. Monopolistic competition therefore has the following features:

1. Significant numbers of sellers in a highly competitive market
2. Differentiated products
3. Sales promotion and advertising
4. Easy entry of new firms in the long run   *the firms are small to get in*

Even a cursory look at the U.S. economy leads to the conclusion that monopolistic competition is an important form of market structure in the United States. Indeed, that is true of all developed economies.

Number of Firms

In a perfectly competitive situation, there is an extremely large number of firms; in pure monopoly, there is only one. In monopolistic competition, there is a large number of firms, but not as many as in perfect competition. This fact has several important implications for a monopolistically competitive industry.

1. *Small share of market.* With so many firms, each firm has a relatively small share of the total market.
2. *Lack of collusion.* With so many firms, it is very difficult for all of them to get together to collude—to cooperate in setting a pure monopoly price (and output).

Collusive pricing in a monopolistically competitive industry is virtually impossible. Also, barriers to entry are minor, and the flow of new firms into the industry makes collusive agreements less likely. The large number of firms makes the monitoring and detection of cheating very costly and extremely difficult. This difficulty is compounded by differentiated products and high rates of innovation; collusive agreements are easier for a homogeneous product than for heterogeneous ones.

3. *Independence.* Because there are so many firms, each one acts independently of the others. No firm attempts to take into account the reaction of all of its rival firms—that would be impossible with so many rivals. Rivals' reactions to output and price changes are largely ignored.

Follow the link at www.econtoday.com/chap26 to *Wall Street Journal* articles about real-world examples of monopolistic competition.

Product Differentiation

Perhaps the most important feature of the monopolistically competitive market is **product differentiation.** We can say that each individual manufacturer of a product has an absolute monopoly over its own product, which is slightly differentiated from other similar products. This means that the firm has some control over the price it charges. Unlike the perfectly competitive firm, it faces a downward-sloping demand curve.

Consider the abundance of brand names for toothpaste, soap, gasoline, vitamins, shampoo, and most other consumer goods and a great many services. We are not obliged to buy just one type of television set, just one type of jeans, or just one type of footwear. We can usually choose from a number of similar but differentiated products. The greater a firm's success at product differentiation, the greater the firm's pricing options.

Toothpastes all perform the same basic function, so why do toothpaste manufacturers go out of their way to convince consumers that their toothpaste is unique?

Product differentiation
The distinguishing of products by brand name, color, and other minor attributes. Product differentiation occurs in other than perfectly competitive markets in which products are, in theory, homogeneous, such as wheat or corn.

E X A M P L E

What Besides Healthier Teeth Do Toothpastes Have to Offer?

Recently, television commercials promoting toothpastes featured a well-known television chef expressing his satisfaction with the latest in toothpaste flavors, including citrus, herbal mint, and cinnamon. U.S. consumers fully understand the health benefits of brushing their teeth, so makers of the various brands sold in the toothpaste market seek to emphasize how good their toothpastes taste.

Manufacturers have also differentiated their toothpastes by promoting them as beauty products. Using names such as

"Whitening Expressions" and "Rejuvenating Effects," toothpaste companies battle in media ads to convince consumers that their great-tasting brands of toothpastes will also produce the brightest smiles.

For Critical Analysis
If a number of consumers become convinced that a particular toothpaste really will "rejuvenate" their teeth, what will happen to the price elasticity of demand for that specific toothpaste?

Each separate differentiated product has numerous similar substitutes. This clearly has an impact on the price elasticity of demand for the individual firm. Recall that one determinant of price elasticity of demand is the availability of substitutes: The greater the number and closeness of substitutes available, other things being equal, the greater the price elasticity of demand. If the consumer has a vast array of alternatives that are just about as good as the product under study, a relatively small increase in the price of that product will lead many consumers to switch to one of the many close substitutes. Thus the ability of a firm to raise the price above the price of *close* substitutes is very small. Even though the demand curve slopes downward, it does so only slightly. In other words, it is relatively elastic (over that small price range) compared to a monopolist's demand curve. In the extreme case, with perfect competition, the substitutes are perfect because we are dealing with only one particular undifferentiated product. In that case, the individual firm has a perfectly elastic demand curve.

Sales Promotion and Advertising

Monopolistic competition differs from perfect competition in that no individual firm in a perfectly competitive market will advertise. A perfectly competitive firm, by definition, can sell all that it wants to sell at the going market price anyway. Why, then, would it spend even one penny on advertising? Furthermore, by definition, the perfect competitor is selling a product that is identical to the product that all other firms in the industry are selling. Any advertisement that induces consumers to buy more of that product will, in effect, be helping all the competitors, too. A perfect competitor therefore cannot be expected to incur any advertising costs (except when all firms in an industry collectively agree to advertise to urge the public to buy more beef or drink more milk).

The monopolistic competitor has, however, at least *some* monopoly power. Because consumers regard the monopolistic competitor's product as distinguishable from the products of the other firms, the firm can search for the price consumers are willing to pay for its differentiated product. Advertising, therefore, may result in increased profits. Advertising is used to increase demand and to differentiate one's product. How much advertising should be undertaken? It should be carried to the point at which the additional revenue from one more dollar of advertising just equals that one dollar of additional cost.

Ease of Entry

For any current monopolistic competitor, potential competition is always lurking in the background. The easier—that is, the less costly—entry is, the more a current monopolistic competitor must worry about losing business.

A good example of a monopolistic competitive industry is the computer software industry. Many small firms provide different programs for many applications. The fixed capital costs required to enter this industry are small; all you need are skilled programmers. In addition, there are few legal restrictions. The firms in this industry also engage in extensive advertising in over 150 computer publications.

How might the movement toward using plastic bottles for soft drinks have helped put extra fizz into the competition among cola brands in Latin America?

International EXAMPLE

In Mexico, "Big" and "Cheap" Promote Soft-Drink Sales

Kola Real, a soft drink manufactured by a Peru-based firm called Industrias Ananos, was invented in the late 1980s by a couple who saw an opportunity to enter Peru's cola market when terrorists routinely hijacked Coca-Cola trucks. Industrias Ananos differentiates Kola Real from competing brands by distributing the soft drink in large bottles and advertising it as "big" and "cheap." During the 1990s, this strategy helped Kola Real emerge as one the top-selling cola brands in Peru, Ecuador, and Venezuela.

Recently, Industrias Ananos decided to enter Mexico, the world's second largest market for soft drinks after the U.S. market. By the late 1990s, a change in production methods had made it easier to enter Mexico's soft-drink market. Previously existing companies in that nation, such as Coca-Cola and Pepsi, had convinced grocery stores to stock drinks bottled in plastic containers instead of glass bottles. This simplified the path to market entry for Kola Real, because in other nations Industrias Ananos already sold Kola Real in large plastic bottles that it promoted as "big" and "cheap." Within a short time, the company's Mexican version of Kola Real, which Industrias Ananos called "Big Cola," had emerged as one of the top-selling Mexican soft drinks.

For Critical Analysis
How might the fact that extra-large plastic bottles cost only a fraction of a penny more to make than other cola firms' plastic bottles have eased the entry of Industrias Ananos into the Mexican soft-drink market?

CONCEPTS in Brief

- In a monopolistically competitive industry, a relatively large number of firms interact in a highly competitive market.

- Because monopolistically competitive firms sell differentiated products, sales promotion and advertising are common features of a monopolistically competitive industry.

- There is easy entry (or exit) of new firms in a monopolistically competitive industry.

To test your understanding of the concepts covered in this section, go to the Online Review at www.myeconlab.com/miller.

PRICE AND OUTPUT FOR THE MONOPOLISTIC COMPETITOR

Now that we are aware of the assumptions underlying the monopolistic competition model, we can analyze the price and output behavior of each firm in a monopolistically competitive industry. We assume in the analysis that follows that the desired product type and quality have been chosen. We further assume that the budget and the type of promotional activity have already been chosen and do not change.

The Individual Firm's Demand and Cost Curves

Because the individual firm is not a perfect competitor, its demand curve slopes downward, as in all three panels of Figure 26-1 (page 622). Hence it faces a marginal revenue curve that is also downward sloping and below the demand curve. To find the profit-maximizing rate of output and the profit-maximizing price, we go to the output where the marginal cost curve intersects the marginal revenue curve from below. That gives us the profit-maximizing output rate. Then we draw a vertical line up to the demand curve. That gives us the price that can be charged to sell exactly that quantity produced. This is what we have done in Figure 26-1. In each panel, a marginal cost curve intersects the marginal revenue curve at A. The profit-maximizing rate of output is q, and the profit-maximizing price is P.

Short-Run Equilibrium

In the short run, it is possible for a monopolistic competitor to make economic profits—profits over and above the normal rate of return or beyond what is necessary to keep that firm in that industry. We show such a situation in panel (a) of Figure 26-1 on page 622.

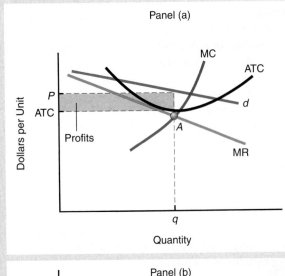

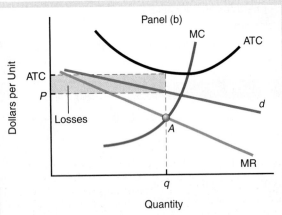

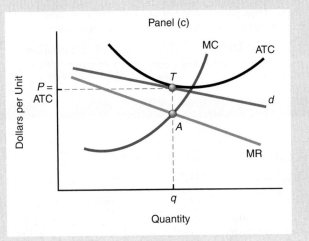

FIGURE 26-1

Short-Run and Long-Run Equilibrium with Monopolistic Competition

In panel (a), the typical monopolistic competitor is shown making economic profits. In this situation, there would be entry into the industry, forcing the demand curve for the individual monopolistic competitor leftward. Eventually, firms would find themselves in the situation depicted in panel (c), where zero economic profits are being made. In panel (b), the typical firm is in a monopolistically competitive industry making economic losses. In this situation, firms would leave the industry. Each remaining firm's demand curve would shift outward to the right. Eventually, the typical firm would find itself in the situation depicted in panel (c).

The average total cost curve is drawn in below the demand curve, *d*, at the profit-maximizing rate of output, *q*. Economic profits are shown by the shaded rectangle in that panel.

Losses in the short run are clearly also possible. They are presented in panel (b) of Figure 26-1. Here the average total cost curve lies everywhere above the individual firm's demand curve, *d*. The losses are marked as the shaded rectangle.

Just as with any market structure or any firm, in the short run it is possible to observe either economic profits or economic losses. (In the long run such is not the case with monopolistic competition, however.) In either case, the price does not equal marginal cost but rather is above it. Therefore, there may be some misallocation of resources, a topic that we will discuss later in this chapter.

The Long Run: Zero Economic Profits

The long run is where the similarity between perfect competition and monopolistic competition becomes more obvious. In the long run, because so many firms produce substitutes for the product in question, any economic profits will disappear with competition. They will be reduced to zero either through entry by new firms seeing a chance to make a higher rate of return than elsewhere or by changes in product quality and advertising outlays by existing firms in the industry. (Profitable products will be imitated by other firms.) As for economic losses in the short run, they will disappear in the long run because the firms that suffer them will leave the industry. They will go into another business where the expected rate of return is at least normal. Panels (a) and (b) of Figure 26-1 therefore represent only short-run situations for a monopolistically competitive firm. In the long run, the individual firm's demand curve *d* will just touch the average total cost curve at the particular price that is profit maximizing for that particular firm. This is shown in panel (c) of Figure 26-1.

A word of warning: This is an idealized, long-run equilibrium situation for each firm in the industry. It does not mean that even in the long run we will observe every single firm in a monopolistically competitive industry making *exactly* zero economic profits or *just* a normal rate of return. We live in a dynamic world. All we are saying is that if this model is correct, the rate of return will *tend toward* normal—economic profits will *tend toward* zero.

COMPARING PERFECT COMPETITION WITH MONOPOLISTIC COMPETITION

If both the monopolistic competitor and the perfect competitor make zero economic profits in the long run, how are they different? The answer lies in the fact that the demand curve for the individual perfect competitor is perfectly elastic. Such is not the case for the individual monopolistic competitor; its demand curve is less than perfectly elastic. This firm has some control over price. Price elasticity of demand is not infinite.

We see the two situations in Figure 26-2. Both panels show average total costs just touching the respective demand curves at the particular price at which the firm is selling

FIGURE 26-2
Comparison of the Perfect Competitor with the Monopolistic Competitor

In panel (a), the perfectly competitive firm has zero economic profits in the long run. The price is set equal to marginal cost, and the price is P_1. The firm's demand curve is just tangent to the minimum point on its average total cost curve. With the monopolistically competitive firm in panel (b), there are also zero economic profits in the long run. The price is greater than marginal cost. The monopolistically competitive firm does not find itself at the minimum point on its average total cost curve. It is operating at a rate of output to the left of the minimum point on the ATC curve.

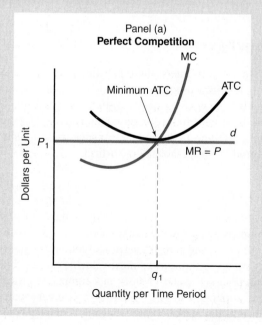

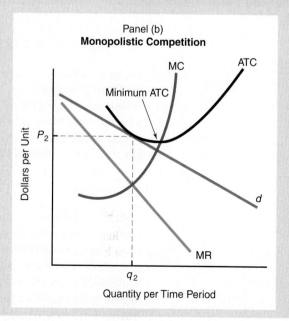

the product. Notice, however, that the perfect competitor's average total costs are at a minimum. This is not the case with the monopolistic competitor. The equilibrium rate of output is to the left of the minimum point on the average total cost curve where price is greater than marginal cost. The monopolistic competitor cannot expand output to the point of minimum costs without lowering price, and then marginal cost would exceed marginal revenue. A monopolistic competitor at profit maximization charges a price that exceeds marginal cost. In this respect it is similar to the monopolist.

It has consequently been argued that monopolistic competition involves *waste* because minimum average total costs are not achieved and price exceeds marginal cost. There are too many firms, each with excess capacity, producing too little output. According to critics of monopolistic competition, society's resources are being wasted.

Chamberlin had an answer to this criticism. He contended that the difference between the average cost of production for a monopolistically competitive firm in an open market and the minimum average total cost represented what he called the cost of producing "differentness." Chamberlin did not consider this difference in cost between perfect competition and monopolistic competition a waste. In fact, he argued that it is rational for consumers to have a taste for differentiation; consumers willingly accept the resultant increased production costs in return for more choice and variety of output.

CONCEPTS in Brief

- In the short run, it is possible for monopolistically competitive firms to make economic profits or economic losses.

- In the long run, monopolistically competitive firms will make zero economic profits—that is, they will make a normal rate of return.

- Because the monopolistic competitor faces a downward-sloping demand curve, it does not produce at the minimum point on its average total cost curve. Hence we say that a monopolistic competitor has higher average total costs per unit than a perfect competitor would have.

- Chamberlin argued that the difference between the average cost of production for a monopolistically competitive firm and the minimum average total cost at which a competitive firm would produce is the cost of producing "differentness."

To test your understanding of the concepts covered in this section, go to the Online Review at www.myeconlab.com/miller.

BRAND NAMES AND ADVERTISING

Because "differentness" has value to consumers, monopolistically competitive firms regard their brand names as valuable. Firms use trademarks—words, symbols, and logos—to distinguish their product brands from goods or services sold by other firms. Consumers associate these trademarks with the firms' products. Consequently, companies regard their brands as valuable private (intellectual) property, and they engage in advertising to maintain the differentiation of their products from those of other firms.

Brand Names and Trademarks

A firm's ongoing sales generate current profits and, as long as the firm is viable, the prospect of future profits. A company's value in the marketplace, or its purchase value, depends largely on its current profitability and perceptions of its future profitability.

Table 26-1 gives the market values of the world's most valuable product brands. Each valuation depends on the market prices of shares of stock in a company times the number of shares traded. Brand names, symbols, and logos relate to consumers' perceptions of product differentiation and hence to the market values of firms. Companies protect their

Brand	Market Value ($ billions)
Coca-Cola	67.4
Microsoft	61.4
International Business Machines (IBM)	53.8
General Electric (GE)	44.1
Intel	33.5
Disney	27.1
McDonald's	25.0
Marlboro	22.1
Nokia	24.0
Toyota	22.7

Source: Interbrand Annual Survey, 2004.

TABLE 26-1
Values of the Top Ten Brands
The market value of a company is equal to the number of shares of stock ownership issued by the company times the market price of each share. To a large extent, the company's value reflects the value of its brand.

trademarks from misuse by registering them with the U.S. Patent and Trademark Office. Once its trademark application is approved, a company has the right to seek legal damages if someone makes unauthorized use of its brand name, spreads false rumors about the company, or engages in other activities that can reduce the value of its brand.

Advertising

To help ensure that consumers differentiate their product brands from those of other firms, monopolistically competitive firms commonly engage in advertising. Advertising comes in various forms, and the nature of advertising can depend considerably on the types of products that firms wish to distinguish from competing brands.

Methods of Advertising. Figure 26-3 shows the current distribution of advertising expenses among the various advertising media. Today, as in the past, firms primarily rely on

Economics Front and Center

For practice thinking about advertising methods, consider the case study, **Will Viral Marketing Work Wonders?,** on page 631.

FIGURE 26-3
Distribution of U.S. Advertising Expenses
Direct marketing accounts for more than half of advertising expenses in the United States.

Sources: *Advertising Today; Direct Marketing Today;* and Internet Advertising Bureau.

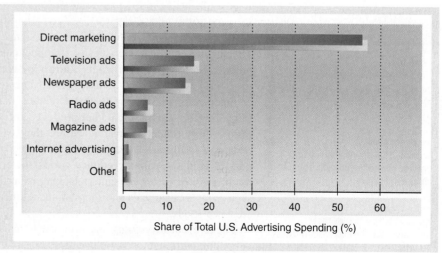

Direct marketing
Advertising targeted at specific consumers, typically in the form of postal mailings, telephone calls, or e-mail messages.

two approaches to advertising their products. One is **direct marketing,** in which firms engage in personalized advertising using postal mailings, phone calls, and e-mail messages (excluding so-called banner and pop-up ads on Web sites). The other is **mass marketing,** in which firms aim advertising messages at as many consumers as possible via media such as television, newspapers, radio, and magazines.

A third advertising method is called **interactive marketing.** This advertising approach allows a consumer to respond directly to an advertising message; often the consumer is able to search for more detailed information and place an order as part of the response. Sales booths and some types of Internet advertising, such as banner ads with links to sellers' Web pages, are forms of interactive marketing.

How might a recent court ruling regarding Web pop-up ads increase the scope of interactivity in Internet advertising?

Mass marketing
Advertising intended to reach as many consumers as possible, typically through television, newspaper, radio, or magazine ads.

Interactive marketing
Advertising that permits a consumer to follow up directly by searching for more information and placing direct product orders.

E-Commerce EXAMPLE

No More Brand Protections from Pop-Up Ads

Since the advent of Internet advertising, courts have ruled that trademark and copyright protections prevent operators of commercial Web sites from engaging in "framing," or including a rival's Web site within their own Web sites. Directing consumers to negative information about a rival by placing its name in "meta tags" that search engines use to locate Web sites has also run afoul of trademark and copyright laws.

Until recently, many firms assumed that it was also illegal to arrange for pop-up ads to show up on a consumer's computer screen just as the consumer is about to click the "order submit" button for a competing product. A federal district judge in Virginia, however, determined that online advertising companies,

such as Claria.com and WhenU.com, could insert pop-up ads into the content of others' Web sites. Thus some consumers on the verge of "checking out" at Amazon.com now receive a pop-up ad from a competing online bookstore offering a lower price. In this way, the legal ruling promises to expand the degree of interactivity in Internet advertising.

For Critical Analysis
Under what circumstances might consumers assign either positive or negative value to the appearance of pop-up ads just as they are about to click the "order submit" button at a seller's Web site?

Search good
A product with characteristics that enable an individual to evaluate the product's quality in advance of a purchase.

Experience good
A product that an individual must consume before the product's quality can be established.

Credence good
A product with qualities that consumers lack the expertise to assess without assistance.

Informational versus Persuasive Advertising. Some ads provide considerable information about products, while others seem designed mainly to attract a consumer's attention. The qualities and characteristics of a product determine how the firm should advertise that product. Some types of products, known as **search goods,** possess qualities that are relatively easy for consumers to assess in advance of their purchase. Clothing and music are common examples of items that have features that a consumer may assess, or perhaps even sample, before purchasing. Other products, known as **experience goods,** are products that people must actually consume before they can determine their qualities. Soft drinks, restaurant meals, and haircutting services are examples of experience goods. A third category of products, called **credence goods,** includes goods and services with qualities that might be difficult for consumers lacking expertise to assess without assistance. Products such as pharmaceuticals and services such as health care and legal advice are examples of credence goods.

The forms of advertising that firms use to market a search good are likely to be considerably different from those employed in the marketing of an experience good. If the item is a search good, a firm is more likely to use **informational advertising** that emphasizes the features of its product. An audio or video ad for the latest CD by a rock group is likely to include snippets of songs that are featured on the CD, which helps potential buyers assess the quality of the music. In contrast, if the product is an experience good, a firm is more likely to engage in **persuasive advertising** intended to induce a consumer to try the product and, as a consequence, discover a previously unknown taste for it. For example, a soft-drink ad is likely to depict happy people drinking the clearly identified product during breaks from enjoyable outdoor activities on a hot day. If a product is a credence good, producers commonly use a mix of informational and persuasive advertising. For instance, an ad for a pharmaceutical product commonly provides both detailed information about the product's curative properties and side effects and suggestions to consumers to ask physicians to help them assess the drug.

Informational advertising
Advertising that emphasizes transmitting knowledge about the features of a product.

Persuasive advertising
Advertising that is intended to induce a consumer to purchase a particular product and discover a previously unknown taste for the item.

Advertising as Signaling Behavior.
Recall from Chapter 24 that *signals* are compact gestures or actions that convey information. For example, high profits in an industry are signals that resources should flow to that industry. Individual companies can explicitly engage in signaling behavior. A firm can do so by establishing brand names or trademarks and then promoting them heavily. This is a signal to prospective consumers that this is a company that plans to stay in business. Before the modern age of advertising, U.S. banks faced a problem in signaling their soundness. To solve this problem, they constructed large, imposing bank buildings using marble and granite. Stone communicated permanence. The effect was to give bank customers confidence that they were not doing business with fly-by-night operations.

When Dell, Inc. advertises its brand name heavily, it incurs substantial costs. The only way it can recoup those costs is by selling many Dell personal computers over a long period of time. Heavy advertising in the company's brand name thereby signals to personal computer buyers that Dell intends to stay in business a long time and wants to develop a loyal customer base—because loyal customers are repeat customers.

CONCEPTS in Brief

- Trademarks such as words, symbols, and logos distinguish firms' products from those of other firms. Firms seek to differentiate their brands through advertising, via direct marketing, mass marketing, or interactive marketing.

- A firm is more likely to use informational advertising that emphasizes the features of its product if the item is a search good with features that consumers can assess in advance.

- A firm is more likely to use persuasive advertising to affect consumers' tastes and preferences if it sells an experience good. This is an item that people must actually consume before they can determine its qualities.

- A firm that sells a credence good, which is an item possessing qualities that consumers lack the expertise to fully assess, typically uses a combination of informational and persuasive advertising.

To test your understanding of the concepts covered in this section, go to the Online Review at www.myeconlab.com/miller.

INFORMATION PRODUCTS AND MONOPOLISTIC COMPETITION

A number of industries sell **information products,** which entail relatively high fixed costs associated with the use of knowledge and other information-intensive inputs as key factors of production. Once the first unit has been produced, however, it is possible to produce additional units at a relatively low per-unit cost. Most information products can be placed

Information product
An item that is produced using information-intensive inputs at a relatively high fixed cost but distributed for sale at a relatively low marginal cost.

into digital form. Good examples are computer games, computer operating systems, digital music and videos, educational and training software, electronic books and encyclopedias, and office productivity software.

Special Cost Characteristics of Information Products

Creating the first copy of an information product often entails incurring a relatively sizable up-front cost. Once the first copy is created, however, making additional copies can be very inexpensive. For instance, a firm that sells a computer game can simply make properly formatted copies of the original digital file of the game on a CD. Alternatively, the firm might make the game available for consumers to download, at a price, via the Internet.

Costs of Producing Information Products. To think about the cost conditions faced by the seller of an information product, consider the production and sale of a computer game. The company that creates a computer game must devote many hours of labor to developing and editing its content. Each hour of labor and each unit of other resources devoted to performing this task entail an opportunity cost. The sum of all these up-front costs constitutes a relatively sizable *fixed cost* that the company must incur to generate the first copy of the computer game.

Once the company has developed the computer game in a form that is readable by personal computers, the marginal cost of making and distributing additional copies is very low. In the case of a computer game, it is simply a matter of incurring a minuscule cost to place the required files on a CD or on the company's Web site.

Cost Curves for an Information Product. Suppose that a manufacturer decides to produce and sell a computer game. Creating the first copy of the game requires incurring a total fixed cost equal to $250,000. The marginal cost that the company incurs to place the computer game on a CD or in downloadable format is a constant amount equal to $2.50 per computer game.

Figure 26-4 displays the firm's cost curves for this information product. By definition, average fixed cost is total fixed cost divided by the quantity produced and sold. Hence the average fixed cost of the first computer game is $250,000. But if the company sells 5,000 copies, the average fixed cost drops to $50 per game. If the total quantity sold is 50,000, average fixed cost declines to $5 per game. The average fixed cost (AFC) curve slopes downward over the entire range of possible quantities of computer games.

Average variable cost equals total variable cost divided by the number of units of a product that a firm sells. If this company sells only one copy, then the total variable cost it incurs is the per-unit cost of $2.50, and this is also the average variable cost of producing one unit. Because the per-unit cost of producing the computer game is a constant $2.50, producing two games entails a total variable cost of $5.00, and the average variable cost of producing two games is $5.00 ÷ 2 = $2.50. Thus, as shown in Figure 26-4, the average variable cost of producing and selling this computer game is always equal to the constant marginal cost of $2.50 per game that the company incurs. The average variable cost (AVC) curve is the same as the marginal cost (MC) curve, which for this company is the horizontal line depicted in Figure 26-4.

Short-Run Economies of Operation. By definition, average total cost equals the sum of average fixed cost and average variable cost. The average total cost (ATC) curve for this computer game company slopes downward over its entire range.

Recall from Chapter 23 that along the downward-sloping range of an individual firm's *long-run* average cost curve, the firm experiences *economies of scale*. For the producer of an information product such as a computer game, the *short-run* average total cost curve slopes downward. Consequently, sellers of information products typically experience

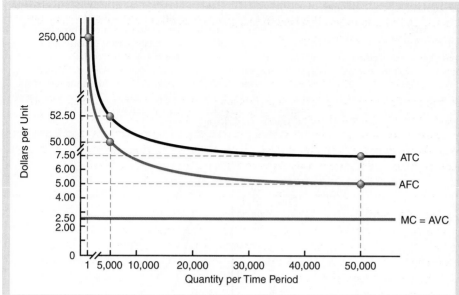

FIGURE 26-4

Cost Curves for a Producer of an Information Product

The total fixed cost of producing a computer game is $250,000. If the producer sells 5,000 copies, average fixed cost falls to $50 per copy. If quantity sold rises to 50,000, average fixed cost decreases to $5 per copy. Thus the producer's average fixed cost (AFC) curve slopes downward. If the per-unit cost of producing each copy of the game is $2.50, then both the marginal cost (MC) and average variable cost (AVC) curves are horizontal at $2.50 per copy. Adding the AFC and AVC curves yields the ATC curve. Because the ATC curve slopes downward, the producer of this information product experiences short-run economies of operation.

short-run economies of operation. The average total cost of producing and selling an information product declines as more units of the product are sold. Short-run economies of operation are a distinguishing characteristic of information products that sets them apart from most other goods and services.

Short-run economies of operation
A distinguishing characteristic of an information product arising from declining short-run average total cost as more units of the product are sold.

Monopolistic Competition and Information Products

In the example depicted in Figure 26-4, the information product is a computer game. There are numerous computer games among which consumers can choose. Hence there are many products that are close substitutes in the market for computer games. Yet no two computer games are exactly the same. This means that the particular computer game product sold by the company in our example is distinguishable from other competing products.

For the sake of argument, therefore, let's suppose that this company participates in a monopolistically competitive market for this computer game. Panels (a) and (b) of Figure 26-5 on the following page display a possible demand curve for the computer game manufactured and sold by this particular company.

Marginal Cost Pricing and Information Products. What if the company making this particular computer game were to behave *as if* it were a perfectly competitive firm by setting the price of its product equal to marginal cost? Panel (a) of Figure 26-5 provides the answer to this question. If the company sets the price of the computer game equal to marginal cost, it will charge only $2.50 per game it sells. Naturally, a relatively larger number of people desire to purchase computer games at this price, and given the demand curve in the figure, the company could sell 20,000 copies of this game.

The company would face a problem, however. At a price of $2.50 per computer game, it would earn $50,000 in revenues on sales of 20,000 copies. The average fixed cost of 20,000 copies equals $250,000/20,000, or $12.50 per computer game. Adding this to the constant $2.50 average variable cost implies an average total cost of selling 20,000 copies of $15 per game. Under marginal cost pricing, therefore, the company would earn an average loss of $12.50 (price − average total cost = $2.50 − $15.00 = −$12.50) per computer game for all 20,000 copies sold. The company's total economic loss from selling 20,000

FIGURE 26-5
The Infeasibility of Marginal Cost Pricing of an Information Product.

In panel (a), if the firm with the average total cost and marginal cost cost curves shown in Figure 26-4 sets the price of the computer game equal to its constant marginal cost of $2.50 per copy, then consumers will purchase 20,000 copies. This yields $50,000 in revenues. The firm's average total cost of 20,000 games is $15 per copy, so its total cost of selling that number of copies is $15 × 20,000 = $300,000. Marginal cost pricing

thereby entails a $250,000 loss, which is the total fixed cost of producing the computer game. Panel (b) illustrates how the price of the game is ultimately determined under monopolistic competition. Setting a price of $27.50 per game induces consumers to buy 10,000 copies, and the average total cost of producing this number of copies is also $27.50. Consequently, total revenues equal $275,000, which just covers the sum of the $250,000 in total fixed costs and $25,000 (the 10,000 copies times the constant $2.50 average variable cost) in total variable costs. The firm earns zero economic profits.

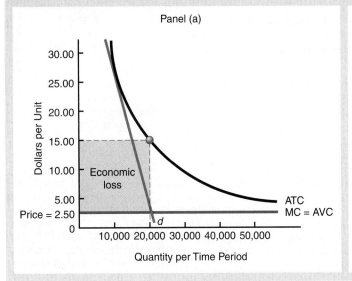

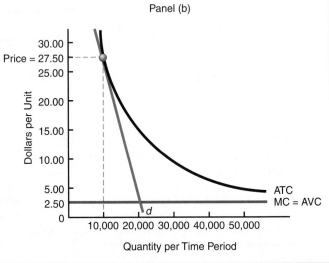

computer games at a price equal to marginal cost would amount to $250,000. Hence the company would fail to recoup the $250,000 total fixed cost of producing the computer game. If the company had planned to set its price equal to the computer game's marginal production cost, it would never have sought to produce the computer game in the first place!

The failure of marginal cost pricing to allow firms selling information products to cover the fixed costs of producing those products is intrinsic to the nature of such products. In the presence of short-run economies of operation in producing information products, marginal cost pricing is simply not feasible in the marketplace.

Recall that marginal cost pricing is associated with perfect competition. An important implication of this example is that markets for information products cannot function as perfectly competitive markets. Imperfect competition is the rule, not the exception, in the market for information products.

The Case in Which Price Equals Average Total Cost. Panel (b) of Figure 26-5 illustrates how the price of the computer game is ultimately determined in a monopolistically competitive market. After all entry or exit from the market has occurred, the price of the computer game will equal the producer's average cost of production, including all implicit opportunity costs. The price charged for the game generates total revenues sufficient to cover all explicit and implicit costs and therefore is consistent with earning a normal return on invested capital.

Given the demand curve depicted in Figure 26-5, at a price of $27.50 per computer game, consumers are willing to purchase 10,000 copies. The company's average total cost of offering 10,000 copies for sale is also equal to $27.50 per computer game. Consequently, the price of each copy equals the average total cost of producing the game.

At a price of $27.50 per computer game, the company's revenues from selling 10,000 copies equal $275,000. This amount of revenues is just sufficient to cover the company's total fixed cost (including the opportunity cost of capital) of $250,000 and the $25,000 total variable cost it incurs in producing 10,000 copies at an average variable cost of $2.50 per game. Thus the company earns zero economic profits.

Long-Run Equilibrium for an Information Product Industry. When the price of an information product equals average total cost, sellers charge the minimum price required to cover their production costs, including the relatively high initial costs they must incur to develop their products in the first place. Consumers thereby pay the lowest price necessary to induce sellers to provide the item.

The situation illustrated in panel (b) of Figure 26-5 corresponds to a long-run equilibrium for this particular firm in a monopolistically competitive market for computer games. If this and other companies face a situation such as the diagram depicts, there is no incentive for additional companies to enter or leave the computer game industry. Consequently, the product price naturally tends to adjust to equality with average total cost as a monopolistically competitive industry composed of sellers of information products moves toward long-run equilibrium.

CONCEPTS in Brief

● Firms that sell information products experience relatively high fixed costs, but once they have produced the first unit, they can sell additional units at a relatively low per-unit cost. Consequently, the manufacturer of an information product experiences short-run economies of operation.

● If a firm sets the price of an information product equal to marginal cost, it earns only sufficient revenues to cover its variable costs. Engaging in marginal cost pricing, therefore, fails to cover the relatively high fixed costs of making an information product.

● In a long-run equilibrium outcome under monopolistic competition, the price of an information product equals average total cost. The seller's total revenues exactly cover total costs, including the opportunity cost of capital.

To test your understanding of the concepts covered in this section, go to the Online Review at www.myeconlab.com/miller.

CASE STUDY: Economics Front and Center

Will Viral Marketing Work Wonders?

Lopez is working on a marketing degree, and she feels fortunate to have obtained a summer job with an advertising firm. At the first meeting she attends with full-time colleagues at the firm, Lopez listens as one promotes a concept known as *viral marketing*, which he suggests would be perfect for one of the firm's clients, a beer manufacturer. The viral marketing plan calls for the beer manufacturer to give away at no charge Web-based e-mail accounts to buyers of six-packs. Then each time someone sends a message from one of these accounts, a simple tag will appear at the bottom stating, "Buy a six-pack of the smoothest beer around, and then get your free e-mail account at [a link to the home page of the beer manufacturer]." This viral marketing approach, the colleague predicts, will induce large numbers of people to give the client's beer a try.

Lopez isn't so sure. Most people, she suspects, already have e-mail accounts providing more features than the beer firm is willing to pay to set up at no charge to the buyer of a single six-pack. Nevertheless, she does see potential in the concept. As her colleague continues to describe his idea, she starts listing her thoughts about how to make subtle changes in his proposal.

Points to Analyze

1. *What type of advertising—direct, mass, or interactive marketing—is Lopez's colleague suggesting?*

2. *Would using this viral marketing approach cause the demand for the first six-pack of beer to be more inelastic? What about the elasticity of demand for additional six-packs?*

Firms have developed a wide variety of formats for obtaining and listening to digital music files. As a consequence, the online music industry has become a monopolistically competitive free-for-all. Some sellers of online music have strived to differentiate their products from those of other firms. At the same time, however, other firms have sought to reduce the extent of product differentiation in the market for online music.

Concepts Applied

- Product Differentiation
- Monopolistic Competition
- Advertising

Same Song, Different Formats

To obtain the songs they sell on the Internet, firms in the online music industry typically must pay between 65 and 75 cents per song. Firms also incur other costs in the form of credit-card processing fees, bandwidth charges, and expenses associated with providing miscellaneous customer services.

The companies' products are highly differentiated, however. If you buy a song from Apple Computer's iTune Web site, it is in a format that allows it to be transferred to a pocket-sized iPod device for storing and playing that song and hundreds or even thousands more. If you purchase the same song from Microsoft, it is formatted to be stored and played on the Windows Media Player that probably came pre-installed on your personal computer. Finally, if you just want to be able to listen to the song any time you want without having to go to the trouble to store it as a digital file, you can pay a company called Rhapsody a monthly subscription fee to listen to this and other tunes in real time via your Internet connection.

The Long Run Arrives Quickly in Online Music

Because online music products are so highly differentiated, prices that consumers pay to obtain music online vary from site to site. Firms that simply offer downloadable songs that consumers must figure out how to store and play themselves, such as Musicmatch, Napster, MusicNow, and BuyMusic, typically charge about 85 to 90 cents per song. Other companies sell music players, such as gadgets offered by Dell, Sony, and Samsung, which play specially formatted songs downloadable from their sites at slightly lower prices.

When online music sales first began in the late 1990s, only a few firms were able to earn a normal profit. By 2000, a number of firms had exited from the industry. Then, in the early 2000s, the fortunes of the industry suddenly brightened with the emergence of so many new technologies for delivering online music. During 2003, the lure of positive economic profits induced Wal-Mart, Yahoo, Amazon, and several others to enter the online music industry. Within a year's time, economic profits from online music sales had fallen dramatically once more.

To maintain their profitability, a number of firms began selling advertising space at their sites and bombarding customers with pop-up ads. In spite of these efforts to generate sufficient revenues to remain profitable, in 2004 a number of online music sellers were failing to earn a normal profit and were contemplating closing down their online music sites.

RealNetworks Seeks to Level the Playing Field

In reaction to the popularity of Apple's iPod player, the online media company RealNetworks temporarily slashed its prices and revamped its software for online music to allow songs downloaded using its system to be playable on iPods devices. In the face of this attack on its efforts to differentiate its product, Apple filed a lawsuit seeking to prevent other online music sellers from offering iPod-compatible songs. How this legal tussle turns out may help determine the extent of product differentiation in the online music industry.

1. Why do you suppose that the sale of online music often entails short-run economies of operation?

2. Why do you suppose that analysts of the online music industry suggest that long-run adjustments in this industry often take place within only a year or two? (Hint: Compared with many other industries, why might the costs of entry or exit in the online music industry be much lower?)

For Critical Analysis

1. To learn about the recent growth in the downloadable music business, follow the link to an article from *PC World* at www.econtoday.com/chap26.

2. For a more downbeat assessment from *BusinessWeek* about the long-run future of the market for downloadable songs, go to www.econtoday.com/chap26.

Web Resources

Evaluate why firms in the online music industry charge widely varying prices to consumers who purchase their products. Explain how it can be that each firm earns zero economic profits in the long run, even though consumers continue to pay some firms more than others to consume their online music products.

Research Project

SUMMARY DISCUSSION of Learning Objectives

1. **The Key Characteristics of a Monopolistically Competitive Industry:** A monopolistically competitive industry consists of a large number of firms that sell differentiated products that are close substitutes. Firms can easily enter or exit a monopolistically competitive industry. Because monopolistically competitive firms can increase their profits if they can successfully distinguish their products from those of their rivals, they have an incentive to engage in sales promotions and advertising.

2. **Contrasting the Output and Pricing Decisions of Monopolistically Competitive Firms with Those of Perfectly Competitive Firms:** In the short run, a monopolistically competitive firm produces output to the point where marginal revenue equals marginal cost. The price it charges for this output, which is the maximum price that people are willing to pay as determined by the demand for its product, can exceed both marginal cost and average total cost in the short run, and the resulting economic profits can induce new firms to enter the industry. As they do, existing firms in the industry experience declines in the demand for their products and reduce their prices to the point at which price equals average total cost. In the long run, therefore, monopolistically competitive firms, like perfectly competitive firms, earn zero economic profits. In contrast to perfectly competitive firms, however, price still exceeds marginal cost in the long-run equilibrium for monopolistically competitive firms.

3. **Why Brand Names and Advertising Are Important Features of Monopolistically Competitive Industries:** Monopolistically competitive firms attempt to boost the demand for their products through product differentiation. They use words, symbols, and logos (trademarks) to distinguish their products from substitute items produced by other firms in the industry. In addition, they engage in advertising, in the form of direct marketing, mass marketing, or interactive marketing. If the product is a search good with features that consumers can evaluate prior to purchase, the seller is more likely to use advertising to transmit information about product features. If the firm is selling an experience good, which has features that are apparent only when consumed, it is more likely to engage in persuasive advertising intended to cause consumers to discover unknown tastes. If the product is a credence good with characteristics that consumers cannot readily assess unaided, then the firm often uses a mix of informational and persuasive advertising.

4. **Properties of Information Products and Determining Their Prices:** Providing an information product entails incurring relatively high fixed costs but a relatively low per-unit cost for additional units of output. Hence the average total cost curve for a firm that sells an information product slopes downward, meaning that the firm experiences economies of operation in the short run. Under marginal cost pricing, the producer of an information product earns only sufficient revenues to cover its variable costs, so it incurs economic losses equal to its total fixed costs. In a long-run monopolistically competitive equilibrium, price adjusts to equality with average total cost. The firm earns sufficient revenues to cover total costs, including the opportunity cost of capital.

KEY TERMS AND CONCEPTS

credence goods (626)

direct marketing (626)

experience goods (626)

informational advertising (627)

information product (627)

interactive marketing (626)

mass marketing (626)

monopolistic competition (618)

persuasive advertising (627)

product differentiation (619)

search good (626)

short-run economies of operation (629)

PROBLEMS

Answers to the odd-numbered problems appear at the back of the book.

26-1. Explain why the following are examples of monopolistic competition.

 a. There are a number of fast-food restaurants in town, and they compete fiercely. Some restaurants cook their hamburgers over open flames. Others fry their hamburgers. In addition, some serve broiled fish sandwiches, while others serve fried fish sandwiches. A few serve ice-cream cones for dessert, while others offer frozen ice-cream pies.

 b. There is a vast number of colleges and universities across the country. Each competes for top students. All offer similar courses and programs, but some have better programs in business, while others have stronger programs in the arts and humanities. Still others are academically stronger in the sciences.

26-2. A father goes to the pharmacy late at night for cold medicine for a sick child. There are many liquid cold medicines, all of which have *almost* exactly the same ingredients. Yet medicines with brand names that the man recognizes from television commercials sell for more than the unadvertised versions. Explain, in economic terms, this perplexing situation to the father.

26-3. The following table depicts the prices and total costs a local used bookstore faces. The bookstore competes with a number of similar stores, but it capitalizes on its location and the word-of-mouth reputation of the coffee it serves to its customers. Calculate the store's total revenue, total profit, marginal revenue, and marginal cost at each level of output, beginning with the first unit. Based on marginal analysis, what is the approximate profit-maximizing level of output for this business?

Output	Price per Book ($)	Total Costs ($)
0	6.00	2.00
1	5.75	5.25
2	5.50	7.50
3	5.25	9.60
4	5.00	12.10
5	4.75	15.80
6	4.50	20.00
7	4.00	24.75

26-4. Calculate total average costs for the bookstore in Problem 26-3. Illustrate the store's short-run equilibrium by plotting demand, marginal revenue, average total costs, and marginal costs. What is its total profit?

26-5. Suppose that after long-run adjustments take place in the used book market, the business in Problem 26-3 ends up producing 4 units of output. What are the market price and economic profits of this monopolistic competitor in the long run?

26-6. Classify each of the following as an example of direct, interactive, and/or mass marketing.

 a. The sales force of a pharmaceutical company visits physicians' offices to promote new medications and to answer physicians' questions about treatment options and possible side effects.

 b. A mortgage company targets a list of specific low-risk borrowers for a barrage of e-mail messages touting its low interest rates and fees.

 c. An online bookseller pays fees to an Internet search engine to post banner ads relating to each search topic chosen by someone conducting a search; in part this helps promote the bookseller's brand, but clicking on the banner ad also directs the person to a Web page displaying books on the topic that are available for purchase.

d. A national rental car chain runs advertisements on all of the nation's major television networks.

26-7. Classify each of the following as an example of direct, interactive, and/or mass marketing.

a. A cosmetics firm pays for full-page display ads in a number of top women's magazines.

b. A magazine distributor mails a fold-out flyer advertising its products to the addresses of all individuals it has identified as possibly interested in magazine subscriptions.

c. An online gambling operation arranges for pop-up ads to appear on the computer screen every time a person uses a media player to listen to digital music or play video files, and clicking on the ads directs an individual to its Web gambling site.

d. A car dealership places advertisements in newspapers throughout the region where potential customers reside.

26-8. Categorize each of the following as an experience good, a search good, or a credence good or service, and justify your answer.

a. A heavy-duty filing cabinet

b. A restaurant meal

c. A wool overcoat

d. Psychotherapy

26-9. Categorize each of the following as an experience good, a search good, or a credence good or service, and justify your answer.

a. Services of a carpet cleaning company

b. A new cancer treatment

c. Athletic socks

d. A silk necktie

26-10. In what ways do credence goods share certain characteristics of both experience goods and search goods? How do credence goods differ from both experience goods and search goods? Explain your answers.

26-11. In light of your answer to Problem 26-10, explain why advertising of credence goods commonly contains both informational and persuasive elements.

26-12. Is each of the following items more likely to be the subject of an informational or a persuasive advertisement? Why?

a. An office copying machine

b. An automobile loan

c. A deodorant

d. A soft drink

26-13. Discuss the special characteristics of an information product, and explain the implications for a producer's short-run average and marginal cost curves.

26-14. Explain why having a price equal to marginal cost is not feasible for the producer of an information product.

26-15. The producer of a downloadable antivirus software program spends exactly $2,850,000 producing the first copy and incurring various costs required to make the software "user-friendly." The firm can produce and distribute additional copies at a per-unit cost of $1. If the company sold as many copies as consumers wished to purchase at a price of $1 per copy, it would sell 300,000 copies. If the company maximizes its economic profits in the short run, it sells 100,000 copies at a price of $35. Finally, the company earns zero economic profits when it sells 150,000 copies.

a. What are the firm's economic profits (or losses) if it sells 300,000 copies of the antivirus software program at a $1 price per copy?

b. What are the maximum economic profits that the firm can earn in the short run?

c. What is marginal revenue when the firm maximizes its short-run economic profits?

d. In the long run, after entry of competing firms, what amount of economic profits will this firm earn?

26-16. A firm that sells e-books—books in digital form downloadable from the Internet—sells all e-books relating to do-it-yourself topics (home plumbing, gardening, and so on) at the same price. At present, the company can earn a maximum annual profit of $25,000 when it sells 10,000 copies within a year's time. The firm incurs a 50-cent expense each time a consumer downloads a copy, but the company must spend $100,000 per year developing new editions of the e-books. The company has determined that it would earn zero economic profits if price were equal to average total cost, and in this case it could sell 20,000 copies. Under marginal cost pricing, it could sell 100,000 copies.

a. In the short run, what is the firm's profit-maximizing price of e-books relating to do-it-yourself topics?

b. At the profit-maximizing quantity, what is the average total cost of producing e-books?

ECONOMICS ON THE NET

Legal Services on the Internet A number of legal firms now offer services on the Internet, and in this application you contemplate features of the market for Web-based legal services.

Title: Nolo.com—Law for All

Navigation: Link to the Nolo.com site via **www.econtoday.com/chap26**.

Application Answer the following questions.

1. In what respects does the market for legal services, such as those provided online by Nolo.com, have the characteristics of a monopolistically competitive industry?

2. How can providers of legal services differentiate their products? How does Nolo.com attempt to do this?

For Group Discussion and Analysis Assign groups to search the Web and compile a list of at least three additional online legal firms and to compare the services these firms offer. Reconvene the entire class and discuss whether it is reasonable to classify the market for online legal services as monopolistically competitive.

If your exam were tomorrow, would you be ready? For each chapter, MyEconLab Practice Tests and Study Plans pinpoint which sections you have mastered and which ones you need to study. That way, you are more efficient with your study time, and you are better prepared for your exams.

In addition to Practice Tests and your personalized Study Plan, you'll find the following media resources in MyEconLab:

1. *Graphs in Motion* animation of Figures 26-2, 26-4, and 26-5.
2. Video featuring the author, Roger LeRoy Miller, on the following subject:
   ● Characteristics of Monopolistic Competition
3. Links to the Web sites cited in the marginal Internet Resources, Issues and Applications feature, and Economics on the Net activity.
4. Audio clips of all key terms, additional practice problems, and a PDF version of the material from the print Study Guide.
5. eThemes of the Times, which is a New York Times article to help you understand the real-world applications of what you are learning.

To see how it works, turn to page 16 and then go to **www.myeconlab.com/miller**.

Get Ahead of the Curve

Chapter 27

Oligopoly and Strategic Behavior

I t is a typical day at United Parcel Service (UPS), in that its 85,000 drivers have transported more than 10 million packages. It is also what is becoming a typical year, in that UPS is in the process of losing one to two percentage points of its share of market sales to FedEx Ground, the ground-delivery arm of the company that has long dominated the market for airborne packages. Together, the two companies now earn nearly three-fourths of all revenues generated in the market for ground package deliveries. The only other nationwide ground-delivery services are the U.S. Postal Service and DHL. By the end of this chapter, you will understand how pricing and production decisions by any one of these companies can affect the choices made by the other firms.

LEARNING OBJECTIVES

After reading this chapter, you should be able to:

1. Outline the fundamental characteristics of oligopoly
2. Understand how to apply game theory to evaluate the pricing strategies of oligopolistic firms
3. Explain the kinked demand theory of oligopolistic price rigidity
4. Describe theories of how firms may deter market entry by potential rivals
5. Illustrate why network effects and market feedback can explain why some industries are oligopolies

Media Resources

Refer to the end of the chapter for a full listing of the multimedia learning materials available in MyEconLab.

Did You Know That **...** 80 percent of all the microprocessor chips used globally as components in personal computers and servers are manufactured by a single company—Intel? Several other companies, such as Sun Microsystems, Fujitsu, and Advanced Micro Devices, produce the remaining 20 percent of the world's output of microprocessor chips. The microprocessor-chip industry cannot be called a monopoly because there is more than one firm in the industry. Nevertheless, it has a single predominant seller.

The microprocessor-chip industry is not the only industry with identifiably predominant firms. In the wireless-phone and defense industries, for instance, the top five firms account for more than 80 percent of all sales. The top three publishers of college textbooks generate well over 70 percent of all textbook sales. In this chapter, you will learn about the special characteristics of industries composed of a few firms.

OLIGOPOLY

An important market structure that we have yet to discuss involves a situation in which a few large firms dominate an entire industry. They are not competitive in the sense that we have used the term; they are not even monopolistically competitive. And because there are several of them, a pure monopoly does not exist. We call such a situation an **oligopoly,** which consists of a small number of *interdependent* sellers. Each firm in the industry knows that other firms will react to its changes in prices, quantities, and qualities. An oligopoly market structure can exist for either a homogeneous or a differentiated product.

Oligopoly
A market situation in which there are very few sellers. Each seller knows that the other sellers will react to its changes in prices and quantities.

Characteristics of Oligopoly

Oligopoly is characterized by a small number of interdependent firms that constitute the entire market.

Small Number of Firms. How many is "a small number of firms"? More than two but less than a hundred? The question is not easy to answer. Basically, though, oligopoly exists when the top few firms in the industry account for an overwhelming percentage of total industry output.

Oligopolies usually involve three to five big companies that produce the bulk of industry output. Between World War II and the 1970s, three firms—General Motors, Chrysler, and Ford—produced and sold nearly all the output of the U.S. automobile industry. Among manufacturers of chewing gum and coin-operated amusement games, four large firms produce and sell essentially the entire output of each industry.

Strategic dependence
A situation in which one firm's actions with respect to price, quality, advertising, and related changes may be strategically countered by the reactions of one or more other firms in the industry. Such dependence can exist only when there are a limited number of major firms in an industry.

Interdependence. All markets and all firms are, in a sense, interdependent. But only when a few large firms produce most of the output in an industry does the question of **strategic dependence** of one on the others' actions arise. In this situation, when any one firm changes its output, its product price, or the quality of its product, other firms notice the effects of its decisions. The firms must recognize that they are interdependent and that any action on the part of one firm with respect to output, price, quality, or product differentiation will cause a reaction on the part of other firms. A model of such mutual interdependence is difficult to build, but examples of such behavior are not hard to find in the real world. Oligopolists in the cigarette industry, for example, are constantly reacting to each other.

Recall that in the model of perfect competition, each firm ignores the behavior of other firms because each firm is able to sell all that it wants at the going market price. At the other extreme, the pure monopolist does not have to worry about the reaction of current rivals because there are none. In an oligopolistic market structure, the managers of firms are like generals in a war: *They must attempt to predict the reaction of rival firms.* It is a strategic game.

Why Oligopoly Occurs

Why are some industries composed chiefly of a few large firms? What causes an industry that might otherwise be competitive to tend toward oligopoly? We can provide some partial answers here.

Follow the link at
www.econtoday.com/chap27 to *Wall Street Journal* articles about real-world examples involving oligopoly.

Economies of Scale. Perhaps the most common reason that has been offered for the existence of oligopoly is economies of scale. Recall that economies of scale are situations in which a doubling of output results in less than a doubling of total costs. When economies of scale exist, the firm's long-run average total cost curve will slope downward as the firm produces more and more output. Average total cost can be reduced by continuing to expand the scale of operation. Smaller firms in such a situation will have a tendency to be inefficient. Their average total costs will be greater than those incurred by large firms. Little by little, they will go out of business or be absorbed into larger firms.

Barriers to Entry. It is possible that certain barriers to entry have prevented more competition in oligopolistic industries. They include legal barriers, such as patents, and control and ownership of critical supplies. Indeed, we can find periods in the past when firms maintained market power because they were able not only to erect a barrier to entry but also to keep it in place year after year. In principle, the chemical, electronics, and aluminum industries have been at one time or another either monopolistic or oligopolistic because of the ownership of patents and the control of strategic inputs by specific firms.

How have two firms maintained a position as the only producers of systems used to scramble and unscramble cable television signals?

E X A M P L E

Sony Tries to Break into the Cable-Signal-Scrambling Duopoly

When two firms produce all of an industry's output, they constitute a special case of oligopoly known as a *duopoly*. Since the early 1980s, two firms, Motorola and Scientific-Atlanta, have functioned as a duopoly in the market for systems used to scramble television signals transmitted by cable companies and then unscramble them in people's homes. Each company uses its own encoding software to perform the scrambling and unscrambling at each end of the cable connection. A cable television company typically chooses to use either Motorola's system or Scientific-Atlanta's system because operating parallel signal-scrambling networks entails incurring twice the expense.

Another company, Sony, has developed a technology that promises to make it much less expensive for cable television companies to use the cable-signal-scrambling services of more than one company at a time. Sony's system makes mul-

tiple digital copies of a single cable television signal, which cable companies can distribute to Motorola, Scientific-Atlanta, and any other firms that care to enter the market. In this way, cable television companies potentially will be able to use the services of multiple firms, thereby breaking up the cable-signal-scrambling duopoly. Two additional firms, NDS and Canal Plus, have already expressed an interest in competing with Motorola and Scientific-Atlanta in the cable-signal-scrambling market.

For Critical Analysis
How would the entry of additional firms into the cable-signal-scrambling industry complicate efforts by Motorola and Scientific-Atlanta to predict the reactions of rival firms in the industry?

Vertical merger
The joining of a firm with another to which it sells an output or from which it buys an input.

Horizontal merger
The joining of firms that are producing or selling a similar product.

Concentration ratio
The percentage of all sales contributed by the leading four or leading eight firms in an industry; sometimes called the *industry concentration ratio.*

Oligopoly by Merger. Another reason that oligopolistic market structures may sometimes develop is that firms merge. A merger is the joining of two or more firms under single ownership or control. The merged firm naturally becomes larger, enjoys greater economies of scale as output increases, and may ultimately have a greater ability to influence the market price for the industry's output.

There are two types of mergers, vertical and horizontal. A **vertical merger** occurs when one firm merges with either a firm from which it purchases an input or a firm to which it sells its output. Vertical mergers occur, for example, when a coal-using electrical utility purchases a coal-mining firm or when a shoe manufacturer purchases retail shoe outlets.

Obviously, vertical mergers cannot create oligopoly as we have defined it. But that can indeed occur via a **horizontal merger,** which involves firms selling a similar product. If two shoe manufacturing firms merge, that is a horizontal merger. If a group of firms, all producing steel, merge into one, that is also a horizontal merger.

So far we have been talking about oligopoly in a theoretical manner. Now it is time to look at the actual oligopoly situation in the United States.

Measuring Industry Concentration

As we have stated, oligopoly is a situation in which a few interdependent firms produce a large part of total output in an industry. This has been called *industry concentration.* Before we show the concentration statistics in the United States, let's determine how industry concentration can be measured.

Concentration Ratio. The most popular way to compute industry concentration is to determine the percentage of total sales or production accounted for by the top four or top eight firms in an industry. This gives the four- or eight-firm **concentration ratio,** also known as the *industry concentration ratio.* An example of an industry with 25 firms is given in Table 27-1. We can see in that table that the four largest firms account for almost 90 percent of total output in the hypothetical industry. That market situation is an example of an oligopoly because a few firms will recognize the interdependence of their output, pricing, and quality decisions.

TABLE 27-1
Computing the Four-Firm Concentration Ratio

Firm	Annual Sales ($ millions)	
1	150 ⎫	
2	100 ⎬ = 400	Total number of firms in industry = 25
3	80	
4	70 ⎭	
5 through 25	50	
Total	450	

Four-firm concentration ratio = $\frac{400}{450}$ = 88.9%

TABLE 27-2
Four-Firm Domestic Concentration Ratios for Selected U.S. Industries

Industry	Share of Value of Total Domestic Shipments Accounted for by the Top Four Firms (%)
Tobacco products	99
Breakfast cereals	83
Domestic motor vehicles	82
Household vacuum cleaners	69
Primary aluminum	59
Soft drinks	47
Computers	45
Printing and publishing	34

Source: U.S. Bureau of the Census.

U.S. Concentration Ratios. Table 27-2 shows the four-firm *domestic* concentration ratios for various industries. Is there any way that we can show or determine which industries to classify as oligopolistic? There is no definite answer. If we arbitrarily picked a four-firm concentration ratio of 75 percent, we could indicate that tobacco products, breakfast cereals, and domestic motor vehicles were oligopolistic. But we would always be dealing with an arbitrary definition.

How can we measure the market shares of Internet search engines, such as Google and Yahoo, that do not charge consumers to use their sites to search the Web?

E-Commerce EXAMPLE

Measuring Concentration in the Internet Search-Engine Industry

Internet search engines such as Google and Yahoo generate revenues by charging firms that post advertisements on their sites relating to search topics that consumers enter. Because search-engine firms enter into so many different types of advertising arrangements, measuring industry concentrations using sales data is a difficult proposition. Therefore, to measure industry concentration in the Internet search-engine industry, economists rely on a production-based measure. They calculate the number of Web searches conducted at each site per unit of time and then divide by the total number of searches during the selected interval. This calculation yields a four-firm (Google, Yahoo, AOL Time Warner, and MSN-Microsoft) concentration ratio of 91 percent. Thus the Internet search-engine industry is highly concentrated.

For Critical Analysis
Why do you think that changes in the formats of search engines operated by Yahoo, AOL Time Warner, and MSN-Microsoft often follow closely on the heels of changes at the Web site of Google, which processes about a third of all Web searches?

Oligopoly, Efficiency, and Resource Allocation

Although oligopoly is not the dominant form of market structure in the United States, oligopolistic industries do exist. To the extent that oligopolists have *market power*—the ability to *individually* affect the *market* price for the industry's output—they lead to resource misallocations, just as monopolies do. Oligopolists charge prices that exceed marginal cost. But what about oligopolies that occur because of economies of scale? Consumers might actually end up paying lower prices than if the industry were composed of numerous smaller firms.

All in all, there is no definite evidence of serious resource misallocation in the United States because of oligopolies. In any event, *the more U.S. firms face competition from the rest of the world, the less any current oligopoly will be able to exercise market power.*

CONCEPTS in Brief

- An oligopoly is a market situation in which there are a small number of interdependent sellers.

- Oligopoly may result from economies of scale, barriers to entry, and mergers.

- Vertical mergers involve the merging of one firm with either the supplier of an input or the purchaser of its output.

- Horizontal mergers involve the joining of firms selling a similar product.

- Industry concentration can be measured by the combined percentage of total sales accounted for by the top four or top eight firms in the industry.

To test your understanding of the concepts covered in this section, go to the Online Review at www.myeconlab.com/miller.

STRATEGIC BEHAVIOR AND GAME THEORY

Reaction function
The manner in which one oligopolist reacts to a change in price, output, or quality made by another oligopolist in the industry.

Game theory
A way of describing the various possible outcomes in any situation involving two or more interacting individuals when those individuals are aware of the interactive nature of their situation and plan accordingly. The plans made by these individuals are known as *game strategies.*

Cooperative game
A game in which the players explicitly cooperate to make themselves better off. As applied to firms, it involves companies colluding in order to make higher than competitive rates of return.

Noncooperative game
A game in which the players neither negotiate nor cooperate in any way. As applied to firms in an industry, this is the common situation in which there are relatively few firms and each has some ability to change price.

At this point, we would like to be able to show oligopoly price and output determination in the way we showed it for perfect competition, pure monopoly, and monopolistic competition, but we cannot. Whenever there are relatively few firms competing in an industry, each can and does react to the price, quantity, quality, and product innovations that the others undertake. In other words, each oligopolist has a **reaction function.** Oligopolistic competitors are interdependent. Consequently, the decision makers in such firms must employ strategies. And we must be able to model their strategic behavior if we wish to predict how prices and outputs are determined in oligopolistic market structures. In general, we can think of reactions of other firms to one firm's actions as part of a *game* that is played by all firms in the industry. Not surprisingly, economists have developed **game theory** models to describe firms' rational interactions. Game theory is the analytical framework in which two or more individuals, companies, or nations compete for certain payoffs that depend on the strategy that the others employ. Poker is such a game situation because it involves a strategy of reacting to the actions of others.

Some Basic Notions About Game Theory

Games can be either cooperative or noncooperative. If firms get together to collude or form a cartel, that is considered a **cooperative game.** Whenever it is too costly for firms to negotiate such collusive agreements and to enforce them, they are in a **noncooperative game** situation. Most strategic behavior in the marketplace is best described as a noncooperative game.

Why would a college or university allow sports rivals to sell merchandise that ridicules its own sports mascot?

E X A M P L E

The Cooperative Game of College Sports Licensing

It is a Saturday in late November, which means that college football teams will be pitted against their most hated rivals. Auburn fans will attend tailgate parties wearing T-shirts depicting the Auburn tiger mascot strangling the Alabama elephant. Ohio State fans will have spent the preceding week working at desktops adorned with paperweights depicting their buckeye mascot squashing Michigan wolverines. Why do the University of Alabama and the University of Michigan give permission for these items to be produced and sold, when the items do not flatter their trademarked sports mascots? The reason is that they share in the revenues generated

from the sale of such items. These and other colleges and universities thereby participate in a cooperative game involving the sale of products ridiculing sports mascots.

For Critical Analysis

If a small manufacturer of T-shirts earns all the revenues from selling unlicensed apparel depicting one college's mascot boiling another's in a big pot, do the T-shirt maker and the two colleges whose mascots are depicted participate in a cooperative game or a noncooperative game?

Games can be classified by whether the payoffs are negative, zero, or positive. In a **zero-sum game,** one player's losses are offset by another player's gains; at any time, sum totals are zero. If two retailers have an absolutely fixed total number of customers, the customers that one retailer wins over are exactly equal to the customers that the other retailer loses. In a **negative-sum game,** players as a group lose at the end of the game (although one perhaps by more than the other, and it's possible for one or more players to win). In a **positive-sum game,** players as a group end up better off. Some economists describe all voluntary exchanges as positive-sum games. After an exchange, both the buyer and the seller are better off than they were prior to the exchange.

Strategies in Noncooperative Games. Players, such as decision makers in oligopolistic firms, have to devise a **strategy,** which is defined as a rule used to make a choice. The goal of the decision maker is to devise a strategy that is more successful than alternative strategies. Whenever a firm's decision makers can come up with certain strategies that are generally successful no matter what actions competitors take, these are called **dominant strategies.** The dominant strategy always yields the unique best action for the decision maker no matter what action the other "players" undertake. Relatively few business decision makers over a long period of time have successfully devised dominant strategies. We know this by observation: Few firms in oligopolistic industries have maintained relatively high profits consistently over time.

How can a real-world situation faced by two captured bank robbers help to illustrate basic principles of game theory?

Zero-sum game
A game in which any gains within the group are exactly offset by equal losses by the end of the game.

Negative-sum game
A game in which players as a group lose at the end of the game.

Positive-sum game
A game in which players as a group are better off at the end of the game.

Strategy
Any rule that is used to make a choice, such as "Always pick heads."

Dominant strategies
Strategies that always yield the highest benefit. Regardless of what other players do, a dominant strategy will yield the most benefit for the player using it.

E X A M P L E

The Prisoners' Dilemma

A real-world example of game theory occurs when two people involved in a bank robbery are caught. What should they

do when questioned by police? The result has been called the **prisoners' dilemma.** The two suspects, Sam and Carol, are interrogated separately (they cannot communicate with each other) and are given various alternatives. The interrogator indicates to Sam and Carol the following:

1. If both confess to the bank robbery, they will both go to prison for five years.
2. If neither confesses, they will each be given a sentence of two years on a lesser charge.
3. If one prisoner turns state's evidence and confesses, that prisoner goes free and the other one, who did not confess, will serve 10 years on bank robbery charges.

You can see the prisoners' alternatives in the **payoff matrix** in Figure 27-1. The two possibilities for each prisoner are "confess" and "don't confess." There are four possibilities:

1. Both confess.
2. Neither confesses.
3. Sam confesses (turns state's evidence) but Carol doesn't.
4. Carol confesses (turns state's evidence) but Sam doesn't.

In Figure 27-1, all of Sam's possible outcomes are shown on the upper half of each rectangle, and all of Carol's possible outcomes are shown on the lower half.

By looking at the payoff matrix, you can see that if Carol confesses, Sam's best strategy is to confess also—he'll get only 5 years instead of 10. Conversely, if Sam confesses, Carol's best strategy is also to confess—she'll get 5 years instead of 10. Now let's say that Sam is being interrogated and Carol doesn't confess. Sam's best strategy is still to confess, because then he goes free instead of serving two years. Conversely, if Carol is being interrogated, her best strategy is still to confess even if Sam hasn't. She'll go free instead of serving 10 years. To confess is a dominant strategy for Sam. To confess is also a dominant strategy for Carol. The situation is exactly symmetrical. So this is the prisoners' dilemma. The prisoners know that both of them will be better off if neither confesses. Yet it is in each individual prisoner's interest to confess, even though the *collective* outcome of each prisoner's pursuing his or her own interest is inferior for both.

For Critical Analysis
Can you apply the prisoners' dilemma to the firms in a two-firm industry that agree to share market sales equally? (Hint: Think about the payoff to cheating on the market-sharing agreement.)

FIGURE 27-1
The Prisoners' Dilemma Payoff Matrix
Regardless of what the other prisoner does, each prisoner is better off if he or she confesses. So confessing is the dominant strategy, and each ends up behind bars for five years.

Prisoners' dilemma
A famous strategic game in which two prisoners have a choice between confessing and not confessing to a crime. If neither confesses, they serve a minimum sentence. If both confess, they serve a longer sentence. If one confesses and the other doesn't, the one who confesses goes free. The dominant strategy is always to confess.

Payoff matrix
A matrix of outcomes, or consequences, of the strategies available to the players in a game.

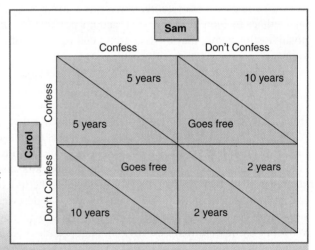

Economics Front and Center

To consider why firms might be tempted to engage in collusive behavior, contemplate the case study, **Confronting the Temptation to Collude,** on page 653.

Applying Game Theory to Pricing Strategies

We can apply game strategy to two firms—oligopolists—that have to decide on their pricing strategy. Each can choose either a high or a low price. Their payoff matrix is shown in Figure 27-2. If they both choose a high price, each will make $6 million, but if they both choose a low price, each will make only $4 million. If one sets a high price and the other a low one, the low-priced firm will make $8 million, but the high-priced firm will make only $2 million. As in the prisoners' dilemma, in the absence of collusion, they will end up choosing low prices.

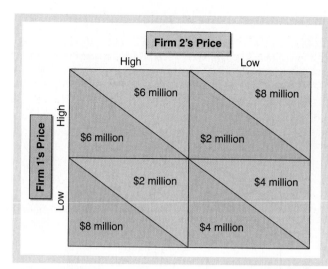

FIGURE 27-2
Game Theory and Pricing Strategies
This payoff matrix shows that if both oligopolists choose a high price, each makes $6 million. If they both choose a low price, each makes $4 million. If one chooses a low price and the other doesn't, the low-priced firm will make $8 million. Unless they collude, they will end up at the low-priced solution, because charging a low price is the dominant strategy.

Opportunistic Behavior

In the prisoners' dilemma, it is clear that cooperative behavior—both parties standing firm without admitting to anything—leads to the best outcome for both players. But each prisoner (player) stands to gain by cheating. Such action is called **opportunistic behavior.** Our daily economic activities involve the equivalent of the prisoners' dilemma all the time. We could engage in opportunistic behavior. You could write a check for a purchase knowing that it is going to bounce because you have just closed that bank account. When you agree to perform a specific task for pay, you could perform your work in a substandard way. When you go to buy an item, the seller might be able to cheat you by selling you a defective item.

In short, if all of us—sellers and buyers—engaged in opportunistic behavior all of the time, we would always end up in the upper right-hand or lower left-hand boxes of the prisoners' dilemma payoff matrix in Figure 27-1. We would constantly be acting in a world of noncooperative behavior. That is not the world in which most of us live, however. Why not? Because most of us engage in *repeat transactions.* Manufacturers would like us to keep purchasing their products. Sellers would like us to keep coming back to their stores. As sellers of labor services, we all would like to keep our jobs, get promotions, or be hired away by another firm at a higher wage rate. We engage in **tit-for-tat strategic behavior.** In tit-for-tat strategy, manufacturers and sellers continue to guarantee their merchandise, even though a small percentage of consumers take advantage of product guarantees to file false claims for refunds.

Opportunistic behavior
Actions that ignore the possible long-run benefits of cooperation and focus solely on short-run gains.

Tit-for-tat strategic behavior
In game theory, cooperation that continues so long as the other players continue to cooperate.

PRICE RIGIDITY AND THE KINKED DEMAND CURVE

Let's hypothesize that the decision makers in an oligopolistic firm assume that rivals will react in the following way: They will match all price decreases (in order not to be undersold) but not price increases (because they want to capture more business). There is no collusion. The implications of this reaction function are rigid prices and a kinked demand curve for each firm.

Nature of the Kinked Demand Curve

In Figure 27-3 on page 646, we draw a kinked demand curve, which is implicit in the assumption that oligopolists match price decreases but not price increases. We start off in

FIGURE 27-3
The Kinked Demand Curve

If the oligopolist firm assumes that rivals will not match price changes, it faces demand curve d_1d_1 and marginal revenue curve MR_1. If it assumes that rivals will match price changes, it faces demand curve d_2d_2 and marginal revenue curve MR_2. If the oligopolist believes that rivals will not re-

act to price increases but will react to price decreases, at prices above P_0, it faces demand curve d_1d_1, and at prices below P_0, it faces the other demand curve, d_2d_2. The overall demand curve will therefore have a kink, as is seen in panel (b) at price P_0. The marginal revenue curve will have a vertical break, as shown by the dashed line in panel (b).

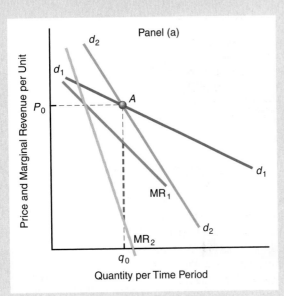

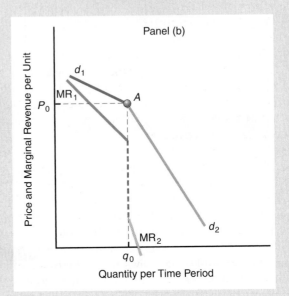

panel (a) at a given price of P_0 and assume that the quantity demanded at the price for this individual oligopolist is q_0. P_0 is usually the stable market price. If the oligopolist assumes that rivals will not react by matching a change in the price of its own product, it faces demand curve d_1d_1 with marginal revenue curve MR_1. Conversely, if it assumes that rivals will react to a change in the price of its product by matching the price change, it faces demand curve d_2d_2 with marginal revenue curve MR_2. More than likely, the oligopolist firm will assume that if it lowers price, rivals will react by matching that reduction to avoid losing their respective shares of the market. The oligopolist that initially lowers its price will not greatly increase its quantity demanded. So, when it lowers its price, it believes that it will face demand curve d_2d_2. But if it increases price above P_0, rivals will probably not follow suit. Thus a higher price than P_0 will cause quantity demanded to decrease rapidly. The demand schedule to the left of and above point A will be relatively elastic, as represented by d_1d_1. At prices above P_0, the relevant demand curve is d_1d_1, whereas below price P_0, the relevant demand curve will be d_2d_2. Consequently, at point A there will be a *kink* in the resulting demand curve. This is shown in panel (b) of Figure 27-3, where the demand curve is labeled d_1d_2. The resulting marginal revenue curve is labeled MR_1MR_2. It has a discontinuous portion, or gap, represented by the boldfaced dashed vertical lines in both panels.

Price Rigidity

The kinked demand curve analysis may help explain why price changes might be infrequent in an oligopolistic industry without collusion. Each oligopolist can see only harm in a price change: If price is increased, the oligopolist will lose many of its customers to rivals that do not raise their prices. That is to say, the oligopolist moves up from point A along demand curve d_1 in panel (b) of Figure 27-3. However, if an oligopolist lowers its price, given that rivals will lower their prices too, its sales will not increase very much. Moving down from point A in panel (b) of Figure 27-3, we see that the demand curve is relatively inelastic. If the elasticity is less than 1, total revenues will fall rather than rise with the lowering of price. Given that the production of a larger output will increase total costs, the oligopolist's profits will fall. The lowering of price by the oligopolist might start a *price war* in which its rival firms will charge an even lower price.

The theoretical reason for price inflexibility under the kinked demand curve model has to do with the discontinuous portion of the marginal revenue curve shown in panel (b) of Figure 27-3, which we reproduce in Figure 27-4. Assume that marginal cost is represented by MC. The profit-maximizing rate of output is q_0, which can be sold at a price of P_0. Now assume that the marginal cost curve shifts upward to MC$'$. What will happen to the profit-maximizing rate of output? Nothing. Both quantity and price will remain the same for this oligopolist.

Remember that the profit-maximizing rate of output is where marginal revenue equals marginal cost. The shift in the marginal cost curve to MC$'$ does not change the profit-maximizing rate of output in Figure 27-4 because MC$'$ still cuts the marginal revenue curve in the latter's discontinuous portion. Thus the equality between marginal revenue and marginal cost still holds at output rate q_0 even when the marginal cost curve shifts upward. What will happen when marginal costs fall to MC$''$? Nothing. This oligopolist will continue to produce at a rate of output q_0 and charge a price of P_0. Whenever the marginal cost curve cuts the discontinuous portion of the marginal revenue curve, fluctuations (within limits) in marginal cost will not affect output or price because the profit-maximizing condition MR $=$ MC will hold. The result is that even when firms in an oligopolistic industry such as this experience increases or decreases in costs, their prices do not change as long as MC cuts MR in the discontinuous portion. Hence prices are seen to be rigid in oligopolistic industries if oligopolists react the way we assume they do in this model.

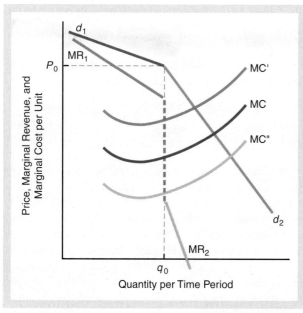

FIGURE 27-4
Changes in Cost May Not Alter the Profit-Maximizing Price and Output

As long as the marginal cost curve intersects the marginal revenue curve in the latter's discontinuous portion, the profit-maximizing price P_0 (and output q_0) will remain unchanged even with changes in MC. (However, the firm's rate of profit will change.)

Criticisms of the Kinked Demand Curve

One of the criticisms directed against the kinked demand curve is that we have no idea how the existing price, P_0, came to be. If every oligopolistic firm faced a kinked demand curve, it would not pay for the firm to change prices. The problem is that the kinked demand curve does not show us how demand and supply originally determine the going price of an oligopolist's product.

As far as the evidence goes, it is not encouraging. Oligopoly prices do not appear to be as rigid, particularly in the upward direction, as the kinked demand curve theory implies. During the 1970s and early 1980s, when prices in the economy were rising overall, oligopolistic producers increased their prices frequently. Evidence of price changes during the Great Depression showed that oligopolies changed prices much more frequently than monopolies.

CONCEPTS in Brief

- Each oligopolist has a reaction function because oligopolistic competitors are interdependent. They must therefore engage in strategic behavior. One way to model this behavior is to use game theory.

- Games can be either cooperative or noncooperative. A cartel is cooperative. When a cartel breaks down and its members start cheating, the industry becomes a noncooperative game. In a zero-sum game, one player's losses are exactly offset by another player's gains. In a negative-sum

game, all players collectively lose, perhaps one player more than the others. In a positive-sum game, the players as a group end up better off.

- Decision makers in oligopolistic firms must devise a strategy. A dominant strategy is one that is generally successful no matter what actions competitors take.

- The kinked demand curve oligopoly model predicts that major shifts in marginal cost will not cause any change in industry price.

To test your understanding of the concepts covered in this section, go to the Online Review at www.myeconlab.com/miller.

STRATEGIC BEHAVIOR WITH IMPLICIT COLLUSION: A MODEL OF PRICE LEADERSHIP

What if oligopolists do not actually collude to raise prices and share markets but do so implicitly? There are no formal cartel arrangements and no formal meetings. Nonetheless, there is *tacit collusion*. One example of this is the model of **price leadership.**

The Theory of Price Leadership

Price leadership
A practice in many oligopolistic industries in which the largest firm publishes its price list ahead of its competitors, who then match those announced prices. Also called *parallel pricing.*

In the theory of price leadership, the basic assumption is that the leading firm, usually the biggest, sets the price and allows other firms to sell all they can at that price. The dominant firm then sells the rest. The leading firm always makes the first move in a price leadership model.

By definition, price leadership requires that one firm be the leader. Because of laws against collusion, firms in an industry cannot communicate this directly. That is why it is often natural for the largest firm to become the price leader. In the automobile industry during the period of General Motors' market leadership (until the 1980s), that company was traditionally the price leader. At various times in the breakfast food industry, Kellogg was the price leader. Some observers have argued that Harvard University was once the price leader among Ivy League schools. In the banking industry, various leading banks have been price leaders in announcing changes in the prime rate, the interest rate charged on loans offered to the best credit risks. One day a large New York–based bank, such as Chase Manhattan, would announce an increase or decrease in its prime rate. Within five or six hours, all other banks would announce the same change in their prime rate.

Price Wars

Price leadership may not always work. If the price leader ends up much better off than the firms that follow, the followers may in fact not set prices according to those set by the leading firm. The result may be a **price war.** The leading firm lowers its prices a little bit, but the other firms lower theirs even more. Price wars have occurred in many industries. Supermarkets within a given locale often engage in price wars, especially during holiday periods. One may offer turkeys at so much per pound on Wednesday; competing stores cut their price on turkeys on Thursday, so the first store cuts its price even more on Friday.

How do you suppose that the rival to the top seller in the disposable diaper industry gained market share when it unexpectedly launched a price war?

Price war
A pricing campaign designed to capture additional market share by repeatedly cutting prices.

E X A M P L E

The Maker of Huggies Struggles to Absorb a Pampers Pricing Punch

In late 2001, Kimberly-Clark Corporation, which manufactures Huggies, the top-selling disposable diaper, quietly launched a plan to raise the price of its product. It left the price of a package of diapers unchanged but removed one diaper from each package, thereby effectively increasing the price per diaper by 5 percent. The company anticipated that Procter & Gamble, the manufacturer of Pampers and Luvs disposable diapers, would react by increasing its diaper prices as well.

Instead, Procter & Gamble responded by launching an unexpected price cut. Procter & Gamble reduced the price of Pampers by 15 percent. It also arranged with supermarket chains to provide purchasers of Huggies with coupons offering $5 off on their next purchase of disposable diapers—as long as they were Pampers instead of Huggies.

During the months that followed, Kimberly-Clark reversed its original strategy and embarked on its own set of steep price reductions. At the end of the great diaper price war, consumers were happier, and so was Procter & Gamble. Kimberly-Clark's share of disposable diaper sales had dropped from 46 to 43 percent, and Procter & Gamble's share had climbed from 33 to 38 percent.

For Critical Analysis
What do you suppose determined how much Procter & Gamble was willing to reduce the price of Pampers disposable diapers in its effort to sharply undercut the price of Huggies?

DETERRING ENTRY INTO AN INDUSTRY

Some economists believe that all decision making by existing firms in a stable industry involves some type of game playing. An important part of game playing does not have to do with how existing competitors might react to a decision by others. Rather, it has to do with how *potential* competitors might react. Strategic decision making requires that existing firms in an industry come up with strategies to deter entrance into that industry. One important way is, of course, to get a local, state, or federal government to restrict entry. Adopting certain pricing and investment strategies may also deter entry.

Increasing Entry Costs

One **entry deterrence strategy** is to raise the cost of entry by a new firm. The threat of a price war is one technique. To be able to sustain a long price war, existing firms might invest in excess capacity so that they can expand output if necessary. When existing firms invest in excess capacity, they are signaling potential competitors that they will engage in a price war.

Entry deterrence strategy
Any strategy undertaken by firms in an industry, either individually or together, with the intent or effect of raising the cost of entry into the industry by a new firm.

Another way that existing domestic firms can raise the entry cost of foreign firms is by getting the U.S. government to pass stringent environmental or health and safety standards. These typically raise costs more for foreign producers, often in developing countries, than for domestic producers.

Limit-Pricing Strategies

Sometimes existing firms will make it clear to potential competitors that the existing firms would not change their output rate if new firms were to enter the industry. Instead, the existing firms would simply lower the market price (moving down their demand curves) enough to sell the same quantity as they currently do. This new price would be below the level at which an entering firm could earn a normal profit, and that prospect effectively discourages entry. This is called the **limit-pricing model.**

Limit-pricing model
A model that hypothesizes that a group of colluding sellers will set the highest common price that they believe they can charge without new firms seeking to enter that industry in search of relatively high profits.

Raising Customers' Switching Costs

If an existing firm can make it more costly for customers to switch from its product or service to a competitor's, the existing firm can deter entry. Existing firms can raise customers' switching costs in a host of ways. Makers of computer equipment have in the past altered their operating systems and software products so that they would not operate on new competitors' computers. Any customer wanting to change from one computer system to another faced a high switching cost.

Why are there good reasons to question the common argument that switching costs help explain the configuration of computer keyboards?

EXAMPLE

Do QWERTY Keyboards Persist Because of High Switching Costs?

The design of your computer keyboard dates back to 1868, when Christopher Sholes patented the QWERTY layout for manual typewriters (the first six letters in the top row of letters are Q, W, E, R, T, Y). It was a strictly mechanical design decision—Sholes placed the keys most likely to be struck in sequence on opposite sides of the typewriter to reduce the chances that the type bars would jam.

In 1936, August Dvorak patented a different keyboard layout, which he claimed permitted more rapid typing without jamming. In spite of a U.S. Navy study concluding that the Dvorak system worked better, no one adopted it. For years since, a number of economists have argued that the QWERTY keyboard is a classic example of a product with switching costs too high to induce consumers to adopt a more efficient alternative.

There are, however, a couple of problems with this interpretation. One is that the Navy's study had a conflict-of-interest problem: It was directed by a lieutenant commander by the name of August Dvorak, the wartime Navy's top expert on laborsaving programs. Another is that careful studies in years since have shown that QWERTY's bad points for typing efficiency may well be outweighed by other benefits. This implies that typists may have simply adopted the better keyboard. Switching costs may not be such an important factor after all.

For Critical Analysis
Can you think of an item with high switching costs that may discourage consumers from purchasing an alternative product?

CONCEPTS in Brief

- One type of strategic behavior involving implicit collusion is price leadership. The dominant firm is assumed to set the price and then allows other firms to sell all that they want to sell at that price. Whatever is left over is sold by the dominant firm. The dominant firm always makes the first move in a price leadership model. If the nondominant firms decide to compete, they may start a price war.

- One strategic decision may be to attempt to raise the cost of entry of new firms into an industry. The threat of a price war is one technique. Another is to lobby the federal government to pass stringent environmental or health and safety standards in an attempt to keep out foreign competition.

- In a limit-pricing model, existing firms limit prices to a level above competitive prices before entry of new firms but are willing to reduce prices.

- Another way to raise the cost to new firms is to make it more costly for customers to switch from one product or service to a competitor's.

To test your understanding of the concepts covered in this section, go to the Online Review at www.myeconlab.com/miller.

NETWORK EFFECTS

A common source of switching costs is a shared understanding among consumers about how to use a product. Such a shared understanding can sometimes generate **network effects,** or situations in which a consumer's willingness to use an item depends on how many others use it. Commonplace examples are telephones and fax machines. Ownership of a phone or fax machine is not particularly useful if no one else has one, but once a number of people own a phone or fax machine, the benefits that others gain from consuming these devices increases.

In like manner, people who commonly work on joint projects within a network of fellow employees, consultants, or clients naturally find it useful to share computer files. Trading digital files is an easier process if all use common word processing and office productivity software. The benefit that each person receives from using word processing and office productivity software increases when others also use the same software.

Network effect
A situation in which a consumer's willingness to purchase a good or service is influenced by how many others also buy or have bought the item.

Network Effects and Market Feedback

On the one hand, industries in which firms produce goods or services subject to network effects can experience sudden surges in growth. On the other hand, the fortunes of such industries can also undergo significant and sometimes sudden reversals.

Positive Market Feedback. When network effects are an important characteristic of an industry's product, an industry can experience **positive market feedback.** This is the potential for a network effect to arise when an industry's product catches on with consumers. Increased use of the product by some consumers then induces other consumers to purchase the product as well.

Positive market feedback can affect the prospects of an entire industry. The market for Internet service provider (ISP) servers is an example. The growth of this industry has roughly paralleled the rapid growth of Internet servers worldwide. Undoubtedly, positive market feedback resulting from network effects associated with Internet communications and interactions resulted in additional people desiring to obtain access to the Internet.

Positive market feedback
A tendency for a good or service to come into favor with additional consumers because other consumers have chosen to buy the item.

Negative Market Feedback. Network effects can also result in **negative market feedback,** in which a speedy downward spiral of product sales occurs for a product subject to network effects. If a sufficient number of consumers cut back on their use of the product,

Negative market feedback
A tendency for a good or service to fall out of favor with more consumers because other consumers have stopped purchasing the item.

others are induced to reduce their consumption as well, and the product can rapidly become a "has-been."

An example of an industry that has experienced negative market feedback of late is the telecommunications industry. Traditional telecommunications firms such as AT&T, WorldCom, and Sprint experienced positive market feedback during the late 1980s and early 1990s as wireless phones and fax machines proliferated and individuals and firms began making long-distance phone calls from cell phones or via fax machines. Since the mid-1990s, as more people have acquired Internet access via local Internet service providers, e-mail communications and e-mail document attachments have supplanted large volumes of phone and fax communications. For the telecommunications industry, the greater use of e-mail and e-mail attachments by some individuals induced others to follow suit. This resulted in negative market feedback that reduced the overall demand for traditional long-distance phone services.

Network Effects and Industry Concentration

In some industries, a few firms can potentially reap most of the benefits of positive market feedback. Suppose that firms in an industry sell differentiated products that are subject to network effects. If the products of two or three firms catch on, these firms will capture the bulk of the sales due to industry network effects.

A good example is the market for online auction services. An individual is more likely to use the services of an auction site if there is a significant likelihood that many other potential buyers or sellers also trade items at that site. Hence there is a network effect present in the online auction industry, in which eBay, Amazon, and Yahoo account for more than 80 percent of total sales. eBay in particular has experienced positive market feedback, and its share of sales of online auction services has increased to more than 50 percent.

Consequently, in an industry that produces and sells products subject to network effects, a small number of firms may be able to secure the bulk of the payoffs resulting from positive market feedback. In such an industry, oligopoly is likely to emerge as the prevailing market structure.

CONCEPTS in Brief

- Network effects exist when a consumer's demand for an item depends in part on how many other consumers also use the product.

- Positive market feedback arises if consumption of a product by a sufficient number of individuals induces others to purchase it. Negative market feedback can take place if a

falloff in usage of a product by some consumers causes others to stop purchasing the item.

- In an industry with differentiated products subject to network effects, an oligopoly may arise if a few firms can reap most of the sales gains resulting from positive market feedback.

To test your understanding of the concepts covered in this section, go to the Online Review at www.myeconlab.com/miller.

COMPARING MARKET STRUCTURES

Now that we have looked at perfect competition, pure monopoly, monopolistic competition, and oligopoly, we are in a position to compare the attributes of these four different market structures. We do this in summary form in Table 27-3, in which we compare the number of sellers, their ability to set price, and the degree of product differentiation and also give some examples of each of the four market structures.

TABLE 27-3
Comparing Market Structures

Market Structure	Number of Sellers	Unrestricted Entry and Exit	Ability to Set Price	Long-Run Economic Profits Possible	Product Differentiation	Nonprice Competition	Examples
Perfect competition	Numerous	Yes	None	No	None	None	Agriculture, roofing nails
Monopolistic competition	Many	Yes	Some	No	Considerable	Yes	Toothpaste, toilet paper, soap, retail trade
Oligopoly	Few	Partial	Some	Yes	Frequent	Yes	Recorded music, college textbooks
Pure monopoly	One	No (for entry)	Considerable	Yes	None (product is unique)	Yes	Some electric companies, some local telephone companies

CASE STUDY: Economics Front and Center

Confronting the Temptation to Collude

Franz, the chief executive officer (CEO) of one of the two largest airline companies in a European nation, faces a dilemma. The CEO of the other predominant airline firm has called to let him know that European Union (EU) authorities charged with enforcing laws against cartels have launched an investigation of their firms. The EU officials suspect that the two companies, which together provide 90 percent of the air service among a few key European cities, have been collusively setting airfares on these routes.

In fact, Franz and the CEO of the other airline *have not* been colluding. The other CEO suggests, however, that perhaps the two companies should arrange a collusive agreement *after* the official investigation is over. At that time, the other CEO points out, the two airlines will be least subject to suspicion. If Franz chooses not to go along with this suggestion, the other CEO promises that her company will do whatever it takes—discounts or direct price cuts—to emerge as the dominant air link among the cities both companies serve. Franz, who had been reviewing bad news about his company's revenue prospects when he took this phone call, pauses to think about how to respond to her statements and consider his own response.

Points to Analyze

1. *In what type of game is Franz now a participant?*

2. *If Franz declines the other CEO's offer to collude, what alternative pricing strategy might he pursue?*

Oligopoly in the Ground-Shipping Business

Concepts Applied
- Concentration Ratio
- Horizontal Merger
- Strategic Dependence

The U.S. ground-shipping industry employs workers, trucks, and vans to transport more than 17 million packages each day. As you can see in Figure 27-5, only four firms—United Parcel Service (UPS), FedEx Ground, the U.S. Postal Service (USPS), and DHL—provide U.S. ground-shipping services. Thus the four-firm concentration ratio in this oligopolistic industry is 100 percent.

A Long-Concentrated Industry

There is nothing new about a 100 percent concentration ratio in the U.S. ground-shipping business. For years, the Interstate Commerce Commission granted only the USPS unhindered rights to ship small packages across state lines. Between the 1950s and 1970s, United Parcel launched a long series of legal actions that ultimately led to its current capability to transport packages on the ground to any address within the 48 contiguous U.S. states.

Until very recently, therefore, the ground-delivery industry had a *two-firm* concentration ratio of 100 percent. During a

1997 teamsters strike that brought UPS delivery services to a halt, FedEx completed a horizontal merger with Roadway Packages Services and launched FedEx Ground as a nationwide company. DHL has provided ground-shipping services since 2001.

Strategic Dependence and Competing on the Basis of Price per Constant-Quality Unit

As you learned in Chapter 3, people evaluate the price of an item per unit of constant quality of the product in question. This fact is particularly important to managers of the four

---

FIGURE 27-5
Shares of Sales Contributed by Firms in the Ground-Shipping Industry
There are only four firms in the U.S. market for transporting and delivering packages using ground vehicles, so the four-firm concentration ratio in this industry is 100 percent.

Source: U.S. Department of Commerce.

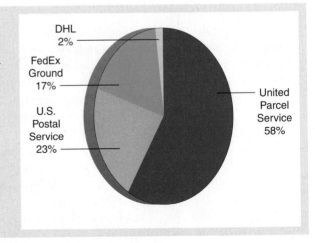

firms competing for business in the ground-shipping business, because customers often are very conscious of both delivery prices *and* delivery schedules. Each of the four firms knows that strategic dependence among the firms exists along both dimensions.

Nonunionized drivers at FedEx Ground function as independent contractors who have proved willing to deliver packages on Saturdays, when unionized USPS and UPS are closed. In an effort to counter this quality advantage possessed by FedEx Ground, the USPS has worked to shave about half a day off its speediest ground-delivery service.

UPS has implemented a streamlined system of networks linking tractor-trailer trucks and trains to move up promised delivery dates. These USPS and UPS schedule enhancements, in turn, set off a chain reaction at FedEx Ground and DHL, which in turn are involved in frenzied efforts to speed the pace of their ground-delivery services.

In this oligopoly, strategic dependence is visible on every major roadway, as drivers hustle their cargoes of packages in their daily efforts to reduce the price per constant-quality unit charged by their companies.

For Critical Analysis

1. Now that many governmentally erected barriers to entry in the ground-shipping business have fallen by the wayside, what entry barriers remain?
2. For some consumers, why might a $15 fee for delivering a package in four days effectively be higher than a $20 fee for getting it to the same location in three days?

Web Resources

1. Use the link at **www.econtoday.com/chap27** to learn more about how UPS ultimately broke down barriers to entry into the market for nationwide package deliveries.
2. Find out about the horizontal merger that created FedEx Ground at **www.econtoday.com/chap27**.

Research Project

Review the theories of oligopoly behavior discussed in this chapter, and discuss how each theory might potentially apply to the ground-shipping industry. Which theory do you feel is likely to best explain the strategic interactions among firms in this industry? Why?

SUMMARY DISCUSSION of Learning Objectives

1. **The Fundamental Characteristics of Oligopoly:** Economies of scale, certain barriers to entry, and horizontal mergers among firms that sell similar products can result in an oligopoly, a situation in which a few firms produce the bulk of an industry's total output. To measure the extent to which a few firms account for an industry's production and sales, economists calculate concentration ratios, which are the percentages of total sales or total production by the top handful of firms in an industry. Strategic dependence is an important characteristic of oligopoly. One firm's decisions concerning price, product quality, or advertising can bring about responses by other firms. Thus one firm's choices can affect the prices charged by other firms in the industry.

2. **Applying Game Theory to Evaluate the Pricing Strategies of Oligopolistic Firms:** Game theory is the analytical framework that economists apply to evaluate how two or more individuals, companies, or nations compete for payoffs that depend on the strategies that others employ. When firms get together to collude or form a cartel, they partici-

pate in cooperative games, but when they cannot work together, they engage in noncooperative games. One important type of game often applied to oligopoly situations is the prisoners' dilemma, in which the inability to cooperate in determining prices of their products can cause firms to choose lower prices than they otherwise would prefer.

3. **The Kinked Demand Theory of Oligopolistic Price Rigidity:** If an oligopolistic firm believes that no other firms selling similar products will raise their prices in response to an increase in the price of its product, it perceives the demand curve for its product to be relatively elastic at prices above the price it currently charges. At the same time, if the firm believes that all other firms would respond to a cut in the price of its product by reducing the prices of their products, it views the demand for its product as relatively inelastic at prices below the current price. Hence, in this situation, the firm perceives the demand for its product to be kinked, which means that its marginal revenue curve has a break at the current price. Changes in the firm's marginal cost will

therefore not necessarily induce the firm to change its production and pricing decisions, so price rigidity may result.

4. **How Firms May Deter Market Entry by Potential Rivals:** To strategically deter market entry by potential competitors, firms in an industry may seek to raise the entry costs that such potential rivals would face. For example, existing firms may invest in excess productive capacity to signal that they could outlast other firms in sustained price wars, or they might engage in lobbying efforts to forestall competition from potential foreign entrants into domestic markets. Existing firms may also engage in limit pricing, signaling to potential entrants that the entry of new rivals would cause them to reduce prices so low that entering the market is no longer economically attractive. Existing firms may also develop ways to make it difficult for current customers to switch to products produced by new entrants.

5. **Why Network Effects and Market Feedback Encourage Oligopoly:** Network effects arise when a consumer's demand for a good or service is affected by how many other consumers also use the item. There is positive market feedback when enough people consume a product to induce others to purchase it as well. Negative market feedback occurs when decreased purchases of a good or service by some consumers give others an incentive to stop buying the item. Oligopoly can develop in an industry with differentiated products subject to network effects because a few firms may be able to capture most growth in demand induced by positive market feedback.

KEY TERMS AND CONCEPTS

concentration ratio (640)

cooperative game (642)

dominant strategies (643)

entry deterrence strategy (649)

game theory (642)

horizontal merger (640)

limit-pricing model (650)

negative market feedback (651)

negative-sum game (643)

network effect (651)

noncooperative game (642)

oligopoly (638)

opportunistic behavior (645)

payoff matrix (644)

positive market feedback (651)

positive-sum game (643)

price leadership (648)

price war (649)

prisoners' dilemma (644)

reaction function (642)

strategic dependence (638)

strategy (643)

tit-for-tat strategic behavior (645)

vertical merger (640)

zero-sum game (643)

PROBLEMS

Answers to the odd-numbered problems appear at the back of the book.

27-1. Suppose that the distribution of sales within an industry is as shown in the table.

    a. What is the four-firm concentration ratio for this industry?

    b. What is the eight-firm concentration ratio for this industry?

Firm	Share of Total Market Sales
A	15%
B	14
C	12
D	11
E	10
F	10
G	8
H	7
All other	13
Total	100%

27-2. Suppose that the distribution of sales within an industry is as follows:

Firm	Share of Total Market Sales
A	25%
B	24
C	13
D	11
E	7
F	7
G	5
H	5
I	3
Total	100%

a. What is the four-firm concentration ratio for this industry?

b. What is the eight-firm concentration ratio for this industry?

27-3. Characterize each of the following as a positive-sum game, a zero-sum game, or a negative-sum game.

a. Office workers contribute $10 each to a pool of funds, and whoever best predicts the winners in a professional sports playoff wins the entire sum.

b. After three years of fighting with large losses of human lives and materiél, neither nation involved in a war is any closer to its objective than it was before the war began.

c. Two collectors who previously owned incomplete and nearly worthless sets of trading cards exchange several cards, and as a result both end up with completed sets with significant market value.

27-4. Characterize each of the following as a positive-sum game, a zero-sum game, or a negative-sum game.

a. You play a card game in your dorm room with three other students. Each player brings $5 to the game to bet on the outcome, winner take all.

b. Two nations exchange goods in a mutually beneficial transaction.

c. A thousand people buy $1 lottery tickets with a single payoff of $800.

27-5. Last weekend, Bob attended the university football game. At the opening kickoff, the crowd stood up. Bob therefore had to stand up as well to see the game. For the crowd (not the football team), explain the outcomes of a cooperative game and a noncooperative game. Explain what Bob's "tit-for-tat strategic behavior" would be.

27-6. One of the three shops on campus that sell university logo clothing has found that if it sells a sweatshirt for $30 or more, the other two shops keep their prices constant and the store loses revenues. If, however, the shop reduces its price below $30, the other stores react by lowering their prices. What kind of market structure does this store face? If the store's marginal costs fluctuate up and down very slightly, how should the store adjust its prices?

27-7. At the beginning of each semester, the university cafeteria posts the prices of its sandwiches. Business students note that as soon as the university posts these prices, the area delis adjust their prices accordingly. The business students argue that this is price collusion and that the university should be prosecuted for collusion. Are the students necessarily correct?

27-8. Explain why network effects can cause the demand for a product *either* to expand *or* to contract relative to what it would be if there were no network effects.

27-9. List three products that you think are subject to network effects. For each product, indicate whether, in your view, all or just a few firms within the industry that produces each product experience market feedback effects. In your view, are any market feedback effects in these industries currently positive or negative?

ECONOMICS ON THE NET

Current Concentration Ratios in U.S. Manufacturing Industries As you learned in this chapter, economists sometimes use concentration ratios to evaluate whether industries are oligopolies. In this application, you will make your own determination using the most recent data available.

Title: Concentration Ratios in Manufacturing

Navigation: Follow the link at www.econtoday.com/chap27 to get to the U.S. Census Bureau's report on Concentration Ratios in Manufacturing.

Application Answer the following questions.

1. Select the report for the most recent year. Find the four-firm concentration ratios for the following industries: fluid milk (311511), women's and girl's cut & sew dresses (315233), envelopes (322232), electronic computers (334111).

2. Which industries are characterized by a high level of competition? Which industries are characterized by a low level of competition? Which industries qualify as oligopolies?

3. Name some of the firms that operate in the industries that qualify as oligopolies.

For Group Study and Analysis Discuss whether the four-firm concentration ratio is a good measure of competition. Consider some of the firms you named in item 3. Do you consider these firms to be "competitive" in their pricing and output decisions? Consider the four-firm concentration ratio for ready-mix concrete (327320). Do you think that on a local basis, this industry is competitive? Why or why not?

Media Resources

If your exam were tomorrow, would you be ready? For each chapter, MyEconLab Practice Tests and Study Plans pinpoint which sections you have mastered and which ones you need to study. That way, you are more efficient with your study time, and you are better prepared for your exams.

In addition to Practice Tests and your personalized Study Plan, you'll find the following media resources in MyEconLab:

1. *Graphs in Motion* animation of Figure 27-4.
2. Videos featuring the author, Roger LeRoy Miller, on the following subjects:
   - Opportunistic Behavior
   - Price Leadership and Price Wars.

3. Links to the Web sites cited in the marginal Internet Resources, Issues and Applications feature, and Economics on the Net activity.
4. Audio clips of all key terms, additional practice problems, and a PDF version of the material from the print Study Guide.
5. eThemes of the Times, which is a New York Times article to help you understand the real-world applications of what you are learning.

To see how it works, turn to page 16 and then go to **www.myeconlab.com/miller**.

Get Ahead of the Curve

Chapter 28
Regulation and Antitrust Policy in a Globalized Economy

Every seat in the large room in a New York City building is taken, and a number of fashion models are present. So are writers for the world's major fashion magazines. These individuals have not come to view the latest clothing styles, however. Instead, they are attending a news conference highlighting the models' allegations of collusive price fixing by the top fashion-modeling agencies. At the same moment, just a few miles away, several grand juries convened by the U.S. Department of Justice are questioning owners and managers of several of these agencies. It will now be up to the courts to determine whether fashion-modeling agencies have violated U.S. antitrust laws, which, as you will learn in this chapter, are the cornerstone of the federal government's efforts to promote competition.

LEARNING OBJECTIVES

After reading this chapter, you should be able to:

1. Distinguish between economic regulation and social regulation
2. Recognize the practical difficulties in regulating the prices charged by natural monopolies
3. Explain the main rationales for regulation of industries that are not inherently monopolistic
4. Identify alternative theories aimed at explaining the behavior of regulators
5. Understand the foundations of antitrust laws and regulations
6. Discuss basic issues in enforcing antitrust laws.

Media Resources

Refer to the end of the chapter for a full listing of the multimedia learning materials available in MyEconLab.

Did You Know That . . . in the early 2000s, following intense lobbying from various advocacy groups, the U.S. Department of Agriculture (USDA) issued rules governing how large the majority of holes must be in each slice of Swiss cheese? Most holes in each slice, the USDA ruled, must be between three-eighths of an inch and thirteen-sixteenths of an inch in diameter. Furthermore, the USDA stated, "The cheese shall be properly set and shall possess well-developed round oval-shaped eyes that are uniformly distributed." These regulations are enforced by a team of USDA Swiss cheese overseers and graders. This group evaluates the holes in Swiss cheese using 22 different classifications, such as cabbage, collapsed, dull, dead, frog mouth, gassy, nesty, one-sided, underset, and uneven.

The Swiss cheese manufacturing industry is just one example of a U.S. industry that faces government regulations. Indeed, all U.S. firms are highly regulated. Consequently, how regulations and other forms of government oversight *should act* to promote greater economic efficiency and how they *actually act* are important topics for understanding how our economy works. Nevertheless, before you can begin your study of the economic effects of regulation, it is important to understand the various ways in which the government oversees the activities of U.S. businesses.

FORMS OF INDUSTRY REGULATION

The U.S. government began regulating social and economic activity early in the nation's history. The amount of government regulation began increasing in the twentieth century and has grown considerably since 1970. Figure 28-1 displays two common measures of regulation in the United States. Panel (a) shows regulatory spending by federal agencies

FIGURE 28-1
Regulation on the Rise
Panel (a) shows that federal government regulatory spending is about $30 billion per year today. State and local spending is not shown. As panel (b)

shows, the number of pages in the *Federal Register* per year rose from 1990 to 2000, dropped off somewhat, and then began to rise once more.

Sources: Institute for University Studies; *Federal Register*, various issues.

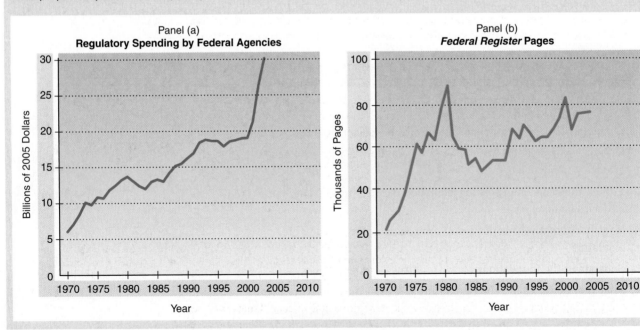

(in 2005 dollars), which has generally trended upward since 1970. Panel (b) depicts the number of pages in the *Federal Register*, a government publication that lists all new regulatory rules. According to this measure, the scope of new federal regulations increased sharply during the 1970s, dropped off in the 1980s, and has generally increased since then.

There are two basic types of government regulation. One is *economic regulation* of natural monopolies and of specific nonmonopolistic industries. For instance, some state commissions regulate the prices and quality of services provided by electric power companies, which are considered natural monopolies that experience lower long-run average costs as their output increases. Financial services industries and interstate transportation industries are examples of nonmonopolistic industries that are subjected to considerable government regulation. The other form of government regulation is *social regulation*, which covers all industries. Examples include various occupational, health, and safety rules that federal and state governments impose on most businesses.

Economic Regulation

Initially, most economic regulation in the United States was aimed at controlling prices in industries considered to be natural monopolies. Over time, federal and state governments have also sought to influence the characteristics of products or processes of firms in a variety of industries without inherently monopolistic features.

Regulation of Natural Monopolies. The regulation of natural monopolies has tended to emphasize restrictions on product prices. Various public utility commissions throughout the United States regulate the rates (prices) of electrical utility companies and some telephone operating companies. This *rate regulation*, as it is usually called, has been aimed at preventing such industries from earning monopoly profits.

Regulation of Nonmonopolistic Industries. The prices charged by firms in many other industries that do not have steadily declining long-run average costs, such as financial services industries, have also been subjected to regulations. Every state in the United States, for instance, has a government agency devoted to regulating the prices that insurance companies charge.

More broadly, government regulations establish rules pertaining to production, product (or service) features, and entry and exit within a number of specific nonmonopolistic industries. The federal government is heavily involved, for instance, in regulating the securities, banking, transportation, and communications industries. The Securities and Exchange Commission regulates securities markets. The Federal Reserve, Office of the Comptroller of the Currency, and Federal Deposit Insurance Corporation regulate commercial banks. The Office of Thrift Supervision regulates savings banks, and the National Credit Union Administration supervises credit unions. The Federal Aviation Administration supervises the airline industry, and the Federal Motor Carrier Safety Administration regulates the trucking industry. The Federal Communications Commission has oversight powers relating to broadcasting and telephone and communications services.

Social Regulation

In contrast to economic regulation, which covers only particular industries, social regulation applies to all firms in the economy. In principle, the aim of social regulation is a better quality of life through improved products, a less polluted environment, and better working conditions. Since the 1970s, an increasing array of government resources has been directed toward regulating product safety, advertising, and environmental effects. Table 28-1 on page 662 lists some major federal agencies involved in these broad regulatory activities.

TABLE 28-1
Federal Agencies Engaged in Social Regulation

Agency	Jurisdiction	Date Formed	Major Regulatory Functions
Federal Trade Commission (FTC)	Product markets	1914	Is responsible for preventing businesses from engaging in misleading advertising, unfair trade practices, and monopolistic actions, as well as for protecting consumer rights.
Food and Drug Administration (FDA)	Food and pharmaceuticals	1927	Regulates the quality and safety of foods, health and medical products, pharmaceuticals, cosmetics, and animal feed.
Equal Employment Opportunity Commission (EEOC)	Labor markets	1964	Investigates complaints of discrimination based on race, religion, sex, or age in hiring, promotion, firing, wages, testing, and all other conditions of employment.
Environmental Protection Agency (EPA)	Environment	1970	Develops and enforces environmental standards for air, water, toxic waste, and noise.
Occupational Safety and Health Administration (OSHA)	Health and safety	1970	Regulates workplace safety and health conditions.
Consumer Product Safety Commission (CPSC)	Consumer product safety	1972	Is responsible for protecting consumers from products posing fire, electrical, chemical, or mechanical hazards or dangers to children.

The essential objectives of social regulation are to protect people from incompetent or unscrupulous producers. The *potential* benefits of more social regulations are many. For example, the water supply in some cities is known to be contaminated with cancer-causing chemicals, and air pollution that contribute to many illnesses. Society would clearly benefit from cleaning up these pollutants. As we shall discuss, however, broad social regulations also entail costs that we all pay, and not just as taxpayers who fund the regulatory activities of agencies such as those listed in Table 28-1.

CONCEPTS in Brief

- Economic regulation applies to specific industries, whereas social regulation applies to businesses throughout the economy.

- Governments commonly regulate the prices and quality of services provided by electric, gas, and other utilities, which are commonly considered natural monopolies. Govern-

ments also single out various nonmonopolistic industries, such as the financial and transportation industries, for special forms of economic regulation.

- Among the common forms of social regulation covering all industries are the occupational, health, and safety rules that federal and state governments impose on producers.

To test your understanding of the concepts covered in this section, go to the Online Review at **www.myeconlab.com/miller.**

REGULATING NATURAL MONOPOLIES

At one time, the major thrust of government regulation of business was directed at dealing generally with the so-called monopoly problem. Of particular concern to governments was the creation of appropriate regulations for natural monopolies.

Natural Monopolies Revisited

You will recall from Chapter 25 that a natural monopoly arises whenever a single firm has the ability to produce all of an industry's output at a lower per-unit cost than other firms attempting to produce less than the total industry. Natural gas and electric utilities are possible examples of industries in which firms' long-run average costs fall as output increases. In a natural monopoly, economies of large-scale production dominate, leading to a single-firm industry.

The Pricing and Output Decisions of the Natural Monopolist. Like any other firm, a natural monopolist will select an output rate at which marginal revenue equals marginal cost. Panel (a) of Figure 28-2 depicts a situation in which a monopoly firm faces the

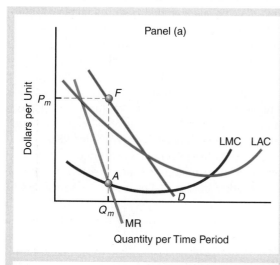

Panel (a)

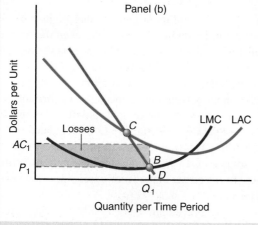

Panel (b)

FIGURE 28-2

Profit Maximization and Regulation Through Marginal Cost Pricing

The profit-maximizing natural monopolist here would produce at the point in panel (a) where marginal costs equal marginal revenue—that is, at point A, which gives the quantity of production Q_m. The price charged would be P_m at point F, which is the price consumers would be willing to pay for the quantity produced. If a regulatory commission attempted to regulate natural monopolies so that price equaled long-run marginal cost, the commission would make the monopolist set production at the point where the marginal cost curve intersects the demand schedule. This is shown in panel (b). The quantity produced would be Q_1, and the price would be P_1. However, average costs at Q_1 are equal to AC_1. Losses would ensue, equal to the shaded area. It would be self-defeating for a regulatory commission to force a natural monopolist to produce at an output rate at which MC $= P$ without subsidizing some of its costs because losses would eventually drive the natural monopolist out of business.

market demand curve, *D*, and the marginal revenue curve, MR. The intersection of the marginal revenue curve and the long-run marginal cost curve, LMC, is at point *A*. The unregulated monopolist would therefore produce the quantity Q_m and charge the price P_m.

What can we say about the monopolist's solution to the price-quantity question? We know that consumers end up paying a higher price for the product than they would in a perfectly competitive situation. At this higher price, consumers buy less than they would purchase under perfect competition. Thus the monopoly situation is economically inefficient from society's point of view. The price charged for the product is higher than the opportunity cost to society, and consequently there is a misallocation of resources. That is, the price P_m does not equal the true marginal cost of producing the item because the true marginal cost is found at point *A*.

Regulating the Natural Monopolist: The Problem of Marginal Cost Pricing. Let's assume that the government wants the natural monopolist to produce at an output at which price equals marginal cost. This outcome, the government recognizes, would ensure that the value of the satisfaction that individuals receive from the last unit produced and purchased is just equal to the marginal cost to society.

Where is that particular solution in panel (b) of Figure 28-2? It is at the intersection of the marginal cost curve and the demand curve, which is point *B*. Recall that the efficient, perfectly competitive output arises when price equals marginal cost. If a regulatory commission requires the natural monopolist to engage in marginal cost pricing by producing the quantity Q_1 and selling the product at the price P_1 at point *B*, how large will the firm's profits be? Profits, of course, are a *positive* difference between total revenues and total costs. In this case, total revenues equal P_1 times Q_1, and total costs equal average cost times the number of units produced. At Q_1, average cost equals AC_1. Average costs, therefore, are higher than the price that the regulatory commission requires the natural monopolist to charge. In this regulatory environment, the firm will earn *negative* economic profits. It sustains economic *losses* equal to the shaded area in panel (b) of Figure 28-2.

Thus regulation that forces a natural monopolist to produce and price as if it were a perfectly competitive firm will also force that monopolist into negative profits, or losses. Obviously, the monopolist would rather go out of business than be subject to such regulation.

Practical Regulation of Natural Monopolies

As a practical matter, regulators cannot force a natural monopolist to engage in marginal cost pricing. Consequently, regulation of natural monopolies has often taken the form of allowing the regulated natural monopolist to set price where LAC intersects the demand curve *D*, which is at point *C* in panel (b) of Figure 28-2. This is called *average cost pricing*. Average cost includes what the regulators deem a "fair" rate of return on investment.

Cost-of-service regulation
Regulation that allows prices to reflect only the actual cost of production and no monopoly profits.

Two conventional methods of natural-monopoly regulation aimed at achieving an average-cost-pricing outcome have been cost-of-service regulation and rate-of-return regulation. A regulatory commission using **cost-of-service regulation** allows regulated utility companies to charge only prices reflecting the actual average cost of providing services to consumers. In a somewhat similar vein, some regulatory commissions use **rate-of-return regulation,** which allows regulated firms to set prices that ensure a normal, or competitive, rate of return on investment in the business.

Rate-of-return regulation
Regulation that seeks to keep the rate of return in an industry at a competitive level by not allowing prices that would produce economic profits.

How might cost-of-service and rate-of-return regulation potentially contribute to a higher probability of big power failures?

Policy E X A M P L E

How Utility Pricing Regulations May Lead to Power Outages

During the weeks and months following the widespread power blackout affecting millions of people in the Northeast and Midwest on August 14, 2003, regulators of public utilities began to rethink their methods of regulating electricity prices. In many locales, regulators using cost-of-service and rate-of-return regulation had allowed utilities to recover costs of past investments only if the utilities agreed to freeze current prices. To keep their current prices low and earn sufficient revenues to cover their current total costs of providing power, utilities had to keep a lid on costs. One way they did this was by cutting back on equipment maintenance and tree

trimming near power lines—both of which were found to have contributed to the big August 2003 blackout. In this way, methods of regulating utilities' prices may expose the nation's electricity grid to a greater risk of local breakdowns or, in rare cases, to more widespread blackouts.

For Critical Analysis
Why might managers of an electric utility determine that it is in the interests of the company's owners to allow some of its equipment to wear out?

CONCEPTS in Brief

- A natural monopoly arises when one firm can produce all of an industry's output at a lower per-unit cost than other firms.

- A natural monopolist that is allowed to maximize profit will produce output to the point at which marginal revenue equals long-run marginal cost; it charges the price that people are willing to pay for that quantity produced.

- A natural monopolist that is forced to set price equal to long-run marginal cost will sustain losses, an outcome that

often leads regulators to allow natural monopolists to charge prices that just cover their average costs or provide a normal rate of return.

- Cost-of-service regulation permits a natural monopoly to charge prices based on its actual cost of production and no monopoly profits. Rate-of-return regulation requres charging prices that yield a rate of return consistent with zero economic profits.

To test your understanding of the concepts covered in this section, go to the Online Review at **www.myeconlab.com/miller.**

REGULATING NONMONOPOLISTIC INDUSTRIES

Traditionally, a fundamental purpose of governments has been to provide a coordinated system of safeguarding the interests of their citizens. Not surprisingly, protecting consumer interests is the main rationale offered for governmental regulatory functions.

Rationales for Consumer Protection in Nonmonopolistic Industries

The Latin phrase *caveat emptor*, or "let the buyer beware," was once the operative principle in most consumer dealings with businesses. The phrase embodies the idea that the buyer alone is ultimately responsible for assessing a producer and the quality of the items it sells before agreeing to purchase the firm's product. Today, various federal agencies require companies to meet specific minimal standards in their dealings with consumers. For instance, a few years ago, the U.S. Federal Trade Commission assessed monetary penalties on Toys "R" Us and KB Toys because they failed to ship goods sold on their Web sites in time for a pre-Christmas delivery. Such a government action would have been unheard of a few decades ago.

In some industries, federal agencies dictate the rules of the game for firms' interactions with consumers. The Federal Aviation Administration (FAA), for example, oversees virtually every aspect of the delivery of services by airline companies. The FAA regulates the process by which tickets for flights are sold and distributed, oversees all flight operations, and even establishes rules governing the procedures for returning luggage after flights are concluded.

Reasons for Government-Orchestrated Consumer Protection.

Two rationales are commonly advanced for heavy government involvement in overseeing and supervising nonmonopolistic industries. One, which you encountered in Chapter 5, is the possibility of *market failures*. For example, the presence of negative externalities such as pollution may induce governments to regulate industries that create such externalities.

The second common rationale is *asymmetric information*. In the context of many producer-consumer interactions, this term refers to situations in which a producer has information about a product that the consumer lacks. For instance, administrators of your college or university may know that another school in your vicinity offers better-quality degree programs in certain fields. If so, it would not be in your college or university's interest to transmit this information to applicants who are interested in pursuing degrees in those fields.

For certain products, asymmetric information problems can pose special difficulties for consumers trying to assess product quality in advance of purchase. In unregulated financial markets, for example, individuals contemplating buying a company's stock, a municipality's bond, or a bank's certificate of deposit might struggle to assess the associated risks of financial loss. If the air transportation industry were unregulated, a person might have trouble determining if one airline's planes were considerably less safe than those of competing airlines. In an unregulated market for pharmaceuticals, parents might worry about whether one company's childhood-asthma medication could have more dangerous side effects than medications sold by other firms.

Asymmetric Information and Product Quality.

In extreme cases, asymmetric information can create situations in which most of the available products are of low quality. A commonly cited example is the market for used automobiles. Current owners of cars that *appear* to be in good condition know the autos' service records. Some owners know that their cars have been well maintained and really do run great. Others, however, have not kept their autos in good repair and thus are aware that they will be susceptible to greater-than-normal mechanical or electrical problems.

Suppose that in your local used-car market, half of all used cars offered for sale are high-quality autos. The other half are low-quality cars, commonly called "lemons," that are likely to break down within a few months or perhaps even weeks. In addition, suppose that a consumer is willing to pay $20,000 for a particular car model if it is in excellent condition but is willing to pay only $10,000 if it is a lemon. Finally, suppose that people who own truly high-quality used cars are only willing to sell at a price of at least $20,000, but people who own lemons are willing to sell at any price at or above $10,000.

Because there is a 50–50 chance that a given car up for sale is of either quality, the average amount that a prospective buyer is willing to pay equals $(\frac{1}{2} \times \$20,000) + (\frac{1}{2} \times \$10,000) = \$15,000$. Owners of low-quality used cars are willing to sell them at this price, but owners of high-quality used cars are not. In this example, only lemons will be traded in the used-car market because most owners of cars in excellent condition will not sell their cars at a price that prospective buyers are willing to pay.

Lemons problem
The potential for asymmetric information to bring about a general decline in product quality in an industry.

The Lemons Problem.

Economists refer to the possibility that asymmetric information can lead to a general reduction in product quality in an industry as the **lemons problem.** This problem does not apply only to the used-car industry. In principle, any product with qualities that are difficult for consumers to fully assess is susceptible to the same problem. *Credence* *goods*, which as you learned in Chapter 26 are items such as pharmaceuticals, health care, and professional services, also may be particularly vulnerable to the lemons problem.

Market Solutions to the Lemons Problem. Firms offering truly high-quality products for sale can address the lemons problem in a variety of ways. They can offer product guarantees and warranties. In addition, to help consumers separate high-quality producers from incompetent or unscrupulous competitors, the high-quality producers may work together to establish industry standards.

In some cases, firms in an industry may even seek external product certification. They may, for example, solicit scientific reports supporting proposed industry standards and bearing witness that products of certain firms in the industry meet those standards. To legitimize a product-certification process, firms may hire outside companies or groups to issue such reports.

Implementing Consumer Protection Regulation

Governments offering asymmetric information and lemons problems as rationales for regulation presumably have concluded that private market solutions such as warranties, industry standards, and product certification are insufficient. To meet this perceived need, governments may offer legal remedies to consumers or enforce licensing requirements in an effort to provide minimum product standards. In some cases, governments go well beyond simple licensing requirements by establishing a regulatory apparatus for overseeing all aspects of an industry's operations.

Liability Laws and Government Licensing. Sometimes liability laws, which specify penalties for product failures, provide consumers with protections similar to guarantees and warranties. When the Federal Trade Commission (FTC) charged Toys "R" Us and KB Toys with failing to meet pre-Christmas delivery dates for Internet toy orders, it operated under a mail-order statute Congress passed in the early 1970s. The mail-order law effectively made the toy companies' delivery guarantees legally enforceable. Although the FTC applied the law in this particular case, any consumer could have filed suit for damages under the terms of the statute.

Federal and state governments also get involved in consumer protection by issuing licenses granting only qualifying firms the legal right to produce and sell certain products. For instance, in an effort to ensure that bodies of deceased individuals are handled with care and dignity, governments of nearly half of the states give only people who have a mortuary license or licensed funeral directors the right to sell caskets.

Although government licensing may successfully limit the sale of low-quality goods, licensing requirements also often limit the number of providers. As you learned in Chapter 25, this can ease efforts by established firms to search for the profit-maximizing price, thereby enabling them to act as monopolists. In addition, if governments rely on the expertise of established firms for assistance in drafting licensing requirements, these firms may have strong incentives to recommend low standards for themselves but high standards for prospective entrants.

Direct Economic and Social Regulation. In some instances, governments determine that liability laws and licensing requirements are insufficient to protect the interests of consumers. A government may decide that lemons problems in banking are so severe that without an extensive banking regulatory apparatus, consumers will lose confidence in banks, and bank runs may ensue. It may rely on similar rationales to establish economic regulation of other financial services industries. Eventually, it may apply consumer

Go to www.econtoday.com/chap28 to see how the Federal Trade Commission imposes regulations intended to protect consumers.

protection rationales to justify the economic regulation of other industries such as trucking or air transportation.

The government may establish an oversight authority to make certain that consumers are protected from incompetent producers of foods and pharmaceuticals. Eventually, the government may determine that a host of other products should meet government consumer protection standards. It may also decide that the people who produce the products also require government agencies to ensure workplace safety. In this way, social regulation emerges, as it has in the United States and most other developed nations.

CONCEPTS in Brief

- Governments tend to regulate industries in which they think market failures and asymmetric information problems are most severe.

- A common justification for government regulation is to protect consumers from adverse effects of asymmetric information.

- To address the lemons problem, or the potential for low-quality products to predominate when asymmetric information is widespread, governments often supplement private firms' guarantees, warranties, and certification standards with liability laws and licensing requirements.

To test your understanding of the concepts covered in this section, go to the Online Review at www.myeconlab.com/miller.

INCENTIVES AND COSTS OF REGULATION

Abiding by government regulations is a costly undertaking for firms. Consequently, businesses engage in a number of activities intended to avoid the true intent of regulations or to bring about changes in the regulations that government agencies establish.

Creative Response and Feedback Effects: Results of Regulation

Creative response
Behavior on the part of a firm that allows it to comply with the letter of the law but violate the spirit, significantly lessening the law's effects.

Sometimes firms respond to a regulation in a way that conforms to the letter of the law but undermines its spirit. When they do so, they engage in **creative response** to regulations.

Consider state laws requiring male-female pay equity: The wages of women must be on a par with those paid to males who are performing the same tasks. Employers that pay the same wages to both males and females are clearly not in violation of the law. Yet wages are only one component of total employee compensation. Another component is fringe benefits, such as on-the-job training. Because on-the-job training is difficult to observe from outside the firm, employers could offer less on-the-job training to women and still not be in technical violation of pay-equity laws. This unobservable difference would mean that males were able to acquire skills that could raise their future income even though males and females were receiving the same current wages, in compliance with the law.

One type of creative response has been labeled a *feedback effect*. Individuals' behaviors may change after a regulation has been put into effect. If regulation requires fluoridated water, then parents know that their children's teeth have significant protection against tooth decay. Consequently, the feedback effect is that parents become less concerned about how many sweets their children eat.

Explaining Regulators' Behavior

Those charged with enforcing government regulations operate outside the market, so their decisions are determined by nonmarket processes. A number of theories have emerged to describe the behavior of regulators. These theories explain how regulation can harm consumers by generating higher prices and fewer product choices while benefiting producers by reducing competitive forces and allowing higher profits. Two of the best-known theories of regulatory behavior are the *capture hypothesis* and the *share-the-gains, share-the-pains theory.*

The Capture Hypothesis. Regulators often end up becoming champions of the firms they are charged with regulating. According to the **capture hypothesis,** regardless of why a regulatory agency was originally established, eventually special interests of the industry it regulates will capture it. After all, the people who know the most about a regulated industry are the people already in the industry. Thus people who have been in the industry and have allegiances and friendships with others in the industry will most likely be asked to regulate the industry.

According to the capture hypothesis, individual consumers of a regulated industry's products and individual taxpayers who finance a regulatory agency have interests too diverse to be greatly concerned with the industry's actions. In contrast, special interests of the industry are well organized and well defined. These interests also have more to offer political entrepreneurs within a regulatory agency, such as future employment with one of the regulated firms. Therefore, regulators have a strong incentive to support the position of a well-organized special-interest group within the regulated industry.

Why do you suppose that Philip Morris, the cigarette manufacturer, has been *seeking* regulatory oversight by the U.S. Food and Drug Administration?

Capture hypothesis
A theory of regulatory behavior that predicts that regulators will eventually be captured by special interests of the industry being regulated.

E X A M P L E

Why This Cigarette Manufacturer Wants to Be Regulated

During the 1990s, the Food and Drug Administration (FDA) launched preliminary efforts to convince Congress to grant the FDA the power to regulate the manufacture and sale of cigarettes. FDA officials argued that it should have this power because nicotine, a key ingredient in cigarettes, is an addictive drug. Initially, tobacco companies unanimously responded by denying that nicotine is addictive.

By 2003, however, one company, Philip Morris, had completely reversed its position. This manufacturer of the top-selling cigarette brand, Marlboro, began *lobbying* to be regulated by the FDA. Regulation, the company decided, would improve the public image of cigarettes. After all, if the company

could market cigarettes with "FDA Approved" printed on the package, more people might be willing to consume cigarettes. In addition, the company reasoned, a pro-regulation position would help it gain favorable treatment from regulators if cigarette manufacturing does eventually become a regulated industry. Favorable treatment from regulators might, in turn, cement Marlboro's position as the number one cigarette brand.

For Critical Analysis
Why might a firm or industry that is particularly cooperative with its regulators have a good chance of "capturing" its regulators?

"Share the Gains, Share the Pains." The **share-the-gains, share-the-pains theory** offers a somewhat different view of regulators' behavior. This theory focuses on the specific aims of regulators. It proposes that a regulator's main objective is simply to continue in the position. To do so, the regulator must obtain the approval of both the legislators who originally established and continue to oversee the regulatory agency and the regulated industry. The regulator must also take into account the views of the industry's customers.

In contrast to the capture hypothesis, which holds that regulators must take into account only industry special interests, the share-the-gains, share-the-pains theory contends that

Share-the-gains, share-the-pains theory
A theory of regulatory behavior that holds that regulators must take account of the demands of three groups: legislators, who established and oversee the regulatory agency; firms in the regulated industry; and consumers of the regulated industry's products.

Economics Front and Center

To contemplate how the alternative theories of regulator behavior might apply in a real-world situation, read the case study, **Time to Take a Stand on Utility Rates,** on page 677.

regulators must worry about legislators and consumers as well. After all, if industry customers who are hurt by improper regulation complain to legislators, the regulators might lose their jobs. Whereas the capture theory predicts that regulators will quickly allow electric utilities to raise their rates in the face of higher fuel costs, the share-the-gains, share-the-pains theory predicts a slower, more measured regulatory response. Ultimately, regulators will permit an increase in utility rates, but the allowed adjustment will not be as speedy or complete as predicted by the capture hypothesis. The regulatory agency is not completely captured by the industry; it also has to consider the views of consumers and legislators.

The Benefits and Costs of Regulation

As noted earlier, regulation offers many *potential* benefits. *Actual* benefits, however, are difficult to measure. Putting a dollar value on safer products, a cleaner environment, and better working conditions is a difficult proposition. Furthermore, the benefits of most regulations accrue to society over a long time.

The Direct Costs of Regulation to Taxpayers.
Measuring the costs of regulation is also a challenging undertaking. After all, about 4,500 new federal regulations are issued each year. One cost, though, is certain: U.S. taxpayers pay about $30 billion per year to staff regulatory agencies with more than 190,000 employees and to fund their various activities. Figure 28-3 displays the distribution of total federal government outlays for economic and social regulation of various areas of the economy.

The *total* cost of regulation is much higher than just the explicit government outlays to fund the administration of various regulations, however. After all, businesses must expend resources complying with regulations, developing creative responses to regulations, and funding special-interest lobbying efforts directed at legislators and regulatory officials. Sometimes companies find that it is impossible to comply with one regulation without violating another, and determining how to avoid the resulting legal entanglements can entail significant expenditures.

The Total Social Cost of Regulation.
According to the Office of Management and Budget, annual expenditures that U.S. businesses must make solely to comply with regulations issued by various federal agencies amount to between $500 billion and $600 billion per

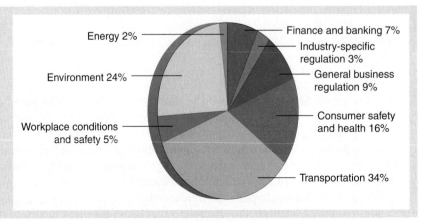

FIGURE 28-3
The Distribution of Federal Regulatory Spending
This figure shows the areas of the economy to which about $30 billion of taxpayer-provided funds are distributed to finance economic and social regulation.

Source: Office of Management and Budget.

Energy 2%
Finance and banking 7%
Industry-specific regulation 3%
Environment 24%
General business regulation 9%
Consumer safety and health 16%
Workplace conditions and safety 5%
Transportation 34%

year. Nevertheless, this estimate encompasses only explicit costs of satisfying regulatory demands placed on businesses. It ignores relevant opportunity costs. After all, owners, managers, and employees of companies could be doing other things with their time and resources than complying with regulations. Economists estimate that the opportunity costs of complying with federal regulations may be as high as $270 billion per year.

All told, therefore, the total social cost associated with satisfying federal regulations in the United States is probably between $800 billion and $900 billion per year. This figure, of course, applies only to federal regulations. It does not include the explicit and implicit opportunity costs associated with regulations issued by 50 different state governments and thousands of municipalities. Undoubtedly, the annual cost of regulation throughout the United States exceeds $1 trillion per year.

Why do you suppose that it is so important to the federal government—and taxpayers—to determine whether having outside experts review proposed federal regulations raises or lowers the regulations' benefits and costs?

Policy EXAMPLE

Peer Review and the Benefits and Costs of Federal Regulations

When a professor or scientist seeks to publish an article detailing an idea or discovery in a professional journal, the editors of the journal normally send the paper to qualified researchers in the relevant field. These outside "peer reviewers" determine if the suggested idea or discovery is really based on sound reasoning and evidence.

The Office of Management and Budget (OMB) has proposed extending the idea of peer reviews to suggested new regulations. Under this proposal, if a regulatory body—for instance, the Consumer Product Safety Commission (CPSC)—wished to impose a new regulation, it could not go into effect until a peer review had been completed by scientists outside the government.

The government would have to pay the scientists to compensate them for their time and effort in conducting the peer review. OMB officials argue, however, that the overall result would be greater social benefits achieved at a lower total cost to the government and businesses. On the one hand, a peer review approving the new CPSC regulation might offer suggestions for improvement that could make it more beneficial to society at a lower total cost. On the other hand, if the peer review dissuaded the CPSC from adopting the proposed regulation, then each year thereafter the government would not have to use tax dollars to implement it, nor would firms have to incur costs to comply.

For Critical Analysis
Why might proponents of a new CPSC regulation concerning, for example, infant toy safety regard the time spent conducting a detailed peer review as a factor that could reduce the proposed regulation's social benefit?

CONCEPTS in Brief

● The capture hypothesis holds that regulatory agencies will eventually be captured by industry special interests because consumers individually are not greatly influenced by regulation, whereas regulated firms are directly affected.

● According to the share-the-gains, share-the-pains theory of regulation, regulators must take into account the interests of three groups: the industry, legislators, and consumers.

● Regulation has benefits that are difficult to quantify in dollars. The costs of regulation include direct government expenditures on regulatory agencies and firms' explicit and implicit opportunity costs of complying.

To test your understanding of the concepts covered in this section, go to the Online Review at www.myeconlab.com/miller.

ANTITRUST POLICY

An expressed aim of the U.S. government is to foster competition. To this end, Congress has made numerous attempts to legislate against business practices it has perceived to be anticompetitive. This is the general idea behind antitrust legislation. If the courts can prevent collusion among sellers of a product, there will be no restriction of output, and monopoly prices will not result. Instead, the perfectly competitive solution to the price-quantity problem will emerge: The competitive output will prevail in each industry, producers will earn zero economic profits in the long run, and the price of each item will equal its marginal social opportunity cost.

Antitrust Policy in the United States

Congress has enacted four key antitrust laws, which Table 28-2 summarizes. The most important of these is the original U.S. antitrust law, called the Sherman Act.

The Sherman Antitrust Act of 1890. The Sherman Antitrust Act, which was passed in 1890, was the first attempt by the federal government to control the growth of monopoly in the United States. The most important provisions of that act are as follows:

TABLE 28-2
Key U.S. Antitrust Laws

Sherman Antitrust Act of 1890	Forbids any contract, combination, or conspiracy to restrain trade or commerce within the United States or across U.S. borders. Holds any person who attempts to monopolize trade or commerce criminally liable.
Clayton Act of 1914	Prohibits specific business practices deemed to restrain trade or commerce. Bans discrimination in prices charged to various purchasers when price differences are not due to actual differences in selling or transportation costs. Also forbids a company from selling goods on the condition that the purchaser must deal exclusively with that company. In addition, prevents corporations from holding stock in other companies when this may lessen competition.
Federal Trade Commission Act of 1914 (and 1938 Amendment)	Outlaws business practices that reduce the extent of competition, such as cutthroat pricing intended to drive rivals from the marketplace. Also established the Federal Trade Commission and empowered it to issue cease and desist orders in situations where it determines "unfair methods of competition in commerce" exist. The 1938 amendment added deceptive business practices to the list of illegal acts.
Robinson-Patman Act of 1936	Bans selected discriminatory price cuts by chain stores that allegedly drive smaller competitors from the marketplace. In addition, forbids price discrimination through special concessions in the form of price or quantity discounts, free advertising, or promotional allowances granted to one buyer but not to others, if these actions substantially reduce competition.

Regulation and Antitrust Policy in a Globalized Economy **673**

Section 1: Every contract, combination in the form of a trust or otherwise, or conspiracy, in restraint of trade or commerce among the several states, or with foreign nations, is hereby declared to be illegal.

Section 2: Every person who shall monopolize, or attempt to monopolize, or combine or conspire with any other person or persons to monopolize any part of the trade or commerce . . . shall be guilty of a misdemeanor.*

Notice how vague this act really is. No definition is given for the terms *restraint of trade* or *monopolize*. Despite this vagueness, however, the act was used to prosecute the infamous Standard Oil Trust of New Jersey. This company was charged with and convicted of violations of Sections 1 and 2 of the Sherman Antitrust Act in 1906. At the time it controlled more than 80 percent of the nation's oil-refining capacity. In addressing the company's legal appeal, the U.S. Supreme Court ruled that Standard Oil's predominance in the oil market created "a *prima facie* presumption of intent and purpose to control and maintain dominancy . . . not as a result from normal methods of industrial development, but by means of combinations." Here the word *combination* meant entering into associations and preferential arrangements with the intent of restraining competition. The Supreme Court forced Standard Oil of New Jersey to break up into many smaller companies that would have no choice but to compete.

The Sherman Act applies today just as it did more than a century ago. In June 2001, the federal Court of Appeals in the District of Columbia determined that Microsoft Corporation had violated the Sherman Act. The court ruled that Microsoft had engaged in anticompetitive conduct in an effort to monopolize the market for operating systems for personal computers. Initially, the U.S. Justice Department proposed a Standard Oil–style remedy: splitting Microsoft into several companies. Ultimately, however, Microsoft reached a settlement that kept the company intact but required it to alter many of its business practices.

For updates on various antitrust cases currently in progress, go to the "Antitrust.org" Web site operated by Alston and Bird, a major U.S. law firm, via the link available at www.econtoday.com/chap28.

Other Important Antitrust Legislation.

Table 28-2 lists three other important antitrust laws. In 1914, Congress passed the Clayton Act to clarify some of the vague provisions of the Sherman Act by identifying specific business practices that were to be legally prohibited.

Congress also passed the Federal Trade Commission Act in 1914. In addition to establishing the Federal Trade Commission to investigate unfair trade practices, this law enumerated certain business practices that, according to Congress, involved overly aggressive competition. A 1938 amendment to this law expressly prohibited "unfair or deceptive acts or practices in commerce" and empowered the FTC to regulate advertising and marketing practices by U.S. firms.

The Robinson-Patman Act of 1936 amended the Clayton Act by singling out specific business practices, such as selected price cuts, aimed at driving smaller competitors out of business. The act is often referred to as the "Chain Store Act" because it was intended to protect *independent* retailers and wholesalers from "unfair competition" by chain stores.

Exemptions from Antitrust Laws.

Numerous laws exempt the following industries and business practices from antitrust legislation:

- Labor unions
- Public utilities—electric, gas, and telephone companies
- Professional baseball
- Cooperative activities among U.S. exporters
- Hospitals

---

*This is now a felony.

- Public transit and water systems
- Suppliers of military equipment
- Joint publishing arrangements in a single city by two or more newspapers

Thus not all U.S. businesses are subject to antitrust laws.

International Discord in Antitrust Policy

What, if anything, should U.S. antitrust authorities do if AT&T decides that it wishes to merge with British Telecommunications or if Germany's Deutsche Telecom wants to acquire Sprint? What, if anything, should they do if Time Warner, the largest U.S. entertainment company, attempts to merge with London-based EMI, one of the world's largest recorded-music companies? These are not just rhetorical questions, as U.S. and European antitrust authorities learned in the early 2000s when these issues actually surfaced. Growing international linkages among markets for many goods and services have increasingly made antitrust policy a global undertaking.

The international dimensions of antitrust pose a problem for U.S. antitrust authorities in the Department of Justice and Federal Trade Commission. In the United States, the overriding goal of antitrust policies has traditionally been protecting the interests of consumers. This is also a formal objective of antitrust efforts of European Union (EU) antitrust authorities. In the EU, however, policymakers are also required to reject any business combination that "creates or strengthens a dominant position as a result of which effective competition would be significantly impeded."

This additional clause is currently creating tension between U.S. and EU policymaking. In the United States, increasing dominance of a market by a single firm arouses the concern of antitrust authorities. Nevertheless, U.S. authorities typically will remain passive if they determine that greater market dominance arises from factors such as exceptional management and greater cost efficiencies that ultimately benefit consumers by reducing prices. In contrast, under EU rules antitrust authorities are obliged to block *any* business combination that increases the dominance of any producer. They must do so irrespective of what factors might have caused the business's preeminence in the marketplace.

CONCEPTS in Brief

- The first national antitrust law was the Sherman Antitrust Act of 1890, which made illegal every contract and combination in restraint of trade; it remains the single most important antitrust law in the United States.

- The Clayton Act of 1914 made illegal various specific business practices, such as price discrimination.

- The Federal Trade Commission Act of 1914 and its 1938 amendment established the Federal Trade Commission and prohibited "unfair or deceptive acts or practices in commerce."

- The Robinson-Patman Act of 1936 aimed to prevent large producers from driving out small competitors by means of selective discriminatory price cuts.

To test your understanding of the concepts covered in this section, go to the Online Review at www.myeconlab.com/miller.

ANTITRUST ENFORCEMENT

Monopolization
The possession of monopoly power in the relevant market and the willful acquisition or maintenance of that power, as distinguished from growth or development as a consequence of a superior product, business acumen, or historical accident.

How are antitrust laws enforced? In the United States, most enforcement continues to be based on the Sherman Act. The Supreme Court has defined the offense of **monopolization** as involving the following elements: "(1) the possession of monopoly power in the relevant market and (2) the willful acquisition or maintenance of that power, as distinguished from growth or development as a consequence of a superior product, business acumen, or historical accident."

Monopoly Power and the Relevant Market

The Sherman Act does not define monopoly. Monopoly need not be a single entity. Also, monopoly is not a function of size alone. For example a "mom and pop" grocery store located in an isolated town can function as a monopolist.

How do you suppose that college bookstore operators in Indianapolis could have gone about attempting to monopolize a local market for textbooks?

Policy E X A M P L E

In Indianapolis, Bookstores Rig the Race for Profits

In addition to being the home of the well-known "500" auto race, Indianapolis is also the location of several medical and other technical schools. In late 2003, a federal grand jury indicted the managers of two college bookstores on charges that they violated antitrust laws by participating in a price-fixing conspiracy involving the sale of medical and other textbooks. Allegedly, managers of the two bookstores met to discuss competition between their bookstores on or near the campus of Indiana University–Purdue University at Indianapolis

(IUPUI). At that meeting, U.S. Justice Department officials alleged, the bookstore operators agreed to eliminate discounts on medical textbooks and to cooperate in raising their markups on all new textbooks from 25 percent to 27 percent.

For Critical Analysis
In light of the fact that college students could have purchased many of their textbooks on the Internet, could the two bookstores on and near IUPUI really have operated an effective monopoly?

It is difficult to define and measure market power precisely. As a workable proxy, courts often look to the firm's percentage share of the "relevant market." This is the so-called **market share test.** A firm is generally considered to have monopoly power if its share of the relevant market is 70 percent or more. This is only a rule of thumb, however, not an absolute dictum. In some cases, a smaller share may be held to constitute monopoly power.

The relevant market consists of two elements: a relevant *product* market and a relevant *geographic* market. What should the relevant product market include? It must include all items produced by different firms that have identical attributes, such as sugar. Yet products that are not identical may sometimes be substituted for one another. Coffee may be substituted for tea, for example. In defining the relevant product market, the key issue is the degree to which products are interchangeable. If one product is sufficiently substitutable for another, then the two products are considered to be part of the same product market.

The second component of the relevant market is the geographic boundaries of the market. For items that are sold nationwide, the geographic boundaries of the market encompass the entire United States. If a producer and its competitors sell in only a limited area (one in which customers have no access to other sources of the product), the geographic market is limited to that area. A national firm may thus compete in several distinct areas and have monopoly power in one area but not in another.

Market share test
The percentage of a market that a particular firm supplies; used as the primary measure of monopoly power.

Product Packaging and Antitrust Enforcement

A particular problem in U.S. antitrust enforcement is determining whether a firm has engaged in "willful acquisition or maintenance" of market power. Unfortunately, actions that appear to some observers to be good business look like antitrust violations to others. To illustrate why quandaries can arise in antitrust enforcement, let's consider two examples: *versioning* and *bundling*.

Versioning
Selling a product in slightly altered forms to different groups of consumers.

Product Versioning. A firm engages in product **versioning** when it sells an item in slightly altered forms to different groups of consumers. A typical method of versioning is to remove certain features from an item and offer what remains as a somewhat stripped-down version of the product at a different price.

Consider an office productivity software program, such as Adobe Acrobat or Microsoft Word. Firms selling such programs typically offer both a "professional" version containing a full range of features and a "standard" version providing only basic functions. One perspective on this practice regards it as a form of price discrimination, or selling essentially the same product at different prices to different consumers. People who desire to use the full range of features in Adobe Acrobat or Microsoft Word are likely to be computing professionals. Compared to most other consumers, their demand for the full-featured version of an office productivity software program is likely to be less elastic. In principle, therefore, Adobe and Microsoft can earn higher profits by offering "professional" versions at higher prices and selling a "standard" version at a lower price.

Price discrimination—charging varying prices to different consumers when the price differences are not a result of different production or transportation costs—is illegal under the Clayton Act of 1914. Are Adobe, Microsoft, and other companies engaging in illegal price discrimination? Another perspective on versioning indicates that they are not. According to this point of view, consumers regard "professional" and "standard" versions of software packages as imperfect substitutes. Consequently, each version is a distinctive product sold in a unique market. If so, versioning increases overall consumer satisfaction because consumers who are not computing professionals are able to utilize certain features of software products at a lower price. So far, antitrust authorities in the United States and elsewhere have been inclined toward this view of the economic effects of versioning, rather than perceiving it as a form of price discrimination.

Bundling
Offering two or more products for sale as a set.

Tie-in sales
Purchases of one product that are permitted by the seller only if the consumer buys another good or service from the same firm.

Product Bundling. Antitrust authorities have been less upbeat concerning another form of product packaging, known as **bundling,** which involves the joint sale of two or more products as a set. Antitrust authorities usually are not concerned if a firm allows consumers to purchase the products either individually or as a set. They are more likely to investigate a firm's business practices, however, when it allows consumers to purchase one product only when it is bundled with another. Antitrust officials often view this form of bundling as a method of price discrimination known as **tie-in sales,** in which a firm requires consumers who wish to buy one of its products to purchase another item the firm sells as well.

To understand their reasoning, consider a situation in which one group of consumers is willing to pay $500 for a computer operating system but only $100 for an Internet-browsing program. A second group of consumers is willing to pay only $250 for the same computer operating system but is willing to pay $350 for the same Internet-browsing program. If the same company that sells both types of software offers the operating system at a price above $250, then only consumers in the first group will buy this software. Likewise, if it sells the Internet-browsing program at a price above $100, then only the second group of consumers will purchase that program.

But if the firm sells both products as a bundled set, it can charge $600 and generate sales of both software products to both groups. One interpretation is that the first group perceives that it pays $500 for the operating system, but to the second group, the operating system's price is $250. At the same time, the first group feels it has paid $100 for the Internet-browsing program, while the second group perceives the price of the program to be $350. Effectively, bundling enables the software company to engage in price discrimination by charging different prices to different groups.

Antitrust enforcers in the Justice Department applied this interpretation in their prosecution of Microsoft, which for years had bundled its Internet-browsing program, Internet

Explorer, together with its Windows operating system. Enforcement officials added another twist by contending that Microsoft also had monopoly power in the market for computer operating systems. By bundling the two products, they argued, Microsoft had sought both to price-discriminate and to extend its monopoly power to the market for Internet-browsing software. The remedy that the courts imposed was for Microsoft to alter some of its business practices. As part of this legal remedy, Microsoft was required to unbundle its Windows and Internet Explorer products.

CONCEPTS in Brief

- As part of the enforcement of antitrust laws, U.S. officials at the Department of Justice and the Federal Trade Commission often apply market share tests to determine if a few firms account for most of industry sales.

- Antitrust enforcers must decide whether producers seek to monopolize the relevant market, which involves determining both the relevant product market and the relevant geographic market.

- Antitrust authorities generally have not considered product versioning, or offering different versions of essentially the same product for sale at different prices, to be illegal price discrimination. Both U.S. and European authorities have, however, raised antitrust concerns about product bundling, which they view as a method of engaging in tie-in sales that require consumers to purchase one product in order to obtain another.

To test your understanding of the concepts covered in this section, go to the Online Review at www.myeconlab.com/miller.

CASE STUDY: Economics Front and Center

Time to Take a Stand on Utility Rates

Simpson, who was once employed by a public utility, has been appointed to the board of regulators for a local power company. She has been on the job only about a week. Yesterday afternoon she and the other members of the regulatory board received a proposal for a 20 percent increase in electricity rates for most residential and business customers. A hastily organized board meeting—in executive session to avoid public media coverage—has just opened.

Simpson listens as other board members offer their views on the proposed rate hike. Most support the price increases, which they argue are justified in light of recent increases in the power company's costs. Simpson's mind races as she contemplates her own stand on the issue. The legislators who recommended her for the job did so because of her strong stand against big rate increases, and she has just finished reading a stack of letters from consumers already unhappy with the prices they pay. At the same time, however, the financial data the power company has provided really do document a 20 percent increase in the company's unit cost of providing electricity.

When her turn to speak arrives, one more thought flashes into Simpson's mind: A key reason she took the position was to gain experience that might help her land an executive position at another public utility. Simpson begins her statement: "I certainly see merit in the company's call for a rate increase, but it seems to me it would be better to begin this year with a rate increase closer to 15 percent than to 20 percent. We can then re-evaluate the situation next year."

Points to Analyze

1. *What elements of Simpson's situation contribute to the potential for her eventually to become a captured regulator?*

2. *Based on Simpson's thinking and her statement, does her behavior better fit the capture hypothesis or the share-the-gains, share-the-pains theory of regulator behavior?*

A Model Case of Collusive Price Fixing?

M any individuals strive to become professional fashion models. They quickly find, however, that getting off to a good start in the modeling business requires more than just the "right look." It requires considerable hard work, plus significant up-front expenses. In recent years, many fashion models have wondered if some of the high expenses they incur might not be due to illegal collusion among the fashion-modeling agencies that help them find jobs.

Concepts Applied

- Regulation
- Antitrust
- Monopolization

Obtaining Photos of Warm Beauty Requires Cold Cash

To handle their job bookings and rate negotiations with photography studios, models use the services of fashion-modeling agencies. For years, the top agencies have arranged identical terms with their models and their photography-studio clients. To book a model for a photo shoot for an advertisement, catalog, or fashion magazine, a photography studio pays a fashion-modeling agency a premium equal to 20 percent of the payment to the model. The model also pays a 20 percent fee to the agency. Thus, if a photography studio hires a supermodel for a one-day shoot for a negotiated payment of $10,000, it pays the fashion-modeling agency representing the model $12,000, and the agency pays the supermodel $8,000.

Of course, most models' earnings for day-long photo shoots are much lower than the rates earned by supermodels. In addition, even if photography studios fail to choose a model for any photo shoots, the model often must reimburse fashion-modeling agencies for other expenses, such as copying services, messenger services, and other incidentals. Thus it is not uncommon for models to find themselves in debt to the agencies.

Is Something Wrong with This Picture?

For years, it was "well known" in the fashion-modeling business that "cutthroat competition" existed among fashion-modeling agencies. Fashion magazines commonly ran stories about feuds between owners of the top agencies, who allegedly could not stand to be in the same room with each other.

Consequently, many observers were surprised to learn that during the 1990s, top fashion-modeling agencies had conducted regular meetings at trendy Manhattan restaurants. A now-defunct organization called the International Model Managers Association coordinated these meetings, and secretaries of the organization took minutes. These minutes summarized broad discussions of models' commissions, agencies' photography-studio clients, and the market conditions the agencies jointly faced. The minutes also showed that member agencies engaged in detailed discussions about the service fees they charged the models, as well as about the uniform terms they developed for models' agency contracts.

Once these minutes became public in 2003, the U.S. Justice Department launched a major antitrust investigation. More than 70 grand juries have investigated alleged efforts by the International Model Managers Association to collusively fix prices and allocate clients among member agencies. In addition, current and former models and clients have filed private lawsuits alleging antitrust violations. All of these investigations and lawsuits promise to keep district attorneys, lawyers, and courts tied up assessing potential antitrust violations in the modeling industry for some years to come.

1. Does the fact that the top fashion-modeling agencies have charged models the same commission rate over the years necessarily imply that they have collusively set prices? (Hint: Do perfectly competitive firms charge different prices?)

2. How might one go about trying to determine the "relevant market" in the fashion-modeling industry?

For Critical Analysis

1. Explore information concerning recent U.S. Justice Department antitrust actions at **www.econtoday.com/chap28**.

2. Learn more about the privately filed legal actions against fashion-modeling agencies via the link to the U.S. District Court of the Southern District of New York available at **www.econtoday.com/chap28**.

Web Resources

Assuming that the allegations concerning collusive price fixing in the fashion-modeling industry turn out to be true, what antitrust law best applies to the situation? What hurdles do you think that antitrust authorities or private individuals would face in trying to apply this antitrust law to obtain a legal remedy?

Research Project

S U M M A R Y   D I S C U S S I O N   of Leaning Objectives

1. **Government Regulation of Business:** There are two basic forms of government regulation of business: economic regulation and social regulation. Economic regulation applies to specific industries; it includes the regulation of prices charged by natural monopolies and the regulation of certain activities of specific nonmonopolistic industries. Social regulations affect nearly all businesses and encompass a broad range of objectives concerning such issues as product safety, environmental quality, and working conditions.

2. **Practical Difficulties in Regulating the Prices Charged by Natural Monopolies:** To try to ensure that a monopolist charges a price consistent with the marginal cost of producing the good or service that it produces, a government regulator might contemplate requiring the firm to set price equal to marginal cost. This is the point where the demand curve the monopolist faces crosses its marginal cost curve. A problem arises, however, in the case of a natural monopoly, for which the long-run average total cost curve and the long-run marginal cost curve slope downward. In this situation, long-run marginal cost is typically less than long-run average total cost, so requiring marginal cost pricing forces the natural monopoly to incur an economic loss. As a practical matter, therefore, regulators normally aim for a natural monopoly to charge a price equal to average total cost so that the firm earns zero economic profits.

3. **Rationales for Regulating Nonmonopolistic Industries:** The two most common rationales for regulation of non-

monopolistic industries relate to addressing market failures and protecting consumers from problems arising from information asymmetries they face in some markets. Asymmetric information can also create a lemons problem, which occurs when uncertainty about product quality leads to markets containing mostly low-quality items. Governments may seek to reduce the lemons problem by establishing liability laws and business licensing requirements.

4. **Regulators' Incentives and the Costs of Regulation:** The capture theory of regulator behavior predicts that because people with expertise about a regulated industry are most likely to be selected to regulate the industry, these regulators will eventually find themselves supporting the positions of the firms that they regulate. An alternative view, called the share-the-gains, share-the pains theory, predicts that a regulator takes into account the preferences of legislators and consumers as well as the regulated firms themselves. Thus a regulator tries to satisfy all constituencies, at least in part. The costs of regulation are easier to quantify in dollar terms than the benefits. These costs include both the direct costs to taxpayers of funding regulatory agencies and the explicit and implicit opportunity costs that businesses must incur to comply with regulations.

5. **Foundations of Antitrust:** There are four key antitrust laws. The Sherman Act of 1890 forbids attempts to monopolize an industry. The Clayton Act of 1914 clarified antitrust law by prohibiting specific types of business

practices that Congress determined were aimed at restraining trade. In addition, the Federal Trade Commission Act of 1914, as amended in 1938, seeks to prohibit deceptive business practices and to prevent "cutthroat pricing," which Congress felt could unfairly eliminate too many competitors. Finally, the Robinson-Patman Act of 1936 outlawed price cuts that Congress had determined to be discriminatory and predatory.

6. **Issues in Enforcing Antitrust Laws:** Antitrust laws are vague, so enforcement of the laws is based on court interpretations of their meaning. The Supreme Court has defined monopolization as possessing or seeking monopoly pricing power in the "relevant market." Authorities charged with enforcing antitrust laws use a market share test, which involves determining the percentage of market production or sales supplied by a firm. A key issue in applying the market share test is defining the relevant market. In recent years, antitrust officials have raised questions about whether product packaging, either in the form of different versions or as bundled sets, is a type of price discrimination. There are alternative views about whether firms truly use product versioning to practice price discrimination, so this business practice has not attracted much antitrust attention. U.S. antitrust authorities have, however, charged that product bundling is a means of engaging in tie-sales, in which a firm price-discriminates by requiring consumers to purchase one product before being able to buy another item.

KEY TERMS AND CONCEPTS

bundling (676)

capture hypothesis (669)

cost-of-service regulation (664)

creative response (668)

lemons problem (666)

market share test (675)

monopolization (674)

rate-of-return regulation (664)

share-the-gains, share-the-pains theory (669)

tie-in sales (676)

versioning (676)

PROBLEMS

Answers to the odd-numbered problems appear at the back of the book.

28-1. Local cable television companies are usually granted monopoly rights to service a particular territory of a metropolitan area. The companies typically pay special taxes and license fees to local municipalities. Why might a municipality give monopoly rights to a cable company?

28-2. A local cable company, the sole provider of cable television service, is regulated by the municipal government. The owner of the company claims that she is normally opposed to regulation by government, but asserts that regulation is necessary because local residents would not want a large number of different cables crisscrossing the city. Why do you think the owner is defending regulation by the city?

28-3. The following table depicts the cost and demand structure a natural monopoly faces. Calculate total revenues, marginal revenue, and marginal cost at each output level. If this firm were allowed to operate as a monopolist, what would be the quantity produced and the price charged by the firm? What would be the amount of monopoly profit?

Quantity	Price($)	Long-Run Total Cost ($)
0	100	0
1	95	92
2	90	177
3	85	255
4	80	331
5	75	406
6	70	480

28-4. If regulators required the firm in Problem 28-3 to practice marginal cost pricing, what quantity would it produce, and what price would it charge? What is the firm's profit under this regulatory framework?

28-5. If regulators required the firm in Problem 28-3 to practice average cost pricing, what quantity would it produce, and what price would it charge? What is the firm's profit under this regulatory framework?

28-6. Discuss the major strength and weakness of the two traditional approaches to regulation of natural monopolies.

28-7. Are lemons problems likely to be more common in some industries and less common in others? Based on your answer to this question, should government regulatory activities designed to reduce the scope of lemons problems take the form of economic regulation or social regulation? Take a stand, and support your reasoning.

28-8. Research into genetically modified crops has led to significant productivity gains for countries such as the United States that employ these techniques. Countries such as the European Union member nations, however, have imposed controls on the import of these products, citing concern for public health. Is the European Union's regulation of genetically modified crops social regulation or economic regulation?

28-9. Using the example in Problem 28-8, do you think this is more likely an example of the capture hypothesis or the share-the-gains, share-the-pains theory? Why?

28-10. In spite of a number of available sites to establish a business, few regulations, and minimum zoning problems, there is only one fast-food restaurant bordering campus. Given the significant potential for entry by other competitors, will this monopoly necessarily be able to charge a price above marginal cost?

28-11. Consider the following fictitious sales data (in thousands of dollars) for books sold both over the Internet and in physical retail establishments. Firms have numbers instead of names, and Firm 1 generates book sales only over the Internet. Antitrust authorities judge that a single firm possesses "monopoly power" if its share of sales in the relevant market exceeds 70 percent.

Internet Book Sales		Book Sales in Physical Stores		Combined Book Sales	
Firm	Sales	Firm	Sales	Firm	Sales
1	$ 750	2	$4,200	2	$ 4,250
2	50	3	2,000	3	2,050
3	50	4	1,950	4	2,000
4	50	5	450	1	750
5	50	6	400	5	500
6	50			6	450
Total	$1,000		$9,000		$10,000

a. Suppose that the antitrust authorities determine that bookselling in physical retail stores and Internet bookselling are individually separate relevant markets. Does any single firm have monopoly power, as defined by the antitrust authorities?

b. Suppose that in fact there is really only a single book industry, in which firms compete both in physical retail stores and via the Internet. According to the antitrust authorities' measure of monopoly power, is there actually cause for concern?

28-12. In recent years, the Internet auction firm eBay has sought to make its auction technology the favorite of software programmers, and it has begun licensing its technology to other Web sites. The company's managers have publicly stated that their goal is for eBay's auction system to become the dominant "operating system" of all auction applications on the Internet. Are there any potential antitrust issues related to the company's efforts?

28-13. Recently, the U.S. Justice Department initiated an antitrust investigation of Homestore.com, a Web site containing the listings of thousands of real estate agents in the United States. In cities and even in local communities, there is considerable rivalry among realtors. Nevertheless, nearly all belong to the National Association of Realtors, which is the majority owner of Homestore.com. In 2000, Homestore.com purchased a rival site, Move.com, which left the Microsoft Network's Homeadvisor.com as its only remaining key rival. Why do you suppose the Justice Department became concerned about the activities of Homestore.com? What factors are likely to affect its decision about whether Homestore.com has violated any antitrust laws?

28-14. A package delivery company provides both overnight and second-day delivery services. It charges almost twice as much to deliver an overnight package to any world location as it does to deliver the same package to the same location in two days. Often, second-day packages arrive at company warehouses in destination cities by the next day, but drivers intentionally do not deliver these packages until the following day. What is this business practice called? Briefly summarize alternative perspectives concerning whether this activity should or should not be viewed as a form of price discrimination.

28-15. A firm that sells both Internet-security software and computer antivirus software will sell the antivirus software as a stand-alone product. It will only sell the Internet-security software to consumers in a bundled package that also includes the antivirus software. What is this business practice called? Briefly explain why an antitrust authority might view this practice as a form of price discrimination.

ECONOMICS ON THE NET

Guidelines for U.S. Antitrust Merger Enforcement How does the U.S. government apply antitrust laws to mergers? This application gives you the opportunity to learn about the standards applied by the Antitrust Division of the U.S. Department of Justice when it evaluates a proposed merger.

Title: U.S. Department of Justice Antitrust Merger Enforcement Guidelines

Navigation: Go to www.econtoday.com/chap28 to access the home page of the Antitrust Division of the U.S. Department of Justice. Click on *Public Documents* and then on *Merger Enforcement*.

Application Answer the following questions.

1. Click on *Horizontal Merger Guidelines*. In section 1, click on *Overview*, and read this section. What factors do U.S. antitrust authorities consider when evaluating the potential for a horizontal merger to "enhance market power"—that is, to place the combination in a monopoly situation?

2. Back up to the page titled *Merger Enforcement Guidelines*, and click on *Non-Horizontal Merger Guidelines*. Read the guidelines. In what situations will the antitrust authorities most likely question a nonhorizontal merger?

For Group Study and Analysis Have three groups of students from the class examine sections 1, 2, and 3 of the Horizontal Merger Guidelines discussed in item 1. After each group reports on all the factors that the antitrust authorities consider when evaluating a horizontal merger, discuss why large teams of lawyers and many economic consultants are typically involved when the Antitrust Division of the Department of Justice alleges that a proposed merger would be "anticompetitive."

If your exam were tomorrow, would you be ready? For each chapter, MyEconLab Practice Tests and Study Plans pinpoint which sections you have mastered and which ones you need to study. That way, you are more efficient with your study time, and you are better prepared for your exams.

In addition to Practice Tests and your personalized Study Plan, you'll find the following media resources in MyEconLab:

1. *Graphs in Motion* animation of Figures 28-1 and 28-2.
2. Videos featuring the author, Roger LeRoy Miller, on the following subjects:
   - Creative Response and Feedback Effects: Results of Regulation
   - Theory of Contestable Markets
   - Antitrust Laws

3. Links to the Web sites cited in the marginal Internet Resources, Issues and Applications feature, and Economics on the Net activity.
4. Audio clips of all key terms, additional practice problems, and a PDF version of the material from the print Study Guide.
5. eThemes of the Times, which is a New York Times article to help you understand the real-world applications of what you are learning.

To see how it works, turn to page 16 and then go to www.myeconlab.com/miller.

Get Ahead of the Curve

Chapter 29

The Labor Market: Demand, Supply, and Outsourcing

Following the end of the recession in 2001, the trucking business began to pick up considerably. Prospects for higher wages and higher employment of truck drivers looked bright. Then the U.S. Department of Transportation established new rules limiting the amount of time that all truck drivers could spend driving their rigs along the nation's highways. After the new rules went into effect, truck drivers did indeed earn higher wages. They also found more jobs, but not as many as the drivers had anticipated a year earlier. In this chapter, you will learn about the factors that can influence the market wage and equilibrium employment level in the market for truck drivers, as well as in the markets for the services of other workers.

LEARNING OBJECTIVES

After reading this chapter, you should be able to:

1. Understand why a firm's marginal revenue product curve is its labor demand curve

2. Explain in what sense the demand for labor is a "derived" demand

3. Identify the key factors influencing the elasticity of demand for inputs

4. Describe how equilibrium wage rates are determined for perfectly competitive firms

5. Explain what labor outsourcing is and how it is ultimately likely to affect U.S. workers' earnings and employment prospects

6. Contrast the demand for labor and wage determination by a product market monopolist with outcomes that would arise under perfect competition

Media Resources

Refer to the end of the chapter for a full listing of the multimedia learning materials available in MyEconLab.

Did You Know That ... about 13 percent of all workers in the United States are part-time employees who work fewer than 30 hours per week? In Switzerland, Japan, and Australia, just over 25 percent of all workers are employed on a part-time basis. In the Netherlands, almost 35 percent of all workers are part-time employees.

Both full- and part-time workers provide labor inputs that firms use to produce goods and services. A firm's demand for inputs can be studied in much the same manner as we studied the demand for output in different market situations. Again, various market situations will be examined. Our analysis will always end with the same conclusion: A firm will hire employees up to the point beyond which it isn't profitable to hire any more. It will hire employees to the point at which the marginal benefit of hiring a worker will just equal the marginal cost. Basically, in every profit-maximizing situation, it is most profitable to carry out an activity up to the point at which the marginal benefit equals the marginal cost. Remembering that guideline will help you in analyzing decision making at the firm level, which is where we will begin our discussion of the demand for labor.

LABOR DEMAND FOR A PERFECTLY COMPETITIVE FIRM

We will start our analysis under the assumption that the market for input factors is perfectly competitive. We will further assume that the output market is perfectly competitive. This provides a benchmark against which to compare other situations in which labor markets or product markets are not perfectly competitive.

Competition in the Product Market

Let's take as our example a firm that sells blank compact discs (CDs) and is in competition with many companies selling the same kind of product. Assume that the laborers hired by our CD manufacturing firm do not need any special skills. This firm sells CD 10-packs in a perfectly competitive market. The CD manufacturer also buys labor (its variable input) in a perfectly competitive market. A firm that hires labor under perfectly competitive conditions hires only a minuscule proportion of all the workers who are potentially available to the firm. By "potentially available," we mean all the workers in a given geographic area who possess the skills demanded by our perfect competitor. In such a market, it is always possible for the individual firm to hire extra workers without having to offer a higher wage. Thus the supply of labor to the firm is perfectly elastic at the going wage rate established by the forces of supply and demand in the entire labor market. The firm is a *price taker* in the labor market.

Marginal Physical Product

Marginal physical product (MPP) of labor
The change in output resulting from the addition of one more worker. The MPP of the worker equals the change in total output accounted for by hiring the worker, holding all other factors of production constant.

Look at panel (a) of Figure 29-1. In column 1, we show the number of workers per week that the firm can hire. In column 2, we show total physical product (TPP) per week, the total *physical* production of packages of 10 CDs that different quantities of the labor input (in combination with a fixed amount of other inputs) will generate in a week's time. In column 3, we show the additional output gained when the CD manufacturing company adds workers to its existing manufacturing facility. This column, the **marginal physical product (MPP) of labor,** represents the extra (additional) output attributed to employing additional units of the variable input factor. If this firm employs seven workers rather than six, the MPP is 118. The law of diminishing marginal returns predicts that additional units of a variable factor will, after some point, cause the MPP to decline, other things held constant.

FIGURE 29-1
Marginal Revenue Product

In panel (a), column 4 shows marginal revenue product (MRP), which is the additional revenue the firm receives for the sale of that additional output. Marginal revenue product is simply the revenue the additional worker brings in—the combination of that worker's contribution to production and the revenue that that production will bring to the firm. For this perfectly competitive firm, marginal revenue is equal to the price of the product, or $10 per unit. At a weekly wage of $830, the profit-maximizing employer will pay for only 12 workers because then the marginal revenue product is just equal to the wage rate or weekly salary.

Panel (a)

(1) Labor Input (workers per week)	(2) Total Physical Product (TPP) (CD packages per week)	(3) Marginal Physical Product (MPP) (CD packages per week)	(4) Marginal Revenue (MR = P = $10) x MPP = Marginal Revenue Product (MRP) ($ per additional worker)	(5) Wage Rate ($ per week) = Marginal Factor Cost (MFC) = Change in Total Costs ÷ Change in Labor
6	882			
7	1,000	118	$1,180	$830
8	1,111	111	1,110	830
9	1,215	104	1,040	830
10	1,312	97	970	830
11	1,402	90	900	830
12	1,485	83	830	830
13	1,561	76	760	830

In panel (b), we find the number of workers the firm will want to hire by observing the wage rate that is established by the forces of supply and demand in the entire labor market. We show that this employer is hiring labor in a perfectly competitive labor market and therefore faces a perfectly elastic supply curve represented by s at $830 per week. As in other situations, we have a supply and demand model; in this example, the demand curve is represented by MRP, and the supply curve is s. Profit maximization occurs at their intersection.

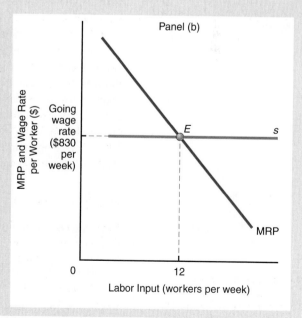

We are assuming that all other nonlabor factors of production are held constant. So, if our CD manufacturing firm wants to add one more worker to its production line, it has to crowd all the existing workers a little closer together because it does not increase its capital stock (the production equipment). Therefore, as we add more workers, each one has a smaller and smaller fraction of the available capital stock with which to work. If one worker uses one machine, adding another worker usually won't double the output because the machine can run only so fast and for so many hours per day. In other words, MPP declines because of the law of diminishing marginal returns.

Marginal Revenue Product

Marginal revenue product (MRP)
The marginal physical product (MPP) times marginal revenue (MR). The MRP gives the additional revenue obtained from a one-unit change in labor input.

We now need to translate into a dollar value the physical product that results from hiring an additional worker. This is done by multiplying the marginal physical product by the marginal revenue of the firm. Because our CD firm is selling its product in a perfectly competitive market, marginal revenue is equal to the price of the product. If employing seven workers rather than six yields an MPP of 118 and the marginal revenue is $10 per package of 10 CDs, the **marginal revenue product (MRP)** is $1,180 (118 × $10). The MRP is shown in column 4 of panel (a) of Figure 29-1 on the previous page. *The marginal revenue product represents the incremental worker's contribution to the firm's total revenues.*

When a firm operates in a competitive product market, the marginal physical product times the product price is also sometimes referred to as the *value of marginal product (VMP)*. Because price and marginal revenue are the same for a perfectly competitive firm, the VMP is also the MRP for such a firm.

Marginal factor cost (MFC)
The cost of using an additional unit of an input. For example, if a firm can hire all the workers it wants at the going wage rate, the marginal factor cost of labor is the wage rate.

In column 5 of panel (a) of Figure 29-1, we show the wage rate, or *marginal factor cost,* of each worker. The marginal cost of workers is the extra cost incurred in employing an additional unit of that factor of production. We call that cost the **marginal factor cost (MFC).** Otherwise stated,

$$\text{Marginal factor cost} = \frac{\text{change in total cost}}{\text{change in amount of resource used}}$$

Because each worker is paid the same competitively determined wage of $830 per week, the MFC is the same for all workers. And because the firm is buying labor in a perfectly competitive labor market, the wage rate of $830 per week really represents the supply curve of labor to the firm. That supply curve is perfectly elastic because the firm can purchase all labor at the same wage rate, considering that it is a minuscule part of the entire labor-purchasing market. (Recall the definition of perfect competition.) We show this perfectly elastic supply curve as *s* in panel (b) of Figure 29-1.

General Rule for Hiring. Virtually every optimizing rule in economics involves comparing marginal benefits with marginal cost. Because the benefit from added workers is extra output and consequently more revenues, the general rule for the hiring decision of a firm is this:

> *The firm hires workers up to the point at which the additional cost associated with hiring the last worker is equal to the additional revenue generated by that worker.*

In a perfectly competitive market, this is the point at which the wage rate just equals the marginal revenue product. If the firm hired more workers, the additional wages would not be covered by additional increases in total revenue. If the firm hired fewer workers, it would be forfeiting the contributions that those workers could make to total profits.

Therefore, referring to columns 4 and 5 in panel (a) of Figure 29-1, we see that this firm would certainly employ at least seven workers because the MRP is $1,180 while the MFC is only $830. The firm would continue to add workers up to the point at which MFC = MRP because as workers are added, they contribute more to revenue than to cost.

The MRP Curve: Demand for Labor. We can also use panel (b) of Figure 29-1 on page 685 to find how many workers our firm should hire. First, we draw a line at the going wage rate, which is determined by demand and supply in the labor market. The line is labeled *s* to indicate that it is the supply curve of labor for the *individual* firm purchasing labor in a perfectly competitive labor market. That firm can purchase all the labor it wants of equal quality at $830 per worker. This perfectly elastic supply curve, *s,* intersects the marginal revenue product curve at 12 workers per week. At the intersection, *E,* the wage rate is equal to the marginal revenue product. The firm maximizes profits where its demand curve for labor, which turns out to be its MRP curve, intersects the firm's supply curve for labor, shown as *s.* The firm in our example would not hire the thirteenth worker, who will add only $760 to revenue but $830 to cost. If the price of labor should fall to, say, $760 per worker per week, it would become profitable for the firm to hire an additional worker; the quantity of labor demanded increases as the wage decreases.

Why is it that even though violinists in an orchestra arguably have a higher marginal physical product—measured by the number of notes played in concerts— than those playing fewer notes on other instruments, they earn lower wages?

International E X A M P L E

Violinists in a German Orchestra Confuse MPP with MRP

In 2004, violinists in the Beethoven Orchestra in Bonn, Germany, filed a lawsuit asking a court to require orchestra managers to raise their pay. Their rationale was that they typically play many more notes in a concert than musicians playing other instruments, such as the oboe or the French horn.

If each violinist really does play more notes per concert than other musicians, then arguably the marginal *physical* product of labor is indeed higher for violinists. What matters to the owners and managers of an orchestra, however, is the marginal *revenue* product of each musician in an orchestra. Indeed, in their response to the violinists' lawsuit, managers of the Beethoven Orchestra used this logic to explain why oboe and French horn soloists who play fewer notes earn higher pay than violinists who play as a group within the orchestra. If the orchestra's violinists play their thousands of notes especially well as a group, they contribute to solid performances by the orchestra that help maintain steady ticket sales. But if an oboe or French horn soloist plays particularly beautifully, the orchestra's concert performances sparkle, which helps boost ticket sales. In other words, it is the additional revenue generated by each musician's contribution to the output of concert performances that determines the musician's value to the orchestra, not how many notes the musician plays.

For Critical Analysis
Why might an orchestra be willing to pay virtuoso violin soloists higher wages for orchestra performances than other violinists, even though the soloists actually play fewer notes in concerts than the rest of those playing the violin?

Derived Demand for Labor

We have identified an individual firm's demand for labor curve, which shows the quantity of labor that the firm will wish to hire at each wage rate, as its MRP curve. Under conditions of perfect competition in both product and labor markets, MRP is determined by

FIGURE 29-2
Demand for Labor, a Derived Demand
The demand for labor is derived from the demand for the final product being produced. Therefore, the marginal revenue product curve will shift whenever the price of the product changes. If we start with the marginal revenue product curve MRP at the going wage rate of $830 per week, 12 workers will be hired. If the price of CDs goes down, the marginal product curve will shift to MRP_1, and the number of workers hired will fall, in this case to 10. If the price of CDs goes up, the marginal revenue product curve will shift to MRP_2, and the number of workers hired will increase, in this case to 15.

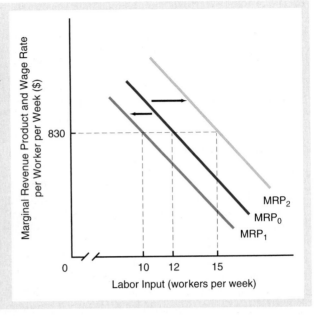

Derived demand
Input factor demand derived from demand for the final product being produced.

multiplying MPP times the product's price. This suggests that the demand for labor is a **derived demand.** Factors of production are rented or purchased not because they give any intrinsic satisfaction to the firms' owners but because they can be used to manufacture output that is expected to be sold at a profit.

We know that an increase in the market demand for a given product raises the product's price (all other things held constant), which in turn increases the marginal revenue product, or demand for the resource. Figure 29-2 illustrates the effective role played by changes in product demand in a perfectly competitive product market. The MRP curve shifts whenever there is a change in the price of the final product that the workers are producing. Suppose, for example, that the market price of blank CDs declines. In that case, the MRP curve will shift to the left from MRP_0 to MRP_1. We know that $MRP \equiv MPP \times MR$. If marginal revenue (here the output price) falls, so does the demand for labor. At the same going wage rate, the firm will hire fewer workers. This is because at various levels of labor use, the marginal revenue product of labor is now lower. At the initial equilibrium, therefore, the price of labor (here the MFC) becomes greater than MRP. Thus the firm would reduce the number of workers hired. Conversely, if the marginal revenue (output price) rises, the demand for labor will also rise, and the firm will want to hire more workers at each and every possible wage rate.

We just pointed out that $MRP \equiv MPP \times MR$. Clearly, then, a change in marginal productivity, or in the marginal physical product of labor, will shift the MRP curve. If the marginal productivity of labor decreases, the MRP curve, or demand curve, for labor will shift inward to the left. Again, this is because at every quantity of labor used, the MRP will be lower. A lower quantity of labor will be demanded at every possible wage rate.

CONCEPTS in Brief

- The change in total output due to a one-unit change in one variable input, holding all other inputs constant, is called the marginal physical product (MPP). When we multiply marginal physical product times marginal revenue, we obtain the marginal revenue product (MRP).

● A firm will hire workers up to the point at which the additional cost of hiring one more worker is equal to the additional revenue generated. For the individual firm, therefore, its MRP of labor curve is also its demand for labor curve.

● The demand for labor is a derived demand, derived from the demand for final output. Therefore, a change in the price of the final output will cause a shift in the MRP curve (which is also the firm's demand for labor curve).

To test your understanding of the concepts covered in this section, go to the Online Review at www.myeconlab.com/miller.

THE MARKET DEMAND FOR LABOR

The downward-sloping portion of each individual firm's marginal revenue product curve is also its demand curve for the one variable factor of production—in our example, labor. When we go to the entire market for a particular type of labor in a particular industry, we will also find that the quantity of labor demanded will vary inversely as the wage rate changes.

Constructing the Market Labor Demand Curve

Given that the market demand curve for labor is made up of the individual firms' downward-sloping demand curves for labor, we can safely infer that the market demand curve for labor will look like D in panel (b) of Figure 29-3: It will slope downward. That market demand curve for labor in the CD industry shows the quantities of labor demanded by all of the firms in the industry at various wage rates.

Nevertheless, the market demand curve for labor is *not* a simple horizontal summation of the labor demand curves of all individual firms. Remember that the demand for labor is

FIGURE 29-3
Derivation of the Market Demand Curve for Labor
The market demand curve for labor is not simply the horizontal summation of each individual firm's demand curve for labor. If wage rates fall from $20 to $10, all 200 firms will increase employment and therefore

output, causing the price of the product to fall. This causes the marginal revenue product curve of each firm to shift inward, from d_0 to d_1 in panel (a). The resulting market demand curve, D, in panel (b) is therefore less elastic around prices from $10 to $20 than it would be if the output price remained constant.

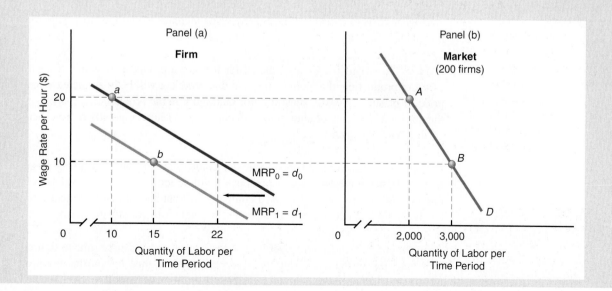

a derived demand. Even if we hold labor productivity constant, the demand for labor still depends on both the wage rate and the price of the final output. Assume that we start at a wage rate of $20 per hour and employment level 10 in panel (a) of Figure 29-3. If we sum all such employment levels—point *a* in panel (a)—across 200 firms, we get a market quantity demanded of 2,000, or point *A* in panel (b), at the wage rate of $20. A decrease in the wage rate to $10 per hour would induce individual firms' employment levels to increase toward a quantity demanded of 22 if price did not change. As all 200 firms simultaneously increase employment, however, there is a shift in the product supply curve such that output increases. Hence the price of the product must fall. The fall in the output price in turn causes a downward shift of each firm's MRP curve (d_0) to MRP_1 (d_1) in panel (a). Thus each firm's employment of labor increases to 15 rather than to 22 at the wage rate of $10 per hour. A summation of all such 200 employment levels gives us 3,000—point *B*— in panel (b).

Determinants of Demand Elasticity for Inputs

Just as we were able to discuss the price elasticity of demand for different commodities in Chapter 21, we can discuss the price elasticity of demand for inputs. The price elasticity of demand for labor is defined in a manner similar to the price elasticity of demand for goods: the percentage change in quantity demanded divided by the percentage change in the price of labor. When the *numerical* value of this ratio is less than 1, demand is inelastic; when it is 1, demand is unit-elastic; and when it is greater than 1, demand is elastic.

There are four principal determinants of the price elasticity of demand for an input. The price elasticity of demand for a variable input will be greater:

1. The greater the price elasticity of demand for the final product
2. The easier it is to employ substitute inputs in production
3. The larger the proportion of total costs accounted for by the particular variable input
4. The longer the time period being considered

Final Product Price Elasticity An individual radish farmer faces an extremely elastic demand for radishes, given the existence of many competing radish growers. If the farmer's laborers tried to obtain a significant wage increase, the farmer couldn't pass on the resultant higher costs to radish buyers. So any wage increase would lead to a large reduction in the quantity of labor demanded by the individual radish farmer.

Ease of Substitution Clearly, the easier it is for a producer to switch to using another factor of production, the more responsive that producer will be to an increase in an input's price. If plastic can easily substitute for aluminum in the production of, say, car bumpers, then a rise in the price of aluminum will cause automakers to greatly reduce their quantity of aluminum demanded.

Portion of Total Cost When a particular input's costs account for a very large share of total costs, any increase in that input's price will affect total costs relatively more. If labor costs are 80 percent of total costs, a company will cut back on employment more aggressively than if labor costs are only 8 percent of total costs, for any given wage increase.

Adjustment Period Finally, over longer periods, firms have more time to figure out ways to economize on the use of inputs whose prices have gone up. Furthermore, over time, technological change will allow for easier substitution in favor of relatively cheaper inputs and against inputs whose prices went up. At first, a pay raise obtained by a strong telephone company union may not result in many layoffs, but over time, the telephone company will use new technology to replace many of the now more expensive workers.

WAGE DETERMINATION IN A PERFECTLY COMPETITIVE LABOR MARKET

Having developed the demand curve for labor (and all other variable inputs) in a particular industry, let's turn to the labor supply curve. By adding supply to the analysis, we can come up with the equilibrium wage rate that workers earn in an industry. We can think in terms of a supply curve for labor that slopes upward in a particular industry. At higher wage rates, more workers will want to enter that particular industry. The individual firm, however, does not face the entire *market* supply curve. Rather, in a perfectly competitive case, the individual firm is such a small part of the market that it can hire all the workers that it wants at the going wage rate. We say, therefore, that the industry faces an upward-sloping supply curve but that the individual *firm* faces a perfectly elastic supply curve for labor.

Labor Market Equilibrium

The demand curve for labor in the CD industry is *D* in Figure 29-4, and the supply curve of labor is *S*. The equilibrium wage rate of $830 a week is established at the intersection of the two curves. The quantity of workers both supplied and demanded at that rate is Q_1. If for some reason the wage rate fell to $800 a week, in our hypothetical example, there would be an excess number of workers demanded at that wage rate. Conversely, if the

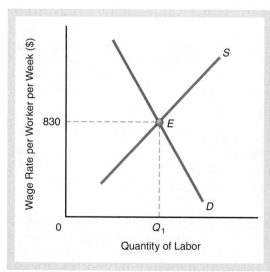

FIGURE 29-4
The Equilibrium Wage Rate and the CD Industry
The industry demand curve for labor is *D*. We put in a hypothetical upward-sloping labor supply curve for the CD industry, *S*. The intersection is at point *E*, giving an equilibrium wage rate of $830 per week and an equilibrium quantity of labor demanded of Q_1. At a wage above $830 per week, there will be an excess quantity of workers supplied. At a wage below $830 per week, there will be an excess quantity of workers demanded.

wage rate rose to $900 a week, there would be an excess quantity of workers supplied at that wage rate. In either case, competition would quickly force the wage back to the equilibrium level.

We have just found the equilibrium wage rate for the entire CD industry. The individual firm must take that equilibrium wage rate as given in the competitive model used here because the individual firm is a very small part of the total demand for labor. Thus each firm purchasing labor in a perfectly competitive market can purchase all of the input it wants at the going market price.

Have you ever wondered how long it takes the average U.S. worker to earn sufficient wages to buy a basic item, such as a burger at a fast-food restaurant, compared with workers in other countries?

International EXAMPLE

How Long Does It Take to Earn a Big Mac?

One way to compare the real purchasing power of market wages in different countries is to determine how long someone would have to work at a job to be able to buy an item that is widely available in most places in the world. One such item is McDonald's Big Mac sandwich, which is sold in the company's restaurants around the globe. In the United States, a typical worker spends about nine minutes on the job before earning market wages sufficient to purchase a Big Mac. In contrast, a Nigerian worker who earns the average market wage and wishes to buy a Big Mac must work about an hour. A worker earning the average market wage rate in Pakistan must spend more than two hours.

In Kenya, three hours of labor are required for a worker who receives the average market wage to be able to purchase a Big Mac. Thus the purchasing power of the average market wage in the United States is considerably higher than in Nigeria, Pakistan, and Kenya.

For Critical Analysis
What factors could cause the purchasing power of the average U.S. market wage rate to be so much higher than the average market wage rate in Nigeria, Pakistan, and Kenya?

Shifts in the Market Demand for and the Supply of Labor

Just as we discussed shifts in the supply curve and the demand curve for various products in Chapter 3, we can discuss the effects of shifts in supply and demand in labor markets.

Reasons for Labor Demand Curve Shifts. Many factors can cause the demand curve for labor to shift. We have already discussed a number of them. Clearly, because the demand for labor or any other variable input is a derived demand, the labor demand curve will shift if there is a shift in the demand for the final product. There are two other important determinants of the position of the demand curve for labor: changes in labor's productivity and changes in the price of related factors of production (substitutes and complements).

1. *Changes in the demand for the final product.* The demand for labor or any other variable input is derived from the demand for the final product. The marginal revenue product is equal to marginal physical product times marginal revenue. Therefore, any change in the price of the final product will change MRP. This happened when we derived the market demand for labor. The rule of thumb is as follows:

   A change in the demand for the final product that labor (or any other variable input) is producing will shift the market demand curve for labor in the same direction.

2. *Changes in labor productivity.* The second part of the MRP equation is MPP, which relates to labor productivity. We can surmise, then, that, other things being equal:

> ***A change in labor productivity will shift the market labor demand curve in the same direction.***

Labor productivity can increase because labor has more capital or land to work with, because of technological improvements, or because labor's quality has improved. Such considerations explain why the real standard of living of workers in the United States is higher than in most other countries. U.S. workers generally work with a larger capital stock, have more natural resources, are in better physical condition, and are better trained than workers in many countries. Hence the demand for labor in the United States, is, other things held constant, greater. Conversely, labor is relatively more scarce in the United States than it is in many other countries. One result of relatively greater demand and relatively smaller supply is a relatively higher wage rate.

3. *Change in the price of related factors.* Labor is not the only resource that firms use. Some resources are substitutes and some are complements. If we hold output constant, we have the following general rule:

> ***A change in the price of a substitute input will cause the demand for labor to change in the same direction. This is typically called the* substitution effect.***

Note, however, that if the cost of production falls sufficiently, the firm will find it more profitable to produce and sell a larger output. If this so-called *output effect* is great enough, it will override the substitution effect just mentioned, and the firm will end up employing not only more of the relatively cheaper variable input but also more labor. This is exactly what happened for many years in the U.S. automobile industry. Auto companies employed more machinery (capital), but employment continued to increase in spite of rising wage rates. The reason: technological improvement caused the marginal physical productivity of labor to rise faster than its wage rate.

Why do you suppose that employment of labor in factories has declined worldwide since the mid-1990s?

International EXAMPLE

Manufacturing Jobs Disappear Worldwide

Political leaders and media commentators often express concern that since 1995, U.S. manufacturing employment has fallen by nearly 12 percent. Their comments commonly imply that other countries must be capturing those lost manufacturing jobs. In fact, many other countries have also experienced declines in manufacturing employment. Since 1995, the number of people making physical goods in factories has also decreased by 12 percent in both Russia and South Korea. The United Kingdom has lost about 13 percent of its manufacturing jobs, and manufacturing employment has declined by 16 percent in both Japan and China. In Brazil, the number of factory jobs has fallen by 20 percent.

Technological improvements experienced worldwide have enabled manufacturing industries to substitute capital for labor as market wages have increased. Many of the approximately 22 million people who used to be employed in the world's factories have obtained jobs in such industries as telecommunications networking and software design and support.

For Critical Analysis
If the global prices of capital goods used by manufacturing industries increase substantially during the next decade, would you expect employment in factories to continue to decline?

With respect to complements, we are referring to inputs that must be used jointly. Assume now that capital and labor are complementary. In general, we predict the following:

> *A change in the price of a complementary input will cause the demand for labor to change in the opposite direction.*

If the cost of machines goes up but they must be used with labor, fewer machines will be purchased and therefore fewer workers will be used.

Determinants of the Supply of Labor. Labor supply curves may shift in a particular industry for a number of reasons. For example, if wage rates for factory workers in the CD industry remain constant while wages for factory workers in the computer industry go up dramatically, the supply curve of factory workers in the CD industry will shift inward to the left as these workers shift to the computer industry.

Changes in working conditions in an industry can also affect its labor supply curve. If employers in the CD industry discover a new production technique that makes working conditions much more pleasant, the supply curve of labor to the CD industry will shift outward to the right.

Job flexibility also determines the position of the labor supply curve. For example, when an industry allows workers more flexibility, such as the ability to work at home via computer, the workers are likely to provide more hours of labor. That is to say, their supply curve will shift outward to the right. Some industries in which firms offer *job sharing,* particularly to people raising families, have found that the supply curve of labor has shifted outward to the right.

CONCEPTS in Brief

- The individual competitive firm faces a perfectly elastic labor supply curve—it can hire all the labor it wants at the going market wage rate. The industry supply curve of labor slopes upward.

- By plotting an industrywide supply curve for labor and an industrywide demand curve for labor on the same

graph, we obtain the equilibrium wage rate in the industry.

- The labor demand curve can shift because the demand for the final product shifts, labor productivity changes, or the price of a related (substitute or complementary) factor of production changes.

To test your understanding of the concepts covered in this section, go to the Online Review at www.myeconlab.com/miller.

LABOR OUTSOURCING, WAGES, AND EMPLOYMENT

In addition to making it easier for people to work at home, computer technology has made it possible for them to provide labor services to companies located in another country. Some companies based in Mexico regularly transmit financial records—often via e-mail and the Internet—to U.S. accountants so that they can process payrolls and compile income statements. Meanwhile, some U.S. manufacturers of personal computers and peripheral devices arrange for customers' calls for assistance to be directed to call centers in India, where English-speaking technical-support specialists help the customers with their problems.

A firm that employs labor located outside the country in which it is located engages in labor **outsourcing.** Mexican companies that hire U.S. accountants outsource accounting services to the United States. U.S. computer manufacturers that employ Indian call-center staff outsource technical-support services to India. How does outsourcing affect employ-

Outsourcing
A firm's employment of labor outside the country in which the firm is located.

ment and wages in the United States? Who loses and who gains from outsourcing? Let's consider each of these questions in turn.

Wage and Employment Effects of Outsourcing

Equilibrium wages and levels of employment in U.S. labor markets are determined by the demands for and supplies of labor in those markets. As you have learned, one of the determinants of the market demand for labor is the price of a substitute input. Availability of a lower-priced substitute, you also learned, causes the demand for labor to fall. Thus the *immediate* economic effects of labor outsourcing are straightforward. When a home industry's firms can obtain *foreign* labor services that are a close substitute for *home* labor services, the demand for labor services provided by foreign workers will increase. The demand for labor services provided by home workers will decrease. What this economic reasoning ultimately implies for U.S. labor markets, however, depends on whether we view the United States as the "home" country or the "foreign" country.

U.S. Labor Market Effects of Outsourcing by U.S. Firms. To begin, let's view the United States as the home country. Developments in computer, communications, and transportation technologies have enabled an increasing number of U.S. firms to regard the labor of foreign workers as a close substitute for labor provided by U.S. workers. Take a look at Figure 29-5. Panel (a) depicts demand and supply curves in the U.S. market for workers who handle calls for technical support for U.S. manufacturers of personal computers. Suppose that before technological change makes foreign labor substitutable for U.S. labor, point E_1 is the initial equilibrium. At this point, the market wage rate in this U.S. labor market is $19 per hour.

FIGURE 29-5

Outsourcing of U.S. Computer Technical-Support Services

Initially, the market wage for U.S. workers providing technical support for customers of U.S. computer manufacturers is $19 per hour at point E_1 in panel (a), while the market wage for Indian workers who provide the same service is $8 per hour in panel (b). This gives U.S. firms an incentive to substitute away from U.S. workers to Indian workers. The market demand for U.S. labor decreases in panel (a), generating a new equilibrium at point E_2 at a lower U.S. market wage and employment level. The market demand for Indian labor increases in panel (b), bringing about higher wages and employment at point E_2.

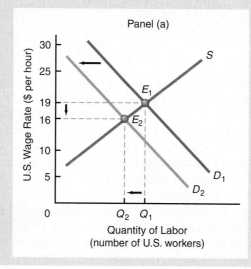
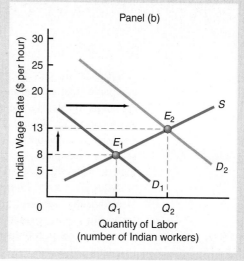

Now suppose that U.S. personal computer manufacturers are able to consider foreign labor as a substitute input for U.S. labor. Panel (b) displays demand and supply curves in a market for substitutable labor services in India. At the initial equilibrium point E_1 the wage rate denominated in U.S. dollars is $8 per hour. Firms in this U.S. industry will respond to the lower price of substitute labor in India by increasing their demand for labor services in that country and reducing their demand for U.S. labor. Thus, in panel (b), the market demand for the substitute labor services available in India rises. The market wage in India rises to $13 per hour, at point E_2, and Indian employment increases. In panel (a), the market demand for U.S. labor services decreases. At the new equilibrium point E_2, the U.S. market wage has fallen to $16 per hour, and equilibrium employment has decreased.

Consequently, when U.S. firms are the home firms engaging in labor outsourcing, the effects are lower wages and decreased employment in the relevant U.S. labor markets. In those nations where workers providing the outsourced labor reside, the effects are higher wages and increased employment.

Why are estimates that at least 3 million U.S. jobs will be outsourced to India within the next 10 years almost certainly too high?

International EXAMPLE

The Missing Factor in Estimates of U.S. Job Losses to India

According to a number of U.S. media commentators and politicians, India's large population of technically trained workers is likely to sap 3 to 4 million jobs from U.S. labor markets by 2015. Some prognosticators have estimated that as many as 10 million U.S. jobs may flow to India. A few estimates have been even higher.

An unstated assumption is implicit in these estimates, however. The estimates are based on the notion that wages in India will remain unchanged. Yet the analysis in Figure 29-5 predicts that as firms in the United States and other nations seek to employ more Indian workers, market wages in India should rise. In fact, between 2003 and 2004 labor-outsourcing companies scrambling for qualified Indian workers faced

market wage increases of 15 to 20 percent *each year*. If equilibrium wages in India's labor markets continue to increase at this pace, the incentive for U.S. firms to substitute Indian labor for home labor will decrease rapidly. Thus it is unlikely that 3 to 4 million U.S. jobs will move to India by 2015, and it is even more improbable that outsourcing to India will replace 10 million or more U.S. jobs.

For Critical Analysis
The analysis in Figure 29-5 also predicts that an immediate effect of U.S. labor outsourcing will be lower wages in affected U.S. labor markets. How will this affect the incentive for U.S. firms to continue outsourcing to India?

U.S. Labor Market Effects of Outsourcing by Foreign Firms. U.S. firms are not the only companies that engage in outsourcing. Consider the Mexican companies that hire U.S. accountants to calculate their payrolls and maintain their financial records. Figure 29-6 shows the effects in the Mexican and U.S. markets for labor services provided by accountants before and after *Mexican* outsourcing of accountants' labor. At point E_1 in panel (a), before any outsourcing takes place, the initial market wage for qualified accountants in Mexico is $29 per hour. In panel (b), the market wage for similarly qualified U.S. accountants is $21 per hour.

After e-mail and Internet access allow companies in Mexico to transfer financial data electronically, the services of U.S. accountants become available as a less expensive substitute for those provided by Mexican accountants. When Mexican firms respond by seeking to hire U.S. accountants, the demand for U.S. accountants' labor services rises in panel (b). This causes the market wage earned by U.S. accountants to increase to $23 per hour.

FIGURE 29-6

Outsourcing of Accounting Services by Mexican Firms

Suppose that the market wage for accounting services in Mexico is initially $29 per hour, at point E_1 in panel (a), but in the United States accountants earn just $21 per hour at point E_1 in panel (b). Mexican firms respond by substituting labor services provided by U.S. accountants for the services of Mexican accountants. The market demand for the services of Mexican accountants decreases in panel (a), and at point E_2 fewer Mexican accountants are employed at a lower market wage. The market demand for U.S. accounting services increases in panel (b). This generates higher wages and employment for U.S. accountants at point E_2.

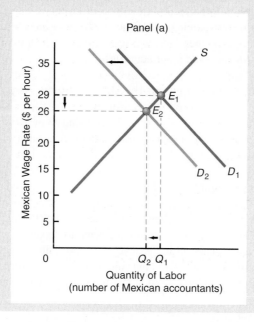
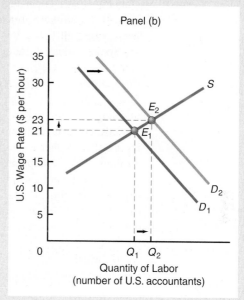

Mexican firms substitute away from the services of Mexican accountants, so in panel (a) the demand for the labor of accountants in Mexico declines. Mexican accountants' wages decline to $26 per hour.

In contrast to the situation in which U.S. firms are the home firms engaging in labor outsourcing, when foreign firms outsource by hiring workers in the United States, wages and employment levels rise in the affected U.S. markets. In the nations where the firms engaging in outsourcing are located, the effects are lower wages and decreased employment.

Gauging the Net Effects of Outsourcing on the U.S. Economy

In the example depicted in Figure 29-5, the market wage and employment level for U.S. technical-support workers declined as a result of outsourcing by U.S. firms. In contrast, in the example shown in Figure 29-6, U.S. accountants earned higher wages and experienced increased employment as a result of outsourcing by Mexican firms. Together, these examples illustrate a fundamental conclusion concerning the effects of global labor outsourcing in U.S. labor markets:

> *Labor outsourcing by U.S. firms tends to reduce U.S. wages and employment. Whenever foreign firms engage in labor outsourcing in the United States, however, U.S. wages and employment increase.*

Consequently, the immediate effects of increased worldwide labor outsourcing are lower wages and employment in some U.S. labor markets and higher wages and employment in others. In this narrow sense, some U.S. workers "lose" from outsourcing while others "gain," just as some Mexican workers "lose" while some Indian workers "gain."

To read a Heritage Foundation lecture about the net effects of outsourcing on U.S. jobs, use the link at www.econtoday.com/chap29.

Short-Run versus Long-Run Effects of Outsourcing. Even in the best of times workers in labor markets experience short-run ups and downs in wages and jobs. In the United States, after all, nearly 4 million jobs come and go every month.

To be sure, in the near term certain groups of U.S. workers, at least for a time, earn lower pay or experience reduced employment opportunities as a result of labor outsourcing. Nevertheless, what really matters when gauging the overall effects of increased global outsourcing of labor is the *long-term* effects on the *overall* levels of wages and employment. If the ultimate effects of outsourcing are higher wages and increased employment levels across all U.S. labor markets, then U.S. workers ultimately benefit from outsourcing. So do workers in India, Mexico, and other countries.

The Long-Term Benefits of Outsourcing for the U.S. Economy. As you will learn in Chapter 33, computer companies' labor outsourcing to India constitutes a form of U.S. spending on imports. Many of the dollars that U.S. firms spend to purchase Indian labor services, however, ultimately flow back into the United States. A number of Indian workers use their higher wages to buy more U.S. export products. Some invest some of their earnings in U.S. companies.

Increased labor outsourcing is part of a broader trend toward increased international trade of goods and services. Engaging in international trade allows residents of a nation to specialize in producing the goods and services that they can produce most efficiently. The resource saving that results expands the ability of a nation's residents to produce more goods and services than they could have produced in the absence of trade. This generates higher incomes, which the nation's residents can use to consume more items as well. On net, therefore, outsourcing makes consumers in the United States and other countries better off.

Benefits of Outsourcing for U.S. Workers. What are the net effects of outsourcing on the well-being of U.S. workers? As you have already seen, the immediate effects are mixed. Initially, some workers gain, and some workers lose.

Nevertheless, in the long run workers must also be better off. After all, if outsourcing allows U.S. firms to operate more efficiently, then those firms can allocate their resource savings to the production of more goods and services. Furthermore, because outsourcing contributes to higher incomes, consumers will buy these goods and services. Thus the expanded production and consumption possibilities made possible by outsourcing and other forms of international trade generate higher total revenues across U.S. firms.

As you learned earlier, the demand for labor is a derived demand determined by each worker's marginal revenue product. In the long run, outsourcing helps boost the overall value of the marginal revenue product in industries throughout the U.S. economy. Consequently, the ultimate long-run effect of outsourcing is an increase in the demand for labor in most industries. Increased labor demand, in turn, pushes up wages and boosts employment. Labor economists have estimated that during the 1990s, labor outsourcing probably created between 20 and 25 million more jobs in the United States than it destroyed. Recent estimates indicate that every $1.00 that U.S. firms spend on outsourcing is matched by an overall benefit to the U.S. economy ranging from $1.12 to $1.14.

Economics Front and Center

To contemplate how outsourcing can eventually raise employment at U.S. firms, read the case study, **Outsourcing Can Be a Win–Win Situation,** on page 703.

CONCEPTS in Brief

- Advances in telecommunications and computer networking are making foreign labor more easily substitutable for home labor, and home firms' substitution of foreign labor for home labor is known as labor outsourcing.

- In the short run, outsourcing by U.S. firms reduces the demand for labor, market wages, and equilibrium employment in U.S. labor markets. Outsourcing by foreign firms that hire U.S. labor increases the demand for labor, market wages, and equilibrium employment in U.S. labor markets. The net short-run effects on U.S. wages and employment are mixed.

● In the long run, outsourcing enables U.S. firms to operate more efficiently, which allows resources to be redirected to other revenue-generating activities that bring about overall increases in U.S. wages and employment.

To test your understanding of the concepts covered in this section, go to the Online Review at www.myeconlab.com/miller.

MONOPOLY IN THE PRODUCT MARKET

So far we've considered only perfectly competitive markets, both in selling the final product and in buying factors of production. We will continue our assumption that the firm purchases its factors of production in a perfectly competitive factor market. Now, however, we will assume that the firm sells its product in an *imperfectly* competitive output market. In other words, we are considering the output market structures of monopoly, oligopoly, and monopolistic competition. In all such cases, the firm, be it a monopolist, an oligopolist, or a monopolistic competitor, faces a downward-sloping demand curve for its product.

Throughout the rest of this chapter, we will simply refer to a monopoly output situation for ease of analysis. The analysis holds for all industry structures that are less than perfectly competitive. In any event, the fact that our firm now faces a downward-sloping demand curve for its product means that if it wants to sell more of its product (at a uniform price), it has to lower the price, *not just on the last unit, but on all preceding units.* The *marginal revenue* received from selling an additional unit is continuously falling (and is less than price) as the firm attempts to sell more and more. This is certainly different from our earlier discussions in this chapter in which the firm could sell all it wanted at a constant price. Why? Because the firm we discussed until now was a perfect competitor.

Constructing the Monopolist's Input Demand Curve

In reconstructing our demand schedule for an input, we must account for the facts that (1) the marginal *physical* product falls because of the law of diminishing returns as more workers are added and (2) the price (and marginal revenue) received for the product sold also falls as more is produced and sold. That is, for the monopolist, we have to account for both the diminishing marginal physical product and the diminishing marginal revenue. Marginal revenue is always less than price for the monopolist. The marginal revenue curve is always below the downward-sloping product demand curve.

Marginal revenue for the perfect competitor is equal to the price of the product because all units can be sold at the going market price. In our CD example, we assumed that the perfect competitor could sell all it wanted at $10 per pack of blank CDs. A one-unit change in sales always led to a $10 change in total revenues. Hence marginal revenue was always equal to $10 for that perfect competitor.

The monopolist, however, cannot simply calculate marginal revenue by looking at the price of the product. To sell the additional output from an additional unit of input, the monopolist has to cut prices on all previous units of output. As output is increasing, then, marginal revenue is falling. The underlying concept is, of course, the same for both the perfect competitor and the monopolist. We are asking exactly the same question in both cases: When an additional worker is hired, what is the benefit? In either case, the benefit is obviously the change in total revenues due to the one-unit change in the variable input, labor. In our discussion of the perfect competitor, we were able simply to look at the marginal physical product and multiply it by the *constant* per-unit price of the product because the price of the product never changed (for the perfect competitor, $P = \text{MR}$).

A single monopolist ends up hiring fewer workers than would all of the competitive firms added together. To see this, we must consider the marginal revenue product for the monopolist, which varies with each one-unit change in the monopolist's labor input. This is what we do in panel (a) of Figure 29-7, where column 5, "Marginal Revenue Product," gives the monopolist a quantitative notion of how additional workers and additional production generate additional revenues. The marginal revenue product curve for this monopolist has been plotted in panel (b) of the figure. To emphasize the lower elasticity of the

---

FIGURE 29-7
A Monopolist's Marginal Revenue Product
The monopolist hires just enough workers to make marginal revenue product equal to the going wage rate. If the going wage rate is $830 per week, as shown by the labor supply curve, *s*, in panel (b), the monopolist would want to hire approximately 10 workers per week. That is the profit-maximizing amount of labor. The MRP curve for a perfect competitor from Figure 29-1 on page 685 is also plotted (MRP_c). The monopolist's MRP curve will always be less elastic around the going wage rate than it would be if marginal revenue were constant.

Panel (a)

(1) Labor Input (workers per week)	(2) Marginal Physical Product (MPP) (CD packages per week)	(3) Price of Product (P)	(4) Marginal Revenue (MR)	(5) Marginal Revenue Product (MRP_m) = (2) x (4)
8	111	$11.60	$9.40	$1,043.40
9	104	11.40	9.00	936.00
10	97	11.20	8.60	834.20
11	90	11.00	8.20	738.00
12	83	10.80	7.80	647.40
13	76	10.60	7.40	562.40

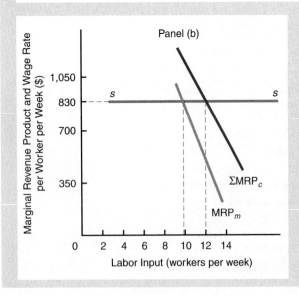

monopolist's MRP curve (MRP_m) around the wage rate $830, the sum of the MRP curves for a perfectly competitive industry (labeled ΣMRP_c), which is the labor demand curve under perfect competition, has been plotted on the same graph in Figure 29-7.

Why does MRP_m represent the monopolist's input demand curve? As always, our profit-maximizing monopolist will continue to hire labor as long as additional profits result. Profits are made as long as the additional cost of more workers is outweighed by the additional revenues made from selling the output of those workers. When the wage rate equals these additional revenues, the monopolist stops hiring. That is, the firm stops hiring when the wage rate is equal to the marginal revenue product because additional workers would add more to cost than to revenue.

Why the Monopolist Hires Fewer Workers

Because we have used the same numbers as in Figure 29-1 on page 685, we can see that the monopolist hires fewer worker-weeks than firms in a perfect competitive market would. That is to say, if we could magically change the CD industry in our example from one in which there is perfect competition in the output market to one in which there is monopoly in the output market, the amount of employment would fall. Why? Because the monopolist must take account of the declining product price that must be charged in order to sell a larger number of CDs. Remember that every firm hires up to the point at which marginal benefit equals marginal cost. The marginal benefit to the monopolist of hiring an additional worker is not simply the additional output times the price of the product. Rather, the monopolist faces a reduction in the price charged on *all* units sold in order to be able to sell more.

So the monopolist ends up hiring fewer workers than all of the perfect competitors taken together, assuming that all other factors remain the same for the two hypothetical examples. But this should not come as a surprise. In considering product markets, by implication we saw that a monopolized CD industry would produce less output than a competitive one. Therefore, the monopolized CD industry would hire fewer workers.

THE UTILIZATION OF OTHER FACTORS OF PRODUCTION

The analysis in this chapter has been given in terms of the demand for the variable input labor. The same analysis holds for any other variable factor input. We could have talked about the demand for fertilizer or the demand for the services of tractors by a farmer instead of the demand for labor and reached the same conclusions. The entrepreneur will hire or buy any variable input up to the point at which its price equals the marginal revenue product.

A further question remains: How much of each variable factor should the firm utilize when all the variable factors are combined to produce the product? We can answer this question by looking at either the profit-maximizing side of the question or the cost-minimizing side.*

---

*Many economic problems involving maximization of profit or other economic variables have *duals*, or precise restatements, in terms of *minimization* rather than maximization. The problem "How do we maximize our output, given fixed resources?" for example, is the dual of the problem "How do we minimize our cost, given fixed output?" Noneconomists sometimes confuse their discussions of economic issues by mistakenly believing that a problem and its dual are two problems rather than one. Asking, for example, "How can we maximize our profits while minimizing our costs?" makes about as much sense as asking, "How can we cross the street while getting to the other side?"

Profit Maximization Revisited

If a firm wants to maximize profits, how much of each factor should be hired (or bought)? As we just saw, the firm will never utilize a factor of production unless the marginal benefit from hiring that factor is at least equal to the marginal cost. What is the marginal benefit? As we have pointed out several times, the marginal benefit is the change in total revenues due to a one-unit change in utilization of the variable input. What is the marginal cost? In the case of a firm buying in a competitive market, it is the price of the variable factor—the wage rate if we are referring to labor.

The profit-maximizing combination of resources for the firm will be where, in a perfectly competitive situation,

MRP of labor = price of labor (wage rates)
MRP of capital = price of capital (cost per unit of service)
MRP of land = price of land (rental rate per unit)

To attain maximum profits, the marginal revenue product of each of a firm's resources must be exactly equal to its price. If the MRP of labor is $20 and its price is only $15, the firm will be underemploying labor.

Cost Minimization and Factor Utilization

From the cost minimization point of view, how can the firm minimize its total costs for a given output? Assume that you are an entrepreneur attempting to minimize costs. Consider a hypothetical situation in which if you spend $1 more on labor, you would get 20 more units of output, but if you spend $1 more on machines, you would get only 10 more units of output. What would you want to do in such a situation? Most likely you would wish to hire more workers or sell off some of your machines, for you are not getting as much output per last dollar spent on machines as you are per last dollar spent on labor. You would want to employ factors of production so that the marginal products per last dollar spent on each are equal. Thus the least-cost, or cost minimization, rule will be as follows:

> *To minimize total costs for a particular rate of production, the firm will hire factors of production up to the point at which the marginal physical product per last dollar spent on each factor of production is equalized.*

That is,

$$\frac{\text{MPP of labor}}{\text{price of labor (wage rate)}} = \frac{\text{MPP of capital}}{\text{price of capital (cost per unit of service)}} = \frac{\text{MPP of land}}{\text{price of land (rental rate per unit)}}$$

All we are saying here is that the profit-maximizing firm will always utilize *all* resources in such combinations that cost will be minimized for any given output rate. This is commonly called the *least-cost combination of resources*. There is an exact match between the profit-maximizing combination of resources and the least-cost combination of resources. In other words, either rule can be used to yield the same cost-minimizing rate of utilization of each variable resource.*

How does the cost-minimizing rule for input utilization help to explain why top managers of U.S. companies earn so much more than other employees?

---

*This can be proved as follows: Profit maximization requires that the price of every input must equal that input's marginal revenue product (the general case). Let i be the input. Then $P_i = \text{MRP}_i$. But MRP is defined as marginal revenue times marginal physical product of the input. Therefore, for every input i, $P_i = \text{MR} \times \text{MPP}_i$. If we divide both sides by MPP_i, we get $P_i/\text{MPP}_i = \text{MR}$. If we take the reciprocal, we obtain $\text{MPP}/P_i = 1/\text{MR}$, which must be true for each and every input. That is another way of stating our cost minimization rule.

E X A M P L E

Why Chief Executive Officers Get Such High Pay

The typical chief executive officer (CEO) of a U.S. company earns more than 400 times the average salary of other employees in the company. Firms minimize their costs when the ratio of a CEO's marginal physical product to the wage paid the CEO equals the ratio of the marginal physical product of another worker to that worker's wage rate. On average, therefore, U.S. firms must consider the marginal physical product of a CEO to be more than 400 times higher than the marginal physical product of other workers.

For Critical Analysis

If firms in Europe are also cost-minimizing firms, then what can you infer from the fact that CEOs of European firms typically earn less than 20 times as much as the average worker in those firms?

CONCEPTS in Brief

- When a firm sells its output in a monopoly market, marginal revenue is less than price.

- Just as the MRP is the perfectly competitive firm's input demand curve, the MRP is also the monopolist's demand curve.

- The profit-maximizing combination of factors will occur when each factor is used up to the point at which its MRP is equal to its unit price.

- To minimize total costs for a given output, the profit-maximizing firm will hire each factor of production up to the point at which the marginal physical product per last dollar spent on each factor is equal to the marginal physical product per last dollar spent on each of the other factors of production.

To test your understanding of the concepts covered in this section, go to the Online Review at www.myeconlab.com/miller.

C A S E   S T U D Y : Economics Front and Center

Outsourcing Can Be a Win–Win Situation

Jackson is a mid-level manager at a U.S. firm that coordinates travel arrangements and provides guided tours for foreign groups visiting the most popular U.S. tourist attractions. As part of its package of travel services, the firm organizes all financial arrangements for the members of each visiting tour group. This can be a complex and time-consuming task because employees must arrange fund transfers involving financial institutions around the globe.

Now, however, Jackson has recommended to the firm's senior officers that the firm should pay workers in South Korea to handle these financial arrangements via e-mail and the Internet. The total cost of outsourcing to the workers in South Korea, Jackson has determined, would be more than 30 percent lower than the wages his firm pays the workers who currently handle this task.

The cost reductions made possible by outsourcing the financial arrangements to South Korean workers will allow the firm to cut the prices of its tour packages by 10 percent. Jackson esti-

mates that this price cut should generate a 20 percent increase in the quantity of travel services demanded and that the firm's revenues should rise. The firm can shift employees who currently handle clients' financial arrangements to jobs as tour guides or bus drivers. Eventually, Jackson's firm may find itself *adding* to its U.S. employees instead of reducing them.

Points to Analyze

1. *Who besides the owners of Jackson's firm will benefit if its senior managers approve Jackson's outsourcing recommendation?*

2. *If outsourcing allows Jackson's firm to reduce its tour package price by 10 percent, how could its demand for labor eventually increase? (Hint: If the travel-services industry is perfectly competitive, then marginal revenue product equals price times marginal physical product.)*

Issues and Applications

How a Federal Labor Rule Boosted Truckers' Wages

One of the duties the U.S. Congress has delegated to the Department of Transportation is the authority to enact highway-safety rules. Among other things, this department has the ability to establish limits on the time that truck drivers spend on the road each day. In an effort to reduce accidents resulting from driver fatigue—estimated to account for about 1,300 of the 4,800 annual fatality-causing U.S. traffic accidents involving large trucks—the department recently implemented the first major change in these limits since 1939. This change had a major impact on the market for labor in the trucking industry. As a consequence, it also affected the shipping costs that all of us pay to purchase items transported via trucks.

Concepts Applied

- Supply of Labor
- Marginal Revenue Product
- Equilibrium Wage Rate

Reducing Labor Supply in the Trucking Industry

Under the old federal work rules, every truck driver could be on duty a maximum of 16 hours per day and had to rest at least 8 hours each day. The new rules, which went into effect at the beginning of 2003, limit daily hours on duty to 14 hours and require at least 10 hours of rest per day.

Of course, these mandates immediately reduced the quantity of labor supplied by truckers to shipping firms at any given wage rate. Thus the direct economic effect of the regulations was a leftward shift in the labor supply curve in the market for labor services provided by truck drivers. The supply of labor declined.

Lower Labor Supply Meets Higher Labor Demand in the Trucking Industry

In 2003, the U.S. economy was already in the midst of an upswing, and so was the demand for the services of trucking firms. Revenues earned by trucking firms were rising, which boosted the marginal revenue product of labor provided by truck drivers. Based on what you have learned in this chapter, you can surmise what happened as a result: There was an increase in the derived demand for labor by trucking firms, as illustrated in Figure 29-8 by the rightward shift in the labor

demand schedule from D_1 to D_2. In the absence of the Department of Transportation's regulatory change, therefore, we would have anticipated an increase in the market wage rate of truck drivers, from W_1 to W_2. We would also have predicted a rise in the equilibrium quantity of labor employed in the trucking industry, from Q_1 to Q_2.

The new rule, however, caused labor supply to fall, from S_1 to S_2, at the same time that labor demand was increasing. The predicted result, a further rise in the market wage rate, to W_3, is exactly what took place. In 2003, the average hourly wage rate earned by drivers of large freight trucks rose by more than 50 cents per hour. Another predicted result is a smaller increase in the equilibrium quantity of truck drivers employed, such as the quantity Q_3 in Figure 29-8. This is also what occurred. Whereas the U.S. Labor Department had estimated in 2002 that employment of drivers of large freight trucks would increase by nearly 50,000 workers in 2003, employment actually rose by only about 27,000 workers.

Before enacting its trucking mandates, the Transportation Department estimated that they would reduce U.S. traffic fatalities by about 400 per year. We can conclude that the regulations also generated higher wage costs for trucking companies and tended to depress employment growth in the trucking industry.

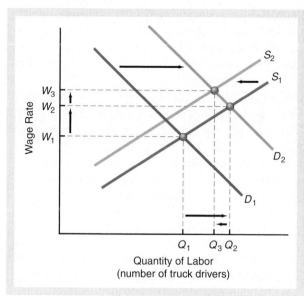

FIGURE 29-8

Higher Labor Demand and Lower Labor Supply in the Market for Truck Drivers
A general increase in the marginal revenue product of services provided by drivers of freight trucks causes the market demand for truck drivers to increase. The market wage rate increases, from W_1 to W_2, and equilibrium employment rises, from Q_1 to Q_2. Regulations that reduce the supply of labor cause a further increase in the market wage rate, to W_3. There is, however, a smaller net increase in equilibrium employment, to Q_3 as a result.

For Critical Analysis

1. Why do you suppose that individuals who own and drive their own freight trucks were opposed to the new Transportation Department regulations?
2. Who potentially bears the highest *opportunity* cost as a result of the new trucking work rules? (Hint: If a newly trained truck driver had anticipated being one of the Q_2 workers depicted in Figure 29-8 but was not among the Q_3 workers actually employed, what did that individual lose during any time spent unemployed during 2003?)

Web Resources

1. For specific labor market information relating to freight trucking from the Bureau of Labor Statistics, go to **www.econtoday.com/chap29**.
2. Bureau of Labor Statistics information about wages paid to and employment of drivers of large freight trucks and for numerous other occupations is available via the link at **www.econtoday.com/chap29**.

Research Project

Evaluate how the rise in marginal factor costs induced by the trucker wage increase generated by the economic upswing and tougher work rules in 2003 must have affected the marginal costs faced by trucking firms. Explain how this could have helped contribute to the nearly 8 percent increase in shipping fees charged by trucking firms in 2003 and the nearly 10 percent fee increase that occurred in 2004. In addition, explain what is likely to happen during the middle and late 2000s to both market wages earned by truck drivers and to shipping fees charged by trucking firms if trucker work-hour requirements remain unchanged and the demand for truck transportation services continues to increase.

SUMMARY DISCUSSION of Learning Objectives

1. **Why a Firm's Marginal Revenue Product Curve Is Its Labor Demand Curve:** The marginal revenue product of labor equals marginal revenue times the marginal physical product of labor. Because of the law of diminishing marginal returns, for a perfectly competitive producer the marginal revenue product curve slopes downward. To maximize profits, a firm hires labor to the point where the marginal factor cost of labor—the addition to total input costs resulting from employing an additional unit of labor—equals the marginal revenue product. For firms

that hire labor in competitive labor markets, the market wage rate is the marginal factor cost of labor, so profit maximization requires hiring labor to the point where the wage rate equals marginal revenue product, which is a point on the marginal revenue product schedule. Thus the marginal revenue product curve gives combinations of wage rates and desired employment of labor for a firm, which means that it is the firm's labor demand curve.

2. **The Demand for Labor as a Derived Demand:** For firms that are perfect competitors in their product markets, marginal revenue equals the market price of their output, so the marginal revenue product of labor equals the product price times the marginal physical product of labor. As conditions in the product market vary and cause the market price at which firms sell their output to change, their marginal revenue product curves shift. Hence the demand for labor by perfectly competitive firms is derived from the demand for the final products these firms produce.

3. **Key Factors Affecting the Elasticity of Demand for Inputs:** The price elasticity of demand for an input, such as labor, is equal to the percentage change in the quantity of the input demanded divided by the percentage change in the price of the input, such as the wage rate. The price elasticity of demand for a particular input is relatively high when any one of the following is true: (a) the price elasticity of demand for the final product is relatively high; (b) it is relatively easy to substitute other inputs in the production process; (c) the proportion of total costs accounted for by the input is relatively large; or (d) the firm has a longer time period to adjust to the change in the input's price.

4. **How Equilibrium Wage Rates at Perfectly Competitive Firms Are Determined:** For perfectly competitive firms, the market labor demand curve is the sum of the individual labor demand curves for all firms, which in turn are the firms' marginal revenue product curves. At the equilibrium wage rate, the quantity of labor demanded by all firms is equal to the quantity of labor supplied by all workers in the marketplace. At this wage rate, each firm looks to its own labor demand curve to determine how much labor to employ.

5. **U.S. Wage and Employment Effects of Labor Outsourcing:** Technological changes are increasingly making foreign labor more readily available as a cheaper substitute for home labor for firms that engage in labor outsourcing. The immediate, short-run effects on wages and employment in U.S. labor markets are mixed. Outsourcing by U.S. firms reduces the demand for labor in affected U.S. labor markets and thereby pushes down wages and employment. Outsourcing by foreign firms that hire U.S. labor, however, raises the demand for labor in related U.S. labor markets, which boosts wages and employment in those labor markets. In the long run, outsourcing allows U.S. firms to operate more efficiently. The resulting resource savings effectively increase U.S. production and consumption possibilities, thereby raising revenues of U.S. firms. This induces an overall rise in U.S. labor demand and a general increase in U.S. wages and employment.

6. **Contrasting the Demand for Labor and Wage Determination Under Monopoly with Outcomes Under Perfect Competition:** If a firm that is a monopolist in its product market competes with firms of other industries for labor in a competitive labor market, it takes the market wage rate as given. Its labor demand curve, however, lies to the left of the labor demand curve for the industry that would have arisen if the industry included a number of perfectly competitive firms. The reason is that marginal revenue is less than price for a monopolist, so the marginal revenue product of the monopolist is lower than under competition. Thus, at the competitively determined wage rate, a monopolized industry employs fewer workers than the industry otherwise would if it were perfectly competitive.

KEY TERMS AND CONCEPTS

derived demand (688)

marginal factor cost (MFC) (686)

marginal physical product (MPP) of labor (684)

marginal revenue product (MRP) (686)

outsourcing (694)

PROBLEMS

Answers to the odd-numbered problems appear at the back of the book.

29-1. The following table depicts the output of a firm that manufactures computer printers. The printers sell for $100 each.

Labor Input (workers per week)	Total Physical Output (printers per week)
10	200
11	218
12	234
13	248
14	260
15	270
16	278

Calculate the marginal physical product and marginal revenue product at each input level above 10 units.

29-2. Suppose that the firm in Problem 29-1 has chosen to hire 15 workers. What is the maximum wage the firm would be willing to pay?

29-3. The weekly wage paid by computer printer manufacturers in a perfectly competitive market is $1,200. Using the information provided in the table that accompanies Problem 29-1, how many workers will the profit-maximizing employer hire?

29-4. Suppose that there is an increase in the demand for personal computer systems. Explain the likely effects on marginal revenue product, marginal factor cost, and the number of workers hired by the firm in Problem 29-1.

29-5. Explain what happens to the elasticity of demand for labor in a given industry after each of the following events.

 a. A new manufacturing technique makes capital easier to substitute for labor.

 b. There is an increase in the number of substitutes for the final product that labor produces.

 c. After a drop in the prices of capital inputs, labor accounts for a larger portion of a firm's factor costs.

29-6. Explain how the following events would affect the demand for labor.

 a. A new education program administered by the company increases labor's marginal product.

 b. The firm completes a new plant with a larger workspace and new machinery.

29-7. The following table depicts the product market and labor market a MP3-player manufacturer faces.

Labor Input (workers per day)	Total Physical Product	Product Price ($)
10	100	50
11	109	49
12	116	48
13	121	47
14	124	46
15	125	45

Calculate the firm's marginal physical product, total revenue, and marginal revenue product at each input level above 10 units.

29-8. The firm in Problem 29-7 competes in a perfectly competitive labor market, and the market wage it faces is $100. How many workers will the profit-maximizing employer hire?

29-9. A firm hires labor in a perfectly competitive labor market. Its current profit-maximizing hourly output is 100 units, which the firm sells at a price of $5 per unit. The marginal physical product of the last unit of labor employed is 5 units per hour. The firm pays each worker an hourly wage of $15.

 a. What marginal revenue does the firm earn from sale of the output produced by the last worker employed?

 b. Does this firm sell its output in a perfectly competitive market?

29-10. Top and mid-level managers of Japanese firms with U.S. offices and plants must travel to the United States several times each month. Most Japanese firms previously employed their own travel staffs to arrange these trips, but increasingly they have been outsourcing this work to U.S. travel agents. Assuming that this trend becomes widespread, what will happen to wages and employment of Japanese and U.S. workers who provide travel services?

29-11. Explain why the short-term effects of outsourcing on U.S. wages and employment tend to be more ambiguous than the long-term effects.

29-12. A profit-maximizing monopolist hires workers in a perfectly competitive labor market. Employing the last worker increased the firm's total weekly output from 110 units to 111 units and caused the firm's weekly revenues to rise from $25,000 to $25,750. What is the currently prevailing weekly wage rate in the labor market?

29-13. A monopoly firm hires workers in a perfectly competitive labor market in which the market wage rate is $20 per day. If the firm maximizes profit, and if the marginal revenue from the last unit of output produced by the last worker hired equals $10, what is the marginal physical product of that worker?

29-14. The current market wage rate is $10, the rental rate of land is $1,000 per unit, and the rental rate of capital is $500. Production managers at a firm find that under their current allocation of factors of production, the marginal revenue product of labor is 100, the marginal revenue product of land is $10,000, and the marginal revenue product of capital is $4,000. Is the firm maximizing profit? Why or why not?

29-15. The current wage rate is $10, and the rental rate of capital is $500. A firm's marginal physical product of labor is 200, and its marginal physical product of capital is 20,000. Is the firm maximizing profits for the given cost outlay? Why or why not?

ECONOMICS ON THE NET

Current Trends in U.S. Labor Markets The Federal Reserve's "Beige Book," which summarizes regional economic conditions around the United States, provides a wealth of information about the current status of U.S. labor markets. This Internet application helps you assess developments in employment and wages in the United States.

Title: The Beige Book–Summary

Navigation: Go to www.econtoday.com/chap29 to access the home page of the Federal Reserve's Board of Governors. Click on *Monetary Policy,* and then click on *Beige Book.* Then select the report for the most recent period.

Application Read the section entitled "Labor Markets" and answer the following questions.

1. Has overall employment been rising or falling during the most recent year? Based on what you learned in this chapter, what factors might account for this pattern? Does the Beige Book summary bear our any of these explanations for changes in U.S. employment?

2. Have U.S. workers' wages been rising or falling during the most recent year?

For Group Study and Analysis: The left-hand margin of the Beige Book site lists the reports of the 12 Federal Reserve districts. Divide the class into two groups, and have each group develop brief summaries of the main conclusions of one district's report concerning employment and wages within that district. Reconvene and compare the reports. Are there pronounced regional differences?

Media Resources

If your exam were tomorrow, would you be ready? For each chapter, MyEconLab Practice Tests and Study Plans pinpoint which sections you have mastered and which ones you need to study. That way, you are more efficient with your study time, and you are better prepared for your exams.

In addition to Practice Tests and your personalized Study Plan, you'll find the following media resources in MyEconLab:
1. *Graphs in Motion* animation of Figures 29-1, 29-2, 29-4, and 29-7.
2. *On Economics in Motion* in-depth animation of Labor.
3. Videos featuring the author, Roger LeRoy Miller, on the following subjects:
   ● Determinants of Demand Elasticity for Inputs
   ● Shifts in the Market Demand for Labor

4. Links to the Web sites cited in the marginal Internet Resources, Issues and Applications feature, and Economics on the Net activity.
5. Audio clips of all key terms, additional practice problems, and a PDF version of the material from the print Study Guide.
6. eThemes of the Times, which is a New York Times article to help you understand the real-world applications of what you are learning.

To see how it works, turn to page 16 and then go to www.myeconlab.com/miller.

Get Ahead of the Curve

Chapter

30

Unions and Labor Market Monopoly Power

I n years past, every eye would have been on the clock. This year, however, the union strike deadline of midnight on August 3 came and went without notice by managers and workers at Verizon Communications. Business went on as usual as negotiators continued their efforts to reach a labor agreement. Even though the average hourly wage rate for Verizon's workers had recently fallen, wages were not the key contract issue. Instead, union officials focused on ensuring job security and health care for Verizon workers. Both sides in the talks knew that resolving these issues would take weeks, if not months. In this chapter, you will learn why marathon talks have become commonplace in U.S. union-management negotiations.

LEARNING OBJECTIVES

After reading this chapter, you should be able to:

1. Outline the essential history of the labor union movement
2. Discuss the current status of labor unions
3. Describe the basic economic goals and strategies of labor unions
4. Evaluate the potential effects of labor unions on wages and productivity
5. Explain how a monopsonist determines how much labor to employ and what wage rate to pay
6. Compare wage and employment decisions by a monopsonistic firm with the choices made by firms in industries with alternative market structures

Media Resources

Refer to the end of the chapter for a full listing of the multimedia learning materials available in MyEconLab.

Labor unions
Worker organizations that seek to secure economic improvements for their members; they also seek to improve the safety, health, and other benefits (such as job security) of their members.

. . . half of the members of U.S. **labor unions**—organizations that seek to secure economic improvements for their members—reside in only six states (California, Illinois, Michigan, New York, Ohio, and Pennsylvania)? These states are homes to a large majority of the private-sector workers who belong to unions. Beyond their borders, the only area experiencing growth in union membership during the past four decades is the public sector. In the early 1960s, only about 10 percent of all government employees in the United States belonged to unions. Now nearly 40 percent of government workers are union members, and 46 percent of *all* U.S. union members work in the public sector.

Clearly, the labor landscape is shifting in the United States. Traditionally, one rationale for forming a union was that members might be able to earn more than they would in a competitive labor market by obtaining a type of monopoly power. Because the entire supply of a particular group of workers is controlled by a single source when a union bargains as a single entity with management, a certain monopoly element enters into the determination of employment. We can no longer talk about a perfectly competitive labor supply situation. Later in the chapter, we will examine the converse—a single employer who is the sole employer of a particular group of workers.

INDUSTRIALIZATION AND LABOR UNIONS

Craft unions
Labor unions composed of workers who engage in a particular trade or skill, such as baking, carpentry, or plumbing.

In most parts of the world, labor movements began with local **craft unions.** These were groups of workers in individual trades, such as shoemaking, printing, or baking. Beginning around the middle of the eighteenth century, new technologies permitted reductions in unit production costs through the formation of larger-scale enterprises that hired dozens or more workers. By the late 1790s, workers in some British craft unions began trying to convince employers to engage in **collective bargaining,** in which business management bargains with representatives of all union members about wages and hours of work.

Collective bargaining
Bargaining between the management of a company or of a group of companies and the management of a union or a group of unions for the purpose of reaching a mutually agreeable contract that sets wages, fringe benefits, and working conditions for all employees in all the unions involved.

In 1799 and 1800, the British Parliament passed laws called the Combination Acts aimed at prohibiting the formation of unions. In 1825, Parliament enacted a replacement Combination Act allowing unions to exist and to engage in limited collective bargaining. Unions on the European continent managed to convince most governments throughout Europe to enact similar laws during the first half of the nineteenth century.

Unions in the United States

The development of unions in the United States lagged several decades behind events in Europe. In the years between the Civil War and the Great Depression (1861–1930s), the Knights of Labor, an organized group of both skilled and unskilled workers, pushed for an eight-hour workday and equal pay for women and men. In 1886, a dissident group from the Knights of Labor formed the American Federation of Labor (AFL) under the leadership of Samuel Gompers. During World War I, union membership increased to more than 5 million. But after the war, the government decided to stop protecting labor's right to organize. Membership began to fall.

The Formation of Industrial Unions. The Great Depression was a landmark event in U.S. labor history. Franklin Roosevelt's National Industrial Recovery Act of 1933 gave labor the federal right to bargain collectively, but that act was declared unconstitutional. The 1935 National Labor Relations Act (NLRA), otherwise known as the Wagner Act, took its place. The NLRA guaranteed workers the right to start unions, to engage in collective bargaining, and to be members in any union.

In 1938, the Congress of Industrial Organizations (CIO) was formed by John L. Lewis, the president of the United Mine Workers. Prior to the formation of the CIO, most labor organizations were craft unions. The CIO was composed of **industrial unions,** which drew their membership from an entire industry such as steel or automobiles. In 1955, the CIO and the AFL merged because the leaders of both associations thought a merger would help organized labor grow faster.

Congressional Control over Labor Unions.

Since the Great Depression, Congress has occasionally altered the relationship between labor and management through significant legislation. One of the most important pieces of legislation was the Taft-Hartley Act of 1947 (the Labor Management Relations Act). In general, the Taft-Hartley Act outlawed certain labor practices of unions, such as make-work rules and forcing unwilling workers to join a particular union. Among other things, it allowed individual states to pass their own **right-to-work laws.** A right-to-work law makes it illegal for union membership to be a requirement for continued employment in any establishment.

More specifically, the Taft-Hartley Act made a **closed shop** illegal; a closed shop requires union membership before employment can be obtained. A **union shop,** however, is legal; a union shop does not require membership as a prerequisite for employment, but it can, and usually does, require that workers join the union after a specified amount of time on the job. (Even a union shop is illegal in states with right-to-work laws.)

Jurisdictional disputes, sympathy strikes, and secondary boycotts were also made illegal by the Taft-Hartley Act. A **jurisdictional dispute** involves two or more unions fighting (and striking) over which should have control in a particular jurisdiction. For example, should a carpenter working for a steel manufacturer be part of the steelworkers' union or the carpenters' union? A **sympathy strike** occurs when one union strikes in sympathy with another union's cause or strike. For example, if the retail clerks' union in an area is striking grocery stores, Teamsters may refuse to deliver products to those stores in sympathy with the retail clerks' demands for higher wages or better working conditions. A **secondary boycott** is the boycotting of a company that deals with a struck company. For example, if union workers strike a baking company, the boycotting of grocery stores that continue to sell that company's products is a secondary boycott. A secondary boycott brings pressure on third parties to force them to stop dealing with an employer who is being struck.

Perhaps the most famous aspect of the Taft-Hartley Act is its provision allowing the president to obtain a court injunction that will stop a strike for an 80-day cooling-off period if the strike is expected to imperil the nation's safety or health.

The Current Status of Labor Unions

Every country has its own rules governing unions and the circumstances under which they can engage in work actions such as strikes. Furthermore, union-organizing efforts have been more successful in some nations than in others. These international differences complicate efforts to compare the status of unions in various nations. Nevertheless, it is possible to assess how widespread union membership is in different countries and to evaluate overall trends in the extent of unionization.

Worldwide Trends in Unionization.

Figure 30-1 on the following page shows union membership as a share of total employment for a diverse set of nations. As the figure indicates, rates of unionization vary considerably from country to country. More than 70 percent of workers belong to unions in Finland and Sweden, while fewer than 20 percent of workers in Japan, Singapore, and South Korea are union members.

In nearly all these countries, the percentages of workers who are union members have been declining steadily during the past several years. Since the 1970s, union membership rates have dropped in every country depicted in Figure 30-1 with the exception of Finland, where the rate of unionization has risen slightly. In all other countries, union membership

Industrial unions
Labor unions that consist of workers from a particular industry, such as automobile manufacturing or steel manufacturing.

Right-to-work laws
Laws that make it illegal to require union membership as a condition of continuing employment in a particular firm.

Closed shop
A business enterprise in which employees must belong to the union before they can be hired and must remain in the union after they are hired.

Union shop
A legal environment in which businesses may hire nonunion members, conditional on their joining the union by some specified date after employment begins.

Jurisdictional dispute
A dispute involving two or more unions over which should have control of a particular jurisdiction, such as a particular craft or skill or a particular firm or industry.

Sympathy strike
A strike by a union in sympathy with another union's strike or cause.

Secondary boycott
A boycott of companies or products sold by companies that are dealing with a company being struck.

Go to www.econtoday.com/chap30 to link to the Legal Information Institute's review all the key U.S. labor laws.

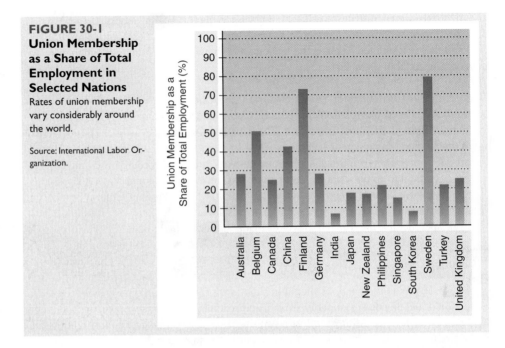

FIGURE 30-1
Union Membership as a Share of Total Employment in Selected Nations
Rates of union membership vary considerably around the world.

Source: International Labor Organization.

rates have dropped by at least 5 percentage points since the 1970s. In Australia, union membership as a share of total employment has fallen by more than 25 percentage points.

U.S. Unionization Trends. Figure 30-2 shows that union membership has also been declining in the United States since the 1970s. Currently, only slightly more than 12 percent

FIGURE 30-2
Decline in Union Membership
Numerically, union membership in the United States has increased dramatically since the 1930s, but as a percentage of the labor force, union membership peaked around 1960 and has been falling ever since. Most recently, the absolute number of union members has also diminished.

Sources: L. Davis et al., *American Economic Growth* (New York: HarperCollins, 1972), p. 220; U.S. Department of Labor, Bureau of Labor Statistics.

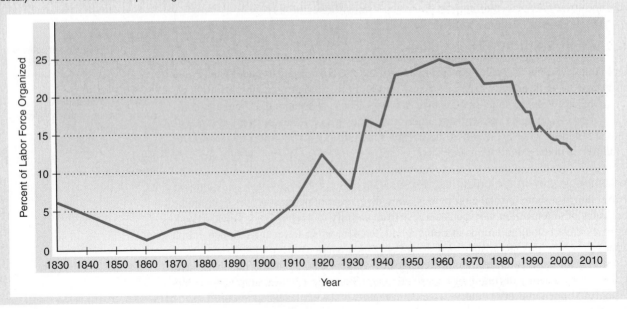

TABLE 30-1
The Ten Largest Unions in the United States
Half of the top ten U.S. unions have members who work in service and government occupations.

Union	Industry	Members
National Education Association	Education	2,668,925
International Brotherhood of Teamsters	Trucking, delivery	1,398,412
United Food and Commercial Workers International Union	Food and grocery services	1,385,043
Service Employees International Union	Health care, public, and janitorial services	1,376,292
American Federation of State, County, and Municipal Employees	Government services	1,300,000
Laborers' International Union of North America	Construction, utilities	795,335
American Federation of Teachers	Education	741,270
International Association of Machinists and Aerospace Workers	Machine and aerospace	722,987
International Brotherhood of Electrical Workers	Electrical	722,095
International Union, United Automobile, Aerospace, and Agricultural Implement Workers of America	Auto, aerospace, and agricultural implements	701,818

Source: U.S. Department of Labor.

of U.S. workers are union members. If we remove labor unions in the public sector—federal, state, and local government workers—only about 9 percent of workers in the private sector belong to unions.

A large part of the explanation for the decline in union membership has to do with the shift away from manufacturing. In 1948, workers in goods-producing industries, transportation, and utilities, which traditionally have been among the most heavily unionized industries, constituted more than half of private nonagricultural employment. Today that fraction is about one-fifth. Manufacturing jobs account for less than 15 percent of all employment in the United States.

The relative decline in manufacturing employment helps explain why most of the largest U.S. unions now draw their members primarily from workers in service industries and governments. As you can see in Table 30-1, five of the ten largest unions now represent workers in these areas. The remaining five largest unions represent the goods-producing industries, transportation, and utilities that once dominated the U.S. union movement.

Although the trend away from manufacturing is the main reason for the decline in unionism, the deregulation of certain industries, such as airlines and trucking, has also contributed, as has increased global competition. In addition, immigration has weakened the power of unions. Much of the unskilled and typically nonunionized work in the United States is done by foreign-born workers, and immigrant workers who are undocumented cannot legally join a union.

How might increased social regulation by the U.S. government have contributed to the decline of U.S. unions?

Who Needs Unions?

One of the key rationales for the development of unions was that by bargaining for shorter hours and higher pay, they would prevent employers from "taking advantage of" lowly paid employees. In modern times, however, the government performs this role. Under new rules issued by the U.S. Department of Labor, people earning as much as $100,000 per year can qualify for overtime pay. Occupations covered by the rules include cooks, paralegals, bookkeepers, inspectors, and bank examiners. Even comparison shoppers can file for time-and-a-half pay for extra hours they spend at shopping malls. No longer do people in these occupations feel obliged to turn to unions to make sure that they get paid more for working longer hours.

For Critical Analysis
How do government actions that toughen workplace-safety rules affect workers' incentives to form unions?

CONCEPTS in Brief

- The American Federation of Labor (AFL), composed of craft unions, was formed in 1886 under the leadership of Samuel Gompers. Membership increased until after World War I, when the government temporarily stopped protecting labor's right to organize.

- During the Great Depression, legislation was passed that allowed for collective bargaining. The National Labor Relations Act of 1935 guaranteed workers the right to form unions. The Congress of Industrial Organizations (CIO), composed of industrial unions, was formed during the Great Depression. The AFL and the CIO merged in 1955.

- Rates of union membership vary considerably across countries. In the United States, union membership as a percentage of the labor force peaked at nearly 25 percent in 1960 and has declined since then to only slightly more than 12 percent.

To test your understanding of the concepts covered in this section, go to the Online Review at www.myeconlab.com/miller.

UNION GOALS AND STRATEGIES

Through collective bargaining, unions establish the wages below which no individual worker can legally offer his or her services. Each year, union representatives and management negotiate collective bargaining contracts covering wages as well as working conditions and fringe benefits for about 6 million workers. If approved by the members, a union labor contract sets wage rates, maximum workdays, working conditions, fringe benefits, and other matters, usually for the next two or three years.

Strike: The Ultimate Bargaining Tool

Whenever union-management negotiations break down, union negotiators may turn to their ultimate bargaining tool, the threat or the reality of a strike. Strikes make headlines, but in less than 2 percent of all labor-management disputes does a strike occur before the contract is signed. In the other 98 percent, contracts are signed without much public fanfare.

The purpose of a strike is to impose costs on recalcitrant management to force it to accept the union's proposed contract terms. Strikes disrupt production and interfere with a company's or an industry's ability to sell goods and services. The strike works both ways, though, because workers receive no wages while on strike (though they may be partly compensated out of union strike funds). Striking union workers may also be eligible to draw state unemployment benefits.

The impact of a strike is closely related to the ability of striking unions to prevent non-striking (and perhaps nonunion) employees from continuing to work for the targeted company or industry. Therefore, steps are usually taken to prevent others from working for the employer. **Strikebreakers** can effectively destroy whatever bargaining power rests behind a strike. Numerous methods have been used to prevent strikebreakers from breaking strikes. Violence has been known to erupt, almost always in connection with union attempts to prevent strikebreaking.

In recent years, companies have had less incentive to hire strikebreakers, because work stoppages have become much less common. From 1945 until 1990, on average more than 200 union strikes took place in the United States each year. Since 1990, however, the average has been closer to 25 strikes per year.

Strikebreakers
Temporary or permanent workers hired by a company to replace union members who are striking.

Union Goals with Direct Wage Setting

We have already pointed out that one of the goals of unions is to set minimum wages. The effects of setting a wage rate higher than a competitive market clearing wage rate can be seen in Figure 30-3. We have a competitive market for labor. The market demand curve is D, and the market supply curve is S. The market clearing wage rate is W_e. The equilibrium quantity of labor is Q_e. If the union establishes by collective bargaining a minimum wage rate that exceeds W_e, an excess quantity of labor will be supplied (assuming no change in the labor demand schedule). If the minimum wage established by union collective bargaining is W_U, the quantity supplied will be Q_S. The quantity demanded will be Q_D. The difference is the excess quantity supplied, or surplus. Hence the following point becomes clear:

> *One of the major roles of a union that establishes a wage rate above the market clearing wage rate is to ration available jobs among the excess number of workers who wish to work in unionized industries.*

Note also that the surplus of labor is equivalent to a shortage of jobs at wage rates above equilibrium.

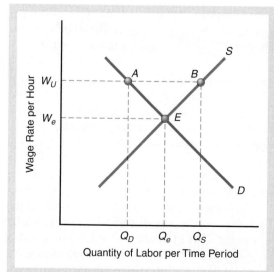

FIGURE 30-3
Unions Must Ration Jobs
If the union succeeds in obtaining wage rate W_U, the quantity of labor demanded will be Q_D, but the quantity of labor supplied will be Q_S. The union must ration a limited number of jobs to a greater number of workers; the surplus of labor is equivalent to a shortage of jobs at that wage rate.

To ration jobs, the union may use a seniority system, lengthen the apprenticeship period to discourage potential members from joining, or institute other rationing methods. This has the effect of shifting the supply of labor curve to the left in order to support the higher wage, W_U.

There is a trade-off here that any union's leadership must face: Higher wages inevitably mean a reduction in total employment—a smaller number of positions. When facing higher wages, management may replace part of the workforce with machinery. In addition, at higher wages, more workers will seek to enter the industry.

How do you suppose that German employers responded to high union wages when the expansion of the European Union (EU) enabled them to move plants and equipment closer to workers willing to accept lower pay?

International EXAMPLE

In Europe, Jobs Can Now Move Farther East

Germany has an extensive system of centralized wage bargaining that involves nearly 60,000 different labor agreements. Furthermore, any German company with more than 2,000 employees must give half the seats on its management board to employee representatives. The result has been steady wage increases. Wages in Germany are higher than in most other European nations. German wages are certainly much higher than wages in all ten of the EU's new members from Eastern Europe, whose borders are now open to factors of production from elsewhere in the EU.

When union workers at German companies recently began pushing for higher wages, managers at several firms pointed out that German wages were already twice as high as the average wage in Slovakia. This big wage differential, the managers noted, could help cover the costs of moving plants and equipment out of Germany and into Slovakia, where willing workers could readily replace German workers. Discussions about big wage boosts for German union workers died out rapidly thereafter.

For Critical Analysis
If EU borders really become fully open to movements in all factors of production, will average German wages remain twice as high as average Slovakian wages?

If we view unions as monopoly sellers of a service, we can identify three different types of goals that they may pursue: ensuring employment for all members of the union, maximizing aggregate income of workers, and maximizing wage rates for some workers.

Employing All Members in the Union. Assume that the union has Q_1 workers. If it faces a labor demand curve such as D in Figure 30-4, the only way it can "sell" all of those workers' services is to accept a wage rate of W_1. This is similar to any other market. The demand curve tells the maximum price that can be charged to sell any particular quantity of a good or service. Here the service happens to be labor.

Maximizing Member Income. If the union is interested in maximizing the gross income of its members, it will normally want a smaller membership than Q_1—namely, Q_2 workers, all employed and paid a wage rate of W_2. The aggregate income to all members of the union is represented by the wages of only the ones who work. Total income earned by union members is maximized where the price elasticity of demand is numerically equal to 1. That occurs where marginal revenue equals zero. In Figure 30-4, marginal revenue equals zero at a quantity of labor Q_2. So we know that if the union obtains a wage rate

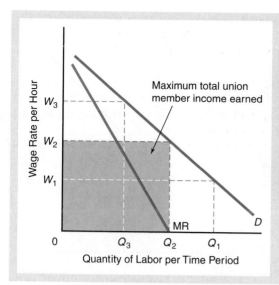

FIGURE 30-4
What Do Unions Maximize?
Assume that the union wants to employ all its Q_1 members. It will attempt to get wage rate W_1. If the union wants to maximize total wage receipts (income), it will do so at wage rate W_2, where the elasticity of the demand for labor is equal to 1. (The shaded area represents the maximum total income that the union would earn at W_2.) If the union wants to maximize the wage rate for a given number of workers, say, Q_3, it will set the wage rate at W_3.

equal to W_2, and therefore Q_2 workers are demanded, the total income to the union membership will be maximized. In other words, $Q_2 \times W_2$ (the shaded area) will be greater than any other combination of wage rates and quantities of union workers demanded. It is, for example, greater than $Q_1 \times W_1$. Note that in this situation, if the union started out with Q_1 members, there would be $Q_1 - Q_2$ members out of *union* work at the wage rate W_2. (Those out of union work either remain unemployed or go to other industries. Such actions have a depressing effect on wages in nonunion industries due to the increase in supply of workers there.)

Maximizing Wage Rates for Certain Workers. Assume that the union wants to maximize the wage rates for some of its workers—perhaps those with the most seniority. If it wants to keep a quantity of Q_3 workers employed, it will seek to obtain a wage rate of W_3. This will require deciding which workers should be unemployed and which workers should work and for how long each week or each year they should be employed.

Union Strategies to Raise Wages Indirectly

One way or another, unions seek above-market wages for some or all of their members. Sometimes unions try to achieve this goal without making wage increases direct features of contract negotiations.

Limiting Entry over Time. One way to raise wage rates without specifically setting wages is for unions to limit the size of their membership to the size of their employed workforce at the time the union was first organized. No workers are put out of work when the union is formed. Over time, as the demand for labor in the industry increases, the union prevents any net increase in membership, so larger wage increases are obtained than would otherwise be the case. We see this in Figure 30-5 on the following page. Union members freeze entry into their union, thereby obtaining a wage rate of $21 per hour instead of allowing a wage rate of $20 per hour with no restriction on labor supply.

Altering the Demand for Union Labor. Another way that unions can increase wages is to shift the demand curve for labor outward to the right. This approach compares favorably

Economics Front and Center

To contemplate alternative union strategies, read the case study, **Time for New Union Members, or Not?** on page 725.

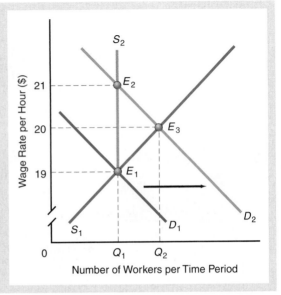

FIGURE 30-5
Restricting Supply over Time
When the union was formed, it didn't affect wage rates or employment, which remained at $19 and Q_1 (the equilibrium wage rate and quantity at point E_1). However, as demand increased—that is, as the demand schedule shifted outward to D_2 from D_1—the union restricted membership to its original level of Q_1. The new supply curve is S_1S_2, which intersects D_2 at E_2, or at a wage rate of $21. Without the union, equilibrium would be at E_3, with a wage rate of $20 and employment of Q_2.

with the supply restriction approach because it increases both wage rates and the employment level. The demand for union labor can be increased by increasing worker productivity, increasing the demand for union-made goods, and decreasing the demand for non-union-made goods.

1. *Increasing worker productivity.* Supporters of unions have argued that unions provide a good system of industrial jurisprudence. The presence of unions may induce workers to feel that they are working in fair and just circumstances. If so, they work harder, increasing labor productivity. Productivity is also increased when unions resolve differences and reduce conflicts between workers and management, thereby providing a more peaceful administrative environment.

2. *Increasing demand for union-made goods.* Because the demand for labor is a derived demand, a rise in the demand for products produced by union labor will increase the demand for union labor itself. One way that unions attempt to increase the demand for goods produced by union labor is by advertising "Look for the union label."

3. *Decreasing the demand for non-union-made goods.* When the demand for goods that are competing with (or are substitutes for) union-made goods is reduced, consumers shift to union-made goods, increasing the demand. The campaigns of various unions against imports are a good example. The United Auto Workers support restrictions on imported cars as strongly as the Textile Workers Unions support restrictions on imported textile goods. The result is greater demand for goods "made in the USA," which in turn presumably increases the demand for U.S. union (and nonunion) labor.

ECONOMIC EFFECTS OF LABOR UNIONS

Figure 30-6 displays the percentages of workers who are union members in the most heavily unionized occupations. Do union members in these and other occupations earn higher wages? Are they more or less productive than nonunionized workers in their industries?

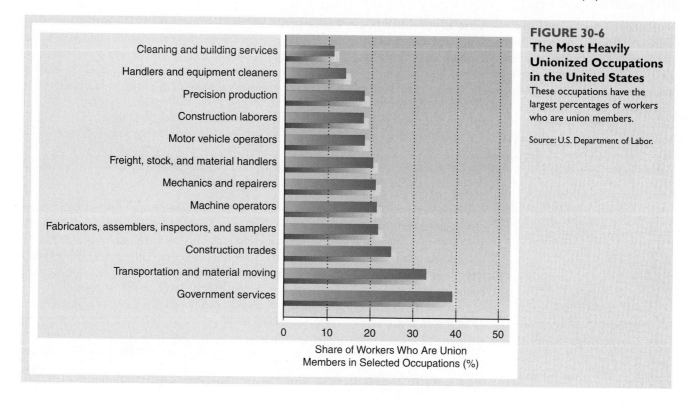

FIGURE 30-6
The Most Heavily Unionized Occupations in the United States
These occupations have the largest percentages of workers who are union members.

Source: U.S. Department of Labor.

Share of Workers Who Are Union Members in Selected Occupations (%)

What are the broader economic effects of unionization? Let's consider each of these questions in turn.

Unions and Wages

You have learned that unions are able to raise the wages of their members if they can successfully limit the supply of labor in a particular industry. Unions are also able to raise wages if they can induce increases in the demand for union labor.

Economists have extensively studied the differences between union wages and nonunion wages. They have found that the average *hourly* wage earned by a typical union worker is about $2.25 higher than the hourly wage earned by a typical worker who is not a union member. Adjusted for inflation, this union-nonunion hourly wage differential is only about half as large as it was two decades ago, however.

How has the ability of unionized auto workers to keep wages above competitive levels influenced the production of autos in the United States?

E X A M P L E

Union Wages Change the U.S. Automotive Landscape

Until the 1970s, the only mass-produced automobiles produced in the United States were made by of General Motors (GM), Ford, Chrysler, and a now-defunct company called American Motors. Furthermore, nearly all of the workers at these companies were unionized. Since the late 1970s, however, foreign-based companies such as Toyota, Nissan, Honda, and Hyundai have built U.S. plants. They have also hired nonunion workers at lower hourly wages.

Higher costs of a unionized workforce have induced GM, Ford, and Chrysler to close dozens of factories and shed thousands of union employees during the 2000s. In the same period, foreign automakers have added nearly as many U.S. plants and hired thousands of nonunion employees. Thus being saddled with higher-priced union workers has generated a shrinkage in the U.S.-based auto industry, while the ability to hire lower-priced nonunion workers has enabled foreign producers to expand their U.S. presence.

For Critical Analysis
Since 2004, the health benefits paid to unionized auto workers have cost producers about $1,000 per car more than those paid to nonunionized auto workers. How is this likely to affect foreign producers' total share of U.S. auto production?

Comparisons of the *annual* earnings of union and nonunion workers indicate that in recent years, unions have not succeeded in raising the annual incomes of their members. In 1985, workers who belonged to unions earned nearly 7 percent more per year than nonunion workers, even though union workers worked fewer hours per week. Today, a typical nonunion employee still works slightly longer each week, but the average nonunion worker also has a higher annual income than the average union worker.

Even the $2.25 hourly wage differential already mentioned is somewhat misleading because it is an average across *all* U.S. workers. In the private sector, union workers earn only about 4 percent more than nonunion workers, or a little less than 60 cents per hour. The hourly wage gain for government workers is nearly six times higher at about $3.55 per hour. A state government employee who belongs to a union currently earns an hourly wage more than 20 percent higher than a state government worker who is not a union member.

Unions and Labor Productivity

A traditional view of union behavior is that unions decrease productivity by artificially shifting the demand curve for union labor outward through excessive staffing and make-work requirements. For example, some economists have traditionally argued that unions tend to bargain for excessive use of workers, as when an airline union requires an engineer on all flights. This is called **featherbedding.** Many painters' unions, for example, resisted the use of paint sprayers and required that their members use only brushes. They even specified the maximum width of the brush. Moreover, whenever a union strikes, productivity drops, and this reduction in productivity in one sector of the economy can spill over into other sectors.

Featherbedding
Any practice that forces employers to use more labor than they would otherwise or to use existing labor in an inefficient manner.

This traditional critical view of unions has been countered by an argument that unions can actually increase productivity. Some labor economists contend that unions act as a collective voice for their members to air grievances and raise concerns about conditions that reduce productivity. As a consequence, these economists suggest, worker turnover is lower in unionized industries, and this stability may contribute to productivity increases. Indeed, there is strong evidence that worker turnover is reduced when unions are present. Of course, this evidence may also be consistent with the fact that wage rates are so attractive to union members that they will not quit unless working conditions become truly intolerable.

Economic Benefits and Costs of Labor Unions

As should be clear by now, there are two opposing views of unions. One sees them as monopolies whose main effect is to raise the wage rate of high-seniority members at the expense of low-seniority members (and nonunion workers). The other contends that unions can increase labor productivity by promoting safer working conditions and generally better work environments and that they contribute to workforce stability by providing arbitration and grievance procedures.

Critics point out that the positive view of unionism overlooks the fact that many of the benefits that unions provide do not require that unions engage in restrictive labor practices, such as the closed shop. Unions could still do positive things for workers without restricting the labor market.

Consequently, a key issue that economists seek to assess when judging the social costs of unions is the extent to which their existence has a negative effect on employment growth. Most evidence indicates that while unions do significantly reduce employment in some of the most heavily unionized occupations, the overall effects on U.S. employment are modest. On the whole, therefore, the social costs of unions in the United States are probably relatively low.

CONCEPTS in Brief

- When unions raise wage rates above market clearing prices, they face the problem of rationing a restricted number of jobs to a worker who desires to earn the higher wages.

- Unions may pursue any one of three goals: (1) to employ all members in the union, (2) to maximize total income of the union's workers, or (3) to maximize wages for certain, usually high-seniority, workers.

- Unions can increase the wage rate of members by engaging in practices that shift the union labor supply curve inward

or shift the demand curve for union labor outward (or both).

- Some economists believe that unions can increase productivity by acting as a collective voice for their members, thereby freeing members from the task of convincing their employers that some change in working arrangements should be made. Unions may reduce turnover, thus improving productivity.

To test your understanding of the concepts covered in this section, go to the Online Review at www.myeconlab.com/miller.

MONOPSONY: A BUYER'S MONOPOLY

Let's assume that a firm is a perfect competitor in the product market. The firm cannot alter the price of the product it sells, and it faces a perfectly elastic demand curve for its product. We also assume that the firm is the only buyer of a particular input. Although this situation may not occur often, it is useful to consider. Let's think in terms of a factory town, like those dominated by textile mills or those in the mining industry. One company not only hires the workers but also owns the businesses in the community, owns the apartments that workers live in, and hires the clerks, waiters, and all other personnel. This buyer of labor is called a **monopsonist,** the only buyer in the market.

What does this situation mean to a monopsonist in terms of the costs of hiring extra workers? It means that if the monopsonist wants to hire more workers, it has to offer higher wages. Our monopsonist firm cannot hire all the labor it wants at the going wage rate. Instead, it faces an upward-sloping supply curve. If it wants to hire more workers, it has to raise wage rates, including the wages of all its current workers (assuming a non-wage-discriminating monopsonist). It therefore has to take account of these increased costs when deciding how many more workers to hire.

Monopsonist
The only buyer in a market.

Marginal Factor Cost

The monopsonist faces an upward-sloping supply curve of the input in question because as the only buyer, it faces the entire market supply curve. Each time the monopsonist buyer of labor, for example, wishes to hire more workers, it must raise wage rates. Thus the marginal cost of another unit of labor is rising. In fact, the marginal cost of increasing its workforce will always be greater than the wage rate. This is because the monopsonist must pay the same wage rate to everyone in order to obtain another unit of labor; thus the higher wage rate has to be offered not only to the last worker but also to *all* its other workers. We call the additional cost to the monopsonist of hiring one more worker the marginal factor cost (MFC).

The marginal factor cost of hiring the last worker is therefore that worker's wages plus the increase in the wages of all other existing workers. As we pointed out in Chapter 29, marginal factor cost is equal to the change in total variable costs due to a one-unit change in the one variable factor of production—in this case, labor. In Chapter 29, marginal factor cost was simply the competitive wage rate because the employer could hire all workers at the same wage rate.

Derivation of a Marginal Factor Cost Curve

Panel (a) of Figure 30-7 shows the quantity of labor purchased, the wage rate per hour, the total cost of the quantity of labor supplied per hour, and the marginal factor cost per hour for the additional labor bought.

We translate the columns from panel (a) to the graph in panel (b) of the figure. We show the supply curve as *S*, which is taken from columns 1 and 2. (Note that this is the same as the *average* factor cost curve; hence you can view Figure 30-7 as showing the relationship between average factor cost and marginal factor cost.) The marginal factor cost curve (MFC) is taken from columns 1 and 4. The MFC curve must be above the supply curve whenever the supply curve is upward sloping. If the supply curve is upward sloping, the firm must pay a higher wage rate in order to attract a larger amount of labor. This higher wage rate must be paid to all workers; thus the increase in total costs due to an increase in the labor input will exceed the wage rate. (Recall from Chapter 29 that in a perfectly competitive input market, the supply curve is perfectly elastic and the marginal factor cost curve is identical to the supply curve.)

Employment and Wages Under Monopsony

To determine the number of workers that a monopsonist desires to hire, we compare the marginal benefit to the marginal cost of each hiring decision. The marginal cost is the marginal factor cost (MFC) curve, and the marginal benefit is the marginal revenue product (MRP) curve. In Figure 30-8 on page 724, we assume competition in the output market and monopsony in the input market. A monopsonist finds its profit-maximizing quantity of labor demanded at *A*, where the marginal revenue product is just equal to the marginal factor cost. The monopsonist will therefore desire to hire exactly Q_m workers.

The Input Price Paid by a Monopsony. How much is the firm going to pay these workers? The monopsonist sets the wage rate so that it will get exactly the quantity, Q_m, supplied to it by its "captive" labor force. We find that wage rate is W_m. There is no reason to pay the workers any more than W_m because at that wage rate, the firm can get exactly the quantity it wants. The actual quantity used is determined by the intersection of the marginal factor cost curve and the marginal revenue product curve for labor—that is, at the point at which the marginal revenue from expanding employment just equals the marginal cost of doing so (point *A* in Figure 30-8).

Notice that the profit-maximizing wage rate paid to workers (W_m) is lower than the marginal revenue product. That is to say, workers are paid a wage that is less than their contribution to the monopsonist's revenues. This is sometimes referred to as **monopsonistic exploitation** of labor. The monopsonist is able to do this because each individual worker has little power in bargaining for a higher wage. (The organization of workers into a union, though, normally creates a monopoly supplier of labor, which gives the union some power to bargain for higher wages.)

Monopsonistic exploitation
Paying a price for the variable input that is less than its marginal revenue product; the difference between marginal revenue product and the wage rate.

Panel (a)

(1) Quantity of Labor Supplied to Management	(2) Required Hourly Wage Rate	(3) Total Wage Bill (3) = (1) x (2)	(4) Marginal Factor Cost $(\text{MFC}) = \dfrac{\text{Change in (3)}}{\text{Change in (1)}}$
0	—	—	
			$12
1	$12	$12	
			16
2	14	28	
			20
3	16	48	
			24
4	18	72	
			28
5	20	100	
			32
6	22	132	

FIGURE 30-7
Derivation of a Marginal Factor Cost Curve

The supply curve, S, in panel (b) is taken from columns 1 and 2 of panel (a). The marginal factor cost curve (MFC) is taken from columns 1 and 4. It is the increase in the total wage bill resulting from a one-unit increase in labor input.

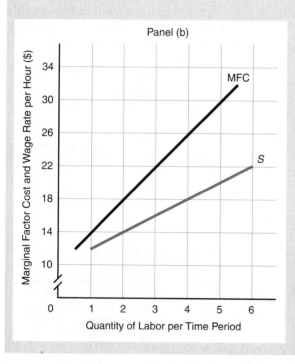

Panel (b)

Bilateral Monopoly. What happens when a monopsonist meets a monopolist? This situation is called **bilateral monopoly,** defined as a market structure in which a single buyer faces a single seller. An example of bilateral monopoly is a county education employer facing a single teachers' union in that labor market. Another example is a players' union facing an organized group of team owners, as has occurred in professional baseball and football. To analyze bilateral monopoly, we would have to look at the interaction of both sides, buyer and seller. The price outcome turns out to be indeterminate.

Bilateral monopoly
A market structure consisting of a monopolist and a monopsonist.

FIGURE 30-8
Wage and Employment Determination for a Monopsonist

The monopsonist firm looks at a marginal cost curve, MFC, that slopes upward and is above its labor supply curve, S. The marginal benefit of hiring additional workers is given by the firm's MRP curve (its demand-for-labor curve). The intersection of MFC with MRP, at point A, determines the number of workers hired. The firm hires Q_m workers but has to pay them only W_m in order to attract them. Compare this with the competitive solution, in which the wage rate would have to be W_e and the quantity of labor would be Q_e.

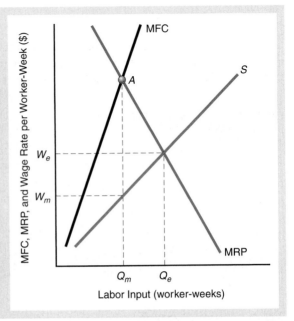

FIGURE 30-9
Pricing and Employment Under Various Market Conditions

In panel (a), the firm operates in perfect competition in both the input and output markets. It purchases labor up to the point where the going rate W_e is equal to MRP_c. It hires quantity Q_e of labor. In panel (b), the firm is a perfect competitor in the input market but has a monopoly in the output market. It purchases labor up to the point where W_e is equal to MRP_m. It hires a smaller quantity of labor, Q_m, than in panel (a). In panel (c), the firm is a monopsonist in the input market and a perfect competitor in the output market. It hires labor up to the point where $MFC = MRP_c$. It will hire quantity Q_1 and pay wage rate W_c. Panel (d) shows a situation in which the firm is both a monopolist in the market for its output and a monopsonist in its labor market. It hires the quantity of labor Q_2 at which $MFC = MRP_m$ and pays the wage rate W_m.

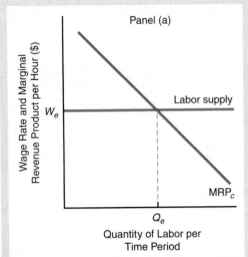

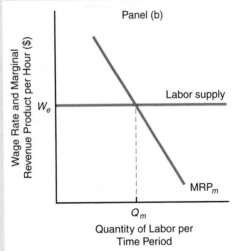

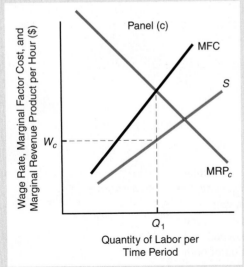

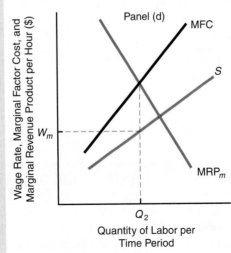

We have studied the pricing of labor in various situations, including perfect competition in both the output and input markets and monopoly in both the output and input markets. Figure 30-9 shows four possible situations graphically.

CONCEPTS in Brief

- A monopsonist is the only buyer in a market. The monopsonist faces an upward-sloping supply curve of labor.

- Because the monopsonist faces an upward-sloping supply curve of labor, the marginal factor cost of increasing the labor input by one unit is greater than the wage rate. Thus the marginal factor cost curve always lies above the supply curve.

- A monopsonist will hire workers up to the point at which marginal factor cost equals marginal revenue product. Then the monopsonist will find what minimal wage is necessary to attract that number of workers, as indicated by the supply curve.

To test your understanding of the concepts covered in this section, go to the Online Review at www.myeconlab.com/miller.

CASE STUDY: Economics Front and Center

Time for New Union Members, or Not?

Jaworski works as an assistant to the leaders of a federation of five large unions that are part of the AFL-CIO. These union leaders are dissatisfied with the AFL-CIO, which they view as overly passive in the face of falling union memberships and declining union-nonunion wage differentials. Jaworski has been assigned to determine how much the combined incomes of unions in this federation would rise if they could attract younger members and increase union membership by 10 percent. She has also been charged with determining how many recruiters and other resources would be required to generate the required membership increase.

As she is completing a first draft of her report to the five-union federation, Jaworksi receives a phone call from a senior AFL-CIO official who has learned about the federation's plans. He demands to know why he and other officials of the AFL-CIO were not consulted about the federation's intention to mount a new recruiting drive. When Jaworksi explains that the federation's planning is only at an early stage, his response is blunt. "Most existing AFL-CIO union members have high seniority and are satisfied with their earnings, and a big effort to recruit young people might well cause their wages to decline," he states. "No one in your federation is to launch any new recruiting efforts without consulting with us first. Goodbye." Jaworski responds in kind, hangs up the phone, and continues working on the concluding section of her report.

Points to Analyze

1. *What strategy is the five-union federation contemplating pursuing?*

2. *What is the current goal of the AFL-CIO?*

Concepts Applied

- Labor Unions
- Collective Bargaining
- Union Wages

I n June 1952, the United Steelworkers of America won one of the biggest union victories in U.S. history, when the Supreme Court ruled that President Harry Truman had illegally ordered army troops to avert a strike by the union. In 2003, the union was set to make history once more. Its contract with Goodyear Tire & Rubber Company had expired in April, and four months of talks had not yet led to an agreement. After a long meeting, the union's leaders announced that there would be no strike. Thus the steelworkers' union had just agreed to the longest period of continued work by unionized workers after a contract had expired.

Wages Take a Back Seat to Job Security

For the United Steelworkers of America, the key issue that had to be ironed out with Goodyear was the fate of several tire factories that the company had announced it might close. The union was willing to let the talks drag on, especially if any additional day, week, or month of discussions might yield management concessions that would prevent another plant closing. Ultimately, Goodyear agreed to close only one facility instead of the three plants that it had hoped to shut down.

Health Benefits Become a New Hot-Button Issue

To prevent the plant closings, the steelworkers' union agreed to keep their members' base wages unchanged during the first year of the new contract. Nevertheless, the union claimed a major victory, because the only change in health benefits appearing in the final union contract was a slight increase in workers' copayments for prescription drugs. Union leaders had drawn a "line in the sand" when it came to health benefits. The union was convinced that the promise of better health benefits, not higher wages, would ultimately be the key to renewed membership growth.

For Critical Analysis

1. In what ways did the choices that the United Steelworkers faced in negotiating with Goodyear reflect the fundamental trade-off that any union must face?
2. From the perspectives of both United Steelworkers members and steel companies, in what ways are increased health benefits similar to or different from wage increases?

Web Resource

Go to www.econtoday.com/chap30 to learn more about the various workers represented by the United Steelworkers of America, including many employed in health care industries and the public sector as well as in mining and steelmaking.

Research Project

Consider the choices that the United Steelworkers of America made in 2003. In light of these decisions, which of the union strategies considered in this chapter do you conclude that this union actually employed in pursuing their ultimate goals?

SUMMARY DISCUSSION of Learning Objectives

1. **Labor Unions:** The first labor unions were craft unions, representing workers in specific trades. In the United States, the American Federation of Labor (AFL) emerged in the late nineteenth century. In 1935, the National Labor Relations Act (or Wagner Act) granted workers the right to form unions and bargain collectively. Industrial unions, which represent workers of specific industries formed the Congress of Industrial Organizations (CIO) in 1938, and in 1955 a merger formed the current AFL-CIO. The Taft-Hartley Act of 1947 placed limitations on unions' rights to organize, strike, and boycott.

2. **The Current Status of Labor Unions:** In some nations, more than half of all workers belong to unions, but in the United States, only about one in eight workers is a union member. A key reason for the decline in U.S. union membership rates is undoubtedly the relative decline in manufacturing jobs as a share of total employment. In addition, in less skilled occupations that would otherwise be attractive to union organizers, many workers are undocumented and foreign-born (i.e. illegal immigrants). Greater domestic and global competition has probably also had a part in bringing about a decline in unions in the United States.

3. **Basic Goals and Strategies of Labor Unions:** A key goal of most unions is to achieve higher wages. Often this entails bargaining for wages above competitive levels, which produces surplus labor. Thus a major task of many unions is to ration available jobs among the excess number of individuals who desire to work at the wages established by collective bargaining agreements. One strategy that unions often use to address this trade-off between wages and the number of jobs is to maximize the total income of members. If the focus of union objectives is the well-being of current members only, the union may bargain for limits on entry of new workers and seek to maximize the wages of current union members only. Another way for unions to try to push up wages is to try to increase worker productivity and lobby consumers to increase their demands for union-produced goods and reduce their demands for goods produced by nonunionized industries.

4. **Effects of Labor Unions on Wages and Productivity:** Economists have found that hourly wages of unionized workers are typically higher than those of workers who are not union members. On average, union hourly wages are about $2.25 higher than wages of nonunionized workers. Because unionized employees typically work fewer hours per year, however, their average annual earnings are lower than those of nonunionized employees. It is less clear how unions affect worker productivity. On the one hand, some collective bargaining rules specifying how jobs are performed appear to reduce productivity. On the other hand, unionization reduces job turnover, which may enhance productivity.

5. **How a Monopsonist Determines How Much Labor to Employ and What Wage Rate to Pay:** A monopsony is the only firm that buys a particular input, such as labor, in a specific market. For a monopsonist in a labor market, paying a higher wage to attract an additional unit of labor increases its total factor costs for all other labor employed. For this reason, the marginal factor cost of labor is always higher than the wage rate, so the marginal factor cost schedule lies above the labor supply schedule. The labor market monopsonist employs labor to the point at which the marginal factor cost of labor equals the marginal revenue product of labor. It then pays the workers it hires the wage at which they are willing to work, as determined by the labor supply curve, which lies below the marginal factor cost curve. As a result, the monopsonist pays workers a wage that is less than their marginal revenue product.

6. **Comparing a Monopsonist's Wage and Employment Decisions with Choices by Firms in Industries with Other Market Structures:** Firms that are perfect competitors or monopolies in their product markets but hire workers in perfectly competitive labor markets take the wage rate as market determined, meaning that their individual actions are unable to influence the market wage rate. A product market monopolist tends to employ fewer workers than would be employed if the monopolist's industry were perfectly competitive, but the product market monopolist nonetheless cannot affect the market wage rate. In contrast, a monopsonist is the only employer of labor, so it searches for the wage rate that maximizes its profit. This wage rate is less than the marginal revenue product of labor. In a situation in which a firm is both a product market monopolist and a labor market monopsonist, the firm's demand for labor is also lower than it would be if the firm's product market were competitive, and hence the firm hires fewer workers as well.

KEY TERMS AND CONCEPTS

bilateral monopoly (723)	industrial unions (711)	right-to-work laws (711)
closed shop (711)	jurisdictional dispute (711)	secondary boycott (711)
collective bargaining (710)	labor unions (710)	strikebreakers (715)
craft unions (710)	monopsonist (721)	sympathy strike (711)
featherbedding (720)	monopsonistic exploitation (722)	union shop (711)

PROBLEMS

Answers to the odd-numbered problems appear at the back of the book.

30-1. Discuss three aspects of collective bargaining that society might deem desirable.

30-2. Give three reasons why a government might seek to limit the power of a union.

30-3. What effect do strikebreakers have on the collective bargaining power of a union or other collective bargaining arrangement?

30-4. Suppose that the objective of a union is to maximize the total dues paid to the union by its membership. Explain the union strategy, in terms of the wage level and employment level, under the following two scenarios.

   a. Union dues are a percentage of total earnings of the union membership.

   b. Union dues are paid as a flat amount per union member employed.

30-5. Explain why, in economic terms, the total income of union membership is maximized when marginal revenue is zero.

30-6. Explain the impact of each of the following events on the market for union labor.

   a. Union-produced TV and radio commercials convince consumers to buy domestically manufactured clothing instead of imported clothing.

   b. The union sponsors periodic training programs that instruct union laborers about the most efficient use of machinery and tools.

30-7. Why are unions in industries in which inputs such as machines are poor substitutes for labor more likely to be able to bargain for wages higher than market levels?

30-8. How is it possible for the average annual earnings of nonunionized workers to exceed those of unionized workers even though unionized workers' hourly wages are more than $2 higher?

30-9. In the short run, a tool manufacturer has a fixed amount of capital. Labor is a variable input. The cost and output structure that the firm faces is depicted in the following table:

Labor Supplied	Total Physical Product	Hourly Wage Rate ($)
10	100	5
11	109	6
12	116	7
13	121	8
14	124	9
15	125	10

Derive, at each level of labor supplied, the firm's total wage costs and marginal factor cost.

30-10. Suppose that for the firm in Problem 30-9, the goods market is perfectly competitive. The market price of the product the firm produces is $4 at each quantity supplied by the firm. What is the amount of labor that this profit-maximizing firm will hire, and what wage rate will it pay?

30-11. A firm finds that the price of its product changes with the rate of output. In addition, the wage it pays its workers varies with the amount of labor it employs. The price and wage structure that the firm faces is depicted in the following table.

Labor Supplied	Total Physical Product	Hourly Wage Rate ($)	Product Price ($)
10	100	5	3.11
11	109	6	3.00
12	116	7	2.95
13	121	8	2.92
14	124	9	2.90
15	125	10	2.89

This firm maximizes profits. How many units of labor will it hire? What wage will it pay?

30-12. What is the amount of monopsonistic exploitation that takes place at the firm examined in Problem 30-11?

30-13. A profit-maximizing clothing producer in a remote area is the only employer of people in that area. It sells its clothing in a perfectly competitive market. The firm pays each worker the same weekly wage rate. The last worker hired raised the firm's total weekly wage expenses from $105,600 to $106,480. What is the marginal revenue product of the last worker hired by this firm if it is maximizing profits?

ECONOMICS ON THE NET

Evaluating Union Goals As discussed in this chapter, unions can pursue any of a number of goals. The AFL-CIO's home page provides links to the Web sites of several unions, and reviewing these sites can help you determine the objectives these unions have selected.

Title: American Federation of Labor–Congress of Industrial Organizations

Navigation: Go to www.econtoday.com/chap30 to visit the AFL-CIO's home page.

Application Perform the indicated operations, and answer the following questions.

1. Click on *About the AFL-CIO* under "What We Stand For," then click on *AFL-CIO's Mission*. Does the AFL-CIO claim to represent the interests of all workers or just workers in specific firms or industries? Can you discern what broad wage and employment strategy the AFL-CIO pursues?

2. Click on *Partners and Links*. Explore two or three of these Web sites. Do these unions appear to represent the interests of all workers or just workers in specific firms or industries? What general wage and employment strategies do these unions appear to pursue?

For Group Study and Analysis Divide up all the unions affiliated with the AFL-CIO among groups, and have each group explore the Web sites listed under *Partners and Links* at the AFL-CIO Web site. Have each group report on the wage and employment strategies that appear to prevail for the unions it examined.

 **Media Resources**

If your exam were tomorrow, would you be ready? For each chapter, MyEconLab Practice Tests and Study Plans pinpoint which sections you have mastered and which ones you need to study. That way, you are more efficient with your study time, and you are better prepared for your exams.

In addition to Practice Tests and your personalized Study Plan, you'll find the following media resources in MyEconLab:

1. *Graphs in Motion* animation of Figures 30-3, 30-4, 30-5, 30-7, and 30-8.

2. Videos featuring the author, Roger LeRoy Miller, on the following subjects:
   - Union Goals
   - The Benefits of Labor Unions
   - A Buyer's Monopoly—Monopsony

3. Links to the Web sites cited in the marginal Internet Resources, Issues and Applications feature, and Economics on the Net activity.

4. Audio clips of all key terms, additional practice problems, and a PDF version of the material from the print Study Guide.

5. eThemes of the Times, which is a New York Times article to help you understand the real-world applications of what you are learning.

 **myeconlab**

Get Ahead of the Curve

To see how it works, turn to page 16 and then go to www.myeconlab.com/miller.

Chapter 31

Income, Poverty, and Health Care

To many observers, it is apparent that the U.S. health care system is in the midst of a crisis. After all, they point out, each year the typical U.S. resident purchases more health care than the resident of any other nation on the planet. In addition, almost every year the average prices of health care services grow faster than the overall rate of inflation. Furthermore, total U.S. spending on health care as a percentage of GDP is higher than in any other country in the world. These observers contend that getting the alleged crisis under control will require the United States to follow Japan, Germany, France, Canada, and the United Kingdom by having the government finance a larger share of health expenditures. After completing this chapter, you will be prepared to evaluate the merits of this argument.

Refer to the end of the chapter for a full listing of the multimedia learning materials available in MyEconLab.

LEARNING OBJECTIVES

After reading this chapter, you should be able to:

1. Describe how to use a Lorenz curve to represent a nation's income distribution
2. Identify the key determinants of income differences across individuals
3. Discuss theories of desired income distribution
4. Distinguish among alternative approaches to measuring and addressing poverty
5. Recognize the major reasons for rising health care costs
6. Describe alternative approaches to paying for health care

...during the 2001–2002 recession, both the highest- and lowest-income U.S. households experienced larger proportionate income declines than all other households? The average annual income of households among the highest 20 percent of income earners fell by 3.3 percent. During the same period, the average annual income of households among the lowest 20 percent of income earners decreased by 4.2 percent. In contrast, the average annual income of the other 60 percent of households with middle incomes fell by only slightly more than 1 percent. Because annual income decreased proportionately less among middle-income households, the **distribution of income,** or the way that income is allocated among the population, became more nearly equalized during the recession.

Distribution of income
The way income is allocated among the population.

What determines the distribution of income? Economists have devised various theories to explain income distribution. We will present some of these theories in this chapter. We will also present some of the more obvious institutional reasons why income is not distributed equally in the United States and examine what might be done about health care problems.

INCOME

Income provides each of us with the means of consuming and saving. Income can be the result of a payment for labor services or a payment for ownership of one of the other factors of production besides labor—land, physical capital, or entrepreneurship. In addition, individuals obtain spendable income from gifts and government transfers. (Some individuals also obtain income by stealing, but we will not treat this matter here.) Right now, let us examine how money income is distributed across classes of income earners within the United States.

Measuring Income Distribution: The Lorenz Curve

We can represent the distribution of money income graphically with what is known as the **Lorenz curve,** named after a U.S.-born statistician, Max Otto Lorenz, who proposed it in 1905. The Lorenz curve shows what portion of total money income is accounted for by different proportions of the nation's households. Look at Figure 31-1 on the next page. On the horizontal axis, we measure the *cumulative* percentage of households, lowest-income households first. Starting at the left corner, there are zero households; at the right corner, we have 100 percent of households; and in the middle, we have 50 percent of households. The vertical axis represents the cumulative percentage of money income. The 45-degree line represents complete equality: 50 percent of the households obtain 50 percent of total income, 60 percent of the households obtain 60 percent of total income, and so on. Of course, in no real-world situation is there such complete equality of income; no actual Lorenz curve would be a straight line. Rather, it would be some curved line, like the one labeled "Actual money income distribution" in Figure 31-1. For example, the bottom 50 percent of households in the United States receive about 23 percent of total money income.

Lorenz curve
A geometric representation of the distribution of income. A Lorenz curve that is perfectly straight represents complete income equality. The more bowed a Lorenz curve, the more unequally income is distributed.

In Figure 31-2 also on the following page, we again show the actual money income distribution Lorenz curve, and we also compare it to the distribution of money income in 1929. Since that year, the Lorenz curve has generally become less bowed; that is, it has moved closer to the line of complete equality.

Criticisms of the Lorenz Curve.
In recent years, economists have placed less and less emphasis on the shape of the Lorenz curve as an indication of the degree of income inequality in a country. There are five basic reasons why the Lorenz curve has been criticized:

FIGURE 31-1
The Lorenz Curve

The horizontal axis measures the cumulative percentage of households, with lowest-income households first, from 0 to 100 percent. The vertical axis measures the cumulative percentage of money income from 0 to 100. A straight line at a 45-degree angle cuts the box in half and represents a line of complete income equality, along which 25 percent of the families get 25 percent of the money income, 50 percent get 50 percent, and so on. The observed Lorenz curve, showing actual money income distribution, is not a straight line but rather a curved line as shown. The difference between complete money income equality and the Lorenz curve is the inequality gap.

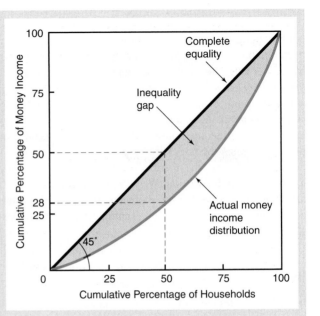

FIGURE 31-2
Lorenz Curves of Income Distribution, 1929 and 2005

Since 1929, the Lorenz curve has moved slightly inward toward the straight line of perfect income equality.

Source: U.S. Department of Commerce.

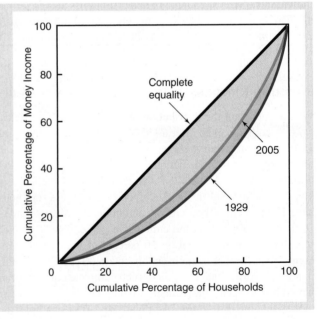

Income in kind
Income received in the form of goods and services, such as housing or medical care; to be contrasted with money income, which is simply income in dollars, or general purchasing power, that can be used to buy *any* goods and services.

1. The Lorenz curve is typically presented in terms of the distribution of *money* income only. It does not include **income in kind,** such as government-provided food stamps, education, or housing aid, and goods or services produced and consumed in the home or on the farm.

2. The Lorenz curve does not account for differences in the size of households or the number of wage earners they contain.

3. It does not account for age differences. Even if all families in the United States had exactly the same *lifetime* incomes, chances are that young families would have modest incomes, middle-aged families would have relatively high incomes, and retired

TABLE 31-1
Percentage Share of Money Income for Households Before Direct Taxes

Income Group	2005	1975	1960	1947
Lowest fifth	4.2	4.4	4.8	5.1
Second fifth	9.2	10.5	12.2	11.8
Third fifth	14.2	17.1	17.8	16.7
Fourth fifth	20.7	24.8	24.0	23.2
Highest fifth	51.7	43.2	41.3	43.3

Source: U.S. Bureau of the Census; author's estimates.
Note: Figures may not sum to 100 percent due to rounding.

families would have low incomes. Because the Lorenz curve is drawn at a moment in time, it could never tell us anything about the inequality of *lifetime* income.

4. The Lorenz curve ordinarily reflects money income *before* taxes.

5. It does not measure unreported income from the underground economy, a substantial source of income for some individuals.

Income Distribution in the United States

We could talk about the percentage of income earners within specific income classes—those earning between $20,001 and $30,000 per year, those earning between $30,001 and $40,000 per year, and so on. The problem with this type of analysis is that we live in a growing economy. Income, with some exceptions, is going up all the time. If we wish to compare the relative shares of total income going to different income classes, we cannot look at specific amounts of money income. Instead, we talk about a distribution of income over five groups. Then we can talk about how much the bottom fifth (or quintile) makes compared with the top fifth, and so on.

In Table 31-1, we see the percentage share of income for households before direct taxes. The table groups households according to whether they are in the lowest 20 percent of the income distribution, the second lowest 20 percent, and so on. We see that in 2005, the estimated lowest 20 percent had a combined money income of 4.2 percent of the total money income of the entire population. This is a little less than the lowest 20 percent had at the end of World War II. Accordingly, some have concluded that the distribution of money income has changed only slightly. *Money* income, however, understates *total* income for individuals who receive in-kind transfers from the government in the form of food stamps, public housing, education, and so on. In particular, since World War II, the share of *total* income—money income plus in-kind benefits—going to the bottom 20 percent of households has more than doubled.

The incomes of the lowest-income U.S. households are not much lower than the incomes of lower-income households in other developed nations. In light of that fact, why is the U.S. income distribution more unequal?

Go to www.econtoday/chap31 to view the U.S. Census Bureau's most recent data on the U.S. income distribution. Click on the most recent year next to "Money Income in the United States."

International EXAMPLE

Why Income Inequality Is Greater in the United States

The U.S. income distribution exhibits greater inequality than income distributions in other developed nations. Figure 31-3 on the following page shows why this is so. It displays average incomes of the highest- and lowest-income households in various countries as percentages of the income at the center of the U.S. income distribution. A key reason that the U.S. income distribution is more unequal is that the highest-income U.S. households earn much more than the highest-income households in other nations.

FIGURE 31-3
Relative Incomes of Rich and Poor Households
This figure shows average incomes in various countries as percentages of the middle U.S. income for the 20 percent of households with highest incomes and the 20 percent of households with lowest incomes.

Source: Organization for Economic Cooperation and Development.

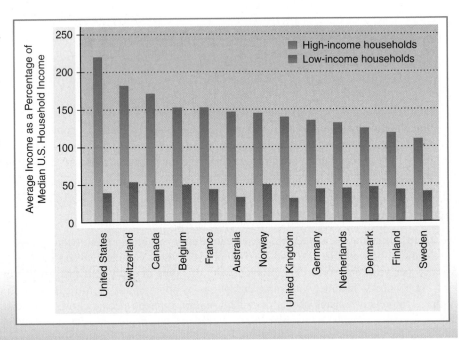

The Distribution of Wealth

When referring to the distribution of income, we must realize that income—a flow—can be viewed as a return on wealth (both human and nonhuman)—a stock. A discussion of the distribution of income is therefore not the same thing as a discussion of the distribution of wealth. A complete concept of wealth would include not only tangible objects, such as buildings, machinery, land, cars, and houses—nonhuman wealth—but also people who have skills, knowledge, initiative, talents, and so on—human wealth. The total of human and nonhuman wealth in the United States makes up our nation's capital stock. (Note that the terms *wealth* and *capital* are sometimes used only with reference to nonhuman wealth.) The capital stock consists of anything that can generate utility to individuals in the future. A fresh ripe tomato is not part of our capital stock. It has to be eaten before it turns rotten and becomes worthless. Once it has been eaten, it can no longer generate satisfaction.

Figure 31-4 shows that the richest 10 percent of U.S. households hold more than two-thirds of all wealth. The problem with those data, gathered by the Federal Reserve System, is that they do not include many important assets. The first of these is workers' claims on private pension plans, which equal at least $4 trillion. If you add the value of these pensions, household wealth increases by almost 25 percent and reveals that the majority of U.S. households are middle-wealth households (popularly known as the *middle class*).

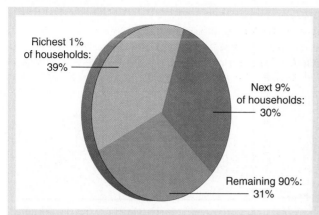

FIGURE 31-4
Measured Total Wealth Distribution
The top 10 percent of households have 69 percent of all measured wealth. This distribution changes dramatically if other nonmeasured components of wealth, such as government-guaranteed Social Security commitments, are taken into account

Source: Board of Governors of the Federal Reserve.

Richest 1% of households: 39%

Next 9% of households: 30%

Remaining 90%: 31%

CONCEPTS in Brief

- The Lorenz curve graphically represents the distribution of income. If it is a straight line, there is complete equality of income. The more it is bowed, the more unequally income is distributed.

- The distribution of wealth is not the same as the distribution of income. Wealth includes assets such as houses, stocks, and bonds. Although the apparent distribution of wealth seems to be more concentrated at the top than income, the data used are not very accurate, and most summary statistics fail to take account of workers' claims on pensions, which are substantial.

To test your understanding of the concepts covered in this section, go to the Online Review at www.myeconlab.com/miller.

DETERMINANTS OF INCOME DIFFERENCES

We know that there are income differences—that is not in dispute. A more important question is why these differences in income occur, for if we know why income differences occur, perhaps we can change public policy, particularly with respect to helping people in the lowest income classes climb the income ladder. What is more, if we know the reasons for income differences, we can ascertain whether any of these determinants have changed over time. We will look at four determinants of income differences: age, marginal productivity, inheritance, and discrimination.

Age

Age turns out to be a determinant of income because with age comes, usually, more education, more training, and more experience. It is not surprising that within every class of income earners, there seem to be regular cycles of earning behavior. Most individuals earn more when they are middle-aged than when they are younger or older. We call this the **age-earnings cycle.**

The Age–Earnings Cycle. Every occupation has its own age-earnings cycle, and every individual will probably experience some variation from the average. Nonetheless, we can characterize the typical age-earnings cycle graphically in Figure 31-5 on the following page. Here we see that at age 18, earnings from wages are relatively low. Earnings gradually rise until they peak at about age 50. Then they fall until retirement, when they become zero (that is, currently earned wages become zero, although retirement payments may then commence). The reason for such a regular cycle in earnings is fairly straightforward.

Age-earnings cycle
The regular earnings profile of an individual throughout his or her lifetime. The age-earnings cycle usually starts with a low income, builds gradually to a peak at around age 50, and then gradually curves down until it approaches zero at retirement.

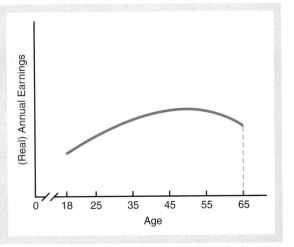

FIGURE 31-5
Typical Age-Earnings Profile
Within every class of income earners there is usually a typical age-earnings profile. Earnings from wages are lowest when starting work at age 18, reach their peak at around age 50, and then taper off until retirement around age 65, when they become zero for most people. The rise in earnings up to age 50 is usually due to increased experience, longer working hours, and better training and schooling. (We abstract from economywide productivity changes that would shift the entire curve upward.)

When individuals start working at a young age, they typically have no work-related experience. Their ability to produce is less than that of more seasoned workers—their productivity is lower. As they become older, they obtain more training and accumulate more experience. Their productivity rises, and they are therefore paid more. They also generally start to work longer hours. As the age of 50 approaches, the productivity of individual workers usually peaks. So, do the number of hours per week that are worked. After this peak in the age-earnings cycle, the effects of aging—decreases in stamina, strength, reaction time, and the like—usually outweigh any increases in training or experience. Also, hours worked usually start to fall for older people. Finally, as a person reaches retirement, both productivity and hours worked diminish rather drastically.

Note that general increases in overall productivity for the entire workforce will result in an upward shift in the typical age-earnings profile depicted in Figure 31-5. Thus, even at the end of the age-earnings cycle, when just about to retire, the worker would receive a relatively high wage compared with the starting wage 45 years earlier. The wage would be higher due to factors that contribute to rising real wages for everyone, regardless of the stage in the age-earnings cycle.

Now we have some idea why specific individuals earn different incomes at different times in their lives, but we have yet to explain why different people are paid different amounts for their labor. One way to explain this is to recall the marginal productivity theory developed in Chapter 29.

Marginal Productivity

When trying to determine how many workers a firm would hire, we had to construct a marginal revenue product curve. We found that as more workers were hired, the marginal revenue product fell due to diminishing marginal returns. If the forces of demand and supply established a certain wage rate, workers would be hired until their marginal physical product times marginal revenue (which equals the market price under perfect competition) was equal to the going wage rate. Then the hiring would stop. This analysis suggests what workers can expect to be paid in the labor market: They can each expect to be paid their marginal revenue product (assuming that there are low-cost information flows and that the labor and product markets are competitive).

In a competitive situation, with mobility of labor resources (at least on the margin), workers who are being paid less than their marginal revenue product will be bid away to better employment opportunities. Either they will seek better employment themselves, or other employers will offer them a higher wage rate. This process will continue until each worker is being paid his or her marginal revenue product.

You may balk at the suggestion that people are paid their marginal revenue product because you may personally know individuals whose MRP is more or less than what they are being paid. Such a situation may exist because we do not live in a world of perfect information or in a world with perfectly competitive input and output markets. Employers cannot always find the most productive employees available. It takes resources to research the past records of potential employees, their training, their education, and their abilities. Nonetheless, competition creates a tendency *toward* equality of wages and MRP.

Determinants of Marginal Productivity. If we accept marginal revenue product theory, we have a way to find out how people can earn higher incomes. If they can increase their marginal physical product, they can expect to be paid more. Some of the determinants of marginal physical product are talent, experience, and training. Most of these are means by which marginal physical product can be increased. Let's examine them in greater detail.

Talent. Talent is the easiest factor to explain, but it is difficult to acquire if you don't have it. Innate abilities and attributes can be very strong, if not overwhelming, determinants of a person's potential productivity. Strength, coordination, and mental alertness are facets of nonacquired human capital and thus have some bearing on the ability to earn income. Someone who is tall and agile has a better chance of being a basketball player than someone who is short and unathletic. A person born with a superior talent for abstract thinking has a better chance of earning a relatively high income as a mathematician or a physicist than someone who is not born with that capability.

Experience. Additional experience at particular tasks is another way to increase productivity. Experience can be linked to the well-known *learning curve* that applies when the same task is done over and over. The worker repeating a task becomes more efficient: The worker can do the same task in less time or in the same amount of time but better. Take an example of a person going to work on an automobile assembly line. At first she is able to fasten only three bolts every two minutes. Then the worker becomes more adept and can fasten four bolts in the same time plus insert a rubber guard on the bumper. After a few more weeks, another task can be added. Experience allows this individual to improve her productivity. The more effectively people learn to do something, the more quickly they can do it and the more efficient they are. Hence we would expect experience to lead to higher productivity. And we would expect people with more experience to be paid more than those with less experience. More experience, however, does not guarantee a higher wage rate. The *demand* for a person's services must also exist. Spending a long time to become a first-rate archer in modern society would probably add very little to a person's income. Experience has value only if the output is demanded by society.

Training. Training is similar to experience but is more formal. Much of a person's increased productivity is due to on-the-job training. Many companies have training programs for new workers.

Investment in Human Capital. Investment in human capital is just like investment in anything else. If you invest in yourself by going to college, rather than going to work after high school and earning more current income, you will presumably be rewarded in the future with a higher income or a more interesting job (or both). This is exactly the motivation that underlies the decision of many college-bound students to obtain a formal higher

For a discussion of how the Organization for Economic Cooperation and Development seeks to measure investments in human capital, go to www.econtoday.com/chap31.

education. Undoubtedly, some students would go to school even if the rate of return on formal education were zero or negative. But we do expect that the higher the rate of return on investing in ourselves, the more such investment there will be. U.S. Labor Department data demonstrate conclusively that on average, high school graduates make more than grade school graduates and that college graduates make more than high school graduates. The estimated annual income of a full-time worker with four years of college in the mid-2000s was about $53,000. That person's high school counterpart was estimated to earn a little less than $32,000, so the "college premium" was just over 65 percent. Generally, the rate of return on investment in human capital is on a par with the rate of return on investment in other areas.

To determine the rate of return on an investment in a college education, we first have to figure out the marginal cost of going to school. The main cost is not what you have to pay for books, fees, and tuition but rather the income you forgo. *The main cost of education is the income forgone—the opportunity cost of not working.* In addition, the direct expenses of college must be paid for. Not all students forgo all income during their college years. Many work part time. Taking account of those who work part time and those who are supported by tuition grants and other scholarships, the average rate of return on going to college ranges between 6 and 10 percent. This is not a bad rate. Of course, this type of computation does leave out all the consumption benefits you get from attending college. Also omitted from the calculations is the change in personality after going to college. You undoubtedly come out a different person. Most people who go through college feel that they have improved themselves both culturally and intellectually in addition to having increased their potential marginal revenue product so that they can make more income. How do we measure the benefit from expanding our horizons and our desire to experience different things in life? This is not easy to measure, and such nonmoney benefits from investing in human capital are not included in normal calculations.

How have differences in the quality of education in urban and rural areas of China affected the gap between the incomes of city and rural residents?

International EXAMPLE

A Widening Urban–Rural Income Gap in China

The best primary and secondary schools in China are located in the major cities. About two-thirds of China's 1.3 billion residents, however, live in rural areas, where schools generally are of much lower quality. Since the mid-1980s, urban schools have been so overcrowded that officials normally have prevented even the best rural students from enrolling in city schools. Hence the training and educational attainments of rural residents have steadily declined relative to those of urban residents. A key economic consequence has been a widening gap between the average incomes of urban and rural residents. In the mid-1980s, a typical urban resident earned about 80 percent more per year than a rural resident. Today, an urban resident earns nearly 215 percent more on average than a rural resident.

For Critical Analysis
What do you think is likely to happen to China's Lorenz curve if the urban-rural income gap continues to widen?

Inheritance

It is not unusual to inherit cash, jewelry, stocks, bonds, homes, or other real estate. Yet only about 10 percent of income inequality in the United States can be traced to differences in inherited wealth. If for some reason the government confiscated all property that had been inherited, the immediate result would be only a modest change in the distribution of income in the United States. In any event, at both federal and state levels substantial inheritance taxes have been levied on the estates of relatively wealthy deceased Americans (although there are some legally valid ways to avoid certain estate taxes).

Discrimination

Economic discrimination occurs whenever workers with the same marginal revenue product receive unequal pay due to some noneconomic factor such as their race, gender, or age. Alternatively, it occurs when there is unequal access to labor markets. It is possible—and indeed quite obvious—that discrimination affects the distribution of income. Certain groups in our society are not paid wages at rates comparable to those received by other groups, even when we correct for productivity. Differences in income remain between whites and nonwhites and between men and women. For example, the median income of black families is about 65 percent that of white families. The median wage rate of women is about 70 percent that of men. Some people argue that all of these differences are due to discrimination against nonwhites and against women.

We cannot simply accept *any* differences in income as due to discrimination, though. What we need to do is discover why differences in income between groups exist and then determine if factors other than discrimination in the labor market can explain them. The unexplained part of income differences can rightfully be considered the result of discrimination.

Access to Education.
African Americans and other minorities have faced discrimination in the acquisition of human capital. The amount and quality of schooling offered black U.S. residents has generally been inferior to that offered whites. Even if minorities attend school as long as whites, their scholastic achievement can be lower because they are typically allotted fewer school resources than their white counterparts. Nonwhite urban individuals are more likely to live in lower-income areas, which have fewer resources to allocate to education due to the lower tax base. One study showed that nonwhite urban males receive between 23 and 27 percent less income than white urban males because of lower-quality education. This would mean that even if employment discrimination were substantially reduced, we would still expect to see a difference between white and nonwhite income because of the low quality of schooling received by the nonwhites and the resulting lower level of productivity. We say, therefore, that among other things, African Americans and certain other minority groups, such as Hispanics, suffer from reduced investment in human capital. Even when this difference in human capital is taken into account, however, there still appears to be an income differential that cannot be explained.

The unexplained income differential between whites and blacks is often attributed to discrimination in the labor market. Because no better explanation is offered, we will stick with the notion that discrimination in the labor market does indeed exist.

The Doctrine of Comparable Worth.
Discrimination against women can occur because of barriers to entry in higher-paying occupations and because of discrimination in the acquisition of human capital, just as has occurred for African Americans. Consider the distribution of the highest-paying and lowest-paying occupations. The lowest-paying jobs are dominated by females, both white and nonwhite. For example, the proportion of women in secretarial, clerical, janitorial, and food service jobs ranges from 70 percent (food service) to 97 percent (secretarial). Proponents of the **comparable-worth doctrine** argue that female secretaries, janitors, and food service workers should be making salaries comparable to those of male truck drivers or construction workers, assuming that the levels of skill and responsibility in these jobs are comparable. These advocates also believe that a

Comparable-worth doctrine
The belief that women should receive the same wages as men if the levels of skill and responsibility in their jobs are equivalent.

comparable-worth policy would benefit the economy overall. They contend that adjusting the wages of workers in female-dominated jobs upward would help to create more efficient and less discriminatory labor markets.

THEORIES OF DESIRED INCOME DISTRIBUTION

We have talked about the factors affecting the distribution of income, but we have not yet mentioned the normative issue of how income *ought* to be distributed. This, of course, requires a value judgment. We are talking about the problem of economic justice. We can never completely resolve this problem because there are always going to be conflicting values. It is impossible to give all people what each thinks is just. Nonetheless, two particular normative standards for the distribution of income have been popular with economists. These are income distribution based on productivity and income distribution based on equality.

Productivity

The *productivity standard* for the distribution of income can be stated simply as "To each according to what he or she produces." This is also called the *contributive standard* because it is based on the principle of rewarding according to the contribution to society's total output. It is also sometimes referred to as the *merit standard* and is one of the oldest concepts of justice. People are rewarded according to merit, and merit is judged by one's ability to produce what is considered useful by society.

Just as any standard is a value judgment, however, so is the productivity standard. It is rooted in the capitalist ethic and has been attacked vigorously by some economists and philosophers, including Karl Marx (1818–1883), who felt that people should be rewarded according to need and not according to productivity.

We measure a person's productive contribution in a capitalist system by the market value of that person's output. We have already referred to this as the marginal revenue product theory of wage determination.

Do not immediately jump to the conclusion that in a world of income distribution determined by productivity, society will necessarily allow the aged, the infirm, and the disabled to die of starvation because they are unproductive. In the United States today, the productivity standard is mixed with a standard based on people's "needs" so that the aged, the disabled, the involuntarily unemployed, the very young, and other unproductive (in the market sense of the word) members of the economy are provided for through private and public transfers.

Equality

The *egalitarian principle* of income distribution is simply "To each exactly the same." Everyone would have exactly the same amount of income. This criterion of income distribution has been debated as far back as biblical times. This system of income distribution has been considered equitable, meaning that presumably everybody is dealt with fairly and equally. There are problems, however, with an income distribution that is completely equal.

Some jobs are more unpleasant or more dangerous than others. Should the people undertaking these jobs be paid exactly the same as everyone else? Indeed, under an equal distribution of income, what incentive would there be for individuals to take risky, hazardous, or unpleasant jobs at all? What about overtime? Who would be willing to work overtime without additional pay? There is another problem: If everyone earned the same income, what incentive would there be for individuals to invest in their own human capital—a costly and time-consuming process?

Just consider the incentive structure within a corporation. Within corporations, much of the differential between, say, the pay of the CEO and the pay of all of the vice presidents is meant to create competition among the vice presidents for the CEO's job. The result is higher productivity. If all incomes were the same, much of this competition would disappear, and productivity would fall.

There is some evidence that differences in income lead to higher rates of economic growth. Future generations are therefore made better off. Elimination of income differences may reduce the rate of economic growth and cause future generations to be poorer than they otherwise might have been.

CONCEPTS in Brief

- Most people follow an age-earnings cycle in which they earn relatively small incomes when they first start working, increase their incomes until about age 50, and then slowly experience a decrease in their real incomes as they approach retirement.

- If we accept the marginal revenue product theory of wages, workers can expect to be paid their marginal revenue product. Full adjustment is never obtained, however, so some workers may be paid more or less than their MRP.

- Marginal physical productivity depends on talent, education, experience, and training.

- Going to school and receiving on-the-job training can be considered an investment in human capital. The main cost of education is the opportunity cost of not working.

- Discrimination is most easily observed in various groups' access to high-paying jobs and to quality education. Minorities and women are disproportionately underrepresented in high-paying jobs. Also, minorities sometimes do not receive access to higher education of the same quality offered to majority-group members.

- Proponents of the comparable-worth doctrine contend that disparate jobs can be compared by examining efforts, skill, and educational training and that wages should therefore be paid on the basis of this comparable worth.

- Two normative standards for income distribution are income distribution based on productivity and income distribution based on equality.

To test your understanding of the concepts covered in this section, go to the Online Review at www.myeconlab.com/miller.

POVERTY AND ATTEMPTS TO ELIMINATE IT

Throughout the history of the world, mass poverty has been accepted as inevitable. This nation and others, particularly in the Western world, however, have sustained enough economic growth in the past several hundred years so that *mass* poverty can no longer be said to be a problem for these fortunate countries. As a matter of fact, the residual of poverty in the United States strikes us as bizarre, an anomaly. How can there still be so much poverty in a nation of such abundance? Having talked about the determinants of the distribution of income, we now have at least some ideas of why some people are destined to remain low-income earners throughout their lives.

Income can be transferred from the relatively well-to-do to the relatively poor by various methods, and as a nation we have been using them for a long time. Today we have a vast array of welfare programs set up for the purpose of redistributing income. As we know, however, these programs have not been entirely successful. Are there alternatives to our current welfare system? Is there a better method of helping the poor? Before we answer these questions, let's look at the concept of poverty in more detail and at the characteristics of the poor. Figure 31-6 on the following page shows that the number of people that the government has classified as poor fell steadily from 1959 to 1969, then leveled off until the recession of 1981–1982. The number then rose dramatically, fell back during the

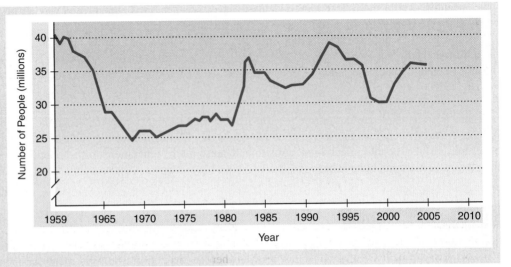

FIGURE 31-6

Official Number of Poor in the United States

The number of individuals classified as poor fell steadily from 1959 through 1969. From 1970 to 1981, the number stayed about the same. It then increased during the 1981–1982 recession, dropped off for a while, rose in the early 1990s, and then fell until it started rising again in the early 2000s. In recent years, it has leveled off.

Source: U.S. Department of Labor.

late 1980s, rose again after the recession in the early 1990s, fell once again thereafter, and then rose in the early 2000s before leveling off in recent years.

How common do you suppose it is for U.S. residents to remain poor throughout their lives?

EXAMPLE

Don't Like Your Position in the Income Distribution? Just Wait

There is considerable "income mobility" in the United States. Between 50 and 80 percent of U.S. residents who at any time earn incomes among the lowest 20 percent of income earners are still part of that category 10 years later. In contrast, within 20 years, 95 percent are no longer classified among the lowest 20 percent of income earners.

Furthermore, many of the lowest-income U.S. residents make dramatic gains in earnings. Nearly half of U.S. residents who began in poverty in the 1980s reached the middle-income 20 percent of the population by the 2000s. Almost a fourth reached the top 20 percent of the U.S. income distribution.

For Critical Analysis

Why do you suppose that some economists argue against using the designations "lower class," "middle class," and "upper class" when discussing the U.S. income distribution?

Defining Poverty

The threshold income level, which is used to determine who falls into the poverty category, was originally based on the cost of a nutritionally adequate food plan designed by the U.S. Department of Agriculture for emergency or temporary use. The threshold was determined by multiplying the food plan cost by 3 on the assumption that food expenses comprise approximately one-third of a poor family's income. Annual revisions of the threshold level were based only on price changes in the food budget. In 1969, a federal interagency committee looked at the calculations of the threshold and decided to set new standards, with adjustments made on the basis of changes in the Consumer Price Index. For example, in 2005, the official poverty level for an urban family of four was around $19,000. It goes up each year to reflect whatever inflation has occurred.

Absolute Poverty

Because the low-income threshold is an absolute measure, we know that if it never changes in real terms, we will reduce poverty even if we do nothing. How can that be? The reasoning is straightforward. Real incomes in the United States have been growing at a compounded annual rate of almost 2 percent per capita for at least the past century and at about 2.5 percent since World War II. If we define the poverty line at a specific real level, more and more individuals will make incomes that exceed that poverty line. Thus, in absolute terms, we will eliminate poverty (assuming continued per capita growth and no change in income distribution).

Go to www.econtoday.com/chap31 to learn about the World Bank's programs intended to combat global poverty.

Relative Poverty

Be careful with this analysis, however. Poverty can also be defined in relative terms; that is, it is defined in terms of the income levels of individuals or families relative to the rest of the population. As long as the distribution of income is not perfectly equal, there will always be some people who make less income than others, even if their relatively low income is high by historical standards. Thus, in a relative sense, the problem of poverty will always exist, although it can be reduced. In any given year, for example, the absolute poverty level *officially* determined by the U.S. government is far above the average income in many countries in the world.

Just how many of the world's countries do you suppose have per capita incomes higher than the official U.S. poverty income threshold?

International EXAMPLE

The U.S. Poverty Level versus Average Incomes Abroad

Each year, the World Bank issues a report that provides the per capita incomes of about 150 nations. Out of all these countries, only 26 currently have per capita incomes higher than the poverty income threshold defined by the U.S. government. This official poverty threshold income level for the United States is *twice* as high as the world's average per capita income level. It is approximately equal to the *average* income of a resident of Slovenia or Portugal.

For Critical Analysis
Does the fact that the U.S. government raises its official poverty threshold income each year imply that it defines poverty in a relative or an absolute sense?

Transfer Payments as Income

The official poverty level is based on pretax income, including cash but not in-kind subsidies—food stamps, housing vouchers, and the like. If we correct poverty levels for such benefits, the percentage of the population that is below the poverty line drops dramatically. Some economists argue that the way the official poverty level is calculated makes no sense in a nation that redistributed over $1.2 trillion in cash and noncash transfers in 2004.

Furthermore, some of the nation's official poor partake in the informal, or underground, sectors of the economy without reporting their income from these sources. And some of the officially defined poor obtain benefits from owning their own home (40 percent of all poor households do own their own homes). Look at Figure 31-7 on the following page for two different views of what has happened to the relative position of this nation's poor. The

FIGURE 31-7

Relative Poverty: Comparing Household Income and Household Spending

This graph shows, on the vertical axis, the ratio of the top 20 percent of income-earning households to the bottom 20 percent. If measured house-

hold income is used, there appears to be increasing income inequality, particularly during the early to mid-1980s. If we look at household *spending*, though, inequality is more nearly constant.

Sources: U.S. Bureau of Labor Statistics; U.S. Bureau of the Census.

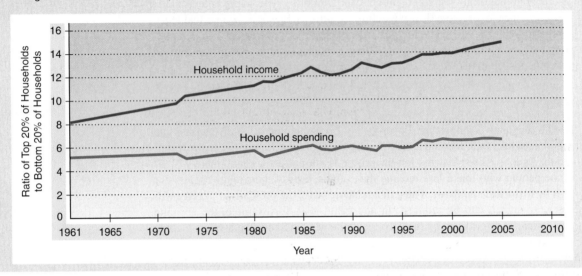

graph shows the ratio of the top fifth of the nation's households to the bottom fifth of the nation's households. If we look only at measured income, it appears that the poor are getting relatively poorer compared to the rich (the top line). If we compare household spending (consumption), however, a different picture emerges. The nation's poorest households are in fact holding their own.

Attacks on Poverty: Major Income Maintenance Programs

There are a variety of income maintenance programs designed to help the poor. We examine a few of them here.

Social Security. For the retired, the unemployed, and the disabled, social insurance programs provide income payments in prescribed situations. The best known is Social Security, which includes what has been called old-age, survivors', and disability insurance (OASDI). As discussed in Chapter 6, this was originally supposed to be a program of compulsory saving financed from payroll taxes levied on both employers and employees. Workers pay for Social Security while working and receive the benefits after retirement. The benefit payments are usually made to people who have reached retirement age. When the insured worker dies, benefits accrue to the survivors, including widows and children. Special benefits provide for disabled workers. Over 90 percent of all employed persons in the United States are covered by OASDI. Today, Social Security is an intergenerational income transfer that is only vaguely related to past earnings. It transfers income from U.S. residents who work—the young through the middle-aged—to those who do not work—older retired persons.

In 2005, more than 45 million people were receiving OASDI checks averaging about $875 a month. Benefit payments from OASDI redistribute income to some degree. Benefit payments, however, are not based on recipient need. Participants' contributions give them the right to benefits even if they would be financially secure without them. Social Security is not really an insurance program because people are not guaranteed that the benefits they receive will be in line with the "contributions" they have made. It is not a personal savings account. The benefits are legislated by Congress. In the future, Congress may not be as sympathetic toward older people as it is today. It could (and probably will have to) legislate for lower real levels of benefits instead of higher ones.

Supplemental Security Income and Temporary Assistance to Needy Families. Many people who are poor but do not qualify for Social Security benefits are assisted through other programs. The federally financed and administered Supplemental Security Income (SSI) program was instituted in 1974. The purpose of SSI is to establish a nationwide minimum income for the aged, the blind, and the disabled. SSI has become one of the fastest-growing transfer programs in the United States. Whereas in 1974 less than $8 billion was spent, the prediction for 2006 is $39 billion. U.S. residents currently eligible for SSI include children and individuals claiming mental disabilities, including drug addicts and alcoholics.

Temporary Assistance to Needy Families (TANF) is a state-administered program, financed in part by federal grants. The program provides aid to families in need. TANF replaced Aid to Families with Dependent Children (AFDC) in 1996. TANF is intended to be temporary. Projected expenditures for TANF are $30 billion in 2005.

Food Stamps. Food stamps are government-issued coupons (or, increasingly, electronic debit cards) that can be used to purchase food. The food stamp program was started in 1964, seemingly, in retrospect, to shore up the nation's agricultural sector by increasing demand for food through retail channels. In 1964, some 367,000 Americans were receiving food stamps. In 2005, the estimate is over 24 million recipients. The annual cost has jumped from $860,000 to more than $23 billion. In 2005, almost one in every nine citizens (including children) was using food stamps. The food stamp program has become a major part of the welfare system in the United States. The program has also become a method of promoting better nutrition among the poor.

Do people tend to value food stamps less than the amount printed on the stamps?

Policy EXAMPLE

What Are Food Stamps Worth?

Most recipients of food stamps qualify because they have relatively low incomes. For the majority of recipients, there are times when they would rather have cash to spend on power bills or clothing, but their billfolds contain food stamps that can only be used to purchase approved food items.

Diane Whitmore of the University of Chicago sought to determine how much value food stamp recipients place on the stamps. She found that 20 to 30 percent of recipients purchase more food with the stamps than they otherwise would if they were to receive cash instead. These individuals, she found, placed an average cash value of 80 cents on each $1 in food stamps they received.

Whitmore also measured the cash-equivalent value of food stamps in the underground market, where some recipients illegally sell their food stamps for cash. She found that food stamps trade for only about 65 percent of their face value in the underground market. This even lower market valuation of food stamps may reflect the fact that people selling them in this market put a particularly low value on the stamps. Thus they are willing to risk breaking the law to trade them for cash.

For Critical Analysis
Who unambiguously gains from the food stamp program? (Hint: Note that many food stamp recipients buy more food than they would if they received cash transfers instead.)

The Earned Income Tax Credit Program. In 1975, the Earned Income Tax Credit Program (EITC) was created to provide rebates of Social Security taxes to low-income workers. Over one-fifth of all tax returns claim an earned-income tax credit; each year the federal government grants more than $36 billion in these credits. In some states, such as Mississippi, nearly half of all families are eligible for EITC. The program works as follows: Single-income households with two children that report income of less than about $34,000 (exclusive of welfare payments) receive EITC benefits up to about $5,000. There is a catch, though. Those with earnings up to threshold of about $11,000 receive higher benefits as their incomes rise. But families earning more than this threshold income are penalized about 18 cents for every dollar they earn above the income threshold. Thus on net the EITC discourages work by low- or moderate-income earners more than it rewards work. In particular, it discourages low-income earners from taking on second jobs. The Government Accountability Office estimates that hours worked by working wives in EITC-beneficiary households have consequently decreased by 15 percent. The average EITC recipient works 1,700 hours a year compared to a normal work year of about 2,000 hours.

No Apparent Reduction in Poverty Rates

In spite of the numerous programs in existence and the hundreds of billions of dollars transferred to the poor, the officially defined rate of poverty in the United States has shown no long-run tendency to decline. From 1945 until the early 1970s, the percentage of U.S. residents in poverty fell steadily every year. It reached a low of around 11 percent in 1973, shot back up beyond 15 percent in 1983, fell to 13.1 percent in 1990, and has since fallen no lower than 12 percent. Why this has happened is a real puzzle. Since the War on Poverty was launched under President Lyndon B. Johnson in 1965, more than $12 trillion has been transferred to the poor, and yet more U.S. residents are poor today than ever before. This fact created the political will to pass the Welfare Reform Act of 1996, putting limits on people's use of welfare. The law's goal has been to get people off welfare and into jobs.

Concepts in Brief

- If poverty is defined in absolute terms, economic growth eventually decreases the number of officially defined poor. If poverty is defined relatively, however, we will never eliminate it.

- Although the relative position of the poor measured by household income seems to have worsened, household spending by the bottom 20 percent of households compared to that of the top 20 percent has shown little change since the 1960s.

- Major attacks on poverty have been made through social insurance programs including Social Security, Supplemental Security Income, Aid to Families with Dependent Children, Temporary Assistance to Needy Families, the earned-income tax credit, and food stamps.

To test your understanding of the concepts covered in this section, go to the Online Review at **www.myeconlab.com/miller.**

HEALTH CARE

It may seem strange to be reading about health care in a chapter on the distribution of income and poverty. Yet health care is in fact intimately related to those two topics. For example, sometimes people become poor because they do not have adequate health insurance (or have none at all), fall ill, and deplete all of their wealth on care. Moreover, some individuals remain in certain jobs simply because their employer's health care package seems so good that they are afraid to change jobs and risk not being covered by health insurance in the process. Finally, as you will see, much of the cause of the increased health care spending in the United States can be attributed to a change in the incentives that U.S. residents face.

The U.S. Health Care Situation

Spending for health care is estimated to account for almost 16 percent of U.S. real GDP. You can see from Figure 31-8 that in 1965, about 6 percent of annual income was spent on health care, but that percentage has been increasing ever since. Per capita spending on health care is greater in the United States than anywhere else in the world today. On a per capita basis, we spend more than twice as much as citizens of Luxembourg, Austria, Australia, Japan, and Denmark. We spend almost three times as much on a per capita basis as citizens of Spain and Ireland.

Why Have Health Care Costs Risen So Much? There are numerous explanations for why health care costs have risen so much. At least one has to do with changing demographics: The U.S. population is getting older.

The Age–Health Care Expenditure Equation. The top 5 percent of health care users incur over 50 percent of all health costs. The bottom 70 percent of health care users account for only 10 percent of health care expenditures. Not surprisingly, the elderly make up most of the top users of health care services. Nursing home expenditures are made primarily by people older than 70. The use of hospitals is also dominated by the aged.

The U.S. population is aging steadily. More than 13 percent of the current 295 million U.S. residents are over 65. It is estimated that by the year 2035, senior citizens will comprise about 22 percent of our population. This aging population stimulates the demand for health care. The elderly consume more than four times as much per capita health care services as the rest of the population. In short, whatever the demand for health care services is today, it is likely to be considerably higher in the future as the U.S. population ages.

New Technologies. Another reason that health care costs have risen so dramatically is advancing technology. Each CT (computerized tomography) scanner costs at least $100,000.

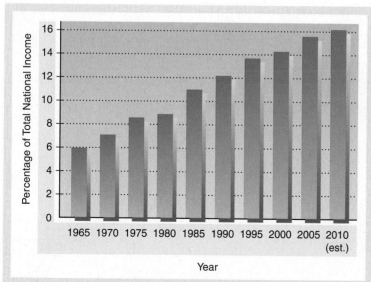

FIGURE 31-8

Percentage of Total National Income Spent on Health Care in the United States

The portion of total national income spent on health care has risen steadily since 1965.

Sources: U.S. Department of Commerce; U.S. Department of Health and Human Services; Deloitte and Touche LLP; VHA, Inc.

An MRI (magnetic resonance imaging) scanner can cost over $2 million. A PET (positron emission tomography) scanner costs around $4 million. All of these machines have become increasingly available in recent decades and are desired throughout the country. Typical fees for procedures using them range from $300 to $400 for a CT scan to as high as $2,000 for a PET scan. The development of new technologies that help physicians and hospitals prolong human life is an ongoing process in an ever-advancing industry. New procedures at even higher prices can be expected in the future.

Third-Party Financing. Currently, government spending on health care constitutes over 40 percent of total health care spending (of which the *federal* government pays about 70 percent). Private insurance accounts for a little over 35 percent of payments for health care. The remainder—less than 20 percent—is paid directly by individuals. Figure 31-9 shows the change in the payment scheme for medical care in the United States since 1930. Medicare and Medicaid are the main sources of hospital and other medical benefits to 35 million U.S. residents, most of whom are over 65. Medicaid—the joint state-federal program—provides long-term health care, particularly for people living in nursing homes. Medicare, Medicaid, and private insurance companies are considered **third parties** in the medical care equation. Caregivers and patients are the two primary parties. When third parties step in to pay for medical care, the quantity demanded for those services increases. For example, when Medicare and Medicaid went into effect in the 1960s, the volume of federal government–reimbursed medical services increased by more than 65 percent.

The availability of third-party payments for costly medical care has generated increases in the availability of hospital beds. Between 1974 and 2005, the number of hospital beds increased by over 50 percent. Present occupancy rates are only around 65 percent.

Price, Quantity Demanded, and the Question of Moral Hazard. Although some people may think that the demand for health care is insensitive to price changes, theory clearly indicates otherwise. Look at Figure 31-10. There you see a hypothetical demand curve for health care services. To the extent that third parties—whether government or private insurance—pay for health care, the out-of-pocket cost, or net price, to the individual decreases. If all medical expenses were paid for by third parties, dropping the price to zero in Figure 31-10, the quantity demanded would skyrocket.

Third parties
Parties who are not directly involved in a given activity or transaction. For example, in the relationship between caregivers and patients, fees may be paid by third parties (insurance companies, government).

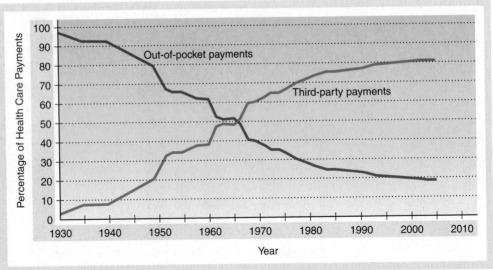

FIGURE 31-9
Third-Party versus Out-of-Pocket Health Care Payments
Out-of-pocket payments for health care services have been falling steadily since the 1930s. In contrast, third-party payments for health care have risen to the point that they account for over 80 percent of all such outlays today.

Sources: Health Care Financing Administration; U.S. Department of Health and Human Services.

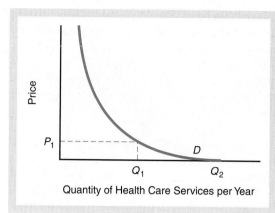

FIGURE 31-10
The Demand for Health Care Services
At price P_1, the quantity of health care services demanded per year would hypothetically be Q_1. If the price fell to zero (third-party payment with zero deductible), the quantity demanded would expand to Q_2.

One of the issues here has to do with the problem of *moral hazard*. Consider two individuals with two different health insurance policies. The first policy pays for all medical expenses, but under the second, the individual has to pay the first $1,000 a year (this amount is known as the *deductible*). Will the behavior of the two individuals be different? Generally, the answer is yes. The individual with no deductible is more likely to seek treatment for health problems after they develop rather than try to avoid them and will generally expect medical attention on a more regular basis. In contrast, the individual who faces the first $1,000 of medical expenses each year will tend to engage in more wellness activities and will be less inclined to seek medical care for minor problems. The moral hazard here is that the individual with the zero deductible for medical care expenses may engage in a lifestyle that is less healthful than will the individual with the $1,000 deductible.

Moral Hazard as It Affects Physicians and Hospitals. The issue of moral hazard also has a direct effect on the behavior of physicians and hospital administrators. Due to third-party payments, patients rarely have to worry about the expense of operations and other medical procedures. As a consequence, both physicians and hospitals order more procedures. Physicians are typically reimbursed on the basis of medical procedures; thus they have no financial interest in trying to keep hospital costs down. Indeed, many have an incentive to raise costs.

Such actions are most evident with terminally ill patients. A physician may order a CT scan and other costly procedures for a terminally ill patient. The physician knows that Medicare or some other type of insurance will pay. Then the physician can charge a fee for analyzing the CT scan. Fully 30 percent of Medicare expenditures are for U.S. residents who are in the last six months of their lives.

Rising Medicare expenditures are one of the most serious problems facing the federal government today. The number of beneficiaries has increased from 19.1 million in 1966 (first year of operation) to more than 36 million in 2005. Figure 31-11 on the following page shows that federal spending on Medicare has been growing at over 10 percent a year, adjusted for inflation. The addition of a Medicare prescription drug benefit in 2003 has set the stage for an even higher rate of growth in Medicare spending.

Is National Health Insurance the Answer?

Proponents of a national health care system believe that the current system relies too heavily on private insurers. They argue in favor of a Canadian-style system. In Canada, the government sets the fees that are paid to each physician for seeing a patient and prohibits

Economics Front and Center

To contemplate the issues faced by health care providers in a largely nationalized health care system such as Canada's, read the case study, **A Canadian Doctor Faces a Tough Career Choice,** on page 752.

FIGURE 31-11
Federal Medicare Spending
Federal spending on Medicare has increased about 10 percent a year, after adjusting for inflation, since its inception in 1966. (All figures expressed in constant 2000 dollars.)

Sources: *Economic Report of the President*; U.S. Bureau of Labor Statistics.

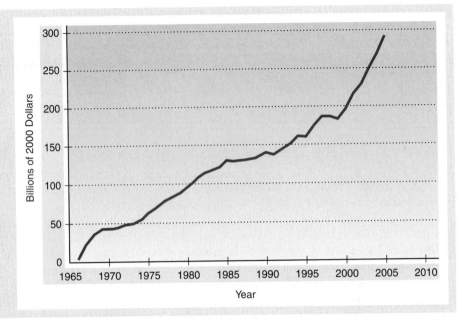

private practice. The Canadian government also imposes a cap on the income that any doctor can receive in a given year. The Canadian federal government provides a specified amount of funding to hospitals, leaving it to them to decide how to allocate the funds. If we were to follow the Canadian model, the average U.S. resident would receive fewer health services than at present. Hospital stays would be longer, but there would be fewer tests and procedures.

Is the publicly provided health care that the Canadian government commonly describes as "free" to all Canadian residents really costless?

International EXAMPLE

Hidden Costs of "Free" Canadian Health Care

Because physicians are unwilling to provide as many services as people wish to purchase at below-market fees dictated by the Canadian government, long waiting lists are a fixture of the Canadian system. The average waiting time to see a specialist after referral by a general practitioner is more than four months. Individuals experiencing debilitating back pain often must wait at least a year for neurosurgery. Even people diagnosed with life-threatening cancers typically have to wait six weeks before they have an initial examination by a cancer specialist.

The high opportunity costs associated with long waits for officially approved health care have led to the establishment of private health care clinics on Native American reservations, where physicians can legally accept private payments. (It is il-

legal for Canadians to purchase private health insurance to pay for care received on these reservations, however.) In addition, rather than wait for years to obtain elective surgeries, about 20,000 Canadians fly to India each year at their own expense and pay physicians in that country to perform surgeries such as hip replacements. In actuality, the "free" Canadian health care system is very costly to that nation's residents.

For Critical Analysis
Why do you suppose that many Canadians who wish to have MRI scans travel to the United States and pay for scans out of their own pockets instead of waiting three months for a "free" MRI scan in Canada?

Alternatives to a national health care policy involve some type of national health insurance, perhaps offered only to people who qualify on the basis of low annual income. A number of politicians have offered variations on such a program. The over 40 million U.S. residents who have no health insurance at some time during each year would almost certainly benefit. The share of annual national income that goes to health care expenditures would rise, however. Also, federal government spending might increase by another $30 billion to $50 billion (or more) per year to pay for the program.

Countering the Moral Hazard Problem: A Health Savings Account

As an alternative to completely changing the U.S. health care industry, in 2003 Congress authorized **health savings accounts (HSAs)**. These accounts replaced experimental *medical savings accounts* that Congress had previously permitted but had limited to 700,000 accounts nationwide. Anyone with a relatively high health insurance deductible—a minimum level of out-of-pocket expenses of $1,000 for an individual or $2,000 for a family—can open an HSA at a financial institution offering such accounts. Individuals younger than 55 can make annual deposits of up to $2,600 per person per year, and families can deposit as much as $5,150 per year. Once a person reaches the age of 55, allowable deposits can be even higher, but contributions must end once the person reaches 65 and becomes eligible for Medicare.

Health savings account (HSA)
A tax-exempt health care account into which individuals can pay on a regular basis and out of which medical expenses can be paid.

People with HSAs may use deposited funds and tax-free interest earnings to cover any out-of-pocket health care expenses. In addition, they can draw on HSAs to pay health insurance premiums if they become unemployed or to cover medical expenses they incur after they have retired. There is a 10 percent penalty for most withdrawals used for nonmedical purposes before retirement, but when a person retires, funds in an HSA may be used to supplement other sources of income. A single person depositing the maximum amount each year with no withdrawals will have hundreds of thousands of dollars in the account after 40 years.

Combating Moral Hazard. A major benefit of an HSA is that the moral hazard problem is reduced. Individuals ultimately pay for their own *minor* medical expenses. They do not have the incentive to seek medical care as frequently for minor problems. In addition, they have an incentive to engage in wellness activities. Finally, for those using an HSA, the physician-patient relationship remains intact because third parties (insurance companies or the government) do not intervene in paying or monitoring medical expenses. Patients with HSAs will not usually allow physicians to routinely order expensive tests for every minor ache or pain because they get to keep any funds saved in the HSA.

Critics' Responses. Some critics argue that because individuals get to keep whatever they don't spend from their HSAs, they will forgo necessary visits to medical care facilities and may develop more serious medical problems as a consequence. Other critics argue that HSAs will sabotage managed care plans. Under managed care plans, deductibles are either reduced or eliminated completely. In exchange, managed health care plan participants are extremely limited in physician choice. Just the opposite is true with HSAs—high deductibles and unlimited choice of physicians.

Concepts in Brief

- Health care costs have risen because (1) our population has been getting older and the elderly use more health care services, (2) new technologies and medicine cost more, and (3) third-party financing—private and government-sponsored health insurance—reduces the incentive for individuals to reduce their spending on health care services.

● National health insurance has been proposed as an answer to our current problems, but it does little to alter the reasons why health care costs continue to rise.

● In 2003, Congress authorized health savings accounts, which allow individuals to set aside funds that are tax-exempt and can be used only for medical care. Whatever is left over becomes a type of retirement account.

To test your understanding of the concepts covered in this section, go to the Online Review at **www.myeconlab.com/miller.**

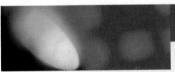

CASE STUDY : Economics Front and Center

A Canadian Doctor Faces a Tough Career Choice

Farraday is a Canadian physician who makes his living as an oncologist specializing in leukemias, or blood cancers. Over the years, his income has grown at a meager pace because most of his patients are covered by the government's national health insurance plan that places legal limits on the fees he can charge. Farraday's job is also more difficult than it used to be. Patients with leukemia who wish to obtain the latest treatments often must wait for weeks or even months before receiving government approval. Consequently, Farraday expends a considerable amount of time and energy trying to find ways to obtain the best possible outcomes with alternative, but less effective, forms of treatment.

Now Farraday faces a tough choice. He has been offered a job with a company in India that provides health care to Canadian cancer patients unwilling to wait for government approval to receive the latest, most expensive treatments. If he accepts the position, Farraday would supervise several Indian oncologists. He and his wife would have to move far from his adult son and daughter and the grandchildren, but his income would be four times higher than it is now. Farraday takes a deep breath, picks up the phone, and begins to punch in the number of the head of the Indian health care firm who has offered him the job. It is time to inform her of his decision.

Points to Analyze

1. *Why are Canadian leukemia patients willing to forgo publicly funded treatments in Canada in favor of treatments in India that they must pay for themselves?*

2. *Why do you suppose that most economists believe that privately provided health care make up a much larger share of Canadians' health care expenditures than the government's official estimate of 25 percent? (Hint: In its tabulation of total health care spending by Canadians, the government includes only their expenses on health care within Canada's borders.)*

Issues and Applications

Should U.S. Health Care Copy Other Nations' Programs?

igure 31-12 shows that total spending on health care as a percentage of total national income is much higher in the United States than in other developed countries. Many media and political commentators have argued that this is evidence of a health care-spending "crisis" in the United States. A solution, many have suggested, is for the U.S. government to follow the examples set by governments in other countries, such as Canada, Japan, and European nations, and increase its expenditures on health care.

Concepts Applied

- Economics of Health Care
- Health Care Expenditures

If There Is a U.S. "Crisis," It Must Be by Choice

These commentators usually fail to mention another fact, however. As Figure 31-12 also indicates, as a percentage of total national income, government spending on health care in the United States is already on a par with that of other developed nations. U.S. government spending on health care as a share of total income is somewhat higher than in Japan and the United Kingdom, and it is only slightly less than in Canada.

As the figure makes clear, total U.S. health care spending amounts to a much higher share of total income than in other nations because U.S. residents *choose* to allocate a larger share of their incomes to health care. *Private* spending on health care in the United States amounts to more than 9

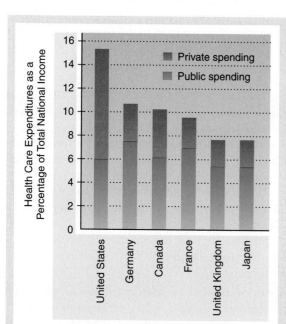

FIGURE 31-12

Private versus Public Expenditures on Health Care in Selected Nations

U.S. government spending on health care as a percentage of total national income is similar to public expenditures as a share of income in other developed nations. *Total* health care spending as a percentage of income is significantly higher in the United States, however. This implies that residents of the United States choose to devote a much larger portion of their incomes to health care expenditures than residents of other developed nations.

Source: Organization for Economic Cooperation and Development.

percent of total national income. In contrast, in Germany private expenditures on health care amount to only slightly over 3 percent of total income.

In Other Countries, Relatively Lower Health Care Expenditures Are Not Necessarily a Choice

Why do individuals in other nations allocate smaller percentages of their incomes to health care expenditures? For residents of many countries, the answer is that their national governments will not allow them to spend more on health care. Even though individuals in these nations might desire to visit physicians more frequently and obtain more treatments for a wider range of ailments, government rules do not permit them to do so. In Canada, for instance, patients who desire CT scans or surgeries must often wait for months or years before obtaining government approval to consume these health care services.

In Germany and France, where, as Figure 31-12 indicates, governments account for the majority of health care expenditures, government agencies coordinate particularly complex rules regulating health care spending. The agencies do this so inefficiently that the costs of providing each unit of health care in these countries are the highest in the world. The German government is currently in the midst of implementing a massive "modernization program" for its health care system. As part of its efforts to repair the system, the German government is *privatizing* many elements of its programs. Therefore, even as U.S. critics continue to argue for modeling the U.S. health care system on government-dominated systems elsewhere, Germany is striving to move closer to the U.S. system.

For Critical Analysis

1. Why do you suppose that a key position in the Canadian health care system is a "triage expert," who decides which people qualify for particular treatments and which do not?
2. How does using waiting lists as rationing devices help governments hold down the costs of providing publicly funded health care?

Web Resources

1. To learn more about the involvement of the federal government in the U.S. markets for health care, go to www.econtoday.com/chap31.
2. For more information about arguments favoring complete U.S. government funding of all health care, use the link at www.econtoday.com/chap31 to go to the home page of "Physicians for a National Health Program."

Research Project

Discuss how market forces that influence prices ration health care in private markets. Contrast this form of rationing with governmental rationing of health care using waiting lists and other nonprice rationing devices. What are the advantages and disadvantages of these alternative approaches to determining who gets access to health care and how that access is funded?

SUMMARY DISCUSSION of Learning Objectives

1. **Using a Lorenz Curve to Represent a Nation's Income Distribution:** A Lorenz curve is a diagram that illustrates the distribution of income geometrically by measuring the percentage of households in relation to the cumulative percentage of income earnings. A perfectly straight Lorenz curve depicts perfect income equality because at each percentage of households measured along a straight-line Lorenz curve, those households earn exactly the same percentage of income. The more bowed a Lorenz curve, the more unequally income is distributed.

2. **Key Determinants of Income Differences Across Individuals:** Because of the age-earnings cycle, in which

people typically begin working at relatively low incomes when young, age is an important factor influencing income differences. So are marginal productivity differences, which arise from differences in talent, experience, and training due to different investments in human capital. Discrimination likely plays a role as well, and economists attribute some of the unexplained portions of income differences across people to factors related to discrimination.

3. **Theories of Desired Income Distribution:** Economists agree that determining how income ought to be distributed is a normative issue influenced by alternative no-

tions of economic justice. Nevertheless, two theories of desired income distribution receive considerable attention. One is the productivity standard (also called the contributive or merit standard), according to which each person receives income according to the value of what the person produces. The other is the egalitarian principle of income distribution, which proposes that each person should receive exactly the same income.

4. **Alternative Approaches to Measuring and Addressing Poverty:** One approach to measuring poverty is to define an absolute poverty standard, such as a specific and unchanging income level. If an absolute measure of poverty is used and the economy experiences persistent real growth, poverty will eventually disappear. Another approach defines poverty in terms of income levels relative to the rest of the population. Under this definition, poverty exists as long as the distribution of incomes is unequal. Official poverty measures are often based on pretax income and fail to take transfer payments into account. Currently, the U.S. government seeks to address poverty via income maintenance programs such as Social Security, Supplemental Security Income, Temporary Assistance to Needy Families, food stamps, and the Earned Income Tax Credit program.

5. **Major Reasons for Rising Health Care Costs:** Spending on health care as a percentage of total U.S. national income has increased during recent decades. One reason is that the U.S. population is aging, and older people typically experience more health problems. Another contributing factor is the adoption of higher-quality but higher-priced technologies for diagnosing and treating health problems. In addition, third-party financing of health care expenditures by private and government insurance programs gives covered individuals an incentive to purchase more health care than they would if they paid all expenses out of pocket. Moral hazard problems can also arise because consumers may be more likely to seek treatment for insured health problems after they develop instead of trying to avoid them, and physicians and hospitals may order more procedures than they otherwise would require.

6. **Alternative Approaches to Paying for Health Care:** An alternative approach to funding health care would be to rely less on private insurers and more on governmental funding of care for all citizens. Under such a system, the government typically sets fees and establishes limits on access to care. Another approach would be to establish an income-based national health insurance program, in which only lower-income people would qualify for government assistance in meeting their health care expenses. Another option, which Congress authorized in 2003, is to provide incentives for people to save some of their income in health savings accounts, from which they can draw funds to pay for health care expenses in the future.

KEY TERMS AND CONCEPTS

PROBLEMS

Answers to the odd-numbered problems appear at the back of the book.

31-1. Consider the accompanying graph, which depicts Lorenz curves for countries X, Y, and Z.

    a. Which country has the least income inequality?

    b. Which country has the most income inequality?

    c. Countries Y and Z are identical in all but one respect: population distribution. The share of the population made up of children below working age is much higher in country Z. Recently, how-

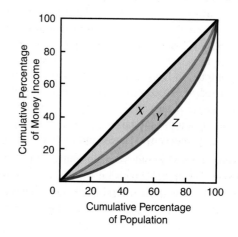

ever, birthrates have declined in country Z and risen in country Y. Assuming that the countries remain identical in all other respects, would you expect that in 20 years the Lorenz curves for the two countries will be closer together or farther apart?

31-2. Consider the following estimates from the 1990s of shares of income to each group. Use graph paper or a hand-drawn diagram to draw rough Lorenz curves for each country. Which has the most nearly equal distribution, based on your diagram?

Country	Poorest 40%	Next 30%	Next 20%	Richest 10%
Bolivia	13	21	26	40
Chile	13	20	26	41
Uruguay	22	26	26	26

31-3. Suppose that the 20 percent of people with the highest incomes decide to increase their annual giving to charities, which pass nearly all the funds on to the 20 percent of people with the lowest incomes. What is the effect on the shape of the Lorenz curve?

31-4. Suppose that a nation has implemented a system for applying a tax rate of 2 percent to the incomes earned by the 10 percent of its residents with the highest incomes. All funds collected are then transferred directly to the 10 percent of the nation's residents with the lowest incomes.

   a. What is the general effect on the shape of a Lorenz curve based on pretax incomes?

   b. What is the general effect on the shape of a Lorenz curve based on after-tax incomes?

31-5. Estimates indicate that during the 1990s, the poorest 40 percent of the population earned about 15 percent of total income in Argentina. In Brazil, the poorest 40 percent earned about 10 percent of total income. The next-highest 30 percent of income earners in Argentina received roughly 25 percent of total income. By contrast, in Brazil, the next-highest 30 percent of income earners received approximately 20 percent of total income. Can you determine, without drawing a diagram (though you can if you wish), which country's Lorenz curve was bowed out farther to the right?

31-6. A retired 68-year-old man currently draws Social Security and a small pension from his previous employment. He is in very good health and would like to take on a new challenge, and he decides to go back to work. He determines that under the rules of Social Security and his pension plan, if he were to work full time, he would face a marginal tax rate of 110 percent for the last hour he works each week. What does this mean?

31-7. In what ways might policies aimed at achieving complete income equality across all households be incompatible with economic efficiency?

31-8. Some economists have argued that if the government wishes to subsidize health care, it should instead provide predetermined sums of payments (based on the type of health care problems experienced) directly to patients, who then would be free to choose their health care providers. Whether or not you agree, can you give an economic rationale for this approach to governmental health care funding?

31-9. Suppose that a government agency guarantees to pay all of an individual's future health care expenses after the end of this year, so that the effective price of health care for the individual will be zero from that date onward. In what ways might this well-intended policy induce the individual to consume "excessive" health care services in future years?

31-10. Suppose that a group of doctors establishes a joint practice in a remote area. This group provides the only health care available to people in the local community, and its objective is to maximize total economic profits for the group's members. Draw a diagram illustrating how the price and quantity of health care will be determined in this community. (Hint: How does a single producer of any service determine its output and price?)

31-11. A government agency determines that the entire community discussed in Problem 31-10 qualifies for a special program in which the government will pay for a number of health care services that most residents previously had not consumed. Many residents immediately make appointments with the community physicians' group. Given the information in Problem 31-10, what is the likely effect on the profit-maximizing price and the equilibrium quantity of health care services provided by the physicians' group in this community?

31-12. A government agency notifies the physicians' group in Problem 31-10 that to continue providing services in the community, the group must document its activities. The resulting paperwork expenses raise the cost of each unit of health care services that the group provides. What is the likely effect on the profit-maximizing price and the equilibrium quantity of health care services provided by the physicians' group in this community?

31-13. As discussed in this chapter, interest-bearing health savings accounts (HSAs) allow individuals with qualifying health insurance plans to use deposited funds to pay out-of-pocket medical expenses. Subject to penalties and taxation, holders of HSAs can use funds in the accounts and tax-free interest earnings to pay non-health-related expenses if they wish. Many people, however, participate in optional *health reimbursement accounts (HRAs)* offered alongside employer-provided health insurance plans. HRAs, into which people typically make payments via tax-free deductions from their weekly or monthly earnings, are non-interest-bearing and can be used only to pay medical expenses. Any funds in HRAs that individuals fail to use for medical expenses within a calendar year revert to the employer at the end of the year. Is an HSA or an HRA more likely to create moral hazard problems? Explain your reasoning.

ECONOMICS ON THE NET

Measuring Poverty Many economists believe that there are problems with the current official measure of poverty. In this application, you will learn about some of these problems and will be able to examine an alternative poverty measure that one group of economists has proposed.

Title: Joint Center for Poverty Research (JCPR)

Navigation: Go to **www.econtoday.com/chap31** to visit the JCPR's home page. Click on *Publications*. Select the complete listing of policy briefs. Click on the *Policy Brief* titled "Measuring Poverty—A New Approach."

Application Read the article; then answer the following questions.

1. How is the current official poverty income level calculated? What is the main problem with this way of calculating the threshold income for classifying impoverished households?

2. What is the alternative conceptual measure of poverty that the authors propose? How does it differ from the current measure?

For Group Study and Analysis Discuss the two measures of poverty discussed in the article. What people would no longer be classified as living in poverty under the proposed measure of poverty? What people would join the ranks of those classified as among the impoverished in the United States? How might adopting the new measure of poverty affect efforts to address the U.S. poverty problem?

Media Resources

If your exam were tomorrow, would you be ready? For each chapter, MyEconLab Practice Tests and Study Plans pinpoint which sections you have mastered and which ones you need to study. That way, you are more efficient with your study time, and you are better prepared for your exams.

In addition to Practice Tests and your personalized Study Plan, you'll find the following media resources in MyEconLab:

1. *Graphs in Motion* animation of Figures 31-1, 31-5, 31-7, and 31-9.
2. Videos featuring the author, Roger LeRoy Miller, on the following subjects:
   - The Determinants of Income Differences
   - Defining Poverty

3. Links to the Web sites cited in the marginal Internet Resources, Issues and Applications feature, and Economics on the Net activity.
4. Audio clips of all key terms, additional practice problems, and a PDF version of the material from the print Study Guide.
5. eThemes of the Times, which is a New York Times article to help you understand the real-world applications of what you are learning.

myeconlab
Get Ahead of the Curve

To see how it works, turn to page 16 and then go to **www.myeconlab.com/miller**.

Chapter 32

Environmental Economics

Indonesia's Komodo island group is like no other place on our planet. Its reefs are home to more coral species than all the islands of the Caribbean Sea. Many rare fish and turtles also inhabit the waters around the islands. The best-known creature of the islands, however, is the Komodo dragon, the world's largest living lizard species. For residents of Indonesia, who have been struggling with a weak economy, finding ways to preserve all these unique species has become a thorny issue. Poachers illegally capture turtles, which are a pricey delicacy. Fishermen routinely use cyanide, even though this poison damages the coral reefs and threatens the entire Komodo ecosystem. In this chapter, you will learn about the economic approach to dissuading people from harming the environment.

Refer to the end of the chapter for a full listing of the multimedia learning materials available in MyEconLab.

LEARNING OBJECTIVES

After reading this chapter, you should be able to:

1. Distinguish between private costs and social costs
2. Understand market externalities and possible ways to correct externalities
3. Describe how economists can conceptually determine the optimal quantity of pollution
4. Explain the roles of private and common property rights in alternative approaches to addressing the problem of pollution
5. Discuss how the assignment of property rights may influence the fates of endangered species
6. Contrast the benefits and costs of recycling scarce resources

...the average home in the United States receives 20 paper bills per month via the U.S. Postal Service? The total amount of paper used in all these bill deliveries weighs in at 771,000 tons per year. If all U.S. households chose to receive and pay all these bills electronically using the Internet, the resulting decrease in paper production could save more than 18 million trees per year and 15 billion gallons of wastewater. About 1.7 billion pounds of solid waste per year, or the equivalent of all the solid waste produced each year in the city of Detroit, would be eliminated. A complete switch to Internet billing and payments would also eliminate more than 2 billion tons of carbon dioxide and other greenhouse gases, or the amount of air pollutants produced by 390,000 autos.

Given the significant resource savings and environmental benefits that electronic billing and payments could generate, why have only a few million people in the United States switched from paper bills to electronic billing? Presumably, the answer is that only these few million have perceived the individual benefits of making this switch to be greater than the individual costs.

The economic way of thinking about the effects of personal choices on natural resources and the environment requires considering the costs of environmental protection. What additional portion of your weekly wages are you willing to give up in exchange for every 1 percent improvement in the average air quality where you live? To some people, framing questions in terms of the dollars-and-cents costs of environmental improvement sounds anti-ecological. But this is not so. Economists want to help citizens and policymakers opt for informed policies that have the maximum possible *net* benefits (benefits minus costs). As you will see, every decision in favor of "the environment" involves a trade-off.

PRIVATE VERSUS SOCIAL COSTS

Human actions often give rise to unwanted side effects—the destruction of our environment is one. Human actions generate pollutants that go into the air and the water. The question that is often asked is, Why can individuals and businesses continue to create pollution without necessarily paying directly for the negative consequences?

Until now, we've been dealing with situations in which the costs of an individual's actions are borne directly by the individual. When a business has to pay wages to workers, it knows exactly what its labor costs are. When it has to buy materials or build a plant, it knows quite well what these will cost. An individual who has to pay for car repairs or a theater ticket knows exactly what the cost will be. These costs are what we term *private costs.* **Private costs** are borne solely by the individuals who incur them. They are *internal* in the sense that the firm or household must explicitly take account of them.

What about a situation in which a business dumps the waste products from its production process into a nearby river or an individual litters a public park or beach? Obviously, a cost is involved in these actions. When the firm pollutes the water, people downstream suffer the consequences. They may not want to swim in or drink the polluted water. They may also be unable to catch as many fish as before because of the pollution. In the case of littering, the people who come along after our litterer has cluttered the park or the beach are the ones who bear the costs. The cost of these actions is borne by people other than those who commit the actions. The creator of the cost is not the sole bearer. The costs are not internalized by the individual or firm; they are external. When we add *external* costs to *internal,* or private, costs, we get **social costs.** Pollution problems—indeed, all problems pertaining to the environment—may be viewed as situations in which social costs exceed private costs. Because some economic participants pay only the smaller private costs of

Private costs
Costs borne solely by the individuals who incur them. Also called *internal costs.*

Social costs
The full costs borne by society whenever a resource use occurs. Social costs can be measured by adding external costs to private, or internal, costs.

their actions, not the full social costs, their actions ultimately contribute to higher spillover costs on the rest of society. In such situations in which social and private costs diverge, we therefore see "too much" steel production, automobile driving, and beach littering, to pick only a few of the many possible examples.

The Costs of Polluted Air

Why is the air in cities so polluted from automobile exhaust fumes? When automobile drivers step into their cars, they bear only the private costs of driving. That is, they must pay for the gas, maintenance, depreciation, and insurance on their automobiles. But they cause an additional cost, that of air pollution, which they are not forced to take account of when they make the decision to drive. Air pollution is a cost because it causes harm to individuals—burning eyes, respiratory ailments, and dirtier clothes, cars, and buildings. The air pollution created by automobile exhaust is a cost that individual operators of automobiles do not yet bear directly. The social cost of driving includes all the private costs plus at least the cost of air pollution, which society bears. Decisions made only on the basis of private costs lead to too much automobile driving or, alternatively, to too few resources spent on the reduction of automobile pollution for a given amount of driving. Clean air is a scarce resource used by automobile drivers free of charge. They will use more of it than they would if they had to pay the full social costs.

Externalities

Externality
A situation in which a private cost (or benefit) diverges from a social cost (or benefit); a situation in which the costs (or benefits) of an action are not fully borne (or gained) by the two parties engaged in exchange or by an individual engaging in a scarce-resource-using activity.

When a private cost differs from a social cost, we say that there is an **externality** because individual decision makers are not paying (internalizing) all the costs. (We briefly covered this topic in Chapter 5.) Some of these costs remain external to the decision-making process. Remember that the full cost of using a scarce resource is borne one way or another by all who live in the society. That is, society must pay the full opportunity cost of any activity that uses scarce resources. The individual decision maker is the firm or the customer, and external costs and benefits will not enter into that individual's or firm's decision-making processes.

We might want to view the problem as it is presented in Figure 32-1. Here we have the market demand curve, D, for the product X and the supply curve, S_1, for product X. The supply curve, S_1, includes only internal, or private, costs. The intersection of the demand and supply curves as drawn will be at price P_1 and quantity Q_1 (at E_1). We now assume that the production of good X involves externalities that the private firms did not take into account. Those externalities could be air pollution, water pollution, scenery destruction, or anything of that nature.

We know that the social costs of producing product X exceed the private costs. We show this by drawing curve S_2. It is above the original supply curve S_1 because it includes the full social costs of producing the product. If firms could be made to bear these costs, the price would be P_2 and the quantity Q_2 (at E_2). The inclusion of external costs in the decision-making process would lead to a higher-priced product and a decline in quantity produced. Thus we see that when social costs are not being fully borne by the creators of those costs, the quantity produced is "excessive" because the price is too low.

Economics Front and Center

To contemplate externality issues facing today's emerging nanotechnology industry, take a look at the case study, **Confronting Potential Nanotechnology Externalities**, on page 771.

CORRECTING FOR EXTERNALITIES

We can see here a method for reducing pollution and environmental degradation. Somehow the signals in the economy must be changed so that decision makers will take into account *all* the costs of their actions. In the case of automobile pollution, we might want to

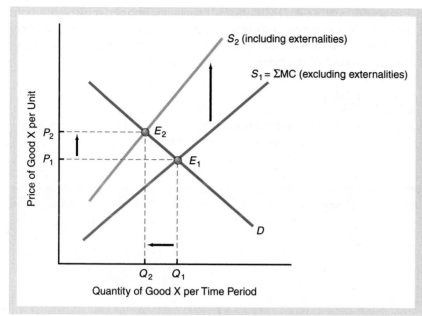

FIGURE 32-1
Reckoning with Full Social Costs
The supply curve, S_1, is equal to the horizontal summation (Σ) of the individual marginal cost curves above the respective minimum average variable costs of all the firms producing good X. These individual marginal cost curves include only internal, or private, costs. If the external costs were included and added to the private costs, we would have social costs. The supply curve would shift upward to S_2. In the uncorrected situation, the equilibrium price is P_1, and the equilibrium quantity is Q_1. In the corrected situation, the equilibrium price would rise to P_2, and the equilibrium quantity would fall to Q_2.

devise some method of taxing motorists according to the amount of pollution they cause. In the case of a firm, we might want to devise a system of taxing businesses according to the amount of pollution for which they are responsible. They would then have an incentive to install pollution abatement equipment.

The Polluters' Choice

Facing an additional private cost for polluting, firms will be induced to (1) install pollution abatement equipment or otherwise change production techniques so as to reduce the amount of pollution, (2) reduce pollution-causing activity, or (3) simply pay the price to pollute. The relative costs and benefits of each option for each polluter will determine which one or combination will be chosen. Allowing the choice is the efficient way to decide who pollutes and who doesn't. In principle, each polluter faces the full social cost of its actions and makes a production decision accordingly.

Is a Uniform Tax Appropriate?

It may not be appropriate to levy a *uniform* tax according to physical quantities of pollution. After all, we're talking about external costs. Such costs are not necessarily the same everywhere in the United States for the same action.

Essentially, we must establish the amount of the *economic damages* rather than the amount of the physical pollution. A polluting electrical plant in New York City will cause much more damage than the same plant in Montana. There are already innumerable demands on the air in New York City, so the pollution from smokestacks will not be cleansed away naturally. Millions of people will breathe the polluted air and thereby incur the costs of sore throats, sickness, emphysema, and even early death. Buildings will become dirtier faster because of the pollution, as will cars and clothes. A given quantity of pollution will cause more harm in concentrated urban environments than it will in less dense rural environments. If we were to establish some form of taxation to align private costs with social costs and to force people to internalize externalities, we would somehow have to come up with a measure of *economic* costs instead of *physical* quantities. But the tax, in any event, would fall on the private sector and modify individuals' and firms' behavior. Therefore, because the economic cost for the same physical quantity of pollution would be different in different locations according to population density, the natural formation of mountains and rivers, and so forth, so-called optimal taxes on pollution would vary from location to location. (Nonetheless, a uniform tax might make sense when administrative costs, particularly the cost of ascertaining the actual economic costs, are relatively high.)

Why do you suppose that U.S. air pollution and fuel economy standards are encouraging auto manufacturers to produce more vehicles with diesel engines?

Policy E X A M P L E

Why Smelly Diesel Engines Are Catching On

The diesel engine, which was invented in 1890, packs more air into its cylinders than a gasoline engine. As a result, the diesel engine creates more powerful internal-combustion explosions per drop of fuel, making it more fuel efficient. Two forms of U.S. regulations are currently making the diesel engine more attractive to companies that produce autos, trucks, and sport utility vehicles (SUVs). On the one hand, producers must meet federal fuel economy standards. Each producer's fleet of autos must average 27.5 miles per gallon, and by 2007 every automaker's fleets of trucks and SUVs must average 22.2 miles per gallon. On the other hand, vehicle manufacturers must also satisfy restrictions on emissions of nitrogen oxide, soot, and other gases that contribute to air pollution.

In years past, diesel engines produced too many pollutants to allow producers to satisfy federal pollution standards, even though more widespread use in vehicles would have assisted in

meeting fuel economy rules. Recent technological advances have changed the outlook for diesels, however. Electronic sensors in diesel engine cylinders can regulate fuel nozzles with less wiggle room than a human hair to produce carefully controlled bursts at forces up to 29,000 pounds per square inch. As a result, a diesel engine can burn fuel much more cleanly while continuing to operate 20 to 30 percent more efficiently than a gasoline engine. Producers of U.S. trucks and SUVs are already introducing numerous new models with diesel engines, which are likely to come into more widespread use by 2010.

For Critical Analysis
How do pollution emission regulations that apply to each producer's entire fleet of SUVs affect its marginal cost of producing these vehicles?

CONCEPTS in Brief

- Private costs are costs that are borne directly by consumers and producers when they engage in any resource-using activity.

- Social costs are private costs plus any other costs that are external to the decision maker. For example, the social

costs of driving include all the private costs plus, at a minimum, any pollution caused.

- When private costs differ from social costs, externalities exist because individual decision makers are not internalizing all the costs that society is bearing.

To test your understanding of the concepts covered in this section, go to the Online Review at www.myeconlab.com/miller.

POLLUTION

The term *pollution* is used quite loosely and can refer to a variety of by-products of any activity. Industrial pollution involves mainly air and water but can also include noise and such concepts as aesthetic pollution, as when a landscape is altered in a negative way. For the most part, we will be analyzing the most common forms—air and water pollution.

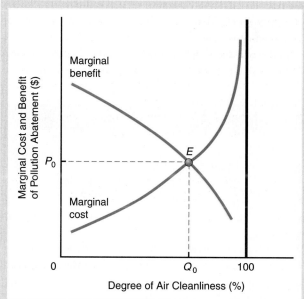

FIGURE 32-2
The Optimal Quantity of Air Pollution
As we attempt to get a greater degree of air cleanliness, the marginal cost rises until even the slightest attempt at increasing air cleanliness leads to a very high marginal cost, as can be seen at the upper right of the graph. Conversely, the marginal benefit curve slopes downward: The more pure air we have, the less we value an additional unit of pure air. Marginal cost and marginal benefit intersect at point E. The optimal degree of air cleanliness is something less than 100 percent at Q_0. The price that we should pay for the last unit of air cleanup is no greater than P_0, for that is where marginal cost equals marginal benefit.

When asked how much pollution there should be in the economy, many people will respond, "None." But if we ask those same people how much starvation or deprivation of consumer products should exist in the economy, many will again say, "None." Growing and distributing food or producing consumer products creates pollution, however. In effect, therefore, there is no correct answer to how much pollution should be in an economy because when we ask how much pollution there *should* be, we are entering the realm of normative economics. We are asking people to express values. There is no way to disprove somebody's value system scientifically. One way we can approach a discussion of the "correct" amount of pollution is to set up the same type of marginal analysis we used in our discussion of a firm's employment and output decisions. That is to say, we should pursue measures to reduce pollution only up to the point at which the marginal benefit from further reduction equals the marginal cost of further reduction.

Look at Figure 32-2. On the horizontal axis, we show the degree of cleanliness of the air. A vertical line is drawn at 100 percent cleanliness—the air cannot become any cleaner. Consider the benefits of obtaining a greater degree of air cleanliness. These benefits are represented by the marginal benefit curve, which slopes downward.

When the air is very dirty, the marginal benefit from air that is a little cleaner appears to be relatively high, as shown on the vertical axis. As the air becomes increasingly cleaner, however, the marginal benefit of a little bit more air cleanliness falls.

Consider the marginal cost of pollution abatement—that is, the marginal cost of obtaining cleaner air. In the 1960s, automobiles had no pollution abatement devices. Eliminating only 20 percent of the pollutants emitted by internal-combustion engines entailed a relatively small cost per unit of pollution removed. The cost of eliminating the next 20 percent rose, though. Finally, as we now get to the upper limits of removal of pollutants from the emissions of internal-combustion engines, we find that the elimination of one more percentage point of the amount of pollutants becomes astronomically expensive. To go from 97 percent cleanliness to 98 percent cleanliness involves a marginal cost that is many times greater than the marginal cost of going from 10 percent cleanliness to 11 percent cleanliness.

Go to **www.econtoday.com/chap32** to see a review by the ACCF Center for Policy Research of possible economic effects of alternative pollution reduction scenarios.

It is realistic, therefore, to draw the marginal cost of pollution abatement as an upward-sloping curve, as shown in Figure 32-2 on the previous page. (The marginal cost curve slopes up because of the law of diminishing returns.)

Why has the cost-benefit trade-off associated with "hybrid" cars and trucks that use less fuel and create less pollution led most consumers to decline to purchase these vehicles?

E X A M P L E

Weighing the Marginal Costs and Benefits of Hybrid Vehicles

For several years, Toyota, General Motors, and other auto manufacturers have offered consumers hybrid automobiles and pickup trucks that combine a downsized internal-combustion engine with an electric motor. This engine configuration allows hybrid vehicles to use less fuel while generating fewer environmentally harmful gases.

Now consider the cost-benefit trade-off that a consumer faces when contemplating purchasing a hybrid vehicle. The price of a hybrid car or truck is typically about $2,500 higher than for a vehicle with a standard internal-combustion engine. The quality-adjusted price is even higher because the engines of hybrid vehicles offer less power than standard engines. At the same time, the consumer's direct dollar benefit from purchasing a hybrid vehicle is relatively small. At a price of about $2 per gallon for fuel, the cost savings from driving a hybrid vehicle average only about $200 per year. The federal government grants a tax deduction to owners of hybrid vehicles, but for most consumers this generates a tax savings of only $500.

Thus a typical individual would have to own a hybrid car or truck for at least 10 years before the dollar benefits would equal the vehicle's higher cost. For most consumers, therefore, the marginal benefit from buying a hybrid vehicle in an effort to contribute to a cleaner environment is always less than the marginal cost. This explains why hybrid cars and trucks have been slow to catch on with U.S. buyers.

For Critical Analysis

What would happen to the quantity of hybrid vehicles sold in the United States if the federal government increased the tax deduction granted to purchasers of these vehicles?

The Optimal Quantity of Pollution

Optimal quantity of pollution
The level of pollution for which the marginal benefit of one additional unit of clean air just equals the marginal cost of that additional unit of clean air.

The **optimal quantity of pollution** is defined as the level of pollution at which the marginal benefit equals the marginal cost of obtaining clean air. This occurs at the intersection of the marginal benefit curve and the marginal cost curve in Figure 32-2, at point *E* (p. 763). This solution is analytically exactly the same as for every other economic activity. If we increased pollution control by one more unit greater than Q_0, the marginal cost of that small increase in the degree of air cleanliness would be greater than the marginal benefit to society.

As is usually the case in economic analysis, the optimal quantity of just about anything occurs when marginal cost equals marginal benefit. That is, the optimal quantity of pollution occurs at the point at which the marginal cost of reducing (or abating) pollution is just equal to the marginal benefit of doing so. The marginal cost of pollution abatement rises as more and more abatement is achieved (as the environment becomes cleaner and cleaner, the *extra* cost of cleansing rises). Early units of pollution abatement are easily achieved (at low cost), but attaining higher and higher levels of environmental quality becomes progressively more difficult (as the extra cost rises to prohibitive levels). At the same time, the marginal benefits of an increasingly cleaner environment fall; the marginal benefit of pollution abatement declines as our notion of a cleaner environment moves from human life-support requirements to recreation to beauty to a perfectly pure environment. The point at which the increasing marginal cost of pollution abatement equals the decreasing marginal benefit of pollution abatement defines the optimal quantity of pollution.

Recognizing that the optimal quantity of pollution is not zero becomes easier when we realize that it takes scarce resources to reduce pollution. A trade-off exists between producing a cleaner environment and producing other goods and services. In that sense, environmental cleanliness is a resource that can be analyzed like any other resource, and a cleaner environment must take its place with other societal wants.

Go to www.econtoday.com/chap32 to learn from the National Center for Policy Analysis about a market-oriented government program for reducing pollution.

CONCEPTS in Brief

- The marginal cost of cleaning up the environment rises as we get closer to 100 percent cleanliness. Indeed, it rises at an increasing rate.
- The marginal benefit of environmental cleanliness falls as we have more of it.

- The optimal quantity of pollution is the quantity at which the marginal cost of cleanup equals the marginal benefit of cleanup.
- Pollution abatement is a trade-off. We trade off goods and services for cleaner air and water, and vice versa.

To test your understanding of the concepts covered in this section, go to the Online Review at www.myeconlab.com/miller.

COMMON PROPERTY

In most cases, you do not have **private property rights,** or exclusive ownership rights, to the air surrounding you, nor does anyone else. Air is a **common property,** or a nonexclusive resource. Therein lies the crux of the problem. When no one owns a particular resource, no one has any incentive (conscience aside) to consider misuse of that resource. If one person decides not to pollute the air, there will normally be no significant effect on the total level of pollution. If one person decides not to pollute the ocean, there will still be approximately the same amount of ocean pollution—provided, of course, that the individual was previously responsible for only a small part of the total amount of ocean pollution.

Basically, pollution occurs when we have poorly defined private property rights, as in air and common bodies of water. We do not, for example, have a visual pollution problem in people's attics. That is their own property, which they choose to keep as clean as they want, given their preferences for cleanliness as weighed against the costs of keeping the attic neat and tidy.

When private property rights exist, individuals have legal recourse for any damages sustained through the misuse of their property. When private property rights are well defined, the use of property—that is, the use of resources—will generally involve contracting between the owners of those resources. If you own land, you might contract with another person who wants to use your land for raising cows. The contract would most likely be written in the form of a lease agreement.

Private property rights
Exclusive rights of ownership that allow the use, transfer, and exchange of property.

Common property
Property that is owned by everyone and therefore by no one. Air and water are examples of common property resources.

Voluntary Agreements and Transaction Costs

Is it possible for externalities to be internalized via voluntary agreement? Take a simple example. You live in a house with a nice view of a lake. The family living below you plants a tree. The tree grows so tall that it eventually starts to cut off your view. In most cities, no one has property rights to views; therefore, you usually cannot go to court to obtain relief. You do have the option of contracting with your neighbors, however.

Voluntary Agreements: Contracting. You have the option of paying your neighbors (contracting) to cut back the tree. You could start out with an offer of a small amount and keep going up until your neighbors agree or until you reach your limit. Your limit will equal the value you place on having an unobstructed view of the lake. Your neighbors will be willing if the payment is at least equal to the reduction in their intrinsic property value due to a stunted tree. Your offering the payment makes your neighbors aware of the social cost of their actions. The social cost here is equal to the care of the tree plus the cost suffered by you from an impeded view of the lake.

In essence, then, your offer of money income to your neighbors indicates to them that there is an opportunity cost to their actions. If they don't comply, they forfeit the payments that you are offering them. The point here is that *opportunity cost always exists, no matter who has property rights.* Therefore, we would expect under some circumstances that voluntary contracting will occur to internalize externalities.[*] The question is, When will voluntary agreements occur?

Transaction Costs. One major condition for the outcome just outlined is that the **transaction costs**—all costs associated with making and enforcing agreements—must be low relative to the expected benefits of reaching an agreement. (We already looked at this topic briefly in Chapter 4.) If we expand our example to a much larger one such as air pollution, the transaction costs of numerous homeowners trying to reach agreements with the individuals and companies that create the pollution are relatively high. Consequently, we don't expect voluntary contracting to be an effective way to internalize the externality of air pollution.

Transaction costs
All costs associated with making, reaching, and enforcing agreements.

Why is it that even though planting trees contributes to better air quality, companies that plant them may have trouble taking credit for the improvement?

Policy E X A M P L E

Trying to Lay Claim to Trees That Sop Up Pollution

American Electric Power (AEP) owns power plants around the United States that together release about 3 percent of U.S. carbon dioxide (CO_2) emissions every year. The company has entered into a voluntary agreement with the U.S. government to cut its CO_2 emissions by 1 percent every year. AEP has determined that building cleaner power plants would cost between $50 and $75 per ton of eliminated CO_2 emissions. In contrast, planting a sufficient number of CO_2-absorbing trees would cost only about $1 to $2 per ton of emissions.

AEP faces two problems in utilizing trees to reduce the polluting effects of its power plants. One is uncertainty about how much CO_2 trees absorb from the air. The company has already spent more than $17 million to reforest nearly 60,000 acres of land near its U.S. power plants, and it has paid more than $7 million to protect an existing 4-million-acre forest in Bolivia. AEP

projects that over several decades the new U.S. trees alone will sop up 11 millions of tons of CO_2, or the amount its power plants release in 16 months. Independent and government scientists disagree, however, about whether these estimates are accurate.

The second problem is that the property rights to CO_2 tree absorptions are poorly defined. It is unclear, for instance, how much pollution-reduction credit AEP will ultimately be able to claim from its investment in Bolivian forests if Bolivian polluters also try to lay claim to the pollution abatement benefits those forests provide.

For Critical Analysis
Under what circumstance could society come out ahead if AEP and other polluters planted trees instead of cleaning up any of their power plants?

---

[*]This analysis is known as the *Coase theorem*, named after its originator, Nobel laureate Ronald Coase, who demonstrated that the potential for negative or positive externalities does not necessarily require government intervention in situations in which property rights are defined and enforceable and transaction costs are relatively low.

Changing Property Rights

We can approach the problem of property rights by assuming that initially in a society, many property rights to resources are not defined. But this situation does not cause a problem as long as no one cares to use the resources for which there are no property rights or resources are available in desired quantities at a zero price. Only if and when a use is found for a resource or the supply of a resource is inadequate at a zero price does a problem develop. The problem requires that something be done about deciding property rights. If not, the resource will be wasted and possibly even destroyed. Property rights can be assigned to individuals who will then assert control; or they may be assigned to government, which can maintain and preserve the resource, charge for its use, or implement some other rationing device. With common property such as air and water, governments have indeed attempted to take over the control of those resources so that they cannot be wasted or destroyed.

Another way of viewing the pollution problem is to argue that property rights are "sacred" and that there are property rights in every resource that exists. We can then say that each individual does not have the right to act on anything that is not his or her property. Hence no individual has the right to pollute because that amounts to using property that the individual does not specifically own.

Clearly, we must fill the gap between private costs and social costs in situations in which property rights are not well defined or assigned. There are three ways to fill this gap: taxation, subsidization, and regulation. Government is involved in all three. Unfortunately, government does not have perfect information and may not pick the appropriate tax, subsidy, or type of regulation. Furthermore, in some situations, taxes are hard to enforce, or subsidies are difficult to give out to "worthy" recipients. In such cases, outright prohibition of the polluting activity may be the optimal solution to a particular pollution problem. For example, if it is difficult to monitor the level of a particular type of pollution that even in small quantities can cause severe environmental damage, outright prohibition of activities that cause such pollution may be the only alternative.

Are There Alternatives to Pollution-Causing Resource Use?

Some people cannot understand why, if pollution is bad, we still use pollution-causing resources such as coal and oil to generate electricity. Why don't we forgo the use of such polluting resources and opt for one that apparently is pollution free, such as solar energy? The plain fact is that the cost of generating solar power in most circumstances is much higher than generating that same power through conventional means. We do not yet have the technology that allows us the luxury of driving solar-powered cars. Moreover, with current technology, the solar panels necessary to generate the electricity for the average town would cover massive sections of the countryside, and the manufacturing of those solar panels would itself generate pollution.

How can some homeowners' use of solar panels to save natural resources and cut down on pollution emissions create negative externalities for other homeowners?

EXAMPLE

Solar Power Is Fine, but Not in My Neighborhood

Solar panels are most cost-effective in locales where there is plenty of sunshine, such as many parts of Arizona. Neverthe-

less, each year about 50 homeowners associations in that state attempt to impose neighborhood restrictions preventing the use of solar panels. According to these associations, ugly solar panels on the roofs of houses detract from a community's aesthetics.

An Arizona state law forbids neighborhood associations from imposing restrictions on solar panels. Nevertheless, homeowners who wish a court to enforce the law must incur legal fees. Many Arizona homeowners have found that the total legal expenses they must incur to enforce their right to install solar panels have exceeded their savings in lower power bills.

For Critical Analysis
Why do you suppose that owners of beachfront homes around the nation have launched legal challenges against the offshore installation of large equipment that harnesses the power of waves and winds to generate electricity?

WILD SPECIES, COMMON PROPERTY, AND TRADE-OFFS

Go to www.econtoday.com/chap32 to contemplate the issue of endangered species via a link to the National Center for Policy Analysis.

One of the most distressing common property problems involves endangered species, usually in the wild. No one is concerned about not having enough dogs, cats, cattle, sheep, and horses. The reason is that virtually all of those species are private property. Spotted owls, bighorn mountain sheep, condors, and the like are typically common property. No one has a vested interest in making sure that they perpetuate in good health.

In 1973, the federal government passed the Endangered Species Act in an attempt to prevent species from dying out. Initially, few individuals were affected by the rulings of the Interior Department regarding which species were listed as endangered. Eventually, however, as more and more species were put on the endangered list, a trade-off became apparent. Nationwide, the trade-off was brought to the public's attention when the spotted owl was declared an endangered species in the Pacific Northwest. Ultimately, thousands of logging jobs were lost when the courts upheld the ban on logging in the areas presumed to be the spotted owl's natural habitat. Then another small bird, the marbled murrelet, was found in an ancient forest, causing the Pacific Lumber Company to cut back its logging practices. In 1995, the U.S. Supreme Court ruled that the federal government did have the right to regulate activities on private land in order to save endangered species.

The issues are not straightforward. Today the earth has only 0.02 percent of all of the species that have ever lived, and nearly all the 99.08 percent of extinct species became extinct before humans appeared. Every year, 1,000 to 3,000 new species are discovered and classified. Estimates of how many species are actually dying out vary from a high of 50,000 a year (based on the assumption that undiscovered insect species are dying off before being discovered) to a low of one every four years.

How has Chinese fish farming helped reduce pressures on global populations of wild fish?

International EXAMPLE

How Chinese Fish Farming Helps Wild Fish Populations

Fish farming, or the growing of edible fish in small freshwater ponds and sea inlets blocked with earthen dams, began in China thousands of years ago. Twenty years ago, Chinese fish farmers were producing about a million tons of fish each year. Since then, the production of farmed fish has increased dramatically. Chinese fish farmers currently produce almost 35 million tons of fish per year, or more than 70 percent of the world's total production of farmed fish. Much of this yield goes for human consumption in China and other Asian nations, where Chinese fish farmers now sell a considerable amount of their fish production. The rest of China's farmed-fish yield is used to produce fishmeal and fish oil. These fish by-products are fed to poultry and pigs—and carnivorous fish such as salmon, eel, cod, and striped bass grown in fish farms.

Back in the 1980s, environmentalists worried that wild fish populations in the world's oceans, lakes, and rivers would eventually be extinguished as the global human population increased. In fact, annual catches of wild fish have been declining since the 1990s. The reason is that consumers in Asia and elsewhere have gradually been substituting farmed fish for wild fish. Current estimates indicate that by 2030 more than half of the fish consumed globally will be grown on farms.

For Critical Analysis
What do you suppose has happened to the market price of wild salmon, shrimp, and other fishes since the 1980s as the farmed-fish share of U.S. fish consumption has risen from less than 10 percent to more than 50 percent? (Hint: What happens to the demand for an item when large numbers of consumers switch to a substitute?)

CONCEPTS in Brief

- A common property resource is one that no one owns— or, otherwise stated, that everyone owns.

- Common property exists when property rights are indefinite or nonexistent.

- When no property rights exist, pollution occurs because no one individual or firm has a sufficient economic incentive to care for the common property in question, be it air, water, or scenery.

- Private costs will equal social costs for common property only if a few individuals or companies are involved and they are able to contract among themselves.

To test your understanding of the concepts covered in this section, go to the Online Review at www.myeconlab.com/miller.

RECYCLING

As part of the overall ecology movement, there has been a major push to save scarce resources via recycling. **Recycling** involves reusing paper products, plastics, glass, and metals rather than putting them into solid waste dumps. Many cities have instituted mandatory recycling programs.

The benefits of recycling are straightforward. Fewer *natural* resources are used. But some economists argue that recycling does not necessarily save *total* resources. For example, recycling paper products may not necessarily save trees, according to a study A. Clark Wiseman conducted for Resources for the Future in Washington, D.C. He argues that an increase in paper recycling will eventually lead to a reduction in the demand for virgin paper and thus for trees. Because most trees are planted specifically to produce paper, a reduction in the demand for trees will mean that certain land now used to grow trees will be put to other uses. The end result may be smaller rather than larger forests, a result that is probably not desired in the long run.

Recycling
The reuse of raw materials derived from manufactured products.

Recycling's Invisible Costs

The recycling of paper can also pollute. Used paper has ink on it that has to be removed during the recycling process. According to the National Wildlife Federation, the production of 100 tons of deinked (bleached) fiber generates 40 tons of sludge. This sludge has to be disposed of, usually in a landfill. In general, recycling creates wastes that must be eliminated.

The use of resources also involves another issue: Recycling requires human effort. The labor resources involved in recycling are often many times more costly than the potential savings in scarce resources *not* used. That means that net resource use, counting all resources, may sometimes be greater with recycling than without it.

Why is it possible that using corn by-products to produce auto fuel may ultimately use more resources than are saved?

Policy EXAMPLE

The Uncertain Economics of Ethanol

For years, farmers have sold corn and corn by-products for use in the production of a fuel called ethanol, which is an alternative to gasoline in powering cars and trucks. The firms that produce ethanol, which yields less pollution than gasoline, receive about $1.4 billion in annual subsidies from the federal government. This translates into a subsidy of about 50 cents for each gallon of ethanol produced. Currently, about 75 U.S. plants produce about 3 billion gallons of this fuel each year.

The U.S. Department of Agriculture's official estimates indicate that ethanol yields 34 percent more energy than is required to produce the fuel. Some scientists contend, however, that these estimates omit about half of the inputs used in corn production. They also point out that in drier climates, most corn must be irrigated, which depletes underground water reserves and uses up natural gas burned to power irrigation pumps. Thus the production of ethanol at currently subsidized levels may entail more social costs than social benefits.

For Critical Analysis
Who provides the funds used to subsidize the production of ethanol?

Landfills

One of the arguments in favor of recycling is to avoid a solid waste "crisis." Some people believe that we are running out of solid waste dump sites in the United States. This is perhaps true in and near major cities, and indeed the most populated areas of the country might ultimately benefit from recycling programs. In the rest of the United States, however, the data do not seem to indicate that we are running out of solid waste landfill sites. Throughout the United States, the disposal price per ton of city garbage has actually fallen. Prices vary, of course, for the 165 million tons of trash disposed of each year. In San Jose, California, it costs $50 a ton to dump, whereas in Morris County, New Jersey, it costs $131 a ton.

Currently, municipal governments can do three things with solid waste: burn it, bury it, or recycle it. The amount of solid waste dumped in landfills is dropping, even as total trash output rises. Consider, though, that the total garbage output of the United States for the entire twenty-first century could be put in a square landfill 10 miles on a side that is 100 yards deep. Recycling to reduce solid waste disposal may end up costing society more resources simply because putting such waste into a landfill may be a less costly alternative.

Should We Save Scarce Resources?

Periodically, the call for recycling focuses on the necessity of saving scarce resources because "we are running out." There is little evidence to back up this claim because virtually every natural resource has fallen in price (corrected for inflation) over the past century. In 1980, the late Julian Simon made a $1,000 bet with well-known environmentalist Paul Erlich. Simon bet $200 per resource that any five natural resources that Erlich picked would decline in price (corrected for inflation) by the end of the 1980s. Simon won. (When Simon asked Erlich to renew the bet for $20,000 for the 1990s, Erlich declined.) From the 1980s into the early 2000s, the price of virtually every natural resource fell (corrected for inflation), and so did the price of every agricultural commodity. The same was true for many forest products. Though few people remember the dire predictions of the 1970s, many noneconomists throughout the world argued at that time that the world's oil reserves were vanishing. These predictions were wrong, which is why the pretax, inflation-corrected price of gasoline is not significantly higher today than it was in the 1950s.

In spite of predictions in the early 1980s by World Watch Institute president Lester Brown, real food prices did not rise. Indeed, the real price of food fell by more than 30 percent for the major agricultural commodities during the 1980s and by even more into the 2000s. A casual knowledge of supply and demand tells you that because the demand for food did not decrease, supply must have increased faster than demand.

With respect to the forests, at least in the United States and Western Europe, there are more forests today than there were 100 years ago. In this country, the major problems of deforestation seem to be on land owned by the U.S. Forest Service for which private timber companies are paid almost $1 billion a year in subsidies to cut down trees.

CONCEPTS in Brief

- Recycling involves reusing paper, glass, and other materials rather than putting them into solid waste dumps. Recycling does have a cost both in the resources used for recycling and in the pollution created during recycling, such as the sludge from bleaching paper for reuse.

- Landfills are an alternative to recycling. Expansion of these solid waste disposal sites is outpacing demand increases.

- Resources may not be getting scarcer. The inflation-corrected price of most resources has been falling for decades.

To test your understanding of the concepts covered in this section, go to the Online Review at www.myeconlab.com/miller.

CASE STUDY: Economics Front and Center

Confronting Potential Nanotechnology Externalities

Yang is an employee of Nanotech Enterprises, a company that manufactures carbon nanotube wires only 10 to 12 atoms in width. The wires are used to strengthen various substances, such as materials used in the bodies of trucks, rail cars, and construction equipment.

Yang has just met with officials of the Environmental Protection Agency (EPA), who informed him that the EPA has launched an effort to assess the potential for nanotechnologies to create future pollution problems. At present, the officials indicated, the EPA is particularly concerned about the potential for people to accidentally inhale large quantities of carbon nanotube wires. The EPA officials also asked whether these substances might chemically bind with poisonous metals and disperse into the atmosphere.

Yang begins drafting notes on his meeting that he will send to the company's senior officers. Although prospects for near-term EPA regulation of his company's operations are slim, he states, it is clear that the company may face an ever-widening array of EPA regulations in future years. In light of this likely future regulatory burden, Yang proposes two possibilities for the company to consider. One is to begin now to develop procedures for minimizing human ingestion of the carbon nanotube wires. This option, he suggests, would enable the company to gradually add the more costly procedures to its production process, thereby potentially reducing future compliance costs. The other is to do nothing now and instead confront the issue only when the EPA actually issues regulatory restrictions. This would minimize current costs but might lead to much higher costs in the future.

Points to Analyze

1. *What does Nanotech Enterprises currently stand to gain from launching efforts to limit the possible negative externality effects associated with its product?*

2. *Why might senior officers of Nanotech Enterprises be tempted to choose to do nothing at present to address the potential externality effects of the firm's product?*

Protecting the Komodo Islands

Concepts Applied
- Common Property
- Private Property Rights

Before 1997, when the bottom fell out of the Indonesian economy, the nation's government spent 80 percent more on environmental conservation efforts than it does today. After the government's spending on enforcing environmental regulations plummeted, a number of Indonesians began openly violating laws aimed at protecting the unique species located on and around the Komodo islands. Poachers openly laid traps that, in addition to killing rare turtles, sometimes caught and killed even rarer baby Komodo dragons instead. Fishermen who had already boosted their harvests by poisoning large quantities of fish with cyanide began tossing dynamite into waters where they spotted schools of fish. After each explosion, they trawled over the surface and scooped up the fish carcasses in their nets. Both cyanide and dynamite fishing were wreaking major damage on the coral reefs ringing the islands.

Desperate to do something to protect these common properties on the Komodo islands from destruction, the Indonesian government tried something radical. It began offering economic inducements that gave residents incentives to protect the environment on their own, instead of relying on public funds to do so.

Removing the Incentive to Use Cyanide and Dynamite

The Indonesians who lived near the Komodo islands had not been trapping turtles and using cyanide and dynamite to kill large quantities of fish for the fun of it. They had done so in an effort to boost their real incomes.

To remove the incentive for local residents to kill off wild turtles and fish, the government established private property rights over some members of these species. It promoted the development of separate turtle and fish farms, which hired many of the people who previously had been illegally killing turtles and fish. Instead of destroying turtles and fish in the wild, the former poachers and fishermen now earn incomes from harvesting members of these species raised on the farms.

Transforming a Publicly Funded Park into a Private Operation

The Indonesian government has also found ways to have private markets fund environmental protection efforts. For instance, the government now allows private companies to operate a number of Komodo nature parks. To encourage tourists to visit, the companies are willing to incur the costs of providing tours, keeping the parklands clean, and guarding against unauthorized tourist incursions into animal habitats. Consequently, private firms have assumed from the government the social costs associated with maintaining park environments. To cover these costs and generate profits for their owners, the companies operating the parks earn revenues from charging tourists $30 entrance fees and selling food and beverages.

Since these privatization programs for environmental protection went into effect beginning in 2001, human economies in the vicinity of the Komodo islands have been boosted by earnings from turtle and fish harvesting and tourism. Taxing these activities has boosted the revenues of the Indonesian government, which previously viewed the Komodo islands as a drain on public funds. At the same time, populations of wild turtles, Komodo dragons, and fish have recovered to levels observed in the early 1990s. The absence of cyanide and dynamite from the waters around the Komodo islands has allowed the coral reefs to regenerate. Because it is now in the self-interest of humans for the environment to flourish, that is what we are observing.

For Critical Analysis

1. How might harvesting some members of a species potentially help to save the species as a whole?
2. Why are private companies willing to spend more than the Indonesian government to keep Komodo parklands clean?

Web Resources

1. Go to www.econtoday.com/chap32 to read about how one private group, The Nature Conservancy, has promoted private property rights to help protect fish species around the Komodo islands.
2. Learn about how The Nature Conservancy has promoted private tourism to help generate funds to protect environments around the world via the link available at www.econtoday.com/chap32.

Research Project

Evaluate the relative merits of public versus private funding of efforts to protect rare and endangered species. Why might governments have an important role even if they choose to promote private-market approaches to keeping species populations from faltering?

SUMMARY DISCUSSION of Learning Objectives

1. **Private Costs versus Social Costs:** Private, or internal, costs are borne solely by individuals who use resources. Social costs are the full costs that society bears whenever resources are used. Problems related to the environment arise when individuals take into account only private costs instead of the broader social costs arising from their use of resources.

2. **Market Externalities and Ways to Correct Them:** A market externality is a situation in which a private cost (or benefit) differs from the social cost (or benefit) associated with a market transaction between two parties or from use of a scarce resource. Correcting an externality arising from differences between private and social costs, such as pollution, requires forcing individuals to take all the social costs of their actions into account. This might be accomplished by taxing those who create externalities, such as polluters.

3. **Determining the Optimal Amount of Pollution:** The marginal benefit of pollution abatement, or the additional benefit to society from reducing pollution, declines as the quality of the environment improves. At the same time, however, the marginal cost of pollution abatement, or the additional cost to society from reducing pollution, increases as more and more resources are devoted to bringing about an improved environment. The optimal quantity of pollution is the amount of pollution for which the marginal benefit of pollution abatement just equals the marginal cost of pollution abatement. Beyond this level of pollution, the additional cost of cleaning the environment exceeds the additional benefit.

4. **Private and Common Property Rights and the Pollution Problem:** Private property rights are exclusive individual rights of ownership that permit the use and exchange of a resource. Common property is owned by everyone and therefore by no single individual. A pollution problem often arises because air and many water resources are common property, and private property rights relating to them are not well defined. Therefore, no one has an individual incentive to take the long-run pernicious effects of excessive pollution into account. This is a

common rationale for using taxes, subsidies, or regulations to address the pollution problem.

5. **Endangered Species and the Assignment of Property Rights:** Many members of such species as dogs, pigs, and horses are the private property of human beings. Thus people have economic incentives—satisfaction derived from pet ownership, the desire for pork as a food product, a preference for animal-borne transport—to protect members of these species. In contrast, most members of species such as spotted owls, condors, or tigers are common property, so no specific individuals have incentives to keep these species in good health. A possible

way to address the endangered species problem is government involvement via taxes, subsidies, or regulations.

6. **Benefits and Costs of Recycling:** Recycling entails reusing paper, glass, and other materials instead of putting them in solid waste dumps. Recycling has a clear benefit of limiting the use of natural resources. It also entails costs, however. One cost might be lost benefits of forests, because a key incentive for perpetuating forests is the future production of paper and other wood-based products. Recycling also requires the use of labor, and the costs of these human resources can exceed the potential savings in scarce resources not used because of recycling.

KEY TERMS AND CONCEPTS

common property (765)

externality (760)

optimal quantity of pollution (764)

private costs (759)

private property rights (765)

recycling (769)

social costs (759)

transaction costs (766)

PROBLEMS

Answers to the odd-numbered problems appear at the back of the book.

32-1. The market price of insecticide is initially $10 per unit. To address a negative externality in this market, the government decides to charge producers of insecticide for the privilege of polluting during the production process. A fee that fully takes into account the social costs of pollution is determined, and once it is put into effect, the market supply curve for insecticide shifts upward by $4 per unit. The market price of insecticide also increases, to $12 per unit. What fee is the government charging insecticide manufacturers?

32-2. A tract of land is found to contain a plant from which drug companies can extract a newly discovered cancer-fighting medicine. This variety of plant does not grow anywhere else in the world. Initially, the many owners of lots within this tract, who had not planned to use the land for anything other than its current use as a scenic locale for small vacation homes, announced that they would put all their holdings up for sale to drug companies. Because the land is also home to an endangered lizard species, however, a government agency decides to limit the number of acres in this tract that drug companies can purchase and use for their drug-producing operations. The gov-

ernment declares that the remaining portion of the land must be left in its current state. What will be the effect of government regulation on the market price of the acreage that is available for extraction of cancer-fighting medicine? What will be the effect on the market price of the land that the government declares to be usable only for existing vacation homes?

32-3. When a government charges firms for the privilege of polluting, a typical result is a rise in the market price of the good or service produced by those firms. Consequently, consumers of the good or service usually have to pay a higher price to obtain it. Why might this be socially desirable?

32-4. Most wild Asian tigers are the common property of the humans and governments that control the lands they inhabit. Why does this pose a significant problem for maintaining the wild tiger population in the future? (Hint: Who currently has an incentive to care about the wild tiger population?)

32-5. In several African countries where the rhinoceros was once a thriving species, the animal is now nearly extinct. In most of these nations, rhinoceros horns are used as traditional ingredients in certain medicines. Why might making rhinoceros farming legal do more to promote preservation of the species than imposing stiff penalties on people who are caught engaging in rhinoceros hunting?

32-6. Why is it possible for recycling of paper or plastics to use up more resources than the activity saves?

32-7. Examine the following marginal costs and marginal benefits associated with water cleanliness in a given locale.

Quantity of Clean Water (%)	Marginal Cost ($)	Marginal Benefit ($)
0	3,000	200,000
20	15,000	120,000
40	50,000	90,000
60	85,000	85,000
80	100,000	40,000
100	Infinite	0

a. What is the optimal degree of water cleanliness?
b. What is the optimal degree of water pollution?
c. Suppose that a company creates a food additive that offsets most of the harmful effects of drinking polluted water. As a result, the marginal benefit of water cleanliness declines by $40,000 at each degree of water cleanliness at or less than 80 percent. What is the optimal degree of water cleanliness after this change?

32-8. Examine the following marginal costs and marginal benefits associated with air cleanliness in a given locale:

Quantity of Clean Air (%)	Marginal Cost ($)	Marginal Benefit ($)
0	50,000	600,000
20	150,000	360,000
40	200,000	200,000
60	300,000	150,000
80	400,000	120,000
100	Infinite	0

a. What is the optimal degree of air cleanliness?
b. What is the optimal degree of air pollution?
c. Suppose that a state provides subsidies for a company to build plants that contribute to air pollution. Cleaning up this pollution causes the marginal cost of air cleanliness to rise by $210,000 at each degree of air cleanliness. What is the optimal degree of air cleanliness after this change?

32-9. The following table displays hypothetical annual total costs and total benefits of conserving wild tigers at several possible worldwide tiger population levels.

Population of Wild Tigers	Total Cost ($ millions)	Total Benefit ($ millions)
0	0	40
2,000	25	90
4,000	35	130
6,000	50	160
8,000	75	185
10,000	110	205
12,000	165	215

a. Calculate the marginal costs and benefits.
b. Given the data, what is the socially optimal world population of wild tigers?
c. Suppose that tiger farming is legalized and that this has the effect of reducing the marginal cost of tiger conservation by $15 million for each 2,000-tiger population increment in the table. What is the new socially optimal population of wild tigers?

32-10. The following table gives hypothetical annual total costs and total benefits of maintaining alternative populations of Asian elephants.

Population of Asian Elephants	Total Cost ($ millions)	Total Benefit ($ millions)
0	0	0
7,500	20	100
15,000	45	185
22,500	90	260
30,000	155	325
37,500	235	375
45,000	330	410

a. Calculate the marginal costs and benefits, and draw marginal benefit and cost schedules.
b. Given the data, what is the socially optimal world population of Asian elephants?
c. Suppose that two events occur simultaneously. Technological development allows machines to do more efficiently much of the work that elephants once did, which reduces by $40 million the marginal benefit of maintaining the elephant population for each 7,500 increment in the elephant

population. In addition, new techniques for breeding, feeding, and protecting elephants reduce the marginal cost by $10 million for each 7,500 incre-

ment in the elephant population. What is the new socially optimal population of Asian elephants?

ECONOMICS ON THE NET

Economic Analysis at the Environmental Protection Agency
In this chapter, you learned how to use economic analysis to think about environmental problems. Does the U.S. government use economic analysis? This application helps you learn the extent to which the government uses economics in its environmental policymaking.

Title: National Center for Environmental Economics (NCEE)

Navigation: Go to www.econtoday.com/chap32 to visit the NCEE's home page. Under *other information,* select *Plain English.* Click on "Environmental Protection: Is It Bad for the Economy? A Non-Technical Summary of the Literature," and view the table of contents. Read "What Do We Spend on Environmental Protection?"

Application Read this section of the article; then answer the following questions.

1. According to the article, what are the key objectives of the EPA? What role does cost-benefit analysis appear to play in the EPA's efforts? Does the EPA appear to take other issues into account in its policymaking?

2. Back up to Table of Contents, and click on "Regardless of the Cost of Environmental Protection, Is It Still Money Well Spent?" In what ways does this discussion help clarify your answers in item 1?

For Group Study and Analysis Have a class discussion of the following question: Should the EPA apply economic analysis in all aspects of its policymaking? If not, why not? If so, in what manner should economic analysis be applied?

If your exam were tomorrow, would you be ready? For each chapter, MyEconLab Practice Tests and Study Plans pinpoint which sections you have mastered and which ones you need to study. That way, you are more efficient with your study time, and you are better prepared for your exams.

In addition to Practice Tests and your personalized Study Plan, you'll find the following media resources in MyEconLab:
1. *Graphs in Motion* animation of Figures 32-1 and 32-2.
2. Videos featuring the author, Roger LeRoy Miller, on the following subjects:
   - Correcting for Externalities
   - Recycling

3. Links to the Web sites cited in the marginal Internet Resources, Issues and Applications feature, and Economics on the Net activity.
4. Audio clips of all key terms, additional practice problems, and a PDF version of the material from the print Study Guide.
5. eThemes of the Times, which is a New York Times article to help you understand the real-world applications of what you are learning.

To see how it works, turn to page 16 and then go to www.myeconlab.com/miller.

Get Ahead of the Curve

Chapter 33

Comparative Advantage and the Open Economy

I t is September 2003, and the global negotiations about international trade have begun in Cancún, Mexico. Representatives from the European Union (EU), the United States, and Japan have high hopes that they will be able to convince developing nations to open their borders to more imports of EU, U.S., and Japanese products. To their dismay, however, representatives of most developing nations have a different agenda. They want big cutbacks in EU, U.S., and Japanese agricultural subsidies. When the EU, U.S., and Japanese representatives balk, the meetings abruptly come to a conclusion, and a shadow has been cast over the future of global trade. In this chapter, you will learn why developing nations view subsidies to EU, U.S., and Japanese farmers as an issue relating to international trade.

LEARNING OBJECTIVES

After reading this chapter, you should be able to:

1. Discuss the worldwide importance of international trade
2. Explain why nations can gain from specializing in production and engaging in international trade
3. Distinguish between comparative advantage and absolute advantage
4. Understand common arguments against free trade
5. Describe ways that nations restrict foreign trade
6. Identify key international agreements and organizations that adjudicate trade disputes among nations

Media Resources

Refer to the end of the chapter for a full listing of the multimedia learning materials available in MyEconLab.

Did You Know That . . . in 2000, Ohio Art Company, the firm that sells Etch A Sketch toys, moved its production facilities from Ohio to China? Likewise, since 2001 Lionel Corporation, which once produced electric toy trains in New York, New Jersey, and Michigan, has manufactured its products in China. The Barbie dolls and other numerous toys that Mattell Corporation sells are no longer produced in the United States. Mattell now makes all of its toys in plants located in China, India, Indonesia, Italy, Malaysia, Mexico, and Thailand.

What economic forces have induced these and most other U.S. toy companies to choose to manufacture their products abroad instead of within the borders of the United States? The first thing you will learn in this chapter is that gains from specialization and international trade provide the fundamental economic motivation for determining where to produce any good or service. These gains ultimately explain why nearly all toys sold in the United States are now imported from other nations.

THE WORLDWIDE IMPORTANCE OF INTERNATIONAL TRADE

Look at panel (a) of Figure 33-1. Since the end of World War II, world output of goods and services (world real gross domestic product, or real GDP) has increased almost every year; it is now almost eight times what it was then. Look at the top line in panel (a). World trade has increased to more than 24 times what it was in 1950.

The United States figured prominently in this expansion of world trade. In panel (b) of Figure 33-1, you see imports and exports expressed as a percentage of total annual yearly income (GDP). Whereas imports added up to barely 4 percent of annual U.S. GDP in 1950, today they account for more than 14 percent. International trade has definitely become more important to the economy of the United States, and it may become even more so as other countries loosen their trade restrictions.

How has the ability of people around the world to buy and sell items using the Internet affected international trade?

Go to www.econtoday.com/chap33 for the World Trade Organization's most recent data on world trade.

E-Commerce EXAMPLE

The Internet Boosts International Trade

Caroline Freund of the World Bank and Diana Weinhold of the London School of Economics have examined how increased Internet use has affected international trade in the United States and 55 other nations. They found that greater Internet use by a nation's residents reduces their costs of engaging in international trade. As a consequence, the immediate effect of the takeoff in commercial sales on the Internet between 1997 and 1999 was a 1 percentage point increase in the average country's international trade. Since then, each 10 percentage point increase in Internet use by a nation's residents has resulted in a further 0.2 percentage point increase in trade with other nations.

For Critical Analysis
How might the ability to buy and sell items using the Internet reduce the costs of trading with other countries?

WHY WE TRADE: COMPARATIVE ADVANTAGE AND MUTUAL GAINS FROM EXCHANGE

You have already been introduced to the concept of specialization and mutual gains from trade in Chapter 2. These concepts are worth repeating because they are essential to under-

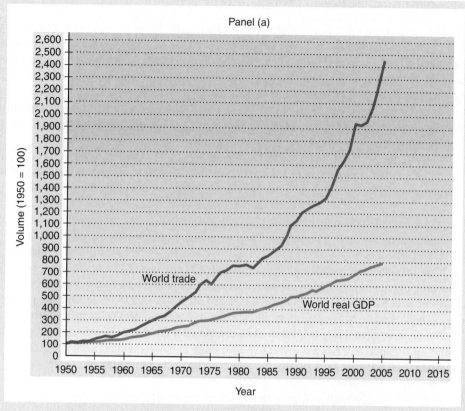

Panel (a)

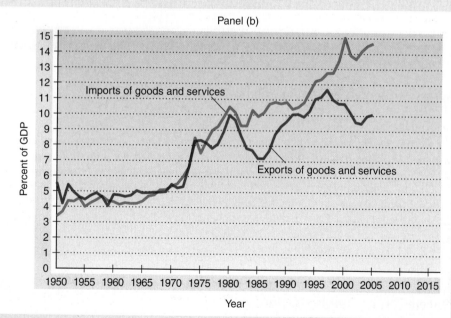

Panel (b)

FIGURE 33-1

The Growth of World Trade

In panel (a), you can see the growth in world trade in relative terms because we use an index of 100 to represent real world trade in 1950. By the mid-2000s, that index had increased to over 2,400. At the same time, the index of world real GDP (annual world real income) had gone up to only around 800. World trade is clearly on the rise: In the United States, both imports and exports, expressed as a percentage of annual national income (GDP) in panel (b), have generally been rising since 1950.

Sources: Steven Husted and Michael Melvin, *International Economics,* 3d ed. (New York: HarperCollins, 1995), p. 11, used with permission; World Trade Organization; Federal Reserve System; U.S. Department of Commerce.

standing why the world is better off because of more international trade. The best way to understand the gains from trade among nations is first to understand the output gains from specialization between individuals.

The Output Gains from Specialization

Suppose that a creative advertising specialist can come up with two pages of ad copy (written words) an hour or generate one computerized art rendering per hour. At the same time, a computer artist can write one page of ad copy per hour or complete one computerized art rendering per hour. Here the ad specialist can come up with more pages of ad copy per hour than the computer specialist and seemingly is just as good as the computer specialist at doing computerized art renderings. Is there any reason for the creative specialist and the computer specialist to "trade"? The answer is yes because such trading will lead to higher output.

Go to www.econtoday.com/chap33 for data on U.S. trade with all other nations of the world.

Consider the scenario of no trading. Assume that during each eight-hour day, the ad specialist and the computer whiz devote half of their day to writing ad copy and half to computerized art rendering. The ad specialist would create eight pages of ad copy (4 hours × 2) and four computerized art renderings (4 × 1). During that same period, the computer specialist would create four pages of ad copy (4 hours × 1) and four computerized art renderings (4 × 1). Each day, the combined output for the ad specialist and the computer specialist would be 12 pages of ad copy and eight computerized art renderings.

If the ad specialist specialized only in writing ad copy and the computer whiz specialized only in creating computerized art renderings, their combined output would rise to 16 pages of ad copy (8 × 2) and eight computerized art renderings (8 × 1). Overall, production would increase by four pages of ad copy per day with no decline in art renderings.

The creative advertising employee has a comparative advantage in writing ad copy, and the computer specialist has a comparative advantage in doing computerized art renderings. **Comparative advantage** is simply the ability to produce something at a lower opportunity cost than other producers, as we pointed out in Chapter 2.

Comparative advantage
The ability to produce a good or service at a lower opportunity cost than other producers.

Why do you suppose that Argentina and Uruguay import electricity from Brazil?

International EXAMPLE

Power Moves Across Borders in South America

Most South American nations produce about half of their electricity by burning natural gas to generate electric power. Natural gas is much easier to find, extract, and put to use in Brazil than in neighboring Argentina and Uruguay. Consequently, the opportunity cost of producing electricity is lower in Brazil. The lower opportunity cost of producing electricity in Brazil explains why both Argentina and Uruguay have been importing electricity from Brazil since early 2004.

For Critical Analysis
Why might Brazil someday import electricity from Argentina if recent discoveries of untapped natural gas in southern Argentina generate large increases in its stocks of this resource?

Specialization Among Nations

To demonstrate the concept of comparative advantage for nations, let's take the example of India and the United States. In Table 33-1, we show the comparative costs of production of commercial software programs and personal computers in terms of worker-days. This is a simple two-country, two-commodity world in which we assume that labor is the only factor of production. As you can see from the table, in the United States, it takes one worker-

Product	United States (worker-days)	India (worker-days)
Software program	1	1
Personal computer	1	2

TABLE 33-1
Comparative Costs of Production

day to produce one software program, and the same is true for one computer. In India, it takes one worker-day to produce one software program but two worker-days to produce one computer. In this sense, U.S. residents appear to be just as good at producing software programs as residents of India and actually have an **absolute advantage** in producing computers.

Trade will still take place, however, which may seem paradoxical. How can trade take place if we can seemingly produce at least as many units of both goods as residents of India can? Why don't we just produce both ourselves? To understand why, let's assume first that there is no trade and no specialization and that the workforce in each country consists of 200 workers. These 200 workers are, by assumption, divided equally in the production of software programs and computers. We see in Table 33-2 that 100 software programs and 100 computers are produced per day in the United States. In India, 100 software programs and 50 computers are produced per day. The total daily world production in our two-country world is 200 software programs and 150 computers.

Now the countries specialize. What can India produce more cheaply? Look at the comparative costs of production expressed in worker-days in Table 33-1. What is the cost of producing one more software program? One worker-day. What is the cost of producing one more computer? Two worker-days. We can say, then, that in terms of the value of computers given up, in India the *opportunity cost* of producing software programs is lower than in the United States. India will specialize in the activity that has the lower opportunity cost. In other words, India will specialize in the activity in which is has a comparative advantage, which is the production of software programs.

According to Table 33-3 (page 782), after specialization, the United States produces 200 computers and India produces 200 software programs. Notice that the total world production per day has gone up from 200 software programs and 150 computers to 200 software programs and 200 computers per day. This was done without any increased use of resources. The gain, 50 "free" computers, results from a more efficient allocation of resources worldwide. World output is greater when countries specialize in producing the goods in which they have a comparative advantage and then engage in foreign trade. An-

Absolute advantage
The ability to produce more output from given inputs of resources than other producers can.

	United States		India		
Product	Workers	Output	Workers	Output	World Output
Software programs	100	100	100	100	200
Personal computers	100	100	100	50	150

TABLE 33-2
Daily World Output Before Specialization
It is assumed that 200 workers are available in each country.

TABLE 33-3
Daily World Output After Specialization
It is assumed that 200 workers are available in each country.

Product	United States		India		
	Workers	Output	Workers	Output	World Output
Software programs	0	0	200	200	200
Personal computers	200	200	0	0	200

other way of looking at this is to consider the choice between two ways of producing a good. Obviously, each country would choose the less costly production process. One way of "producing" a good is to import it, so if in fact the imported good is cheaper than the domestically produced good, we will "produce" it by importing it. Not everybody, of course, is better off when free trade occurs. In our example, U.S. software producers and Indian computer makers are worse off because those two *domestic* industries have disappeared.

Some people are worried that the United States (or any country, for that matter) might someday "run out of exports" because of overaggressive foreign competition. The analysis of comparative advantage tells us the contrary. No matter how much other countries compete for our business, the United States (or any other country) will always have a comparative advantage in something that it can export. In 10 or 20 years, that something may not be what we export today, but it will be exportable nonetheless because we will have a comparative advantage in producing it. Consequently, the significant flows of world trade shown in Figure 33-2 will continue because the United States and other nations will retain comparative advantages in producing various goods and services.

Why has the island nation of Mauritius recently experienced a significant drop in exports of the key item it specializes in producing?

International E X A M P L E

Mauritius Searches for a New Comparative Advantage

For years, Mauritius, a nation located on an island in the Indian Ocean off the coast of Madagascar, specialized in the production of sugarcane. Beginning in the 1970s, however, textile firms discovered that the costs of hiring unskilled workers in Mauritius to operate clothing manufacturing equipment were very low. Textile companies rushed to establish factories on the island. By the mid-1990s one out of every five Mauritian workers had a job in the textile industry, and the Mauritian per capita income level had nearly doubled.

During the late 1990s and early 2000s, however, China and India emerged as new centers of clothing production. The Mauritian textile industry was unable to match these nations'

low production costs, and it began to shrink. By the mid-2000s, thousands of the island's residents, amounting to nearly 10 percent of its labor force, were out of work. Now Mauritian leaders are hoping that the improved education that accompanied higher incomes ultimately will help many unemployed workers find jobs in two new export industries: tourism and financial services.

For Critical Analysis
Why do changing relative opportunity costs across the world's nations cause comparative advantages to shift among nations over time?

FIGURE 33-2
World Trade Flows

International merchandise trade amounts to more than $7.5 trillion worldwide. The percentage figures show the proportion of trade flowing in the various directions throughout the globe.

Sources: World Trade Organization and author's estimates (data are for 2005).

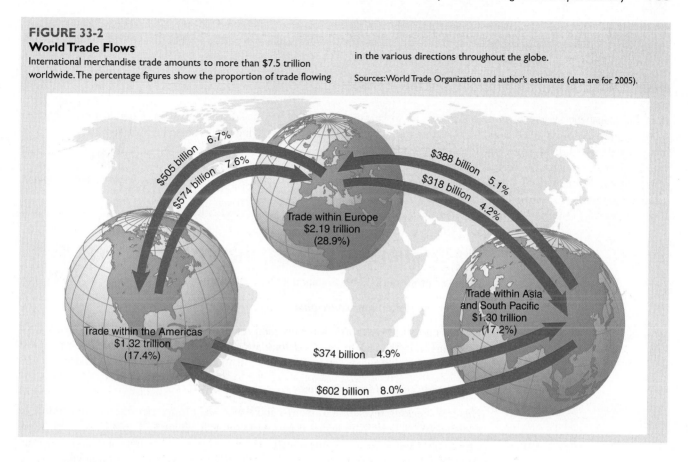

Other Benefits from International Trade: The Transmission of Ideas

Beyond the fact that comparative advantage results in an overall increase in the output of goods produced and consumed, there is another benefit to international trade. International trade bestows benefits on countries through the international transmission of ideas. According to economic historians, international trade has been the principal means by which new goods, services, and processes have spread around the world. For example, coffee was initially grown in Arabia near the Red Sea. Around A.D. 675, it began to be roasted and consumed as a beverage. Eventually, it was exported to other parts of the world, and the Dutch started cultivating it in their colonies during the seventeenth century and the French in the eighteenth century. The lowly potato is native to the Peruvian Andes. In the sixteenth century, it was brought to Europe by Spanish explorers. Thereafter, its cultivation and consumption spread rapidly. It became part of the North American agricultural scene in the early eighteenth century.

New processes have been transmitted through international trade. One of those involves the Japanese manufacturing innovation that emphasized redesigning the system rather than running the existing system in the best possible way. Inventories were reduced to just-in-time levels by reengineering machine setup methods.

All of the *intellectual property* that has been introduced throughout the world is a result of international trade. This includes new music, such as rock and roll in the 1950s and 1960s and hip-hop in the 1990s and 2000s. It includes the software applications and computer communications tools that are common for computer users everywhere.

How did international trade contribute to the development of the alphabet?

International EXAMPLE

International Trade and the Alphabet

Even the alphabetic system of writing that appears to be the source of most alphabets in the world today was spread through international trade. According to some scholars, the Phoenicians, who lived on the long, narrow strip of Mediterranean coast north of Israel from the ninth century B.C. to around 300 B.C., created the first true alphabet. It is thought that they developed the alpha-bet so that they could keep international trading records on their ships without having to take along highly trained scribes.

For Critical Analysis
Before alphabets were used, how might people have communicated in written form?

THE RELATIONSHIP BETWEEN IMPORTS AND EXPORTS

The basic proposition in understanding all of international trade is this:

> *In the long run, imports are paid for by exports.*[*]

Go to www.econtoday.com/chap33 to view the most recent trade statistics for the United States.

The reason that imports are ultimately paid for by exports is that foreign residents want something in exchange for the goods that are shipped to the United States. For the most part, they want U.S.-made goods. From this truism comes a remarkable corollary:

> *Any restriction of imports ultimately reduces exports.*

This is a shocking revelation to many people who want to restrict foreign competition to protect domestic jobs. Although it is possible to protect certain U.S. jobs by restricting foreign competition, it is impossible to make *everyone* better off by imposing import restrictions. Why? Because ultimately such restrictions lead to a reduction in employment in the export industries of the nation.

INTERNATIONAL COMPETITIVENESS

"The United States is falling behind." "We need to stay competitive internationally." Statements such as these are often heard in government circles when the subject of international trade comes up. There are two problems with such talk. The first has to do with a simple definition. What does "global competitiveness" really mean? When one company competes against another, it is in competition. Is the United States like one big corporation, in competition with other countries? Certainly not. The standard of living in each country is almost solely a function of how well the economy functions *within that country*, not relative to other countries.

Another problem arises with respect to the real world. According to the Institute for Management Development in Lausanne, Switzerland, the United States continues to lead the pack in overall productive efficiency, ahead of Japan, Germany, and the rest of the European Union. According to the report, the top-class ranking of the United States has

---

*We have to modify this rule by adding that in the short run, imports can also be paid for by the sale (or export) of real and financial assets, such as land, stocks, and bonds, or through an extension of credit from other countries.

been due to widespread entrepreneurship, more than a decade of economic restructuring, and information-technology investments. Other factors include the sophisticated U.S. financial system and large investments in scientific research.

How have information-technology investments affected the mix of exports in the United States?

E X A M P L E

U.S. Service Exports Gain on Merchandise Exports

Investments in new information technologies have increased U.S. efficiency in the production of many goods and services. Nevertheless, the most significant effect has been to reduce the opportunity cost of producing services in the United States relative to other nations. Figure 33-3 shows that a consequence has been considerable growth in the nation's exports of commercial services relative to its *merchandise exports*, or exports of physical goods. In 1980, U.S. exports of commercial services amounted to less than 18 percent of

U.S. merchandise exports. Today, U.S. exports of commercial services are more than 40 percent of U.S. merchandise exports.

For Critical Analysis
What would happen to U.S. exports of commercial services as a percentage of merchandise exports if nations such as India and Singapore were to gain a comparative advantage in providing commercial services?

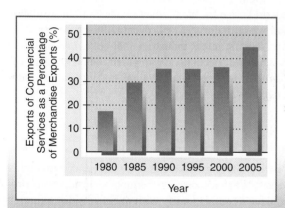

FIGURE 33-3
U.S. Exports of Commercial Services in Relation to U.S. Merchandise Exports
Since 1980, commercial service exports from the United States have more than doubled as a fraction of U.S. merchandise exports.

Source: U.S. Bureau of Economic Analysis.

CONCEPTS in Brief

- Countries can be better off materially if they specialize in producing goods for which they have a comparative advantage.

- It is important to distinguish between absolute and comparative advantage; the former refers to the ability to produce a unit of output with fewer physical units of input; the latter refers to producing output that has the lowest opportunity cost for a nation.

- Different nations will always have different comparative advantages because of differing opportunity costs due to different resource mixes.

To test your understanding of the concepts covered in this section, go to the Online Review at **www.myeconlab.com/miller**.

ARGUMENTS AGAINST FREE TRADE

Numerous arguments are raised against free trade. They mainly focus on the costs of trade; they do not consider the benefits or the possible alternatives for reducing the costs of free trade while still reaping benefits.

The Infant Industry Argument

Infant industry argument
The contention that tariffs should be imposed to protect from import competition an industry that is trying to get started. Presumably, after the industry becomes technologically efficient, the tariff can be lifted.

A nation may feel that if a particular industry is allowed to develop domestically, it will eventually become efficient enough to compete effectively in the world market. Therefore, the nation may impose some restrictions on imports in order to give domestic producers the time they need to develop their efficiency to the point where they can compete in the domestic market without any restrictions on imports. In graphic terminology, we would expect that if the protected industry truly does experience improvements in production techniques or technological breakthroughs toward greater efficiency in the future, the supply curve will shift outward to the right so that the domestic industry can produce larger quantities at each and every price. National policymakers often assert that this **infant industry argument** has some merit in the short run. They have used it to protect a number of industries in their infancy around the world.

Such a policy can be abused, however. Often the protective import-restricting arrangements remain even after the infant has matured. If other countries can still produce more cheaply, the people who benefit from this type of situation are obviously the stockholders (and specialized factors of production that will earn economic rents) in the industry that is still being protected from world competition. The people who lose out are the consumers, who must pay a price higher than the world price for the product in question. In any event, it is very difficult to know beforehand which industries will eventually survive. In other words, we cannot predict very well the specific infant industries that policymakers might deem worthy of protection. Note that when we speculate about which industries "should" be protected, we are in the realm of *normative economics.* We are making a value judgment, a subjective statement of what *ought to be.*

Countering Foreign Subsidies and Dumping

Go to www.econtoday.com/chap33 for a Congressional Budget Office review of antidumping actions in the United States and around the world.

Another strong argument against unrestricted foreign trade has to do with countering other nations' subsidies to their own producers. When a foreign government subsidizes its producers, our producers claim that they cannot compete fairly with these subsidized foreign producers. To the extent that such subsidies fluctuate, it can be argued that unrestricted free trade will seriously disrupt domestic producers. They will not know when foreign governments are going to subsidize their producers and when they are not. Our competing industries will be expanding and contracting too frequently.

Dumping
Selling a good or a service abroad below the price charged in the home market or at a price below its cost of production.

The phenomenon called *dumping* is also used as an argument against unrestricted trade. **Dumping** is said to occur when a producer sells its products abroad below the price that is charged in the home market or at a price below its cost of production. When a foreign producer is accused of dumping, further investigation usually reveals that the foreign nation is in the throes of a recession. The foreign producer does not want to slow down its production at home. Because it anticipates an end to the recession and doesn't want to hold large inventories, it dumps its products abroad at prices below home prices. U.S. competitors may also allege that it sells its output at prices below its full costs in an effort to cover at least part of its variable costs of production.

Protecting Domestic Jobs

Perhaps the argument used most often against free trade is that unrestrained competition from other countries will eliminate jobs in the United States because other countries have lower-cost labor than we do. (Less restrictive environmental standards in other countries might also lower their private costs relative to ours.) This is a compelling argument, particularly for politicians from areas that might be threatened by foreign competition. For example, a representative from an area with shoe factories would certainly be upset about the possibility of constituents' losing their jobs because of competition from lower-priced shoe manufacturers in Brazil and Italy. But of course this argument against free trade is equally applicable to trade between the states within the United States.

Economists David Gould, G. L. Woodbridge, and Roy Ruffin examined the data on the relationship between increases in imports and the rate of unemployment. Their conclusion was that there is no causal link between the two. Indeed, in half the cases they studied, when imports increased, unemployment fell.

Another issue has to do with the cost of protecting U.S. jobs by restricting international trade. The Institute for International Economics examined just the restrictions on foreign textiles and apparel goods. U.S. consumers pay $9 billion a year more to protect jobs in those industries. That comes out to $50,000 *a year* for each job saved in an industry in which the average job pays only $20,000 a year. Similar studies have yielded similar results: Restrictions on imports of Japanese cars have cost $160,000 *per year* for every job saved in the auto industry. Every job preserved in the glass industry has cost $200,000 each and every year. Every job preserved in the U.S. steel industry has cost an astounding $750,000 per year.

> ### Economics Front and Center
>
> To contemplate how a nation's government might use product quality control as a pretext for restricting international trade in an effort to protect domestic jobs, read the case study, **A Looming Tequila Battle,** on page 792.

Emerging Arguments Against Free Trade

In recent years, two new antitrade arguments have been advanced. One of these focuses on environmental concerns. For instance, many environmentalists have suggested that genetic engineering of plants and animals could lead to accidental production of new diseases. These worries have induced the European Union to restrain trade in such products.

Another argument against free trade arises from national defense concerns. Major espionage successes by China in the late 1990s and early 2000s led some U.S. strategic experts to propose sweeping restrictions on exports of new technology.

Free trade proponents counter that at best these are arguments for the judicious regulation of trade. They continue to argue that by and large, broad trade restrictions mainly harm the interests of the nations that impose them.

CONCEPTS in Brief

- The infant industry argument against free trade contends that new industries should be protected against world competition so that they can become technologically efficient in the long run.

- Unrestricted foreign trade may allow foreign governments to subsidize exports or foreign producers to engage in dumping—selling products in other countries below their cost of production. To the extent that foreign export subsidies and dumping create more instability in domestic production, they may impair our well-being.

To test your understanding of the concepts covered in this section, go to the Online Review at www.myeconlab.com/miller.

WAYS TO RESTRICT FOREIGN TRADE

International trade can be stopped or at least stifled in many ways. These include quotas and taxes (the latter are usually called *tariffs* when applied to internationally traded items). Let's talk first about quotas.

Quotas

Quota system
A government-imposed restriction on the quantity of a specific good that another country is allowed to sell in the United States. In other words, quotas are restrictions on imports. These restrictions are usually applied to one or several specific countries.

Under a **quota system,** individual countries or groups of foreign producers are restricted to a certain amount of trade. An import quota specifies the maximum amount of a commodity that may be imported during a specified period of time. For example, the government might not allow more than 50 million barrels of foreign crude oil to enter the United States in a particular month.

Consider the example of quotas on textiles. Figure 33-4 presents the demand and supply curves for imported textiles. In an unrestricted import market, the equilibrium quantity imported is 900 million yards at a price of $1 per yard (expressed in constant-quality units). When an import quota is imposed, the supply curve is no longer S. Instead, the supply curve becomes vertical at some amount less than the equilibrium quantity—here, 800 million yards per year. The price to the U.S. consumer increases from $1.00 to $1.50. Thus the output restriction induced by the textile quota also has the effect of influencing the price that domestic suppliers can charge for their goods. This benefits domestic textile producers by raising their revenues and therefore their profits.

Voluntary restraint agreement (VRA)
An official agreement with another country that "voluntarily" restricts the quantity of its exports to the United States.

Voluntary Quotas. Quotas do not have to be explicit and defined by law. They can be "voluntary." Such a quota is called a **voluntary restraint agreement (VRA).** In the early 1980s, Japanese automakers voluntarily restrained exports to the United States. These restraints stayed in place into the 1990s. Today, there are VRAs on machine tools and textiles.

Voluntary import expansion (VIE)
An official agreement with another country in which it agrees to import more from the United States.

The opposite of a VRA is a **voluntary import expansion (VIE).** Under a VIE, a foreign government agrees to have its companies import more foreign goods from another

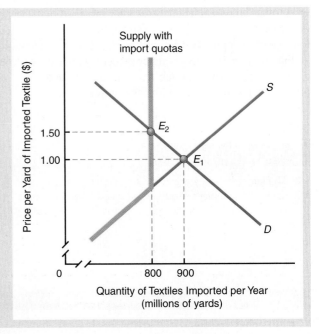

FIGURE 33-4
The Effect of Quotas on Textile Imports
Without restrictions, at point E_1, 900 million yards of textiles would be imported each year into the United States at the world price of $1.00 per yard. If the federal government imposes a quota of only 800 million yards, the effective supply curve becomes vertical at that quantity. It intersects the demand curve at point E_2, so the new equilibrium price is $1.50 per yard.

country. The United States almost started a major international trade war with Japan in 1995 over just such an issue. The U.S. government wanted Japanese automobile manufacturers voluntarily to increase their imports of U.S.-made automobile parts. Ultimately, Japanese companies did make a token increase in their imports of U.S. auto parts.

Tariffs

We can analyze tariffs by using standard supply and demand diagrams. Let's use as our commodity laptop computers, some of which are made in Japan and some of which are made domestically. In panel (a) of Figure 33-5, you see the demand and supply of Japanese laptops. The equilibrium price is $1,000 per constant-quality unit, and the equilibrium quantity is 10 million per year. In panel (b), you see the same equilibrium price of $1,000, and the *domestic* equilibrium quantity is 5 million units per year.

Now a tariff of $500 is imposed on all imported Japanese laptops. The supply curve shifts upward by $500 to S_2. For purchasers of Japanese laptops, the price increases to $1,250. The quantity demanded falls to 8 million per year. In panel (b), you see that at the higher price of imported Japanese laptops, the demand curve for U.S.-made laptops shifts outward to the right to D_2. The equilibrium price increases to $1,250, but the equilibrium quantity increases to 6.5 million units per year. So the tariff benefits domestic laptop producers because it increases the demand for their products due to the higher price of a close

Go to www.econtoday.com/chap33 to take a look at the U.S. State Department's reports on economic policy and trade practices.

FIGURE 33-5

The Effect of a Tariff on Japanese-Made Laptop Computers

Without a tariff, the United States buys 10 million Japanese laptops per year at an average price of $1,000, at point E_1 in panel (a). U.S. producers sell 5 million domestically made laptops, also at $1,000 each, at point E_1 in panel (b). A $500-per-laptop tariff will shift the Japanese import supply curve to S_2 in panel (a), so that the new equilibrium is at E_2, with price increased to $1,250 and quantity sold reduced to 8 million per year. The demand curve for U.S.-made laptops (for which there is no tariff) shifts to D_2, in panel (b). Domestic sales increase to 6.5 million per year, at point E_2.

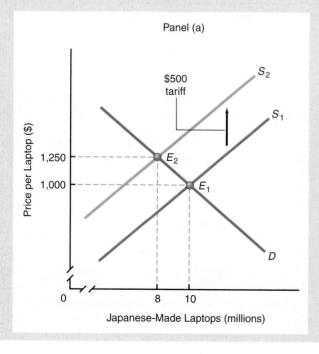

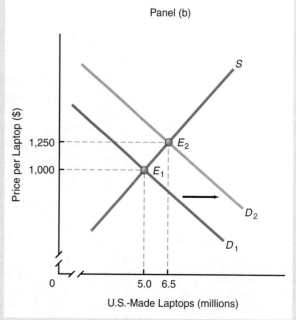

FIGURE 33-6

Tariff Rates in the United States Since 1820
Tariff rates in the United States have bounced around like a football; in-deed, in Congress, tariffs are a political football. Import-competing indus-tries prefer high tariffs. In the twentieth century, the highest tariff was the Smoot-Hawley Tariff of 1930, which was about as high as the "tariff of abominations" in 1828.

Source: U.S. Department of Commerce.

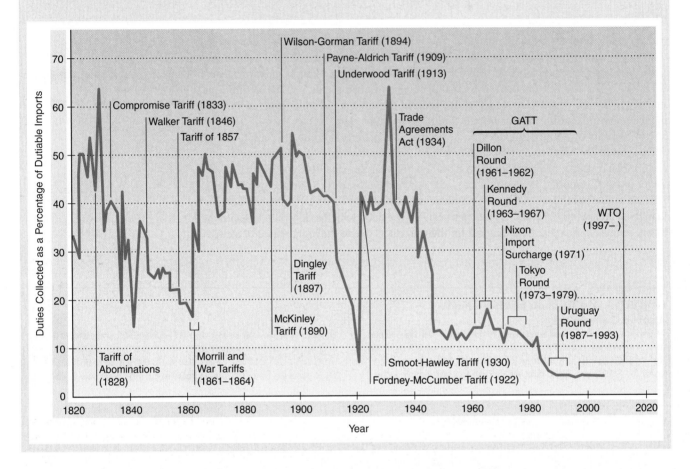

substitute, Japanese laptops. This causes a redistribution of income from Japanese produc-ers and U.S. consumers of laptops to U.S. producers of laptops.

Tariffs in the United States. In Figure 33-6, we see that tariffs on all imported goods have varied widely. The highest rates in the twentieth century occurred with the passage of the Smoot-Hawley Tariff in 1930.

Current Tariff Laws. The Trade Expansion Act of 1962 gave the president the authority to reduce tariffs by up to 50 percent. Subsequently, tariffs were reduced by about 35 per-cent. In 1974, the Trade Reform Act allowed the president to reduce tariffs further. In 1984, the Trade and Tariff Act resulted in the lowest tariff rates ever. All such trade agree-ment obligations of the United States were carried out under the auspices of the **General Agreement on Tariffs and Trade (GATT),** which was signed in 1947. Member nations of GATT account for more than 85 percent of world trade. As you can see in Figure 33-6, there have been a number of rounds of negotiations to reduce tariffs. In 2002, the U.S. government proposed eliminating all tariffs on manufactured goods by 2015.

General Agreement on Tariffs and Trade (GATT)
An international agreement established in 1947 to further world trade by reducing barriers and tariffs. GATT was replaced by the World Trade Organization in 1995.

INTERNATIONAL TRADE ORGANIZATIONS

The widespread effort to reduce tariffs around the world has generated interest among nations in joining various international trade organizations. These organizations promote trade by granting preferences in the form of reduced or eliminated tariffs, duties, or quotas.

The World Trade Organization (WTO)

The most important international trade organization with the largest membership is the **World Trade Organization (WTO),** which was ratified by the Uruguay Round of the General Agreement on Tariffs and Trade at the end of 1993. The WTO, which as of 2005 had 147 member nations and included 33 observer governments, began operations on January 1, 1995. WTO decisions have concerned such topics as special U.S. steel tariffs imposed in the early 2000s, which the U.S. government withdrew after the WTO determined that they violated its rules. The WTO also adjudicated the European Union's "banana wars" and determined that the EU's policies unfairly favored many former European colonies in Africa, the Caribbean, and the Pacific at the expense of banana-exporting countries in Latin America. Now those former colonies no longer have a privileged position in European markets.

Why do you suppose that European nations continue to dispute WTO rules regarding the international trade of products that originated in those countries?

World Trade Organization (WTO)
The successor organization to GATT that handles trade disputes among its member nations.

International E X A M P L E

The European Union Starts a Food Fight

The European Union (EU) has pressed the WTO to create a global register of "geographically defined" food products it believes should be protected from alleged copycat products outside the EU. If the EU gets its way, firms around the globe will violate WTO rules if they sell food products named for European locales where the products first originated. Dairy products such as parmesan cheese and cheddar cheese and alcoholic bev-

erages such as champagne, sherry, and madeira are among the 41 products on the EU's proposed list.

For Critical Analysis
Who would stand to benefit from the EU's efforts to prevent free trade of products with names originally derived from European locales?

On a larger scale, the WTO fostered the most important and far-reaching global trade agreement ever covering financial institutions, including banks, insurers, and investment companies. The more than 100 signatories to this new treaty have legally committed themselves to giving foreign residents more freedom to own and operate companies in virtually all segments of the financial services industry.

Regional Trade Agreements

Numerous other international trade organizations exist alongside the WTO. Sometimes known as **regional trade blocs,** these organizations are created by special deals among groups of countries that grant trade preferences only to countries within their groups. Currently, more than 140 bilateral or regional trade agreements are in effect around the globe. Examples include groups of industrial powerhouses, such the European Union, the North American Free Trade Agreement, and the Association of Southeast Asian Nations. Nations in South America with per capita real GDP nearer the world average have also formed re-

Regional trade bloc
A group of nations that grants members special trade privileges.

gional trade blocs called Mercosur and the Andean Community. Less developed nations have also formed regional trade blocs, such as the Economic Community of West African States and the Community of East and Southern Africa.

Some economists have worried that the formation of regional trade blocs could result in a reduction in members' trade with nations outside their own blocs. If more trade is diverted from a bloc than is created within it, then on net a regional trade agreement reduces trade. So far, however, most evidence indicates that regional trade blocs have promoted trade instead of hindering it. Numerous studies have found that as countries around the world have become more open to trade, they have tended to join regional trade blocs that promote even more openness.

CONCEPTS in Brief

- One means of restricting foreign trade is a quota system. An import quota specifies a maximum amount of a good that may be imported during a certain period.

- Another means of restricting imports is a tariff, which is a tax on imports only. An import tariff benefits import-competing industries and harms consumers by raising prices.

- The main international institution created to improve trade among nations was the General Agreement on Tariffs and

Trade (GATT). The last round of trade talks under GATT, the Uruguay Round, led to the creation of the World Trade Organization.

- Regional trade agreements among numerous nations of the world have established more than 140 regional trade blocs, which grant special trade privileges such as reduced tariff barriers and quota exemptions to member nations.

To test your understanding of the concepts covered in this section, go to the Online Review at www.myeconlab.com/miller.

CASE STUDY: Economics Front and Center

A Looming Tequila Battle

Corso is a mid-level official of the American Distilled Spirits Council (ADSC), a trade group composed of U.S. sellers of wines and other distilled alcoholic beverages. She has been assigned to investigate recent efforts by the Mexican government to regulate U.S. sales of tequila. At present, more than 80 percent of all tequila sold in the United States is transported from Mexico in bulk and then placed in containers by individual U.S. bottlers that wholesale it in their local areas.

Mexico's quasi-governmental Tequila Regulatory Council (TRC) has notified Corso that it has discovered evidence that bulk handlers on both sides of the border have tampered with tequila products. Some Mexican handlers, the TRC contends, have added water to certain tequilas, and a few U.S. handlers have blended different tequilas. In light of these alleged threats to the quality of tequilas, Corso has learned, the TRC is recommending to the Mexican government that it ban all bulk tequila shipments and require that tequila be bottled in Mexico.

After meeting with her superiors, Corso begins drafting a response to the TRC's claims and recommendation. "The TRC's recommendation," her draft response begins, "has less to do with quality control than with protecting jobs south of the U.S. border. If the Mexican government follows the TRC's recommendation, the ADSC will ask the U.S. government to file formal complaints with both the North American Free Trade Agreement and the World Trade Organization."

Points to Analyze

1. *Of the ways of restricting international trade discussed in this chapter, which method has the TRC recommended to the Mexican government?*

2. *How could the Mexican government discourage the cross-border shipment of bulk tequila without resorting to an outright ban on such shipments?*

Issues and Applications

Agricultural Subsidies Derail the WTO

A s shown in Figure 33-7, by the mid-2000s membership of the World Trade Organization had grown to include about 50 percent more nations than had participated in the General Agreement on Tariffs and Trade in 1985. Global trade had more than tripled during the same period.

As trade among nations increased into the early 2000s, however, a dark cloud began to hover over the global trading system administered by the WTO. Developing nations were becoming increasingly skeptical of developed nations' true commitment to open trade. Even as the United States, the European Union, and Japan were pushing developing countries to lift tariff and quota barriers to U.S., EU, and Japanese exports, the governments of the developed nations were boosting subsidies to their domestic farmers producing agricultural goods. The subsidies allowed these farmers to sell their products at lower prices than they otherwise would have accepted. This, of course, gave agricultural producers in these developed nations an artificial advantage in world markets.

Concepts Applied

- World Trade Organization
- General Agreement on Tariffs and Trade
- Protectionism

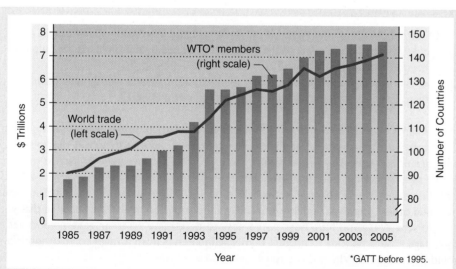

FIGURE 33-7

Growth in the World Trade Organization's Membership and in Global Trade

Both membership in the World Trade Organization and total international trade have increased considerably since the mid-1980s.

Source: World Trade Organization.

The Problem with Agricultural Subsidies

Naturally, those who have most to lose from agricultural subsidies are farmers residing in nations without government agricultural subsidies. By and large, these farmers live in developing countries. From their perspective, the U.S., EU, and Japanese subsidies amount to protectionist policies.

Consider, for instance, who is harmed by U.S. cotton subsidies. In 2002, Congress raised subsidies paid to U.S. cotton growers to nearly $4 billion per year. This gave U.S. cotton producers a significant advantage over their competitors elsewhere in the world. A number of these were farmers residing in poverty-stricken West Africa. Many of them were forced out of business by the lower cotton prices resulting from the influx of subsidized cotton exported by growers in the United States.

Agricultural Protectionism Slows the World Trade Locomotive

In 2003, U.S. agricultural subsidies were equal to nearly 20 percent of the total value of U.S. farming production. In the EU, subsidies amounted to 35 percent of the market value of agricultural output. The share of Japan's subsidies was even higher, at nearly 60 percent.

That year, many of the developing nations placed at a competitive disadvantage by these whopping agricultural subsidies drew a line in the sand. Most of these nations pulled out of WTO-sponsored global trade talks in Cancún, Mexico. More openness to trade on their part, they said, would depend on whether the developed nations slashed protectionist subsidies of agricultural production.

In late 2003, the U.S. government offered a proposal for joint reductions in agricultural subsidies by the United States, the European Union, and Japan. The governments of EU nations and Japan expressed some interest in considering the idea. Within months, however, negotiators faced a stalemate concerning exactly how to reduce subsidies without harming their U.S., EU, and Japanese farmers. As a consequence, so far the developed nations have not cut subsidies to their farmers, even though some economists estimate that eliminating the subsidies would add at least $100 billion annually to global GDP.

For Critical Analysis

1. Why do subsidies to U.S. cotton producers induce them to increase their supply of cotton for export to other nations? (Hint: How does a per-unit subsidy affect the marginal cost, and hence the short-run supply curve, of a perfectly competitive cotton producer?)
2. Who else besides West African cotton producers are harmed by U.S. government subsidies to cotton producers? (Hint: Who provides the funds for all the subsidies received by U.S. farmers?)

Web Resources

1. To learn more about why West African nations regard U.S. cotton subsidies as a protectionist policy, go to a link to the discussion provided by the Global Policy Forum at www.econtoday.com/chap33.
2. The Australia-Japan Research Foundation's analysis of Japan's world-leading agricultural subsidies is available at www.econtoday.com/chap33.

Research Project

Governments of developed nations typically argue that agricultural subsidies are domestic policies aimed solely at helping their farmers. Spillover effects in world markets, they claim, are not intentionally protectionist. Likewise, the U.S. government justifies its rules barring sales of certain European-manufactured pharmaceuticals as necessary to protect consumer safety. The EU bans all genetically modified U.S. crops on the same grounds. Yet these and other "domestic" policies adversely affect international trade. Suppose that you work for the WTO. You have been asked how to determine whether governments actually engage in such policies to protect domestic industries from foreign competition. How would you proceed? Why is this a tough question to answer?

SUMMARY DISCUSSION of Learning Objectives

1. **The Worldwide Importance of International Trade:** Total trade among nations has been growing faster than total world GDP. The growth of U.S. exports and imports relative to U.S. GDP parallels this global trend. Together, exports and imports now equal about one-fourth of total national production. In some countries, trade accounts for a much higher share of total economic activity.

2. **Why Nations Can Gain from Specializing in Production and Engaging in Trade:** A country has a comparative advantage in producing a good if it can produce that good at a lower opportunity cost, in terms of forgone production of a second good, than another nation. Because the other nation has a comparative advantage in producing the second good, both nations can gain by specializing in producing the goods in which they have a comparative advantage and engaging in international trade. Together they can then produce and consume more than they would have produced and consumed in the absence of specialization and trade.

3. **Comparative Advantage versus Absolute Advantage:** Whereas a nation has a comparative advantage in producing a good when it can produce the good at a lower opportunity cost relative to the opportunity cost of producing the good in another nation, a nation has an absolute advantage when it can produce more output with a given set of inputs than can be produced in the other country. Trade can still take place if both nations have a comparative advantage in producing goods that they can agree to exchange. The reason is that it can still benefit the nation with an absolute advantage to specialize in production.

4. **Arguments Against Free Trade:** One argument against free trade is that temporary import restrictions might permit an "infant industry" to develop to the point at which it could compete without such restrictions. Another argument concerns dumping, in which foreign companies allegedly sell some of their output in domestic markets at prices below the prices in the companies' home markets or even below the companies' costs of production. In addition, some environmentalists contend that nations should restrain foreign trade to prevent exposing their countries to environmental hazards to plants, animals, or even humans. Finally, some contend that countries should limit exports of technologies that could pose a threat to their national defense.

5. **Ways That Nations Restrict Foreign Trade:** One way to restrain trade is to impose a quota, or a limit on imports of a good. This action restricts the supply of the good in the domestic market, thereby pushing up the equilibrium price of the good. Another way to reduce trade is to place a tariff on imported goods. This reduces the supply of foreign-made goods and increases the demand for domestically produced goods, thereby bringing about a rise in the price of the good.

6. **Key International Trade Agreements and Organizations:** From 1947 to 1995, nations agreed to abide by the General Agreement on Tariffs and Trade (GATT), which laid an international legal foundation for relaxing quotas and reducing tariffs. Since 1995, the World Trade Organization (WTO) has adjudicated trade disputes that arise between or among nations. Now there are also more than 140 regional trade blocs that provide special trade preferences to member nations.

KEY TERMS AND CONCEPTS

absolute advantage (781)

comparative advantage (780)

dumping (786)

General Agreement on Tariffs and Trade (GATT) (780)

infant industry argument (786)

quota system (788)

regional trade bloc (791)

voluntary import expansion (VIE) (788)

voluntary restraint agreement (VRA) (788)

World Trade Organization (WTO) (791)

PROBLEMS

Answers to the odd-numbered problems appear at the back of the book.

33-1. The following hypothetical example depicts the number of calculators and books that Norway and Sweden can produce with one unit of labor.

Country	Calculators	Books
Norway	2	1
Sweden	4	1

If each country has 100 units of labor and the country splits its labor force evenly between the two industries, how much of each good can the nations produce individually and jointly? Which nation has an absolute advantage in calculators, and which nation has an absolute advantage in books?

33-2. Suppose that the two nations in Problem 33-1 do not trade.

    a. What would be the price of books in terms of calculators in each nation?

    b. What is the opportunity cost of producing one calculator in each nation?

    c. What is the opportunity cost of producing one book in each nation?

33-3. Consider the nations in Problem 33-1 when answering the following questions.

    a. Which country has a comparative advantage in calculators, and which has a comparative advantage in books?

    b. What is the total or joint output if the two nations specialize in the good for which they have a comparative advantage?

33-4. Illustrate possible production possibilities curves (PPCs, see Chapter 2) for the two nations in Problem 33-1 in a graph with books depicted on the vertical axis and calculators on the horizontal axis. What do the differing slopes of the PPCs for these two nations indicate about the opportunity costs of producing calculators and books in the two countries? What are the implications for the comparative advantage of producing calculators or books in Norway and Sweden?

33-5. Suppose that initially the two nations in Problem 33-1 do not engage in international trade. Now they have decided to trade with each other at a rate where one

book exchanges for three calculators. Using this rate of exchange, explain, in economic terms, whether their exchange is a zero-sum game, a positive-sum game, or a negative-sum game. (Hint: Review Chapter 27 if necessary to answer this question.)

33-6. The marginal physical product of a worker in an advanced nation (MPP_A) is 100, and the wage (W_A) is $25. The marginal physical product of a worker in a developing nation (MPP_D) is 15, and the wage (W_D) is $5. Product prices are equal in all nations. As a cost-minimizing business manager in the advanced nation, would you be enticed to move your business to the developing nation to take advantage of the lower wage?

33-7. Consider the following table, which shows unspecialized productive capabilities of sets of workers in South Shore and neighboring East Isle, when answering the questions that follow.

Product	South Shore		East Isle	
	Workers	Output	Workers	Output
Modems	100	25	100	45
DVD drives	100	50	100	15

    a. Which country has an absolute advantage in producing modems? DVD drives?

    b. Which country has a comparative advantage in producing modems? DVD drives?

33-8. Refer to the table in Problem 33-7 to answer the following questions.

    a. If each country has a total of 200 workers to devote to production of modems and DVD drives, what are the combined outputs of the two goods if these countries do not specialize in production according to comparative advantage?

    b. What are the combined outputs if the two countries completely specialize in production according to comparative advantage? Measured in terms of outputs of modems and DVD drives, what are the gains from trade?

33-9. Consider the following table, which shows unspecialized productive capabilities of sets of workers in Northern Kingdom and Western Republic, neighboring countries that share a border, when answering the questions that follow.

Product	Northern Kingdom		Western Republic	
	Workers	Output	Workers	Output
Bushels of wheat	100	55	100	20
Surfboards	100	30	100	45

a. Which country has an absolute advantage in producing bushels of wheat? Surfboards?

b. Which country has a comparative advantage in producing bushels of wheat? Surfboards?

33-10. Suppose that each nation in Problem 33-9 currently specializes according to its comparative advantage, maximizes its production given the 200 workers each has available, and engages in trade with the other country. What do the two nations lose, in terms of outputs of bushels of wheat and surfboards, if one nation's government implements a law banning international trade?

33-11. You are a policymaker of a major exporting nation. Your main export good has a price elasticity of demand of −0.50. Is there any economic reason why you would voluntarily agree to export restraints?

33-12. The following table depicts the bicycle industry before and after a nation has imposed quota restraints.

	Before Quota	After Quota
Quantity imported	1,000,000	900,000
Price paid	$50	$60

Draw a diagram illustrating conditions in the imported bicycle market before and after the quota, and answer the following questions.

a. What are the total expenditures of consumers before and after the quota?

b. What is the price elasticity of demand for bicycles?

c. Who benefits from the imposition of the quota?

33-13 The following diagrams illustrate the markets for imported Korean-made and U.S.-manufactured televisions before and after a tariff is imposed on imported TVs.

a. What was the amount of the tariff per TV?

b. What was the total revenue of Korean television exports before the tariff? After the tariff?

c. What is the tariff revenue earned by the U.S. government?

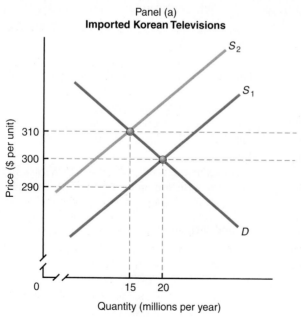

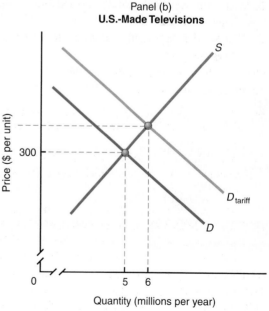

33-14. Base your answers to the following questions on the graphs accompanying Problem 33-13.

    a. What was the revenue of U.S. television manufacturers before the tariff was imposed?

    b. What is their total revenue after the tariff?

    c. Who has gained from the tariff, and who is worse off?

ECONOMICS ON THE NET

How the World Trade Organization Settles Trade Disputes A key function of the WTO is to adjudicate trade disagreements that arise among nations. This application helps you learn about the process that the WTO follows when considering international trade disputes.

Title: The World Trade Organization: Settling Trade Disputes

Navigation: Go to www.econtoday.com/chap33 to access the WTO's Web page titled *Trading into the Future*, and click on *3. Settling Disputes*, in the left-hand margin.

Application Read the article; then answer the following questions.

1. As the article discusses, settling trade disputes often takes at least a year. What aspects of the WTO's dispute settlement process take the longest time?

2. Does the WTO actually "punish" a country it finds has broken international trading agreements? If not, who does impose sanctions?

For **Group Study and Analysis** Back up to *Trading into the Future*, and click on *4. Beyond the Agreements*. Have a class discussion of the pros and cons of WTO involvement in each of the areas discussed in this article. Which are most important for promoting world trade? Which are least important?

Media Resources

If your exam were tomorrow, would you be ready? For each chapter, MyEconLab Practice Tests and Study Plans pinpoint which sections you have mastered and which ones you need to study. That way, you are more efficient with your study time, and you are better prepared for your exams.

In addition to Practice Tests and your personalized Study Plan, you'll find the following media resources in MyEconLab:

1. *Graphs in Motion* animation of Figures 33-1, 33-4, and 33-5.
2. Videos featuring the author, Roger LeRoy Miller, on the following subjects:
   - The Gains from Trade
   - Arguments Against Free Trade

3. Links to the Web sites cited in the marginal Internet Resources, Issues and Applications feature, and Economics on the Net activity.
4. Audio clips of all key terms, additional practice problems, and a PDF version of the material from the print Study Guide.
5. eThemes of the Times, which is a New York Times article to help you understand the real-world applications of what you are learning.

To see how it works, turn to page 16 and then go to www.myeconlab.com/miller.

Get Ahead of the Curve

Chapter 34

Exchange Rates and the Balance of Payments

On this particular day, as on many others in the 2000s, the Japanese yen's value was rising relative to the U.S. dollar. Because yen were more expensive to obtain with dollars, U.S. residents faced higher dollar prices when they considered purchasing Japanese-made goods. In an effort to prevent a fall in exports to the United States that would weaken total spending on Japanese goods and services, the Japanese Finance Ministry hurriedly placed a very large order with a private Japanese bank to sell yen for dollars on its behalf. About 30 minutes later, the Finance Ministry canceled the order. Nevertheless, exactly as the Finance Ministry had planned, the yen's dollar value fell. Why did the Japanese Finance Ministry's apparent reversal of its sale of yen encourage a fall in the yen's dollar value? In this chapter, you will learn the answer to this question.

LEARNING OBJECTIVES

After reading this chapter, you should be able to:

1. Distinguish between the balance of trade and the balance of payments
2. Identify the key accounts within the balance of payments
3. Outline how exchange rates are determined in the markets for foreign exchange
4. Discuss factors that can induce changes in equilibrium exchange rates
5. Understand how policymakers can go about attempting to fix exchange rates
6. Explain alternative approaches to limiting exchange rate variability

Media Resources

Refer to the end of the chapter for a full listing of the multimedia learning materials available in MyEconLab.

. . . when the value of the U.S. dollar in terms of other nations' currencies declines, foreign automakers often respond by shifting more of their production to the United States? For instance, when the dollar's world value declined between 2002 and 2004, Toyota cut back on vehicle output in Japan and increased production at its five U.S. plants. Likewise, DaimlerChrysler reduced its Mercedes output in Germany but nearly doubled production of Mercedes sport utility vehicles at its Alabama factory. Vehicles that these companies continued producing in Japan and Germany were priced in terms of yen and euros. Thus the 2002–2004 decline in the value of the dollar in terms of yen and euros caused vehicles still produced in those nations to be more expensive to U.S. consumers using dollars to buy them. By shifting production of more vehicles to the United States, Toyota, Daimler-Chrysler, and other foreign producers were able to avoid higher dollar prices that would have reduced their U.S. sales.

In this chapter, you will learn more about how changes in the dollar's value affect decisions of both sellers *and* buyers, both abroad *and* in the United States. Before we consider what causes variations in the value of the dollar and the more than 170 other currencies in circulation around the world, however, we will examine how we keep track of the international financial transactions that these currencies facilitate.

THE BALANCE OF PAYMENTS AND INTERNATIONAL CAPITAL MOVEMENTS

Governments typically keep track of each year's economic activities by calculating the gross domestic product—the total of expenditures on all newly produced final domestic goods and services—and its components. A summary information system has also been developed for international trade. It covers the balance of trade and the balance of payments. The **balance of trade** refers specifically to exports and imports of goods as discussed in Chapter 33. When international trade is in balance, the value of exports equals the value of imports. When the value of imports exceeds the value of exports, we are running a deficit in the balance of trade. When the value of exports exceeds the value of imports, we are running a surplus.

The **balance of payments** is a more general concept that expresses the total of all economic transactions between a nation and the rest of the world, usually for a period of one year. Each country's balance of payments summarizes information about that country's exports, imports, earnings by domestic residents on assets located abroad, earnings on domestic assets owned by foreign residents, international capital movements, and official transactions by central banks and governments. In essence, then, the balance of payments is a record of all the transactions between households, firms, and the government of one country and the rest of the world. Any transaction that leads to a *payment* by a country's residents (or government) is a deficit item, identified by a negative sign (−) when the actual numbers are given for the items listed in the second column of Table 34-1. Any transaction that leads to a *receipt* by a country's residents (or government) is a surplus item and is identified by a plus sign (+) when actual numbers are considered. Table 34-1 gives a listing of the surplus and deficit items on international accounts.

Accounting Identities

Accounting identities—definitions of equivalent values—exist for financial institutions and other businesses. We begin with simple accounting identities that must hold for families and then go on to describe international accounting identities.

Balance of trade
The difference between exports and imports of goods.

Balance of payments
A system of accounts that measures transactions of goods, services, income, and financial assets between domestic households, businesses, and governments and residents of the rest of the world during a specific time period.

Accounting identities
Values that are equivalent by definition.

Surplus Items (+)	Deficit Items (−)
Exports of merchandise	Imports of merchandise
Private and governmental gifts from foreign residents	Private and governmental gifts to foreign residents
Foreign use of domestically owned transportation	Use of foreign-owned transportation
Foreign tourists' expenditures in this country	U.S. tourists' expenditures abroad
Foreign military spending in this country	Military spending abroad
Interest and dividend receipts from foreign entities	Interest and dividends paid to foreign residents
Sales of domestic assets to foreign residents	Purchases of foreign assets
Funds deposited in this country by foreign residents	Funds placed in foreign depository institutions
Sales of gold to foreign residents	Purchases of gold from foreign residents
Sales of domestic currency to foreign residents	Purchases of foreign currency

If a family unit is spending more than its current income, such a situation necessarily implies that the family unit must be doing one of the following:

1. Reducing its money holdings or selling stocks, bonds, or other assets
2. Borrowing
3. Receiving gifts from friends or relatives
4. Receiving public transfers from a government, which obtained the funds by taxing others (a transfer is a payment, in money or in goods or services, made without receiving goods or services in return)

We can use this information to derive an identity: If a family unit is currently spending more than it is earning, it must draw on previously acquired wealth, borrow, or receive either private or public aid. Similarly, an identity exists for a family unit that is currently spending less than it is earning: It must be increasing its money holdings or be lending and acquiring other financial assets, or it must pay taxes or bestow gifts on others. When we consider businesses and governments, each unit in each group faces its own identities or constraints. Ultimately, net lending by households must equal net borrowing by businesses and governments.

Disequilibrium. Even though our individual family unit's accounts must balance, in the sense that the identity discussed previously must hold, sometimes the item that brings about the balance cannot continue indefinitely. *If family expenditures exceed family income and this situation is financed by borrowing, the household may be considered to be in disequilibrium because such a situation cannot continue indefinitely.* If such a deficit is financed by drawing on previously accumulated assets, the family may also be in disequilibrium because it cannot continue indefinitely to draw on its wealth; eventually, it will become impossible for that family to continue such a lifestyle. (Of course, if the family members are retired, they may well be in equilibrium by drawing on previously acquired assets to finance current deficits; this example illustrates that it is necessary to understand circumstances fully before pronouncing an economic unit in disequilibrium.)

Equilibrium. Individual households, businesses, and governments, as well as the entire group of households, businesses, and governments, must eventually reach equilibrium. Certain economic adjustment mechanisms have evolved to ensure equilibrium. Deficit households must eventually increase their income or decrease their expenditures. They will find that they have to pay higher interest rates if they wish to borrow to finance their deficits. Eventually, their credit sources will dry up, and they will be forced into equilibrium. Businesses, on occasion, must lower costs or prices—or go bankrupt—to reach equilibrium.

An Accounting Identity Among Nations. When people from different nations trade or interact, certain identities or constraints must also hold. People buy goods from people in other nations; they also lend to and present gifts to people in other nations. If residents of a nation interact with residents of other nations, an accounting identity ensures a balance (but not an equilibrium, as will soon become clear). Let's look at the three categories of balance of payments transactions: current account transactions, capital account transactions, and official reserve account transactions.

Current Account Transactions

During any designated period, all payments and gifts that are related to the purchase or sale of both goods and services constitute the **current account** in international trade. Major types of current account transactions include the exchange of merchandise, the exchange of services, and unilateral transfers.

Current account
A category of balance of payments transactions that measures the exchange of merchandise, the exchange of services, and unilateral transfers.

Merchandise Trade Exports and Imports. The largest portion of any nation's balance of payments current account is typically the importing and exporting of merchandise goods. During 2004, for example, as can be seen in lines 1 and 2 of Table 34-2, the United States exported an estimated $813.7 billion of merchandise and imported $1,406.5 billion. The balance of merchandise trade is defined as the difference between the value of merchandise exports and the value of merchandise imports. For 2004, the United States had a balance of merchandise trade deficit because the value of its merchandise imports exceeded the value of its merchandise exports. This deficit was about $592.8 billion (line 3).

Service Exports and Imports. The balance of (merchandise) trade has to do with tangible items—things you can feel, touch, and see. Service exports and imports have to do with invisible or intangible items that are bought and sold, such as shipping, insurance, tourist expenditures, and banking services. Also, income earned by foreign residents on U.S. investments and income earned by U.S. residents on foreign investments are part of service imports and exports. As can be seen in lines 4 and 5 of Table 34-2, in 2004, service exports were $336.7 billion and service imports were $255.0 billion. Thus the balance of services was about $81.7 billion in 2004 (line 6). Exports constitute receipts or inflows into the United States and are positive; imports constitute payments abroad or outflows of money and are negative.

When we combine the balance of merchandise trade with the balance of services, we obtain a balance on goods and services equal to −$511.1 billion in 2004 (line 7).

How much different would the balance on goods and services be if it was based on the locations of the owners of the firms that produce traded goods and services?

TABLE 34-2
U.S. Balance of Payments Account, 2004 (in billions of dollars)

Current Account

(1)	Exports of goods	+ 813.7	
(2)	Imports of goods	− 1,406.5	
(3)	Balance of trade		− 592.8
(4)	Exports of services	+ 336.7	
(5)	Imports of services	− 255.0	
(6)	Balance of services		+ 81.7
(7)	Balance on goods and services [(3) + (6)]		− 511.1
(8)	Net unilateral transfers	− 70.1	
(9)	Balance on current account		− 581.2

Capital Account

(10)	U.S. private capital going abroad	− 795.1	
(11)	Foreign private capital coming into the United States	+ 1,137.4	
(12)	Balance on capital account [(10) + (11)]		+ 342.3
(13)	Balance on current account plus balance on capital account [(9) + (12)]		− 238.9

Official Reserve Transactions Account

(14)	Official transactions balance		+ 238.9
(15)	Total (balance)		0

Sources: U.S. Department of Commerce, Bureau of Economic Analysis; author's estimates.

*Includes an approximately $25 billion statistical discrepancy, probably uncounted capital inflows, many of which relate to the illegal drug trade.

E X A M P L E

Taking Multinational Firms into Account in Trade Statistics

The U.S. balance on goods and services tracks the net flow of international trade of goods and services based on where traded items are produced. Thus the statisticians who tabulate this balance add only exports of goods and services *produced* within U.S. borders and subtract only U.S. imports of for-eign-*produced* goods and services. But this accounting does not include all activities of U.S. firms. Consider, for example, a U.S. multinational firm that owns a plant in Mexico where it produces a good or service that it sells to Canadian residents. Because the item is produced in Mexico and purchased by

Canadians, this transaction is not included in the U.S. balance on goods and services even though a U.S. firm was involved.

Recently, the U.S. Department of Commerce began report-ing a measure of the balance on goods and services based on the locations of the companies that own the resources utilized to produce internationally traded goods and services. This *ownership-based* U.S. balance on goods and services adjusts exports and imports to account for purchases and sales in-volving foreign affiliates of U.S. firms. Annual net receipts that U.S. parent companies derive from trade conducted by their foreign affiliates are always much larger than the net receipts foreign firms receive from their U.S. affiliates that engage in international trade. Consequently, the deficit in the ownership-based balance on goods and services averages about $60 billion per year less than the deficit in the official, production-based measure of this balance.

For Critical Analysis
Why might the fact that the balance of payments accounts were designed before multinational firms were very common help explain why the balances in these accounts are not based on ownership?

Unilateral Transfers. U.S. residents give gifts to relatives and others abroad, the federal government grants gifts to foreign nations, foreign residents give gifts to U.S. residents, and some foreign governments have granted funds to the U.S. government. In the current account, we see that net unilateral transfers—the total amount of gifts given by U.S. residents and the government minus the total amount received from abroad by U.S. residents and the government—came to an estimated −$70.1 billion in 2004 (line 8). The fact that there is a minus sign before the number for unilateral transfers means that U.S. residents gave more to foreign residents than foreign residents gave to U.S. residents.

Balancing the Current Account. The balance on current account tracks the value of a country's exports of goods and services (including military receipts plus income on investments abroad) and transfer payments (private and government) relative to the value of that country's imports of goods and services and transfer payments (private and government). In 2004, it was estimated to be −$581.2 billion.

Go to www.econtoday.com/chap34 for the latest U.S. balance of payments data from the Bureau of Economic Analysis.

If the sum of net exports of goods and services plus net unilateral transfers plus net investment income exceeds zero, a **current account surplus** *is said to exist; if this sum is negative, a* **current account deficit** *is said to exist. A* **current account deficit** *means that we are importing more goods and services than we are exporting. Such a deficit must be paid for by the export of money or money equivalent, which means a capital account surplus.*

Capital Account Transactions

Capital account
A category of balance of payments transactions that measures flows of real and financial assets.

In world markets, it is possible to buy and sell not only goods and services but also real and financial assets. These are the international transactions measured in the **capital accounts**. Capital account transactions occur because of foreign investments—either by foreign residents investing in the United States or by U.S. residents investing in other countries. The purchase of shares of stock in British firms on the London stock market by a U.S. resident causes an outflow of funds from the United States to Britain. The building of a Japanese automobile factory in the United States causes an inflow of funds from Japan to the United States. Any time foreign residents buy U.S. government securities, there is an inflow of funds from other countries to the United States. Any time U.S. residents buy foreign government securities, there is an outflow of funds from the United States to other countries. Loans to and from foreign residents cause outflows and inflows.

Line 10 of Table 34-2 on the previous page indicates that in 2004, the value of private capital going out of the United States was an estimated −$795.1 billion, and line 11 shows that the value of private capital coming into the United States (including a statistical discrepancy) was $1,137.4 billion. U.S. capital going abroad constitutes payments or outflows and is therefore negative. Foreign capital coming into the United States constitutes receipts or inflows and is therefore positive. Thus there was a positive net capital movement of $342.3 billion into the United States (line 12). This net private flow of capital is also called the balance on capital account.

There is a relationship between the current account and the capital account, assuming no interventions by the finance ministries or central banks of nations.

In the absence of interventions by finance ministries or central banks, the current account and the capital account must sum to zero. Stated differently, the current account deficit must equal the capital account surplus when governments or central banks do not engage in foreign exchange interventions. In this situation, any nation experiencing a current account deficit, such as the United States, must also be running a capital account surplus.

This basic relationship is apparent in the United States, as you can see in Figure 34-1.

FIGURE 34-1
The Relationship Between the Current Account and the Capital Account

To some extent, the capital account is the mirror image of the current account. We can see this in the years since 1970. When the current account was in surplus, the capital account was in deficit. When the current ac-

count was in deficit, the capital account was in surplus. Indeed, virtually the only time foreign residents can invest in the United States is when the current account is in deficit.

Sources: International Monetary Fund; *Economic Indicators*.

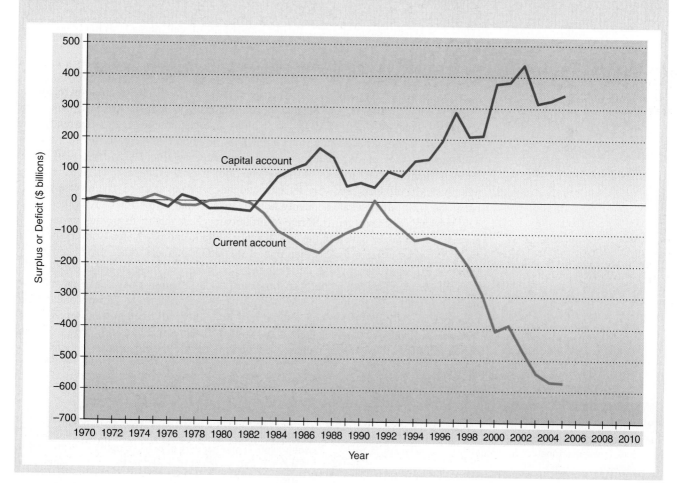

Official Reserve Account Transactions

The third type of balance of payments transaction concerns official reserve assets, which consist of the following:

Special drawing rights (SDRs)
Reserve assets created by the International Monetary Fund for countries to use in settling international payment obligations.

International Monetary Fund
An agency founded to administer an international foreign exchange system and to lend to member countries that had balance of payments problems. The IMF now functions as a lender of last resort for national governments.

1. Foreign currencies
2. Gold
3. **Special drawing rights (SDRs),** which are reserve assets that the **International Monetary Fund** created to be used by countries to settle international payment obligations
4. The reserve position in the International Monetary Fund
5. Financial assets held by an official agency, such as the U.S. Treasury Department

To consider how official reserve account transactions occur, look again at Table 34-2 on page 803. The surplus in the U.S. capital account was $342.3 billion. But the deficit in the U.S. current account was −$581.2 billion, so the United States had a net deficit on the combined accounts (line 13) of −$238.9 billion. In other words, the United States obtained less in foreign funds in all its international transactions than it used. How is this deficiency made up? By foreign central banks adding to their U.S. funds, shown by the +$238.9 billion in official transactions on line 14 in Table 34-2. There is a plus sign on line 14 because this represents an *inflow* of foreign exchange in our international transactions.

The balance (line 15) in Table 34-2 is zero, as it must be with double-entry bookkeeping. The U.S. balance of payments deficit is measured by the official transactions figure on line 14.

What Affects the Balance of Payments?

A major factor affecting any nation's balance of payments is its rate of inflation relative to that of its trading partners. Assume that the rates of inflation in the United States and in the European Monetary Union (EMU)—the nations that use the euro as their currency—are equal. Now suppose that all of a sudden, the U.S. inflation rate increases. EMU residents will find that U.S. products are becoming more expensive, and U.S. firms will export fewer of them to EMU nations. At the current dollar-euro exchange rate, U.S. residents will find EMU products relatively cheaper, and they will import more. The reverse will occur if the U.S. inflation rate suddenly falls relative to that of the EMU. All other things held constant, whenever the U.S. rate of inflation exceeds that of its trading partners, we expect to see a larger deficit in the U.S. balance of trade and payments. Conversely, when the U.S. rate of inflation is less than that of its trading partners, other things being constant, we expect to see a smaller deficit in the U.S. balance of trade and payments.

Another important factor that sometimes influences a nation's balance of payments is its relative political stability. Political instability causes *capital flight.* Owners of capital in countries anticipating or experiencing political instability will often move assets to countries that are politically stable, such as the United States. Hence the U.S. capital account balance is likely to increase whenever political instability looms in other nations in the world.

CONCEPTS in Brief

- The balance of payments reflects the value of all transactions in international trade, including goods, services, financial assets, and gifts.

- The merchandise trade balance gives us the difference between exports and imports of tangible items. Merchandise trade transactions are represented by exports and imports of tangible items.

- Included in the current account along with merchandise trade are service exports and imports relating to commerce in intangible items, such as shipping, insurance, and tourist expenditures. The current account also includes income earned by foreign residents on U.S. investments and income earned by U.S. residents on foreign investments.

- Unilateral transfers involve international private gifts and federal government grants or gifts to foreign nations.

- When we add the balance of merchandise trade and the balance of services and take account of net unilateral transfers and net investment income, we come up with the balance on the current account, a summary statistic.

- There are also capital account transactions that relate to the buying and selling of financial and real assets. Foreign capital is always entering the United States, and U.S. capital is always flowing abroad. The difference is called the balance on capital account.

- Another type of balance of payments transaction concerns the official reserve assets of individual countries, or what is often simply called official transactions. By standard accounting convention, official transactions are exactly equal to a nation's balance of payments but opposite in sign.

- A nation's balance of payments can be affected by its relative rate of inflation and by its political stability relative to other nations.

To test your understanding of the concepts covered in this section, go to the Online Review at www.myeconlab.com/miller.

DETERMINING FOREIGN EXCHANGE RATES

When you buy foreign products, such as a Japanese-made laptop computer, you have dollars with which to pay the Japanese manufacturer. The Japanese manufacturer, however, cannot pay workers in dollars. The workers are Japanese, they live in Japan, and they must have yen to buy goods and services in that country. There must therefore be some way of exchanging dollars for yen that the computer manufacturer will accept. That exchange occurs in a **foreign exchange market,** which in this case involves the exchange of yen and dollars.

The particular **exchange rate** between yen and dollars that prevails—the dollar price of the yen—depends on the current demand for and supply of yen and dollars. In a sense, then, our analysis of the exchange rate between dollars and yen will be familiar, for we have used supply and demand throughout this book. If it costs you 1 cent to buy 1 yen, that is the foreign exchange rate determined by the current demand for and supply of yen in the foreign exchange market. The Japanese person going to the foreign exchange market would need 100 yen to buy 1 dollar.

Now let's consider what determines the demand for and supply of foreign currency in the foreign exchange market. We will continue to assume that the only two countries in the world are Japan and the United States.

Foreign exchange market
A market in which households, firms, and governments buy and sell national currencies.

Exchange rate
The price of one nation's currency in terms of the currency of another country.

Demand for and Supply of Foreign Currency

You wish to purchase a Japanese-made laptop computer directly from the manufacturer. To do so, you must have Japanese yen. You go to the foreign exchange market (or your U.S. bank). Your desire to buy the Japanese laptop computer therefore causes you to offer (supply) dollars to the foreign exchange market. Your demand for Japanese yen is equivalent to your supply of U.S. dollars to the foreign exchange market.

Every U.S. transaction involving the importation of foreign goods constitutes a supply of dollars and a demand for some foreign currency, and the opposite is true for export transactions.

In this case, the import transaction constitutes a demand for Japanese yen.

In our example, we will assume that only two goods are being traded, Japanese laptop computers and U.S. microprocessors. The U.S. demand for Japanese laptop computers

Flexible exchange rates
Exchange rates that are allowed to fluctuate in the open market in response to changes in supply and demand. Sometimes called *floating exchange rates*.

creates a supply of dollars and demand for yen in the foreign exchange market. Similarly, the Japanese demand for U.S. microprocessors creates a supply of yen and a demand for dollars in the foreign exchange market. Under a system of **flexible exchange rates,** the supply of and demand for dollars and yen in the foreign exchange market will determine the equilibrium foreign exchange rate. The equilibrium exchange rate will tell us how many yen a dollar can be exchanged for—that is, the dollar price of yen—or how many dollars (or fractions of a dollar) a yen can be exchanged for—the yen price of dollars.

The Equilibrium Foreign Exchange Rate

To determine the equilibrium foreign exchange rate, we have to find out what determines the demand for and supply of foreign exchange. We will ignore for the moment any speculative aspect of buying foreign exchange. That is, we assume that there are no individuals who wish to buy yen simply because they think that their price will go up in the future.

The idea of an exchange rate is no different from the idea of paying a certain price for something you want to buy. If you like coffee, you know you have to pay about 75 cents a cup. If the price went up to $2.50, you would probably buy fewer cups. If the price went down to 25 cents, you might buy more. In other words, the demand curve for cups of coffee, expressed in terms of dollars, slopes downward following the law of demand. The demand curve for yen slopes downward also, and we will see why.

Go to www.econtoday.com/chap34 for recent data from the Federal Reserve Bank of St. Louis on the exchange value of the U.S. dollar relative to the major currencies of the world.

Let's think more closely about the demand schedule for yen. Let's say that it costs you 1 cent to purchase 1 yen; that is the exchange rate between dollars and yen. If tomorrow you had to pay $1\frac{1}{4}$ cents ($0.0125) for the same yen, the exchange rate would have changed. Looking at such a change, we would say that there has been an **appreciation** in the value of the yen in the foreign exchange market. But another way to view this increase in the value of the yen is to say that there has been a **depreciation** in the value of the dollar in the foreign exchange market. The dollar used to buy 100 yen; tomorrow, the dollar will be able to buy only 80 yen at a price of $1\frac{1}{4}$ cents per yen. If the dollar price of yen rises, you will probably demand fewer yen. Why? The answer lies in looking at the reason you and others demand yen in the first place.

Appreciation
An increase in the exchange value of one nation's currency in terms of the currency of another nation.

Depreciation
A decrease in the exchange value of one nation's currency in terms of the currency of another nation.

How do you suppose that a significant appreciation of the euro relative to the dollar affects U.S. imports of French wines?

International EXAMPLE

The Euro's Value Is Up, So French Wine Exports Are Down

Between 2002 and 2005, French wine exports to the United States dropped by nearly 18 percent. Some wine experts blamed part of the decline on what they perceived to be a drop in the overall quality of French wines. Others argued that during the 2001–2002 recession, U.S. residents seeking lower-priced wines had developed a taste for less expensive home-grown varieties. A few media commentators even attributed the drop to U.S. residents' unhappiness with the French government's foreign policies.

Economists offered a more fundamental explanation. During 2003, the dollar depreciated by almost 20 percent relative to the euro. Even if the euro price of a bottle of an elite

French Bordeaux wine held steady at around €200 between 2002 and 2003, U.S. residents had to give up nearly 20 percent more dollars to purchase it. The effective increase in the U.S. price of French wines generated a reduction in the quantity demanded by U.S. residents. Thus French wine exports to the United States declined.

For Critical Analysis
What do you predict will happen, other things being equal, to French exports of wine to the United States if the dollar appreciates considerably in relation to the euro?

Appreciation and Depreciation of Japanese Yen. Recall that in our example, you and others demand yen to buy Japanese laptop computers. The demand curve for Japanese laptop computers, we will assume, follows the law of demand and therefore slopes downward. If it costs more U.S. dollars to buy the same quantity of Japanese laptop computers, presumably you and other U.S. residents will not buy the same quantity; your quantity demanded will be less. We say that your demand for Japanese yen is *derived from* your demand for Japanese laptop computers. In panel (a) of Figure 34-2 on the next page, we present the hypothetical demand schedule for Japanese laptop computers by a representative set of U.S. consumers during a typical week. In panel (b), we show graphically the U.S. demand curve for Japanese yen in terms of U.S. dollars taken from panel (a).

An Example of Derived Demand. Let us assume that the price of a Japanese laptop computer in Japan is 100,000 yen. Given that price, we can find the number of yen required to purchase up to 500 Japanese laptop computers. That information is given in panel (c) of Figure 34-2. If purchasing one laptop computer requires 100,000 yen, 500 laptop computers require 50 million yen. Now we have enough information to determine the derived demand curve for Japanese yen. If 1 yen costs 1 cent, a laptop computer would cost $1,000 (100,000 yen per computer $\times$ 1 cent per yen = $1,000 per computer). At $1,000 per computer, the representative group of U.S. consumers would, we see from panel (a) of Figure 34-2, demand 500 laptop computers.

From panel (c), we see that 50 million yen would be demanded to buy the 500 laptop computers. We show this quantity demanded in panel (d). In panel (e), we draw the derived demand curve for yen. Now consider what happens if the price of yen goes up to $1\frac{1}{4}$ cents ($0.0125). A Japanese laptop computer priced at 100,000 yen in Japan would now cost $1,250. From panel (a), we see that at $1,250 per computer, 300 laptop computers will be imported from Japan into the United States by our representative group of U.S. consumers. From panel (c), we see that 300 computers would require 30 million yen to be purchased; thus, in panels (d) and (e), we see that at a price of $1\frac{1}{4}$ cents per yen, the quantity demanded will be 30 million yen.

We continue similar calculations all the way up to a price of $1\frac{1}{2}$ cents ($0.0150) per yen. At that price, a Japanese laptop computer costing 100,000 yen in Japan would cost $1,500, and our representative U.S. consumers would import only 100 laptop computers.

Downward-Sloping Derived Demand. As can be expected, as the price of yen rises, the quantity demanded will fall. The only difference here from the standard demand analysis developed in Chapter 3 and used throughout this text is that the demand for yen is derived from the demand for a final product—Japanese laptop computers in our example.

Supply of Japanese Yen. Assume that Japanese laptop manufacturers buy U.S. microprocessors. The supply of Japanese yen is a derived supply in that it is derived from the Japanese demand for U.S. microprocessors. We could go through an example similar to the one for laptop computers to come up with a supply schedule of Japanese yen in Japan. It slopes upward. Obviously, the Japanese want dollars to purchase U.S. goods. Japanese residents will be willing to supply more yen when the dollar price of yen goes up, because they can then buy more U.S. goods with the same quantity of yen. That is, the yen would be worth more in exchange for U.S. goods than when the dollar price for yen was lower.

An Example. Let's take an example. Suppose a U.S.-produced microprocessor costs $200. If the exchange rate is 1 cent per yen, a Japanese resident will have to come up with 20,000 yen (= $200 at $0.0100 per yen) to buy one microprocessor. If, however, the exchange rate goes up to $1\frac{1}{4}$ cents for yen, a Japanese resident must come up with only

Panel (a)
Demand Schedule for Japanese Laptop Computers in the United States per Week

Price per Unit	Quantity Demanded
$1,500	100
1,250	300
1,000	500
750	700

Panel (b)
U.S. Demand Curve for Japanese Laptop Computers

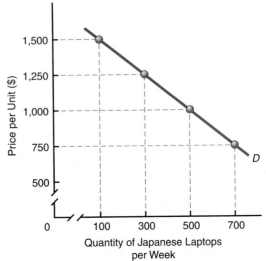

Panel (c)
Yen Required to Purchase Quantity Demanded (at P = 100,000 yen per computer)

Quantity Demanded	Yen Required (millions)
100	10
300	30
500	50
700	70

Panel (d)
Derived Demand Schedule for Yen in the United States with Which to Pay for Imports of Laptops

Dollar Price of One Yen	Dollar Price of Computers	Quantity of Computers Demanded	Quantity of Yen Demanded per Week (millions)
$ 0.0150	$1,500	100	10
0.0125	1,250	300	30
0.0100	1,000	500	50
0.0075	750	700	70

Panel (e)
U.S. Derived Demand for Yen

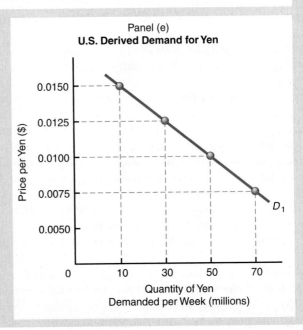

FIGURE 34-2
Deriving the Demand for Yen
In panel (a), we show the demand schedule for Japanese laptop computers in the United States, expressed in terms of dollars per computer. In panel (b), we show the demand curve, D, which slopes downward. In panel (c), we show the number of yen required to purchase up to 700 laptop computers. If the price per laptop computer in Japan is 100,000 yen, we can now find the quantity of yen needed to pay for the various quantities demanded. In panel (d), we see the derived demand for yen in the United States in order to purchase the various quantities of computers given in panel (a). The resultant demand curve, D_1, is shown in panel (e). This is the U.S. derived demand for yen.

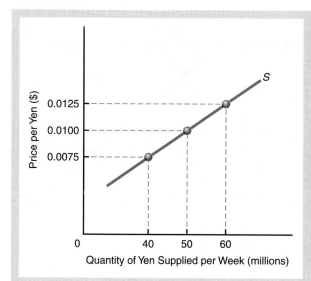

FIGURE 34-3
The Supply of Japanese Yen
If the market price of a U.S.-produced microprocessor is $200, then at an exchange rate of $0.0100 per yen (1 cent per yen), the price of the microprocessor to a Japanese consumer is 20,000 yen. If the exchange rate rises to $0.0125 per yen, the Japanese price of the microprocessor falls to 16,000 yen. This induces an increase in the quantity of microprocessors demanded by Japanese consumers and consequently an increase in the quantity of yen supplied in exchange for dollars in the foreign exchange market. In contrast, if the exchange rate falls to $0.0075 per yen, the Japanese price of the microprocessor rises to 26,667 yen. This causes a decrease in the quantity of microprocessors demanded by Japanese consumers. As a result, there is a decline in the quantity of yen supplied in exchange for dollars in the foreign exchange market.

16,000 yen (= $200 at $0.0125 per yen) to buy a U.S. microprocessor. At this lower price (in yen) of U.S. microprocessors, the Japanese will demand a larger quantity. In other words, as the price of yen goes up in terms of dollars, the quantity of U.S. microprocessors demanded will go up, and hence the quantity of yen supplied will go up. Therefore, the supply schedule of yen, which is derived from the Japanese demand for U.S. goods, will slope upward.*

We could easily work through a detailed numerical example to show that the supply curve of Japanese yen slopes upward. Rather than do that, we will simply draw it as upward sloping in Figure 34-3.

Total Demand for and Supply of Japanese Yen. Let us now look at the total demand for and supply of Japanese yen. We take all consumers of Japanese laptop computer and of U.S. microprocessors and put their demands for and supplies of yen together into one diagram. Thus we are showing the total demand for and total supply of Japanese yen. The horizontal axis in Figure 34-4 on the following page represents the quantity of foreign exchange—the number of yen per year. The vertical axis represents the exchange rate—the price of foreign currency (yen) expressed in dollars (per yen). The foreign currency price of $0.0125 per yen means it will cost you $1\frac{1}{4}$ cents to buy 1 yen. At the foreign currency price of $0.0100 per yen, you know that it will cost you 1 cent to buy 1 yen. The equilibrium, *E*, is again established at 1 cent for 1 yen.

In our hypothetical example, assuming that there are only representative groups of laptop computer consumers in the United States and microprocessor consumers in Japan, the equilibrium exchange rate will be set at 1 cent per yen, or 100 yen to one dollar.

---

*Actually, the supply schedule of foreign currency will be upward sloping if we assume that the demand for U.S. imported microprocessors on the part of the Japanese is price-elastic. If the demand schedule for microprocessors is inelastic, the supply schedule will be negatively sloped. In the case of unit elasticity of demand, the supply schedule for yen will be a vertical line. Throughout the rest of this chapter, we will assume that demand is price-elastic. It turns out that the price elasticity of demand tells us whether total expenditures by microprocessors purchasers in Japan will rise or fall when the yen drops in value. In the long run, it is quite realistic to think that the price elasticity of demand for imports is numerically greater than 1 anyway.

FIGURE 34-4
Total Demand for and Supply of Japanese Yen
The market supply curve for Japanese yen results from the total demand for U.S. microprocessors. The demand curve, D, slopes downward like most demand curves, and the supply curve, S, slopes upward. The foreign exchange price, or the U.S. dollar price of yen, is given on the vertical axis. The number of yen is represented on the horizontal axis. If the foreign exchange rate is $0.0125—that is, if it takes 1¼ cents to buy 1 yen—U.S. residents will demand 2 trillion yen. The equilibrium exchange rate is at the intersection of D and S, or point E. The equilibrium exchange rate is $0.0100 (1 cent). At this point, 3 trillion yen are both demanded and supplied each year.

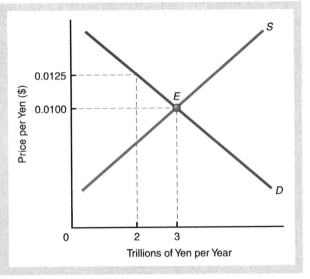

This equilibrium is not established because U.S. residents like to buy yen or because the Japanese like to buy dollars. Rather, the equilibrium exchange rate depends on how many microprocessors the Japanese want and how many Japanese laptop computers U.S. residents want (given their respective incomes, their tastes, and the relative price of laptop computers and microprocessors).*

A Shift in Demand. Assume that a successful advertising campaign by U.S. computer importers has caused U.S. demand for Japanese laptop computers to rise. U.S. residents demand more laptop computers at all prices. Their demand curve for Japanese laptop computers has shifted outward to the right.

The increased demand for Japanese laptop computers can be translated into an increased demand for yen. All U.S. residents clamoring for Japanese laptop computers will supply more dollars to the foreign exchange market while demanding more Japanese yen to pay for the computers. Figure 34-5 presents a new demand schedule, D_2, for Japanese yen; this demand schedule is to the right of the original demand schedule. If the Japanese do not change their desire for U.S. microprocessors, the supply schedule for Japanese yen will remain stable.

A new equilibrium will be established at a higher exchange rate. In our particular example, the new equilibrium is established at an exchange rate of $0.0120 per yen. It now takes 1.2 cents to buy 1 Japanese yen, whereas formerly it took 1 cent. This will be translated into an increase in the price of Japanese laptop computers to U.S. residents and as a decrease in the price of U.S. microprocessors to the Japanese. For example, a Japanese laptop computer priced at 100,000 yen that sold for $1,000 in the United States will now be priced at $1,200. Conversely, a U.S. microprocessor priced at $50 that previously sold for 5,000 yen in Japan will now sell for 4,167 yen.

What do you think has happened to the dollar price of South Africa's currency, the rand, as a result of increases in world demand for South African goods and financial assets?

---

*Remember that we are dealing with a two-country world in which we are considering only the exchange of U.S. microprocessors and Japanese laptop computers. In the real world, more than just goods and services are exchanged among countries. Some U.S. residents buy Japanese financial assets; some Japanese residents buy U.S. financial assets. We are ignoring such transactions for the moment.

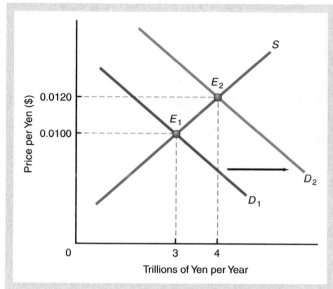

FIGURE 34-5
A Shift in the Demand Schedule
The demand schedule for Japanese laptop computers shifts to the right, causing the derived demand schedule for yen to shift to the right also. We have shown this as a shift from D_1 to D_2. We have assumed that the Japanese supply schedule for yen has remained stable—that is, Japanese demand for U.S. microprocessors has remained constant. The old equilibrium foreign exchange rate was $0.0100 (1 cent). The new equilibrium exchange rate will be E_2. It will now cost $0.0120 (1.2 cents) to buy 1 yen. The higher price of yen will be translated into a higher U.S. dollar price for Japanese laptop computers and a lower Japanese yen price for U.S. microprocessors.

International E X A M P L E

South Africa's Currency Appreciation

The global demand for gold and platinum, which are key South African export goods, has increased significantly since the end of 2001. In addition, South African interest rates rose relative to many other nations' interest rates after 2001, which induced residents of other nations to hold more South African financial assets. As people outside South Africa have sought to acquire more of its gold, platinum, and financial assets, the demand for its currency, the rand, has also increased. The result has been an increase in the dollar price of the rand. At the end of 2001, the rand's dollar price was only about $7\frac{1}{2}$ cents. Today, it is more than twice as high, at nearly $15\frac{1}{2}$ cents.

For Critical Analysis
As the rand's dollar price has increased, what has happened to the dollar price of gold and platinum produced in South Africa?

A Shift in Supply. We just assumed that the U.S. demand for Japanese laptop computers had shifted due to a successful ad campaign. Because the demand for Japanese yen is a derived demand by U.S. residents for laptop computers, this is translated into a shift in the demand curve for yen. As an alternative exercise, we might assume that the supply curve of Japanese yen shifts outward to the right. Such a supply shift could occur for many reasons, one of which is a relative rise in the Japanese price level. For example, if the prices of all Japanese-manufactured computer components went up 100 percent in yen, U.S. microprocessors would become relatively cheaper. That would mean that Japanese residents would want to buy more U.S. microprocessors. But remember that when they want to buy more U.S. microprocessors, they supply more yen to the foreign exchange market.

Thus we see in Figure 34-6 (p. 814) that the supply curve of Japanese yen moves from S to S_1. In the absence of restrictions—that is, in a system of flexible exchange rates—the new equilibrium exchange rate will be 1 yen equals $0.0050, or $\frac{1}{2}$ cent equals 1 yen. The quantity of yen demanded and supplied will increase from 3 trillion per year to 5 trillion

> **Economics Front and Center**
>
> To contemplate whether governments' announcements of their *preferred* levels of exchange rates can influence *actual* levels of exchange rates, read the case study, **Can Government Statements Move Exchange Rates?** on page 820.

FIGURE 34-6
A Shift in the Supply of Japanese Yen
There has been a shift in the supply curve for Japanese yen. The new equilibrium will occur at E_1, meaning that $0.0050 ($\frac{1}{2}$ cent), rather than $0.0100 (1 cent), will now buy 1 yen. After the exchange rate adjustment, the annual amount of yen demanded and supplied will increase from 3 trillion to 5 trillion.

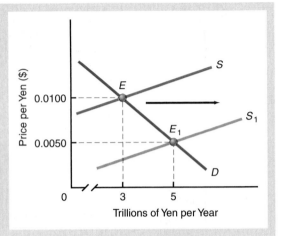

per year. We say, then, that in a flexible international exchange rate system, shifts in the demand for and supply of foreign currencies will cause changes in the equilibrium foreign exchange rates. Those rates will remain in effect until supply or demand shifts.

Market Determinants of Exchange Rates

The foreign exchange market is affected by many other variables in addition to changes in relative price levels, including the following:

- *Changes in real interest rates.* If the U.S. interest rate, corrected for people's expectations of inflation, abruptly increases relative to the rest of the world, international investors elsewhere will increase their demand for dollar-denominated assets, thereby increasing the demand for dollars in foreign exchange markets. An increased demand for dollars in foreign exchange markets, other things held constant, will cause the dollar to appreciate and other currencies to depreciate.
- *Changes in productivity.* Whenever one country's productivity increases relative to another's, the former country will become more price-competitive in world markets. At lower prices, the quantity of its exports demanded will increase. Thus there will be an increase in the demand for its currency.
- *Changes in consumer preferences.* If Germany's citizens suddenly develop a taste for U.S.-made automobiles, this will increase the derived demand for U.S. dollars in foreign exchange markets.
- *Perceptions of economic stability.* As already mentioned, if the United States looks economically and politically more stable relative to other countries, more foreign residents will want to put their savings into U.S. assets than in their own domestic assets. This will increase the demand for dollars.

CONCEPTS in Brief

- The foreign exchange rate is the rate at which one country's currency can be exchanged for another's.
- The demand for foreign exchange is a derived demand; it is derived from the demand for foreign goods and services

(and financial assets). The supply of foreign exchange is derived from foreign residents' demands for domestic goods and services.

- The demand curve of foreign exchange slopes downward, and the supply curve of foreign exchange slopes upward. The equilibrium foreign exchange rate occurs at the intersection of the demand and supply curves for a currency.

- A shift in the demand for foreign goods will result in a shift in the demand for foreign exchange, thereby changing the equilibrium foreign exchange rate. A shift in the supply of foreign currency will also cause a change in the equilibrium exchange rate.

To test your understanding of the concepts covered in this section, go to the Online Review at www.myeconlab.com/miller.

THE GOLD STANDARD AND THE INTERNATIONAL MONETARY FUND

The current system of more or less freely floating exchange rates is a recent development. We have had, in the past, periods of a gold standard, fixed exchange rates under the International Monetary Fund, and variants of the two.

The Gold Standard

Until the 1930s, many nations were on a gold standard. The value of their domestic currency was tied directly to gold. Nations operating under this gold standard agreed to redeem their currencies for a fixed amount of gold at the request of any holder of that currency. Although gold was not necessarily the means of exchange for world trade, it was the unit to which all currencies under the gold standard were pegged. And because all currencies in the system were linked to gold, exchange rates between those currencies were fixed. Indeed, the gold standard has been offered as the prototype of a fixed exchange rate system. The heyday of the gold standard was from about 1870 to 1914.

There was (and always is) a relationship between the balance of payments and changes in domestic money supplies throughout the world. Under a gold standard, the international financial market reached equilibrium through the effect of gold flows on each country's money supply. When a nation suffered a deficit in its balance of payments, more gold would flow out than in. Because the domestic money supply was based on gold, an outflow of gold to foreign residents caused an automatic reduction in the domestic money supply. This caused several things to happen. Interest rates rose, thereby attracting foreign capital and reducing any deficit in the balance of payments. At the same time, the reduction in the money supply was equivalent to a restrictive monetary policy, which caused national output and prices to fall. Imports were discouraged and exports were encouraged, thereby again increasing net exports.

Two problems plagued the gold standard. One was that by varying the value of its currency in response to changes in the quantity of gold, a nation gave up control of its domestic monetary policy. Another was that the world's commerce was at the mercy of gold discoveries. Throughout history, each time new veins of gold were found, desired expenditures on goods and services increased. If production of goods and services failed to increase proportionately, inflation resulted.

Bretton Woods and the International Monetary Fund

In 1944, as World War II was ending, representatives from the world's capitalist countries met in Bretton Woods, New Hampshire, to create a new international payment system to replace the gold standard, which had collapsed during the 1930s. The Bretton Woods Agreement Act was signed on July 31, 1945, by President Harry Truman. It created a new permanent institution, the International Monetary Fund (IMF), to administer the agreement and to lend to member countries that were experiencing significant balance of payments deficits. The arrangements thus provided are now called the old IMF system or the Bretton Woods system.

Par value
The officially determined value of a currency.

Member governments maintained the value of their currencies within 1 percent of the declared **par value**—the officially determined value. The United States, which owned most of the world's gold stock, was similarly obligated to maintain gold prices within a 1 percent margin of the official rate of $35 an ounce. Except for a transitional arrangement permitting a one-time adjustment of up to 10 percent in par value, members could alter exchange rates thereafter only with the approval of the IMF.

On August 15, 1971, President Richard Nixon suspended the convertibility of the dollar into gold. On December 18, 1971, the United States officially devalued the dollar—that is, lowered its official value—relative to the currencies of 14 major industrial nations. Finally, on March 16, 1973, the finance ministers of the European Economic Community (now the European Union) announced that they would let their currencies float against the dollar, something Japan had already begun doing with its yen. Since 1973, the United States and most other trading countries have had either freely floating exchange rates or managed ("dirty") floating exchange rates, in which their governments or central banks intervene from time to time to try to influence world market exchange rates.

FIXED VERSUS FLOATING EXCHANGE RATES

The United States went off the Bretton Woods system of fixed exchange rates in 1973. As Figure 34-7 indicates, many other nations of the world have been less willing to permit the values of their currencies to vary in the foreign exchange markets.

Fixing the Exchange Rate

How did nations fix their exchange rates in years past? How do many countries accomplish this today? Figure 34-8 shows the market for ringgit, the currency of Malaysia. At the initial equilibrium point E_1, U.S. residents had to give up $0.263 (26.3 cents) to obtain 1 ringgit. Suppose now that there is an increase in the supply of ringgit for dollars, perhaps because Malaysian residents wish to buy more U.S. goods. Other things being equal, the result would be a movement to point E_2 in Figure 34-8. The dollar value of the ringgit would fall to $0.200 (20 cents).

FIGURE 34-7
Current Foreign Exchange Rate Arrangements
Currently, 22 percent of the member nations of the International Monetary Fund have an independent float, and just over 22 percent have a managed float exchange rate arrangement. Among countries with a fixed exchange rate, more than 33 percent uses a fixed U.S. dollar exchange rate. Slightly over 21 percent of all nations use the currencies of other nations instead of issuing their own currencies.

Source: International Monetary Fund.

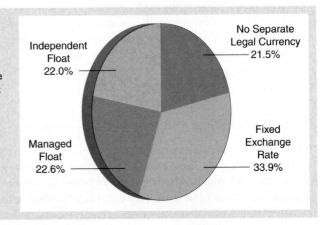

Independent Float 22.0%

No Separate Legal Currency 21.5%

Managed Float 22.6%

Fixed Exchange Rate 33.9%

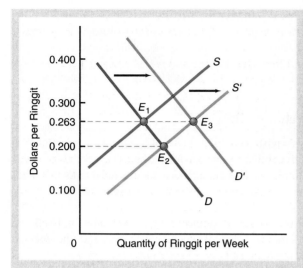

FIGURE 34-8
A Fixed Exchange Rate
This figure illustrates how the Bank of Malaysia could fix the dollar-ringgit exchange rate in the face of an increase in the supply of ringgit caused by a rise in the demand for U.S. goods by Malaysian residents. In the absence of any action by the Bank of Malaysia, the result would be a movement from point E_1 to point E_2. The dollar value of the ringgit would fall from $0.263 to $0.200. The Bank of Malaysia can prevent this exchange rate change by purchasing ringgit with dollars in the foreign exchange market, thereby raising the demand for ringgit. At the new equilibrium point, E_3, the ringgit's value remains at $0.263.

To prevent a ringgit depreciation from occurring, however, the Bank of Malaysia, the central bank, could increase the demand for ringgit in the foreign exchange market by purchasing ringgit with dollars. The Bank of Malaysia can do this using dollars that it has on hand as part of its *foreign exchange reserves.* All central banks hold reserves of foreign currencies. Because the U.S. dollar is a key international currency, the Bank of Malaysia and other central banks typically hold billions of dollars in reserve so that they can make transactions such as the one in this example. Note that a sufficiently large purchase of ringgit could, as shown in Figure 34-8, cause the demand curve to shift rightward to achieve the new equilibrium point E_3, at which the ringgit's value remains at $0.263. Provided that it has enough dollar reserves on hand, the Bank of Malaysia could maintain—effectively fix—the exchange rate in the face of the fall in the demand for ringgit.

This is the manner in which the Bank of Malaysia has maintained the dollar-ringgit exchange rate since 1999. This basic approach—varying the amount of the national currency demanded at any given exchange rate in foreign exchange markets when necessary—is also the way that *any* central bank seeks to keep its nation's currency value unchanged in light of changing market forces.

Central banks can keep exchange rates fixed as long as they have enough foreign exchange reserves to deal with potentially long-lasting changes in the demand for or supply of their nation's currency.

What currencies do central banks most prefer to hold?

International E X A M P L E

Central Banks' Currencies of Choice

A central bank allocates its foreign exchange reserves based on its perception of which currencies are likely to prove most useful in altering the demand for its own nation's currency. Nearly 20 percent of all foreign exchange reserves held by all central

banks are euros. Just over 15 percent of their foreign exchange reserves are Japanese yen, British pounds, and miscellaneous other currencies not including the U.S. dollar. Dollars account for the remaining 65 percent of all the foreign exchange reserves of all central banks. Clearly, central banks view the dollar as the most useful currency to utilize if they should desire to alter the demand for their respective currencies in the world's foreign exchange markets.

For Critical Analysis
Why might the extent of a foreign currency's use in global trade and finance affect a central bank's willingness to include it among its foreign exchange reserves?

Pros and Cons of a Fixed Exchange Rate

Why might a nation such as Malaysia wish to keep the value of its currency from fluctuating? One reason is that changes in the exchange rate can affect the market values of assets that are denominated in foreign currencies. This can increase the financial risks that a nation's residents face, thereby forcing them to incur costs to avoid these risks.

Foreign exchange risk
The possibility that changes in the value of a nation's currency will result in variations in the market value of assets.

Hedge
A financial strategy that reduces the chance of suffering losses arising from foreign exchange risk.

Foreign Exchange Risk. The possibility that variations in the market value of assets can take place as a result of changes in the value of a nation's currency is the **foreign exchange risk** that residents of a country face because their nation's currency value can vary. For instance, if companies in Malaysia had many loans denominated in dollars but earned nearly all their revenues in ringgit from sales within Malaysia, a decline in the dollar value of the ringgit would mean that Malaysian companies would have to allocate a larger portion of their earnings to make the same *dollar* loan payments as before. Thus a fall in the ringgit's value would increase the operating costs of these companies, thereby reducing their profitability and raising the likelihood of eventual bankruptcy.

Limiting foreign exchange risk is a classic rationale for adopting a fixed exchange rate. Nevertheless, a country's residents are not defenseless against foreign exchange risk. In what is known as a **hedge,** they can adopt strategies intended to offset the risk arising from exchange rate variations. For example, a company in Malaysia that has significant euro earnings from sales in Germany but sizable loans from U.S. investors could arrange to convert its euro earnings into dollars via special types of foreign exchange contracts called *currency swaps.* The Malaysian company could likewise avoid holdings of ringgit and shield itself—*hedge*—against variations in the ringgit's value.

The Exchange Rate as a Shock Absorber. If fixing the exchange rate limits foreign exchange risk, why do so many nations allow the exchange rates to float? The answer must be that there are potential drawbacks associated with fixing exchange rates. One is that exchange rate variations can actually perform a valuable service for a nation's economy. Consider a situation in which residents of a nation speak only their own nation's language. As a result, the country's residents are very *immobile:* They cannot trade their labor skills outside their own nation's borders.

Now think about what happens if this nation chooses to fix its exchange rate. Imagine a situation in which other countries begin to sell products that are close substitutes for the products its people specialize in producing, causing a sizable drop in worldwide demand for the nation's goods. Over a short-run period in which prices and wages cannot adjust, the result will be a sharp decline in production of goods and services, a falloff in national income, and higher unemployment. Contrast this situation with one in which the exchange rate floats. In this case, a sizable decline in outside demand for the nation's products will cause it to experience a trade deficit, which will lead to a significant drop in the demand for that nation's currency. As a result, the nation's currency will experience a sizable depreciation, making the goods that the nation offers to sell abroad much less expensive in other countries. People abroad who continue to consume the nation's products will increase their purchases, and the nation's exports will increase. Its production will begin to recover somewhat, as will its residents' incomes. Unemployment will begin to fall.

This example illustrates how exchange rate variations can be beneficial, especially if a nation's residents are relatively immobile. It can be difficult, for example, for a Polish resident who has never studied Portuguese to make a move to Lisbon, even if she is highly qualified for available jobs there. If many residents of Poland face similar linguistic or cultural barriers, Poland could be better off with a floating exchange rate even if its residents must incur significant costs hedging against foreign exchange risk as a result.

Splitting the Difference: Dirty Floats and Target Zones

In recent years, national policymakers have tried to soften the choice between adopting a fixed exchange rate and allowing exchange rates full flexibility in the foreign exchange markets by "splitting the difference" between the two extremes.

A Dirty Float.
One way to split the difference is to let exchange rates float most of the time but "manage" exchange rate movements part of the time. U.S. policymakers have occasionally engaged in what is called a **dirty float,** the active management of flexible exchange rates. The management of flexible exchange rates has usually come about through international policy cooperation.

Dirty float
Active management of a floating exchange rate on the part of a country's government, often in cooperation with other nations.

Is it possible for nations to "manage" foreign exchange rates? Some economists do not think so. For example, economists Michael Bordo and Anna Schwartz studied the foreign exchange intervention actions coordinated by the Federal Reserve and the U.S. Treasury during the second half of the 1980s. Besides showing that such interventions were sporadic and variable, Bordo and Schwartz came to an even more compelling conclusion: Exchange rate interventions were trivial relative to the total trading of foreign exchange on a daily basis. For example, in April 1989, total foreign exchange trading amounted to $129 billion per day, yet the U.S. central bank purchased only $100 million in deutsche marks and yen during that entire month (and did so on a single day). For all of 1989, Fed purchases of marks and yen were only $17.7 billion, or the equivalent of less than 13 percent of the amount of an average day's trading in April of that year. Their conclusion is that foreign exchange market interventions by the U.S. central bank or the central banks of the other nations do not influence exchange rates in the long run.

Crawling Pegs.
Another approach to splitting the difference between fixed and floating exchange rates is called a **crawling peg.** This is an automatically adjusting target for the value of a nation's currency. For instance, a central bank might announce that it wants the value of its currency relative to the U.S. dollar to decline at an annual rate of 5 percent, a rate of depreciation that it feels is consistent with long-run market forces. The central bank would then try to buy or sell foreign exchange reserves in sufficient quantities to be sure that the currency depreciation takes place gradually, thereby reducing the foreign exchange risk faced by the nation's residents. In this way, a crawling peg functions like a floating exchange rate in the sense that the exchange rate can change over time. But it is like a fixed exchange rate in the sense that the central bank always tries to keep the exchange rate close to a target value. In this way, a crawling peg has elements of both kinds of exchange rate systems.

Crawling peg
An exchange rate arrangement in which a country pegs the value of its currency to the exchange value of another nation's currency but allows the par value to change at regular intervals.

Target Zones.
A third way to try to split the difference between fixed and floating exchange rates is to adopt an exchange rate **target zone.** Under this policy, a central bank announces that there are specific upper and lower *bands,* or limits, for permissible values for the exchange rate. Within those limits, which define the exchange rate target zone, the central bank permits the exchange rate to move flexibly. The central bank commits itself, however, to intervene in the foreign exchange markets to ensure that its nation's currency value will not rise above the upper band or fall below the lower band. For instance, if the

Target zone
A range of permitted exchange rate variations between upper and lower exchange rate bands that a central bank defends by selling or buying foreign exchange reserves.

exchange rate approaches the upper band, the central bank must sell foreign exchange reserves in sufficient quantities to prevent additional depreciation of its nation's currency. If the exchange rate approaches the lower band, the central bank must purchase sufficient amounts of foreign exchange reserves to halt any further currency appreciation.

In 1999, officials from the European Union attempted to get the U.S. and Japanese governments to agree to target zones for the exchange rate between the newly created euro, the dollar, and the yen. So far, however, no target zones have been created, and the euro has floated freely.

Concepts in Brief

- The International Monetary Fund was developed after World War II as an institution to maintain fixed exchange rates in the world. Since 1973, however, fixed exchange rates have disappeared in most major trading countries. For these nations, exchange rates are largely determined by the forces of demand and supply in foreign exchange markets.

- Many other nations, however, have tried to fix their exchange rates, with varying degrees of success. Although fixing the exchange rate helps protect a nation's residents from foreign exchange risk, this policy makes less mobile residents susceptible to greater volatility in income and employment. It can also expose the central bank to spo-

radic currency crises arising from unpredictable changes in world capital flows.

- Countries have experimented with exchange rate systems between the extremes of fixed and floating exchange rates. Under a dirty float, a central bank permits the value of its nation's currency to float in foreign exchange markets but intervenes from time to time to influence the exchange rate. Under a crawling peg, a central bank tries to push its nation's currency value in a desired direction. Pursuing a target zone policy, a central bank aims to keep the exchange rate between upper and lower bands, intervening only when the exchange rate approaches either limit.

To test your understanding of the concepts covered in this section, go to the Online Review at www.myeconlab.com/miller.

CASE STUDY: Economics Front and Center

Can Government Statements Move Exchange Rates?

Martin is an employee of the U.S. Department of the Treasury. He has been assigned to assist the Group of Seven (G-7) finance ministers representing the governments of the United States, Japan, Germany, France, the United Kingdom, Italy, and Canada.

The latest G-7 meeting is under way. The German, French, and Italian finance ministers have proposed that the group issue a joint statement calling on China to allow its currency, the yuan, to rise in value relative to the dollar and the euro. These three finance ministers contend that making this statement will signal to traders in foreign exchange markets that the G-7 governments are serious in their view that there is a need for yuan appreciation. Traders, the finance ministers argue, will respond by purchasing yuan in anticipation of a future increase in the currency's value. Thus the market demand for China's currency will rise, and it will appreciate. In this way, the G-7 nations can bring about the desired outcome without actually having to sell dollars and euros for yuan in foreign exchange markets.

Martin thinks back to 2004, when the G-7 issued an essentially identical statement. What actually occurred afterward was an appreciation of the *euro* relative to both Asian currencies *and* the dollar. Martin wonders if the German, French, and Italian foreign ministers really understand that exchange rates are determined by demand and supply, rather than by politicians' whims.

Points to Analyze

1. *If the German, French, and Italian governments could convince the European Central Bank (ECB) to try to bring about an appreciation of Asian currencies relative to the euro, what would the ECB have to do?*

2. *How might the ECB and the Federal Reserve coordinate efforts to induce appreciations of Asian currencies relative to both the euro and the dollar?*

Issues and Applications

Japan's Finance Ministry Learns a New Currency Trick

Since 2002, there has been a general tendency for the U.S. dollar to lose value relative to the Japanese yen. This decline in the dollar's value vis-à-vis the yen has effectively raised the prices that U.S. consumers must pay to purchase Japanese goods and services. To try to keep this from occurring, the Japanese government has added billions of dollars to its foreign exchange reserves. The aim of purchasing dollars has been to raise the demand for dollars, increase the dollar's value in terms of yen, and reduce the U.S. prices of Japanese goods and services.

Traditionally, it was easy for economists to tell when the Japanese government was engaging in efforts to prop up the dollar's value in terms of yen. Lately, however, the Japanese government has found ways to hide its efforts to prevent the yen from appreciating.

Concepts Applied

- Exchange Rate
- Foreign Exchange Reserves
- Foreign Exchange Market

Selling Yen to Keep the Dollar-Yen Exchange Rate from Dropping

At first, Japanese efforts to prevent the yen's value from rising relative to the dollar entailed adding more dollars to the nation's roughly $700 billion in total foreign exchange reserves. Offering more yen in exchange for dollars increased the supply of yen in the foreign exchange market, which pushed the equilibrium dollar-yen exchange rate back downward. As a consequence, fewer dollars were required in exchange for yen so that the effective prices that U.S. residents paid for Japanese goods and services were lower once more.

Actions to sell Japanese yen for dollars in the foreign exchange market were coordinated by the Japanese government's Finance Ministry. Sometimes the Finance Ministry would instruct the Bank of Japan to purchase dollars directly on its behalf. At other times, it would direct the Bank of Japan to ask a private Japanese bank to buy dollars on its behalf. After the private bank had completed the transaction, the Finance Ministry would transmit more yen to the bank in exchange for the dollars than the bank had paid for the dollars in the foreign exchange market. In this way, the bank would profit from purchasing the dollars, and the Finance Ministry

would accomplish its aim of increasing the supply of yen in the foreign exchange market.

Inducing Private Banks to Prevent the Yen from Appreciating

In the face of ongoing pressure for a yen appreciation, the Japanese Finance Ministry found itself on the verge of buying dollars, through its accounts with the Bank of Japan or with private banks, almost continually. Because Japan officially had a floating exchange rate, the Finance Ministry did not want to give the impression that it was trying to fix the dollar-yen exchange rate. Therefore, it searched for a way to disguise its efforts to prevent the yen from appreciating.

The method Finance Ministry found entailed operating solely through private banks instead of the Bank of Japan. As before, the Finance Ministry would place an order with a private bank to purchase dollars with yen. It would place a very large order so that other banks would know that the government had to be involved. This caused the other Japanese banks to anticipate a decline in the value of the yen generated by the government's action, which encouraged them to buy dollars in hopes of profiting from selling them after the yen's value had declined. When numerous banks purchased dollars with yen, the yen started to depreciate against the dollar, just as the Finance Ministry desired. In the meantime, the Finance Ministry would cancel its order for the original bank to purchase dollars with yen. This bank would go along because it also would be able to profit from selling dollars for yen after the yen's depreciation.

In this way, neither the Japanese Finance Ministry nor the Bank of Japan was *officially* involved in efforts to prevent a yen appreciation. Foreign exchange market traders knew better, of course, but as long as private banks could profit from the Finance Ministry's actions, they were willing to participate in its not-so-transparent scheme to hide its activities.

For Critical Analysis

1. Why do you suppose that the Japanese Finance Ministry wished to keep the U.S. prices of Japanese-produced goods and services from increasing?
2. Why do you suppose economists commonly argue that actions to move exchange rates in desired directions are successful only if a government and the central bank or private banks operating on its behalf are able to profit from their efforts? (Hint: Would Japanese banks have been willing to sell yen for dollars if they expected that the yen would appreciate in the future?)

Web Resources

1. To read about the Bank of Japan's own perspective on its numerous foreign exchange interventions over the years, go to www.econtoday.com/chap34.
2. Go to the link available at www.econtoday.com/chap34 to learn more about U.S. interventions in foreign exchange markets from the Federal Reserve Bank of New York.

Research Project

Make a list of factors that are likely to influence whether a government's effort to alter the exchange value of its currency is likely to succeed in the near term. Why are the short-run effects of such efforts likely to be more pronounced than the long-run effects? Explain.

SUMMARY DISCUSSION of Learning Objectives

1. **The Balance of Trade versus the Balance of Payments:** The balance of trade is the difference between exports of goods and imports of goods during a given period. The balance of payments is a system of accounts for all transactions between a nation's residents and the residents of other countries of the world. In addition to exports and imports, therefore, the balance of payments includes cross-border exchanges of services and financial assets within a given time interval.

2. **The Key Accounts Within the Balance of Payments:** There are three important accounts within the balance of payments. The current account measures net exchanges of goods and services, transfers, and income flows across a nation's borders. The capital account measures net flows of financial assets. The official reserve transactions account tabulates cross-border exchanges of financial assets involving the home nation's government and central bank as well as foreign governments and central banks.

Because each international exchange generates both an inflow and an outflow, the sum of the balances on all three accounts must equal zero.

3. **Exchange Rate Determination in the Market for Foreign Exchange:** From the perspective of the United States, the demand for a nation's currency by U.S. residents is derived largely from the demand for imports from that nation. Likewise, the supply of a nation's currency is derived mainly from the supply of U.S. exports to that country. The equilibrium exchange rate is the rate of exchange between the dollar and the other nation's currency at which the quantity of the currency demanded is equal to the quantity supplied.

4. **Factors That Can Induce Changes in Equilibrium Exchange Rates:** The equilibrium exchange rate changes in response to changes in the demand for or supply of another nation's currency. Changes in desired flows of exports or imports, real interest rates, productivity in one

nation relative to productivity in another nation, tastes and preferences of consumers, and perceptions of economic stability are key factors that can affect the positions of the demand and supply curves in foreign exchange markets. Thus changes in these factors can induce variations in equilibrium exchange rates.

5. **How Policymakers Can Attempt to Keep Exchange Rates Fixed:** If the current price of another nation's currency in terms of the home currency starts to fall below the level where the home country wants it to remain, the home country's central bank can use reserves of the other nation's currency to purchase the home currency in foreign exchange markets. This raises the demand for the home currency and thereby pushes up the currency's value in terms of the other nation's currency. In this way, the home country can keep the exchange rate fixed at a desired value, as long as it has sufficient reserves of the other currency to use for this purpose.

6. **Alternative Approaches to Limiting Exchange Rate Variability:** Today, many nations permit their exchange rates to vary in foreign exchange markets. Others pursue policies that limit the variability of exchange rates. Some engage in a dirty float, in which they manage exchange rates, often in cooperation with other nations. Some establish crawling pegs, in which the target value of the exchange rate is adjusted automatically over time. And some establish target zones, with upper and lower limits on the extent to which exchange rates are allowed to vary.

KEY TERMS AND CONCEPTS

accounting identities (800)

appreciation (808)

balance of payments (800)

balance of trade (800)

capital account (804)

crawling peg (819)

current account (802)

depreciation (808)

dirty float (819)

exchange rate (807)

flexible exchange rates (808)

foreign exchange market (807)

foreign exchange risk (818)

hedge (818)

International Monetary Fund (806)

par value (816)

special drawing rights (SDRs) (806)

target zone (820)

PROBLEMS

Answers to the odd-numbered problems appear at the back of the book.

34-1. Over the course of a year, a nation tracked its foreign transactions and arrived at the following amounts:

Merchandise exports	500
Service exports	75
Net unilateral transfers	10
Domestic assets abroad (capital outflows)	−200
Foreign assets at home (capital inflows)	300
Changes in official reserves	−35
Merchandise imports	600
Service imports	50

What is this nation's balance of trade, current account balance, and capital account balance?

34-2. Whenever the United States reaches record levels on its current account deficit, Congress flirts with the idea of restricting imported goods. Would trade restrictions like those studied in Chapter 33 be appropriate if Congress desires mutual gains from trade?

34-3. Explain how the following events would affect the market for the Mexican peso.

a. Improvements in Mexican production technology yield superior guitars, and many musicians around the world desire these guitars.

b. Perceptions of political instability surrounding regular elections in Mexico make international investors nervous about future business prospects in Mexico.

34-4. Explain how the following events would affect the market for South Africa's currency, the rand.

a. A rise in U.S. inflation causes many U.S. residents to seek to buy gold, which is a major South African export good, as a hedge against inflation.

b. Major discoveries of the highest-quality diamonds ever found occur in Russia and Central Asia, causing a significant decline in purchases of South African diamonds.

34-5. Explain how the following events would affect the market for Thailand's currency, the baht.

a. Market interest rates on financial assets denominated in baht decline relative to market interest rates on financial assets denominated in other nations' currencies.

b. Thailand's productivity increases relative to productivity in other countries.

34-6. Suppose that the following two events take place in the market for Kuwait's currency, the dinar: The U.S. demand for oil, Kuwait's main export good, declines, and market interest rates on financial assets denominated in dinar decrease relative to U.S. interest rates. What happens to the dollar price of the dinar? Does the dinar appreciate or depreciate relative to the dollar?

34-7. Suppose that the following two events take place in the market for China's currency, the yuan: U.S. parents are more willing than before to buy action figures and other Chinese toy exports, and China's government tightens restrictions on the amount of U.S. dollar–denominated financial assets that Chinese residents may legally purchase. What happens to the dollar price of the yuan? Does the yuan appreciate or depreciate relative to the dollar?

34-8. On Wednesday, the exchange rate between the euro and the U.S. dollar was $1.20 per euro. On Thursday, it was $1.18. Did the dollar appreciate or depreciate against the euro? By how much?

34-9. On Wednesday, the exchange rate between the euro and the U.S. dollar was $1.17 per euro and the exchange rate between the Canadian dollar and the U.S. dollar was U.S. $0.79 per Canadian dollar. What is the exchange rate between the Canadian dollar and the euro?

34-10. Suppose that signs of an improvement in the Japanese economy lead international investors to resume lending to the Japanese government and businesses. Poli-

cymakers, however, are worried about how this will influence the yen. How would this event affect the market for the yen? How should the central bank, the Bank of Japan, respond to this event if it wants to keep the value of the yen unchanged?

34-11. Briefly explain the differences between a flexible exchange rate system, a fixed exchange rate system, a dirty float, and the use of target zones.

34-12. Explain how each of the following would affect Canada's balance of payments.

a. Canada's rate of inflation falls below that of the United States, its main trading partner.

b. The possibility of Quebec's separating from the federation frightens international investors.

34-13. Suppose that under a gold standard, the U.S. dollar is pegged to gold at a rate of $35 per ounce and the pound sterling is pegged to gold at a rate of £17.50 per ounce. Explain how the gold standard constitutes an exchange rate arrangement between the dollar and the pound. What is the exchange rate between the U.S. dollar and the pound sterling?

34-14. Suppose that under the Bretton Woods system, the dollar is pegged to gold at a rate of $35 per ounce and the pound sterling is pegged to the dollar at a rate of $2 = £1. If the dollar is devalued against gold and the pegged rate is changed to $40 per ounce, what does this imply for the exchange value of the pound?

34-15. Suppose that the Bank of China wishes to peg the rate of exchange of its currency, the yuan, in terms of the U.S. dollar. In each of the following situations, should it add to or subtract from its dollar foreign exchange reserves? Why?

a. U.S. parents begin buying fewer Chinese-manufactured toys for their children.

b. U.S. interest rates rise relative to interest rates in China, so Chinese residents seek to purchase additional U.S. financial assets.

c. Chinese furniture manufacturers produce high-quality early American furniture and successfully export large quantities of the furniture to the United States.

ECONOMICS ON THE NET

Daily Exchange Rates It is an easy matter to keep up with changes in exchange rates every day using the Web site of the Federal Reserve Bank of New York. In this application, you will learn how hard it is to predict exchange rate movements, and you will get some practice thinking about what factors can cause exchange rates to change.

Title: The Federal Reserve Bank of New York: Foreign Exchange 12 Noon Rates

Navigation: Go to **www.econtoday.com/chap34** to visit the Federal Reserve Bank of New York's Statistics home page. Click on *Foreign Exchange 12 Noon Rates.*

Application Answer the following questions.

1. For each currency listed, how many dollars does it take to purchase a unit of the currency in the spot foreign exchange market?

2. For each day during a given week (or month), choose a currency from those listed and keep track of its value rel-

ative to the dollar. Based on your tabulations, try to predict the value of the currency at the end of the week *following* your data collections. Use any information you may have, or just do your best without any additional information. How far off did your prediction turn out to be?

For Group Study and Analysis Each day, you can also click on a report titled "Foreign Exchange 10 A.M. Rates," which shows exchange rates for a subset of countries listed in the noon report. Assign each country in the 10 A.M. report to a group. Ask the group to determine whether the currency's value appreciated or depreciated relative to the dollar between 10 A.M. and noon. In addition, ask each group to discuss what kinds of demand or supply shifts could have caused the change that occurred during this interval.

If your exam were tomorrow, would you be ready? For each chapter, MyEconLab Practice Tests and Study Plans pinpoint which sections you have mastered and which ones you need to study. That way, you are more efficient with your study time, and you are better prepared for your exams.

In addition to Practice Tests and your personalized Study Plan, you'll find the following media resources in MyEconLab:

1. *Graphs in Motion* animation of Figures 34-1, 34-3, 34-4, 34-5, and 34-6.
2. An Economics in Motion in-depth animation of Exchange Rates.
3. Videos featuring the author, Roger LeRoy Miller, on the following subjects:
   - Market Determinants of Foreign Exchange Rates
   - Pros and Cons of a Fixed Exchange Rate

4. Links to the Web sites cited in the marginal Internet Resources, Issues and Applications feature, and Economics on the Net activity.
5. Audio clips of all key terms, additional practice problems, and a PDF version of the material from the print Study Guide.
6. eThemes of the Times, which is a New York Times article to help you understand the real-world applications of what you are learning.

To see how it works, turn to page 16 and then go to **www.myeconlab.com/miller**.

Get Ahead of the Curve

Answers to Odd-Numbered Problems

CHAPTER 1

1-1. Economics is the study of how individuals allocate limited resources to satisfy unlimited wants.

  a. Among the factors that a rational, self-interested student will take into account are her income, the price of the textbook, her anticipation of how much she is likely to study the textbook, and how much studying the book is likely to affect her grade.

  b. A rational, self-interested government official will, for example, recognize that higher taxes will raise more funds for mass transit while making more voters, who have limited resources, willing to select replacement officials.

  c. A municipality's rational, self-interested government will, for instance, take into account that higher hotel taxes will produce more funds if as many visitors continue to stay at hotels, but the higher taxes will also discourage some visitors from spending nights at hotels.

1-3. Because wants are unlimited, the phrase applies to very high-income households as well as low- and middle-income households. Consider, for instance, a household that has a low income and unlimited wants at the beginning of the year. The household's wants will remain unlimited if it becomes a high-income household later in the year.

1-5. Sally is displaying rational behavior if all of these activities are in her self-interest. For example, Sally likely derives intrinsic value from volunteer and extracurricular activities and may believe that these activities, along with good grades, improve her prospects of finding a job after she completes her studies. Hence, these activities are in her self-interest even though they take away some study time.

1-7. If, for instance, your model indicates that each hour of study results in a 15 percentage-point gain on each test, you should spend 6 hours ($6 \times 15 = 90$) studying economics and 4 hours ($4 \times 15 = 60$) studying French.

1-9. **a.** Yes
  b. No
  c. Yes

1-11. Positive economic analysis deals with economics models with predictions that are statements of fact, which can be objectively proven or disproven. Normative analysis takes into account subjective personal or social values concerning the way things *ought* to be.

1-13. **a.** An increase in the supply of laptop computers, perhaps because of the entry of new computer manufacturers into the market, pushes their price back down.

  b. Another factor, such as higher hotel taxes at popular vacation destinations, makes vacation travel more expensive.

  c. Some other factor, such as a fall in market wages that workers can earn, discourages people from working additional hours.

APPENDIX A

A-1. **a.** Independent: price of a notebook; Dependent: quantity of notebooks
  b. Independent: work-study hours; Dependent: credit hours
  c. Independent: hours of study; Dependent: economics grade

A-3. **a.** above x axis; left of y axis
  b. below x axis, right of y axis
  c. on x axis; to right of y axis

A-5.

y	x
−20	−4
−10	−2
0	0
10	2
20	4

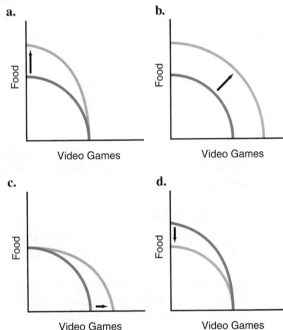

A-7. Each one-unit increase in *x* yields a 5-unit increase in *y*, so the slope given by the change in *y* corresponding to the change in *x* is equal to 5.

A-9. **a.** positive; each 1-unit rise in *x* induces a 5-unit increase in *y*.

  b. positive; each 1-unit rise in *x* induces a 1-unit increase in *y*.

  c. negative; each 1-unit rise in *x* induces a 3-unit decline in *y*.

CHAPTER 2

2-1. The opportunity cost of attending a class at 11:00 A.M. is the next-best use of that hour of the day. Likewise, the opportunity cost of attending an 8:00 A.M. class is the next-best use of that particular hour of the day. If you are an early riser, it is arguable that the opportunity cost of the 8:00 A.M. hour is lower, because you will already be up at that time but have fewer choices compared with the 11:00 A.M. hour when shops, recreation centers, and the like are open. If you are a late riser, it may be that the opportunity cost of the 8:00 A.M. hour is higher, because you place a relatively high value on an additional hour of sleep in the morning.

2-3. Each additional 10 points earned in economics costs 10 additional points in biology, so this PPC illustrates *constant* opportunity costs.

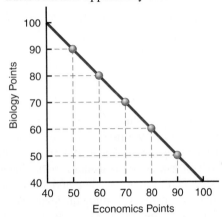

2-5. The $4,500 paid for tuition, room and board, and books are explicit costs and not opportunity costs. The $3,000 in forgone after-tax wages is the opportunity cost that the student incurs.

2-7.

a.

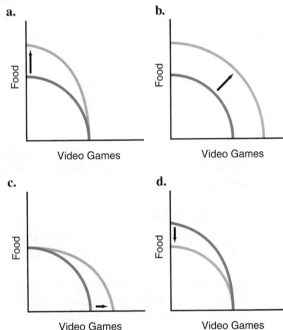

Food / Video Games

b.

Food / Video Games

c.

Food / Video Games

d.

Food / Video Games

2-9. Because it takes you less time to do laundry, you have an absolute advantage in laundry. Neither you nor your roommate has an absolute advantage in meal preparation. You require 2 hours to fold a basket of laundry, so your opportunity cost of folding a basket of laundry is 2 meals. Your roommate's opportunity cost of folding a basket of laundry is 3 meals. Hence, you have a comparative advantage in laundry, and your roommate has a comparative advantage in meal preparation.

2-11. If countries produce the goods for which they have a comparative advantage and trade for those for which they are at a comparative disadvantage, then the distribution of resources is more efficient in each nation, yielding gains for both. Artificially restraining trade that otherwise would yield such gains thereby imposes social losses on residents of both nations.

2-13. **a.** If the two nations have the same production possibilities, then they face the same opportunity costs of producing consumption goods and capital goods. Thus, at present neither has a comparative advantage in producing either good.

    b. Because country B produces more capital goods today, it will be able to produce more of both goods in the future. Thus, country B's PPC will shift outward by a greater amount next.

    c. Country B now has a comparative advantage in producing capital goods, and country A now has a comparative advantage in producing consumption goods.

2-15. D

CHAPTER 3

3-1. The equilibrium price is $11 per CD, and the equilibrium quantity is 80 million CDs. At a price of $10 per CD, the quantity of CDs demanded is 90 million, and the quantity of CDs supplied is 60 million. Hence, there is a shortage of 30 million CDs at a price of $10 per CD.

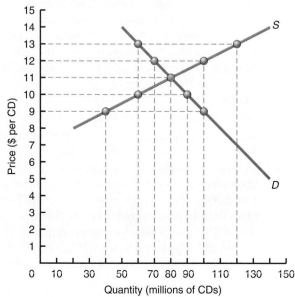

3-3. **a.** DSL and cable Internet access services are substitutes, so a reduction in the price of cable Internet access services causes a decrease in the demand for DSL high-speed Internet access services.

    b. A decrease in the price of DSL Internet access services generates an increase in the quantity of these services demanded.

    c. DSL high-speed Internet access services are a normal good, so a fall in the incomes of consumers reduces the demand for these services.

    d. If consumers expect that the price of DSL high-speed Internet services will fall in the future, then the demand for these services will tend to decrease today.

3-5. **a.** Complement: eggs; substitute: sausage

    b. Complement: tennis balls; substitute: racquetball racquets

    c. Complement: cream; substitute: tea

    d. Complement: gasoline; substitute: city bus

3-7. The increase in the market price of Roquefort cheese causes the demand for blue cheese to increase, so the demand curve for blue cheese shifts to the right. The market price of blue cheese increases, and the equilibrium quantity of blue cheese rises.

3-9. **a.** Because memory chips are an input in the production of laptop computers, a decrease in the price of memory chips causes an increase in the supply of laptop computers. The market supply curve shifts to the right, which causes the market price of laptop computers to fall and the equilibrium quantity of laptop computers to increase.

    b. Machinery used to produce laptop computers is an input in the production of these devices, so an increase in the price of machinery generates a decrease in the supply of laptop computers. The market supply curve shifts to the left, which causes the market price of laptop computers to rise and the equilibrium quantity of laptop computers to decrease.

    c. An increase in the number of manufacturers of laptop computers causes an increase in the supply of laptop computers. The market supply curve shifts rightward. The market price of laptop computers declines, and the equilibrium quantity of laptop computers increases.

    d. The demand curve for laptop computers shifts to the left along the supply curve, so there is a decrease in the quantity supplied. The market price falls, and the equilibrium quantity declines.

3-11. a. The demand for tickets declines, and there will be a surplus of tickets.
  b. The demand for tickets rises, and there will be a shortage of tickets.
  c. The demand for tickets rises, and there will be a shortage of tickets.
  d. The demand for tickets declines, and there will be a surplus of tickets.

3-13. Ethanol producers will respond to the subsidy by producing more ethanol at any given price, so the supply of ethanol will increase, thereby generating a decrease in the price of ethanol.
  a. Producers striving to supply more ethanol will consume more corn, an input in ethanol production. Hence, the demand for corn will increase, so the market price of corn will rise, and the equilibrium quantity of corn will increase.
  b. A decline in the market price of ethanol, a substitute for gasoline, will cause the demand for gasoline to decline. The market price of gasoline will fall, and the equilibrium quantity of gasoline will decrease.
  c. Ethanol and automobiles are complements, so a decline in the price of ethanol will cause an increase in the demand for autos. The market price of autos will rise, and the equilibrium quantity of autos will increase.

3-15. Aluminum is an input in the production of canned soft drinks, so an increase in the price of aluminum reduces the supply of canned soft drinks (option c). The resulting rise in the market price of canned soft drinks brings about an decrease in the quantity of canned soft drinks demanded (option b). In equilibrium, the quantity of soft drinks supplied decreases (option d) to an amount equal to the quantity demanded. The demand curve does not shift, however, so option b does not apply.

CHAPTER 4

4-1. To the band, its producer, and consumers, the market price of the CD provides an indication of the popularity of the band's music. If the market price rises relative to other CDs, then this signals that the band should continue to record its music for sale. If the market price falls relative to other CDs, then this signals that members of the band may want to consider leaving the recording industry.

4-3. The market rental rate is $500 per apartment, and the equilibrium quantity of apartments rented to ten-

ants is 2,000. At a ceiling price of $450 per month, the number of apartments that students wishing to live off campus wish to rent increases to 2,500 apartments. At the ceiling price, the number of apartments that owners are willing to supply decreases to 1,800 apartments. Thus, there is a shortage of 700 apartments at the ceiling price, and only 1,800 are rented at the ceiling price.

4-5. At the above-market price of sugar in the U.S. sugar market, U.S. chocolate manufacturers that use sugar as an input face higher costs. Thus, they supply less chocolate at any given price of chocolate, and the market supply curve shifts leftward. This pushes up the market price of chocolate products and reduces the equilibrium quantity of chocolate. U.S. sugar producers also sell surplus sugar in foreign sugar markets, which causes the supply curve for sugar in foreign markets to shift rightward. This reduces the market price of foreign sugar and raises the equilibrium quantity in the foreign market.

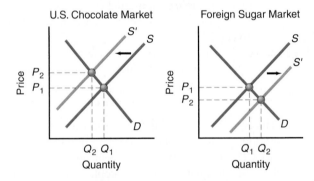

4-7. The market price is $400, and the equilibrium quantity of seats is 1,600. If airlines cannot sell tickets to more than 1,200 passengers, then passengers are willing to pay $600 per seat. Normally airlines would be willing to sell each ticket for $200, but they will be able to charge a price as high as $600 for each of the 1,200 tickets they sell. Hence, the quantity of tickets sold declines from 1,600, and the price of a ticket rises from $400 to as high as $600.

4-9. Before the price support program, total revenue for farmers was $5 million (the equilibrium price of $1.00 per bushel times the equilibrium quantity of 5 million bushels). After the program, total revenue is $10 million (the support price of $1.25 per bushel times the 8 million bushels demanded at the support price). The cost of the program for taxpayers is $5 million (the support price of $1.25 per bushel times the 4 million bushels the government must purchase that consumers do not wish to buy at the higher support price).

4-11. **a.** Because the minimum wage is above the equilibrium wage, more individuals who are currently now employed at fast-food restaurants will seek to work, but fast-food restaurants will desire to employ fewer workers than before. Consequently, there will be a surplus of labor, or unemployed workers, at the above-market minimum wage.

b. The wage rate is the price of an input, labor, so a rise in the wage pushes up the price of this input. This induces fast-food restaurants to reduce the quantity of hamburgers supplied at any given price of hamburgers, so the market supply curve shifts leftward. This brings about an increase in the market price of hamburgers and a reduction in the equilibrium quantity of hamburgers produced and consumed.

4-13. **a.** The rise in the number of wheat producers causes the market supply curve to shift rightward, so more wheat is supplied at the support price.

b. The quantity of wheat demanded at the same support price is unchanged.

c. Because quantity demanded is unchanged while quantity supplied has increased, the amount of surplus wheat that the government must purchase has risen.

CHAPTER 5

5-1. In the absence of laws forbidding cigar smoking in public places, people who are bothered by the odor of cigar smoke will experience costs not borne by cigar producers. Because the supply of cigars will not reflect these costs, the market cigar supply curve will likely be too far to the right from the perspective of society. The market price of cigars will be too low, and too many cigars will be produced and consumed.

5-3. Imposing the tax on pesticides causes an increase in the price of pesticides, which are an input in the production of oranges. Hence, the supply curve in the orange market shifts leftward. The market price of oranges increases, and the equilibrium quantity of oranges declines. Hence, orange consumers indirectly help to pay for dealing with the spillover costs of pesticide production by paying more for oranges.

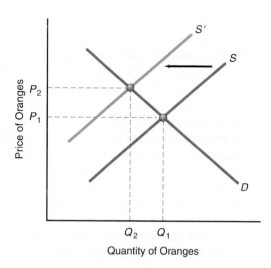

5-5. **a.** If the social benefits associated with bus ridership were taken into account, the demand for bus ridership would be greater, and the market price would be higher. The equilibrium quantity of bus rides would be higher.

b. The government could pay commuters a subsidy to ride the bus, thereby increasing the demand for bus ridership. This would increase the market price and equilibrium number of bus rides.

5-7. The government could provide schools and parents with subsidies to pay for computers and Internet access. This would increase the market price of Internet access and the equilibrium number of people, including children, with access to the Internet.

5-9. The problem is that although most people around the lighthouse will benefit from its presence, there is no incentive for people to voluntarily contribute if they believe that others ultimately will pay for it. That is, the city is likely to face a free-rider problem in its efforts to raise its share of the funds required for the lighthouse.

5-11. Because the marginal tax rate increases as workers' earnings decline, this tax system is regressive.

5-13. Seeking to increase budget allocations in future years and to make workers' jobs more interesting can be consistent with the profit-maximizing objectives of firms in private markets. Also, the government agency is promoting competition, which is analogous to behaving like a firm in a private market. Achieving these goals via majority rule and regulatory coercion, however, are aspects that are specific to the public sector.

CHAPTER 6

6-1. 1997: $300 million; 1999: $350 million; 2001: $400 million; 2004: $400 million; 2005: $420 million

6-3. During 2004 the tax base was an amount of income equal to $20 million/0.05 = $400 million. During 2005 the income tax base was equal to $19.2 million/0.06 = $320 million. Although various factors could have contributed to the fall in taxable income, dynamic tax analysis suggests that the higher income tax rate induced people to reduce their reported income. For instance, some people might have earned less income subject to city income taxes, and others might have even moved outside the city to avoid paying the higher income tax rate.

6-5. a. As shown in the diagram, if the supply and demand curves have their normal shapes, then the $2 per month tax on DSL Internet access services shifts the market supply curve upward by $2. The equilibrium quantity of DSL access services produced and consumed declines. In addition, the monthly market price of DSL access increases by an amount less than $2 per month. Consequently, consumers and producers share in paying the tax on each unit.

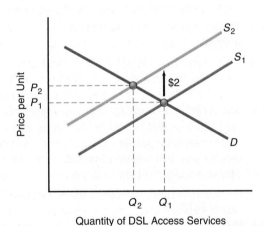

Quantity of DSL Access Services

b. If the market price of DSL Internet access for households rises by the full amount of the tax, then as shown in the diagram below, over the relevant range the demand for DSL access services by households is vertical. The quantity of services demanded by households is completely unresponsive to the tax, so households pay a monthly access rate that is exactly $2 higher, so they pay all of the tax.

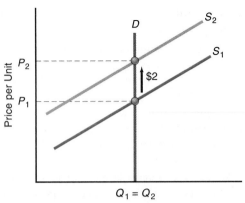

Quantity of DSL Access Services

c. If the market price of DSL access for businesses does not change, then as shown in the diagram below, over the relevant range the demand for Internet access services by businesses is horizontal. The quantity of services demanded by businesses is very highly responsive to the tax, so DSL access providers must bear the tax in the form of higher costs. Providers of DSL access services pay all of the tax.

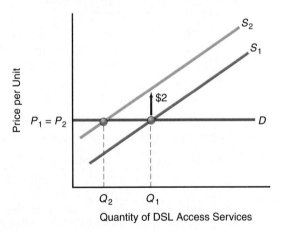

Quantity of DSL Access Services

6-7. Yes, public schools will lose students to private schools. The prices that public schools receive will also decline. Both of these changes will result in lower revenues for public schools.

6-9. a. $40 million
   b. The effective price of a DVD drive to consumers will be lower after the government pays the subsidy, so people will purchase a larger quantity.
   c. $60 million
   d. $90 million

6-11. a. 50 percent
b. -20 percent

CHAPTER 20

20-1. The campus pizzeria indicates by its pricing policy that it recognizes the principle of diminishing marginal utility. Because a customer's marginal utility of the second pizza is typically lower than the first, the customer is likely to value the second less and, therefore, willing to pay less for it.

20-3. The total utility of the third, fourth, and fifth cheeseburger is 48, 56, and 60, respectively. The marginal utility of the first and second cheeseburger is 20 and 16, respectively. The total utility of the first, second, and third bag of French fries is 8, 14, and 18, respectively. The marginal utility of the fourth and fifth bag of French fries is 2 and 0, respectively.

20-5. When total utility is rising, the only thing we can say about marginal utility for certain is that it is positive.

20-7. The student should compare the marginal utility per tuition dollar spent at the two universities. Assuming that a "unit" of college is a degree, the student should divide the additional satisfaction derived from a degree at each university by the total tuition it would take to earn a degree at each institution. The university with the higher marginal utility per tuition dollar is the one the student should attend.

20-9. The new utility maximizing combination is four cheeseburgers and two orders of French fries. The substitution effect is shown by the increase in the relatively less expensive good, cheeseburgers, relative to French fries. The income effect is illustrated by greater total consumption.

20-11. If the student spends 2 hours playing Web computer games, his marginal utility per dollar spent is 20 utils/$10 per hour, or 2 utils per dollar for each hour he plays. If he spends 2 hours at a baseball game, his marginal utility per dollar spent is 40 utils/$40 per 2-hour period spent at a game or 40 utils/$20 for each hour at the game, or 2 utils per hour. Hence, he spends 2 hours playing computer games and spends 2 hours at a baseball game.

20-13. Now if the student spends 6 hours playing Web computer games, he derives 6 utils per $3 per hour, or 2 utils per dollar for each hour he plays.

20-15. The marginal utility of good Y is 9 utils.

APPENDIX E

E-1. The indifference curve is convex to the origin because of a diminishing marginal rate of substitution. As an individual consumes more and more of an item, the less the individual is willing to forgo of the other item. The diminishing marginal rate of substitution is due to a diminishing marginal utility.

E-3. Sue's marginal rate of substitution is calculated below:

Combination of Bottled Water and Soft Drinks	Bottled Water per Month	Soft Drinks Per Month	MRS
A	5	11	
B	10	7	5:4
C	15	4	5:3
D	20	2	5:2
E	25	1	5:1

The diminishing marginal rate of substitution of soft drinks for water shows Sue's diminishing marginal utility of bottled water. She is willing to forgo fewer and fewer soft drinks to get an additional five bottles of water.

E-5. Given that water is on the horizontal axis and soft drinks on the vertical axis, the slope of Sue's budget constraint is the price of water divided by the price of soft drinks, or $P_W/P_S = \frac{1}{2}$. The only combination of bottled water and soft drinks that is on Sue's indifference curve and budget constraint is combination C. For this combination, total expenditures on water and soft drinks are $23.

E-7. With the quantity of bottled water measured along the horizontal axis and the quantity of soft drinks measured along the vertical axis, the slope of Sue's budget constraint is the price of water divided by the price of soft drinks. This ratio equals $\frac{1}{2}$. The only combination of bottled water and soft drinks that is on Sue's indifference curve and budget constraint is combination C, where expenditures on water and soft drinks total to $23.

E-9. Yes, Sue's revealed preferences indicate that her demand for soft drinks obeys the law of demand. When the price of soft drinks declines from $2 to $1, her quantity demanded rises from 4 to 8.

CHAPTER 21

21-1. |[(200 − 150)/(350/2)]/[(9 − 10)/(19/2)]|, which is approximately equal to 2.7

21-3. |[(100 − 200)/(300/2)]/[($2 − $1)/($3/2)]| = 1.0. Demand is unit-elastic.

21-5. |[(80 − 120)/(200/2)]/[($22.50 − $17.50)/($40/2)]| = 1.6. Demand is elastic.

21-7. Because price and total revenue move in the same direction, the craftsman faces inelastic demand for his guitars.

21-9. **a.** More inelastic, because it represents a smaller portion of the budget.
   b. More elastic, because there are many close substitutes.
   c. More elastic, because there are a number of substitutes.
   d. More inelastic, because there are few close substitutes.
   e. More inelastic, because it represents a small portion of the budget.

21-11. Let X denote the percentage change in the quantity of bacon. Then X/10 percent = −0.5. X, therefore, is −5 percent.

21-13. [(125,000 − 75,000)/(200,000/2)]/[($35,000 − $25,000)/($60,000/2)] = 1.5. Supply is elastic.

21-15. The short-run price elasticity of supply is 0.5, and the long-run price elasticity of supply is 2.0.

CHAPTER 22

22-1. **a.** Bob earns a high economic rent. With a specialized skill that is in great demand his income is likely to be high and his opportunity cost relatively low.
   b. Sally earns a high economic rent. As a supermodel her income likely to be high and, without any education, her opportunity cost relatively low.
   c. If Tim were to leave teaching, not a relatively high paying occupation, he could sell insurance full time. Hence, his opportunity cost is high relative to his income and his economic rent low.

22-3. The economic rents that Michael Jordan was able to earn as a basketball player relative to those he could earn as a baseball player surely played a large role in his decision to return to basketball. Hence, they helped direct his resources (athletic talents) to their most efficient uses.

22-5. A sole proprietorships is a business entity owned by a single individual, whereas a partnership is a business entity owned by more than one individual. A corporation, in contrast, is a legal entity that is owned by shareholders, who own shares of the profits of the entity. Sole proprietorships and partnerships do not face double taxation as do corporations. The owners of corporations, however, enjoy limited liability, whereas the sole proprietor or partner does not.

22-7. Accounting profit is total revenue, $77,250, minus explicit costs, $37,000, for a total of $40,250. Economic profit is total revenue, $77,250, less explicit costs, $37,000, and implicit costs, $40,250, for a total equal to zero.

22-9. **a.** Physical capital.
   b. Financial capital.
   c. Financial capital.
   d. Physical capital.

22-11. **a.** The owner of WebCity faces both tax rates if the firm is a corporation, but if it is a proprietorship the owner faces only the 30 percent personal income tax rate. Thus it should choose to be a proprietorship.
   b. If WebCity is a corporation, the $100,000 in corporate earnings is taxed at a 20 percent rate, so that after-tax dividends are $80,000, and these are taxed at the personal income tax rate of 30 percent, leaving $56,000 in after-tax income for the owner. Hence, the firm should be organized as a proprietorship, so that the after-tax earnings are $70,000.
   c. Yes. In this case, incorporation raises earnings to $150,000, which are taxed at a rate of 20 percent, yielding after-tax dividends of $120,000 that are taxed at the personal rate of 30 percent. This leaves an after-tax income for the owner of $84,000, which is higher than the after-tax earnings of $70,000 if WebCity is a proprietorship that earns lower pre-tax income taxed at the personal rate.
   d. After-tax profits rise from $56,000 to $84,000, or by $28,000.
   e. This policy change would only increase the incentive to incorporate.
   f. A corporate structure provides limited liability for owners, which can be a major advantage. Furthermore, owners may believe that the corporate structure will yield higher pre-tax earnings, as in the above example.

22-13. The real rate of interest in Japan is 2% − 0.5% = 1.5%. The real rate of interest in the United States is

4% − 3% = 1%. Japan, therefore, has the higher *real* rate of interest.

22-15. Ownership of common stock provides voting rights within the firm but also entails immediate loss if assets fall below the value of the firm's liabilities. Preferred stockholders are repaid prior to owners of common stock but preferred stockholders do not have voting rights.

22-17. You should point out to your classmate that stock prices tend to follow a random walk. That is, yesterday's price is the best guide to today's price and, therefore, there are no predictable trends that can be used to "beat" the market.

CHAPTER 23

23-1. The short run is a time period in which the professor cannot enter the job market and find employment elsewhere. This is the nine-month period from August 15 through May 15. The professor can find employment elsewhere after the contract has been fulfilled, so the short run is nine months and the long run is greater than nine months,.

23-3.

Input of Labor (workers per month)	Total Output of DVD Drives	Marginal Physical Product
0	0	—
1	25	25
2	60	35
3	85	25
4	105	20
5	115	10
6	120	5

23-5. Variable costs are equal to total costs, $5 million, less fixed costs, $2 million. Variable costs, therefore, are equal to $3 million. Average variable costs are equal to total variable costs divided by the number of units produced. Average variable costs, therefore, equal $3 million divided by 10,000, or $300.

23-7. Increasing marginal costs occur as the firm moves from producing 50 cable modems to 75 cable modems.

Output (cable modems per month)	Total Cost of Output ($ thousands)	Marginal Costs ($ per unit)
0	10	—
25	60	2.00
50	95	1.40
75	150	2.20
100	220	2.80
125	325	4.20
150	465	5.60

23-9. **a.** Average total costs are $20 per unit plus $30 per unit, or $50 per unit, and total costs divided by average total costs equal output, which thus is $2,500/$50 per unit, or 50 units.

b. TVC = AVC × Q = $20 per unit × 50 units = $1,000.

c. TFC = AFC × Q = $30 per unit × 50 units = $1,500; or TFC = TC − TVC = $2,500 − $1,000 = $1,500.

23-11. Hiring 1 more unit of labor at a wage rate of $20 to increase output by 1 unit causes total costs to rise by $20, so the marginal cost of the 251st unit is $20.

23-13. **a.** $2 per unit

b. 1,000 units

c. $2,000

23-15. **a.** plant size E

b. leftward movement

CHAPTER 24

24-1. **a.** The single firm producing much of the industry's output can affect price. Therefore, this is currently not a competitive industry.

b. The output of each firm is not homogeneous, so this is not a competitive industry.

c. Firms cannot easily enter the industry, so this is not a competitive industry.

24-3. During the course of a week the barber cuts hair for 15 × 5 = 75 people. His total revenue for a week is 75 × $6 = $450. Because this is a competitive market, marginal revenue and average revenue equal the market price, $6.

24-5. The profit-maximizing rate of output is where marginal cost equals marginal revenue, which occurs at 8 pizzas.

Total Output and Sales of Pizzas	Total Cost ($)	Marginal Cost ($ per unit)	Marginal Revenue ($ per unit)
0	5	—	10
1	9	4	10
2	11	2	10
3	12	1	10
4	14	2	10
5	18	4	10
6	24	6	10
7	32	8	10
8	42	10	10
9	54	12	10
10	68	14	10

24-7. Even though the price of pizzas, and hence marginal revenue, falls to only $5, this covers average variable costs. Thus, the shop should stay open.

24-9. Marginal revenue equals marginal cost at 1,500 units of output. The average variable cost of producing this output exceeds the market price at this output level, however, so the firm should shut down in the short run. Then it minimizes its short-run economic losses at the amount of its total fixed costs, which equal $0.50 times 1,500, or $750.

24-11. If marginal cost is below average total cost, then total cost is declining. Because marginal revenue is above the minimum point of average total costs, the marginal revenue curve will intersect marginal revenue in the area where average total costs are rising. Hence, the firm is not maximizing profit and it should increase its rate of production.

24-13. a. There was a significant increase in market supply as more firms entered the industry. A consequence for the typical firm was that the market price fell below the minimum average total cost, resulting in negative economic profits.
b. Firms will consider leaving the industry, and some firms probably *will* leave the industry.

CHAPTER 25

25-1. Because the objective of each cartel member is to maximize economic profits, there is an incentive for an individual member to cheat. Preventing members from cheating becomes harder and harder as the number of members grows. Hence, the large number of coffee growers that exists today makes it unlikely that the cartel will be effective in the long run.

25-3. a. The total revenue and total profits of the drycleaner are as follows.

Output (suits cleaned)	Price ($ per unit)	Total Costs ($)	Total Revenue ($)	Total Profit ($)
0	8.00	3.00	0	−3.00
1	7.50	6.00	7.50	1.50
2	7.00	8.50	14.00	5.50
3	6.50	10.50	19.50	9.00
4	6.00	11.50	24.00	12.50
5	5.50	13.50	27.50	14.00
6	5.00	16.00	30.00	14.00
7	4.50	19.00	31.50	12.50
8	4.00	24.00	32.00	8.00

b. The profit-maximizing rate of output is between 5 and 6 units.

25-5. This statement is not true. Profit maximization occurs at the output rate where marginal revenue and marginal cost are equal. This rate of output may well occur at a point above and to the left of the point of minimum average total cost.

25-7. In a perfectly competitive market, price would equal marginal cost at $4.50, at which the quantity is 8,000. Because the monopolist produces less and charges a higher price than under perfect competition, price exceeds marginal cost at the profit-maximizing level of output. The difference between the price and marginal cost is the per-unit cost to society of a monopolized industry.

25-9. At the 1 million-unit output rate at which marginal revenue equals marginal cost, average variable cost is $31 per unit, which exceeds price. Hence, producing 1 million units of output would generate total variable costs in excess of total revenues. The monopolist should halt its operations in the short run.

25-11. If price varies positively with total revenue, then the monopolist is operating on the inelastic portion of the demand curve. This corresponds to the range where marginal revenue is negative. The monopolist cannot, therefore, be at the point where its profits are maximized. In other words, the monopolist is not producing where marginal cost equals marginal revenue.

25-13. Because marginal cost has risen, the monopolist will be operating at a lower rate of output and charging a higher price. Economic profits are likely to decline because even though the price is higher, its output will be more than proportionately lower.

CHAPTER 26

26-1. a. There are many fast food restaurants producing and selling distinguishable products. Both of these features of this industry are consistent with the theory of monopolistic competition.

b. There are numerous colleges and universities, but each specializes in different academic areas and hence produces heterogeneous products, as in the theory of monopolistic competition.

26-3. The values for marginal cost and marginal revenue appear below. Marginal revenue equals marginal cost at approximately the fifth unit of output, so marginal analysis indicates that five units is the profit-maximizing production level.

Output	Price ($ per unit)	Total Costs ($)	Total Revenue ($)	Marginal Cost ($ per unit)	Marginal Revenue ($ per unit)	Total Profit ($)
0	6.00	2.00	0	—	—	−2.00
1	5.75	5.25	5.75	3.25	5.75	0.00
2	5.50	7.50	11.00	2.25	5.25	3.50
3	5.25	9.60	15.75	2.10	4.75	6.15
4	5.00	12.10	20.00	2.50	4.25	7.90
5	4.75	15.80	23.75	3.70	3.75	7.95
6	4.50	20.00	27.00	4.20	3.25	7.00
7	4.00	24.75	28.00	4.75	1.00	3.25

26-5. After these long-run adjustments have occurred, the demand curve will have shifted to tangency with the average total cost curve at 4 units of output. At this production level, average total cost is $3.03, so this will be the long-run equilibrium price. Because price and average total cost will be equal, the firm will earn zero economic profits.

26-7. a. mass
b. direct
c. mass and interactive
d. mass

26-9. a. experience good. How well the company's employees clean a carpet can only be assessed by observing the cleanliness of the carpet after they have concluded work.

b. credence good. The effectiveness of a new cancer treatment is difficult for a typical consumer to assess without assistance of health care providers possessing expertise that the consumer lacks.

c. search good. A consumer can evaluate the features of athletic socks without actually wearing them while walking, running, or participating in sports.

d. search good. Given knowledge that the necktie is made of silk, a photo and description are sufficient to determine its characteristics.

26-11. The fact that consumers can evaluate certain aspects of a credence good in advance of purchase, as in the case of a search good, explains why ads for credence goods, such as pharmaceuticals, often have informational elements. At the same time, however, the fact that consumers cannot truly evaluate credence goods until after purchase, and even then only with assistance, explains why ads for credence goods also commonly include persuasive elements.

26-13. Typically the fixed costs of producing an information product are relatively high, while average variable cost is equal to a very small per-unit amount. As a consequence, the average total cost curve slopes downward with increased output, and average variable cost equals marginal cost at a low, constant amount irrespective of the quantity produced.

26-15. a. Total costs of producing 300,000 units equal total fixed costs of $2,850,000 plus total variable costs of $300,000, which are $3,150,000. If each copy is sold at a price of $1, then total revenues are $300,000, so economic losses are equal to −$2,850,000.

b. At the profit-maximizing price of $35 per unit, the firm sells 100,000 units and earns total revenues equal to $3,500,000. Its total costs equal total variable costs of $100,000 plus total fixed costs of $2,850,000, or $2,950,000 so the maximum possible short-run economic profit is equal to $3,500,000 − $2,950,000 = $550,000.

c. When the firm maximizes its economic profits, marginal revenue equals marginal cost, which is $1 per unit.

d. $0; in the long run the firm earns zero economic profits, so there is no incentive for other firms to enter the industry.

CHAPTER 27

27-1. a. 15 percent + 14 percent + 12 percent + 11 percent = 52 percent.

    b. 52 percent + 10 percent + 10 percent + 8 percent + 7 percent = 87 percent; or 100 percent − 13 percent = 87 percent.

27-3. a. zero-sum game

    b. negative-sum game

    c. positive-sum game

27-5. Bob is currently a participant in a noncooperative game, in which some people stand and block his view of the football game. His tit-for-tat strategy is to stand up as well. If he stands, however, he will block the view of another spectator. In a cooperative game, all would sit or stand up simultaneously, so that no individual's view is blocked.

27-7. This could be evidence of tacit collusion, with the university cafeteria engaging in price leadership. Nevertheless, prices also adjust across all firms under perfect competition, so it may be a coincidence that the delis' prices change just after variations in the prices at the university cafeteria.

27-9. Possible examples include office productivity software, online auction services, telecommunications services, and Internet payment services. In each case, more people are likely to choose to consume the item when others do, because the inherent usefulness of consuming the item for each person increases with as the number of consumers rises.

CHAPTER 28

28-1. If cable service is an industry that experiences diminishing long-run average total costs, then the city may determine that it is more efficient to have a single, large firm that produces at a lower long-run average cost. The city could then regulate the activity of the firm.

28-3. As the table indicates, long-run average cost and long-run marginal cost decline with greater output. If the firm were allowed to operate as a monopolist, it would produce to the point at which marginal cost equals marginal revenue, which is 2 units of output. The price that consumers are willing to pay for this quantity is $90 per unit, and maximum economic profits are $180 − $175 = $5.

Quantity	Price ($ per unit)	Long-Run Total Cost ($)	LRAC ($ per unit)	LRMC ($ per unit)	MR ($ per unit)
0	100	$0	—	—	
1	95	92	$92.00	$92	$95
2	90	177	88.50	85	85
3	85	255	85.00	78	75
4	80	331	82.75	76	65
5	75	406	81.20	75	55
6	70	480	80.00	74	45

28-5. Long-run average cost and price both equal $85 per unit at 3 units of output. At a price of $80 per unit, the firm's economic profits equal $255 − $255 = $0.

28-7. The main concern of economic regulation is to balance the trade-off between service and price. Economic regulation seeks to keep price lower than the price a profit-maximizing monopolist would charge. Social regulation seeks to improve working conditions and minimize adverse spillovers of production.

28-9. If European regulation is designed to protect domestic industries, then this is an example of the capture hypothesis. If, on the other hand, there are legitimate health concerns, then this is an example of share-the-pain, share-the-gain hypothesis.

28-11. a. In this case, Firm 1 makes 75.0 percent of the sales in the Internet book market, and Firm 2 makes 46.7 percent of the sales in physical retail stores. By the antitrust authority's definition, there is a monopoly situation in the Internet book market.

    b. In the combined market, Firm 2 accounts for 42.5 percent of all sales, and Firm 1's share drops to 7.5 percent, so under this alternative definition there is no cause for concern about monopoly.

28-13. If the Justice Department viewed Internet realtor listing services as a "relevant market" for antitrust policy, then the growing concentration of ownership among this single retailing association might be a concern. Control over Internet listings by this group could help promote cartel-type behavior. A key issue is whether the Internet marketplace for realtor listings is separate from the physical market.

28-15. This is an example of bundling. Because consumers who purchase the bundled product perceive that they have effectively paid different prices for the bundled products based on their willingness to pay, an antitrust authority might view this practice as charging consumers different prices for the same products, or price discrimination.

CHAPTER 29

29-1.

Labor Input (workers per week)	Total Physical Output (printers per day)	Marginal Physical Product	Marginal Revenue Product ($)
10	200	—	—
11	218	18	1,800
12	234	16	1,600
13	248	14	1,400
14	260	12	1,200
15	270	10	1,000
16	278	8	800

29-3. The profit-maximizing employer will hire 14 workers, because this is the level of employment at which marginal revenue product equals marginal factor cost.

29-5. a. The greater is the substitutability of capital, the more elastic is demand for labor.
b. Because the demand for labor is a derived demand, the greater is the elasticity of demand for the final product, the greater is the elasticity of demand for labor.
c. The larger is the portion of factor costs accounted for by labor, the larger is the price elasticity of demand for labor.

29-7.

Labor Input (workers per week)	Total Physical Product	Product Price ($ per unit)	Marginal Physical Product	Total Revenue ($)	Marginal Revenue Product ($)
10	100	50	—	5,000	—
11	109	49	9	5,341	341
12	116	48	7	5,568	227
13	121	47	5	5,687	119
14	124	46	3	5,704	17
15	125	45	1	5,625	−79

29-9. a. The firm maximizes profits, so marginal revenue product (the 5-unit marginal physical product multiplied by marginal revenue) equals the wage rate of $15. Hence, marginal revenue equals $3.
b. At the profit-maximizing output, marginal revenue of $3 is less than the price of $5, so this firm does not sell its output in a perfectly competitive market.

29-11. Labor outsourcing by U.S. firms tends to push down market wages and employment in affected U.S. labor markets, but labor outsourcing by foreign firms who hire U.S. workers tends to push up market wages and employment in affected U.S. labor markets. Consequently, the overall wage and employment effects are ambiguous in the short run. In the long run, however, outsourcing enables U.S. and foreign firms to specialize in producing the goods and services that they can produce most efficiently. The resulting resource saving ultimately expands the ability of U.S. residents to consume more goods and services than they could have otherwise, which raises revenues of U.S. firms and boosts their demands for U.S. workers. In the long run, therefore, outsourcing tends to generate higher U.S. wages and employment.

29-13. The marginal physical product of labor is 2 units of output per unit of labor.

29-15. In order to maximize profits, the firm should hire inputs up to the point at which the marginal physical product per dollar spent on the input is equalized across all inputs. This is not the case in this example. The marginal physical product of labor per dollar spent on wages is 200/$10 = 20 units of output per dollar spent on labor, which is less than the marginal physical product of capital per dollar spent on capital, which is 20,000/$500 or 40 units of output per dollar spent on capital. Thus the firm should reduce the number of labor units it hires to increase the additional output per dollar spent on labor and increase its use of capital to reduce the additional output per dollar spent on capital, to the point where these amounts are equalized.

CHAPTER 30

30-1. Individual workers can air grievances to the collective voice who then takes the issue to the employer. The individual does not run the risk of being singled out by an employer. The individual employee does not waste work time trying to convince employers that changes are needed in the workplace.

30-3. Because strikebreakers can replace union employees, they diminish the collective bargaining power of a union.

30-5. When marginal revenue is zero, the price elasticity of demand is equal to unity. At this point, total revenue is neither rising nor falling. Hence, it is at a maximum point.

30-7. When unions in these industries attempt to bargain for higher than market levels of wages, the firms who employ members of these unions will not be able to readily substitute to alternative inputs. Hence these unions are more likely to be able to achieve their wage objectives.

30-9.

Quantity of Labor Supplied	Total Physical Product	Required Hourly Wage Rate ($ per unit of labor)	Total Wage Bill ($)	Marginal Factor Cost ($ per unit of labor)
10	100	5	50	—
11	109	6	66	16
12	116	7	84	18
13	121	8	104	20
14	124	9	126	22
15	125	10	150	24

30-11. At 11 units of labor the marginal revenue product of labor equals $16. This is equal to the marginal factor cost at this level of employment. The firm, therefore, will hire 11 units of labor and pay a wage of $6 an hour.

Quantity of Labor Supplied	Required Hourly Wage Rate ($ per unit of labor)	Total Factor Cost ($)	Marginal Factor Cost ($ per unit of labor)	Total Physical Product	Product Price ($ per unit)	Total Revenue ($)	Marginal Revenue Product ($ per unit of labor)
10	5	50	—	100	3.11	311.00	—
11	6	66	16.00	109	3.00	327.00	16.00
12	7	84	18.00	116	2.95	342.20	15.20
13	8	104	20.00	121	2.92	353.32	11.12
14	9	126	22.00	124	2.90	359.60	6.28
15	10	150	24.00	125	2.89	361.25	1.65

30-13. The marginal factor cost of the last worker hired was $106,480 − $105,600 = $880, so this is the marginal product of this worker if the firms is maximizing its profits.

CHAPTER 31

31-1.

   a. X, because for this country the Lorenz curve implies complete income equality.

   b. Z, because this country's Lorenz curve is bowed farthest away from the case of complete income equality.

   c. Closer, because if all other things including aggregate income remain unchanged, when more people in country Y are children below working age the share of incomes to people this age will decline, while the reverse will occur in country Z as more of its people reach working age and begin to earn incomes.

31-3. If the Lorenz curve is based on incomes net of transfer payments, then the Lorenz curve will become less bowed. But if the Lorenz curve does not account for transfer payments, its shape will remain unaffected.

31-5. Brazil

31-7. To achieve complete equality of incomes, such policies would remove individual gains from maximizing the economic value of resources and minimizing production costs. Thus, enacting policies aimed at complete income equality could significantly reduce overall efficiency in an economy.

31-9. First, a moral hazard problem will exist, because government action would reduce the individual's incentive to continue a healthy lifestyle, thereby increasing the likelihood of greater health problems that will require future treatment. Second, an individual who currently has health problems will have an incentive to substitute future care that will be available at a zero price for current care that the individual must purchase at a positive price. Finally, in future years the patient will no longer have an incentive to contain health-care expenses, nor will health-care providers have an incentive to minimize their costs.

31-11. The demand for health care will increase, and the marginal revenue curve will shift rightward. Hence, the profit-maximizing price and equilibrium quantity of health-care services will increase.

31-13. Because funds in HRAs earn no interest, can be used to pay only medical expenses, and revert back to the employer at the end of the year if unused, an individual faces incentives to spend all these funds on every possible health care expense. In contrast, because funds in HSAs earn interest and can be used (subject to penalties and taxation) for other types of expenses, an individual has at least some incentive not to try to spend all the funds on health care expenses. Consequently, moral hazard problems are greater with HRAs than with HSAs.

CHAPTER 32

31-1. $4 per unit, which exactly accounts for the per-unit social cost of pollution.

32-3. At the previous, lower market price, consumers failed to pay a price that reflected the social costs, including those relating to pollution, of resources that the firms use to produce the good or service.

32-5. Penalizing rhino hunting discourages most people from engaging in the activity, which reduces the supply of rhino horns and drives up their market price. This, in turn, makes illegal poaching a more lucrative activity, which can lead to an increase in illegal hunting of the few remaining rhinos. If raising rhinos as stock animals were legalized, then more rhino horns would be produced via an increase in the number of rhinos on farms and the market price of rhino horns would decline. This would reduce the incentive for poaching of wild rhinos.

32-7. **a.** 60 percent
b. 40 percent
c. 40 percent

32-9. **a.** The marginal costs and benefits are tabulated below:

Population of Wild Tigers	Marginal Cost ($)	Marginal Benefit ($)
0	—	—
2,000	25	50
4,000	10	40
6,000	15	30
8,000	25	25
10,000	35	20
12,000	50	10

b. 8,000
c. 10,000

CHAPTER 33

33-1. Residents of Norway can produce 100 calculators and 50 books, while residents of Sweden can produce 200 calculators and 50 books. Their total output, therefore, is 300 calculators and 100 books. Sweden has an absolute advantage in calculators. Neither country has an absolute advantage in books.

33-3. **a.** Norway has a comparative advantage in the production of books, and Sweden has a comparative advantage in the production of calculators.
b. If residents of both nations specialize, total production is 400 calculators and 100 books.

33-5. Without trade, Norway would have to forgo 1/2 of a book to obtain 1 calculator. With trade, however, Norway can obtain 1 calculator for 1/3 of a book. Without trade, Sweden would have to forgo 4 calculators to obtain 1 book. With trade, however, Sweden can obtain 1 book for 3 calculators. By trading, both nations can obtain the good at a price that is less than the opportunity cost of producing it. They are both better off with trade, so this is a positive-sum game.

33-7. **a.** East Isle has an absolute advantage in producing modems, and South Shore has an absolute advantage in producing DVD drives.
b. The opportunity cost of producing one modem in South Shore is 2 DVD drives, and the opportunity cost of producing one modem in East Isle is 1/3 DVD drive. The opportunity cost of producing one DVD drive in South Shore is 1/2 modem, and the opportunity cost of producing one DVD drive in East Isle is 3 modems. Consequently, East Isle has a comparative advantage in producing modems, and South Shore has a comparative advantage in producing DVD drives.

33-9. **a.** Northern Kingdom has an absolute advantage in producing wheat, and Western Republic has an absolute advantage in producing surfboards.
b. The opportunity cost of producing one surfboard in Northern Kingdom equals 1.83 bushels of wheat, but it is only 0.45 bushels of wheat in Western Republic, so Western Republic has a comparative advantage in producing surfboards. The opportunity cost of producing one bushel of wheat in Northern Kingdom is 0.55 surfboard,

but in Western Republic it is 2.25 surfboards, so Northern Kingdom has a comparative advantage in wheat production.

33-11. A price elasticity of demand less than unity indicates inelastic demand and, therefore, price and total revenue move in the same direction. If the nation restricts its exports, the price of the product rises and so does total revenue, even though the nation sells fewer units of output abroad.

33-13. **a.** Because the supply curve shifts by the amount of the tariff, the tariff is $20 per television.

b. Total revenue was $300 per unit times 20 million units, or $6 billion, before the tariff and $310 per unit times 15 million units, or $4.65 billion, after the tariff.

c. U.S. tariff revenue is $20 per unit times 15 million units, or $300 million.

CHAPTER 34

34-1. The trade balance is merchandise exports minus merchandise imports, which equals $500 - 600 = -100$, or a deficit of 100. Adding service exports of 75 and subtracting net unilateral transfers of 10 and service imports of 50 yields $-100 + 75 - 10 - 50 = -85$, or a current account balance of -85. The capital account balance equals the difference between capital inflows and capital outflows, or $300 - 200 = +100$, or a capital account surplus of 100.

34-3. **a.** The increase in demand for Mexican made guitars increases the demand for Mexican pesos, and the peso appreciates.

b. International investors will remove some of their financial capital from Mexico. The increase in the supply of the peso in the foreign exchange market will cause the peso to depreciate.

34-5. **a.** Investors shift their funds from Thailand to other nations where interest returns are higher, so the demand for the baht declines. The dollar-baht exchange rate falls, so the dollar appreciates. The baht depreciates.

b. The rise in Thai productivity reduces the price of Thai goods relative to goods in the United States, so U.S. residents purchase more Thai goods. This increases the demand for baht in the foreign exchange market, so the dollar-baht exchange rate increases. The dollar depreciates, and the baht appreciates.

34-7. The demand for Chinese yuan increases, and the supply of yuan decreases. The dollar-yuan exchange rate rises, so the yuan appreciates.

34-9. The Canadian dollar-euro exchange rate is found by dividing the U.S. dollar-euro exchange rate by the U.S. dollar-Canadian dollar exchange rate, or (1.17 $US/euro)/(0.79 $US/$C) = 1.48 $C/euro, or 1.48 Canadian dollars per euro.

34-11. A flexible exchange rate system allows the exchange value of a currency to be determined freely in the foreign exchange market with no intervention by the government. A fixed exchange rate pegs the value of the currency, and the authorities responsible for the value of the currency intervene in foreign exchange markets to maintain this value. A dirty float involves occasional intervention by the exchange authorities. A target zone allows the exchange value to fluctuate, but only within a given range of values.

34-13. When the U.S. dollar is pegged to gold at a rate of $35 and the pound at a rate of $17.50, the dollar-pound exchange rate equals $35/£17.50 = 2 ($/£).

34-15. **a.** The demand for yuan will decrease, which would begin to cause the equilibrium dollar-yuan exchange rate to decline. To prevent a yuan depreciation from occurring, the Bank of China can purchase yuan with dollars, thereby raising the demand for yuan to its previous level at the original exchange rate. Hence the Bank of China should reduce its dollar reserves.

b. To purchase more U.S. financial assets, Chinese residents must obtain more dollars, so they will increase the quantity of yuan supplied at each exchange rate. This would begin to cause the equilibrium dollar-yuan exchange rate to decline. To prevent a yuan depreciation from occurring, the bank of China can purchase yuan with dollars, thereby causing the demand for yuan to increase sufficiently to push the equilibrium exchange rate back to its original level. Thus the Bank of China should reduce its dollar reserves.

c. U.S. residents increase the quantity of yuan demanded at any given exchange rate in order to purchase Chinese furniture, so the demand for yuan increases. This would tend to cause the equilibrium dollar-yuan exchange rate to rise, resulting in a yuan appreciation. To keep this from happening, the Bank of China can purchase dollars with yuan, thereby increasing the supply of yuan and pushing back down the equilibrium exchange rate. Consequently, the Bank of China should increase its dollar reserves.

A

Absolute advantage The ability to produce more units of a good or service using a given quantity of labor or resource inputs. Equivalently, the ability to produce the same quantity of a good or service using fewer units of labor or resource inputs.

Accounting identities Values that are equivalent by definition.

Accounting profit Total revenues minus total explicit costs.

Action time lag The time between recognizing an economic problem and implementing policy to solve it. The action time lag is quite long for fiscal policy, which requires congressional approval.

Active (discretionary) policymaking All actions on the part of monetary and fiscal policymakers that are undertaken in response to or in anticipation of some change in the overall economy.

Ad valorem **taxation** Assessing taxes by charging a tax rate equal to a fraction of the market price of each unit purchased.

Adverse selection The likelihood that individuals who seek to borrow money may use the funds that they receive for unworthy, high-risk projects.

Age-earnings cycle The regular earnings profile of an individual throughout his or her lifetime. The age-earnings cycle usually starts with a low income, builds gradually to a peak at around age 50, and then gradually curves down until it approaches zero at retirement.

Aggregate demand The total of all planned expenditures in the entire economy.

Aggregate demand curve A curve showing planned purchase rates for all final goods and services in the economy at various price levels, all other things held constant.

Aggregate demand shock Any event that causes the aggregate demand curve to shift inward or outward.

Aggregate supply The total of all planned production for the economy.

Aggregate supply shock Any event that causes the aggregate supply curve to shift inward or outward.

Aggregates Total amounts or quantities; aggregate demand, for example, is total planned expenditures throughout a nation.

Anticipated inflation The inflation rate that we believe will occur; when it does, we are in a situation of fully anticipated inflation.

Antitrust legislation Laws that restrict the formation of monopolies and regulate certain anticompetitive business practices.

Appreciation An increase in the exchange value of one nation's currency in terms of the currency of another nation.

Asset demand Holding money as a store of value instead of other assets such as certificates of deposit, corporate bonds, and stocks.

Assets Amounts owned; all items to which a business or household holds legal claim.

Asymmetric information Information possessed by one party in a financial transaction but not by the other party.

Automatic, or built-in, stabilizers Special provisions of certain federal programs that cause changes in desired aggregate expenditures without the action of Congress and the president. Examples are the federal progressive tax system and unemployment compensation.

Autonomous consumption The part of consumption that is independent of (does not depend on) the level of disposable income. Changes in autonomous consumption shift the consumption function.

Average fixed costs Total fixed costs divided by the number of units produced.

Average physical product Total product divided by the variable input.

Average propensity to consume (APC) Real consumption divided by real disposable income; for any given level of real income, the proportion of total real disposable income that is consumed.

Average propensity to save (APS) Real saving divided by real disposable income; for any given level of real income, the proportion of total real disposable income that is saved.

Average tax rate The total tax payment divided by total income. It is the proportion of total income paid in taxes.

Average total costs Total costs divided by the number of units produced; sometimes called *average per-unit total costs.*

Average variable costs Total variable costs divided by the number of units produced.

B

Balance of payments A system of accounts that measures transactions of goods, services, income, and financial assets between domestic households, businesses, and governments and residents of the rest of the world during a specific time period.

Balance of trade The difference between exports and imports of goods.

Balance sheet A statement of the assets and liabilities of any business entity, including financial institutions and the Federal Reserve System. Assets are what is owned; liabilities are what is owed.

Balanced budget A situation in which the government's spending is exactly equal to the total taxes and other revenues it collects during a given period of time.

Bank runs Attempts by many of a bank's depositors to convert checkable and time deposits into currency out of fear that the bank's liabilities may exceed its assets.

Barter The direct exchange of goods and services for other goods and services without the use of money.

Base year The year that is chosen as the point of reference for comparison of prices in other years.

Bilateral monopoly A market structure consisting of a monopolist and a monopsonist.

Black market A market in which goods are traded at prices above their legal maximum prices or in which illegal goods are sold.

Bond A legal claim against a firm, usually entitling the owner of the bond to receive a fixed annual coupon payment, plus a lump-sum payment at the bond's maturity date. Bonds are issued in return for funds lent to the firm.

Budget constraint All of the possible combinations of goods that can be purchased (at fixed prices) with a specific budget.

Bundling Offering two or more products for sale as a set.

Business fluctuations The ups and downs in business activity throughout the economy.

C

Capital account A category of balance of payments transactions that measures flows of real and financial assets.

Capital consumption allowance Another name for depreciation, the amount that businesses would have to save in order to take care of the deterioration of machines and other equipment.

Capital controls Legal restrictions on the ability of a nation's residents to hold and trade assets denominated in foreign currencies.

Capital gain The positive difference between the purchase price and the sale price of an asset. If a share of stock is bought for $5 and then sold for $15, the capital gain is $10.

Capital goods Producer durables; nonconsumable goods that firms use to make other goods.

Capital loss The negative difference between the purchase price and the sale price of an asset.

Capture hypothesis A theory of regulatory behavior that predicts that regulators will eventually be captured by special interests of the industry being regulated.

Cartel An association of producers in an industry that agree to set common prices and output quotas to prevent competition.

Central bank A banker's bank, usually an official institution that also serves as a country's treasury's bank. Central banks normally regulate commercial banks.

Certificate of deposit (CD) A time deposit with a fixed maturity date offered by banks and other financial institutions.

Ceteris paribus **[KAY-ter-us PEAR-uh-bus] assumption** The assumption that nothing changes except the factor or factors being studied.

Ceteris paribus **conditions** Determinants of the relationship between price and quantity that are unchanged along a curve; changes in these factors cause the curve to shift.

Checkable deposits Any deposits in a thrift institution or a commercial bank on which a check may be written, for all intents and purposes, a transactions account.

Closed shop A business enterprise in which employees must belong to the union before they can be hired and must remain in the union after they are hired.

Collective bargaining Bargaining between the management of a company or of a group of companies and the management of a union or a group of unions for the purpose of reaching a mutually agreeable contract that sets wages, fringe benefits, and working conditions for all employees in all the unions involved.

Collective decision making How voters, politicians, and other interested parties act and how these actions influence nonmarket decisions.

Common property Property that is owned by everyone and therefore by no one. Air and water are examples of common property resources.

Comparable-worth doctrine The belief that women should receive the same wages as men if the levels of skill and responsibility in their jobs are equivalent.

Comparative advantage The ability to produce a good or service at a lower opportunity cost than other producers.

Complements Two goods are complements if both are used together for consumption or enjoyment—for example, coffee and cream. The more you buy of one, the more you buy of the other. For complements, a change in the price of one causes an opposite shift in the demand for the other.

Concentration ratio The percentage of all sales contributed by the leading four or leading eight firms in an industry; sometimes called the *industry concentration ratio.*

Constant dollars Dollars expressed in terms of real purchasing power using a particular year as the base or standard of comparison, in contrast to current dollars.

Constant returns to scale No change in long-run average costs when output increases.

Constant-cost industry An industry whose total output can be increased without an increase in long-run per-unit costs; its long-run supply curve is horizontal.

Consumer optimum A choice of a set of goods and services that maximizes the level of satisfaction for each consumer, subject to limited income.

Consumer Price Index (CPI) A statistical measure of a weighted average of prices of a specified set of goods and services purchased by typical consumers in urban areas.

Consumption Spending on new goods and services out of a household's current income. Whatever is not consumed is saved. Consumption includes such things as buying food and going to a concert.

Consumption function The relationship between amount consumed and disposable income. A consumption function tells us how much people plan to consume at various levels of disposable income.

Consumption goods Goods bought by households to use up, such as food and movies.

Contraction A business fluctuation during which the pace of national economic activity is slowing down.

Cooperative game A game in which the players explicitly cooperate to make themselves better off. As applied to firms, it involves companies colluding in order to make higher than competitive rates of return.

Corporation A legal entity that may conduct business in its own name just as an individual does; the owners of a corporation, called shareholders, own shares of the firm's profits and enjoy the protection of limited liability.

Cost-of-living adjustments (COLAs) Clauses in contracts that allow for increases in specified nominal values to take account of changes in the cost of living.

Cost-of-service regulation Regulation that allows prices to reflect only the ac-

tual cost of production and no monopoly profits.

Cost-push inflation Inflation caused by decreases in short-run aggregate supply.

Craft unions Labor unions composed of workers who engage in a particular trade or skill, such as baking, carpentry, or plumbing.

Crawling peg An exchange rate arrangement in which a country pegs the value of its currency to the exchange value of another nation's currency but allows the par value to change at regular intervals.

Creative response Behavior on the part of a firm that allows it to comply with the letter of the law but violate the spirit, significantly lessening the law's effects.

Credence good A product with qualities that consumers lack the expertise to assess without assistance.

Cross price elasticity of demand (E_{xy}) The percentage change in the demand for one good (holding its price constant) divided by the percentage change in the price of a related good.

Crowding-out effect The tendency of expansionary fiscal policy to cause a decrease in planned investment or planned consumption in the private sector; this decrease normally results from the rise in interest rates.

Current account A category of balance of payments transactions that measures the exchange of merchandise, the exchange of services, and unilateral transfers.

Cyclical unemployment Unemployment resulting from business recessions that occur when aggregate (total) demand is insufficient to create full employment.

D

Dead capital Any capital resource that lacks clear title of ownership.

Decreasing-cost industry An industry in which an increase in output leads to a reduction in long-run per-unit costs,

such that the long-run industry supply curve slopes downward.

Deflation A sustained decrease in the average of all prices of goods and services in an economy.

Demand A schedule of how much of a good or service people will purchase at any price during a specified time period, other things being constant.

Demand curve A graphical representation of the demand schedule; a negatively sloped line showing the inverse relationship between the price and the quantity demanded (other things being equal).

Demand-pull inflation Inflation caused by increases in aggregate demand not matched by increases in aggregate supply.

Demerit good A good that has been deemed socially undesirable through the political process. Heroin is an example.

Dependent variable A variable whose value changes according to changes in the value of one or more independent variables.

Depository institutions Financial institutions that accept deposits from savers and lend those deposits out at interest.

Depreciation A decrease in the exchange value of one nation's currency in terms of the currency of another nation; also, a reduction in the value of capital goods over a one-year period due to physical wear and tear and also to obsolescence.

Depression An extremely severe recession.

Derived demand Input factor demand derived from demand for the final product being produced.

Development economics The study of factors that contribute to the economic development of a country.

Diminishing marginal utility The principle that as more of any good or service is consumed, its extra benefit declines. Otherwise stated, increases in total utility from the consumption of a good or service become smaller and smaller as more is consumed during a given time period.

Direct expenditure offsets Actions on the part of the private sector in spending income that offset government fiscal policy actions. Any increase in government spending in an area that competes with the private sector will have some direct expenditure offset.

Direct marketing Advertising targeted at specific consumers, typically in the form of postal mailings, telephone calls, or e-mail messages.

Direct relationship A relationship between two variables that is positive, meaning that an increase in one variable is associated with an increase in the other and a decrease in one variable is associated with a decrease in the other.

Dirty float Active management of a floating exchange rate on the part of a country's government, often in cooperation with other nations.

Discount rate The interest rate that the Federal Reserve charges for reserves that it lends to depository institutions. It is sometimes referred to as the *rediscount rate* or, in Canada and England, as the *bank rate*.

Discounting The method by which the present value of a future sum or a future stream of sums is obtained.

Discouraged workers Individuals who have stopped looking for a job because they are convinced that they will not find a suitable one.

Diseconomies of scale Increases in long-run average costs that occur as output increases.

Disposable personal income (DPI) Personal income after personal income taxes have been paid.

Dissaving Negative saving; a situation in which spending exceeds income. Dissaving can occur when a household is able to borrow or use up existing assets.

Distribution of income The way income is allocated among the population.

Dividends Portion of a corporation's profits paid to its owners (shareholders).

Division of labor The segregation of a resource into different specific tasks; for example, one automobile worker puts on bumpers, another doors, and so on.

Dominant strategies Strategies that always yield the highest benefit. Regardless of what other players do, a dominant strategy will yield the most benefit for the player using it.

Dumping Selling a good or a service abroad below the price charged in the home market or at a price below its cost of production.

Durable consumer goods Consumer goods that have a life span of more than three years.

Dynamic tax analysis Economic evaluation of tax rate changes that recognizes that the tax base eventually declines with ever-higher tax rates, so that tax revenues may eventually decline if the tax rate is raised sufficiently.

E

Economic freedom The rights to own private property and to exchange goods, services, and financial assets with minimal government interference.

Economic goods Goods that are scarce, for which the quantity demanded exceeds the quantity supplied at a zero price.

Economic growth Increases in per capita real GDP measured by its rate of change per year.

Economic profits Total revenues minus total opportunity costs of all inputs used, or the total of all implicit and explicit costs.

Economic rent A payment for the use of any resource over and above its opportunity cost.

Economics The study of how people allocate their limited resources to satisfy their unlimited wants.

Economies of scale Decreases in long-run average costs resulting from increases in output.

Effect time lag The time that elapses between the implementation of a policy and the results of that policy.

Efficiency The case in which a given level of inputs is used to produce the maximum output possible. Alternatively, the situation in which a given output is produced at minimum cost.

Efficiency wage The optimal wage that firms must pay to maintain worker productivity.

Effluent fee A charge to a polluter that gives the right to discharge into the air or water a certain amount of pollution; also called a *pollution tax.*

Elastic demand A demand relationship in which a given percentage change in price will result in a larger percentage change in quantity demanded. Total expenditures and price changes are inversely related in the elastic region of the demand curve.

Empirical Relying on real-world data in evaluating the usefulness of a model.

Endowments The various resources in an economy, including both physical resources and such human resources as ingenuity and management skills.

Entitlements Guaranteed benefits under a government program such as Social Security, Medicare, or Medicaid.

Entrepreneurship The factor of production involving human resources that perform the functions of raising capital, organizing, managing, assembling other factors of production, and making basic business policy decisions. The entrepreneur is a risk taker.

Entry deterrence strategy Any strategy undertaken by firms in an industry, either individually or together, with the intent or effect of raising the cost of entry into the industry by a new firm.

Equation of exchange The formula indicating that the number of monetary units times the number of times each unit is spent on final goods and services is identical to the price level times nominal GDP.

Equilibrium The situation when quantity supplied equals quantity demanded at a particular price.

Excess reserves The difference between legal reserves and required reserves.

Exchange rate The price of one nation's currency in terms of the currency of another country.

Excise tax A tax levied on purchases of a particular good or service.

Exclusion principle The principle that no one can be excluded from the benefits of a public good, even if that person has not paid for it.

Expansion A business fluctuation in which the pace of national economic activity is speeding up.

Expenditure approach Computing GDP by adding up the dollar value at current market prices of all final goods and services.

Experience good A product that an individual must consume before the product's quality can be established.

Explicit costs Costs that business managers must take account of because they must be paid; examples are wages, taxes, and rent.

Externality A consequence of an economic activity that spills over to affect third parties; a situation in which a private cost (or benefit) diverges from a social cost (or benefit); a situation in which the costs (or benefits) of an action are not fully borne (or gained) by the two parties engaged in exchange or by an individual engaging in a scarce-resource-using activity.

F

Featherbedding Any practice that forces employers to use more labor than they would otherwise or to use existing labor in an inefficient manner.

Federal Deposit Insurance Corporation (FDIC) A government agency that insures the deposits held in banks and most other depository institutions; all U.S. banks are insured this way.

Federal funds market A private market (made up mostly of banks) in which banks can borrow reserves from other banks that want to lend them. Federal funds are usually lent for overnight use.

Federal funds rate The interest rate that depository institutions pay to borrow reserves in the interbank federal funds market.

Fiduciary monetary system A system in which money is issued by the government and its value is based uniquely on the public's faith that the currency represents command over goods and services.

Final goods and services Goods and services that are at their final stage of production and will not be transformed into yet other goods or services. For example, wheat is not ordinarily considered a final good because it is usually used to make a final good, bread.

Financial capital Funds used to purchase physical capital goods, such as buildings and equipment, and patents and trademarks.

Financial intermediaries Institutions that transfer funds between ultimate lenders (savers) and ultimate borrowers.

Financial intermediation The process by which financial institutions accept savings from businesses, households, and governments and lend the savings to other businesses, households, and governments.

Firm A business organization that employs resources to produce goods or services for profit. A firm normally owns and operates at least one "plant" in order to produce.

Fiscal policy The discretionary changing of government expenditures or taxes to achieve national economic goals, such as high employment with price stability.

Fixed costs Costs that do not vary with output. Fixed costs typically include such things as rent on a building. These costs are fixed for a certain period of time (in the long run, though, they are variable).

Fixed investment Purchases by businesses of newly produced producer durables, or capital goods, such as production machinery and office equipment.

Flexible exchange rates Exchange rates that are allowed to fluctuate in the open market in response to changes in supply and demand. Sometimes called *floating exchange rates.*

Flow A quantity measured per unit of time; something that occurs over time, such as the income you make per week or per year or the number of individuals who are fired every month.

Foreign direct investment The acquisition of more than 10 percent of the shares of ownership in a company in another nation.

Foreign exchange market A market in which households, firms, and governments buy and sell national currencies.

Foreign exchange rate The price of one currency in terms of another.

Foreign exchange risk The possibility that changes in the value of a nation's currency will result in variations in the market value of assets.

45-degree reference line The line along which planned real expenditures equal real GDP per year.

Fractional reserve banking A system in which depository institutions hold reserves that are less than the amount of total deposits.

Free-rider problem A problem that arises when individuals presume that others will pay for public goods so that, individually, they can escape paying for their portion without causing a reduction in production.

Frictional unemployment Unemployment due to the fact that workers must search for appropriate job offers. This takes time, and so they remain temporarily unemployed.

Full employment An arbitrary level of unemployment that corresponds to "normal" friction in the labor market. In 1986, a 6.5 percent rate of unemployment was considered full employment. Today, it is assumed to be around 5 percent.

G

Game theory A way of describing the various possible outcomes in any situation involving two or more interacting individuals when those individuals are aware of the interactive nature of their situation and plan accordingly. The plans made by these individuals are known as *game strategies.*

GDP deflator A price index measuring the changes in prices of all new goods and services produced in the economy.

General Agreement on Tariffs and Trade (GATT) An international agreement established in 1947 to further world trade by reducing barriers and tariffs. GATT was replaced by the World Trade Organization in 1995.

Goods All things from which individuals derive satisfaction or happiness.

Government budget constraint The limit on government spending and transfers imposed by the fact that every dollar the government spends, transfers, or uses to repay borrowed funds must ultimately be provided by the taxes it collects.

Government budget deficit An excess of government spending over government revenues during a given period of time.

Government budget surplus An excess of government revenues over government spending during a given period of time.

Government, or political, goods Goods (and services) provided by the public sector; they can be either private or public goods.

Gross domestic income (GDI) The sum of all income—wages, interest, rent, and profits—paid to the four factors of production.

Gross domestic product (GDP) The total market value of all final goods and services produced by factors of production located within a nation's borders.

Gross private domestic investment The creation of capital goods, such as factories and machines, that can yield production and hence consumption in the future. Also included in this definition are changes in business inventories and repairs made to machines or buildings.

Gross public debt All federal government debt irrespective of who owns it.

H

Health savings account (HSA) A tax-exempt health care account into which individuals can pay on a regular basis and out of which medical expenses can be paid.

Hedge A financial strategy that reduces the chance of suffering losses arising from foreign exchange risk.

Horizontal merger The joining of firms that are producing or selling a similar product.

Human capital The accumulated training and education of workers.

I

Implicit costs Expenses that managers do not have to pay out of pocket and hence do not normally explicitly calculate, such as the opportunity cost of factors of production that are owned; examples are owner-provided capital and owner-provided labor.

Import quota A physical supply restriction on imports of a particular good, such as sugar. Foreign exporters are unable to sell in the United States more than the quantity specified in the import quota.

Incentive structure The system of rewards and punishments individuals face with respect to their own actions.

Incentives Rewards for engaging in a particular activity.

Income approach Measuring GDP by adding up all components of national income, including wages, interest, rent, and profits.

Income elasticity of demand (E_i) The percentage change in demand for any good, holding its price constant, divided by the percentage change in income; the responsiveness of demand to changes in income, holding the good's relative price constant.

Income in kind Income received in the form of goods and services, such as housing or medical care; to be contrasted with money income, which is simply income in dollars, or general purchasing power, that can be used to buy *any* goods and services.

Income velocity of money The number of times per year a dollar is spent on fi-

nal goods and services; equal to nominal GDP divided by the money supply.

Income-consumption curve The set of optimal consumption points that would occur if income were increased, relative prices remaining constant.

Increasing-cost industry An industry in which an increase in industry output is accompanied by an increase in long-run per-unit costs, such that the long-run industry supply curve slopes upward.

Independent variable A variable whose value is determined independently of, or outside, the equation under study.

Indifference curve A curve composed of a set of consumption alternatives, each of which yields the same total amount of satisfaction.

Indirect business taxes All business taxes except the tax on corporate profits. Indirect business taxes include sales and business property taxes.

Industrial unions Labor unions that consist of workers from a particular industry, such as automobile manufacturing or steel manufacturing.

Industry supply curve The locus of points showing the minimum prices at which given quantities will be forthcoming; also called the *market supply curve.*

Inefficient point Any point below the production possibilities curve at which the use of resources is not generating the maximum possible output.

Inelastic demand A demand relationship in which a given percentage change in price will result in a less than proportionate percentage change in the quantity demanded. Total expenditures and price are directly related in the inelastic region of the demand curve.

Infant industry argument The contention that tariffs should be imposed to protect from import competition an industry that is trying to get started. Presumably, after the industry becomes technologically efficient, the tariff can be lifted.

Inferior goods Goods for which demand falls as income rises.

Inflation A sustained increase in the average of all prices of goods and services in an economy.

Inflation-adjusted return A rate of return that is measured in terms of real goods and services; that is, after the effects of inflation have been factored out.

Inflationary gap The gap that exists whenever equilibrium real GDP per year is greater than full-employment real GDP as shown by the position of the long-run aggregate supply curve.

Information product An item that is produced using information-intensive inputs at a relatively high fixed cost but distributed for sale at a relatively low marginal cost.

Informational advertising Advertising that emphasizes transmitting knowledge about the features of a product.

Innovation Transforming an invention into something that is useful to humans.

Inside information Information that is not available to the general public about what is happening in a corporation.

Interactive marketing Advertising that permits a consumer to follow up directly by searching for more information and placing direct product orders.

Interest The payment for current rather than future command over resources; the cost of obtaining credit. Also, the return paid to owners of capital.

Interest rate effect One of the reasons that the aggregate demand curve slopes downward: Higher price levels increase the interest rate, which in turn causes businesses and consumers to reduce desired spending due to the higher cost of borrowing.

Intermediate goods Goods used up entirely in the production of final goods.

International financial crisis The rapid withdrawal of foreign investments and loans from a nation.

International financial diversification Financing investment projects in more than one country.

International Monetary Fund An agency founded to administer an international foreign exchange system and to lend to member countries that had balance of payments problems. The IMF now functions as a lender of last resort for national governments.

Inventory investment Changes in the stocks of finished goods and goods in process, as well as changes in the raw materials that businesses keep on hand. Whenever inventories are decreasing, inventory investment is negative; whenever they are increasing, inventory investment is positive.

Inverse relationship A relationship between two variables that is negative, meaning that an increase in one variable is associated with a decrease in the other and a decrease in one variable is associated with an increase in the other.

Investment Any use of today's resources to expand tomorrow's production or consumption; spending by businesses on things such as machines and buildings, which can be used to produce goods and services in the future. The investment part of real GDP is the portion that will be used in the process of producing goods in the future.

J

Job leaver An individual in the labor force who quits voluntarily.

Job loser An individual in the labor force whose employment was involuntarily terminated.

Jurisdictional dispute A dispute involving two or more unions over which should have control of a particular jurisdiction, such as a particular craft or skill or a particular firm or industry.

K

Keynesian short-run aggregate supply curve The horizontal portion of the aggregate supply curve in which there is excessive unemployment and unused capacity in the economy.

L

Labor Productive contributions of humans who work, involving both mental and physical activities.

Labor force Individuals aged 16 years or older who either have jobs or who are looking and available for jobs; the number of employed plus the number of unemployed.

Labor force participation rate The percentage of noninstitutionalized working-age individuals who are employed or seeking employment.

Labor productivity Total real domestic output (real GDP) divided by the number of workers (output per worker).

Labor unions Worker organizations that seek to secure economic improvements for their members; they also seek to improve the safety, health and other benefits (such as job security) of their members.

Land The natural resources that are available from nature. Land as a resource includes location, original fertility and mineral deposits, topography, climate, water, and vegetation.

Law of demand The observation that there is a negative, or inverse, relationship between the price of any good or service and the quantity demanded, holding other factors constant.

Law of diminishing (marginal) returns The observation that after some point, successive equal-sized increases in a variable factor of production, such as labor, added to fixed factors of production, will result in smaller increases in output.

Law of increasing relative cost The observation that the opportunity cost of additional units of a good generally increases as society attempts to produce more of that good. This accounts for the bowed-out shape of the production possibilities curve.

Law of supply The observation that the higher the price of a good, the more of that good sellers will make available over a specified time period, other things being equal.

Leading indicators Events that have been found to exhibit changes before changes in business activity.

Legal reserves Reserves that depository institutions are allowed by law to claim as reserves—for example, deposits held at Federal Reserve district banks and vault cash.

Lemons problem The potential for asymmetric information to bring about a general decline in product quality in an industry.

Liabilities Amounts owed; the legal claims against a business or household by nonowners.

Limited liability A legal concept whereby the responsibility, or liability, of the owners of a corporation is limited to the value of the shares in the firm that they own.

Limit-pricing model A model that hypothesizes that a group of colluding sellers will set the highest common price that they believe they can charge without new firms seeking to enter that industry in search of relatively high profits.

Liquidity The degree to which an asset can be acquired or disposed of without much danger of any intervening loss in nominal value and with small transaction costs. Money is the most liquid asset.

Liquidity approach A method of measuring the money supply by looking at money as a temporary store of value.

Long run The time period during which all factors of production can be varied.

Long-run aggregate supply curve A vertical line representing the real output of goods and services after full adjustment has occurred. It can also be viewed as representing the real GDP of the economy under conditions of full employment—the full-employment level of real GDP.

Long-run average cost curve The locus of points representing the minimum unit cost of producing any given rate of output, given current technology and resource prices.

Long-run industry supply curve A market supply curve showing the relationship between prices and quantities after firms have been allowed the time to enter into or exit from an industry, depending on whether there have been positive or negative economic profits.

Lorenz curve A geometric representation of the distribution of income. A Lorenz curve that is perfectly straight represents complete income equality. The more bowed a Lorenz curve, the more unequally income is distributed.

Lump-sum tax A tax that does not depend on income. An example is a $1,000 tax that every household must pay, irrespective of its economic situation.

M

M1 The money supply, taken as the total value of currency plus checkable deposits plus traveler's checks not issued by banks.

M2 M1 plus (1) savings and small-denomination time deposits at all depository institutions, (2) balances in retail money market mutual funds, and (3) money market deposit accounts (MMDAs).

Macroeconomics The study of the behavior of the economy as a whole, including such economywide phenomena as changes in unemployment, the general price level, and national income.

Majority rule A collective decision-making system in which group decisions are made on the basis of more than 50 percent of the vote. In other words, whatever more than half of the electorate votes for, the entire electorate has to accept.

Marginal cost pricing A system of pricing in which the price charged is equal to the opportunity cost to society of producing one more unit of the good or service in question. The opportunity cost is the marginal cost to society.

Marginal costs The change in total costs due to a one-unit change in production rate.

Marginal factor cost (MFC) The cost of using an additional unit of an input. For example, if a firm can hire all the workers it wants at the going wage rate, the marginal factor cost of labor is the wage rate.

Marginal physical product The physical output that is due to the addition of one more unit of a variable factor of production; the change in total product occurring when a variable input is increased and all other inputs are held constant; also called *marginal product* or *marginal return.*

Marginal physical product (MPP) of labor The change in output resulting from the addition of one more worker. The MPP of the worker equals the change in total output accounted for by hiring the worker, holding all other factors of production constant.

Marginal propensity to consume (MPC) The ratio of the change in consumption to the change in disposable income. A marginal propensity to consume of 0.8 tells us that an additional $100 in take-home pay will lead to an additional $80 consumed.

Marginal propensity to save (MPS) The ratio of the change in saving to the change in disposable income. A marginal propensity to save of 0.2 indicates that out of an additional $100 in take-home pay, $20 will be saved. Whatever is not saved is consumed. The marginal propensity to save plus the marginal propensity to consume must always equal 1, by definition.

Marginal revenue The change in total revenues resulting from a change in output (and sale) of one unit of the product in question.

Marginal revenue product (MRP) The marginal physical product (MPP) times marginal revenue (MR). The MRP gives the additional revenue obtained from a one-unit change in labor input.

Marginal tax rate The change in the tax payment divided by the change in income, or the percentage of additional dollars that must be paid in taxes. The marginal tax rate is applied to the highest tax bracket of taxable income reached.

Marginal utility The change in total utility due to a one-unit change in the quantity of a good or service consumed.

Market All of the arrangements that individuals have for exchanging with one another. Thus, for example, we can speak of the labor market, the automobile market, and the credit market.

Market clearing, or equilibrium, price The price that clears the market, at which quantity demanded equals quantity supplied; the price where the demand curve intersects the supply curve.

Market demand The demand of all consumers in the marketplace for a particular good or service. The summation at each price of the quantity demanded by each individual.

Market failure A situation in which an unrestrained market operation leads to either too few or too many resources going to a specific economic activity.

Market share test The percentage of a market that a particular firm supplies; used as the primary measure of monopoly power.

Mass marketing Advertising intended to reach as many consumers as possible, typically through television, newspaper, radio, or magazine ads.

Medium of exchange Any asset that sellers will accept as payment.

Merit good A good that has been deemed socially desirable through the political process. Museums are an example.

Microeconomics The study of decision making undertaken by individuals (or households) and by firms.

Minimum efficient scale (MES) The lowest rate of output per unit time at which long-run average costs for a particular firm are at a minimum.

Minimum wage A wage floor, legislated by government, setting the lowest hourly rate that firms may legally pay workers.

Models, or theories Simplified representations of the real world used as the basis for predictions or explanations.

Monetarists Macroeconomists who believe that inflation in the long run is always caused by excessive monetary growth and that changes in the money supply affect aggregate demand both directly and indirectly.

Monetary rule A monetary policy that incorporates a rule specifying the annual rate of growth of some monetary aggregate.

Money Any medium that is universally accepted in an economy both by sellers of goods and services as payment for those goods and services and by creditors as payment for debts.

Money balances Synonymous with money, money stock, money holdings.

Money illusion Reacting to changes in money prices rather than relative prices. If a worker whose wages double when the price level also doubles thinks he or she is better off, that worker is suffering from money illusion.

Money market deposit accounts (MMDAs) Accounts issued by banks yielding a market rate of interest with a minimum balance requirement and a limit on transactions. They have no minimum maturity.

Money market mutual funds Funds of investment companies that obtain money from the public that is held in common and used to acquire short-maturity credit instruments, such as certificates of deposit and securities sold by the U.S. government.

Money multiplier The reciprocal of the required reserve ratio, assuming no leakages into currency and no excess reserves. It is equal to 1 divided by the required reserve ratio.

Money price The price that we observe today, expressed in today's dollars; also called the *absolute* or *nominal price.*

Money supply The amount of money in circulation.

Monopolist The single supplier of a good or service for which there is no close substitute. The monopolist therefore constitutes its entire industry.

Monopolistic competition A market situation in which a large number of firms produce similar but not identical products. Entry into the industry is relatively easy.

Monopolization The possession of monopoly power in the relevant market and the willful acquisition or maintenance of

that power, as distinguished from growth or development as a consequence of a superior product, business acumen, or historical accident.

Monopoly A firm that has control over the price of a good. In the extreme case, a monopoly is the only seller of a good or service.

Monopsonist The only buyer in a market.

Monopsonistic exploitation Paying a price for the variable input that is less than its marginal revenue product; the difference between marginal revenue product and the wage rate.

Moral hazard The possibility that a borrower might engage in riskier behavior after a loan has been obtained.

Multiplier The ratio of the change in the equilibrium level of real GDP to the change in autonomous real expenditures; the number by which a change in autonomous real investment or autonomous real consumption, for example, is multiplied to get the change in equilibrium real GDP.

N

National income (NI) The total of all factor payments to resource owners. It can be obtained by subtracting indirect business taxes from NDP.

National income accounting A measurement system used to estimate national income and its components; one approach to measuring an economy's aggregate performance.

Natural monopoly A monopoly that arises from the peculiar production characteristics in an industry. It usually arises when there are large economies of scale relative to the industry's demand such that one firm can produce at a lower average cost than can be achieved by multiple firms.

Natural rate of unemployment The rate of unemployment that is estimated to prevail in long-run macroeconomic equilibrium, when all workers and employers have fully adjusted to any changes in the economy.

Near moneys Assets that are almost money. They have a high degree of liquidity and thus can be easily converted into money without loss in value. Time deposits and short-term U.S. government securities are examples.

Negative market feedback A tendency for a good or service to fall out of favor with more consumers because other consumers have stopped purchasing the item.

Negative-sum game A game in which players as a group lose at the end of the game.

Net domestic product (NDP) GDP minus depreciation.

Net investment Gross private domestic investment minus an estimate of the wear and tear on the existing capital stock. Net investment therefore measures the change in capital stock over a one-year period.

Net public debt Gross public debt minus all government interagency borrowing.

Net worth The difference between assets and liabilities.

Network effect A situation in which a consumer's willingness to purchase a good or service is influenced by how many others also buy or have bought the item.

New entrant An individual who has never held a full-time job lasting two weeks or longer but is now seeking employment.

New growth theory A theory of economic growth that examines the factors that determine why technology, research, innovation, and the like are undertaken and how they interact.

Nominal rate of interest The market rate of interest expressed in today's dollars.

Nominal values The values of variables such as GDP and investment expressed in current dollars, also called *money values;* measurement in terms of the actual market prices at which goods and services are sold.

Nonaccelerating inflation rate of unemployment (NAIRU) The rate of unemployment below which the rate of inflation tends to rise and above which the rate of inflation tends to fall.

Noncontrollable expenditures Government spending that changes automatically without action by Congress.

Noncooperative game A game in which the players neither negotiate nor cooperate in any way. As applied to firms in an industry, this is the common situation in which there are relatively few firms and each has some ability to change price.

Nondurable consumer goods Consumer goods that are used up within three years.

Nonincome expense items The total of indirect business taxes and depreciation.

Nonprice rationing devices All methods used to ration scarce goods that are price-controlled. Whenever the price system is not allowed to work, nonprice rationing devices will evolve to ration the affected goods and services.

Normal goods Goods for which demand rises as income rises. Most goods are normal goods.

Normal rate of return The amount that must be paid to an investor to induce investment in a business; also known as the *opportunity cost of capital.*

Normative economics Analysis involving value judgments about economic policies; relates to whether things are good or bad. A statement of *what ought to be.*

Number line A line that can be divided into segments of equal length, each associated with a number.

O

Oligopoly A market situation in which there are very few sellers. Each seller knows that the other sellers will react to its changes in prices and quantities.

Open economy effect One of the reasons that the aggregate demand curve slopes downward: Higher price levels result in foreign residents desiring to buy fewer U.S.-made goods, while U.S. residents now desire more foreign-made goods, thereby reducing net exports. This is equivalent to a reduction in the amount of real goods and services purchased in the United States.

Open market operations The purchase and sale of existing U.S. government securities (such as bonds) in the open private market by the Federal Reserve System.

Opportunistic behavior Actions that ignore the possible long-run benefits of cooperation and focus solely on short-run gains.

Opportunity cost The highest-valued, next-best alternative that must be sacrificed to obtain something or to satisfy a want.

Opportunity cost of capital The normal rate of return, or the available return on the next-best alternative investment. Economists consider this a cost of production, and it is included in our cost examples.

Optimal quantity of pollution The level of pollution for which the marginal benefit of one additional unit of clean air just equals the marginal cost of that additional unit of clean air.

Origin The intersection of the *y* axis and the *x* axis in a graph.

Outsourcing A firm's employment of labor outside the country in which the firm is located.

P

Par value The officially determined value of a currency.

Partnership A business owned by two or more joint owners, or partners, who share the responsibilities and the profits of the firm and are individually liable for all the debts of the partnership.

Passive (nondiscretionary) policymaking Policymaking that is carried out in response to a rule. It is therefore not in response to an actual or potential change in overall economic activity.

Patent A government protection that gives an inventor the exclusive right to make, use, or sell an invention for a limited period of time (currently, 20 years).

Payoff matrix A matrix of outcomes, or consequences, of the strategies available to the players in a game.

Perfect competition A market structure in which the decisions of *individual* buyers and sellers have no effect on market price.

Perfectly competitive firm A firm that is such a small part of the total *industry* that it cannot affect the price of the product it sells.

Perfectly elastic demand A demand that has the characteristic that even the slightest increase in price will lead to zero quantity demanded.

Perfectly elastic supply A supply characterized by a reduction in quantity supplied to zero when there is the slightest decrease in price.

Perfectly inelastic demand A demand that exhibits zero responsiveness to price changes; no matter what the price is, the quantity demanded remains the same.

Perfectly inelastic supply A supply for which quantity supplied remains constant, no matter what happens to price.

Personal Consumption Expenditure (PCE) Index. A statistical measure of average price using annually updated weights based on surveys of consumer spending.

Personal income (PI) The amount of income that households actually receive before they pay personal income taxes.

Persuasive advertising Advertising that is intended to induce a consumer to purchase a particular product and discover a previously unknown taste for the item.

Phillips curve A curve showing the relationship between unemployment and changes in wages or prices. It was long thought to reflect a trade-off between unemployment and inflation.

Physical capital All manufactured resources, including buildings, equipment, machines, and improvements to land that is used for production.

Planning curve The long-run average cost curve.

Planning horizon The long run, during which all inputs are variable.

Plant size The physical size of the factories that a firm owns and operates to produce its output. Plant size can be defined by square footage, maximum physical capacity, and other physical measures.

Policy irrelevance proposition The conclusion that policy actions have no real effects in the short run if the policy actions are anticipated and none in the long run even if the policy actions are unanticipated.

Portfolio investment The purchase of less than 10 percent of the shares of ownership in a company in another nation.

Positive economics Analysis that is strictly limited to making either purely descriptive statements or scientific predictions; for example, "If A, then B." A statement of *what is.*

Positive market feedback A tendency for a good or service to come into favor with additional consumers because other consumers have chosen to buy the item.

Positive-sum game A game in which players as a group are better off at the end of the game.

Precautionary demand Holding money to meet unplanned expenditures and emergencies.

Present value The value of a future amount expressed in today's dollars; the most that someone would pay today to receive a certain sum at some point in the future.

Price ceiling A legal maximum price that may be charged for a particular good or service.

Price controls Government-mandated minimum or maximum prices that may be charged for goods and services.

Price differentiation Establishing different prices for similar products to reflect differences in marginal cost in providing those commodities to different groups of buyers.

Price discrimination Selling a given product at more than one price, with the price difference being unrelated to differences in marginal cost.

Price elasticity of demand (E_p) The responsiveness of the quantity demanded of a commodity to changes in its price; defined as the percentage change in quantity demanded divided by the percentage change in price.

Price elasticity of supply (E_s) The responsiveness of the quantity supplied of a commodity to a change in its price; the percentage change in quantity supplied divided by the percentage change in price.

Price floor A legal minimum price below which a good or service may not be sold. Legal minimum wages are an example.

Price index The cost of today's market basket of goods expressed as a percentage of the cost of the same market basket during a base year.

Price leadership A practice in many oligopolistic industries in which the largest firm publishes its price list ahead of its competitors, who then match those announced prices. Also called *parallel pricing.*

Price searcher A firm that must determine the price-output combination that maximizes profit because it faces a downward-sloping demand curve.

Price system An economic system in which relative prices are constantly changing to reflect changes in supply and demand for different commodities. The prices of those commodities are signals to everyone within the system as to what is relatively scarce and what is relatively abundant.

Price taker A competitive firm that must take the price of its product as given because the firm cannot influence its price.

Price war A pricing campaign designed to capture additional market share by repeatedly cutting prices.

Price-consumption curve The set of consumer-optimum combinations of two goods that the consumer would choose as the price of one good changes, while money income and the price of the other good remain constant.

Principle of rival consumption The recognition that individuals are rivals in consuming private goods because one person's consumption reduces the amount available for others to consume.

Principle of substitution The principle that consumers and producers shift away from goods and resources that become priced relatively higher in favor of goods and resources that are now priced relatively lower.

Prisoners' dilemma A famous strategic game in which two prisoners have a choice between confessing and not confessing to a crime. If neither confesses, they serve a minimum sentence. If both confess, they serve a longer sentence. If one confesses and the other doesn't, the one who confesses goes free. The dominant strategy is always to confess.

Private costs Costs borne solely by the individuals who incur them. Also called *internal costs*.

Private goods Goods that can be consumed by only one individual at a time. Private goods are subject to the principle of rival consumption.

Private property rights Exclusive rights of ownership that allow the use, transfer, and exchange of property.

Producer durables, or capital goods Durable goods having an expected service life of more than three years that are used by businesses to produce other goods and services.

Producer Price Index (PPI) A statistical measure of a weighted average of prices of goods and services that firms produce and sell.

Product differentiation The distinguishing of products by brand name, color, and other minor attributes. Product differentiation occurs in other than perfectly competitive markets in which products are, in theory, homogeneous, such as wheat or corn.

Production Any activity that results in the conversion of resources into products that can be used in consumption.

Production function The relationship between inputs and maximum physical output. A production function is a technological, not an economic, relationship.

Production possibilities curve (PPC) A curve representing all possible combinations of total output that could be produced assuming (1) a fixed amount of productive resources of a given quality and (2) the efficient use of those resources.

Profit-maximizing rate of production The rate of production that maximizes total profits, or the difference between total revenues and total costs; also, the rate of production at which marginal revenue equals marginal cost.

Progressive taxation A tax system in which, as income increases, a higher percentage of the additional income is taxed. The marginal tax rate exceeds the average tax rate as income rises.

Property rights The rights of an owner to use and to exchange property.

Proportional rule A decision-making system in which actions are based on the proportion of the "votes" cast and are in proportion to them. In a market system, if 10 percent of the "dollar votes" are cast for blue cars, 10 percent of the output will be blue cars.

Proportional taxation A tax system in which, regardless of an individual's income, the tax bill comprises exactly the same proportion.

Proprietorship A business owned by one individual who makes the business decisions, receives all the profits, and is legally responsible for the debts of the firm.

Public debt The total value of all outstanding federal government securities.

Public goods Goods for which the principle of rival consumption does not apply; they can be jointly consumed by many individuals simultaneously at no additional cost and with no reduction in quality or quantity. Also no one who fails to help pay for the good can be denied the benefit of the good.

Purchasing power The value of money for buying goods and services. If your

money income stays the same but the price of one good that you are buying goes up, your effective purchasing power falls, and vice versa.

Purchasing power parity Adjustment in exchange rate conversions that takes into account differences in the true cost of living across countries.

Q

Quantity theory of money and prices The hypothesis that changes in the money supply lead to proportional changes in the price level.

Quota subscription A nation's account with the International Monetary Fund, denominated in special drawing rights.

Quota system A government-imposed restriction on the quantity of a specific good that another country is allowed to sell in the United States. In other words, quotas are restrictions on imports. These restrictions are usually applied to one or several specific countries.

R

Random walk theory The theory that there are no predictable trends in securities prices that can be used to "get rich quick."

Rate of discount The rate of interest used to discount future sums back to present value.

Rate of return The future financial benefit to making a current investment.

Rate-of-return regulation Regulation that seeks to keep the rate of return in an industry at a competitive level by not allowing prices that would produce economic profits.

Rational expectations hypothesis A theory stating that people combine the effects of past policy changes on important economic variables with their own judgment about the future effects of current and future policy changes.

Rationality assumption The assumption that people do not intentionally make decisions that would leave them worse off.

Reaction function The manner in which one oligopolist reacts to a change in price, output, or quality made by another oligopolist in the industry.

Real rate of interest The nominal rate of interest minus the anticipated rate of inflation.

Real values Measurement of economic values after adjustments have been made for changes in the average of prices between years.

Real-balance effect The change in expenditures resulting from a change in the real value of money balances when the price level changes, all other things held constant; also called the *wealth effect.*

Real-income effect The change in people's purchasing power that occurs when, other things being constant, the price of one good that they purchase changes. When that price goes up, real income, or purchasing power, falls, and when that price goes down, real income increases.

Recession A period of time during which the rate of growth of business activity is consistently less than its long-term trend or is negative.

Recessionary gap The gap that exists whenever equilibrium real GDP per year is less than full-employment real GDP as shown by the position of the long-run aggregate supply curve.

Recognition time lag The time required to gather information about the current state of the economy.

Recycling The reuse of raw materials derived from manufactured products.

Reentrant An individual who used to work full time but left the labor force and has now reentered it looking for a job.

Regional trade bloc A group of nations that grants members special trade privileges.

Regressive taxation A tax system in which as more dollars are earned, the percentage of tax paid on them falls. The marginal tax rate is less than the average tax rate as income rises.

Reinvestment Profits (or depreciation reserves) used to purchase new capital equipment.

Relative price The price of one commodity divided by the price of another commodity; the number of units of one commodity that must be sacrificed to purchase one unit of another commodity.

Rent control The placement of price ceilings on rents in particular cities.

Repricing, or menu, cost of inflation The cost associated with recalculating prices and printing new price lists when there is inflation.

Required reserve ratio The percentage of total deposits that the Fed requires depository institutions to hold in the form of vault cash or deposits with the Fed.

Required reserves The value of reserves that a depository institution must hold in the form of vault cash or deposits with the Fed.

Reserves In the U.S. Federal Reserve System, deposits held by Federal Reserve district banks for depository institutions, plus depository institutions' vault cash.

Resources Things used to produce other things to satisfy people's wants.

Retained earnings Earnings that a corporation saves, or retains, for investment in other productive activities; earnings that are not distributed to stockholders.

Ricardian equivalence theorem The proposition that an increase in the government budget deficit has no effect on aggregate demand.

Right-to-work laws Laws that make it illegal to require union membership as a condition of continuing employment in a particular firm.

S

Sales taxes Taxes assessed on the prices paid on a large set of goods and services.

Saving The act of not consuming all of one's current income. Whatever is not consumed out of spendable income is, by definition, saved. *Saving* is an action measured over time (a flow), whereas *savings* are a stock, an accumulation resulting from the act of saving in the past.

Savings deposits Interest-earning funds that can be withdrawn at any time without payment of a penalty.

Say's law A dictum of economist J. B. Say that supply creates its own demand; producing goods and services generates the means and the willingness to purchase other goods and services.

Scarcity A situation in which the ingredients for producing the things that people desire are insufficient to satisfy all wants.

Search good A product with characteristics that enable an individual to evaluate the product's quality in advance of a purchase.

Seasonal unemployment Unemployment resulting from the seasonal pattern of work in specific industries. It is usually due to seasonal fluctuations in demand or to changing weather conditions, rendering work difficult, if not impossible, as in the agriculture, construction, and tourist industries.

Secondary boycott A boycott of companies or products sold by companies that are dealing with a company being struck.

Secular deflation A persistent decline in prices resulting from economic growth in the presence of stable aggregate demand.

Securities Stocks and bonds.

Services Mental or physical labor or help purchased by consumers. Examples are the assistance of physicians, lawyers, dentists, repair personnel, housecleaners, educators, retailers, and wholesalers; things purchased or used by consumers that do not have physical characteristics.

Share of stock A legal claim to a share of a corporation's future profits; if it is *common stock,* it incorporates certain voting rights regarding major policy decisions of the corporation; if it is *preferred stock,* its owners are accorded preferential treatment in the payment of dividends.

Share-the-gains, share-the-pains theory A theory of regulatory behavior that holds that regulators must take account of the demands of three groups: legislators, who established and oversee the regulatory agency; firms in the regulated industry; and consumers of the regulated industry's products.

Short run The time period during which at least one input, such as plant size, cannot be changed.

Shortage A situation in which quantity demanded is greater than quantity supplied at a price below the market clearing price.

Short-run aggregate supply curve The relationship between total planned economywide production and the price level in the short run, all other things held constant. If prices adjust incompletely in the short run, the curve is positively sloped.

Short-run break-even price The price at which a firm's total revenues equal its total costs. At the break-even price, the firm is just making a normal rate of return on its capital investment. (It is covering its explicit and implicit costs.)

Short-run economies of operation A distinguishing characteristic of an information product arising from declining short-run average total cost as more units of the product are sold.

Short-run shutdown price The price that covers average variable costs. It occurs just below the intersection of the marginal cost curve and the average variable cost curve.

Signals Compact ways of conveying to economic decision makers information needed to make decisions. A true signal not only conveys information but also provides the incentive to react appropriately. Economic profits and economic losses are such signals.

Slope The change in the y value divided by the corresponding change in the x value of a curve; the "incline" of the curve.

Small menu costs Costs that deter firms from changing prices in response to demand changes—for example, the costs of renegotiating contracts or printing new price lists.

Social costs The full costs borne by society whenever a resource use occurs. Social costs can be measured by adding external costs to private, or internal, costs.

Social Security contributions The mandatory taxes paid out of workers' wages and salaries. Although half are supposedly paid by employers, in fact the net wages of employees are lower by the full amount.

Special drawing rights (SDRs) Reserve assets created by the International Monetary Fund for countries to use in settling international payment obligations.

Specialization The division of productive activities among persons and regions so that no one individual or one area is totally self-sufficient. An individual may specialize, for example, in law or medicine. A nation may specialize in the production of coffee, computers, or cameras.

Standard of deferred payment A property of an asset that makes it desirable for use as a means of settling debts maturing in the future; an essential property of money.

Static tax analysis Economic evaluation of the effects of tax rate changes under the assumption that there is no effect on the tax base, so that there is an unambiguous positive relationship between tax rates and tax revenues.

Stock The quantity of something, measured at a given point in time—for example, an inventory of goods or a bank account. Stocks are defined independently of time, although they are assessed at a point in time.

Store of value The ability to hold value over time; a necessary property of money.

Strategic dependence A situation in which one firm's actions with respect to price, quality, advertising, and related changes may be strategically countered by the reactions of one or more other firms in the industry. Such dependence can exist only when there are a limited number of major firms in an industry.

Strategy Any rule that is used to make a choice, such as "Always pick heads."

Strikebreakers Temporary or permanent workers hired by a company to replace union members who are striking.

Structural unemployment Unemployment resulting from a poor match of workers' abilities and skills with current requirements of employers.

Subsidy A negative tax; a payment to a producer from the government, usually in the form of a cash grant per unit.

Substitutes Two goods are substitutes when either one can be used for consumption to satisfy a similar want—for example, coffee and tea. The more you buy of one, the less you buy of the other. For substitutes, the change in the price of one causes a shift in demand for the other in the same direction as the price change.

Substitution effect The tendency of people to substitute cheaper commodities for more expensive commodities.

Supply A schedule showing the relationship between price and quantity supplied for a specified period of time, other things being equal.

Supply curve The graphical representation of the supply schedule; a line (curve) showing the supply schedule, which generally slopes upward (has a positive slope), other things being equal.

Supply-side economics The suggestion that creating incentives for individuals and firms to increase productivity will cause the aggregate supply curve to shift outward.

Surplus A situation in which quantity supplied is greater than quantity demanded at a price above the market clearing price.

Sweep account A depository institution account that entails regular shifts of funds from checkable deposits that are subject to reserve requirements to savings deposits that are exempt from reserve requirements.

Sympathy strike A strike by a union in sympathy with another union's strike or cause.

T

Target zone A range of permitted exchange rate variations between upper and lower exchange rate bands that a central bank defends by selling or buying foreign exchange reserves.

Tariffs Taxes on imported goods.

Tax base The value of goods, services, incomes, or wealth subject to taxation.

Tax bracket A specified interval of income to which a specific and unique marginal tax rate is applied.

Tax incidence The distribution of tax burdens among various groups in society.

Technology Society's pool of applied knowledge concerning how goods and services can be produced.

Terms of exchange The conditions under which trading takes place. Usually, the terms of exchange are equal to the price at which a good is traded.

The Fed The Federal Reserve System; the central bank of the United States.

Theory of public choice The study of collective decision making.

Third parties Parties who are not directly involved in a given activity or transaction.

Thrift institutions Financial institutions that receive most of their funds from the savings of the public; they include mutual savings banks, savings and loan associations, and credit unions.

Tie-in sales Purchases of one product that are permitted by the seller only if the consumer buys another good or service from the same firm.

Time deposit A deposit in a financial institution that requires notice of intent to withdraw or must be left for an agreed period. Withdrawal of funds prior to the end of the agreed period may result in a penalty.

Tit-for-tat strategic behavior In game theory, cooperation that continues so long as the other players continue to cooperate.

Total costs The sum of total fixed costs and total variable costs.

Total income The yearly amount earned by the nation's resources (factors of production). Total income therefore includes wages, rent, interest payments, and profits that are received by workers, landowners, capital owners, and entrepreneurs, respectively.

Total revenues The price per unit times the total quantity sold.

Transaction costs All costs associated with making, reaching, and enforcing agreements.

Transactions accounts Checking account balances in commercial banks and other types of financial institutions, such as credit unions and mutual savings banks; any accounts in financial institutions on which you can easily write checks without many restrictions.

Transactions approach A method of measuring the money supply by looking at money as a medium of exchange.

Transactions demand Holding money as a medium of exchange to make payments. The level varies directly with nominal GDP.

Transfer payments Money payments made by governments to individuals for which in return no services or goods are rendered. Examples are welfare, Social Security, and unemployment insurance benefits.

Transfers in kind Payments that are in the form of actual goods and services, such as food stamps, subsidized public housing, and medical care, and for which in return no goods or services are rendered concurrently.

Traveler's checks Financial instruments purchased from a bank or a non-

banking organization and signed during purchase that can be used as cash upon a second signature by the purchaser.

U

Unanticipated inflation Inflation at a rate that comes as a surprise, either higher or lower than the rate anticipated.

Unemployment The total number of adults (aged 16 years or older) who are willing and able to work and who are actively looking for work but have not found a job.

Union shop A legal environment in which businesses may hire nonunion members, conditional on their joining the union by some specified date after employment begins.

Unit elasticity of demand A demand relationship in which the quantity demanded changes exactly in proportion to the change in price. Total expenditures are invariant to price changes in the unit-elastic region of the demand curve.

Unit of accounting A measure by which prices are expressed; the common denominator of the price system; a central property of money.

Unit tax A constant tax assessed on each unit of a good that consumers purchase.

Universal banking An environment in which banks face few or no restrictions on their powers to offer a full range of financial services and to own shares of stock in corporations.

Unlimited liability A legal concept whereby the personal assets of the owner of a firm can be seized to pay off the firm's debts.

Util A representative unit by which utility is measured.

Utility The want-satisfying power of a good or service.

Utility analysis The analysis of consumer decision making based on utility maximization.

V

Value added The dollar value of an industry's sales minus the value of intermediate goods (for example, raw materials and parts) used in production.

Variable costs Costs that vary with the rate of production. They include wages paid to workers and purchases of materials.

Versioning Selling a product in slightly altered forms to different groups of consumers.

Vertical merger The joining of a firm with another to which it sells an output or from which it buys an input.

Voluntary exchange An act of trading, done on a voluntary basis, in which both parties to the trade are subjectively better off after the exchange.

Voluntary import expansion (VIE) An official agreement with another country in which it agrees to import more from the United States.

Voluntary restraint agreement (VRA) An official agreement with another country that "voluntarily" restricts the quantity of its exports to the United States.

W

Wants What people would buy if their incomes were unlimited.

Wealth The stock of assets owned by a person, household, firm, or nation. For a household, wealth can consist of a house, cars, personal belongings, stocks, bonds, bank accounts, and cash.

World Bank A multinational agency that specializes in making loans to about 100 developing nations in an effort to promote their long-term development and growth.

World index fund A portfolio of bonds issued in various nations whose individual yields generally move in offsetting directions, thereby reducing the overall risk of losses.

World Trade Organization (WTO) The successor organization to GATT that handles trade disputes among its member nations.

X

x axis The horizontal axis in a graph.

Y

y axis The vertical axis in a graph.

Z

Zero-sum game A game in which any gains within the group are exactly offset by equal losses by the end of the game.